WARBIRDS
WORLDWIDE
HELLCAT
UPDATE
TWENTY
Fw190 RECOVERY
FLYING THE YAK-11
KALAMAZOO JUG
D0505570
TWO
SPITFIRE
UPDATE
THUNDERBOLT SURVIVORS
JET HERITAGE

An International Survey of the World's Warbird Population

WARBIRDS DIRECTORY
WORLDWIDE

A Russian Officer inspects the wreck of a P-40 Kittyhawk in Northern Russia in 1991. These are exciting times! *via Mark Sheppard*

John Chapman & Geoff Goodall

Edited by Paul Coggan

Published by
WARBIRDS WORLDWIDE LTD
P.O. Box 99
Mansfield
Notts NG19 9GU
GREAT BRITAIN

ISBN 1 870601 27 0

- Design by Paul Coggan
- First Published in December 1989

- Reprographics by *Studiograph,* Unit 1, Gauntley Court, Ward Street, Nottingham NG7 5HD (0602 423812)
- Printed by *Linneys Colour Print,* 121 Newgate Lane, Mansfield, Notts NG18 2PA (0623) 656565

Worldwide Trade Distribution by
Warbirds Worldwide, P.O. Box 99, Mansfield, Notts NG19 9GU, ENGLAND.
Tel: +44 623 24288
Fax +44 623 22659

United States Trade Distribution by
Motorbooks International
Box 2, 729 Prospect Avenue,
OSCEOLA,
WI 54020,
USA
Tel: (715) 294 3345
Fax (715) 294 4448

Front Cover Photograph: *John Dibbs captured three aircraft of* ***The Old Flying Machine Company*** *over Cambridgeshire in November 1992. Our special thanks to Ray and Mark Hanna for their generosity in putting these aircraft in the air for our cover shot.*

PRINTED IN GREAT BRITAIN

- ***Originated and Printed exclusively in Sherwood Forest, Nottinghamshire, Robin Hood Country.***

Foreward

I am delighted, and privileged to present the second edition of the Warbirds Worldwide Directory. This new volume represents an achievement parallel to that of rebuilding a warbird. In terms of effort John Chapman and Geoff Goodall have spent several thousand hours inputting the information, checking and collating - and all this after having done the initial research, to present raw data for me to edit and manipulate into the publication you have in your hand. It is a magnificent achievement and John and Geoff deserve congratulations of the highest order To put this into perspective there are some 136,000 words in this book, the majority of which have been typed into the system by the authors. This requires a discipline and dedication that only those closely associated with the production of this publication will truly appreciate.

From the last edition the list of types has been increased from 62 to 172 . The origination and editing of the second edition has involved some healthy debate between the authors and myself. I reluctantly had to chop the Lockheed PV-1 and PV-2 airframes, but am pleased to present a new listing of North American T-6s and associated variants. Both John and Geoff inputted some considerable data on the type, but were not keen that it should appear in this edition. I took the decision to bring the list as up to date as my files would allow, and even now there are some areas of it which need a little more work; we need your help! After spending some two weeks of solid 'T-6 ing' I never want to see another T-6 data file ever again. It gave me a small insight into the sheer logistics of preparing the rest of the data files. Picture content has suffered as a result of this increased amount of data, but this is primarily a data saturated reference work and we are sure you will appreciate this.

There will no doubt also be some healthy debate between readers about which types should have been included in this edition, and those that should have been chopped. I know from experience that it is impossible to please all of the people all of the time. And yes. T-34 owners, we are looking at including your aircraft in the next edition. Stearmans have also been suggested, and we may *consider* this *if* the aircraft concerned is utilised as a true warbird. Otherwise we could be faced with listing several hundred airframes currently employed for crop dusting! We need your feedback, in the form of *constructive* criticism please. Additionally, if you see what you believe is an error or an omission we'd be delighted to hear from you. Owners in particular can help by checking serials and construction numbers on the original makers plates, particularly where T-6s are concerned.

The importance of the *Warbirds Worldwide Directory* was brought home to me shortly after the first edition was published. A well known warbird collector telephoned me from Yugoslavia to say we had two airframes listed in one location and he could only find one. Where on earth was the other? This certainly hammered home the responsibility we shoulder when we put something like this together! We do take it seriously, but we are human and though the computer has taken the brunt of the punishment in manipulating all this data the machine is only as good as the operator. Rest assured however that we have taken every possible care in the preparation of this second edition.

So here we are. You can put the first edition in the archives and begin looking through this second edition which will no doubt replace it as the true 'Bible' of the Warbirds Industry. Before you go any further I urge you to read the section entitled "Using the Warbirds Worldwide Directory" as it explains how you can get the best out of this new book. Enjoy it - and happy hunting! Paul Coggan November 1992.

Corrections and additional data is most welcome. Please write or fax:

Paul Coggan
Editor, WARBIRDS DIRECTORY
P.O. Box 99,
Mansfield,
NOTTS NG19 9GU
ENGLAND

FAX (0623) 22659 Int'l + 446 23 22659

Dedicated to the memory of John R. Sandberg, co-founder of Warbirds Worldwide, warbird owner and engineer.

Contents

JETS SECTION

Introduction

On 24th August 1992 Hurricane Andrew came ashore in Florida and in one fell swoop devastated one of the world's most valuable and interesting collections of warbirds. Many aviation journals reported that the Weeks Air Museum had been totally destroyed, but fortunately this is not the case. Shown here is B-17G 44-83525/N83525 which was actually picked up and transported by the Hurricane! several of the aircraft were damaged however, some quite badly. **Photo By Hermann Buttigieg**

This second edition of the *Warbirds Worldwide Directory* presents a listing of all the major military combat aircraft flown under civil registration markings since the warbird restoration movement came of age around the world. Also listed are some of the known survivors of the earlier World War Two era types - those which may not have received civil markings but still exist as static museum pieces, in storage, or even derelict on some remote airfield but still considered restorable.

The individual aircraft histories outlined in this work *do not* pretend to be the whole story but give known owners and accident details obtained from a variety of official and unofficial sources. When known, details of delivery flights and other significant events are listed, The authors and Editor are well aware, from many years of aircraft research, that the full story of any airframe is unlikely to be found except by first-hand contact with every owner. This is particularly true with warbirds, given the often clandestine source of the original airframes when acquired by various air arms. These now form the backbone of today's restored showpieces. Even those with less colourful backgrounds often come from such hardworking careers as firebombers or aerial sprayers, prone to major accidents and rebuilding, sometimes losing their true 'identities' along the way. Experience has shown that access to original files and even the aircraft's own logbooks still may fail to reveal the true story.

Restorations using components from other aircraft and emerging with a new identity; swapping or even creating Manufacturer's Data Plates; warbirds seemingly destroyed in severe accidents which reappear only months later as pristine restorations - such is the warbird fraternity's mystique and fascination; but also it's frustration for the researcher from afar attempting to document the lives of each aircraft. Thus the histories in this Directory are largely the 'official' version as extracted from the records of Government civil and military aviation authorities. Where there is doubt over the identity, or conflicting information, a notation appears at the end of the aircraft history. **John Chapman & Geoff Goodall October 92**

Acknowledgements

The authors have referred to a wide range of aviation specialist publications to compile this Directory, with continuing base data coming from *Air Britain* and *Aviation Letter* as well (of course) as the regular *Warbirds Worldwide* Quarterly and special *Warbirds Today* series on the Spitfire and Mustang.

After publication of the first edition of the *Directory*, the following wrote with amendments and extra information; Alan Allen, William Carmody, Rick Cooke, Alan Gruening, Lars Gynner, Paul Janicki, Lawrence Jones, Bill Larkins, Christopher Kugler, Martin Kyburz, Gerard Manning, Robert Rudhall, N.D.Welch, Ian Whitney and Rose Zalesky.

The authors also wish to thank fellow Australian researches for their continuing support and sharing of information; Melvyn Davis, Bruce Hoy, Dick Hourigan, David Prossor and Gordon Reid. Finally our special appreciation for their extensive assistance goes to Peter Anderson (Australia), Jerry Vernon (Canada), Larry Webster and Gary Killion (USA). All information was gratefully received and can be seen in the greatly expanded aircraft histories presented in this edition.

The Editor wishes to thank a number of people, all of whom were closely associated with the final production of this major project. Ian Thirsk, Bruce Gordon, Graham Trant, Gary Brown, Philip Warner, James Kightly, Dwight Barnell, Derek Macphail, Alain Capel and Michael Shreeve all did speedy last minute checking on various types for us. John Dibbs gave us considerable support in the design and photographic department.Thierry Thomassin and Gary Brown also gave us access to considerable numbers of pictures.

A very special thank you to Ray, Mark and Sarah Hanna and the engineers at *The Old Flying Machine Company,* Duxford for their support in putting the aircraft in the air for our cover picture, and to John Romain of *The Aircraft Restoration Company* (also at Duxford) for skillfully piloting the camera ship from which our hero John Dibbs hung to capture the pictures.

Without our advertisers the Directory would have been very much thinner and we thank them for their contribution. Please mention this publication when you respond to their advertisements.

The *Warbirds Directory* production 'team' is particularly proud to have utilised the local services of a number of companies with a national reputation for excellence. *Linneys Colour Print* (celebrating their recent acquisition of BS5750) and in particular Kevin Rogers who stuck with my rapid changes of plan with regard to the number of pages we were going to produce with little complaint. On the reprographic side, Phil Walsh and Terry Radford and the entire staff at *Studiograph* in Nottingham handled the burden of actual production of 504 pages. as well as the large amount of work required pre-publication.

Our thanks also to *AppleCentre, Leeds* and the support staff at *Typetronics AppleCentre* at Wetherby who answered our pleas for help when the computers caused us problems (which was not very often), to the technical advisory staff at *Computers Unlimited* for their quick fire answers regarding *Quark Express* software. Amanda Coggan took the brunt of support administrative work processing large amounts of paper and advance orders for this new book

Most of all, I take off my hat to both John and Geoff for the huge effort and sheer dedication they have put into this remarkable work.

Information. on all the colour plates featured in this Directory is on Page 100

How to use this Directory

The *Warbirds Worldwide Directory* covers the history of each aircraft following its disposal by the military. From left to right, the following details are given: Manufacturer's Construction Number (when this is immediately followed by a dot, the aircraft is believed to be still extant); the aircraft's type designation or model; the military serial number; the civil registration; owners and details; and in the extreme right column the relevant dates. With regard to the black dot system, don't assume that an aircraft is no longer extant if there is not a black dot; airframes 'disappear' - there are aircraft to be discovered out there!

Dates are presented in English format: Day/Month/Year. Ownership is usually based on perusal of civil aircraft registers for the year or period quoted. "63/75" signifies that ownership 'by' 1963 and until; 1975 at least, whereas ".63/75" indicates that the aircraft was acquired by that owner 'during' 1963 and still with the same owner by 1975. "5.63" means the change of ownership or event occurred during May 1963.

When looking for a particular aircraft, changes of ownership and registration are listed in chronological date order and so the most recent or current registration and owner will be at the *bottom* of each aircraft's history. Because many warbirds, while painted in authentic military colour schemes, do not carry the correct serial for that airframe, where space permits this is covered by a note in each entry. However, paint schemes often change when the owner changes so be prepared to investigate further!

When a (1 or (2 appears after a civil registration, it refers to more than one allocation of the same registration to that particular aircraft type only.

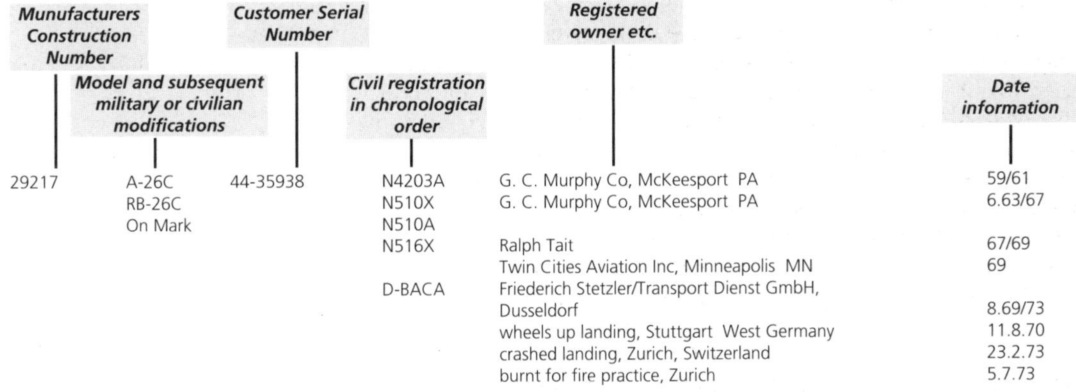

1 **FOCKE WULF Fw189**

2 **NORTH AMERICAN P-51 MUSTANG**

3 **Douglas A-26 Invader**

Page/Type headings are divided into three basic types. Type 1 shows a major type that is extant only in a small number or as a unique warbird. For reasons of space it seemed undesirable to have the type title taking up more space than the entry! Type 2 shows a major type in large numbers and Type 3 is simply a continuation bar, usually on a left hand page or where entries have been interrupted with advertising or a colour section.

Abbreviations

Canada:	BC	British Columbia
	ALTA	Alberta
	SASK	Saskatchewan
	MAN	Manitoba
	ONT	Ontario
	NB	New Brunswick
	NFLD	Newfoundland
Australia:	WA	Western Australia
	SA	South Australia
	VIC	Victoria
	NSW	New South Wales
	QLD	Queensland
	NT	Northern Territory
	TAS	Tasmania
General:	NZ	New Zealand
	PNG	Papua New Guinea
	HKG	Hong Kong
	PI	Philippine Islands
	PR	Puerto Rico
	USVI	U.S. Virgin Islands
	RCAF	Royal Canadian Air Force
	RCN	Royal Canadian Navy
	RAAF	Royal Australian Airforce
	RAN	Royal Australian Navy
	IDFAF	Israeli Defence Force Air Force
	ROKAF	Republic of Korea Air Force
	TNI-AU	Indonesian Air Force
	AURI	Indonesian Air Force
	SAAF	South African Air Force
	USAF	U.S. Air Force
	USAAF	U.S. Army Air Force
	USN	U.S. Navy
	USMC	U.S. Marine Corps
	USANG	U.S. Air National Guard
	RAF	Royal Air Force
	RNFAA	Royal Navy Fleet Air Arm
	NASM	National Air & Space Museum/Smithsonian Institute
	USNAM	U.S. Navy Aviation Museum
	USAFM	U.S.Air Force Museum
	NASA	National Aeronautics & Space Administration
	NACA	National Advisory Committee for Aeronautics
	BOC	Brought on Charge/Date added to air force inventory
	SOC	Struck off Charge/Date deleted from air force inventory
	AFB	U.S. Air Force Base
	ANG	Air National Guard Base
	FAA	Federal Aviation Administration (USA)
	USCAR	U.S. Civil Aircraft Register
	TFA	Trans Florida Aviation
	CAF	Confederate Air Force
	arr.	arrived: usually refers to transport by sea/road
	c/n	Manufacturer's Construction Number or Serial Number
	CofA	Certificate of Air worthiness
	conv.	converted, conversion
	cr.	crashed
	del.	delivered by air
	dep.	depart, departed
	dest.	destroyed
	dism.	dismantled
	displ.	displayed
	ex.	from, previous
	fcd.ldg.	forced landing
	ff	first flight: including after rebuild or transporting

fuse.	fuselage
Govt.	Government
id	identity
inst.	instructional as in airframe
k.	killed
mod.	modified, modification
Mus.	Museum
ntu	registration not taken up
orig.	original, originally
op.	operated by , operator
pres.	presumed
recov.	recovered, salvaged
reg.	registration
rep.	reported
res.	reserved
ret.	returned
tfd.	transferred
u/c	undercarriage
wfu	withdrawn from use, retired

CIVIL REGISTRATION PREFIX / COUNTRY CODE

AP-	Pakistan
B-	Taiwan, Republic of China
C- & CF-	Canada
CC-	Chile
CP-	Bolivia
CS-	Portugal
CU-	Cuba
CX-	Uruguay
EC-	Spain
EI-	Eire
EP-	Iran
F-O	French Overseas Protectorates
F-	France
G-	Great Britain
HB-	Switzerland
HC-	Ecuador
HH-	Haiti
HI-	Dominican Republic
HK-	Colombia
HP-	Panama
HR-	Honduras
HS-	Thailand
I-	Italy
JA-	Japan
LN-	Norway
LV-	Argentina
N & NC	USA
OB-	Peru
OE-	Austria
OO-	Belgium
OY-	Denmark
PH-	Netherlands
PK-	Indonesia
PP- & PT-	Brazil
RP- & PI-	Philippines
SE-	Sweden
TG-	Guatemala
TI-	Costa Rica
TR-	Gabon
VH-	Australia
VR-B	Bermuda
VR-H	Hong Kong
VT-	India
XA-,XB-,XC-	Mexico
YS-	El Salvador
YV-	Venezuela
ZK-	New Zealand
ZP-	Paraguay
XS-	South Africa
4X-	Israel

U.S.A. TWO LETTER STATE ABBREVIATIONS

AL	Alabama
AK	Alaska
AR	Arkansas
AZ	Arizona
CA	California
CO	Colorado
CT	Connecticut
DE	Delaware
DC	District of Columbia
FL	Florida
GA	Georgia
HI	Hawaii
ID	Idaho
IL	Illinois
IN	Indiana
IA	Iowa
KS	Kansas
KY	Kentucky
LA	Louisiana
ME	Maine
MD	Maryland
MA	Massachusetts
MI	Michigan
MN	Minnesota
MS	Mississippi
MO	Missouri
MT	Montana
NE	Nebraska
NV	Nevada
NH	New Hampshire
NJ	New Jersey
NM	New Mexico
NY	New York
NC	North Carolina
ND	North Dakota
OH	Ohio
OK	Oklahoma
OR	Oregon
PA	Pennsylvania
RI	Rhode Island
SC	South Carolina
SD	South Dakota
TN	Tennessee
TX	Texas
UT	Utah
VT	Vermont
VA	Virginia
WA	Washington
WV	West Virgina
WI	Wisconsin
WY	Wyoming

AICHI D2A "Val"

3105 •	D3A2-22			Admiral Nimitz State Historical Park,	
				Fredericksburg TX	.73/91
				recov. ex Gasmata, New Britain	.73
				shipped to USA on carrier HMAS Melbourne	.74
				(displ. as bomb-blasted wreck)	
3179 •	D3A2			Bob Diemert, Carman MAN	.69/73
				recov. ex Ballale Island, Bougainville	.69
			CF-TZT	(rebuilt Carman, Wright R2600 Cyclone	
				engine : ff Carman .72)	
				CNAC, Rockcliffe ONT: del.	.73/84
				Planes of Fame Museum, Chino	1.84/91
			N3131G	The Air Museum, Chino CA	11.91/92
				(displ. as "BII-201"; rest. to fly Chino 91/92,	
				(P&W R1830 engine)	

AICHI M6A

-	M6A1	47		NAS Alameda CA	60
	Floatplane			NASM, Silver Hill MD	66/91
				(under rest. for static displ. 91)	

ARADO Ar.196

Nr623183•	Ar 196A-3	Nr623183		captured on board "Prinz Eugen"	
				displ. NAS Willow Grove PA	57/58
				NASM, displ. as "GA+DX"	65
				NASM, loaned to USNAM, Pensacola FL	72
				NASM, Silver Hill MD	88
- •	Ar 196A-3	-		captured on board "Prince Eugen"	
				NAS Willow Grove PA	65/88
				(displ. as "T3+HK")	
- •	Ar 196A-3	-		Morski Muzei, Varna, Bulgaria	74/84

ARADO Ar.234 "Blitz"

Nr140312•	Ar 234B-2	Nr623167		KG76; captured by RAF,Stavangar, Norway	
				shipped to USA on HMS Reaper	7.45
				(USA trials as FE-1010; T2-1010)	
				Smithsonian Institute, stored Park Ridge IL	.46
				NASM, Silver Hill MD	72/90

- •	B Mk. I	R5868		(83 Sqn/467 Sqn: PO-S : flew 137 sorties)	
				RAF Wroughton : arr. for storage	1.9.47/58
				RAF Scampton : gate guard	.58/70
				RAF Bicester : rest. for RAF Museum	24.8.70/72
				RAF Museum, Hendon : arr.	20.3.72/92
- •	B Mk. 1	W4783		(to RAAF as A66-2: ex 460 Sqdn AR-G)	10.44
				Australian War Memorial, Canberra ACT	60/92
				(displ. as "W4783/AR-G")	
-	B Mk. 1	W4964		(9 Sqdn WS-J/ "Jonnie Walker")	
				Newark Aviation Museum , Newark UK	86/90
				(rear fuselage only "WS-J")	
-	B Mk. I	DV372		(467 Sqdn. RAAF : PO-F) SOC	4.10.45
				fuselage noted in Vendair Hangar, Croydon	5.58
				Imperial War Museum, London (nose only)	58/90
- •	B Mk. X 10 (MR)	FM104		(to RCAF as FM104) BOC 10.6.45 : SOC	10.9.64
				Canadian Nat. Exhibition Grounds, Toronto ONT	65/91
				(displ. on pole as "GA-R")	
- •	B Mk. X 10 (MR)	FM118		(to RCAF as FM118) BOC 10.8.45	
				BCATP Museum, Brandon BC	86
				(derelict hulk recov. from RCAF gunnery range)	
				Nanton Lancaster Society, Nanton ALTA	90/91
				(derelict remains only)	
- •	B Mk. X 10 (MR)	FM136		(to RCAF as FM136) BOC 29.8.45 : SOC	10.4.61
			CF-NJQ	ntu	
				Centennial Planetarium, Calgary ALTA	.61/90
				(displ. on pole as "VN-N", later "NA-P")	
				Aero Space Museum, Airport, Calgary ALTA	90/92
				(removed from pole 4.92: poss. rest. to fly)	
- •	B Mk. X 10 (MR)	FM159		(to RCAF as FM159) BOC 30.8.45 : SOC	4.10.60
				G. White, H. Armstrong, F. Garratt/	
				Nanton Lancaster Society, Nanton ALTA	4.8.60/91
				arr. Nanton by road ex Vulcan AB	28.9.60
				(displ. as "RX-159", later "RJ-N")	
				moved to new hangar Nanton, for static rest.	22.5.91
- •	B Mk. X	FM212		(to RCAF as FM212) SOC	9.10.64
				Jackson Park Sunken Gardens, Windsor ONT	.65/90
				(displ. as "CF-S")	
- •	B Mk. X 10 (MR)	FM213		(to RCAF FM213) SOC	30.6.64
				displ. on pole as "VR-A", Goderich ONT	14.6.64/77
				Canadian Warplane Heritage, Mount Hope ONT	.77/88
			C-GVRA	Canadian Warplane Heritage, Mount Hope ONT	1.9.88/90
				(ff 11.9.88: flies as "KB726/VR-A")	
- •	B Mk. X	KB839		(to RCAF as KB839) BOC 5.6.45	
				CFB Greenwood NS	65/90
				(displ. as "KB976/107" later "FM107/AF-K")	
	B Mk. X 10(AR)	KB848		(to RCAF as KB848) BOC 2.6.45 SOC	3.4.64
				Canadian National Aviation Mus., Ottawa ONT	86/90
				(nose section only)	
- •	B Mk. X 10(AR)	KB882		(to RCAF as KB882) BOC 2.6.45 SOC	26.5.64
				displ. St Jacques Airport, Edmunston NB	7.64/92
- •	B Mk. X	KB889		(to RCAF as KB889) BOC 5.6.46 SOC	21.5.65
				Age of Flight Museum, Niagara Falls ONT	65
				Lancaster Club, Oshawa ONT	73/84

				under restoration, Markham ONT	73/77
				Doug Arnold/Warbirds of GB Ltd, Blackbushe	.84
				(shipped Canada - UK .84)	
			G-LANC	Doug Arnold/Warbirds of GB Ltd, Bitteswell	31.1.85/86
				Imperial War Museum, Duxford : arr. dism.	14.5.86/92
				(under rest. Duxford for static displ.)	
-	B Mk. X	KB941		(to RCAF as KB941) BOC 14.6.45 : SOC	22.1.47
				Mr. Spinks, Lethbridge ALTA	86
				Charles Church Ltd, Manchester UK	90
				(centre section only)	
- •	B Mk. X	KB944		(to RCAF as KB944) BOC	15.6.45
				National Aviation Museum, Rockcliffe, ONT	.64/90
				(displ. as "KB944/NA-P")	
277 •	B Mk X	KB976		(to RCAF as KB976) BOC 17.6.45 : SOC	26.5.64
	10(AR)			Dr. E. Johnson, Calgary ALB : del.	.64/69
				Air Museum of Canada, Calgary ALTA	65
			CF-AMD	Northwestern Air Lease, St Albert ALB	.69/73
			CF-TQC	conv. to fire tanker not completed	
			G-BCOH	Sir W. J. D. Roberts/Strathallan Collection	24.9.74/87
				del. Strathallan by air ex Edmonton : arr.	11.6.75
				Charles Church Ltd, Manchester	.87/90
				trucked to BAe Woodford for rest. to fly: arr	9.4.87
				badly dam. by falling hangar roof, Woodford	12.8.87
				Doug Arnold/Warbirds of GB Ltd, Biggin Hill	8.90
				(under rebuild .92)	
- •	B Mk. X	KB994		(to RCAF as KB994) BOC 15.6.45 : SOC	22.1.47
				derelict on farm Pidgeon Lake, Edmonton	
				ALTA (fuselage only: coded "EQ-K")	72/77
				Northwest Air Lease, St Albert ALB	74
				408th Tactical Helicopter Squadron Museum	
				CFB Edmonton ALTA (under rest.)	86/88
				Charles Church Ltd, Manchester : arr. UK	8.88/90
				Doug Arnold/Warbird of GB Ltd,Biggin Hill	8.90
				Aces High Ltd, North Weald	2.91
				(stored dism. Bedford, Biggin Hill; fuselage	
				to be used in rebuild of G-BCOH)	
- •	B Mk. X	KB999		(to RCAF as KB999) BOC 19.6.45 : SOC	27.6.48
				derelict in Manitoba	86/90
- •	B Mk. 7	NX611		(to Aeronavale as WU-15, New Caledonia)	6.52/64
				del. Noumea-Sydney,Australia for HAPS	8.64
			G-ASXX	Malcolm D. N. Fisher/Historic Aircraft	
				Preservation Society, Biggin Hill	22.10.64
				del. Biggin Hill ex Sydney,Australia : arr.	13.5.65/67
				Reflectaire Museum, Lavenham/Squires Gate	19.5.67/72
				last flight: del. Lavenham to Squires Gate	26.6.70
				Lord Lilford	4.72/84
				RAF Scampton : loan, del. dism.	8.73/88
				(gate guard, displ. as "YF-C")	
				Lincolnshire Aviation Heritage Centre,	
				East Kirby	84/91
				(del. by road Scampton - East Kirby 4.88)	
- •	B Mk. 7	NX622		(to Aeronavale as WU-16, New Caledonia)	6.52/62
				RAAFA, displ. Perth Airport WA : del.	12.62/75
				Air Force Association Aviation Museum,	
				Bullcreek, Perth WA	.75/91
				advertised for sale (again)	.91
- •	B Mk. 7	NX664		(to Aeronavale as WU-21, New Caledonia)	8.52/63

Continued on Page 23

G-SWIF
2
C
238050
U

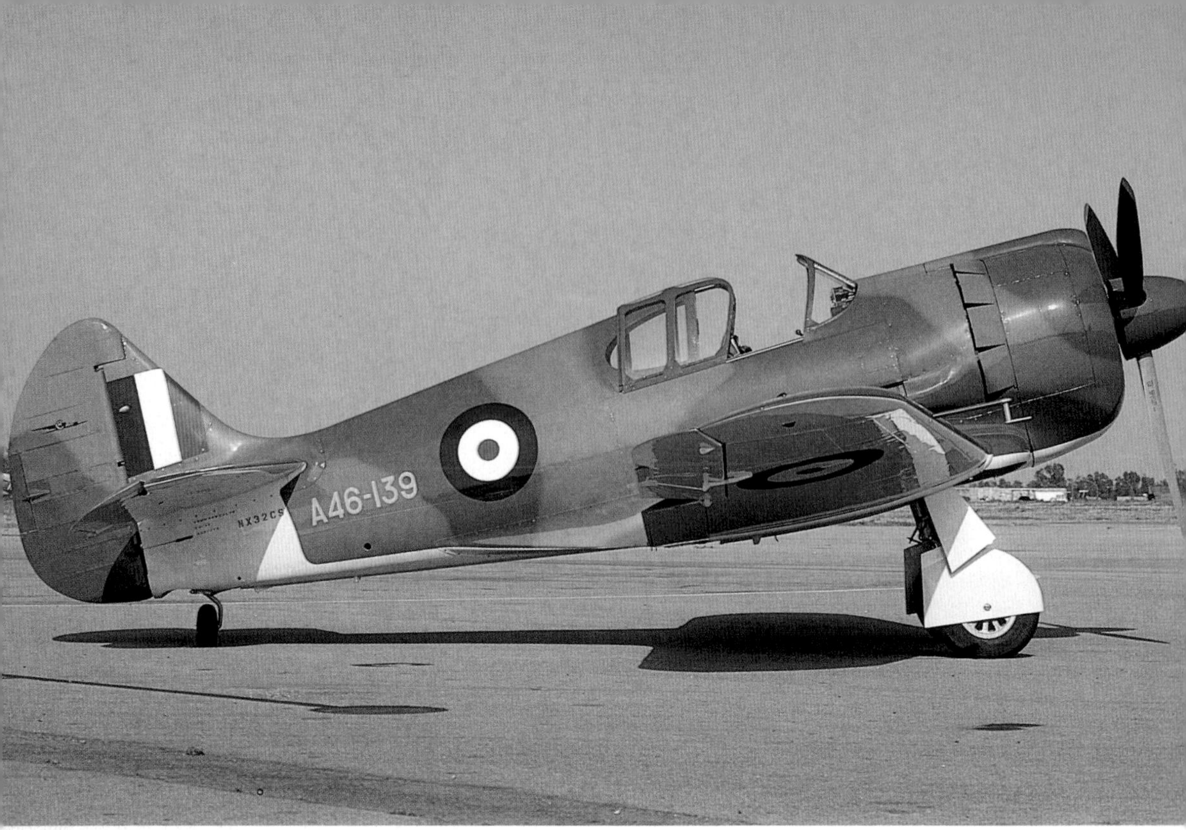
A46-139
NX32CS

GM
D
N1232N
AK845

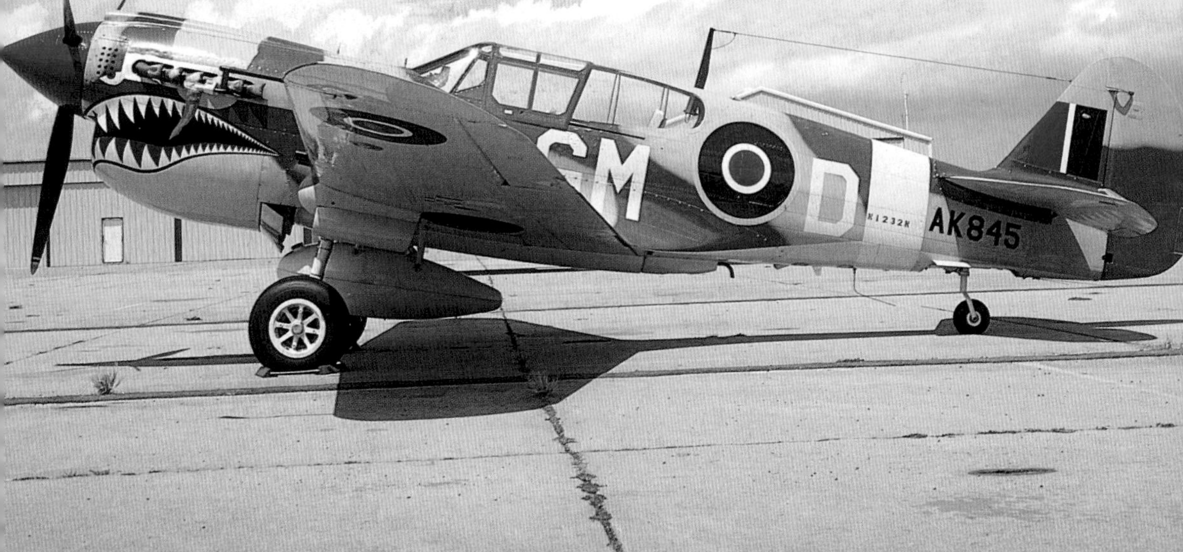

E HT
RR299

PROPELLER
MARINES
VMFN 513

NL3025

Continued from Page 18

				dam. landing, Mata Uti, Wallis Islands,	
				South West Pacific : stripped & abandoned	21.1.63
				recov. derelict, Wallis Islands	.84
				Ailes Ancienne, Le Bourget, Paris	.84/92
				displ. Musee de l'Air, Le Bourget	
- •	B Mk. 7	NX665		(to Aeronavale as WU-13 New Caledonia)	5.52/63
				Museum of Transport & Technology,	
				Auckland NZ : del.	4.64/90
				(displ. as "ND752 & PB457")	
- •	B Mk. I	PA474		Royal Aircraft Establishment/College of	
				Aeronautics, Cranfield : aerofoil flight trials	3.54/62
				RAF Museum, RAF Henlow : del. for storage	25.9.64/65
				RAF Waddington : rest. to fly	18.8.65/68
				RAF Battle of Britain Memorial Flight	68/92
				(flies as "PA474/"PM-M")	

AVRO LINCOLN

1414 •	B Mk. 2	RE408		(to FA Argentina as B-010)	
				Museo Nacional de Aeronautica, Aeroparque,	
				Buenos Aires, Argentina	.68/90
- •	B Mk. 2	RF342	G-APRJ	D. Napier & Sons Ltd, Luton	12.58
				College of Aeronautics, Cranfield	11.62/67
				Historic Aircraft Museum,Southend : del.	9.5.67/83
				Doug Arnold/Warbirds of GB Ltd, Blackbushe	10.5.83/86
				Aces High Ltd, North Weald, UK: arr. dism.	10.9.86/88
				Charles Church Ltd, Manchester: arr. dism.	6.12.88/90
				Doug Arnold/Warbirds of GB Ltd, Biggin Hill	8.90/91
				Aces High Ltd, North Weald	15.2.91
				(to be used in rebuild of Lancaster G-BCOH)	
- •	B Mk. 2	RF398		RAF Watton	63
				RAF Museum, RAF Henlow : del.	30.4.63
				RAF Museum, RAF Cosford	77/92
- •	B Mk. 2	-		(to FA Argentina as B-017)	
				rep. displ. Villa Reynolds AB, Argentina	90

BELL P-39 AIRACOBRA

141 •	P-39D	41-6802		shot down by Japanese, PNG	12.5.42
				William G. Chapman/Air Museum of PNG	70/72
				Kokoda Track War Museum, PNG	.72
				N. M. Armstrong, Auckland NZ : loaned to	
				Museum of Transport & Technology, Auckland	79
				N. M. Armstrong, Melbourne VIC	88
290 •	P-39D	41-6951		forced landing nr Weipa QLD : abandoned	1.5.42/72
				recov. by Cairns Aircraft Recovery Group	9.72
				Sid Beck/Townsville Aero Museum QLD	.72/87
				Sid Beck, Mareeba QLD : static rest.	.87/92
309	P-39D	41-6970		William G. Chapman/Air Museum of PNG	.69
				(recov. ex Gaire PNG, stored Port Moresby)	
				broken up and buried as junk, Port Moresby	c72
554 •	P-39F	41-7215		forced landing nr Weipa QLD : abandoned	1.5.42/72
				recov. by Cairns Aircraft Recovery Group	9.72
				Nick Watling/CARG, Cairns QLD : stored	72/75
				stored Mount Isa, later Mossman QLD	87/92
				(static rest., to be displ. Townsville QLD)	
- •	P-39K	42-4312		Bob Jarrett/South Australian Aviation Museum,	
				Port Adelaide SA	.82/91

Continued on Page 25

Continued from Page 23

				(recov. ex Woodlark Island PNG by Jarrett .82, includes parts from 42-4368)	
				Weeks Air Museum,Tamiami FL	.91/92
- •	P-39N	42-4949		Military Aircraft Restoration Corp, Chino CA	71/79
				(recov. from crash site, Fort Nelson BC 11.71)	
- •	P-39N	42-8740	N81575	Yankee Air Corps, Chino CA	12.90/92
- •	P-39N	42-8881		Yankee Air Corps, Chino CA : rest. to fly	88/91
- •	P-39N	42-18403		Military Aircraft Restoration Corp, Chino CA	.74/88
				(recov. by d'E. C. Darby & N. M. Armstrong for YAF from Tsili Tsili, PNG .74)	
- •	P-39N	42-18408		Military Aircraft Restoration Corp, Chino CA	.74/88
				(recov. by d'E. C. Darby & N. M. Armstrong for YAF from Tsili Tsili, PNG .74)	
- •	P-39N	42-18811		Military Aircraft Restoration Corp, Chino CA	.74/88
				(recov. by d'E. C. Darby & N. M. Armstrong for YAF from Tsili Tsili, PNG .74)	
- •	P-39N	42-18814		Military Aircraft Restoration Corp, Chino CA	.74/90
				(recov. by d'E. C. Darby & N. M. Armstrong for YAF from Tadji, West Sepik PNG .74)	
				noted stored Tallichet compound Chino CA	88
- •	P-39N	42-19027		Military Aircraft Restoration Corp, Chino CA	.74/87
				(recov. by d'E. C. Darby & N. M. Armstrong for YAF from Tadji PNG .74: "Small Fry")	
				Frederick A. Johnsen/Museum Aeronautica, Tacoma WA	.87/90
				(trucked Tacoma ex Chino .87, rest. to fly)	
- •	P-39N	42-19034		Military Aircraft Restoration Corp, Chino CA	.74/90
				(recov. by d'E. C. Darby & N. M. Armstrong for YAF from Tadji, West Sepik PNG .74)	
				noted stored MARC compound Chino CA	88
- •	P-39N	42-19039		J. K. McCarthy Museum, Goroka PNG	72/85
				(displ. on pole as "USAAC 039")	
- •	P-39Q	42-19597		forced landing, Hobbs NM: abandoned by USAF	c46
				dism. derelict, held by Joe Brown, Hobbs NM	c67
			N6968	Don Hull, Sugarland TX	69/74
				Confederate Air Force, Harlingen TX	3.12.74/91
				American Airpower Heritage Flying Museum, Midland TX (flies in Soviet AF scheme)	9.91/92
- •	P-39Q	42-19991		Military Aircraft Restoration Corp, Chino CA	.74/88
				(recov. by d'E. C. Darby & N. M. Armstrong for YAF from Tadji, West Sepik PNG .74)	
- •	P-39Q	42-19993		d'E. C. Darby & N. M. Armstong, Auckland NZ	.74
				(recov. from Tadji, West Sepik PNG .74)	
				stored Auckland NZ	.74/76
				N. M. Armstrong/Australian Aerospace Museum, Essendon Airport, Melbourne VIC	82/88
				(static rest., displ. as "Brooklyn Bum 2nd")	
				Whittington Bros, Ft. Lauderdale FL	.89/90
			N139DP	Museum of Flying, Santa Monica CA	.92
				(arr. Santa Monica from FL .92, rest. to fly)	
- •	P-39Q	42-19995		(8th FG/36th FS: Maj. William A. Shomo : "Snooks 2nd")	

				Military Aircraft Restoration Corp, Chino CA (recov. by d'E. C. Darby & N. M. Armstrong for YAF from Tadji, West Sepik PNG .74)	.74/92
				lsd. Air Heritage Inc, Beaver Falls PA (rebuild to fly, Beaver Falls PA: see unidentified a/c listed at end)	91/92
- •	P-39Q	42-20007		Military Aircraft Restoration Corp, Chino CA (recov. by d'E. C. Darby & N. M. Armstrong for YAF from Tadji, West Sepik PNG .74)	.74/88
				noted stored Tallichet compound Chino CA	88
- •	P-39Q	42-20339		Military Aircraft Restoration Corp, Chino CA (recov. by d'E. C. Darby & N. M. Armstrong for YAF from Tadji, West Sepik PNG .74)	.74/88
- •	P-39Q	44-2433	NX57591	Charles W. Bing (Bendix racer #12/"Juba")	.46
				Elizabeth (Betty) Hass, Scarsdale NY (race #12/"Galloping Gertie")	47/54
			N57591	NASM: loan EAA Museum, Hales Corner WI	70/84
				NASM, Silver Hill MD (displ. as "Galloping Gertie") (FAA quote id."5015015-456L"; also rep. as "26E-433/44-32533)	87/90
- •	P-39Q	44-2438		Military Aircraft Restoration Corp, Chino CA (recov. by d'E. C. Darby & N. M. Armstrong for YAF from Tadji, West Sepik PNG .74)	.74/90
				noted stored Tallichet compound Chino CA	88
- •	P-39Q	44-2485		(to Soviet AF as ....)	
				ditched, del. flight, Carpenter Lake BC	c44
				Garry R. Larkins, Auburn CA (recov. from lake by Garry Larkins 7.90; rebuild to fly, Auburn CA : to go to BC museum)	.90/91
- •	P-39Q	44-2664		(to Soviet AF as 26)	
				shot down over Finland, captured	6.44
				Aviation Museum of Central Finland, Luonetjarvi AB	79/90
- •	P-39Q	44-3291	N56HA	US Historic Aircraft Preservation Museum, Anchorage AK : reg. res.	3.85
- •	P-39Q TP-39Q	44-3887		Jack B. Hardwick/Hardwick Aircraft Co, El Monte CA (stored, derelict, Hardwick Yard, El Monte CA	
				USAFM, Wright-Patterson AFB, Dayton OH (displ. as "887"; later "17073")	7.66/90
- •	RP-39Q TP-39Q	44-3908	NX4829N	W. H. Ostenberg, Scotts Bluff NE (Bendix racer #15)	c46
				Paul Addy, Fosturia OH	c50
			N40A	Archie Baldocchi, San Salvador, El Salvador	54
				E. D. Weiner, Hayward CA (stored, not flown, Orange County CA 59/71)	57
				Robert M. Lindquist, Santa Ana CA	63
				Donald D. Randall, Santa Ana CA	66/69
				Mira Slovak, Van Nuys (rest. as race #21/"Mr Mennen; later #39)	.71/75
				Rebco Inc/Confederate AF, San Antonio TX	29.7.75/82
				Preston Parish/Kalamazoo Aviation History Museum, Kalamazoo MI	1.82/92
- •	P-39Q	44-71500	N57697	US Historical Aircraft Museum, Anchorage AK	10.84/86
				wartime crash : purchased in situ ex USAF	10.10.84

				American Vets Memorial Museum, Denver CO	6.88/92
- •	P-400	AP335		(USAAF) forced landing, LG Bulldog,	
				Lakekamu River PNG : abandoned	2.8.43/84
				recov. by RAAF Chinook for Jack Taft	30.11.84
				Jack N. Taft/US Military Aircraft Museum,	
				Jackson MI	.85/90
- •	P-400	AP347		(USAAC) forced landing, LG Bulldog,	
				Lakekamu River PNG : abandoned	20.8.43/84
				recov. by RAAF Chinook for Jack Taft	29.11.84
				Jack N. Taft/US Military Aircraft Museum,	
				Jackson MI (in deal with PNG Govt.)	.84
				National Museum, Port Moresby PNG	.85/90
				stored, unrest. Pt.Moresby-Jacksons Airport	90
- •	P-400	BW157		(USAAC 67th PS, New Caledonia)	
				fuselage recov. Henderson Field, Guadalcanal	.74
				War Museum, Guadalcanal	.74/79
- •	P-39D	-		(to Soviet AF)	
				Central Armed Forces Museum, Moscow	50s
				Zhukovsky Memorial Museum, Moscow	85
- •	P-39N	-		Military Aircraft Restoration Corp, Chino CA	.74/88
				(recov. by d'E. C. Darby & N. M. Armstrong	
				for YAF from Tsili Tsili, PNG .74)	
				(id. not found when recov: P-39N-5 model)	
- •	P-39N	-		Military Aircraft Restoration Corp, Chino CA	.74
				USAFM: March AFB CA : static rest.	82/92
- •	P-39N	-		Military Aircraft Restoration Corp, Chino CA	74
				Ed Maloney/The Air Museum, Chino CA	84/91
				(static rest. as "42-19027 Little Sir Echo")	
				(id. rep. as 42-18547)	
- •	P-39Q	-		Military Aircraft Restoration Corp, Chino CA	.74/80
				(recov. by d'E. C. Darby & N. M. Armstrong	
				for YAF from Tadji, West Sepik PNG .74)	
				Bell Textron Inc, Buffalo NY : static rest.	.80
				displ. Servicemans Park, Buffalo NY	12.80/92
				(displ. as "219995/Snooks 2nd/Betty Lou 3rd":	
				same aircraft as one of those listed above)	

BELL P-63 KINGCOBRA

- •	P-63A	42-68895		Walter Soplata Collection, Newbury OH	85
				(incomplete fuselage, recov. ex Buffalo NY)	
33-11 •	P-63A	42-68941	NX75488	Steven H. Christenson, Houston TX	47/54
				open storage, Dallas-Love Field TX	c50/c65
			N191H	Olin C. Crabtree, Mercedes TX	.66/72
				M. D. Johnson, Rolling Fork/Grenda MS	73/91
				American Airpower Heritage Flying Museum,	
				Midland TX	9.91/92
- •	P-63A	42-69021	NX90805	stored in open, Van Nuys CA	.46/65
			N90805	Ronald Hasz, Scott City KS	72
				noted dism. in hangar, Van Nuys CA	2.73
				under rebuild Van Nuys CA	87/88
- •	P-63A	42-69080	NX32750	Cal Aero Technical Institute, Glendale CA	
				The Air Museum, Claremont CA	.53/69
			N32750	The Air Museum, Ontario CA	69
			N94501	Planes of Fame, Chino CA	76/79
				(rebuilt to fly, Palomar CA .79)	
				Yankee Air Corps, Chino CA	82/92
				(flies as "269080/"Fatal Fang")	

33-397 •	P-63A	42-69097	NX52113	Alfred Whiteside	.47/49
				(Bendix racer #87/"Kismet")	
				retired, stored	.52
			N52113	Jack Becker, Switzerland	54
				Johan M. Larsen, Minneapolis MN	66/72
				Military Aircraft restoration Corp, Chino CA	73/88
				Warbirds of GB Ltd, Biggin Hill	5.88/90
				(shipped to UK 5.88, stored dism.)	
				Old Flying Machine Co, Duxford	5.90/91
			G-BTWR	The Fighter Collection, Duxford	7.10.91/92
				(rebuild to fly, Duxford)	
				(id. also reported as 33-37: 42-68897)	
- •	RP-63A	42-70255		NASM, Silver Hill MD	65/87
- •	RP-63C	43-11117		USAFM: Yesterdays Air Force, Chino CA	76/79
				USAFM: Bradley Air Museum/New England	
				Air Museum, Windsor Locks CT	11.79/89
				(rest. project, Mooresville NC 82/88:	
				majority of airframe sold to YAC, Chino CA)	
				remaining parts of 43-11117 taken back by	
				USAFM, plus two wrecks recov. ex crash sites:	
				composite static rest., Malmstrom AFB MT	.89/92
				Yankee Air Corps, Chino CA	85/92
				(rebuild to fly Chino, using parts and adopting	
				id. of 44-4181/N9009)	
- •	P-63F	43-11719	NX1719	H. L. Pemberton (Bendix racer #21)	.46
			N443	Trans American Aviation Service, Chicago IL	54/63
				A. T. George, Atlanta GA	66/69
			N447AG	A. T. George, Atlanta GA	69
				Dr. Smith, Sarasota FL	69
			N6763	Jack Flaherty/Flaherty Factors Inc,	
				Hollistreet CA (race #28; #4; later #6)	74/77
				Whittington Brothers, Fort Lauderdale FL	77/81
				Confederate Air Force, Harlingen TX	10.8.81/91
				American Airpower Heritage Flying Museum,	
				Midland TX (flies as "411719")	9.91/92
				(FAA quote id. 296E11)	
- •	P-63E	43-11727		(to FA Hondurena as FAH 400) del.	15.10.48
			N9003R	Bob Bean Aircraft, Hawthorne CA	2.2.60/69
				stored Moseley Field, Phoenix AZ	69
				USAFM, Pima County Air Museum, Tucson AZ	73/88
				(displ. as "311727")	
- •	P-63E	43-11728		(to FA Hondurena as FAH 401) del.	10.48
			N41964	damaged landing, delivery flight, Tegucigalpa	15.10.48
				Bell Aircraft Corp (second cockpit mod.)	57
				USAFM, Wright-Patterson AFB, Dayton OH	1.58/90
				(displ. as "Moonlight Serenade")	
- •	P-63E	43-11729		(to FA Hondurena as FAH 402) del.	13.12.48
				crash landing FAH service	
				hulk on heap, Tegucigalpa FAHB	50s
			N9001R	ntu: Bob Bean Aircraft, Hawthorne CA	2.2.60
				displ. on pole,Tegucigalpa AB as "FAH402"	83/92
- •	P-63E	43-11730		(to FA Hondurena as FAH 403) del.	9.7.49
				damaged in FAH service	
			N9002R	ntu: Bob Bean Aircraft, Hawthorne CA	2.2.60
				rep. with Dan Chvatal, Jordan MN	83
_	P-63E	43-11731		(to FA Hondurena as FAH404) del.	9.7.49
			N9004R	Bob Bean Aircraft, Hawthorne CA	2.2.60
				Rufus E. Shackleford/CAF, Mercedes TX: del.	10.3.63/64
				destroyed by fire, TX	6.3.64

33-766 •	P-63C	44-4181	NX73744	Frank Singer, (Bendix racer #53)	47/49
			N73744	Harry R. Snoke, Fort Wayne IN	54
				Bruce Madison, Phoenix AZ	63/66
				crashed, Chicago IL	6.68
				Darryl Greenamyer, Las Vegas NV	69
			N9009	Larry H. Havens/Pylon Air, Long Beach CA	72
				(rebuilt Long Beach as highly modified racer, using several airframes : race #90)	
				crashed in Pacific Ocean on test flight from Long Beach CA : pilot baled out	7.9.72
				Don Anklin, Mooresville NC: salvaged wreck	84
				Yankee Air Corps, Chino CA	85/92
				(parts used in rest. of 43-11117)	
33-978	P-63C	44-4393	NX62822	Bird Airways, Long Beach CA	.46/48
	RP-63C			(Bendix racer #17)	
			N62822	Galen F. Bartmus, Kingman AZ	54
				Bruce M. Madison, Phoenix AZ	66
				John R. Sandberg, Minneapolis MN	69/75
				(race #28/"Tipsy Miss")	
				Mike Smith, Johnson KS	12.75
				Charles F Nichols/Yankee Air Corps, Chino CA	78
				(flew as "270134/What Price Speed")	
				Bob Reiser, San Francisco CA	81/84
				(flew in all red scheme as "44393/Cobra")	
				Southport Aviation Inc, Reno NV	.84/90
				The Fighter Collection, Duxford	.87/90
				(shipped ex Chino, arr. Duxford 6.1.88)	
				crashed, dest., nr La Ferte-Alais, France	4.6.90
_ •	RP-63G	45-57295		USAFM, Lackland AFB TX	65/92
	QF-63G			(displ. as "557295")	
-	P-63	-	N13350	reg. pending (id. "296A-5-3")	84/92
- •	RP-63C	-		displ. in park as memorial	50/60
				Confederate Air Force, Harlingen TX	84/86
				(hulk stored dism., Mesa AZ & Harlingen TX)	
				Planes of Fame East, Chino CA	89/92
				(rebuild to fly, Chino CA: due to fly .92)	
- •	RP-63C	-		displ. on pole, Fresno Air Terminal CA	50/68
				Yankee Air Corps, Chino CA	85/89
				(rest. to fly, Chino CA)	

BLACKBURN SKUA

- •	Mk. II	L2940		forced landing, sank, Lake Grotli, Norway	27.4.40
				Fleet Air Arm Museum, RNAS Yeovilton	.74/92
				(recov. from lake by RN team 8.74, displ. as recov., frozen lake diorama from 11.83)	

BLOHM VOSS Bv 155

V-3 •	Bv 155B	-		captured by RAF, Finkenwerder	5.45
				Royal Aircraft Establishment, Farnborough	.45
				(shipped to USA for trials as FE-505;T2-505)	
				Smithsonian Institute, stored Park Ridge IL	.46
				NASM, stored Silver Hill MD	66/89 _

2125 •	B-17D	40-3097		(19th BG, Philippines: "The Swoose") BOC	25.4.41
	RB-17D			(personal aircraft, General George H. Brett,	
				Australia & South America 42/44)	
				City of Los Angeles CA : displ. LA Airport	6.4.46/49
				Smithsonian Institution, Washington DC	3.49/61
				(stored Park Ridge IL, Pyote TX, Andrews AFB)	
				NASM, stored dism., Silver Hill MD	4.61/89
2257 •	B-17E	41-2446		(7th BG/22nd BS) BOC	6.12.41
				forced landing, Agaiambo Swamp PNG	23.2.42/91
				USAFM, Travis AFB CA (planned recov.)	85/91
2406 •	B-17E	41-2595		(conv. to XC-108A, to Africa/India .44)	
	XC-108A			sold as scrap, Dow Field, Bangor ME	c12.45
				stored, cut-up in sections, on local farm	45/85
				Steve Alex, Bangor ME	.85
				Michael W. Kellner, Crystal Lake IL: recov.	.85
				stored Galt Airport IL, long-term rest.	.85/90
2682 •	B-17E	41-9210		University of Minnesota - memorial displ.	8.11.45/52
			N5842N	Lysdale Flying Service, St. Paul MN	29.8.52
				Leeward Aeronautical Service, Ft. Wayne IN	3.12.52/55
			CF-ICB	Kenting Aviation, Toronto ONT	4.3.55/64
			N9720F	Four Star Aviation Inc, Miami FL	22.6.64
			CP-753	Compania Boliviana de Aviacion, La Paz	23.7.64
				Frigorificos Reyes, La Paz, Bolivia	74/90
				port u/c collapsed taxying La Paz	3.1.74
				crashed, landing San Borja	8.76
				(noted being rebuilt La Paz, Bolivia 80/90)	
			N8WJ	Whittington Brothers/World Jet Inc,	
				Fort Lauderdale FL: del.	3.90
				Scott D. Smith, Colorado Springs CO	92
2706 •	B-17E	41-9234		(for RAF as FL461: retained USAAF as FL461)	
				forced landed, Black Cat Pass PNG	
				planned recov.	c91
3170 •	B-17F	41-24485		(324th BS/"Memphis Belle")	
	TB-17F			City of Memphis TN : displ. Memphis	3.46/60
				displ. in open, Memphis Airport	65/84
				(complete static rest., Memphis ANGB 84/87)	
				Mud Island Museum, Memphis TN	5.87/92
				(displ. as "124485/DF-A/Memphis Belle")	
8310 •	B-17F	42-3374		MGM Studios, Culver City CA : dism.	.45/70
	(-DL)			Planes of Fame, Chino CA : dism.	.70/81
	RB-17F			USAFM, Beale AFB CA : rest. and displ.	.81/89
				USAFM, Offutt AFB NE : stored dism.	5.89/91
6403	B-17F	42-6107		Dept of Public Institutions, Clarkston WA	.46
	(-VE)	TB-17F		(instructional airframe - became derelict)	
			N1340N	Columbia Airmotive, Troutdale OR	18.11.53
				Aero Enterprises, Troutdale OR (tanker #35) 54/63	
				King Baker/Aero Enterprises Inc, Willows CA	
				& Fresno CA (tanker #E34)	13.9.64
				Aero Flite Inc, Cody WY (tanker #A34)	19.1.68/70
				(re-engined with 4 x RR Dart turboprops .69)	
				cr. fire bombing, Dubois, Yellowstone Pk. WY	18.8.70
				(note: crash date also quoted as 10.70)	
4896 •	B-17F	42-29782		City of Stuttgart AR : war memorial	9.46/53
	RB-17F			Gerald C. Francis, Stuttgart AR	.53
	B-17F		N6015V	Max & John Biegert, Lincoln NE	4.53
			N17W	Max L. Biegert, Lincoln NE : sprayer	3.54/61
				Central Aircraft Corp, Yakima WA : lease	54/55

				Abe Sellard, Stafford AZ : lease	60/61
				(conv. to fire tanker 5.60, tanker #E84)	
				Abe's Aerial Service, Stafford AZ	10.61/63
				Aircraft Specialties Inc, Mesa AZ	17.4.63/81
				(tanker #C84, #C44, #44, #04)	
				(flew in movie "1000 Plane Raid" .68, ferried to Hawaii for movie "Tora Tora Tora" 1.69)	
				Globe Air Inc, Mesa AZ (tanker #04)	18.2.81/84
				Bob Richardson/Portage Bay Inc, Seattle WA	11.6.85/90
				del. Mesa - Boeing Field, Seattle	20.6.85
				arr. Duxford UK for movie "Memphis Belle"	27.6.89
				Museum of Flight, Boeing Field, Seattle WA	9.90/92
5291	B-17F	42-30177		(388th BG USAAF)	
				to Free French Air Force; later French AF	
				("Charlene/ Bir Hakiem"), Wahn, W. Germany	-54
			F-BGSG	Institut Geographique National, Creil	55
				unconv., spares use only, scrapped Wahn	8.73
7190 •	B-17G	42-32076		91st BG/401st BS/ "Shoo Shoo Shoo Baby"	
				interned, Bulltofta, Malmo, Sweden	29.5.44
			SE-BAP	SAAB, reg. for flight test	2.11.45
			OY-DFA	DDL-Danish Airlines "Stig Viking"	5.11.45
				belly landing Blackbushe, UK	27.11.45
				(repaired, del. DDL Copenhagen 25.2.46) wfu	25.6.47
				(to R. Danish Army Air Corps as 67-672: "Store Bjoern")	31.3.48
				(to R. Danish Navy as 67-672)	1.12.49
				(to R. Danish AF as 67-672)	24.10.52
				retired, stored	1.10.53
				Babb Co Inc, New York NY	2.2.55
			F-BGSH	Institut Geographique National, Creil: del.	6.4.55/72
				last flight: retired Creil, became derelict	15.7.61/72
				USAFM : hulk donated by French Government	23.1.72/92
				dism., airfreighted to Wright Patterson AFB	4.2.72/78
				arr. dism. for rest., Dover AFB DE	7.72/88
				USAFM, Wright Patterson AFB, Dayton OH	10.88/92
				(del. Dover AFB-Wright Patterson AFB 13.10.88, displ. as "232076/91st BG/Shoo Shoo Baby")	
8946	B-17G	42-38160		recov. from Lake Zug, Switzerland	c47
				displ. St Gallen, Switzerland	68
				displ. St Moritz, Switzerland	.70/73
				(displ. as "238160/Lonesome Polecat/G")	
				rep. scrapped	c73
8217	B-17G	42-102715		Boy Scouts, Polo IL (memorial "Polo Queen")	9.46/52
	TB-17G		N66573	California Atlantic Airways, St Petersburg FL	12.4.52
				Fairchild Aerial Surveys ("Batmobile #33")	8.9.53
				Ewing Aviation, Los Angeles CA (#E85)	20.11.61
				Black Hills Aviation, Spearfish SD, later Alamogordo NM (tanker #A10,#B10, #10)	15.7.64/79
				crashed, fire bombing, Cayuse Saddle MT	7.79
				(FAA quote id. 32226)	
9300	B-17G	43-38322		Oklahoma Mil. Academy, Rogers County OK	46
				Frank J. Abel	5.1.48
				Alvin B. Graff, Dallas TX	11.5.49
			N66568	California Atlantic Airways, St Petersburg FL	18.1.51
			CB-80	Lloyd Aero Boliviano - LAB, La Paz	5.8.51
			CP-580	Lloyd Aero Boliviano - LAB, La Paz	1.10.54
				crashed La Paz, Bolivia	7.2.65
				rebuilt at La Paz	
			CP-936	Frigorificos Reyes, La Paz	.71
				crashed, San Ignacio de Moxos, Bolivia	11.2.72
9613 •	B-17G	43-38635	N3702G	National Metals Company, Phoenix AZ	31.7.59
	TB-17G			Louis A. Kordish, Long Beach CA	14.11.59

	EB-17G			Chas J. Fischer, Los Angeles CA	22.4.60
	ETB-17G			Edgar A. Neely/Fast-Way Air Service,	
	TB-17G			Long Beach CA	21.7.60/67
				(conv. to fire tanker .60, tanker #E61)	
				TBM Inc, Tulare CA (tanker #E61; #61)	25.4.67/79
				Aero Union Corp, Chico CA	1.11.79
				USAFM, Castle AFB CA : del.	26.11.79
				(displ. as "38635/A-N/Virgin's Delight")	10.80/92
22616 •	B-17G	44-6393		Government of Bolivia: ex Davis Monthan AFB	6.56
(-DL)	CB-17G			(civil conv. by Hamilton Aircraft, Tucson AZ)	
	VB-17G		CP-627	Lloyd Aero Boliviano - LAB, La Paz	1.57
	CB-17G			crashed, La Paz-El Alto	27.8.68
	VB-17G			(rebuilt, using parts of CP-580/43-38322)	
			CP-891	Frigorifico Reyes, La Paz	9.69/80
				USAFM, March AFB CA: del. ex La Paz	10.1.81/91
				(rest., displ. as "230092/Second Patches")	
7943 •	B-17G	44-8543		Federal Telecommunications Corporation,	
(-VE)					
	TB-17G			Teterboro NJ : leased ex USAF	.52/59
	ETB-17G			wfu, del. Teterboro-Davis Monthan AFB AZ	3.59
	JTB-17G		N3701G (2	American Compressed Steel, Cincinatti OH	18.8.59/60
				Aero American Corp, Tucson AZ	9.5.60/61
				Albany Building Corp, Fort Lauderdale FL	6.2.61
				John B. Gregory, Fort Lauderdale FL	15.5.62
				Dothan Aviation Corp, Dothan AL : sprayer	7.3.63/79
				Dr. William D. Hospers/B.C. Vintage Flying	
				Machines, Fort Worth TX	4.10.79/92
				(rest., flies as "48543/Chuckie")	
8246 •	B-17G	44-8846		(351st BG Polebrook, 305th BG Chelveston)	
(-VE)	RB-17G		F-BGSP	Institut Geographique National, Creil	9.12.54/85
			ZS-DXM	ntu: South African survey operations	.65
			F-BGSP	Institut Geographique National, Creil	65/85
			F-AZDX	IGN/Association GMF/Amicale Jean Salis	5.85
				IGN/Forteresse Toujours Volante Association	88/91
				(flew as "48846/W/Lucky Lady")	
				(based UK 6.89 for movie "Memphis Belle",	
				as "25703/DF-S/Mother & Country")	
				(now flies in camouflage, "22960/Pink Lady")	
8289 •	B-17G	44-8889	F-BGSO	Institut Geographique National, Creil	12.8.54
(-VE)				Musee de l'Air, Le Bourget, Paris	8.9.76/90
31957	B-17G	44-83316		retired to Davis Monthan AFB AZ	12.56/59
(-DL)	VB-17G			Norton AFB CA : del. for planned museum	4.59/64
				20th Century Fox Studios : dism.	.64/66
				(fuselage used as film prop. for TV series	
				"12 O'Clock High" as "11868", Chino CA)	
				badly dam. by movie "special effects", Chino	.66
				Black Hills Aviation, Spearfish SD	c67
				(forward fuse. used to rebuild B-17 N6694C)	
				fuse. hulk to Weeks Air Museum, Tamiami FL	c83/90
				fuse. sections stored Borrego Springs CA	88/90
32103 •	B-17G	44-83462		(to FA Braziliera as B17-5408)	.54
(-DL)	SB-17G			displ. Natal AB, Brazil	
				Museu Aerospacial da FA, Rio de Janeiro	81/85
				(44-83718 also quoted)	
32153 •	B-17G	44-83512		USAFM, Lackland AFB, San Antonio TX	.56/92
(-DL)	TB-17G			(displ. as "483512/Heavens Above/H-T")	
32155 •	B-17G	44-83514		retired to Davis-Monthan AFB AZ	27.1.59

(-DL)	RB-17G		N9323Z	Acme Aircraft Parts, Compton CA	31.7.59/60
	DB-17G			Western Air Industries, Anderson CA	11.60/62
	DB-17P			(conv. Anderson CA .60 to fire tanker #E17)	
				Aero Union Corp, Chico CA (#C17, #17)	6.6.62/78
				(rest. to USAAF "483514/Class of 44" .77)	
				Confederate Air Force, Mesa AZ	17.1.78/91
				dam. landing Burbank CA : later repaired	11.88
				American Airpower Heritage Flying Museum, Midland TX	9.91/92
				(flies as "483514/Sentimental Journey")	
32166 •	B-17G	44-83525		retired to Davis-Monthan AFB, Tucson AZ	4.59
(-DL)	DB-17G			last B-17 held at Davis Monthan AFB: displ.	64/67
			N83525	Tallmantz Aviation, Orange County CA: del.	12.1.68
				(flew in movie "1000 Plane Raid", Santa Maria CA 1.68 as "25053/KY-L/Balls of Fire")	
			N4250	ntu: Tallmantz Aviation	
			N83525	Tallmantz/International Flight & Space Museum, Orange County CA	68/72
				I. N. Burchinall Jnr, Paris TX	10.72/83
				(flew for movie "MacArthur" as "KY-L/Suzy Q")	
				(displ. in museums Kissimmee FL & Eloy AZ)	
				Weeks Air Museum, Tamiami FL	11.4.83/92
				(del. Tamiami FL 6.6.87, ex storage Paris TX, static displ. as "KY-L/Suzy Q")	
				Picked up and damaged Hurricane Andrew	24.8.92
32183	B-17G	44-83542	N9324Z	Acme Aircraft Parts, Compton CA	10.9.59
(-DL)	DB-17G			Western Air Industries, Anderson CA	11.60/62
	DB-17P			(conv. to fire tanker 10.61, tanker #E16)	
				Aero Union Corp, Anderson, later Chico CA	6.6.62/71
				(tanker #C18, #E18)	
				crashed firebombing, near Benson AZ	12.7.71
				Desert Air Parts, Tucson AZ : wreck	75/82
				New England Air Museum CT : not collected	
				Weeks Air Museum, Tamiami FL	87/90
				(stored dism., Borrego Springs CA)	
32187 •	B-17G	44-83546		stored Davis-Monthan AFB AZ	10.54/59
(-DL)	CB-17G		N3703G	National Metals Company, Phoenix AZ	31.7.59
	VB-17G			Edgar A. Neely/Fast-Way Air Service, Long Beach CA	11.9.59/67
				(conv. to fire tanker 7.60, #E75, later #E78)	
				TBM Inc, Tulare CA	25.4.67/82
				(tanker #E78; #E68; #68)	
				Military Aircraft Restoration Corp, Chino CA	9.82/92
				(flew as camouflaged "230604/LN-T")	
				loaned: USAFM, March AFB CA	83/91
				(rest. Chino 88/89 as "124485/Memphis Belle")	
				arr. Duxford UK for movie "Memphis Belle"	20.6.89
32200 •	B-17G	44-83559		USAFM, Offutt AFB NE : del.	5.59/91
(-DL)	DB-17G			(displ. as "23474/EP-B/King Bee")	
	DB-17P				
32204 •	B-17G	44-83563		American Compressed Steel, Cincinatti OH	18.8.59
(-DL)	CB-17G		N9563Z	Aero American Corp, Tucson AZ	9.5.60/63
	VB-17G			Columbia Pictures Inc NY : lease	11.10.61
				(arr. Gatwick 8.10.61 for movie "The War Lover" flew as"127742/DF-T")	
				(dep. UK 16.5.62: stored Ryan Field AZ)	
				Aircraft Specialties Inc, Mesa AZ	2.2.63/81
				(tanker #E24, #C24, #24, #89)	
				(flew to Hawaii for movie "Tora Tora Tora" 1.69)	
				Globe Air Inc, Mesa AZ (tanker #89)	18.2.81/85
				National Warplane Museum, Geneseo NY	10.85/92
				(flies as "297400/Fuddy Duddy/K-E")	

32216 •	B-17G	44-83575		USAF: atomic tests Yucca Flats NV	.52
(-DL)	TB-17H			Valley Scrap Metal, Phoenix AZ	4.65
	SB-17G		N93012	Aircraft Specialities Inc, Mesa AZ	5.5.65/81
				(rebuilt test site NV, ferried to Mesa 14.5.65)	
				stored unconv., Mesa : stripped for spares	69/77
				(conv. to tanker, Mesa .77, #99/"Lady Yukka")	
				Globe Air Inc, Mesa AZ (tanker #99)	4.81/85
				Bob Collings/Collings Foundation, Stowe MA	10.85/92
				del. Mesa AZ-Kissimmee FL for military rest.	28.1.87
				crashed, landing Beaver County PA	23.8.87
				(repaired, del. Kissimmee 1.91 for full rest.)	
				(flies as "231909/Nine-O-Nine/A-R")	
32265 •	B-17G	44-83624		USAFM, Wright-Patterson AFB OH : del.	17.6.57/89
(-DL)	MB-17G			(displ. as "483624/VE")	
	TB-17P			USAFM, Dover AFB DE : arr. dism. for rest.	16.6.89/91
DB-17P					
32304 •	B-17G	44-83663		(to FA Brasileira as B17-5400)	5.51
(-DL)	TB-17G			USAFM, Wright-Patterson AFB OH : stored	10.68/73
				(arr. Wright-Patterson on del. ex Brazil 5.10.68)	
			N47780	USAFM: loan Yesterdays Air Force, Chino CA	15.6.73/86
				displ. Combat Air Museum, Topeka KS : del.	.77/80
				displ. Yesterdays AF, St. Petersburg FL : del.	13.7.80/86
				USAFM, Hill AFB UT : arr. dism.	11.86/91
				(rest., displ. as "483663/Short Bier")	
32325 •	B-17G	44-83684		last operational USAF B-17, retired to	
	DB-17G			Davis Monthan AFB AZ	8.59
	DB-17P		N3713G	Ed Maloney/The Air Museum, Claremont CA	24.9.59/70
				The Air Museum, Ontario, later Chino CA	.63/71
				(used in TV series "12 O'Clock High", Chino CA	
				64/66 as "23921/Piccadilly Lily/HP-V")	
				Planes of Fame, Chino CA	71/92
				(static displ. Chino as "483684/Picadilly Lily")	
32331 •	B-17G	44-83690		USAFM, Grissom AFB IN	.61/91
(-DL)	DB-17G			(displ. as "48385/Tarnished Angel/WF-Y, later	
	DB-17P			displ. as "231255/Miss Liberty Belle/XK-D")	
32359 •	B-17G	44-83718		(to FA Brazil as B17-5408)	.55
(-DL)	TB-17H			displ. Natal AB, Brazil	70
	SB-17G			displ. Museu do FAB, Rio de Janeiro	80/90
32363	B-17G	44-83722		atomic tests, Yucca Flats NV, badly damaged	.52/65
(-DL)	B-17H			Valley Scrap Metal, Phoenix AZ : hulk	.65
	TB-17H			Aircraft Specialities Inc, Mesa AZ	.65/81
	SB-17G			(trucked NV-Mesa 5.65, stripped for spares)	
				Globe Air, Mesa AZ : stored hulk	2.81/85
				Weeks Air Museum, Tamiami FL	.85/90
				(dism. hulk stored, Borrego Springs CA)	
32370	B-17G	44-83729		Institut Geographique National, Creil	10.12.47
(-DL)			F-BEED	Institut Geographique National, Creil "Denise"	11.6.48
				wfu and broken-up for spares, Creil	.62
				hulk rep. still at Creil	70/73
32376 •	B-17G	44-83735	NL68269	Transocean Air Lines Inc, Oakland CA	17.2.47
(-DL)				(conv. to executive configuration)	
				Col. Andres Soriano/ Phil. A/L "San Miguel"	12.1.49
				Assembly of God Inc, Springfield MO	4.10.49
			N68629	Leeward Aeronautical, Fort Wayne IN	7.11.51
			F-BDRS	Institut Geographique National, Creil	23.8.52/75
				wfu : noted as hulk, Creil by	72
				Euroworld Ltd, Duxford UK	24.5.75/78
				Imperial War Museum, Duxford	.78/90

				(displ. as "231983/Mary Alice/IY-G")	
32398	B-17G	44-83757	N5198N	SECA, Le Bourget	
(-DL)				Institut Geographique National, Creil	25.7.50
			F-BDRR	Institut Geographique National, Creil	16.9.50/72
				retired, Creil	.62
				noted as derelict hulk, Creil	72
32426 •	B-17G	44-83785	N809Z	Atlantic General Enterprises, Washington DC	1.9.60/62
(-DL)	CB-17G			Intermountain Aviation Inc, Phoenix AZ	4.10.62/75
	VB-17G			(CIA operations,"Skyhook" in nose; conv. to	
				fire tanker, Marana 7.69, #22, #C71, #B71)	
				Evergreen Helicopters, Marana AZ	1.3.75/78
				(tanker #71)	
			N207EV	Evergreen Helicopters, Marana AZ	6.3.79/92
				(tanker #22)	
				Evergreen Equity/747 Inc, McMinnville OR	19.7.85/92
				(rest. to military config., Marana AZ .89/90,	
				flies as USAF "483785/K")	
				(note: id. changed by Atlantic General	
				from 44-85531 to 44-83785 in 5.61)	
32431 •	B-17G	44-83790		forced landed, Newfoundland	24.12.47
(-DL)				located almost intact (5429N/6612W)	.70
32455 •	B-17G	44-83814		North Dakota Public School District, Hazen ND	.47/51
(-DL)			N66571	California Atlantic Airways, St Petersburg FL	20.6.51/53
			CF-HBP	Kenting Aviation Ltd, Toronto ONT: del.	12.5.53/71
				Photographic Survey Corp, Toronto ONT	15.5.57/60
				Hunting Survey Corp, Toronto ONT	11.2.60/62
				Kenting Aviation Ltd, Toronto ONT	9.4.62/71
			N66571	Arnold Kolb/Black Hills Aviation,	
				Spearfish SD, later Alamogordo NM	1.4.71/82
				(conv. to tanker #A18,#18,#C13,#09)	
				NASM, Washington DC	19.1.82/92
				displ. Pima Air Museum AZ (as "483814")	82/84
				del. to Washington-Dulles for NASM : stored	25.4.84/92
32504 •	B-17G	44-83863		(to USN as Bu 77231) BOC 16.7.45 SOC	25.8.55
(-DL)	PB-1W		N5233V	American Compressed Steel Corp, Dallas TX	12.57
			N6464D	ntu: Von E. Carstedt/Carstedt Air,	
				Long Beach CA : sale not completed	
			N5233V	Marson Equipment & Salvage Co, Tucson AZ	26.2.60/61
				Aero Union Corp, Anderson CA	27.9.61
				Rogue Flying Services, Medford OR	3.1.62/63
				(conv. to fire tanker 7.62, tanker #F71)	
				Aero Ag Inc, Medford OR (tanker #F71)	1.4.63/69
				Idaho Aircraft Corp, Boise ID	71
				Aero Union Corp, Chico CA (tanker #D1,#18)	6.6.71/75
				USAFM, Eglin AFB FL : del.	19.6.75/91
				(displ. as "4-83863", later "46106/X")	
32505	B-17G	44-83864		(to USN as Bu 77232) BOC	14.7.45
(-DL)	PB-1W		N5234V	American Compressed Steel Corp/	
				Henry L. Seale Aviation Supply Co, Dallas TX	11.12.57
			N6465D	ntu: Von E. Carstedt/Carstedt Air,	
				Long Beach CA : sale not completed	
			XB-BOE	CIA Mexicana Aero Foto, Mexico City	3.1.58/63
			N73648	Cal Nat Airways, Grass Valley CA	66
				(rebuilt Grass Valley, conv. to tanker #B11)	
				Black Hills Aviation, Spearfish SD (#E56)	69/72
				crashed, Silver City NM	12.7.72
				(note: N73648 rep. rebuilt Spearfish .69 as	
				composite using parts from several aircraft:	
				see 44-83814/N66571)	
32509 •	B-17G	44-83868		(to USN as Bu 77233) BOC	14.7.45
(-DL)	PB-1W		N5237V	American Compressed Steel Corp, Dallas TX	12.57/60

			N6466D	ntu: Von E. Carstedt/Carstedt Air,	
				Long Beach CA : sale not completed	
				(unconv., USN "XD-2", Dallas-Love .58/60)	
			N5237V	Aero Union Corp, Chico CA	.60
				Calvin J. Butler/Butler Farm Air,	
				Redmond OR (tanker #E15)	63/69
				Butler Aircraft Co, Redmond OR	74/77
				(tanker #F15; #65)	
				TBM Inc, Sequoia CA (tanker #65)	79/83
				RAF Museum, Hendon : arr.	9.12.83/92
				(conv. back to military config. as "483868" at	
				Sequoia CA, del. to RAF Bize Norton 3-13.10.83)	
32513 •	B-17G	44-83872		(to USN as Bu 77235) BOC 16.7.45 : SOC	25.8.55
(-DL)	PB-1W			arr. Litchfield Park NAS AZ for storage	15.1.55/58
			N7227C	Aero Service Corp, Philadelphia PA	1.10.57/67
				op. on survey work, by Aeroflex : wfu	10.63
				Confederate Air Force, Mercedes TX , later	
				Harlingen TX	13.4.67/91
				(flew as "124592/Texas Raiders")	
				American Airpower Heritage Flying Museum,	
				Midland TX	9.91/92
				(flies as "483872/Texas Raiders/VP-X")	
32525 •	B-17G	44-83884		(to USN as Bu 77244) BOC 25.7.45 SOC	10.7.56
(-DL)	PB-1W		N5230V	American Compressed Steel Corp, Dallas TX	2.12.57/60
			N6471D	ntu: Von E. Carstedt/Carstedt Air,	
				Long Beach CA : sale not completed	
				(unconv., USN "XD-10", Dallas-Love 58/61)	
			N5230V	Marson Equipment & Salvage Co, Tucson AZ	18.10.60
				Aero Union Corp, Chico CA	27.9.61/79
				(tanker #C19; #E19, #19)	
				USAFM, Barksdale AFB LA	.80/91
				(displ. as "338289/Yankee Doodle II")	
8492 •	B-17G	44-85583		(to FA Brazil as B17-5402)	6.53
(-VE)	TB-17H			displ. Recife AB, Brazil	3.73/89
	SB-17G				
8503	B-17G	44-85594		Institut Geographique National, Creil	28.9.54
(-VE)			F-BGSQ	Institut Geographique National, Creil	7.10.54/72
				scrapped Creil	.72
8508 •	B-17G	44-85599		USAF, retired to Davis Monthan AFB AZ	8.59
(-VE)	EDB-17G			96th BG Memorial Association, Abilene	
	DB-17G			Municiple Airport, Abilene TX : del.	10.60/74
	DB-17P			(displ. as "0-5599/X/Black Hawk")	
				USAFM, Dyess AFB, Abilene TX	.74/90
				(rest., displ. as "485599/A")	
8552	B-17G	44-85643		Institut Geographique National, Creil	12.12.47
(-VE)			F-BEEA	Institut Geographique National, Creil	22.6.48/89
				"Chateau de Verneuil"	
				(based UK for movie "Memphis Belle" 6.89)	
				crashed and dest. by fire, RAF Binbrook UK	25.7.89
8627 •	B-17G	44-85718		Institut Geographique National, Creil	10.12.47
(-VE)			F-BEEC	Institut Geographique National, Creil	3.8.48
			ZS-EEC	I.G.N., "Charlotte"	8.65/66
			F-BEEC	Institut Geographique National, Creil	8.66/84
				wfu Creil	.78/84
			G-FORT	Warbirds of GB, Blackbushe: del.	8.6.84/86
				Patina Ltd, Duxford	.86/87
			N900RW	Robert L.Waltrip/Air SRV Inc, Anderson TX	9.6.87
				(del. ex Duxford, arr. Houston TX 16.7.87)	
				Lone Star Flight Museum, Galveston TX	11.87/92

				(flies as "238050/U-BN/Thunderbird")	
8637	B-17G	44-85728	NX4600	Trans World Airlines, Kansas City MO	26.6.46
(-VE)	Model			executive conversion, by Boeing at Seattle	.46
	299AB		NL1B	TWA (Fleet #242)	2.12.46/47
			EP-HIM	Shah of Persia, Tehran	4.47
			F-BGOE	SECA, Le Bourget, Paris	
				Institut Geographique National, Creil	12.7.52/70
				last flight 22.8.67 : broken-up, Creil	.70
				(note: F-BGOE also quoted as 44-83728)	
8643 •	B-17G	44-85734		Esperado Mining Co, Altus OK : for scrap	25.6.47
(-VE)	Model		N5111N	Pratt & Whitney Engines, Hartford CT	11.47/67
	299Z			(civil conv. by Boeing, Seattle .48, 5th engine in	
				nose, tested P&W T34 & T64 turboprops)	
				Bradley Air Museum, Windsor Locks CT: del.	16.6.67/81
				badly damaged at museum, by tornado	3.10.79
				New England Air Museum CT : wreck stored	81/87
				Tom Reilly Vintage Aircraft, Kissimmee FL	.87/91
				(stored dam. Windsor Locks CT 79/92,	
				planned rebuild to fly, using parts of N6694C)	
8647 •	B-17G	44-85738		AMVETS Chapter 56, Tulare CA: del.	4.8.58/92
(-VE)	DB-17G			displ. Perry's Coffee House, Tulare CA	.71/81
	EDB-17G			displ. AMVETS compound, Tulare CA	.81/92
	DB-17G			dam. by truck running off highway (repaired)	8.82
				(displ. as "0-85738/K")	
8649 •	B-17G	44-85740		Metal Products Inc, Amarillo TX : scrap	17.6.47
(-VE)			NL5017N	Universal Aviation Inc, Tulsa OK	10.7.47
				Charles T. Winters, Miami FL	2.8.47
				Vero Beach Export & Imp. Co, Vero Beach FL	16.8.47/49
			N5017N	Aero Services Corp, Philadelphia PA	27.6.49/62
				Chris D. Stoltzfus & Assoc., Coatesville PA	10.8.62/66
				Dothan Aviation Corp, Dothan AL : sprayer	12.66/78
				William E. Harrison, Tulsa OK	20.2.78/80
				EAA Aviation Foundation, Oshkosh WI	8.80/92
				(flies as "85740/Aluminum Overcast/FU-D")	
8683	B-17G	44-85774		Government of Bolivia: ex Davis Monthan AFB	22.6.56
(-VE)	VB-17G			(civil conv. by Hamilton Aircraft, Tucson AZ)	
			CP-621	Lloyd Aero Boliviano, La Paz	12.56/68
			N621L	Aircraft Specialties Inc, Mesa AZ	12.68/75
				(flew to Hawaii for movie "Tora Tora Tora" 1.69)	
				(tanker #C64, #64)	
				crashed, dest.	7.75
8687 •	B-17G	44-85778	N3509G	Ace Smelting Inc, Phoenix AZ	14.8.59
(-VE)	TB-17G			Sonora Flying Service, Columbia CA	20.9.60/61
	VB-17G			Leo J. Demers, Madras OR (tanker #97)	25.5.61/66
				Aero Union Corp, Chico CA (tanker #E16)	29.4.66/72
				William A. Dempsay/Central Air Service,	
				Rantoul KS (tanker #F42,#42,#102)	2.6.72/78
				Western Air Contractors, American Fork UT	6.7.78/81
				Westernair of Albuquerque, Albuquerque NM	15.6.81/82
				Richard Vartanian/Aircraft Component	
				Equipment Supplies Inc, Klamath Falls OR	28.3.82/90
				(stored, Stockton CA 84/91)	
				Arthur W. McDonnell, Mojave CA	7.90
				Florida Aircraft Leasing Corp, Miami FL	2.91
				Robert L. Waltrip/Lone Star Flight Museum,	
				Galveston TX & Don Whittington/World Jet	
				International, Fort Lauderdale FL	4.91/92
				(flies as "4485778/Miss Museum of Flying")	
				Warbirds of Great Britain, Bournemouth	10.92
				(to fly as "Sally A")	
8693 •	B-17G	44-85784		General Electric Flight Test Center,	

c/n	Type	Serial	Reg.	History	Date
(-VE)	EB-17G			Schenectady NY : leased ex USAF	9.50/54
	ETB-17G		F-BGSR	Institut Geographique National, Creil	10.54/75
			N17TE	Ted White & Duane Egli/Euroworld Inc,	
				Biggin Hill/Duxford UK: del. ex Creil	16.3.75
			G-BEDF	M. H. Campbell, Duxford	5.8.76/79
				B-17 Preservation Trust Ltd, Duxford	.79/92
				(flies as "24485/Sally B")	
8699 •	B-17G	44-85790		Art Lacey, Portland OR	5.3.47/92
(-VE)				(del. flight ex Altus AFB OK 8-10.3.47)	
				displ. Lacy's gas station, Oregon City OR	.47/92
8721	B-17G	44-85812		(to USCG as Bu 77246)	
(-VE)	PB-1G		N4710C	Delta Leasing Corp, Charlotte NC	16.5.58
				Leroy Brown, Miami FL	23.1.59
				M. E. Brown Inc, Bowling Green FL	13.1.60/61
				Challenger Leasing Corp, Fort Lauderdale FL	4.4.61/63
				Dothan Aviation Corp, Dothan AL : sprayer	16.4.63/76
				in-flight fire, crashed Blakeley GA	5.8.76
8722	B-17G	44-85813		Curtiss-Wright Corp, Caldwell NJ : leased	10.45/57
(-VE)	EB-17G			(conv. Boeing,Wichita KS .46: 5th engine in nose)	
	JB-17G		N6694C	Curtiss-Wright Corp, Woodbridge CT	30.8.57/66
	Model			Ewing Aviation Co, San Ramon CA	1.12.66/69
	299Z			Ewing-Kolb Aircraft, Spearfish SD	15.8.69/70
				Arnold Kolb/Black Hills Aviation,	
				Spearfish SD, later Alamogordo NM	30.7.70/80
				(rebuilt Spearfish .69/70, fitted standard	
				forward fuse. ex 44-83316: tanker #C12,#12)	
				crashed, firebombing, Bear Pen NC	16.4.80
				Tom Reilly Vintage Aircraft, Kissimmee FL	85/90
				(wreck parts to be used to rebuild N5111N)	
8737 •	B-17G	44-85828		(to USCG as Bu 77254) BOC 14.8.45 SOC	10.59
(-VE)	PB-1G			disposal ex NAS Elizabeth City NC	10.59
			N9323R	Joe E. Marrs, Opa Locka FL	8.3.60
				Serv-Air Inc, Westchester NY	9.4.60/62
				Tropical Export Trading Co, Ft. Lauderdale FL	23.5.62
				Hugh Wheelus/Dothan Aviation, Dothan AL	17.7.62
				Black Hills Aviation, Spearfish SD	4.10.62/69
				(tanker #B30)	
				Aeroflite Inc, Cody WY (tanker #B30,#37)	71/75
				Bruce Kinney/Kinney Air Tankers, Richey MT	12.75/78
				Aircraft Specialties Inc, Mesa AZ (#37)	18.5.78/80
				USAFM, Pima County Air Museum, Tucson AZ	7.12.80/92
				(displ. as "485828", later "231892/I'll Be Around")	
8738 •	B-17G	44-85829		(to USCG as Bu 77255) BOC 9.46 SOC	5.59
(-VE)	PB-1G			disposal ex NAS Elizabeth City NC	5.59
			N3193G	Ace Smelting Inc, Phoenix AZ	11.5.59
				Fairchild Aerial Surveys, Los Angeles CA	11.59/65
				Aero Service Corp, Philadelphia PA	2.8.65
				Biegert Bros, Shickley NE : sprayer	1.10.65/66
				Aircraft Specialties Inc, Mesa AZ	19.3.66/81
				(tanker #C34; #34)	
				(flew to Hawaii for movie "Tora Tora Tora" 1.69)	
				Globe Air Inc, Mesa AZ (tanker #34)	18.2.81/86
				Yankee Air Force Inc, Willow Run MI : del.	2.7.86/92
				(rest. to fly as "485829/Yankee Lady")	
8749	B-17G	44-85840		Government of Bolivia: ex Davis Monthan AFB	22.6.56
(-VE)				(civil conv. Tucson AZ by Hamilton Aircraft)	
			CP-620	Lloyd Aero Boliviano, La Paz	11.56/68
			N620L	Aircraft Specialties Inc, Mesa AZ	12.68/73
				(flew to Hawaii for movie "Tora Tora Tora" 1.69)	
				damaged landing during filming, Honolulu HI	c3.69

				(tanker #C54, #54) crashed firebombing, near Elko NV	 12.7.73
- •	B-17	-		fuselage and nose section, noted Universal Studios, Hollywood CA	 9.88

BOEING B-29 SUPERFORTRESS

4452	B-29	42-24791		stored NAS China Lake CA (ground target) USAFM, Beale AFB CA (nose only, grafted to museum building)	60/80 86/89
7287	B-29	42-93880		stored NAS China Lake CA	60/75
7384 •	B-29A	42-93967		War Veterans Memorial, Cordele GA	79/85
10561 •	B-29	44-69729		stored NAS China Lake CA USAFM, Lowry AFB CO	56/85 .86/88
10789	B-29	44-69957		stored NAS China Lake CA removed by	60/75 85
10815 •	B-29	44-69983		stored NAS China Lake CA Sandia Atomic Museum, Kirtland AFB NM derelict, dismantled (museum failed) by USAFM, Travis AFB CA (parts only) USAFM, Saipan, Marianas	60/68 74/76 76 86 85
10816	B-29	44-69984		rep. NAS China Lake CA	75
10848 •	B-29 TB-29	44-70016		displ. MASDC, Davis-Monthan AFB AZ USAFM, Pima County Air Museum, Tucson AZ	65/69 .69/92
10881 •	B-29	44-70049		stored NAS China Lake CA listed by USAFM, Travis AFB CA Weeks Air Museum, Tamiami FL stored dism. at Borrego Springs CA	60/85 87 87/91 87/91
10896	B-29	44-70064		stored NAS China Lake CA USAFM, Castle AFB CA (used in composite rebuild with 44-61535: displ. as "461535/"Raz'n Hell")	57/80 .80
10934	B-29	44-70102		stored NAS China Lake CA removed by	60/75 85
10945 •	B-29 TB-29	44-70113		stored Aberdeen Proving Grounds MD Florence Air & Missile Museum, Florence SC stored dism. Florence as "Z-58"	60/73 .73/90 90
11012	B-29A	44-61535		stored NAS China Lake CA : del. USAFM, Castle AFB CA (composite rebuild with 44-70064: displ. as "461535/Raz'n Hell")	2.57/80 .80/92
11146 •	B-29A SB-29A	44-61669	 N3299F	stored NAS China Lake CA USAFM: loaned David C. Tallichet/ Yesterdays Air Force : stored Barstow CA USAFM, March AFB CA : del.	60/75 74/81 5.8.81/92
11148 •	B-29A	44-61671		stored Aberdeen Proving Grounds MD USAFM, Pease AFB NH	60/74 79/90
11216 •	B-29A	44-61739		stored Aberdeen Proving Grounds MD	60/85
11225 •	B-29A TB-29A	44-61748	 G-BHDK	stored NAS China Lake CA : del. Imperial War Museum, Duxford (ferried China Lake-Tucson AZ 11.79:	11.56/79 27.9.79/92

					del. Tucson-Duxford 17.2.80 to 2.3.80)	
					(displ. as "461748/"Hawg Wild")	
11434		B-29A	44-61957		stored NAS China Lake CA	60/75
11452	•	B-29A	44-61975		stored Aberdeen Proving Grounds MD	60/73
		TB-29A			Bradley Air Museum, Windsor Locks CT: arr.	21.6.73/85
					badly damaged by tornado at museum	3.10.79
					New England Air Museum, Windsor Locks CT	84/92
					(displayed as "461975")	
11469		B-29A	44-61992		stored NAS China Lake CA	60/75
11499	•	B-29A	44-62022		stored NAS China Lake CA	60/75
					Fred E. Weisbrod Aircraft Museum, Pueblo CO	78/90
					(displ. as "62022/18/Peachy")	
11532		B-29A	44-62055		stored NAS China Lake CA	60/75
11547	•	B-29A	44-62070		stored NAS China Lake CA	58/71
				N4249	Confederate Air Force, Harlingen TX	23.3.71/81
					(del. China Lake-Harlingen 3.8.71)	
				N529B	Confederate Air Force, Harlingen TX	8.81/91
					American Airpower Heritage Flying Museum, Midland TX (flies as "Fifi")	9.91/92
11565		B-29A	44-62088		stored NAS China Lake CA	60/75
11589	•	B-29A	44-62112		Pima County Air Museum, Tucson AZ	83/85
					(forward fuselage only; rear to Disney studios)	
11616	•	B-29A	44-62139		USAFM, Wright-Patterson AFB, Dayton OH	90/92
					(fuselage only: displ. as "Command Decision")	
11680	•	B-29A	44-62203		stored Aberdeen Proving Grounds MD	60/85
11697	•	B-29A	44-62220		stored Aberdeen Proving Grounds MD	60/85
					USAFM, Kelly AFB TX	88
11699	•	B-29A	44-62222		stored NAS China Lake CA	60/75
					Pima County Air Museum, Tucson AZ (forward fuselage only; rear Disney studios)	83/85
12430	•	B-29	44-87627		stored Aberdeen Proving Grounds MD	60/85
12582	•	B-29	44-87779		stored NAS China Lake CA	56/85
					USAFM, Ellsworth AFB SD	.85/88
13633	•	B-29	45-21739		stored NAS China Lake CA	60/68
					Korean War Museum, Seoul, South Korea	72/87
13643	•	B-29A	45-21749		USAFM, Chanute AFB IL	65/88
13657	•	B-29	45-21763		("Kee Bird"): forced landing in snow, 200m north of Thule, Greenland	.47
					rediscovered, complete	72/85
13681	•	B-29	45-21787		(to USN as Bu84029: NACA 137 "Fertile Myrtle")	
		P2B-1S			retired to NAS Litchfield Park AZ	10.59/69
				N91329	American Air Museum, Oakland CA	.69/84
					(rest. Tucson AZ, del. to Oakland CA 11.69)	
					stored in open, Oakland CA	77/89
					(aborted del. flight Oakland-Stockton CA .84)	
					Kermit A. Weeks, Tamiami FL	7.84
				N29KW	Weeks Air Museum,Tamiami FL	8.85/92
					(trucked Oakland-FL .89, stored dism.)	

c/n		Type	Serial	History	Date
-	•	B-29	42-65281	stored NAS China Lake CA ("Miss America")	60/85 SB-29
				USAFM, Travis AFB CA	86/90
				(del. dism. by C-5A: many parts missing)	
				(displ. as "Miss America")	
-	•	B-29	44-27297	(509th CG/ 393rd CS: "Bockscar")	
				stored Davis- Monthan AFB AZ	48/61
				USAFM, Wright-Patterson AFB OH: del.	26.9.61/92
-	•	B-29	44-27343	stored Aberdeen Proving Grounds MD	60/85
				USAFM, Tinker AFB SD	88
-	•	B-29B TB-29B	44-84053	stored Aberdeen Proving Grounds MD	60/74
				USAFM, Robins AFB GA	85/91
-	•	B-29B TB-29B	44-84076	USAFM, Offutt AFB NE	65/91
				(displ. as "0-484076/Man-o-War")	
-	•	B-29B SB-29B	44-84084	stored NAS China Lake CA	60/85
				listed by USAFM, Travis AFB CA	87
				Weeks Air Museum, Tamiami FL	87/91
				stored dism., Borrego Springs CA	87/91
-	•	B-29	44-86292	(509th CG / 393rd CS: "Enola Gay")	
				NASM, open storage, Andrews AFB MD	59
				NASM, stored dism., Silver Hill MD	65/92
				(under rest. for display)	
-		B-29	44-86402	Aircraft Industries Museum, Louisville KY	c73
-	•	B-29	44-86408	USAFM, Hill AFB UT	88/90
-	•	B-29	-	USAF: forced landing, wheels-up, in snow	
				Elizabeth Islands, near North Pole : abandoned	.47/90
				recov. project, planned to fly out	90
225008	•	Tu-4		(Chinese AF 41048) : turboprop conv.	
				Chinese AF Museum, Datangshan, Beijing	90
2208501	•	Tu-4		(Chinese AF 4114) : turboprop conv.	
				Chinese AF Museum, Datangshan, Beijing	90
2805103	•	Tu-4	-	(Soviet AF ......)	
				Soviet AF Museum, Monino AB, Moscow	90
				(displ. as "01")	

BOULTON PAUL DEFIANT

c/n		Type	Serial	History	Date
-	•	Mk. I	N1671	RAF St.Athan : displ. as "N1617"	61/67
				RAF Museum, Hendon	74/91
				(displ. as "N1671/DE-W")	

BREWSTER BUCCANEER

c/n		Type	Serial	History	Date
-	•	A-34 Mk. I	FF860	abandoned on airfield dump, Tullahoma TN	45/73
				Military Aircraft Restoration Corp, Chino CA	.73/88
-	•	A-34 Mk. I	-	abandoned on airfield dump, Tullahoma TN	45/73
				Military Aircraft Restoration Corp, Chino CA	.73/88
-	•	A-34 Mk. I	-	abandoned on airfield dump, Tullahoma TN	45/73
				Military Aircraft Restoration Corp, Chino CA	.73/80
				Brewster Restoration Project/Naval Air Development Center, Warminster PA	.80/90
				(under rest.)	
-	•	A-34 Mk. I	-	abandoned on airfield dump, Tullahoma TN	c53/73
				hulk displ., Tullahoma TN	84/88

EAA EAGLE HANGAR

Money to build this magnificent museum was raised in part by members of the EAA Warbirds of America – a Division of the Experimental Aircraft Association. If you like military aircraft, you'll find many friends among EAA Warbirds. You'll like the company, the airplanes, the activities! Annual membership $30. (EAA membership required)

For more information call:
1-800-322-2412
(in Canada call 1-800-843-3612)
(overseas call 1-414-426-4800)
Fax (414) 426-4873

EAA Warbirds of America
EAA Aviation Center
Oshkosh, WI 54903-3065

A Tribute to Heroes

Aviation history is on display in the fabulous EAA Eagle Hangar – a 44,000 ft. addition to the world-class EAA Air Adventure Museum. Dedicated to the men, women and aircraft who served our country in World War II, the EAA Eagle Hangar displays legendary airplanes such as the immortal B-17 Flying Fortress, prototype XP-51 Mustang, P-38 Lightning, DeHavilland Mosquito, and many other rare aircraft. Impressive exhibits, audio/visual presentations and a great gift shop provide the entire family with an experience they'll not soon forget. Also see the world's largest private collection of aircraft in the EAA Air Adventure Museum. Over 95 full size aircraft, displays, theaters, gift shop – even an operating airport where antiques and classics are flown on weekends during the summer.

- •	Mk.1c	T5049		(to RAAF as A19-43) BOC 6.42 SOC	9.10.47
				to inst. airframe, RAAF Nhill VIC	20.10.44
				Keith Oldfield, Nhill VIC : moved to farm	.47/71
				Moorabbin Aircraft Museum, Melbourne VIC	1.71/87
				(hulk recov. from farm nr Nhill VIC 10.1.71)	
				Roger Cloy USA	.87
				USAFM, Wright-Patterson AFB, Dayton OH	.88/91
				(static rest., Lowry AFB CO 90)	
- •	Mk. 1F	X7688		RAF Halton : engine test rig	63/67
				(front half of airframe, attached to hut)	
				RAF Museum: stored dism. Halton	70/87
				Tim E. Moore/Skysport Engineering, Bedford	12.87/91
			G-DINT	Tim E. Moore, Hatch	17.6.91/92
				(rebuild to fly using parts ex Australia)	
- •	Mk. XIc	JL946		(to RAAF as A19-148) BOC	11.7.43
				crashed landing, RAAF Drysdale WA	22.1.44
				hulk recov. from Drysdale Strip, Kalumburu WA	
				by Robert Greinert & assoc., Sydney NSW	.80
				Robert Greinert & Martin Mednis/Historic	
				Aircraft Restoration Society, Sydney NSW	80/92
				(composite rest. to fly, Sydney: with A19-144)	
- •	Mk. XI	JM135		(to RAAF as A19-144) BOC	2.7.43
				crashed landing, RAAF Drysdale WA	3.1.44
				hulk recov. from Drysdale Strip, Kalumburu WA	
				by Robert Greiner & assoc., Sydney NSW	.80
				Robert Greinert & Martin Mednis/Historic	
				Aircraft Restoration Society, Sydney NSW	80/92
				(composite rest. to fly, Sydney: with A19-148)	
- •	TF Mk. X	RD253		(to FA Portuguesa as BF-13) : del.	17.3.45
				Lisbon Technical Institute, Lisbon, Portugal	50/65
				RAF Museum, RAF Bicester: static rest.	.65/72
				RAF Museum, RAF Henlow	.67/72
				RAF Museum, Hendon	.72/92
- •	TF Mk. X TT Mk.10	RD867		RAF Museum	.64/69
				(recov. derelict ex RAF Takali, Malta .64;	
				composite rebuild with RD253 at RAF Bicester,	
				remains to RAF St.Athan .67 for static rest.)	
				RAF Museum, RAF Abingdon : displ. as "BQ-I"	.68
				Canadian National Aeronautical Collection	.69
				National Aviation Museum, Rockcliffe ONT	.69/90
- •	TF Mk. X TT Mk.10	-		(to FA Portuguesa as BF-10)	
				Lisbon Technical Institute, Lisbon Portugal	50/65
				Museo do Ar, Alverca, Portugal	66/79
				rep. to SAAF Museum	84
- •	Mk. 21	A8-186		RAAF Wagga NSW: inst. airframe	20.1.47/50
				G. Strong, Boree Creek NSW: moved to farm	.50/65
				Harold Thomas/Camden Museum of Aviation,	
				Camden, later Narellan NSW	.65/92
				(recov. from farm near Wagga NSW 3.60)	
				(displ. as "A8-186/Beaugunsville")	
- •	Mk. 21	A8-324		Robert Greinert & Martin Mednis/Historic	
				Aircraft Restoration Society, Sydney NSW	85/91
				(fuselage only, recov. ex backyard storeshed,	
				Balwyn, Melbourne VIC)	
				The Fighter Collection,	
				Duxford UK : shipped	.91/92
				(rebuild to fly, Duxford)	

- •	Mk. 21 TT	A8-328	Lord Mayors Childrens Camp, Portsea VIC Moorabbin Air Museum, Melbourne VIC (recov. derelict ex camp playground, rest. as "A8-328", later "A8-39": engines run up)	11.56/62 4.62/92
- •	Mk. 21	A8-371	Moorabbin Aircraft Museum, Melbourne VIC (fuselage only, recov. ex backyard storeshed, Frankston, Melbourne VIC 17.5.87) Roger Cloy USA USAFM, Wright-Patterson AFB, Dayton OH	.87 .87 .88/90

BRISTOL BEAUFORT

- •	Mk.V	T9552	(to RAAF as A9-13) BOC recov. by d'E. C. Darby & N. M. Armstong from Tadji, West Sepik PNG : "A9-13/FX-B" N. M. Armstrong/Australian Aerospace Museum, Melbourne VIC : static rest. Jack McDonald, Melbourne VIC loan: Museum of Army Flying, Oakey QLD	1.42 .74 .74/89 89/91 .90/91
- •	Mk.VII	A9-141	damaged RAAF Tocumwal NSW: written off Pearce Dunn/Warbirds Aviation Museum, Mildura VIC : displ. unrest. Ralph Cusack, Brisbane QLD (rebuild to fly, Eagle Farm, Brisbane: using rear fuselage ex A9-485 recov. from Gorrie Strip NT)	1.44 70/85 12.85/92
- •	Mk.VIII	A9-210	Military Aircraft Restoration Corp, Chino CA (recov. by d'E. C. Darby & N. M. Armstrong for YAF from Tadji, West Sepik PNG .74, "QH-D": comprised forward fuselage FF210; centre section RF220 when recov.)	.74/89
- •	Mk.VIII	A9-414	Military Aircraft Restoration Corp, Chino CA (recov. by d'E. C. Darby & N. M. Armstrong for YAF from Tadji, West Sepik PNG .74,"UV-Q": comprised forward fuselage FF414; centre section RF418 when recov.)	.74/89
- •	Mk.VIII	A9-501	dam. landing RAAF Gove NT : abandoned displ. in compound, Gove NT	3.45/80 80/91
- •	Mk.VIII	A9-535	Military Aircraft Restoration Corp, Chino CA (recov. by d'E. C. Darby & N. M. Armstrong for YAF from Tadji, West Sepik PNG .74 : comprised forward fuselage FF537; centre section RF533 when recov.)	.74/89
- •	Mk.VIII	A9-557	crashed landing Tadji PNG (100 Sqdn/QH-L) recov. from Tadji, West Sepik PNG Ian Whitney, Melbourne VIC (comprised forward fuselage FF559; centre section RF555; rear fuselage SF561 at time of recovery) rest. commenced at RAAF Point Cook VIC, fitted with rear fuselage A9-639 Robert Greinert & Martin Mednis/Historic Aircraft Restoration Society, Sydney NSW Australian War Memorial, Canberra ACT (arr. dism. Canberra 15.2.91, stored unrest.)	20.1.45 .74 .74/90 78 .90/91 .91
- •	Mk.VIII	A9-559	Military Aircraft Restoration Corp, Chino CA (recov. by d'E. C. Darby & N. M. Armstrong for YAF from Tadji, West Sepik PNG .74, "QH-F": comprised forward fuselage FF561; c/section RF557; rear fuselage SF563 when recov.)	.74/89

- •	Mk.VIII	A9-637	Military Aircraft Restoration Corp, Chino CA (recov. by d'E. C. Darby & N. M. Armstrong for YAF from Tadji, West Sepik PNG .74, "KT-B": comprised centre section RF635; rear fuselage SF641 when recov.)	.74/89
- •	Mk.VIII	-	Military Aircraft Restoration Corp, Chino CA RAF Museum Store, Cardington : arr. (static rest. as Blenheim "DD931") RAF Museum, Hendon: arr.	.74/91 .91 10.12.91

Certainly the most famous twin Bristol is The Aircraft Restoration Company's G-BPIV ex RCAF 10201; Duxford summer 1992 **(John Dibbs)**

BRISTOL BLENHEIM/FAIRCHILD BOLINGBROKE

- •	Mk. I	-	(to Finnish AF as ....) Tampereen Teknillinen Museo, Tampere, Finland (front fuselage only)	 79/88
- •	Mk. IV	-	(to Finnish AF as BL-200) Tampereen Teknillinen Museo, Tampere, Finland stored Tikkakoski	 79/88 91
- •	Mk. IV	RCAF9041	disposal RCAF Calgary: to farmer for parts John Hutchinson, Cochrane ALTA: to farm Jonathan Spinks, Lethbridge ALTA (hulk recov. ex farm .88: rest. project; displ. Nanton Lancaster Society, Nanton ALTA)	.46 .47/88 .88/92
- •	Mk. IV	RCAF9048	Wes Agnew, Hartney MAN Military Aircraft Restoration Corp, Chino CA Yankee Air Corps Museum, Chino CA (static rest. almost complete, YACM Chino by 84)	 72 81/84
- •	Mk. IV	RCAF9059	Wes Agnew, Hartney MAN Commonwealth Air Training Plan Museum, Brandon MAN	75 88/91
- •	Mk. IVD	RCAF9073	Wes Agnew, Hartney MAN Weeks Air Museum,Tamiami FL	 88/91

			N4260C	Kermit A. Weeks, Tamiami FL (FAA quote id. "11-880-203")	6.91/92
- •	Mk. IV	RCAF9093		Art Best, Victoria BC B. C. Aviation Museum, Victoria BC : parts	46/60 90
- •	Mk. IV	RCAF9104		George Maude, Salt Spring Island BC (disposal ex RCAF Patricia Bay, barged in .46) M. Lacy, Salt Spring Island BC David Maude/North American Interplanetary Society, Sidney BC B. C. Aviation Museum, Sidney BC (static rest., Victoria Airport BC)	.46 .46/80 .80/81 84/92
- •	Mk. IVT	RCAF9869		Western Canada Aviation Museum, Winnipeg MAN	79/91
- •	Mk. IVT	RCAF9883		Commonwealth Air Training Plan Museum, Brandon MAN	88/91
- •	Mk. IVT	RCAF9887		disposal RCAF MacDonald: to farmer for parts George Morris, MacDonald MAN : on farm	.46 .46/92
- •	Mk. IVTD	RCAF9889		Bart Bourne, Winnipeg MAN Canadian Warplane Heritage, Hamilton ONT	76/79 88/91
- •	Mk. IVT	RCAF9892		George Maude, Salt Spring Island BC RCAF Collection : recov. for static rest. Canadian National Aviation Museum, Rockcliffe ONT (displ. as "9892/YO-X")	48/63 5.63/64 6.6.64/92
- •	Mk. IVT	RCAF9893		Wes Agnew, Hartney MAN Ormond Haydon-Baillie, Vancouver BC Ormond Haydon-Baillie, Duxford UK: shipped Graham A. Warner/British Aerial Museum, Duxford Imperial War Museum, Duxford	 .72 .74/78 .79/84 88/90
- •	Mk. IVT	RCAF9895		Wes Agnew, Hartney MAN Musee Royal de L'Armee Koninklijk Legermuseum, Brussels (rebuild of 9895/10038 commenced .88)	69/71 .71/91
- •	Mk. IVT	RCAF9896		R. Yancie, Legend ALTA: to farm Canadian Museum of Flight & Transportation, Vancouver BC : arr. dism. (complete aircraft, stored dism.)	c46/81 10.81/92
- •	Mk. IVT	RCAF9897		disposal ex RCAF Vulcan ALTA: to farmer G.Thomson, Nanton ALTA Jonathan Spinks, Lethbridge ALTA : hulk	c46 c46/80 88/92
- •	Mk. IVT	RCAF9904		Wes Agnew, Hartney MAN Stan Reynolds/Reynolds Aviation Museum, Wetaskwin ALTA	 88/91
- •	Mk. IVT	RCAF9911		Wes Agnew, Hartney MAN Harry Whereatt/Whereatt's Warbirds, Assiniboia SASK	 88/91
- •	Mk. IVT	RCAF9937		Bart Bourne, Winnipeg MAN Canadian Warplane Heritage, Hamilton ONT	76/79 88/91
- •	Mk. IVT	RCAF9940		Wes Agnew, Hartney MAN Sir W. J. D. Roberts/Strathallan Aircraft	

				Collection, Auchterader, Scotland	12.72/79
				Museum of Flight, East Fortune	14.7.81/91
-	Mk. IVT	RCAF9947		Robert Diemert, Carman MAN	73/75
				Eric Vormezeele, Brasschaat, Belgium	84/85
				Musee de l'Air, Paris-Le Bourget	21.8.85/90
				dest. in museum hangar fire, Le Bourget	17.5.90
- •	Mk. IVT	RCAF9949		Bart Bourne, Winnipeg MAN	76/79
				Canadian Warplane Heritage, Hamilton ONT	88/91
- •	Mk. IVT	RCAF9981		Western Canada Aviation Museum,	
				Winnipeg MAN	79
				Jonathan Spinks, Lethbridge ALTA	.83/90
				Canadian Warplane Heritage, Hamilton ONT	91
- •	Mk. IVTT	RCAF9983		Wes Agnew, Hartney MAN	
				Commonwealth Air Training Plan Museum,	
				Brandon MAN	88
				Weeks Air Museum,Tamiami FL	88/91
			N4311Z	Kermit A. Weeks, Tamiami FL	6.91/92
				(FAA quote id. "11-880-202")	
- •	Mk. IVTT	RCAF9987		Wes Agnew, Hartney MAN	
				Harry Whereatt/Whereatt's Warbirds,	
				Assiniboia SASK	88/91
- •	Mk. IVT	RCAF9989		Canadian Warplane Heritage, Hamilton ONT	91
- •	Mk. IVT	RCAF9990		Stan Reynolds/Reynolds Aviation Museum,	
				Wetaskwin ALTA	91/92
- •	Mk. IVTT	RCAF9991		John Coussens, Springfield MO	91
- •	Mk. IVT	RCAF10001		Canadian National Aeronautical Collection,	
				Rockcliffe ONT	
				RAF Museum store, RAF Henlow	.69
				RAF Boscombe Down : rest.	72
				RAF Museum, Hendon	.78/92
				(displ. as Blenheim "L8756/XD-E")	
-	Mk. IVT	RCAFI0038		derelict on farm, Winnipeg MAN	
				recov. by Wes Agnew, Hartney MAN	.69
				(some parts to Brussels with 9895 .71)	
				Ormond Haydon-Baillie, Vancouver BC	.72/78
				shipped to UK, stored Duxford	.74/78
			G-BLHM	ntu: Graham A. Warner/British Aerial Museum,	
				Duxford	.79
			G-MKIV	British Aerial Museum, Duxford	26.3.82/87
				(rest. Duxford, ff. 22.5.87 as "V6028/GB-D")	
				crashed Denham	21.6.87
				(wreck stored Duxford: parts to 10201 rebuild)	
- •	Mk. IVT	RCAF10040		Western Canada Aviation Museum,	
				Winnipeg MAN	76/79
				Canadian Warplane Heritage, Hamilton ONT	.83/91
- •	Mk. IVT	RCAF10070		Wes Agnew, Hartney MAN	75
				John Coussens, Springfield MO	88/91
- •	Mk. IVT	RCAF10073		Military Aircraft Restoration Corp, Chino CA	72/91
				(noted stored MARC compound, Chino 87/91)	
- •	Mk. IVT	RCAF10074		RCAF disposal: A. Beauman, to farm	c46/70
				Jonathan Spinks, Lethbridge ALTA : hulk	91
- •	Mk. IVTT	RCAF10076		Military Aircraft Restoration Corp, Chino CA	72/91
				(noted stored MARC compound, Chino 87)	

- •	Mk. IVT	RCAF10078		Wes Agnew, Hartney MAN Vince O'Connor, Uxbridge ONT	75 88/91
- •	Mk. IVT	RCAF10107		Commonwealth Air Training Plan Museum, Brandon MAN	 88/91
- •	Mk. IVT	RCAF10117		Bart Bourne, Winnipeg MAN Canadian Warplane Heritage, Hamilton ONT (rest. project)	76/79 88/91
- •	Mk. IVT	RCAF10120		Stan Reynolds/Reynolds Aviation Museum, Wetaskwin ALTA	 88/92
- •	Mk. IVT	RCAF10121		Tony Kucher, Dauphin MAN : derelict on farm Canadian Museum of Flight & Transportation, Vancouver BC (static rest., displ. as "RCAF 9120")	70/82 7.82/92
- •	Mk. IVT	RCAF10122		Gerry Schook, Assiniboia SASK: to farm Frank Thompson, Readlyn SASK (recov. ex farm Assiniboia, for static rest.)	.46/92 .92
- •	Mk. IVTT	RCAF10163		B. C. Aviation Museum, Sidney BC	88/91
- •	Mk. IVT	RCAF10184		Western Canada Aviation Museum, Winnipeg MAN Canadian Warplane Heritage, Hamilton ONT	 76/79 .83/91
- •	Mk. IVT	RCAF10201	 G-BPIV	Wes Agnew, Hartney MAN Sir W. J. D. Roberts/Strathallan Aircraft Collection, Scotland : rest. project, arr. Graham A. Warner/British Aerial Museum, Duxford : arr. by road for rest. Graham Warner/The Aircraft Restoration Co, Duxford (rebuild to fly, Duxford)	 .84/88 28.1.88 15.2.89/92
- •	Mk. IVT	RCAF10223		disposal ex RCAF MacDonald ALTA: to farmer J. Weibe ALTA J Coussens, Springfield MO	c46 c46/70 91
- •	Mk. IVT	RCAF..........		Stan Reynolds/Reynolds Aviation Museum, Wetaskwin ALTA	 91/92

826	•	CA-12	A46-3		South Australian Air Museum, Adelaide SA (cockpit area only, recov. ex scrap dump, Tocumwal NSW)	91
848	•	CA-12	A46-25		Les Arthur/Toowoomba Aero Museum QLD (hulk recov. from farm, Oakey QLD)	72/89
					CAC, Fishermans Bend, Melbourne VIC (fuselage only, static rest. project)	.89/91
853	•	CA-12	A46-30		(flew in movie "Smithy", as Lockheed Altair rep. "VH-USB/Lady Southern Cross" .46)	
					Australian Air League, Blacktown NSW	8.46/64
					RAAF Williamtown NSW : gate guard (static rest. by CAC Melbourne VIC .77/80)	.64/76
					Australian War Memorial, Canberra ACT (displ. as "A46-30/SH-B")	.81/92
877	•	CA-12	A46-54		Les Arthur/Toowoomba Aero Museum QLD (hulk recov. from farm, Oakey QLD)	70/77
				VH-MHB	Greg Batts, Brisbane QLD (rebuild to fly, as "A46-54/MH-B")	c77/92
878	•	CA-12	A46-55		Richard E. Hourigan, Melbourne VIC (hulk recov. from farm, Nhill VIC 3.3.69)	3.69/75
					Ron Lee, Melbourne VIC (composite rest. project)	75/91
900	•	CA-12	A46-77		Greg Batts, Brisbane QLD (fuselage only: stored, rest. project)	91
924	•	CA-12	A46-101		fuselage frame recov. ex Tocumwal NSW	
					Dennis Baxter, Sydney NSW (rest. project)	90
945	•	CA-13	A46-122		hulk recov. from farm, Oakey QLD	
					John Hill, Springbrook QLD	
				VH-MHR	Matthew Denning, Brisbane QLD (rebuild to fly, as "A46-122/MH-R")	8.75/92
946	•	CA-13	A46-124		Peter Sledge, Sydney NSW (under rest. Nowra NAS NSW .87)	86/87
					Darwin Aviation Museum, Darwin NT (static rest. project)	90/92
952	•	CA-13	A46-129		recov. ex farm, Oakey QLD	c64
					Camden Museum of Aviation, Camden NSW later Narellan NSW : fuselage only	65/92
962	•	CA-13	A46-139		Les Arthur/Toowoomba Aero Museum QLD (hulk recov. from farm, Oakey QLD)	
					Guido Zuccoli, Toowoomba QLD	
					Dennis Sanders & Dale Clarke, Chino CA	.84/91
				N32CS	Dennis Sanders & Dale Clarke, Chino CA (T-6 rebuilt Chino as Boomerang replica, using parts from A46-139, ff Chino 20.7.91; flies as RAAF "A46-139/Phooey")	8.91/92
965	•	CA-13	A46-142		Les Arthur/Toowoomba Aero Museum QLD (hulk recov. from farm, Toowoomba QLD)	72/79
					Jeff Trappett, RAAF Point Cook VIC	.89
					Don Brown, Konowak, Leongatha VIC (fuselage only, rest. project)	.91/92
988	•	CA-13	A46-165		Ralph Cusack, Brisbane QLD	
					Robert Greinert, Sydney NSW (under rest. at Nowra NAS NSW .86)	78/90

				Weeks Air Museum, Tamiami FL	91
				(fuselage frame only: rest. project)	
997 •	CA-13	A46-174		crashed Cape Gloucester PNG	18.5.44
				shipped to Lae for rebuild, abandoned Nadzab	.44
				d'E. C. Darby & N. M. Armstrong, Auckland NZ	.74
				(hulk recov. from Nadzab PNG .74)	
				Weeks Air Museum, Tamiami FL	88/91
				(fuselage frame & wing centre-section)	
1029 •	CA-19	A46-206		noted Oakey AB QLD, partially rest. fuselage	5.88
				Guido Zuccoli, Toowoomba QLD	89/92
			N4234K	Guido Zuccoli c/o Sanders Aircraft, Chino CA	.91/92
				(rebuild Chino CA: A46-206 fuselage frame rebuilt with modified T-6 mainplane and tail)	
			VH-BOM	Guido Zuccoli, Toowoomba QLD	.92
				(ff due Chino 5.92, to be shipped to Australia, to fly as "A46-206/MH-Y/Milingimbi Ghost")	
1073 •	CA-19	A46-249		Richard E. Hourigan, Melbourne VIC	10.61/92
				(fuse. recov ex farm, Colac VIC 22.10.61)	
				(static rest. project : using parts recov. from A46-21, 55, 81, 147, 219 and wings ex A46-87 recov. ex crash site Cape York QLD)	

Sanders Aircraft of Chino, California rebuilt what is effectively a CAC Boomerang replica, though it does utilise some original parts from A46-139, which was recovered from a farm as a hulk by Les Arthur. It is now owned by Dennis Sanders and Dale Clarke (Thierry Thomassin)

NOTED AN ERROR OR OMISSION? PLEASE TELL US ABOUT IT BY WRITING TO:

WARBIRDS WORLDWIDE, P.O. Box 99, Mansfield, Notts NG19 9GU ENGLAND,

17	•	CA-1 Mk.1	A20-9		recov. ex farm, Tocumwal NSW	c78
					Ashley Briggs, Melbourne VIC	87/92
					(rest. project, using parts ex A20-722,731 id. unknown, will use plate ex A20-9)	
8	•	CA-1 Mk.1	A20-10		Commonwealth Aircraft Corp, Melbourne VIC	31.5.60/63
					Moorabbin Air Museum, Melbourne VIC	1.11.63/91
					(displ. as "A20-10/10")	
11	•	CA-1 Mk.1	A20-13		Commonwealth Aircraft Corp, Melbourne VIC	5.60/63
					W. Gordon Scrap Metals, Werribee VIC	11.63
					Tom King, Melbourne VIC	11.63/66
					National Museum, Port Moresby PNG	68/90
97	•	CA-3 Mk.II	A20-99		Ralph Moyle, Kenmare VIC : dism. on farm	60/74
					loan: RAAF Air Training Corps, Ballarat VIC	70/74
				VH-JML	Eric Lundberg, Richmond NSW	.74/91
					(rebuild to fly, RAAF Richmond & Bankstown NSW)	
103	•	CA-5 Mk.II	A20-103		Australian War Memorial, Canberra ACT	.59/91
					(shot down Zero, Rabaul PNG 12.42)	
136	•	CA-7 Mk.II	A20-136		noted stripped, RAAF Tocumwal NSW	4.62
					Pearce Dunn/Warbirds Aviation Museum, Mildura VIC	70/82
					Jack McDonald, Melbourne VIC	.82
				VH-CAC	ntu: Peter N. Anderson, Sydney NSW	84/92
					(rest. project, Bankstown NSW)	
223	•	CA-7 Mk.II	A20-223		Commonwealth Aircraft Corp, Melbourne VIC	6.60/63
					W. Gordon Scrap Metals, Werribee VIC	11.63
					Mark Pilkington, Lara VIC	85/90
					(rest. project, using parts A20-601, -605)	
224	•	CA-7 Mk.II	A20-224		Commonwealth Aircraft Corp, Melbourne VIC	3.60/63
					W. Gordon Scrap Metals, Werribee VIC	11.63
					Bob Hogg, Noble Park, Melbourne VIC	
					(fuselage mod. to home-made flight training simulator)	
					Robert Greinert & John White/Historical Aircraft Restoration Society, Sydney NSW	85/91
					(rest. project)	
703	•	CA-9 Mk.II	A20-502		Richard E. Hourigan & Ron Lee, Melbourne VIC	70/91
					loan: Warbirds Aviation Museum, Mildura VIC	71/76
					loan: Ballarat Aviation Museum, Ballarat VIC	85/91
					(displ. as "A20-502/BF-O")	
807		CA-9 Mk.II	A20-606		Commonwealth Aircraft Corp, Melbourne VIC	4.60/63
					Airfarm Associates, Tamworth NSW	11.63/67
					Les Arthur/Toowoomba Aero Museum QLD	70/80
					Murray Griffiths, Deniliquin NSW: stripped	
1101	•	CA-16 Mk.III	A20-649		Commonwealth Aircraft Corp, Melbourne VIC	12.58/71
					(Ceres engine testrig, Fishermans Bend factory)	
					Moorabbin Air Museum, Melbourne VIC	.71/88
				VH-WIR	ntu: Moorabbin Air Museum	8.74/88
					(planned rest. to fly, engine runs RAAF Point Cook VIC 8.74: not testflown, stored Point Cook)	
					Alan Searle, Melbourne VIC	2.88
					Weeks Air Museum, Tamiami FL	.88/91
1103	•	CA-16 Mk.III	A20-651		Commonwealth Aircraft Corp, Melbourne VIC	5.60/64
					(rest. by CAC, stored Fishermans Bend 64)	
					Institute of Applied Science, Melbourne VIC	64/68

c/n	Type	Mil. serial	Civil reg.	Owner / history	Date
				Science Museum of Victoria, Melbourne VIC	70/92
				loan: Hawker deHavilland, Pt. Melbourne VIC	86/88
				(stored pending displ., Museum of Victoria)	
1104 •	CA-16 Mk.III	A20-652		Commonwealth Aircraft Corp, Melbourne VIC	4.60/63
				J. A. Frierson, Fleetwings Service Station, Laverton VIC	11.63
				displ. garage, Pascoe Vale, Melbourne VIC	65/69
				displ. garage, Preston, Melbourne	72
				Geoff Milne & Vin Thomas, Albury NSW	.83
			VH-WIR	Geoff Milne, Albury NSW/Bright VIC	26.8.86/92
				(rebuilt Essendon VIC, ff 19.9.86 as "A20-652")	
1108	CA-16 Mk.III	A20-656		Commonwealth Aircraft Corp, Melbourne VIC	6.60/63
				Airland Improvements, Cootamundra NSW	11.63/70
				Richard Hourigan & Ron Lee, Melbourne VIC	.70/91
				(stored dism. Moorabbin 70/91)	
				Rob Black, Brian Jones & Graham Waddington, Melbourne VIC	.91
				(moved to Tyabb VIC .91, rest. project)	
1122 •	CA-16 Mk.III	A20-670		Commonwealth Aircraft Corp, Melbourne VIC	3.60/63
				W. Gordon Scrap Metals, Werribee VIC	11.63
				Ken Baird, Geelong VIC	75/88
				loan: RAAF Museum, RAAF Point Cook VIC	87/88
				(displ. as rest. fuselage only)	
1137 •	CA-16 Mk.III	A20-685		disposal : RAAF Tocumwal NSW	9.59
				Marshall Spreading Service, Albury NSW	3.60/67
				(rest. to taxying condition, Albury .64)	
				Camden Museum of Aviation, Camden NSW later Narellan NSW (displ. as "A20-685")	.67/92
1139 •	CA-16 Mk.III	A20-687		disposal : RAAF Tocumwal NSW	9.59
				Marshalls Spreading Service, Albury NSW	.60/67
				Ken Baird, Geelong VIC	.67/68
				Richard Hourigan, Pat Capron & Ron Lee, Melbourne VIC : arr. Moorabbin dism.	18.8.68/92
				(rest. Moorabbin VIC .67 as "A20-561/QE-B")	
				loan: RAAF Museum, RAAF Point Cook VIC	.77/92
1140 •	CA-16 Mk.III	A20-688		Midland Technical College, Perth Airport WA	5.59/71
				(inst. airframe : del. ex RAAF Pearce 27.5.59)	
				RAAF Association Museum, Perth WA	.71/92
				(displ. as "A20-688/BF-R")	
1147 •	CA-16 Mk.III	A20-695		Commonwealth Aircraft Corp, Melbourne VIC	3.60/63
				W. Gordon Scrap Metals, Werribee VIC	11.63
				Pearce Dunn/Warbirds Aviation Museum, Mildura VIC	70/82
				Jack McDonald, Melbourne VIC	.82
				Ed Field & David Jones, Melbourne VIC	86/91
				(rebuild to fly, RAAF Point Cook VIC)	
1156 •	CA-16 Mk.III	A20-704		owner, Bankstown NSW: del. ex RAAF Mallala	21.2.60/62
				Airfarm Associates, Tamworth NSW	67
				Les Arthur/Toowoomba Aero Museum QLD	74/85
				Murray Griffiths, Deniliquin NSW	9.85/92
				(long-term rest. to fly, Deniliquin NSW)	
1171 •	CA-16 Mk.III	A20-719		Commonwealth Aircraft Corp, Melbourne VIC	3.60/63
				W. Gordon Scrap Metals, Werribee VIC	11.63
				Pearce Dunn/Warbirds Aviation Museum, Mildura VIC	67/82
				Jack McDonald, Melbourne VIC	.82/88
				(rest. to fly, RAAF Point Cook VIC)	

				Robert Greinert/Historical Aircraft Restoration	
				Society, Sydney NSW	91/92
				(rest. to fly, Bankstown NSW)	
1174 •	CA-16	A20-722		Nelson Wilson, Wandin VIC	
	Mk.III			(recov. ex farm near Horsham VIC)	
			VH-CAC	Borg Sorenson, Melbourne VIC	85/92
				(rebuild to fly, Moorabbin VIC, using parts from	
				A20-512 ex farm Horsham VIC, & A20-731)	
28-14 •	CA-28			Channel Seven Vintage Museum, Perth WA	72/87
	Ceres			(conv. back to Wirraway from CA-28 Ceres	
				VH-DAT, displ. as "A20-47/GA-B")	
				WA Museum of Aviation, Perth WA	87/90
				(stored dism., Jandakot Airport WA)	
				moved to Sydney for Wirraway rest. project	.91/92
- •	CA-3	-		Pearce Dunn/Warbirds Aviation Museum,	75/80
	Mk.II			Mildura VIC	
				Michael Muelders, Adelaide SA	85
				Peter Sledge, Sydney NSW	.85/91
				(rest. to fly, Essendon VIC 87/89)	
				Ed Field, Melbourne VIC & Hong Kong	.91/92
				(rest. to fly, Bankstown Airport NSW)	
				(id. unknown, will use id. A20-81)	
- •	CA-16	-	VH-BFF	Geoff Schutt & Ron Lee, Melbourne VIC	5.12.75/80
	Mk.III			(composite rebuild Moorabbin VIC, adopted id.	
				c/n 1105/A20-653, ff Moorabbin 4.12.75)	
				Malcolm Long & Ron Lee, Coolangatta QLD	10.6.80/92
				displ. Chewing Gum Field Air Museum QLD	83/88
				displ. Drage Air World, Wangaratta VIC	.88/91
				(flies as "A20-653/BF-F")	
-	-	-		Pearce Dunn/Warbirds Aviation Museum,	
				Mildura VIC	70/81
				Flygvapnets Flygmuseum, Malmslatt Sweden	.81
				(complete composite aircraft, for rest. by FFM	
				to represent a R.Swedish AF SAAB Sk.14A)	
				(note: wings & centre-section later traded to	
				Peter Sledge, Sydney NSW for A20-81 project)	
- •	-	-		W. Gordon Scrap Metals, Werribee VIC	
				Ian A. Whitney, Romsey VIC	80/92
				(rest. to fly, RAAF Point Cook, Essendon &	
				Romsey VIC : to be flown as "A20-395")	

CAC WINJEEL

1526 •	CA-22	A85-618		first prototype, ff. Fishermans Bend VIC	3.2.51
				RAAF Wagga NSW : inst. airframe	.57/77
				RAAF Museum, RAAF Point Cook VIC	.77/92
1527 •	CA-22	A85-364		2nd prototype	7.51
				RAAF Wagga NSW : inst. airframe	.57/77
				RAAF Museum, RAAF Point Cook VIC	.77/92
25-1 •	CA-25	A85-401		first production aircraft, ff.	23.2.55
				RAAF Museum, RAAF Point Cook VIC	83/88
			VH-NTY	RAAF Museum, RAAF Point Cook VIC	18.1.88/92
				(rest. Point Cook, ff 1.88 as "A85-401")	
25-2 •	CA-25	A85-402		disposal ex RAAF Point Cook (TT7207 hrs)	2.5.79
				Malcolm J. Long, Melbourne VIC	.79
			VH-BFX	Malcolm J. Long, Melbourne VIC	8.4.82/91
				Ron Lee, Melbourne VIC	.91/92
25-3 •	CA-25	A85-403		RAAF Wagga NSW : inst. airframe	80/86
				RAAF Wagga NSW : gate guard	87/92

25-4 •	CA-25	A85-404		disposal ex RAAF Point Cook VIC (TT4234)	2.5.79
				Noel R. Vinson/Aviation Salvage Pty Ltd, Bankstown NSW	6.79
			VH-WHZ	John Weymouth/Heli-Muster Pty Ltd, Sydney NSW & "Victoria River Downs" NT	20.3.81/92
25-5 •	CA-25	A85-405		RAAF East Sale VIC : gate guard	90/92
25-7 •	CA-25	A85-407		RAAF Wagga NSW : inst. airframe	80/89
			VH-NTJ	Winrye Aviation, Bankstown NSW	.89/92
				(rest. Bankstown, ff 20.9.91 as "A85-443")	
25-17 •	CA-25	A85-417		disposal ex RAAF Point Cook VIC	26.5.70
				Peninsula Air Services, Moorabbin VIC	.70/72
				(open storage, dism., Moorabbin)	
				Robert L. Eastgate, Melbourne VIC : stored	74/79
				Don Brown, Korumburra VIC (rest. to fly)	91/92
25-18 •	CA-25	A85-418		disposal ex RAAF Pt. Cook VIC (TT 5623)	2.5.79
				Mike Wansey/Confederate Air Force, Newcastle NSW	6.79
				Moorabbin Air Museum, Moorabbin VIC	6.79/92
25-21 •	CA-25	A85-421		disposal ex RAAF Point Cook VIC	26.5.70
				Peninsula Air Services, Moorabbin VIC	.70/72
				(open storage, dism., Moorabbin)	
				Robert L. Eastgate, Melbourne VIC : stored	74/92
25-22 •	CA-25	A85-422		disposal ex RAAF Point Cook VIC (TT4635)	2.5.79
				Robert Eastgate & Ed Field, Melbourne VIC	6.79
			VH-SOB	Robert L. Eastgate, Melbourne VIC	12.81/92
25-28 •	CA-25	A85-428		RAAF Wagga NSW : inst. airframe	80/87
				private: under rebuild	90
25-29 •	CA-25	A85-429		disposal ex RAAF Point Cook VIC	26.5.70
				Nelson R. Wilson, Coldstream VIC	78/82
				Matthew Onslow, Walcha NSW	90/92
				(rest. to fly, Bankstown NSW)	
25-30 •	CA-25	A85-430		disposal ex RAAF Point Cook VIC	26.5.70
				Noel R. Vinson/Aviation Salvage Pty Ltd, Bankstown NSW: open storage	70/72
				"Adventureland" Playground, Casula NSW	73/78
				Camden Museum of Aviation, Narellan NSW	84/88
				South Australian Historical Aviation Museum, Port Adelaide SA	89/92
25-32 •	CA-25	A85-432		Museum of Army Flying, Oakey AB QLD	5.78/92
				(flies as "A85-432")	
25-34 •	CA-25	A85-434		disposal ex RAAF Point Cook VIC	26.5.70
				Jeff Trappett, Morwell VIC	.70/83
				(stored Essendon VIC 74)	
			VH-AGP	Jeff Trappett, Morwell VIC	25.8.83/89
				Roger Richards, Melbourne VIC	5.4.89/92
25-36 •	CA-25	A85-436		disposal ex RAAF Point Cook VIC (TT4429)	2.5.79
				Noel R. Vinson/Aviation Salvage Pty Ltd, Bankstown NSW	6.79
			VH-WIJ	Noel R. Vinson, Bankstown NSW	6.11.80/84
				Roger Richards, Melbourne VIC	19.9.84/92
25-38 •	CA-25	A85-438	VH-IOX	disposal ex RAAF Point Cook VIC (TT4489)	2.5.79
				William J. McMonagle, Brisbane QLD	19.3.81/92

25-40 •	CA-25	A85-440		RAAF Air Training Corps, Cambridge TAS	.76/85
			VH-HFM	Alf Medley, Horsham, later Donald VIC : del.	25.4.85/92
25-41	CA-25	A85-441		crashed RAAF Point Cook VIC, after midair	
				collision with A85-408	5.6.64
				wreck to Aeronautical Research Laboratory,	
				Fishermans Bend, Melbourne	10.64
				Australian War Memorial, Canberra ACT	90/92
				(rear fuse & parts in storage Duntroon .90)	
25-44 •	CA-25	A85-444		disposal ex RAAF Point Cook VIC	26.5.70
				Noel Vinson/Aviation Salvage Pty Ltd,	
				Bankstown NSW	.70
				displ. auto wreckers yard, Casula NSW	72/73
				Nick Challinor, Murwillumbah NSW	.73/77
				Chewing Gum Field Air Museum,	
				Tallebudgera QLD : stripped, derelict	8.77/86
			VH-AGR	Jeff Trappett, Adelaide SA	12.90/91
				(rebuild to fly, Morwell VIC 90)	
25-45 •	CA-25	A85-445		disposal ex RAAF Point Cook VIC (TT 4137)	2.5.79
				Noel R. Vinson/Aviation Salvage Pty Ltd,	
				Bankstown NSW	6.79/83
			VH-JJG	Murray Griffiths, Deniliquin NSW	9.83/88
				(rebuilt Tocumwal NSW, ff 6.4.84)	
				Doug Hamilton, Wangaratta VIC	12.88/91
				(flies in FAC camouflage as "A85-445")	
25-47 •	CA-25	A85-447		disposal ex RAAF Point Cook VIC	26.5.70
				Pensinsula Air Services, Moorabbin VIC	.70
				(open storage, dism., Moorabbin)	
				playground, Bacchus Marsh Lion Park VIC	74/82
				David Spring-Brown, Monegeeta VIC: derelict	.83
				Rod Swallow, Gisborne VIC : rest. project	90/91
25-48 •	CA-25	A85-448		disposal ex RAAF Pt.Cook VIC	26.5.70
				open storage, dism., Moorabbin VIC	71/73
				playground, Bacchus Marsh Lion Park VIC	74/82
				David Spring-Brown, Monegeeta VIC: derelict	.83
				Rod Swallow, Gisborne VIC: rest. project	90/91
25-49 •	CA-25	A85-449		Port Moresby Technical College PNG : del.	6.78
				National Museum, Port Moresby PNG	90/92
				(stored dism., Jacksons Airport, Pt. Moresby 90)	
25-50 •	CA-25	A85-450		disposal ex RAAF Point Cook VIC	26.5.70
				Noel R. Vinson/Aviation Salvage Pty Ltd,	
				Bankstown NSW	.70
				open storage, dism., Moorabbin VIC	71
				Robert L. Eastgate, Melbourne VIC : stored	74
				Jack McDonald, Melbourne VIC	
				Pearce Dunn/Warbirds Aviation Museum,	
				Mildura VIC	80/82
				Richard E. Hourigan, Melbourne VIC	15.5.82
			VH-HOY	Richard E. Hourigan, Harkaway VIC	22.9.86/92
				(ff Moorabbin 20.9.86, flies as "A85-450")	
25-57 •	CA-25	A85-457		disposal ex RAAF Point Cook VIC (TT6026)	2.5.79
				Nelson R. Wilson, Coldstream VIC	3.80
			VH-HFE	Nelson R. Wilson, Lilydale VIC	10.86/91
25-60 •	CA-25	A85-460		Dept. of Aviation, Essendon VIC : inst. airfr.	8.79/86
			VH-HWI	John Dorward, Melbourne VIC	14.3.89/92
25-61 •	CA-25	A85-461		disposal ex RAAF Point Cook VIC (TT 3674)	2.5.79
				Blayney Airfarmers, Blayney NSW: arr dism	7.79/80
			VH-WIU	John Weymouth/Helimuster Pty Ltd,	

			Sydney NSW & "Victoria River Downs", NT	9.7.82/85
			Don Williamson/Banneret Pty Ltd, Perth WA	29.8.85/92
			(flies in FAC camouflage as "A85-461")	
25-62 •	CA-25	A85-462	last production aircraft : ff.	21.11.57
			RAAF Point Cook : displ. Cadets Mess	75/92

PHOTO PAGES P56 & P57

Duxford's B-17 'Sally B' dressed as 'Ginger Rogers' for the London Weekend television series 'We'll Meet Again' seen on September 11th 1983 The B-17 Preservation Trust Fortress has been seen in a number of interesting paint schemes, including those she wore for the Puttnam film 'Memphis Belle' also filmed at Duxford. The aircraft participation and flying sequences were orchestrated by The Old Flying Machine Company, also based at Duxford (Gary R. Brown archives)

Evocative shot of the IGN's B-17 taken at La Ferte Alais in 1986. Sadly this aircraft crashed and was destroyed by fire during a sortie from RAF Binbrook in Lincolnshire during the filming of 'Memphis Belle'. It was B-17G 44-85643 (Gary R. Brown archives)

The British Air Reserve was an ill fated organisation and once the owner of Hawker Sea Fury FB.11 WJ288, registered in the UK as G-SALY. Eventually purchased by Warbirds of Great Britain the aircraft passed through Duxford en route to the United States where it went into the hands of Pacific Fighters for rebuild for its new owner, Ed Stanley. Unfortunately Ed was killed in a flying accident before the aircraft flew. Now registered to Maria Stanley the Sea Fury is on the USCAR as N15S. (Gary R. Brown archives)

Formerly an airfield decoy at Poona AB, India Hawker Tempest Mk II PR538 was recovered by Warbirds of Great Britain in 1979 and stored for a short time at Blackbushe before passing to Nick Grace of the Tangmere Flight. In 1987 the machine passed into the hands of the RAF Museum and was later restored by The Fighter Collection for the RAF Museum. (Gary R. Brown)

18 •	LB-30A	AM927		damaged in Canada: not delivered to RAF	.41
	RLB-30			op: Consolidated Vultee Corp, San Diego CA	.41/47
			NL24927	Consolidated Vultee Corp, San Diego CA	1.4.47
			N1503	Continental Can Co, Morristown NJ	11.48/59
				Petroleos Mexicanos - PEMEX	11.4.59
			XC-CAY	Petroleos Mexicanos - PEMEX	11.59
			N12905	Confederate Air Force, Harlingen TX	.67/90
				(del. ex Mexico 5.68; flies as "Diamond Lil")	
			N24927	Confederate Air Force, Midland TX	10.90/91
				American Airpower Heritage Flying Museum,	
				Midland TX	9.91/92
25 •	B-24D	40-2367		forced landing, Bechevin Bay, Atka AK	9.12.42
			N58246	US Historical Aircraft Preservation Museum,	
				Anchorage AK	7.84/88
				American Vets Memorial Museum, Denver CO	6.88/90
				(awaiting recov., Atka AK)	
55 •	LB-30	AL557	G-AGZI	Scottish Aviation Ltd, Prestwick	21.9.46/48
			SX-DAA	Hellenic Airlines, Athens "Maid of Athens"	2.48/51
			N9981F	Morrison Knudson Construction Co	.51
			N68735	Morrison Knudson Construction Co	12.51/53
			N92MK	Morrison Knudson Construction Co	
				crashed landing, nr Anchorage AK: abandoned	.58
				Alaska Aviation Heritage Museum,	
				Anchorage AK (planned recov. for rest.)	10.86/90
-	B-24D	42-40461		(to RAF as BZ734: RCAF 599)	
				Yesterdays Air Force, Chino CA	
				recov. ex farm ALTA Canada	.72
				arr. dism. by train, badly damaged in transit	2.72
				broken-up, only nose retained Chino	76/90
				(nose "T1" displ. USAFM, March AFB CA 85)	
-	B-24D	42-40557		(to RAF as BZ755: RCAF 600)	
				Yesterdays Air Force, Chino CA	
				recov. ex farm ALTA Canada	.72
				arr. dism. by train, badly damaged in transit	2.72
				broken-up, nose only retained Chino	76/90
2413 •	B-24D	42-72843		(512nd BS, "Strawberry Bitch")	
				USAFM: stored Davis-Monthan AFB AZ	46/59
				USAFM, Wright-Patterson AFB, OH: del.	18.5.59/92
				(displ. as "Strawberry Bitch")	
5852 •	B-24M	44-41916		(to USN as Bu90165)	
	PB4Y-1		N5141N		
			N4K	Salem Engineering Co, Salem NY	c50
			N4907L		
			CB-76	Compania Boliviana de Aviacion, La Paz	22.3.51
			CP-576	Bolivian Overseas Airways, La Paz, Bolivia	
				wfu stripped for spares, La Paz, Bolivia	73/75
				Frigorifico Reyes, La Paz (held u/s)	80
				La Mercantil de Seguros, La Paz, Bolivia	82
				USAFM, Castle AFB CA	5.82/92
				(arr. dism. 29.5.82, static rest. Castle 82/89;	
				displ. as "441916/RE-H/Shady Lady")	
				(note: id. also quoted as 44-41906/Bu90155)	
- •	B-24M	44-41956		(to RAAF as A72-176) BOC 1.45 SOC	3.48
				George Toye, Moe VIC : as scrap	.48/90
				complete fuselage stored in yard, Moe VIC	.48/90
				Liberator Memorial Fund, Melbourne VIC	.90/92
				(planned static rest. using mainplane from	
				B-24D 42-41091, to be recov. ex Faita PNG)	
-	B-24M	44-42067		(to USN as Bu90232)	69

PB4Y-1			PT-AZX	Frigopar, Rio de Janeiro	69
				abandoned, derelict Belem by	75
1347 •	B-24J	44-44052		(to RAF as KH191: Indian AF 'T-18')	
	B. VII			Indian AF Technical College, Jalahalli, India	72
				Warbirds of GB Ltd, Blackbushe	82/86
				(airfreighted to UK by Heavylift Belfast 6.5.82)	
				(stored dism. Blackbushe 82/86)	
				Collings Foundation, Stowe MA	.86/90
				(shipped USA .86; rebuild Kissimee FL: ff 8.8.89)	
			N224J	Collings Foundation, Stowe MA	6.89/92
				(flies as "All American")	
1470 •	B-24J	44-44175		(to RAF as KH304: Indian AF as HE877)	
	B. VII			retired IAF, stored Poona AB	31.12.68
			N7866	Pima County Air Museum, Tucson AZ	.69/90
				dep. Poona AB on del. flight to Tucson	28.3.69
				(displ. as "444175/HE877/"Paisano" &	
				"Shoot You're Covered")	
1508 •	B-24J	44-44213		(to RAF as KH...... : Indian AF as HE924/L)	
	B. VII			retired IAF, stored Poona AB	31.12.68
				Indian AF Museum, Palam AB, New Delhi	79/90
1567 •	B-24J	44-44272		(to RAF as KH401: Indian AF as HE771)	
	B.VII			retired IAF, stored Poona AB	31.12.68
			N94459	Yesterdays Air Force, Chino CA	
				del. to Duxford UK ex Poona	28.10.73
				del. ex Duxford to USA, via Prestwick	27.8.75
				Military Aircraft Restoration Corp, Chino CA	9.6.80/92
				loan: USAFM, March AFB CA	84/85
				loan: Liberal Air Museum, Liberal KS	.87/88
				(flies as "250551/RR/Delectable Doris")	
1603	B-24J	44-44308		(to RCAF as KK237) BOC 22.11.44: SOC	8.10.46
	B. VII			recov. from farm, adv. for sale, Chase BC	.71
3636 •	B-24J	44-48781		Spartan School of Aeronautics, Tulsa OK	.46/60
				(instr. airframe: later stripped and derelict)	
				stored derelict, airport Tulsa OK	74
				USAFM, Barksdale AFB LA	12.78/89
				(del. by CH-54: displ. as "Laden Maiden")	
-	B-24J	44-49001		The Air Museum, Ontario CA	67/73
				(fuselage only)	
-	B-24L	44-49112		(to RCAF as 11120) BOC 26.3.45: SOC	7.10.46
	B. VII			recov. from farm, adv. for sale, Chase BC	.71
5009 •	B-24L	44-50154		(to RAF as KN820: Indian AF as HE773)	
				Canadian National Aeronautical Collection,	
				Rockcliffe ONT: del. Poona AB,India-Canada	5-17.6.68
				National Aviation Museum, Rockcliffe ONT	68/92
				(displ. as "RCAF 11130")	
6707L •	B-24L	44-50206		(to RAF as KN751: Indian AF as HE807)	
				retired IAF, stored Poona AB	31.12.68
				del. by air Poona - RAF Cosford : arr.	11.7.74
				RAF Museum, RAF Colerne	74/76
				RAF Museum, RAF Cosford	1.76/91
-	B-24M	44-50801	N299A		
	C-87		CP-611	Boliviana de Aviacion, La Paz	4.56
				damaged, Trinidad, Bolivia	27.3.64
			CP-787	Compania Boliviana de Aviacion, La Paz	
				wfu and broken-up, La Paz, Bolivia	.75
6083 •	B-24M	44-51228		USAF Aero Icing Research Laboratory	

		EZB-24M			retired, stored Lackland AFB TX	.53/56
					USAFM, Lackland AFB TX	.56/92
					(displ. as "The Blasted Event/RE")	
-	•	B-24	-		(to Chinese AF as ......)	
					personal aircraft for Chinese Premier	
					rep. retired, Air Base, Northern China	88/90
-	•	B-24D	-		(to RCAF as ....)	
					recov. ex crash site Labrador	c90
					Tom Reilly Vintage Aircraft, Kissimmee FL	.90
					(to be used in rebuild of P4Y-2 to fly)	

CONSOLIDATED PBY CATALINA

-		PBN-1	Bu02838		MGM Studios, Hollywood CA	50/70
					(stored dism., storage lot Culver City CA)	
					broken up	.70
110	•	PBY-5A	Bu05021	N33301	(also rep. as NC18444?)	
				VP-BAR	Caribbean International Airways Ltd, Nassau	8.50
				VP-JAU	Caribbean International Airways Ltd, Kingston	26.2.51
				CF-HFL	Eastern Provincial Airways, Halifax NS	11.53/57
					fcd. ldg. & abandoned, near Goose Bay LAB	1.10.57
					Atlantic Canada Aviation Museum, Halifax NS	.86
					recov. complete, by helicopter	27.10.86
					Western Canada Aviation Mus., Winnipeg MAN	88
117	•	PBY-5A	Bu05028		(rep. for RAF as PBY-5B FP216, but not del.)	
					NAS Pensacola, Land Survival Training Centre	.45/92
					(airframe built into wall of building)	
301	•	PBY-5 Mk.IIA	VA718		(intended for RCAF but del to RAF)	
					beached in foul weather, dam., Diego Garcia	16.9.44
					rep. derelict, Diego Garcia	91/92
382	•	PBY-5A	RCAF9734		(intended for RNEIF as Y-51)	
					(to RAAF as A24-19) : BOC 3.42 SOC	1.46
					Kingsford Smith Aviation Services,	
					Bankstown NSW	10.46
					rebuild for static displ., Wallan VIC	86/90
					(id. also quoted as 317)	
407	•	PBY-5A Landseaire	RCAF9742	N68740	Southern California Aircraft Corp, Ontario CA	52
					(conv. to "Landseaire" air yacht by 52)	
					Crocket & Gamboy Inc, Fresno CA	54
					Flying Bonefish Inc, Carson City NV	63
					Geraldine Cromack, New York NY	66
					Freeport Indonesia Inc, New York NY	68/70
					(op. Darwin NT-West Irian, mining courier run)	
					Lee Otterson, Colusa CA	72/78
					University of Hawaii, Honolulu HI	81/88
					(stored by Aero Nostalgia, Stockton CA 83/89)	
					Gary R. Larkins, Auburn CA	90
					(stored USNAM, NAS Pensacola FL 90)	
					Lone Star Flight Museum, Galveston TX	.91/92
417	•	PBY-5A Landseaire Bird Innovator	RCAF 9746	N59D	reg.	10.56
				N5907	rereg.	11.58
					The Bird Corporation, Palm Springs CA	.62/69
					"The Wandering Albatross"	
					dam. wheels-up landing, Memphis TN	6.12.63
					(two Lycoming GSO-480 engines added .67)	
				N81RD	The Bird Corporation, Richmond CA	4.69/76
				N5907	Madden Aircraft Sales Inc,	7.76
					Atlas Aircraft Corp, Long Beach CA	78

Continued on Page 62

Continued from Page 60

				Pyramid Aviation, Cotati CA	10.78/81
				Research Data Inc, Miami FL	9.81/90
				Dick Durand/Westernair Inc, Albuquerque NM	.90/91
			N5PY	Westernair Inc, Albuquerque NM	9.91/92
427 •	PBY-5A			RCAF9750	
			CF-DIL		3.46
				Wheeler Airlines, St Jovite Station QUE	65
				Wheeler Northland Airways, St Jean QUE	70
			C-FDIL	Ilford Riverton Airways, Winnipeg MAN	72/73
				Can Air, Vancouver BC "Fisherman's Special"	.74/81
				Flying Fireman, Victoria BC	83/88
				(tanker #5; #775)	
				Awood Air Ltd, Victoria BC	.88/89
920	PBY-5A	Bu08101	N5588V	Troy G. Hawkins, Wichita Falls TX	66
				Bird Aircraft, Palm Springs CA	
				Antilles Air Boats, St Thomas USVI	68/74
				Victor W. Newman	10.1.75
928 •	PBY-5A	Bu08109		(to RDAF as 82-857, later L-857)	
				RDAF Museum Collection, Vaerlose AB	79/89
				Flyhistorisk Museum, Sola, Norway : del.	17.11.89/92
1166 •	PBY-5A	Bu08272		(to RAAF as A24-46) SOC	3.43
				C. K. Campbell, Sydney NSW	11.47
				(not conv., broken-up RAAF Lake Boga VIC)	
				Pearce Dunn/Warbirds Aviation Museum, Mildura VIC	68/89
				(dism. hulk, recov. from farm, Lake Boga VIC)	
				John Bell/Whaling Museum, Albany WA	.89/92
				(static rest. using parts recov. from farms)	
1211 •	PBY-5	Bu08317		stored, NAS Norfolk VA	65
				NASM, Silver Hill MD	73/92
				loan: USNAM, NAS Pensacola FL	73/92
- •	PBY-5A	Bu21232	N5609V	Paul Mantz Aviation	.47/49
	Steward-			International Aviation Corp, Glendale CA	.49/51
	Davis		CF-GHU	Queen Charlotte Airlines, Vancouver BC	.51/57
	Super Cat.			"Kitmat Queen"	
				Pacific Western Airlines, Vancouver BC	.57
			N2763A	Alaska Coastal - Ellis Airlines, Juneau AK	.57/63
				Alaska Coastal Airlines, Juneau AK	66
				Alaska Airlines Inc, Seattle WA	69
				Antilles Air Boats Inc, St Thomas USVI	70/73
				Marine Associates, Worcester MA	78
				wfu stripped: Watsonville CA	78/80
				Gerald W. Todd, Santa Cruz CA	8.4.81
				Robert P. Schlaefli/SLAFCO, Moses Lake WA	84/92
1520 •	PBY-5A	Bu33966		(to USCG) BOC 23.8.43 : SOC	.52
			N3936A	used by DEW-lIne contractor, Philadelphia PA	c52
				wfu, Bradley Field, Windsor Locks CT	c55
				J. B. Terrill, Tulsa OK	58
				(remained derelict, Bradley Field 55/88)	
				Americada Corp, New York NY	c60/64
				Bradley Air Museum, Windsor Locks CT	29.5.64/81
				New England Air Museum, Windsor Locks CT	81/89
				Weeks Air Museum, Tamiami FL	11.89/92
				(rest. project)	
1522 •	PBY-5A	Bu33968	N5582V	Troy G. Hawkins, Wichita Falls TX	66/69
			C-GVTF	ntu	
			N84857	Diversified Drilling Muds, Cheyenne WY	10.10.80
				IDFAF Museum, Hazerim AB, Israel	5.85
				fell down steep slope, taxiing Lewistown MT	

c/n	Type	Serial	Reg.	History	Date
				during del. flight : badly damaged	9.5.85
				Ben Kalka, Oakland CA	
				Ray Cox, Renton WA	90/92
				(rebuild to fly, Lewistown MT)	
1547 •	PBY-5A	Bu33993		(to USAAF as 43-43847)	
	OA-10A		N4760C	Alaska Coastal Airlines Inc, Juneau AK	54/66
	Steward-			Alaska Airlines Inc, Seattle WA	69
	Davis			Stan Burnstein, Tulsa OK	72
	Super Cat			Lee Maples/Maples Aviation Co/Geoterrex,	
				Vichy MO	74/84
				op. by Terra Surveys/Geoterrex, Ottawa ONT	82/85
				forced landing, crashed, Lynn WI	22.3.83
				Military Aircraft Restoration Corp, Chino CA	87
				in damaged cond.	87
				USAFM, McChord AFB WA : arr. dism.	12.87/92
				(rest., displ. as OA-10A "434033")	
1566	PBY-5A	Bu34012	N1947M		
			CF-IEE	Transair Ltd, Winnipeg MAN	53/67
				Austin Airways, Toronto ONT	.67/70
				sunk during storm, Sugluk QUE	.70
1570 •	PBY-5A	Bu34016	N5583V	H & F Flying Club, Carlsbad CA	66/69
				reg. pending (noted Haywood CA 6.73)	72
				sank, Infernillo Reservoir, Mexico	19.3.74
				(scuttled in course of drug interception)	
				wreckage located, may be recov.	92
1581 •	PBY-5A	Bu34027	N9505C	Alcan Airways, Kingman AZ (tanker #9)	66
	Super Cat			Intercapital Inc, Las Vegas NV	69
				Robert P. Schlaefli/SLAFCO, Moses Lake WA	72/92
				(tanker #53)	
1584	PBY-5A	Bu34030	N5804N	Remmert Werner Inc, St Louis MO	54
				Monsanto Chemical Co, St. Louis MO	55
				("The Pelican", lifeboats hung under wings)	
			N19Q	re-reg.	57
				Edgar M. Querny, St. Louis MO	63
				Alfran Corp, Milwaukee WI	66/70
				James Stewart/Stewart Enterprises,	
				Minneapolis MN	72
				crashed into Mediterranean, nr Monte Carlo	15.8.72
1637	PBY-5A	Bu48275	N1586M	Air Corp of Miami, Miami FL	54
			CF-NTJ		
			CF-HTN	Transair Ltd, St James MAN	56/65
				Field Aviation Co Ltd, Toronto ONT	70/71
				cr. firebombing, 500m north Edmonton ALTA	3.9.71
1643	PBY-5A	Bu48281	N1540M	Charlotte Aircraft Corp, Charlotte NC	54
			CF-IHJ	Dorval Air Transport, Montreal QUE	56
			N68623	stripped hulk, noted Long Beach CA	67/68
				broken up, Long Beach CA	70
1649 •	PBY-5A	Bu48287	N10017		
	Steward-		CF-JMS	Questor Surveys Ltd, Toronto ONT	
	Davis		VH-UMS	Selco Exploration/Australian Selection P/L	24.4.64
	Super Cat.		CF-JMS	Questor Surveys Ltd, Toronto ONT	11.64/70
			N16647	Questor Surveys	73/74
			C-GGDW	Austin Airways, Timmins ONT	8.75/77
				Geoterrex Ltd/Terra Surveys Ltd, Ottawa	80/85
			N16647	Jack Leavis, Davie FL	8.85/90
				open storage, Opa Locka FL	87/90
				Jim Dent/Air Adventures, Ft. Lauderdale FL	2.90
				Super Three Inc, Fort Lauderdale FL	7.90/91
			N287	Super Three Inc, Fort Lauderdale FL	7.91/92
				(rest. to military config., "Black Cat" scheme)	

1656 •	PBY-5A	Bu48294	N9521C	O. W. Noble, North Little Rock AR	66
				V. & N. Enterprises Inc, North Little Rock AR	69/72
				Two Jacks Inc, Olive Branch MS	78
				Buddy Woods, Palmer AK	.78
				Catalina Flying Inc, Anchorage AK	8.83/87
				Galen S. Vincent, Zephyr Cove NV	88/92
				(based Santa Rosa CA, flies in USN scheme)	
1658	PBY-5A	Bu48296	N68746	Southern California Aircraft Corp, Ontario CA	54
				James N. Routh, Long Beach CA	63
			CF-AAD	Austin Airways, Toronto ONT	.66/73
				crashed, Great Whale QUE	24.9.72
1679 •	PBY-5A	Bu48317	N1495V	(to MLD/Dutch Navy as 16-212)	.47
				loan Bosbad Amusement Pk, Hoeven, Holland	2.8.57/83
				Militaire Luchtvaart Museum, Soesterburg AB	84/92
				(also rep. as c/n1885 and c/n 28109)	
1735	PBY-5A	Bu48373	N10018		
			N95R	Remmert Werner Inc, St Louis MO	58/59
			VH-BRI	Ansett Flying Boat Services, Rose Bay NSW	10.59/62
				"Golden Islander"	
				(del. St Louis MO to Sydney 10-19.10.59)	
				sank at moorings, Hayman Island QLD	8.7.62
				Vic O'Hara, Proserpine QLD: salvaged and	
				hull conv. to houseboat "Henrietta Hoh"	
				in use as houseboat, Shute Harbour QLD	85/92
1736	PBY-5A	Bu48374	N9507C	George B. Alder, Chatanooga TN	63
				Carolina Aircraft Corp, Miami FL	
				Orinoco Mining Co, Pittsburgh PA	.65
			YV-P-DPZ	Orinoco Mining Co, Puerto Ordaz, Venezuela	.65
			YV-O-CFO	Corporacion Ferrominera de Orinoco CA,	.75
				Puerto Ordaz, Venezuela (act. YV-O-CFO-2)	
			YV-584CP	Corporacion Ferrominera de Orinoco CA,	
				Puerto Ordaz, Venezuela	3.83
			YV-63CP	ntu:	
1750	PBY-5A	Bu48388	N1521V		
			HK-1020	Lineas Aereas Interiores de Catalina - LAICA	73
				crashed, Villavicencio, Colombia	11.6.73
1759 •	PBY-5A	Bu48397	N5593V	Thomas W. Kendall, La Verne CA	58/63
				ran on to beach reef, Ash Shaykh Humayd, Aqaba,	
				Saudi Arabia, while under machine-gun fire	
				from bedouins, 300 bullet holes : abandoned	22.3.60
				still on beach Aqaba, complete but derelict	84/92
1768 •	PBY-5A	Bu48406	N5590V	Thomas W. Kendall/Catalina Ltd, La Verne CA	.56/78
				lsd: Catalina Enterprise "Tiare Tahiti"	c60
				(open storage, Van Nuys CA 78/86)	
				International Centre for Environmental Research,	
				Wilmington DE	84
				Thomas W. Kendall, Laguna Beach CA	86
				San Diego Aerospace Museum, San Diego CA	1.86/92
				(del. by air Van Nuys - San Diego 12.86,	
				displ. on pole as USN "48406")	
1774 •	PBY-5A	Bu48412	N10024	Trade Ayer, Linden NJ (USN surplus) reg.	4.9.56
				Cole Brock Inc PA	7.5.57/59
			N96R	Remert Werner Inc, St Louis MO	.59
			YV-P-EPX	Orinoco Mining Co, Puerto Ordaz, Venezuela	10.59/61
			YV-P-EPZ	Orinoco Mining Co, Puerto Ordaz, Venezuela	7.61/75
			YV-O-CFO	Corporacion Ferrominera de Orinoco CA,	.75/83
				Puerto Ordaz, Venezuela (act. YV-O-CFO-4)	

			YV-585CP	Corporacion Ferrominera de Orinoco CA, Puerto Ordaz, Venezuela	3.83/92
			YV-56CP	ntu:	
1781	PBY-5A	Bu48419	PP-ABC	(to FA Brasileira as FAB C-10A 65....)	
			PP-PDR	lsd: Panair do Brazil, Sao Paulo, Brazil	65/71
				(to FA Brasileira as FAB C-10A-65...)	12.71
				Museu Aeroespacial, Rio de Janeiro	82/85
1785 •	PBY-5A	Bu48423	N4002A		
			CF-JJG	Survair Ltd, Ottawa ONT	65
				Canadian Aero Service Ltd, Ottawa ONT	70
				(magnetometer equiped) "Explorer"	60/69
				Spartan Air Services, Ottawa ONT	73/74
			C-FJJG	Kenting Earth Sciences, Ottawa ONT	76/86
			N423RS	Red Stevenson, Jenks OK	6.86
				Bruce Redding, Reno NV : del.	7.86
				APEXX Company Inc, Canby OR	8.86/87
				Northern Air Inc, Dallas TX	12.87/92
1788 •	PBY-5A Steward-Davis Super Cat.	Bu48426	N31235	USN Dept., Washington DC	52/55
				op. by Transocean Airlines, Oakland CA	4.52
				op. for: Trust Territory Air Services, Guam	52/55
				forced landing 275m w. San Francisco CA	30.9.55
				recov. by ship and badly damaged	
				Long Beach Aeromotive Inc CA : rebuilt	56
				C. S. Bearson	.56
				R. Lyle Golding, Long Beach CA	.56/58
				Pacific Airlines, San Francisco CA	.58/61
				Alaska Coastal - Ellis Airlines, Juneau AK	.61
				Alaska Coastal Airlines Inc, Juneau AK	63/66
				Alaska Airlines Inc, Seattle WA	69
				Robert P. Schlaefli/SLAFCO, Moses Lake WA	72/92
				(tanker #80; #98)	
1791 •	PBY-5A	Bu48429	N1565M	Charlotte Aircraft Corp, Charlotte NC	54
			CF-IGJ	Province of Newfoundland & Labrador, St Johns NFLD	65/74
			C-FIGJ	Prov. of Newfoundland & Labrador, St Johns	79/80
				(tanker #2)	
				crashed forced landing, Sherbrooke QUE	19.12.80
				struck-off 8.81: wreckage noted, St Jean QUE	9.82/92
1808	PBY-5A	Bu48446	N5591V	Ellwood L. Schultz, Los Angeles CA	63/69
				Transamerica Trade, Mableton GA	78
			YV-209CP	Peter Bottome, Caracas	.78/85
			N285NJ	Thaddeus B. Bruno Jr, Fort Lauderdale FL	8.85/89
				Enrico Recchi, Turin, Italy	.87
				(del. to Italy, via Reykjavik 1.9.87)	
				crashed and dest., Turin, Italy	21.5.89
1820 •	PBY-5A	Bu46456		(to FA Brasileira as FAB C-10A 6509)	
			N4582T	Military Aircraft Restoration Corp, Chino CA	12.83/90
				USNAM, MCAS Cherry Point NC	88/92
1821 •	PBY-5A	Bu46457		(to FA Brasileira as FAB C-10A 6510)	
			N4582U	Military Aircraft Restoration Corp, Chino CA	12.83/90
				USAFM, Kirtland AFB NM	.84/92
				(displ. as "OA-10A 434077")	
1846	PBY-5A Steward-Davis Super Cat.	Bu46482	N5584V	Thomas W. Kendall/Catalina Ltd, La Verne CA	.56
				Steward-Davis Inc, Long Beach CA	c58
				Alaska Coastal- Ellis Airlines, Juneau AK	c63/66
				Alaska Airlines Inc, Seattle WA	69
				Antilles Air Boats, St Thomas USVI	70/71
				wfu St Croix USVI	7.71
1868 •	PBY-5A	Bu46504	N1513V		

			OB-LBA-251		
			OB-M-251		
			OB-T-251	Loretana de Aviacion - LORASA, Iquitos, Peru	
				ops. ceased: wfu stored Iquitos, Peru	8.76/77
				derelict, Lima-Jorge Chavez	83/87
				rep. broken-up, Lima	c87
				(also rep. extant, Lima 92)	
1886 •	PBY-5A	Bu46522	N5585V	Summer Institute of Linguistics, Glendale CA	63/66
				Jungle Aviation & Radio Service, Waxhaw NC	69
			CF-FFA	Richard L. Rude/Flying Fireman, Sidney BC	.72
			C-FFFA	Flying Fireman Ltd, Sidney BC	.77/88
				(tanker #7; #777)	
				Awood Air Ltd, Victoria BC	.88/90
			N2172N	Erickson Air Crane Co, Central Point OR	1.90/92
1891	PBY-5A	Bu46527	N6473C	noted derelict, unconv., Fort Worth TX	68
				reg. res., USCR (rep. extant 92)	83/92
1903 •	PBY-5A	Bu46539	N1563M	Charlotte Aircraft Corp, Charlotte NC (USCR)	54/69
				not conv., derelict in open, Elizabeth City NC	.47/85
				Gary R. Larkins, Auburn CA	.85/90
				(under rebuild to fly, Auburn CA: not flown)	
				Darryl Greenamyer, Van Nuys CA	.90
				TNI-AU/Indonesian AF Museum, Jakarta	.90/92
1946 •	PBY-5A	Bu46582		(to FA Brasileira as FAB C-10A 6520)	
			N4583A	Military Aircraft Restoration Corp, Chino CA	12.83
				USNAM, NAS Jacksonville FL	86/92
				(displ. as "4934", later "6582")	
				(FAA quotes incorrect id. "46852")	
1954 •	PBY-5A Landseaire	Bu46590	N68756	Southern California Aircraft Corp, Ontario CA	.50
				Fullerton Oil Co, Pasadena CA	.50/60
				Herbert A. Schriner, Larchmont NY	.60/69
				Endicot P. Davison, New Canaan CT	.69/77
				Quebec Labrador Mission Found., Ipswitch MA	9.77/79
				Michael Wansey/Australian Wing CAF	18.9.79/88
				op: Confederate Air Force, Camarillo CA	83/91
				American Airpower Heritage Flying Museum Midland TX	9.91/92
				(flies as RAAF "A24-387/Sea Bitch/NB-N")	
1959 •	PBY-5A	Bu46595	N9501C		
			PT-AXM		
				(to FA Brasileira as FAB C-10A 6551)	
			N4583B	Military Aircraft Restoration Corp, Chino CA	12.83/84
				USAFM, Wright-Patterson AFB OH : del.	7.84/92
				(nose gear collapsed on landing W-P 7.84	
				displ. as "OA-10A 433879/Snafu Snatchers")	
1960 •	PBY-5A Super Canso	Bu46596	N6070C		
			N45998		
			CF-FFW	Flying Fireman Ltd, Sidney BC	68/76
				(tanker #4)	
			C-FFFW	Flying Fireman Ltd, Sidney BC	81/88
				(tanker #774)	
				(sank Silver Lake ONT 5.84: returned to service)	
				Awood Air Ltd, Victoria BC	88/89
1966 •	PBY-5A	Bu46602	N6071C		
			CF-FFZ	Flying Fireman Ltd, Sidney BC	70/76
			C-FFFZ	Flying Fireman Ltd, Sidney BC	81/86
				(tanker #3; #773)	
			N4NC (1	ntu: Wilson C. Edwards, Big Spring TX	3.86
			N607CC	AP Inc, Auburn CA	6.86/90

				USNAM, NAS Pensacola FL	90
				(displ. as "46602/45-P-3")	
				FL Aircraft Leasing Corp, Fort Lauderdale FL	1.91/92
1988 •	PBY-5A	Bu46624	N9502C	Southland Flying Service, Tohula MS	66/69
				Military Aircraft Restoration Corp, Chino CA	79
				sale reported, Long Beach CA	84/92
				(rep. the PBY displayed at 94 Aero Squadron	
				Restaurant, Clearwater FL 81)	
1997 •	PBY-5A	Bu46633	N10023	Trade Ayer Inc, Linden NJ	.56
	Super		CF-MIR	Miron & Freres Ltd, Cartierville QUE	7.57/61
	Canso			(conv. to Super Canso by Noorduyn Aircraft,	
	1000			Montreal QUE, completed 9.12.60)	
				Laurentian Air Services Ltd, Ottawa ONT	9.64/65
				Survair Ltd, Ottawa ONT	9.65
			N608FF	Firefly Inc, Portland OR	
				Aeroservice Corp, Philadelphia PA	
				Barringer Research	
				Equitable Leasing Co Corp, Burbank CA	7.67/69
			C-FMIR	Geoterrex Ltd/Terra Surveys, Ottawa ONT	.70/84
			G-BLSC	Plane Sailing Air Displays Ltd, Duxford	12.84/92
				(del. Johannesburg to UK 14-20.2.85)	
				(flies as "RAF JV928/Y")	
2007 •	PBY-6A	Bu46643	N9556C	Aircraft Instrument Corp, Miami FL (USCR)	66/69
				(to FA Brasiliera as FAB CA-10 6552)	
			PT-BBQ		
			PP-PEB	lsd. from FAB: Panair do Brazil, Sao Paulo	65
				lsd. from FAB: Cruzeiro do Sul, Rio de Janeiro	1.7.65/71
				(ret. to FAB as CA-10-6552): struck-off reg.	17.12.71
				displ. Belem, Brazil	90/92
2008 •	PBY-6A	Bu46644	N6458C	Farmers Air Service, Klamath Falls OR	63
				Liston Aircraft, Klamath Falls OR	63/66
				(tanker #F46)	
				Hemet Valley Flying Service, Hemet CA	69/78
				(tanker #E83)	
			C-GFFH	Flying Fireman Ltd, Sidney BC	5.79/88
				(tanker #8; #778)	
				Atwood Air Ltd, Victoria BC	88/89
			EC-359	ICONA, Cuatro Vientos	.89
			EC-EVK	Servicios Aereos Espanoles SA - SAESA,	
				Cuatro Vientos : op. by ICONA	5.7.90/91
2009 •	PBY-6A	Bu46645	N10013	reg.	5.56
			CF-IZO	Montreal Air Service, Montreal QUE	30.6.56/64
				Sakatchewan Govt., Sakatoon SASK	29.5.64
				North Canada Air Ltd, Prince Albert SASK	3.9.65/73
				(tanker #12)	
			C-FIZO	Norcanair Ltd, Prince Albert SASK	76/81
				Avalon Aviation, Parry Sound ONT	4.8.81/89
				(tanker #8; #798) : fitted PBY-5 tailplane	
				retired, Parry Sound ONT	28.2.88/89
				B. Johnson/Tech Air System, Toronto ONT	.89
				Militaire Luchtvaart Museum, Soesterberg	.89
				del. by air, Oshawa-Eindhoven : arr	28.9.89
				op: Flight Support Europe, Eindhoven	89/91
				Forsvarsmuseet, Akershus Castle, Oslo	.91/92
				(under rest. Gardermoen: to be displ. in RNoAF sc.)	
2017	PBY-6A	Bu46653	N6459C	Farmers Air Service, Klamath Falls OR	63
				Liston Aircraft, Klamath Falls OR	63/66
				(tanker #F11)	
				Hemet Valley Flying Service, Hemet CA	69/70
				(tanker #77)	
				crashed, Columbia CA	18.7.70
2019 •	PBY-6A	Bu46655	N10014		
			CF-IZU	World Wide Airways	56

				Montreal Air Service, Montreal QUE	65
				Province of Newfoundland & Labrador, St Johns NFLD	70/74
			C-FIZU	Province of Newfoundland & Labrador, St Johns NFLD (tanker #4)	79/90
2026 •	PBY-6A	Bu46662	N9588C		
			CF-VIG		
			N788C	Carl H. Ingwer, Tucson AZ	63
				Mural Rearment Inc, New York NY	66
			CF-VIG	Great Lakes Paper Co, Orilla ONT	.67/73
				Avalon Aviation Ltd, Red Deer ALTA	75
			N1022G		3.79
			N999AR	Anchor & Cattle Corp, Grundy VA	6.80
				Red Stevenson, Leonard OK: "The Searcher"	84
				Wilson C. Edwards, Big Spring TX	.84/86
			N4NC (2	Wilson C. Edwards, Big Spring TX	3.86/92
2029 •	PBY-6A	Bu46665	N9555C		
			CC-CNG	TRANSA, Santiago, Chile (stored only)	.57/59
			CC-CNP	Roberto Parrague/Aeroservicios Parrague Ltda, Santiago, Chile "Manutara II"	.59/92
				(ferried to Canada .70 for firebomber conv., tanker #65, later #35)	
				ICONA/Spanish Ministry of Land & Forest Management: lease, del. Spain ex Chile	7.88/92
2043 •	PBY-6A	Bu46679	N9562C	Aircraft Instrument Corp, Miami FL (USCR)	66/69
			CC-CNF	TRANSA, Santiago, Chile	.57/59
				Roberto Parrague/Aeroservicios Parrague Ltda, Santiago : stored 59-80	.59/80
			CC-CCS	Roberto Parrague/Aeroservicios Parrague Ltda, Santiago, Chile (tanker #34)	4.80/92
				sank, landing, Lago Gotierrez, Argentina	27.1.86
				salvaged, returned to service	.88/92
				ICONA/Spanish Ministry of Land & Forest Management : leased, del. Spain ex Chile	7.6.91/92
2063 •	PBY-6A	Bu63993		(to RDAF as 82-866, later L-866)	
				RAF Museum, RAF Colerne UK : del.	30.5.74/75
				RAF Museum, RAF Cosford	10.75/92
2066	PBY-6A	Bu63996	N6456C	Sonora Flying Service, Columbia CA (tanker #E38)	62/66
				Jack R. Urich, Chiloquin OR	69
				Hemet Valley Flying Service, Hemet CA (tanker #E84; #84)	72/78
				dam. by fire on ground, Stockton CA	.77
			C-GFFJ	Flying Fireman Ltd, Sidney BC (tanker #9)	6.80
				cr. & dest., water pick-up, Sioux Lookout ONT	12.7.81
2068	PBY-6A	Bu63998		(to RDAF as 82-863: later L-863) : del.	8.57
			N16KL	Larkin Aircraft Corp, Monterey CA : del.	13.7.72
				American Air Mus. Society, San Fransisco CA	72
				Confederate Air Force, Harlingen TX	10.82/84
				cr and dest., Gulf of Mexico, nr Harlingen TX	13.10.84
2070	PBY-6A	Bu64000		(to RDAF as 82-868: later L-868)	
			N15KL	Larkin Aircraft Corp, Monterey CA : del.	9.6.72
				John Church, Monterey CA	.72
				Confederate Air Force, Harlingen TX	12.72/75
				crashed, dest. near Harlingen TX	18.8.75
2072	PBY-6A	Bu64002	N331RS	Rolled Steel Corp, Skokie IL	69
				Victory Air Museum, Mundelein IL	72/76

2087 •	PBY-6A	Bu64017	N2846D	Jaydon Enterprises, Riverside CA	62/63
				(tanker #E87)	
				Air Tankers Inc, Seattle WA	.63
				(tanker #E87)	
			N5555H		
			F-ZBAV	Protection Civile, Marseilles	.64/73
				("Green Pelican")	
			CF-HNH	Avalon Aviation Ltd, Red Deer ALTA	74/79
			C-FHNH	Avalon Aviation Ltd, Parry Sound ONT	.79/88
				(tanker #6; #796)	
				lsd. Haydn Air, Oslo, Norway	77/85
				wfu East Midlands 9.85 : stored Exeter UK	86/88
			G-BPFY	Aces High Ltd, North Weald	25.10.88
			N212DM	Consolidated Aviation Ent., Burlington VT	25.10.88
			G-BPFY	Aces High Ltd, North Weald	23.12.88
			N212DM	Universal Aviation Corp, Dover DE	6.6.89
			G-BPFY	Aces High Ltd, North Weald	5.3.90
				Warbirds of GB, Biggin Hill : del	15.3.90/92
2104 •	PBY-6A	Bu64034	N2886D	Burson Associates Inc, Columbia CA	63/66
				Sis-Q Flying Service Inc, Santa Rosa CA	69/72
				(tanker #E49)	
				Robert P. Schlaefli/SLAFCO, Pt. Orchard WA	78/92
				(tanker #E49)	
				sank in lake, Northport WA	29.7.85
2105 •	PBY-5A	Bu64035		(to RDAF as 82-861, later L-861)	
				stored dism., Vaerlose AB	70/85
				RDAF Museum Collection, Engagergard AB	79/88
				Flyvevabnets Historik Mseum, Vaerlose AB	91/92
2111 •	PBY-6A	Bu64041	N6453C	Leo J. Demers, Salem OR	
				Rosenbalm Aviation, Medford OR	c59
				Sonora Flying Service, Columbia CA	
				B.B. Burson Associates Inc, Columbia CA	63/66
				(tanker #E54)	
				Hemet Valley Flying Service, Hemet CA	68/78
				(tanker #E54, #54)	
			C-GFFI	Flying Fireman Ltd, Victoria BC	5.79
				(tanker #9)	
			N85U	Flying Fireman Inc, Spanaway WA	3.86/88
				(tanker #85)	
				Awood Air Ltd, Spanaway WA	.88/89
				Flying Fireman Inc, Spanaway WA	90/92
2133	PBY-6A	Bu64063	PT-BBP	Servicios Aerotaxie Abast do Vale, Belem	83
2134 •	PBY-6A	Bu64064	CF-IZZ	World Wide Airways	56
				Montreal Air Service, Montreal QUE	65
				Kenting Aviation Ltd, Toronto ONT	66
			F-ZBAZ	Protection Civile, Marseilles	5.66/73
				(del via Dublin 20.5.66; "Black Pelican")	
			CF-IZZ	Field Aviation Co Ltd, Toronto ONT del.	6.73
			C-FIZZ	Avalon Aviation Ltd, Red Deer ALTA	77/79
				Avalon Aviation Ltd, Parry Sound ONT	.79/86
				(tanker #5; #795: rebuilt with PBY-5A tailplane)	
				retired Parry Sound ONT	28.2.88/89
				Servicios Aereos Espanoles SA/SAESA,	
				Cuatro Vientos, Spain : del. ex Canada	4.7.91/92
			EC-940	Servicios Aereos Espanoles SA/SAESA,	
				Cuatro Vientos, Spain (tanker #795)	.92
2141 •	PBY-6A	Bu64071	NC48129		45
			N6457C	Sonora Flying Service, Columbia CA	62/63
				(tanker #E49)	
				Calypso Air Charters Inc, Miami FL	.63/69
			N48129	Interport Inc	.68

				del. Arizona - Dominican Rep.	2.68
				Carl H. Jurgens, Dominican Republic	69
				(open storage, Fort Lauderdale FL 71/74)	
			N101CS	American Equipment Funding, Wilmington DE	75
				Cousteau Society Inc, Los Angeles CA	.76/78
				crashed and sank, River Tagus, Portugal	28.6.79
				(wreckage rep. Museo do Ar, Alverca AB 92)	
2142 •	PBY-6A	Bu64072	N7057C	George J. Priester, Wheeling IL	63
				John W. Dorr, Malibu CA	66/69
				Aeroborne Enterprises, Davie FL	78
				P & P Charters Inc, Fort Lauderdale FL	84
				Hill Air Company Inc, Fort Lauderdale FL	6.85/87
				National Warplane Museum Inc, Geneseo NY	88/92
				(flies as 'USN/70-P')	
2162 •	PBY-6A	Bu64092	N6881C	Carstedt Sales Corp, Long Beach CA	63
			CF-PIU	Northward Air Service Ltd, Calgary ALTA	65
				Midwest Airlines Ltd, Winnipeg MAN	70
				Ilford Riverton Airways, Winnipeg MAN	73
				St Felicien Air Service, Robervale QUE	.73/76
			C-FPIU	Avalon Aviation Ltd, Parry Sound ONT	.79/89
				(tanker #7; #797)	
				retired, stored Parry Sound ONT	28.2.88/92
2167 •	PBY-6A	Bu64097	N7082C	James Routh/Routh Aircraft, Long Beach CA	63
				(tanker #E94)	
				Multiple Management Corp, Long Beach CA	.63
			F-ZBAW	Protection Civile, Marseilles	c63/73
				("Yellow Pelican")	
			C-FHNF	Avalon Aviation Ltd, Red Deer ALTA	76/79
				Avalon Aviation Ltd, Parry Sound ONT	.79/89
				(tanker #4; #794) : lsd. Haydn Air, Norway	76/77
				retired Parry Sound ONT	28.2.88/89
			N7179Y	Aircraft Marketing Inc, Albuquerque NM	3.91/92
				(flies in blue USN scheme)	
				stored, Fort Lauderdale FL	91/92
				(DoT & FAA quote id. as '225')	
2177 •	PBY-6A	Bu64107		NASM, Washington DC : listed as stored	65
			N9825Z	Florida Forestry Board, Tallahassee FL	66/72
				Robert P. Schlaefli/SLAFCO, Moses Lake WA 78/92	
				(tanker #158)	
				(note: FAA quote id. "235")	
21981 •	PBY-5A	RCAF9752		(to F. A. Brasileira as FAB C10A-6527)	
				Museu Aeroespacial do FAB, Rio de Janeiro	82/92
21986	PBY-5A	RCAF9757		BOC 21.1.43: SOC	18.11.46
			CF-SAT	reg.	11.46
				Transair Ltd, St James MAN	56/65
				William P. Bernard, Edmonton ALB	70/73
				Can-Air Services Ltd, Edmonton ALTA	76/86
				crashed and sank, landing, Maui HI	14.4.86
				wreck recov. by Ray Cox, Renton WA	.86
				(major parts to Alaska Hist. Society for CV.465)	
21996 •	PBY-5A	RCAF9767		BOC 4.3.43: SOC	1.4.46
				(162 Sqn, Reykjavik: sank U-342 17.4.44)	
			CF-CRR	Canadian Pacific Airlines, Vancouver BC	1.4.46/60
				dam. Torrance BC	23.4.59
				Northland Airlines Ltd, Winnipeg MAN	.60
				Midwest Airlines Ltd, Winnipeg MAN	.70
				Ilford Riverton Airways, Winnipeg, Manitoba	73
			C-FCRR	Avalon Aviation Ltd, Red Deer ALTA	77/79
				Avalon Aviation Ltd, Parry Sound ONT	.79/89

Continued on Page 73

G
27002
NAVY
VA 216
618

Continued from Page 70

				(tanker #1; #791)	
				sank, water pick-up, Complex Lake SASK	27.5.78
				sank, water pick-up, Complex Lake SASK	30.5.81
				(salvaged, returned to service)	
				retired Parry Sound ONT	28.2.88/92
22018 •	PBY-5A	RCAF9789		crashed, Bella Bella BC	7.43
				remains rep. extant, Bella Bella BC	92
22022 •	PBY-5A	RCAF9793		BOC 10.5.43: SOC	8.4.46
			YV-P-APE	Texas Petroleum Co/TEXACO Ltda	55
			OB-LDM-349		2.55
			HK-996X		60
			HP-289	Southern Air Transport, Miami FL	60/61
				op. for C.I.A. as communications ship during	
				'Bay of Pigs' attempted Cuban invasion.	4.61
				Turismo Aero : struck-off reg.	13.8.63
			VP-KUD	stored Fort Lauderdale FL	64
			5Y-KUD	Atlantic General Enterprises	65
			HR-236	Caribbean Seafood Production Corp	66
			N6108	Steward- Davis Inc, Long Beach CA	7.68/69
				(flew in movie "Tora Tora Tora", Hawaii .69)	
				Aviation Contractors of Boca Chica,	
				Wenatchee WA	72
				Bombers Inc	
				JK Flying Service	
				Paloma Air Oklahoma, Tulsa OK	78
				(based Costa Rica 77/78)	
			TG-BIV	Troya SA, Guatemala	11.80/86
				Meldy Fernandez, La Aurora, Guatamala	86/88
			N5404J	Alan Preston, Houston TX	10.88
				Tailwinds Aviation, Houston TX	1.89
				Aircraft Marketing Inc, Albuquerque NM	1.90
				Henry L. Hancock/Tropical Sea Air,	
				Harrisburg IL	8.90/92
				(flies in USN scheme) : stored, St Louis MO	91
61154 • Mk.VI	PB2B-2	Bu44248		(to RAF JX630)	
				(to RAAF A24-385) BOC 3.9.45 : SOC	22.8.50
			VH-AGB	ntu: Captain P.G. Taylor, Sydney NSW	1.51
			VH-ASA	P. G. Taylor, Sydney NSW "Frigate Bird II"	12.3.51/61
				(stored RAAF Rathmines & Sydney 4.53/74)	
				Museum of Arts & Applied Sciences, Sydney	.61/92
				loan: Camden Museum of Aviation NSW : arr.	6.4.74/83
				Power House Museum, Sydney NSW : displ.	87/92
CV-240	PBV-1A	RCAF9806		BOC 5.4.43: SOC	18.11.46
				(to FA Brasileira as FAB CA-10 65...)	
			PP-PCX	Panair do Brazil, Sao Paulo	71
				(ret. to FAB): struck-off reg.	17.12.71
CV-244 •	PBV-1A	RCAF9810		(to R Swedish AF as Fv47001)	
				Flygvapnets Flygmuseum, Linkoping, Sweden	72/92
				(displ. as RSwAF "79")	
CV-249 •	PBV-1A	RCAF9815		BOC 2.6.43: SOC	25.5.61
			CF-NJB	Kenting Aviation Ltd, Toronto ONT	20.6.63/66
			F-ZBAR	lsd: Protection Civile, Marseilles : del.	6.5.66
			CF-NJB	Kenting Aviation : returned	11.66
			F-ZBBC	lsd: Protection Civile, Marseilles : del.	5.68
			CF-NJB	Kenting Aviation : del. via Dublin	18.9.68/74
			C-FNJB	Norcanair Ltd, Prince Albert SASK	26.4.74/79
				Province of Saskatchewan, La Ronge SASK	23.6.80/91
				(tanker #9)	
CV-264 •	PBV-1A	RCAF9830		BOC 31.7.43: SOC	26.9.61

			CF-PQK	Dept. of Transport & Communications QUE	73
			C-FPQK	Govt of Quebec, Quebec QUE	79/90
				(tanker #12)	
CV-271 •	PBV-1A	RCAF9837		BOC 7.9.43: SOC	29.11.45
			CF-CRP	Canadian Pacific Airlines, Vancouver BC	11.45/57
				Trans Labrador Airlines	9.5.57
				Eastern Provincial Airways Ltd, Gander NFLD	70
				Province of Newfoundland & Labrador	73
			C-FCRP	Province of Newfoundland & Labrador, St Johns NFLD (tanker #6)	79/6.90
				North Atlantic Aviation Museum, Gander NFLD	.90/92
CV-272 •	PBV-1A	RCAF9838		BOC 20.9.43: SOC	31.10.46
				(to FA Brasiliera as FAB C-10A 6525)	
			N4934H	Airplane Sales International, Beverly Hills CA	5.85
				(del. as N4934H Belem-Albuquerque NM 7.84)	
				USNAM, NAS Corpus Christi TX	88/92
				(displ. as USN "6525")	
CV-281	PBV-1A	RCAF11003		BOC 16.11.43: SOC	6.1.61
			CF-UKR	Kenting Aviation Aircraft Ltd, Toronto ONT	66
			F-ZBAX	Protection Civile, Marseilles : del.	20.5.66
				(to French Aeronavale as No.81/F-YEIC)	
				(del. to Tahiti, via Bahrein 12.4.68)	
				retired Papeete, Tahiti	.71/73
			CC-CDS	Roberto Parrague/Aeroservicios Parrague Ltda, Santiago-Los Cerillos (tanker #31)	8.73
				crashed fire bombing, nr Chiguayante, Chile	8.4.79
CV-283 •	PBV-1A	RCAF11005		BOC 27.10.43: SOC	25.5.61
			CF-NJF	Kenting Aviation Ltd, Toronto ONT	.63/74
			F-ZBAY	lsd: Protection Civile, Marseilles : del.	6.5.66
			CF-NJF	Kenting Aviation Ltd : returned	11.66
			F-ZBBD	lsd: Protection Civile, Marseilles : del.	6.5.68
			CF-NJF	Kenting Aviation Ltd : returned via Dublin	21.9.68/74
			C-FNJF	Norcanair Ltd, Prince Albert SASK	26.4.74/79
				Province of Saskatchewan, La Ronge SASK	23.6.80/91
				(tanker #7)	
CV-285 •	PBV-1A	RCAF11007		BOC 30.10.43 SOC	14.4.45
				fcd. ldg. Tofino, Vancouver Island: abandoned	8.2.45
				Commonwealth Military Aviation Museum, Sidney BC (to be recov. by helicopter)	c92
CV-300 •	PBV-1A	RCAF11022		BOC 4.12.43: SOC	10.1.45
			N18446		
			CF-HHR	Transair Ltd, St James MAN	65
				Field Aviation Co Ltd, Calgary ALTA	70
			C-FHHR	Avalon Aviation Ltd, Red Deer ALTA	77/79
				Avalon Aviation Ltd, Parry Sound ONT	.79/89
				(tanker #3; #793)	
				into receivership, stored Parry Sound ONT	28.2.88/89
				(also rep. c/n 300: Bu2459/VA719/RCAF 9719)	
CV-302 •	PBV-1A	RCAF11024		BOC 7.12.43: SOC	20.10.61
			CF-NTN	ntu	
			CF-UAW	Kenting Aircraft Ltd, Toronto ONT	22.4.66/71
			C-FUAW	Norcanair Ltd, Prince Albert SASK	12.5.71/80
				Province of Saskatchewan, La Ronge SASK	.80/92
				(tanker #8)	
CV-311	PBV-1A	RCAF11029		BOC 30.12.43: SOC	2.2.47
			CF-IDS	Northland Airlines Ltd, Winnipeg MAN	65
				North Canada Air Ltd, Prince Albert SASK	70
				Norcanair Ltd, Prince Albert SASK	73

CV-332 •	PBV-1A	Bu67844		(to USAAF as 44-33880)	
	OA-10A		TF-RVR	Icelandair/Flugfelag Islands, Keflavik	
			CF-FKV	Wheeler Airlines, St Jovite Station QUE	65
			F-BMKS	Unions de Transports Aeriens - UTA, Tahiti	24.2.66
				(to French Aeronavale as No. 32/F-YCHB)	
				retired Papeete, Tahiti	.71/73
			CC-CDT	Roberto Parrague/Aeroservicios Parrague Ltda,	
				Santiago-Los Cerillos (tanker #32)	8.73/92
				ICONA/Spanish Ministry of Land & Forest	
				Management: lease, del. Spain ex Chile	7.88/92
CV-333 •	PBV-1A	RCAF11042		BOC 12.2.44: SOC	15.12.60
			CF-PQF	Province de Quebec, Quebec QUE	65/73
			C-FPQF	Govt of Quebec, Quebec QUE (tanker #11)	79/92
CV-343 •	PBV-1A	RCAF11047		BOC 24.2.44: SOC	26.4.62
			CF-OFI	Province of Newfoundland & Labrador	65/73
			C-FOFI	Government of Newfoundland & Labrador,	
				St Johns NFLD	79/90
				withdrawn from use, St Johns NFLD	90
CV-353	PBV-1A	RCAF11052		BOC 11.3.44: SOC	27.6.47
			CF-FVE	Wheeler Airlines, St Jovite Station QUE	65
				Wheeler Northland Airways, St Jean QUE	70/73
				struck-off reg.	6.73
CV-357 •	PBV-1A	RCAF11054		BOC 20.3.44: SOC	27.6.47
				Lee Crutchell, San Jose, Costa Rica	.54/55
				(civil conv. by SALA, San Jose, Costa Rica .55)	
			CF-JCV	Eastern Canada Stevedoring Co, Montreal QUE	7.56/60
				Austin Airways, Toronto ONT	5.60/76
			C-FJCV	Aero Trades Western Ltd, Winnepeg MAN	9.76/82
				stored, Reno-Stead NV	80/82
				Air Caledonia, Vancouver BC	3.82/86
				The Catalina Safari Co, Solano CA	.87/90
				(for Eastern African tours, based Cairo:	
				del. US - Victoria Falls 9.88)	
			Z-CAT	The Catalina Safari Co, Harare, Zimbabwe	7.90/92
CV-369 •	PBV-1A	RCAF11060		BOC 5.4.44: SOC	25.5.61
			N609FF	Firefly Inc, Portland OR	66/72
				(tanker #E40)	
				Terra Surveys Ltd, Ottawa ONT: lsd.	68/72
			VH-EXG	Terra Surveys Ltd, Ottawa ONT	.72/89
				op: Executive Air Services, Essendon VIC	6.72/89
				RAAF Museum, RAAF Point Cook VIC	.89/92
				(awaiting del. from Essendon)	
CV-383	PBV-1A	RCAF11067		BOC 14.4.44: SOC	20.10.61
			CF-NTL	National Tankers Ltd, Calgary ALTA	65
				Leaseway Ltd, Toronto ONT	70
				Flying Fireman Ltd, Sidney BC	71/78
				crashed fire bombing, Snow Lake, MAN	21.5.78
CV-397 •	PBV-1A	RCAF11074		BOC 5.5.44: SOC	7.11.61
			CF-OWE	Ontario Central Airlines, Kenora ONT	65/70
			C-FOWE	Ilford Riverton Airways, Winnipeg MAN	77/83
				Northland Outdoors of Canada	83
			N691RF	Robert J. Franks, Los Angeles CA	6.84
			C-FOWE	Jonathon Seagull Holdings, Vancouver BC	9.85
				damaged landing, Plymouth Harbour UK	30.5.86
				repaired : dep. on ret. flight to Canada	8.10.86
			N69RF	Robert J. Franks, Los Angeles CA	3.89
				Flying Catalina Corp, Los Angeles CA	6.90/92
CV-399	PBV-1A	RCAF11075		BOC 5.5.44: SOC	7.6.62
			CF-OMO		
			N610FF	Firefly Inc, Portland OR	66/69

				Barringer Research Co, Toronto ONT: lsd	65/70
				crashed on survey flt, Rhinelander WI	15.10.70
CV-407	PBV-1A	RCAF11079		BOC 23.5.44: SOC	29.11.62
			CF-PQP	Province of Quebec, Quebec QUE	.64/74
			C-FPQP	Govt of Quebec, Quebec QUE	86/87
				crashed and wo., landing, La Cache QUE	18.7.87
CV-417 •	PBV-1A	RCAF11084		BOC 24.5.44: SOC	26.9.61
			CF-PQL	Province of Quebec, Quebec QUE	.63/73
			C-FPQL	Govt. of Quebec, Quebec QUE (tanker #13)	79/92
CV-420	PBV-1A	Bu67888		(to USAAF as 44-33924)	OA-10A
			CF-NCJ	Government of Newfoundland & Lab., St Johns	73
CV-421 •	PBV-1A	RCAF11086		dam., 25m e. Ucluelet, Vancouver Island BC	2.12.44
				abandoned: remains rep. extant, Ucluelet	92
CV-423 •	PBV-1A	RCAF11087		BOC 5.6.44	
				Canadian National Aeronautical Collection,	65/90
				National Aviation Museum, Rockcliffe ONT	65/92
CV-425 •	PBV-1A	RCAF11088		BOC 5.6.44: SOC	12.12.60
			CF-GMS		
			CF-PQM	Province of Quebec, Quebec QUE	65/73
			C-FPQM	Govt. of Quebec, Quebec QUE (tanker #14)	79/92
CV-427 •	PBV-1A	RCAF11089		BOC 3.6.44: SOC (last RCAF PBY op. 8.4.63)	29.11.62
			CF-PQO	Province of Quebec, Quebec QUE	.63/73
			C-FPQO	Govt. of Quebec, Quebec QUE (tanker #15)	79/92
CV-430	PBV-1A	Bu67893		(to USAAF as 44-33929)	
	OA-10A		CF-NJC	Eastern Provincial Airways, Gander NFLD	65
				Province of Newfoundland & Labrador	70/74
			C-FNJC	Province of Newfoundland & Labrador,	
				St Johns NFLD (tanker #5)	85/92
CV-435 •	PBV-1A	RCAF11093		BOC 16.6.44: SOC	10.4.61
			CF-NJL	David T. Dorosh, Edmonton ALTA	70/80
CV-437 •	PBV-1A	RCAF11094		BOC 22.6.44: SOC	25.5.61
			CF-NJE	Chiupka Airways Ltd, Lynn Lake MAN	65
				Midwest Airlines Ltd, Winnipeg MAN	70/71
				Nordair Airways Ltd, Winnipeg MAN	2.9.71/72
				Ilford Riverton Airways, Winnipeg, Manitoba	73
				St Felicien Air Service, Roberval QUE	.73/76
				op. by Survair Ltd	77
			C-FNJE	Province of Newfoundland & Labrador,	
				St Johns NFLD (tanker #7)	5.78/92
CV-441	PBV-1A	RCAF11096		BOC 23.6.44: SOC	4.10.46
			CF-IHN	Northern Wings Ltd, Quebec QUE	65
				Flying Fireman Ltd, Sidney BC	70/74
			C-GFFD	Flying Fireman Ltd, Sidney BC	5.75/84
				crashed, Thunder Bay ONT	14.5.84
CV-449	PBV-1A	RCAF11100		BOC 3.7.44: SOC	10.4.61
			CF-NJP		
			F-ZBAR	Securite Civile, Marseille-Merignane	
				nose section, noted Marseille-Merignane	77
				nose to Escadrille Pegase, Aix-Les Milles	89
				rep. subsequently broken-up	
CV-465 •	PBV-1A	Bu67918		(to USAAF as 44-33954 ; 10th ARS)	
	OA-10A			forced landing, abandoned, Dago Lake AK	30.9.47
				R. S. Richards, Anchorage AK (salv. rights)	10.48/78

				Alaska Hist. Aircraft Soc., Anchorage AK	.78
			N44BY	Alaska Historical Aircraft Society	5.84
				uplifted from Dago Lake, by CH-54	30.9.84
			N57875	U.S. Historical Aircraft Preservation Museum, Anchorage AK	5.85
				Alaska Aviation Heritage Mus., Anchorage AK	88
				sale rep., Juneau AK : USCR	90/92
				(long term static rest. project)	
CV-483 •	PBV-1A	Bu67936		(to USAAF as 44-33972)	
	OA-10A		CF-IIW	reg.	.55
				Northern Wings Ltd, Quebec QUE	65
			N3202	Universal Air Leasing Co, Grand Blanc MI	.69
			C-GFFC	Flying Fireman, Victoria BC (tanker #6)	6.75/88
				Awood Air Ltd, Victoria BC	88/89
				lsd. SLAFCO Inc, Moses Lake WA	91/92
CV-520 •	PBV-1A	Bu67973		(to USAAF as 44-34009)	
	OA-10A		N62043		
			CF-IHC	Wheeler Airlines, St Jovite Station QUE	.55/56
				Leasair Ltd, Ottawa ONT	65
			F-BMKR	Union de Transports Aerien, Tahiti	9.2.66
				(to French Aeronavale as No. 20/F-YCHA)	
				retired stored, Tahiti	.71/73
			CC-CDU	Roberto Parrague/Aeroservicios Parrague Ltda, Santiago	5.73
			CC-CGY	Aeroservicios Parrague Ltda, Santiago	80
				(allocated tanker #33)	
				wfu and stripped for spares, Los Cerillos	.80/92
				(unconv., in faded Aeronavale scheme)	
CV-560 •	PBV-1A	Bu68013		(to USAAF as 44-34049)	
	OA-10A		CF-GLX	Queen Charlotte Airlines, Vancouver BC	.51
				Pacific Western Airlines, Vancouver BC	60
				Northland Airlines Ltd, Winnipeg MAN	65
				Midwest Airlines Ltd, Winnipeg MAN	70
				Transair Ltd, St.James MAN	72
				Ilford Riverton Airways, Winnipeg, MAN	74
			C-FGLX	Avalon Aviation Ltd, Red Deer ALTA	77/79
				Avalon Aviation Ltd, Parry Sound ONT	.79/89
				(tanker #2; #792)	
				retired, stored Parry Sound ONT	28.2.88/89
			N3000T	ntu	89
CV-592 •	PBV-1A	Bu68045		(to USAAF as 44-34081)	
	OA-10A		VR-HDH	Cathay Pacific Airways Ltd, Hong Kong	11.46
				Macau Air Transport, Macau	
				Trans Australian Airlines - TAA	6.7.62
			VH-SBV	Trans Australian Airlines - TAA	.63/66
				last flight, Port Moresby PNG	5.1.66
				dam. during fire practice, Port Moresby PNG	
				shipped dism. PNG -Auckland	9.75
				MOTAT/D.F. Keith Memorial Park, Auckland	76/86
				RNZAF Museum, RNZAF Whenuapai	87/89
				(under static rest.)	
CV-605 •	PBV-1A	Bu68058		(to USAAF as 44-34094)	
	OA-10A		NC65715		
			TF-RVG	Icelandair/Flugflelag Islands, Keflavik	.49/52
			CF-DFB	Aero Magnetic Surveys Ltd, Toronto ONT	.52/56
				Kenting Aviation Ltd, Toronto ONT	56/59
				Hunting Survey Corp, Toronto ONT	.60
				Kenting Aviation Ltd, Toronto ONT	4.62
				Wheeler Airlines, St Jovite Station QUE	65
				Wheeler Northland Airways Ltd, St Jean QUE	70/71
				Austin Airways, Timmins ONT	2.6.71/76
				Wheeler Northland Airways Ltd, St Jean QUE	1.3.76
			C-FDFB	Province of Newfoundland & Labrador,	

				St. Johns NFLD (tanker #1)	10.78/8.90
				displ., Botwood NFLD	91/92
-	PBY-5A	-	F-ZBAQ	Protection Civile, Marseilles	73
-	PBY-5A	-	F-ZBBO	Protection Civile, Marseilles	
				wreckage noted Marseilles-Merignane	9.72/73
-	PBY-6A	-	HK-957X	Aerotarzoo Ltda, Bogota: wfu at Bogota by	9.72
-	PBY-5	-		Hemet Valley Flying Service, Hemet CA	
				fus. noted unconv. USN "204", Hemet CA	10.78
-	PBY-5	-	ZP-CBA	Aereas de Transportes Nacional Corp "Mixta"	
		L.A.T.N.		retired Asuncion, Paraguay : derelict by	70/72
- •	PBY-5A	-		(to RAAF as A24-.....)	
				war memorial displ., Lake Boga VIC	88/92
				(complete static rest. from several aircraft)	
- •	PBY-5A	-		(to FA Colombiana as FAC 619)	
				rep. displ. Cundinamaica, Barroblanco AB,	
				Madrid, Colombia	92
- •	PBY-5A	-		(to R Danish AF as 82-857, later L-857)	
				RDAF Museum, Vaerlose AB (stored)	85
- •	PBY-5A	-		(to FA Ecuatoriana as 53602)	
				Museo Aero de FAE, Mariscal Sucre AB, Quito	77/88
- •	PBY-5A	-		(to FA Mexicana as ....)	
				Museo de La FAM, stored Mexico City	79
- •	PBY-5A	-		(FA Panama as ....)	
				rep. possibly stored, Iquitos AB, Panama	92
- •	PBY-5A	-		(to FA Paraguaya as T-29: FAP-2002)	
				rep. poss. ex Argentine Navy	
				stored, Asuncion Airport	77/88
				rest. to flying condition, NuGuazau AB	c12.88/92
				Campo Grande AB, Asuncion	92
- •	PBY-	-		fuselage and wings, rep. stored, Ephrata WA	92
- •	PBY-	-		derelict fuselage, rep. stored, Hawkins TX	92

CULVER PQ-14

N-256 •	PQ-14A	-	N4744N	James E. Bass, College Park GA	63
				Spencer B. Miller, Winnsboro TX	3.64/92
N-427 •	PQ-14A	-	N75380	Ransom J. Heath, Deridder LA	63
				D. J. Wilkins, Gooding ID	66/69
				sale rep.	84/92
N-763 •	PQ-14A	44-21819	N1063M	Michael Leach, Jessup PA	63
				Albert W. Mosley, Pennsauken NJ	66
				William Smela, Washington Crossing PA	69
				Pima County Air Museum, Tucson AZ	72/92
				(displ. as "421819")	
N-839 •	PQ-14A	-	N89573	Howard C. Martin, Hayward CA	69
			N15HM	Ed Maloney/The Air Museum, Chino CA	6.79/92
N-917 •	PQ-14B		N5526A	Dial Wilson, Sarasota FL	63
				Ronald A. Billib, Sarasota FL	66
				Robert V. Campbell, Oskaloosa IA	69/72
				Airpower Museum, Blakesburg IA	12.74/92

- •	PQ-14A PQ-14B	44-68334	N10146	USAF, Wright-Patterson AFB, Dayton OH	63
				EAA Air Museum, Hales Corner WI	67/76
			N999ML	Morton W. Lester, Martinsville VA	12.86/88
				EAA Air Museum, Oshkosh WI	.88/92
N-1059 •	PQ-14B	44-68462	N5389N	Kenneth L. Farris, Bedias TX	63/69
				Robert E. Parcell, Fort Worth TX	76/84
				USAFM, Wright-Patterson AFB, Dayton OH	87/88
N-2402 •	PQ-14A	-	N5092V	D. C. Lawton, San Antonio TX	66/69
				sale rep., San Antonio TX	72/92
N-2432	PQ-14A	-	N4648V	Serge T. Winkler, Tucson AZ	63
				D. J. Wilkins, Gooding ID	66
				George B. Harris, Hickory NC	1.68/92
N-2804	PQ-14A	-	N1676M	Glen D. Martin, Pacoima CA	66/84
-	PQ-14A	43-44439	N5281N	Robert Hoskins, Oklahoma City OK	66/84
- •	PQ-14B TD2C-1	45-58816		(to USN as Bu120035)	
				NASM, Silver Hill MD	65/88
- •	PQ-14B TD2C-1	45-58863		(to USN as Bu120082)	
				NAS Norfolk VA (stored)	65
				USNAM, NAS Pensacola FL	65/91
- •	PQ-14B TD2C-1	45-59043		(to USN as Bu120262)	
			N2775	The Air Museum, Claremont CA	.58
				Leon Brodie, Los Angeles CA	66
				Mack S. Johnson, Kalispell MT	69
				David L. Cronk, Glendora CA	2.71/92

CURTISS F-16C

- •	XF15C-1	Bu01215		New England Air Museum, Windsor Locks CT	87/92
				(fully rest. : displ. as USN "NATC/215")	

CURTISS O-52 OWL

14279 •	0-52	40-2746		Confederate Air Force, Harlingen TX	74/84
				Yankee Air Corps, Chino CA	.84/87
				(arr. unconv. from TX, Chino CA .86)	
				Military Aircraft Restoration Corp, Chino CA	.87/88
				(awaiting rest. in Tallichet yard, Chino 88)	
14296 •	0-52	40-2763		USAFM, Wright-Patterson AFB, Dayton OH	65/89
				(displ. as "119")	
14302 •	0-52	40-2769	N61241	B & F Aircraft Inc, Oaklawn IL	66
				M. Foose & G. Courtwright, Oaklawn IL	
				EAA Air Museum, Milwaukee WI	67/76
				Yankee Air Corps, Chino CA	81/92
				(rest., ff Chino CA 6.82: flies as "02769")	
- •	0-52	-		Walter Soplata Collection, Newbury OH	76/85

c/n	type	mil. serial	reg.	history	date
2380 •	P-40B	-		(to Soviet AF as .....)	
				recovered in Russia	92s
				The Fighter Collection, Duxford	92
16073 •	P-40B	41-13297		lost on patrol Hawaii	1.42
				Curtiss Wright Historical Association,	
				Torrance, CA: wreck recov.	c89/90
				(rest. project to flying condition, using parts	
				from P-40 39-287: crashed Hawaii 10.41)	
- •	P-40C	-		(to Soviet AF as .....)	
				Armed Forces Central Museum, Moscow	50s
				Zhukovsky Institute, Moscow	85
15133 •	P-40E Mk.1a	AK752		(to RCAF as 1028)	
				surplus, Vulcan AB ALTA ; to local farm	.47
				stripped by farmer, later buried on farm	.53
				excavated, recov. by John Paul	.75
			N96045	John R. Paul, Alamo CA	.75
				Steve Seghetti, Vacaville CA	76/85
				Col Pay, Scone NSW (rest. project)	.85
			VH-KTH	Col Pay, Scone NSW	12.89/92
				(rebuilt Scone, ff 15.12.89 as "AK752/ZR-J")	
				dam. landing Coolangatta QLD (repaired)	2.91
15184 •	P-40E Mk.1a	AK803		(to RCAF as 1034)	
				George Maude, Fulford Harbour BC	8.46
				(disposal ex Patricia Bay AB, Vancouver Island,	
				by raft to Maude's home Salt Spring Island .46)	
				stored in open, Salt Spring Island BC	46/74
			C-GHTM	George Maude, Victoria BC	.74/89
				(to Victoria BC for rest. to fly 8.74, fitted	
				with new mainplane ex RCAF 1057)	
				Commonwealth Military Aviation Museum,	
				Sidney BC	89
15208 •	P-40E Mk.1a	AK827		(to RCAF as 1038)	
			N1223N	Fred Dyson, Boeing Field, Seattle WA	13.9.47/49
				(disposal ex Patricia Bay AB, Vancouver Island,	
				barged to Boeing Field, Seattle WA .47)	
				Bob Sturges, Troutdale OR	.49
				Leo J. Demers, Salem OR	
				Rogue River Water Association, Medford OR	54
				Weather Modification Co, Redlands CA	.54/57
				Bill Ruch, Pompano Beach FL	.59
				David B. Robinson, Miami Fl	.59/69
				(advertising display at drive-in theatre, then	
				parked derelict Pompano Beach Airport 60/64)	
				William Ross, Chicago IL (dism.)	.69
				Robert L. Goodman, Litte Rock AR (dism.)	.70
				Charles F. Nichols, Covina CA (dism.)	76/86
			N40245	Yankee Air Corps, Chino CA	4.83/92
				(rebuilt Chino, flies as "136483")	
15244 •	P-40E Mk.1a	AK863		(to RCAF as 1044)	
				John Stansall, Hartney MAN : on farm	.47
				John R. Paul, Alamo CA later Boise ID	.76/92
				(recov. ex farm near Tabor ALTA .76 by	
				John Paul; rest. project, Caldwell ID)	
15370 •	P-40E Mk.1a	AK899		(to RCAF as 1051)	
				Fred Dyson, Boeing Field, Seattle WA	23.10.47
				(disposal ex Patricia Bay AB, Vancouver Island,	
				barged to Boeing Field, Seattle WA .47)	
				displ. gas station roof, Everett WA	54/73
				Military Aircraft restoration Corp, Chino CA	.73

Seen in the UK for the first time in September 1992 The Fighter Collection's rare Curtiss P-40B was recovered from Russia and is a rare machine indeed. Several other aircraft have been recovered for the Fighter Collection including two Hurricanes and a Spitfire from the same source. (Gary R. Brown)

			N9837A	Military Aircraft restoration Corp, Chino CA	79/85
				John D. Pearl/Rudulphs Flying Circus,	
				Chino CA	15.1.85
				Richard W. Hansen, Batavia IL	87/92
				(rebuild Rock County IL, first flight Spring .92)	
				(FAA quote id. "15280")	
15376 •	P-40E	AK905		(to RCAF as 1052)	
	Mk.1a		CF-OGZ	Bob Warden, Calgary ALTA	c56/68
			N11122	William Ross, Chicago IL	.68/72
				Don Plumb,Windsor, ONT	75
				Max Hoffman	76
			N40PE	Rudolf A. Frasca, Champaign IL	78/92
				(FAA orig. quote id."15286", later AK905)	
15404 •	P-40E	AK933		(to RCAF as 1057)	
	Mk.1a			recov. ex farm ALTA by Bob Warden, Calgary	
				hulk stored, Half Moon Bay CA	66
				(mainplane to George Maude, BC for RCAF 1034)	
			N94466	John R. Paul, Alamo CA	66/89
				(rebuilt using mainplane recov. by George Maude	
				ex Cutbank MT .59 : ff. Livermore CA .70)	
				lsd. Old Flying Machine Co, Duxford UK	17.6.84/89
				John R. Paul, Boise ID	4.89/92
				(FAA quotes id. as "AK899")	
15411 •	P-40E	AK940		(to RCAF as 1058) "Vancouver VIII; Popeye X"	
	Mk.1a			surplus at Vulcan ALTA	46
				displ. service station, Red Deer ALTA	46/c67
				Bob Warden Calgary ALTA	c67
				Bob Diemert, Carman MAN	70
			N940AK	Stewart Schwartz & Bill Pryor, Pontiac MI	
				Norton Aero Ltd, Athol ID	84
				William Anderson/Rangoon Airways Inc,	
				Las Vegas NV	84/88
				William Anderson/National Warplane	
				Museum, Geneseo NY	88/91
				(FAA quotes id. 15321; flies as "115321")	
15346 •	P-40E	AK875		(to RCAF as 1047)	
	Mk.1a		NX1048N	Fred Dyson, Boeing Field, Seattle WA	23.10.47
				(disposal ex Patricia Bay AB, Vancouver Island,	
				barged to Boeing Field, Seattle WA .47)	
			N1048N	Ellis R. Meaker, Albany NY	2.4.48/49
				Ken Van Buren, Newfield NJ	8.2.49/51
				Munsey E. Crost, Ashbury Park NJ	6.3.51/52
				James W. Boy, West Durham NC	20.4.52
				Choctaw Area Boy Scouts, Meridian MS	6.8.52/64

				NASM, Silver Hill MD : del. dism. by C-119	.64/74
				(static rest. Andrews AFB .74/76)	
				NASM, Washington DC, displ. as "194"	2.76/88
18723 •	P-40E	AK979		(to RCAF as 1064)	
	Mk.1a			Fred Dyson, Boeing Field, Seattle WA	13.9.47
				(disposal ex Patricia Bay AB, Vancouver Island,	
				barged to Boeing Field, Seattle WA .47)	
				Duane W. Myler, Fostoria OH	.47
			N5672N	Joseph L. Ulman, Fostoria OH	2.48
				Van's Air Service, St Cloud MN	49/50
				B.H. Roberts/Continental Steel Buildings,	
				Burbank CA	11.50/56
				(rebuilt as mod. cockpit 2 seater; ff. 7.51)	
				Shelby H. Curlee, St Louis MO	.56/63
				Bruce Goessling, Monterey CA	63
				crashed landing, Hollister CA	.63
			N151U	Gilbert N. Macy, Monterey CA	63/67
			N151U	Gilbert N. Macy, Monterey CA	
				(to Hawaii on carrier "Yorktown" for movie	
				"Tora Tora Tora", dam. during filming .69)	
				loaned to EAA Museum, Hales Corner WI	69/73
				Thomas L. Camp, Livermore CA	11.72/78
				(trucked to Livermore CA: ff. 13.12.73)	
			N9DA		
			N41JR	Tiger International Inc, Los Angeles CA	
			N41JA	Tiger International Inc, Los Angeles CA	9.80
			N40FT	Flying Tiger Line /Tiger International Inc,	
				Los Angeles CA (flew in camouflage "67")	12.83/89
				loan: San Diego Aerospace Museum CA	87/91
				Federal Express Corp, Memphis TN	10.89/92
18731 •	P-40E	AK987		(to RCAF as 1068)	
	Mk.1a		N1237N	Fred Dyson, Boeing Field, Seattle WA	13.9.47
				(disposal ex Patricia Bay AB, Vancouver Island,	
				barged to Boeing Field, Seattle WA .47)	
			N5673N	Duane W. Myler, Fostoria OH	48
				Robert L. Holderman, Fostoria OH	8.6.48
				Harrison E. Rogers, Quincy MI	8.9.49
				Charles Finkenbine, Coldwater MI	11.52/57
				Frank G. Tallman, Glenview IL	9.9.57
				Walter H. Erikson Jr, Minneapolis MN	.58
				Charles P. Doyle, Rosemount MN	11.58/65
				crashed on ferry flight, nr Fostoria OH	1.12.58
				USAFM, Wright-Patterson AFB OH	c65/90
				(static rest., displ. as "104")	
				(USAFM quotes id."AK987, P-40N 42-65406")	
18779 •	P-40E	AL135		(to RCAF as 1076)	
	Mk.1a			stored Vulcan AB, Chater AB, MacDonald AB	47/60
				Canadian National Aviation Museum,	
				Rockcliffe ONT	.64/92
18781	P-40E	AL137		(to RCAF as 1078)	
	Mk.1a			Fred Dyson, Boeing Field, Seattle WA	23.10.47
				(disposal ex Patricia Bay AB, Vancouver Island,	
				barged to Boeing Field, Seattle WA .47)	
				H. William Porter, Herscher IL	10.1.48
				Jimmie Fulcher, Las Vegas NV (deal aborted)	.48
				aircraft stolen from Boeing Field	c49
			N88917	H. William Porter, Kilgore TX/Herscher IL	.73/92
				(rep. still reg. in hope aircraft located!)	
18796 •	P-40E	AL152		(to RCAF as 1082)	
	Mk.1a		N1207V	Fred Dyson, Boeing Field, Seattle WA	13.9.47/48
				(disposal ex Patricia Bay AB, Vancouver Island,	

				barged to Boeing Field, Seattle WA .47)	
				Charles Wenzel, Flushing NY	6.2.48/50
				Bradley J. Hurd/ Washington County Crop	
				Protective Association, Akron CO	14.6.50
				Burt Mushkin, Moosic CT	
				Gordon C. Clouser, Norman OK	53
				K. C. Benbow/American Aviation Service,	
				Greenville NC	25.3.53
				(stored Wilkes-Barre PA c50/54)	
				Walter H. Erickson, Minneapolis MN	13.9.54/58
				(trucked to Minneapolis, rebuilt, ff .57)	
				Frank G. Tallman, Glenview IL	31.1.58
				Tallmantz Aviation/Movieland of the Air	
				Riverside CA, then Orange County CA	.59/66
				Rosen-Novak Auto Co, Omaha NE	18.2.66
				(displayed Tallmantz, until auctioned 29.5.68)	
				A. R. Dick Woodson, Livermore CA	29.5.68/78
				(used in movie "Tora Tora Tora" .68)	
				(rebuild Livermore CA, ff 15.12.73)	
				Eric Mingledorff, Monroe LA	12.77/85
				(trucked CA to LA 2.78, rest. to fly)	
			N95JB	John MacGuire, El Paso TX	7.86/90
				War Eagles Air Museum, Santa Teresa NM	90/92
18815 •	P-40E Mk.1a	AL171		(to RCAF1084)	
				surplus at Vulcan AB ALTA: "Vancouver IV"	46
				Walter Harris Motors, Champion ALTA	
				fuselage hulk recov. by Bob Warden, Calgary	
				Neil M. Rose, Vancouver WA (fuselage)	
				The Air Museum, Ontario CA	65/73
				John R. Paul, Alamo CA : rest. project	.73
			N62435	John R. Paul, Livermore CA	76/79
				(rebuilt to fly, Livermore CA)	
				Weeks Air Museum, Tamiami FL	82/92
				(flies as "428370/42")	
				dam. landing Tamiami FL (repaired)	3.90
				(FAA quotes c/n 28370: ie. 42-104608)	
- •	P-40E Mk.1a	41-5336		(to RAAF as A29-28) BOC 3.42: SOC	9.47
				Pearce Dunn/Warbirds Aviation Museum,	
				Mildura VIC	68/85
				(fuselage only, recov. from farm Mildura)	
				Jack McDonald, Essendon, VIC	.85/92
				(fuselage rest. completed, stored Oakey QLD)	
16738 •	P-40E Mk.1a	41-13522		(to RAAF as A29-53) BOC 3.42: SOC	2.49
				RAAF disposal, RAAF Werribee VIC	c48
				B. Lang, Beeac via Colac VIC:	c48/66
				Moorabbin Air Museum, Melbourne VIC	12.66/92
				(fus. recov. ex farm, Colac VIC 10.12.66:	
				rest., displ. as"A29-53" using Mustang mainplane)	
19128 •	P-40E Mk.1a	41-25109		(to RAF as ET433: RNZAF as NZ3094)	
				recov. from Rukuhia NZ	.59
				noted at Asplin's Supplies, Hamilton NZ	71
				John Chambers, Dairy Flat NZ (stored)	c71/92
19177 •	P-40E Mk.1a	41-25158		(to RAF as ET482: RNZAF as NZ3009)	
				impressed : USAAC 68th PG, Tonga	
				recov. from Rukuhia NZ	59
				displ. Museum of Transport & Technology,	
				Auckland NZ	64/87
				d'E. C. Darby & R. H. McGarry, Auckland NZ	87/89
				(stored Auckland NZ 87/89)	
18605 •	P-40E Mk.1a	41-36084		(to RAAF as A29-133) BOC 6.42 SOC	8.2.49
				Nelson R. Wilson, Wandin VIC	.60
				(recov. derelict ex orchard, Melbourne VIC)	

			VH-NRW	Nelson R. Wilson, Wandin VIC	87/92
				(long-term rebuild to fly, almost complete)	
18931 •	P-40E	41-36410		(to RAF as EV156: RNZAF as NZ3043)	
	Mk.1a			recov. from Rukuhia NZ	c66
				John R. Smith, Nelson NZ : stored	67/89
- •	P-40F	41-14112		fcd. ldg. Errumango Island, Vanuatu	20.12.42
				(hulk recov. by Robert Grienert & Martin Mednis,	
				Sydney NSW 11.89 : shipped to Australia)	
				Judy E. Pay, Tyabb VIC (rest. project)	.90/92
- •	P-40F	41-14205		fcd. ldg. Errumango Island, Vanuatu	20.12.42
				(hulk recov. by Robert Grienert & Martin Mednis,	
				Sydney NSW 11.89 : shipped to Australia)	
				Ian A. Whitney, Romsey VIC	.89/91
				Graham Hoskings, Tyabb VIC (rest. project)	.91/92
				(id. rep. correct)	
21117 •	P-40K	42-9733		abandoned Amchitka Island, Aleutians	
				recov. by Bob Sturges, Troutdale OR	.69
			N4363	Joseph A. Morasky, Guildford CT	72/74
				Wolcott Air Services, Wolcott CT	78/84
				Bob Byrne, Bloomfield Hills MI : stored	86/88
			ZK-FRE	ntu;Tim Wallis/Alpine Fighter Collection, Wanaka	.88/92
			ZK-PXL	Alpine Fighter Collection, Wanaka	
				(rebuilt Wanaka NZ 88/92, ff 18 4.92)	
21133 •	P-40K	42-9749		crashed Port Heiden AK: to salvage yard	
				recov. by Al Redick & Steve Myers	c78
				David Boyd (stored)	
			N67253	Airpower Inc, Chelan WA	76/84
			N293FR	Bob Byrne, Bloomfield Hills MI	5.86/87
				(rebuilt, ff. 5.86)	
				William Clark, State College PA	.87
				Major Ben Preston (flew as "47071")	85
				Repatria Inc	88/90
				Evergreen International Airlines/747 Inc,	
				McMinnville OR	5.90/92
				(FAA quotes id. "FR293" for N293FR;	
				"23-4275" for N67253)	
				(flies as "FR293", later "21-05006/53,	
				later "Rascal")	
21650 •	P-40K	42-10266		recov. ex Fairbanks crash site by Red Berry	
			N40K	Bill Stebbins, Louisville KY (rest. project)	76/89
27466	P-40M	43-5788		(to RCAF as 832)	
	Mk.III		N1228N	Fred Dyson, Boeing Field, Seattle WA	13.9.47
				(disposal ex Patricia Bay AB, Vancouver Island,	
				barged to Boeing Field, Seattle WA .47)	
				Bill March, Phoenix AZ	51
				Lloyd P. Nolen, Mercedes TX	.51
				Jim Cook, Jacksboro TX (weather mods.)	.53
				Leo J. Demers, Salem OR	55
				W. Keith Larkin/Weather Modification Company,	
				Redlands CA	.55/60
				del. by Larkin to museum, Ocala FL	.60/61
				Joe E. Jones/Confederate AF, Rio Hondo TX	10.6.61
				(del. Ocala FL to TX, by Lefty Gardner 10.6.61)	
				Lloyd P. Nolen/Confederate AF, Mercedes TX	63/65
				crashed, dest. Rebel Field, Mercedes TX	13.3.65
27483 •	P-40M	43-5795		(to RCAF as 845)	
	Mk.III		N1232N	Vance B. Roberts, Seattle WA	27.9.47/50
				(disposal ex Patricia Bay AB, Vancouver Island,	

				barged to Boeing Field, Seattle WA .47)	
				Art J. Bell/Bell Air Services,Boeing Field WA	21.7.50/51
				Jerry L. McMullin, Marysville CA	13.1.51
				John W. Davis/Davis Dusters, Colusa CA	18.9.51/56
				Clyde R. Mallory, Clatskanie OR	9.3.56/57
				W. Keith Larkin/Weather Modification Company, San Jose CA	12.6.57/61
				M. N. Farr & Larry.W. Hamilton, Sonoma CA	10.6.61/64
				Morrill Farr, Sonoma CA	27.3.64
				Harrah's Automobile & Aircraft Collection, Reno NV : static displ.	8.12.64/82
				Bill Destefani, Bakersfield CA	6.82/89
				(rebuilt Shafter CA, ff .83 as "AK845/GM-D")	
				John R. Sandberg, Scottsdale AZ	90
				Bill Destefani, Bakersfield CA	91
				Lone Star Flight Museum, Galveston TX	.91/92
27490 •	P-40M Mk.III	43-5802		(to RCAF as 840)	
			N1233N	Vance B. Roberts, Seattle WA	27.9.47/50
				(disposal ex Patricia Bay AB, Vancouver Island, barged to Boeing Field, Seattle WA .47)	
				Art J. Bell/Bell Air Services,Boeing Field WA	21.7.50
				Oregon State University : inst. airframe	.51/54
				Bob Sturges/Columbia Airmotive, Troutdale OR	.54/66
				(advertising displ., Troutdale Airport 54/61)	
			N1009N(2	Columbia Airmotive, Troutdale OR	2.67/79
				(stored dism. Troutdale, adopted paperwork id. scrapped P-40N N1009N (43-23494/RCAF 877) from Earl Reinert IL 19.2.67)	
				Thomas L. Camp, Livermore CA/Las Vegas NV	.79/92
				(ex stock military: rest. Livermore CA, ff .82)	
				The Fighter Collection, Duxford	2.85/92
				(arr. dism. Duxford 14.2.85, ff 27.2.85; flies as "FR870/GA-S")	
27501 •	P-40M Mk.III	43-5813		(to RNZAF as NZ3119)	
				recov. from Rekuhia NZ	c69
				John Chambers, Dairy Flat, Auckland NZ	c69/92
				(rest. to fly)	
-	P-40N Mk.IV	-		(to RCAF as 850)	
			N.........N	Vance B. Roberts, Seattle WA	27.9.47
				(disposal ex Patricia Bay AB, Vancouver Island, barged to Boeing Field, Seattle WA .47)	
				Babb Co, Burbank CA	c49
28492 •	P-40N Mk.IV	42-104730		(to RAAF A29-448/A29-1050)	8.43
				crashed landing, Tadji Strip PNG	5.44
				recov. by d'E. C. Darby & N. M. Armstrong from Tadji, West Sepik PNG	.74
				d'E. C. Darby, Auckland NZ : stored	.74/89
28580 •	P-40N Mk.IV	42-104818		(to RAAF A29-405/A29-1068)	7.43
				damaged in collision at Tadji Strip	4.44
				Military Aircraft restoration Corp, Chino CA	.74/89
				(recov. by d'E. C. Darby & N. M. Armstrong for YAF from Tadji, West Sepik PNG .74)	
28721 •	P-40N	42-104959		Military Aircraft restoration Corp, Chino CA	.74/89
				(recov. by d'E. C. Darby & N. M. Armstrong for YAF from Finschaffen, PNG .74: wing/cockpit section: shipped to YAF with fuselage of 42-105861 from Dumpu & tail surfaces of 42-105526 from Finschhafen)	
28723 •	P-40N	42-104961		Military Aircraft restoration Corp, Chino CA	.74/89
				(recov. by d'E. C. Darby & N. M. Armstrong	

				for YAF from Tsili Tsili, PNG 9.73)	
28813 •	P-40N	42-105051		(to RAAF as A29-462) BOC	8.43
	Mk.IV			forced landed, Rattlesnake Island QLD	7.45
				Keith W. Hopper, Townsville QLD	86/92
				(recov. from Rattlesnake Island, rebuild to fly)	
28954 •	P-40N	42-105192		(to RCAF as 858)	
	Mk.IV		N1197N	Fred Dyson, Boeing Field, Seattle WA	23.10.47
				(disposal ex Patricia Bay AB, Vancouver Island,	
				barged to Boeing Field, Seattle WA .47)	
				W. P. Bridges, Jackson MS	.52/54
				Louis Rice, Maysville CA	.54
				Richard B. Rowlette, Riverside CA	.54
				Walter Brockin, Riverside CA	55
				W. Keith Larkin/Weather Modification Company,	
				San Jose CA	.55/59
				dam., wheels-up landing near Denver CO	.58
				The Air Museum, Ontario CA	c59/70
				(wreck purchased, rest. for static displ.)	
			N85104	Planes of Fame, Chino CA	10.80/92
				(rest. Chino 77/81,ff .81 as USAAC "47")	
29269 •	P-40N	42-105513		Ian A. Whitney/Australian Aerospace Museum,	
				Melbourne VIC	87/92
				(recov. from Finschhafen PNG by Whitney)	
				(rest. project, Essendon & Romsey VIC)	
29282	P-40N	42-105526		Ian A. Whitney, Romsey VIC	.74/89
				(recov. by d'E. C. Darby & N. M. Armstrong,	
				rear fuselage from Finschhafen PNG .74 ;	
				being used in rest. of 42-105513)	
29472 •	P-40N	42-105710		(to RAAF as A29-528 /A29-1134)	
	Mk.IV			crashed Keningau Strip PNG	6.45
				Military Aircraft restoration Corp, Chino CA	.74/89
				(recov. by d'E. C. Darby & N. M. Armstrong	
				for YAF from Tadji, West Sepik PNG .74)	
29606 •	P-40N	42-105844		(to RCAF as 864)	
	Mk.IV			Canadian Museum of Flight & Transportation,	
				Vancouver BC	88/91
				(wing & parts: recov. ex farm, Courtenay BC)	
29629 •	P-40N	42-105867		(to RCAF as 867)	
	Mk.IV			Robert H. Farrington, Seattle WA	12.8.47
				(disposal ex Patricia Bay AB, Vancouver Island,	
				barged to Boeing Field, Seattle WA .47)	
			N1226N	Jim P. Swann/Universal Aircraft, Seattle WA	29.9.47/51
				Robert B. Harmon, Nabnasset MA	24.2.51
				Gordon Clouser, Norman OK: weather mods	1.6.51/57
				Isaac Newton Burchinall Jnr, Paris TX	27.7.57/58
				dam. landing, Paris TX	.58
				Glen Parker Jr, Nederland TX : dism.	11.11.58
				Mike Dillon, Phoenix AZ	c62/65
				Confederate AF, Mercedes/Harlingen TX	5.65/91
				American Airpower Heritage Flying Museum,	
				Midland TX	9.91/92
				(flies as "29629/48")	
29677 •	P-40N	42-105915		(for del. to Chinese AF: impressed USAAF)	
				recov. from Tadji, West Sepik PNG	.74
				Malcolm Long Collection, Melbourne VIC	.74/88
				displ. RAAF Museum, RAAF Point Cook VIC	77
				displ. Chewing Gum Field Museum,	
				Tallebudgera QLD	80/85

				displ. Drage Air World, Wangaratta VIC	.85/91
				Jack McDonald & John Rayner, Melbourne VIC	.91/92
				(rebuild to fly)	
29689 •	TP-40N	42-105927		NAS Willow Grove PA	58
				NASM, Silver Hill MD	65
				USAFM, Peterson AFB CO	76/88
29713 •	P-40N	42-105951		recov. by d'E. C. Darby & N. M. Armstrong	
				from Tadji, West Sepik PNG	.74
				Military Aircraft restoration Corp, Chino CA	.74/89
				(wings held by d' E.C.Darby, Auckland NZ:	
				fuselage rep. stored, Barstow CA)	
29858 •	P-40N	42-106096		rep. recov. from PNG (id. poss. 42-106196)	
				Dave Chvatal MN	
				Neil Bird, Jacksonville, FL	85/92
29863 •	P-40N Mk.IV	42-106101		(to RAAF as A29-556/A29-1134: BU) BOC	10.43
				hit by landing aircraft, Tadji Strip	5.44
				recov. by d'E. C. Darby & N. M. Armstrong	
				from Tadji, West Sepik PNG	.74
				Military Aircraft restoration Corp, Chino CA	.74/89
				(rep. stored, Barstow CA)	
30158 •	P-40N Mk.IV	42-106396		(to RCAF as 880)	
			NL1195N	Fred Dyson, Boeing Field, Seattle WA	23.10.47
				(disposal ex Patricia Bay AB, Vancouver Island,	
				barged to Boeing Field, Seattle WA .47)	
			N1195N	Jack B. Hardwick/Hardwick Aircraft,	
				Rosemead CA	53/54
				dam. wheels-up landing	
				stored in Hardwick's yard, El Monte CA	55/76
				John R. Paul, Alamo CA (stored dism.)	.76/77
				John R. Paul, Hamilton MT later Boise ID	84/92
				(rebuilt, flew as"130158", later"2106396";	
				race #77,#17)	
30901 •	P-40N Mk.IV	43-22962		(to RNZAF as NZ3220/FE-T "Gloria Lyons")	
				recov. from Rukuhia NZ	c66
				John R. Smith, Maheno/Oamaru NZ	67/89
32824 •	TP-40N	44-7084		NASM, Washington DC	
				USAFM, Wright-Patterson AFB, Dayton OH	61/65
				Charles P. Doyle, Rosemount MN	.65/78
			N999CD	Charles P. Doyle, Rosemount MN	.78
				Planes of Fame East, Spring Park MN	80/92
				(flies as "Miss Josephine")	
32932 •	P-40N	44-7192		Paul Mantz, Glendale CA	19.2.46/60
				(USAAF disposal ex Stillwater AFB OK 19.2.46)	
				displ. Griffith Park, Los Angeles CA	
				Tallmantz Collection, Orange County CA	60/67
			N4161K	San Diego Aerospace Museum, San Diego CA	67/72
				(displ. as "14192")	
			N10626	Doug Champlin/Windward Aviation, Enid OK	.72/80
				Champlin Fighter Museum, Mesa AZ	81/92
				(FAA quotes id. "4192"; also quoted as	
				33097/44-7357)	
32943	P-40N	44-7203		Paul Mantz, Glendale CA	19.2.46/60
				(USAAF disposal ex Stillwater AFB OK 19.2.46)	
				rep. displayed Chino CA	c72
33109 •	P-40N	44-7369		Cal Aero Technical Institute, Glendale CA	
				Ed Maloney/The Air Museum, Claremont CA	c57/70
			N94500	Lou Kauffman (rebuild Van Nuys CA .71)	.71/72
			C-GTGR	Don Plumb/Spitfire Ltd,Windsor ONT	1.74

				Max Hoffman, Fort Collins CO	76
			N40PN	John Williams	76/77
				Joseph G. Mabee, Midland TX	78/92
33359 •	P-40N	44-7619	N5038V	Chowchilla High School, Chowchilla CA	
				Caroll Collier (car dealer's display)	
				George Mokski/Avia-Union, Montebello CA	.54
			N1251N (2	Avia-Union, Montebello CA	.54
				(adopted id. of crashed P-40E N1251N of Avia-Union: c/n 18757, AL113/RCAF 1073)	
				(racer mods., cut-down F-80 canopy)	
				The Air Museum, Ontario CA	11.59/73
			N222SU	Suzanne Parish/Kalamazoo Aviation History Museum, Kalamazoo MI	.73/91
				(flies as "47619")	
32440 •	P-40N	44-7700		(to FA Brasiliera as 4064)	
				Museum Aerospacial da Forca Aera Brasiliera	79
33723 •	P-40N	44-7983		Paul Mantz, Glendale CA	19.2.46/60
				(USAAF disposal ex Stillwater AFB OK 19.2.46)	
				Frank G. Tallman/Movieland of the Air, Orange County CA	60/70
				(stored Tallmantz Collection, USAAF sc. 60/70)	
			N9950	Military Aircraft restoration Corp, Chino CA	7.70/89
				Warbirds of Great Britain, Biggin Hill UK	.89/91
				(rebuild Chino 89/91, shipped to UK 7.91)	
				(FAA quotes id. "2-6-149")	
33915 •	TP-40N	44-47923	N923	H. L. Pemberton, Niles MI	
				Paul Mantz, Los Angeles CA	.59
				Frank G. Tallman/ Movieland of the Air, Orange County CA	69/84
				Weeks Air Museum, Tamiami FL	.85/92
				Damaged Hurricane Andrew, Miami, FL	24.8.92
- •	P-40K	-	N67254	Airpower Inc, Chelan WA	76/84
				rep. awaiting recov. from Aleutians	
				(FAA quote id. "23-4279")	
- •	P-40N Mk.IV	-		(to SAAF as 5067)	
				crashed in swamp near Umkomaas, Natal	30.3.44
				recov. planned	89
- •	P-40E Mk.1a	-		(to RCAF as 10....)	
				Granger Taylor, Duncan BC	77
				(static rest. of several scrapyard hulks)	
				Bob Diemert, Carman MAN	82/87
- •	P-40K	-		Al Reddick	c88
				rep. recov. ex Alaska, stored unrestored	
				Wolcott Air Services at Aero Trader, Chino CA	88/91
				Neil Bird, Jacksonville, FL	92
	P-40N			Neil Bird, Jacksonville, FL	86/92
- •	P-40N	-		Hal Thompson, Arcadia FL	.86/91
				recov. from swap, Florida	.86
				(static rest. project)	
- •	P-40N	-		Ian A. Whitney, Romsey VIC	76
				(hulk recov. ex Iron Range QLD .76)	
				Ron Lee, Melbourne VIC	90/91
				Graham Hoskings, Tyabb VIC	.91/92
				(stored Tyabb, pending rest.)	

-	•	P-40N	-		forced landing, Everglades FL	.43
					recov., Hal Thompson, Arcadia FL	.86/91

CURTISS SB-2 HELLDIVER

-	•	SB2C-3	Bu19075		The Air Museum, Ontario CA	67/78
					Yesterdays Air Force, Chino CA	79/81
				N4250Y	Military Aircraft Restoration Corp, Chino CA	7.81/87
					Yankee Air Corps, Chino CA	.87/89
					(stored unconv., Chino CA)	
-	•	SB2C-1	Bu75552		(A-25A diverted to USMC)	
					ditched, Lake Washington, Seattle WA	
					recov. by Mike Rawson, Minneapolis MN	90
-	•	SB2C-1	Bu76805		(A-25A 42-80449 ntu: diverted to USMC)	
					ditched, Lake Washington, Seattle WA	
					recov. by Mike Rawson, Minneapolis MN	90
-	•	SB2C-5	Bu83321		(to R. Hellenic AF as 83321)	
					displ. Polemico Moussio, Athens	67/91
366	•	SB2C-5	Bu83410		(to R Thai AF as 3-4/97)	
					RTAF Museum, Don Muang, Bangkok	67/90
-	•	SB2C-5	Bu83479		NASM, stored at Silver Hill MD	65/75
					loaned: USNAM, NAS Pensacola FL	.76/91
					(displ. as "H-212")	
-	•	SB2C-5	Bu83589		(NAS Glenview: "VA-103")	
					Trade School MT, ferried to Ontario CA	.62
					The Air Museum, Ontario CA	c62/70
				N92879	Confederate AF, Harlingen TX (del. 11.71)	.70/91
					(flew as USN "5"): crashed Harlingen TX	c8.85
					(rebuilt Breckenridge TX: ff 9.88)	
					American Airpower Heritage Flying Museum,	
					Midland TX (flies as USN "83589/32")	9.91/92
-	•	SB2C-1	-		ditched, Lake Washington, Seattle WA	
					recov. by Mike Rawson, Minneapolis MN	90
-	•	SB2C-1	-		Ted Darcy, Kailua HI : recov. from dump	c87
-	•	SB2C-1	-		Ted Darcy, Kailua HI : recov. from dump	c87
-	•	SB2C-3	-		Sea-Air-Space Museum, New York NY	91
					(displ. as USN "44" on board USS Intrepid)	

98001 •	Prototype	W4050		first flight (as prototype E-0234)	25.11.40
				De Havilland Technical School, Salisbury Hall	.46
				stored Hatfield, Panshanger, Hawarden	
				W. J. S. Baird	58
				Mosquito Aircraft Museum, London Colney	9.58/91
- •	NF Mk. II	HJ711		RAF Air Training Corps, Chingford: fwd fuse.	60s
				Reflectaire auction, Blackpool	29.4.72
				Tony Agar/Night Fighter Preservation Team,	
				Elvington	29.4.72/91
				(static rest. project, major components of	
				PF498, VA878, RS715: "VI-C")	
- •	FB Mk. VI	HR339		(to RNZAF as NZ2382)	
				Ferrymead Aeronautical Society, Christchurch,	
				New Zealand : substantial remains	79/90
- •	FB Mk. VI	HR621		Camden Museum of Aviation, Camden NSW	
				later Narellan NSW	10.68/92
				(recov. from farm Tomingley NSW, static rest.	
				project, using parts from other farm hulks)	
- •	FB Mk. 25	KA114		(to RCAF as KA114) BOC	22.2.45
				disposal at RCAF Vulcan ALTA	3.4.48
				to farmer Milo ALTA: stripped for parts	c4.48/78
				Canadian Museum of Flight & Transportation,	
				Vancouver BC	79/91
				(derelict hulk only, rest. project)	
- •	B Mk. XX	KB336		(to RCAF as KB336) BOC	12.6.44
				Canadian National Aircraft Collection	.51/64
				(stored Chater, McDonald & Calgary)	
				Canadian National Aviation Museum,	
				Rockcliffe ONT (displ. as "KB336/U")	6.2.64/91
- •	PR Mk. IX	LR480		(to SAAF as LR480)	12.44
				South African National Museum of Military	
				History, Saxonwold	.46/91
				(displ. as "LR480/"Lovely Lady")	
- •	PR Mk. XVI	NS631		(to RAAF as A52-600) del.	13.12.44
				RAAF Air Training Corps, Ballarat VIC	50/54
				E. Vollaire, Mildura VIC : stored on farm	11.54/66
				Pearce Dunn/Warbirds Aviation Museum,	
				Mildura VIC : stored dism. "SU-A"	12.66/83
			VH-JUX	ntu: Vincent Thomas, Alan Lane, Geoff Milne,	
				Albury NSW : stored dism.	9.83/87
				RAAF Museum, RAAF Point Cook VIC	.87/92
				(rebuild to fly, 36 Squadron, RAAF Richmond NSW)	
- •	FB Mk. VI	PZ474		(to RNZAF as NZ2384) : BOC	15.4.47
				Bob Bean & Arthur Kaplan/Aircraft Sales Inc,	
				Los Angeles CA	.53
			ZK-BCV	Aircraft Supplies (NZ) Ltd, Palmerston North	7.53
				(on behalf of Aircraft Sales Inc) : del. to USA	2.55
			N9909F	Insurance Finance Corp, Studio City CA	c55/66
				(rep. used in South America by CIA)	
				Marvin E. Whiteman, Whiteman Air Park CA	70
				The Air Museum, Ontario CA	65/67
				(derelict, Whiteman Air Park CA 59/70)	
				parts held John Caler, Sun Valley CA	75
				Jim Merizan, Placentia/Yorba Linda CA	.70/91
				(under rest. Chino CA for static displ.)	
-	FB Mk. VI	RF670	N9868F	Jack Amman/Photogrammetric Engineers Inc,	
				San Antonio TX	1.57

Home of the De Havilland Aircraft Heritage

De Havilland Mosquito B.35 serial TA634 on view at the Mosquito Aircraft Museum, Salisbury Hall

Mosquito Aircraft Museum

Salisbury Hall, London Colney, Nr. St. Albans, Hertfordshire England

Over 20 De Havilland aircraft types are located at the historic site of the Mosquito Aircraft Museum including the original *Wooden Wonder* - Mosquito prototype W4050, Mosquito B.35 TA634 and FB VI TA122. Also on view is a 1918 Be2e, DH82 Tiger Moth, DH94 Moth Minor, Vampire FB6, Venom NF3, and Sea Vixen FAW 2 as well as the Comet 1 and Trident 2 airliners

TA634 outside one of the Museum buildings at Salisbury Hall and work going ahead in the museum restoration facility on FBVI TA122

Open from March to the end of October

					(del. Hatfield - Tripoli 10.57 for survey work)	
					(del. Libya - USA, via Prestwick 5.11.57)	
					Jack Amman/IREX Survey Co, San Antonio TX	66
					derelict San Antonio TX, wrecked during	
					recov. by Confederate Air Force	c66
					remains with Confederate AF, Harlingen TX	70/88
-	•	NF Mk. 30	RK952		(to RBAF as MB-24) : del.	23.10.53
					Musee Royal de l'Armee, Brussels	17.3.57/91
-	•	T Mk. 3	RR299		Hawker Siddeley Aviation Ltd, Hawarden	10.7.63
				G-ASKH	Hawker Siddeley Aviation Ltd, Hawarden	10.9.65/84
					(flew in movie "Mosquito Squadron" 6.68)	
					British Aerospace, Hatfield/Hawarden	84/92
					dam. landing, Hawarden	7.7.88
					(repaired & rest. Hawarden, due to fly .92)	
-	•	B Mk. 35	RS700	CF-HMS	Spartan Air Services Ltd, Ottawa ONT	9.12.54/70
		PR. Mk.35			(del. to Burnaston for civil conv. 12.54)	
					(del. to Canada, via Prestwick 28.6.56)	
					C of A expired	13.5.61
					Centennial Planetarium, Calgary ALTA	70/88
					(stored dism., good condition)	
					Calgary Aero Space Museum, Calgary ALTA	90/92
					(rebuild to fly, CFB Cold Lake ALTA 91)	
-	•	B Mk. 35	RS709		(3 CAACU coded "47") SOC	16.5.63
		TT Mk. 35		G-ASKA	Mirisch Films Ltd, Bovington	11.7.63
					(flew in movie "633 Squadron":"HR113/HT-D/G")	
					Peter Thomas/Skyfame Museum, Staverton	12.63/69
					(flew in movie "Mosquito Squadron")	68
					Ed A. Jurist/Vintage Aircraft International,	
					Nyack NY	.69/71
				N9797	Confederate Air Force, Harlingen TX	12.71/75
					(del. Luton to Harlingen TX 11.12.71-2.1.72)	
					Yesterdays Air Force, Chino CA	4.75/79
					Combat Air Museum, Topeka KS : loan	.76/79
					Warbirds of GB, Blackbushe	28.11.79
					(del. Topeka-Blackbushe, arr. 28.11.79)	
				G-MOSI	Warbirds of GB, Blackbushe	10.11.81
					(rebuild at Blackbushe : ff 9.83)	.81/83
					David Zeuschel, Van Nuys CA	.84
					USAFM, Wright-Patterson AFB, Dayton OH	7.84/91
					(del. to USAFM via Prestwick 22.7.84,	
					displ. as USAAF Mk.PR.XVI "NS519/P")	
-	•	B Mk. 35	RS712	G-ASKB	Mirisch Films, Exeter	30.8.63
		TT Mk.35			(flew in movie "633 Squadron" as "RF580/HT-F")	
					Grp. Capt. H.A Mahaddie, Bovingdon & Henlow	8.64
					(flew in movie "Mosquito Squadron" .68)	
					stored at West Malling	70/72
					Sir William Roberts/Strathallan Collection,	
					Auchterader Scotland : del.	8.11.72/81
					Kermit A. Weeks, Tamiami FL	14.6.81
				N35MK	Kermit A. Weeks, Tamiami FL	17.6.83
				G-ASKB	rest. Auchterader, flown to Booker	21.12.84
					(rebuilt Booker, ferried UK - Tamiami 10.87)	
				N35MK	Weeks Air Museum,Tamiami FL	.87/91
					displ. EAA Museum, Oshkosh WI	91
					(flies as "RS712/EG-F")	
-		B Mk. 35	RS715		(3 CAACU) : noted withdrawn, Exeter	8.62
		TT Mk. 35			Mirisch Films Ltd, Bovingdon	.63
					(fus. & wings used ground scenes "633 Sqdn")	
					transported to MGM Studios, Borehamwood	.63/73
					fuselage hulk to Tony Agar, York	.73

	Type	Serial	Reg	History	Date
				(used in static rest. of HJ711)	
- •	FB Mk. VI	TA122		stored in hangar at RAF Celle, West Germany	6.50/51
				Delft Technical University, Delft, Holland	6.51
				(wings destroyed in 58)	
				RNAF Museum, fus. stored Woensdrecht AB,	
				stored at Gilze-Rijen AB	
				Mosquito Aircraft Museum, London Colney	26.2.78/91
				(rest. with wings of TW233 recov. ex Israel)	
				(displ. as 4 Sqdn RAF "TA122/UP-G")	
- •	B Mk. 35	TA634		City of Liverpool Corporation, Speke	6.11.63/70
	TT Mk. 35			(planned display, but stored in hangar)	
			G-AWJV	City of Liverpool Corporation	21.5.68
				(flew in movie "Mosquito Squadron" .68)	
				Mosquito Aircraft Museum, London Colney	7.10.70/92
				(displ. as "HX922/EF-G", later "8K-K")	
- •	B Mk. 35	TA639		Mirisch Films Ltd, Bovingdon : loan ex RAF	.63
				(flew in movie "633 Squadron": "HJ682/HT-B")	
				RAF Museum Store, Henlow	5.7.67
				RAF Museum, RAF Cosford	70/91
				(displ. camouflaged as "TA639/AZ-E")	
-	B Mk. 35	TA717	N9911F	Fotogrametric Engineers Inc, Los Angeles CA	5.56
				(del. to USA, via Prestwick 5.56)	
			XB-TOX	McIntyre & Quiros, Mexico City	14.6.56
			N6867C	McIntyre & Quiros, Los Angeles CA	5.57
			XB-TOX	McIntyre & Quiros, Mexico City	7.57
				open storage, derelict, Mexico City Airport	66/79
				Mike Meeker, Mission City BC	.79/88
				(hulk recov. ex Mexico City, parts used in	
				rebuild of VR796/CF-HML)	
				Jim Merizan, Yorba Linda CA :	.88/90
				(parts only, for rebuild of PZ474/N9909F)	
- •	B Mk. 35	TA719	G-ASKC	P. F. M. Thomas/Skyfame Museum, Staverton	19.8.63/78
	TT Mk.35			Film Aviation Services, Elstree : loan	.63
				(flew in movie "633 Squadron": "HJ898/HT-G")	
				badly dam., crash landing Staverton	27.7.64
				(ground scenes, movie "Mosquito Squadron"	
				at MGM Borehamwood Studios .68)	
				Imperial War Museum, Duxford	.78/92
				(static displ.)	
- •	FB Mk. VI	TE758		(to RNZAF as NZ2328) : BOC	3.4.47
				surplus at RNZAF Woodbourne	.55
				Jas W. Clarke Syndicate, Totara, nr Oamaru	.55/72
				(fuselage & major components stored on farm)	
				Ferrymead Aeronautical Soc., Christchurch	9.72/91
				(rest. project with HR339/NZ2382)	
- •	FB Mk. VI	TE863		(to RNZAF as NZ2355) : BOC	c7.47
				surplus at RNZAF Woodbourne	.55
				Cliff Horrel, Ashburton NZ	.55
				Ted Packer (rest. project)	
				RNZAF Museum, RNZAF Wigram (rest. project)88/91	
- •	FB Mk. VI	TE910		(to RNZAF as NZ2336) : BOC	24.4.47
				surplus, RNZAF Woodbourne (75 Sqn "YC-B")	.56
				John Smith, Mapua NZ	7.56/91
				(stored under cover, still "YC-B")	
- •	B Mk. 35	TH998		NASM, Washington DC: donated by RAF	31.8.62
	TT Mk.35			(airfreighted by C-124C Duxford - USA)	
				NASM, stored Silver Hill MD	63/88
-	B Mk. 35	TJ118		(3 CAACU) : written-off	18.9.61

	TT Mk. 35			noted withdrawn at 3 CAACU, Exeter	8.62
				Mirisch Films Ltd, Bovingdon	.63
				(used in ground scenes, movie "633 Squadron")	
				transported to MGM Studios, Borehamwood	.63/73
				hulk recov. by Eddie Reynolds	.73
				fus. remains to Mosquito Aircraft Museum and	
				Dave Elvidge, Begbroke, Oxford	.73
				Mosquito Aircraft Museum, London Colney:	.73/92
				(displ. as rest. cockpit section)	
- •	B Mk. 35	TJ138		RAF Bicester: travelling displ. as "VO-L"	7.59
	TT Mk. 35			RAF Museum, RAF Colerne	67/75
				RAF Museum Store, RAF Finningley	.75
				RAF Museum Store, RAF Swinderby	84/86
				RAF Museum, RAF St Athan	11.86/92
				RAF Museum, Hendon	2.92
- •	T Mk. 3	TV959		Mirisch Films, Bovingdon : loan	.63
				(ground scenes "633 Squadron": "MM398/HT-P")	
				Imperial War Museum, Lambeth, London	8.63/88
				(displ. as "TV959/AF-V")	
				Imperial War Museum, Duxford : stored	89/91
				The Fighter Collection, Duxford	8.92
- •	T Mk. 3	TW117		RAF Museum Store, Henlow	30.5.63/67
				Mirisch Films, Bovingdon : loan	.63
				(flew in movie "633 Squadron": "HR155/HT-M")	
				RAF Museum, Hendon	.72/91
				Tacair Systems, Toronto ONT	11.91/92
				loan: Royal Norwegian Air Force Museum,	
				Gardermoen AB: shipped ex UK , arr.	3.2.92
				last reported California	10.92
- •	B Mk. 35	VP189	CF-HMQ	Spartan Air Services Ltd, Ottawa ONT	9.12.54/57
				(civil conv. Burnaston UK 54/55)	
				(del. to Canada, arr. Ottawa 2.6.55)	
			VP-KOM	ntu: Spartan Air Services (Eastern) Ltd	11.57
				(del. Ottawa - Nairobi, Kenya 11.57)	
			CF-HMQ	Spartan Air Services Ltd, Ottawa ONT	.57/67
				(returned to Canada, via Prestwick 4.5.58)	
				last flight, Grand Prairie - Uplands ONT	7.10.63
				J. K. Campbell, Edmonton ALTA	14.9.67
				CFB Edmonton: displ. as "TH-F"	68/70
				City of Edmonton, Artifacts Centre, Edmonton	.75/91
				(stored dism., pending rest.)	
- •	B Mk. 35	VR796	CF-HML	Spartan Air Services Ltd, Ottawa ONT	11.54/66
				(del. Burnaston - Ottawa 2.5.55)	
				last flight, retired at Uplands, Ottawa ONT	10.6.63
				Don Campbell, Kapuskasing ONT	12.66/86
				(rebuild commenced CFB Kapuskasing .67/79,	
				moved to Matsqui BC .79 for continued rest.	
				by Mike Meeker, using parts ex TA717)	
				Ed & Rose Zalesky, Surrey BC	.86/92
				(rest. to fly, Surrey BC)	
- •	FB Mk.40	A52-1053		(A52-19 ntu: to RNZAF as NZ2305)	18.12.46
	T Mk. 43			disposal to farmer, Mr Galpin, Marton NZ	c53
				Museum of Transport & Technology, Auckland	.64/90
DH.3236•	FB Mk.40	A52-319		(A52-210 ntu) BOC 18.2.48 : SOC	20.3.53
	PR Mk.41			Capt. James Woods, Perth WA	20.3.53
				(del. to Perth 10.9.53, for London to	
				Christchurch Air Race: entry withdrawn)	
			VH-WAD	James Woods, Perth WA "The Quokka"	23.9.53/69
				C of A suspended and struck-off reg.	12.10.53

				stored in hangar, Perth Airport WA	.53/63
				Air Force Association, Perth Airport : displ.	1.63/67
				became derelict, moved to airport dump	7.67/69
				James A. Harwood, Perth WA	1.69
				fuselage badly damaged during dismantling	8.1.69
				stored dism. in warehouse, Perth WA	1.69/72
				Ed A. Jurist/Vintage Aircraft International, Nyack NJ	.69
				David M. Kubista, Tucson AZ	6.71
				crated aboard SS Manora, ex Fremantle	23.5.72
				stored Port Melbourne, pending transit USA	72/79
				auctioned to recover shipping costs	22.1.79
				Australian War Memorial, Canberra ACT	22.1.79/91
				(static rest., Bankstown NSW)	
- •	-	-	-	Chinese AF Museum, Datongshon	90

DORNIER Do24

Nr467 •	Do 24T-3	-		(to Spanish AF as HD.5-... later HR.5-...)	
			N99240	Dolph Overton, Kenley NC	77
				sale rep., Los Angeles CA	90
Nr1101 •	Do 24T-3	Nr1101		(Luftwaffe W4+DH)	
				recovered from Lake Biscarosse, France	2.80
				Association de Protection des Epaves du Lac du Biscarosse, Biscarosse, France	80/89
				(recov. from Lake Biscarrosse 2.80)	
Nr1107 •	Do 24T-3	Nr1107		(Luftwaffe W4+BH)	
				Association de Protection des Epaves du Lac du Biscarosse, Biscarosse, France	80/89
				(recov. from Lake Biscarrosse 9.81)	
Nr5341 •	Do 24T-3	Nr5341		(to Spanish AF as 65-2)	12.44
				later reserialled HR.5-2, HD.5-2)	
				Museo del Aire, Cuatro Vientos AB, Madrid	.71/91
				(displ. on artificial lake as "HD.5-2/SAR/58-2")	
Nr5342 •	Do 24T-3	Nr5342		(to Spanish AF as HR.5-1 later HD.5-1)	12.44
			N99225	Dolph Overton, Kenley NC	2.77
				not collected, stored Pollensa, Majorca	78
				RAF Museum, Hendon UK : arr. dism.	30.6.82/91
				Militaire Luchvaart Museum, Soesterberg AB Netherlands	11.91
Nr5344 •	Do 24T-3	Nr5344		(to Spanish AF as HR.5-3 later HD.5-3)	12.44
			N99222	Dolph Overton, Kenley NC: not del.	70
				Dornier Research Centre, Immenstaad	.71/74
				del. by air to Lake Constance WG	28.8.71
				Dornier Werke Museum, Oberpfaffenhofen	84/86
				(fitted with wings from Nr5345/HR.5-4)	
Nr5345 •	Do 24T-3	Nr5345		(to Spanish AF as HD.5-4 later HR.5-4)	12.44
				Dornier Research centre, Immenstaad	.71
				del. by air to Lake Constance	.71
				Dornierwerke GmbH, Immenstaad WG	76
	Do 24TT		D-CATD	Dornierwerke GmbH, Oberpfaffenhofen	4.83
				(prototype experimental Do24TT: ff 25.4.83)	
				Dornier Werke Museum, Oberpfaffenhofen	86

DORNIER Do335 Pfiel

Nr240102•	Do 335A-02	Nr240102		VG+PH: captured Oberpfaffenhofen	22.4.45
				shipped to USA on HMS Reaper	7.45
				(to USN for trials as FE-1012)	
				NASM, stored NAS Norfolk VA	.47/74
				Deutsches Museum, Munich (loan)	84/86
				NASM, Silver Hill MD	90

Mosquito T Mk III TV959 hung from the ceiling of the Imperial War Museum at Lambeth in a very undignified way, less the majority of its starboard wing (which fortunately was not discarded) for many years before being removed and placed into store. With Mosquito airframes in less than plentiful supply (the majority, ironically being in North America!) Stephen Grey of The Fighter Collection masterminded a trade with the IWM and now has TV959 ready for rebuild to flying condition. A Mossie never looks undignified in the air! (Gary Brown archives)

At The Royal Air Force Museum at Hendon Messerschmitt Bf110G-4 sits on permanent display (for the time being at least). Captured at Knokke, Belgium it went to the RAF for trials as AX772. (Gary R. Brown)

Fw190-A8 Wr Nr 733682 is seen here at Duxford before it was restored by The Aircraft Restoration company and taken to the IWM main building at Lambeth where it is suspended from the roof. Formerly with KG200 the aircraft was captured and taken to Farnborough for trials as AM.75 in 1945 (Gary R. Brown)

DOUGLAS O-46

1441 •	O-46A	35-179		USAAC: crashed nr. Harlingen TX	c42/70
				Antique Airplane Association, Ottumwa IA	.70/73
				(recov. ex storage dism. Ottumwa)	
				USAFM, Wright-Patterson AFB, Dayton OH	.73/90
				(rest. and displayed)	

DOUGLAS A-20 HAVOC

3839 •	DB-7B Boston III	AL907		(to Kon Marine 240) : diverted to Australia	1.42
				(to RAAF as A28-8) : 22 Sqn " DU-J "	29.3.42
				crashed landing, Goodenough Island PNG	12.9.43
				RAAF Museum: recov. ex Goodenough Island	2.87/92
				(static rest., RAAF Wagga NSW)	
- •	A-20G	42-86615		(417th BG/675th BS) fcd. ldg., Saidor PNG	16.4.44
				RAAF Museum: recov. ex Yamai, Saidor	21.11.84
				static rest. project, RAAF Wagga NSW	88/91
- •	A-20G	42-86786		(388th BS) forced landing, Amiamon PNG	16.4.44
				RAAF Museum: recov. ex Amaimon	11.84/91
				(static rest. RAAF Wagga NSW, for	
				PNG National Museum, Port Moresby)	
- •	A-20G	43-9401		(417th BG/675th BS) fcd. ldg., Saidor PNG	16.4.44
				RAAF Museum: recov.ex Yamai, Saidor	22.11.84
				static rest. project, RAAF Wagga NSW	88/91
- •	A-20G	43-9686		(417th BG) forced landing, Wabusarik PNG	.44
				RAAF Museum: recov. ex Wabusarik	26.11.84
				static rest. project, RAAF Wagga NSW	88/92
21274 •	A-20G	43-21627		(312th BG/387th BS)	
				recov. by d'E. C. Darby & N. M. Armstrong	
				for YAF, from Tadji, West Sepik PNG	.74
				Military Aircraft Restoration Corp, Chino CA	.74/89
21356 •	A-20G	43-21709		Paul Mantz, Burbank CA (ex Altus AFB OK)	19.2.46
			NC67932	Paul Mantz Air Service, Burbank CA	10.5.48/51
			N67932	Potter Aircraft Service Inc, Burbank CA	11.4.51
			N22M	Glen L. McCarthy, Houston TX	11.51/54
				Valley Hail Suppression, Scottsbluff NE	15.2.54/55
				James M. Cook Co., Jacksboro TX	15.3.55
				C. T. McLaughlin, Snyder TX	31.8.55/59
				Vest Aircraft & Finance Co, Denver CO	23.11.59
				Jack Adams Aircraft Sales, Memphis TN	12.59/60
				George Treadwell, Shelby TN	62
				Billy Hicks, McGehee AR	21.2.62/67
				Jupiter Inc, Houston TX	9.1.67/68
				I. N. Burchinall Jr, Paris TX	12.68/70
				William F. Farah, El Paso TX	6.8.70/74
			N3WF	William F. Farah, El Paso TX	.74/89
				NASM, Washington DC (donated)	25.9.89/91
				ret. by Court Order, to Farah estate	24.3.91
				Lone Star Flight Museum, Galveston TX	16.9.91/92
				(arr. Galveston on del. 11.91)	
21844 •	A-20G	43-22197	N34920	Hughes Aircraft Co, Culver City CA	c50/72
				retired, parked at Culver City CA	63/70
				Antelope Valley Aero Museum, Lancaster CA	c73/86
				Milestones of Flight Museum, Lancaster CA	.86/91
				(stored dism., Lancaster-Fox Field CA 73/91)	
				Weeks Air Museum, Tamiami FL	.91/92
21847 •	A-20G	43-22200	NL63004	H. L. Gogerty, Los Angeles CA	22.1.46
				J. G. Hurst Jr, Miami FL	10.47/49
				William M. Ambrose, Miami FL	13.9.49/50

			N63004	W. R. Robinson, Miami FL	16.1.50/51
				Grant Foster, Falcon, Venezuela	20.9.51/53
				(adv. for sale by Potter Aircraft Service,	
				Burbank CA 6.52: 6 seat executive conv.)	
				L. B. Smith Aircraft Corp, Miami FL	17.2.53/55
				Florida Aircraft Corp, Miami FL	22.8.55/60
				American Airmotive Corp, Miami FL	19.9.60
				Bankers Life & Casualty Co, Chicago IL	20.9.60
				USAFM, Wright-Patterson AFB, Dayton OH	30.9.61/92
				(displ. as "0-22200; later "322200")	
21857	A-20G	43-22210		Hearst Magazines Inc, San Francisco CA	3.6.46/48
			NL67921	Hearst Magazines Inc, San Francisco CA	12.2.48/50
			N67921	W. G. Spillman, Burbank CA	30.1.50/52
				Thorne Engineering Corp, Las Vegas NV	9.1.52/56
				Roberts Aircraft Co, Reno NV	27.4.56/58
				W. Lynn Roberts/Roberts Aircraft Co,	
				Boise ID (sprayer)	12.5.58/59
				Ray C. Wilcox, Boise ID	8.7.59/65
				Donald C. Magnuson & Ralph E. Knight Aircraft	
				Service and Repair Co, Boise ID	14.4.65
				(retired, parked at Boise c59/66)	
				Confederate Air Force, Harlingen TX	5.10.65/88
				(ferried Boise-Harlingen TX 12.9.66,	
				rest. 71/76: ff .76 as "322210/T")	
				crashed and dest., near Harlingen TX	8.10.88
23243 •	A-20H	44-20	N5066N	Delta Drilling Co/Texas Engineering &	
				Manufacturing Co, Dallas TX	25.6.47
				Texas Aircraft Trading Co, Tyler TX	20.8.47
				Universal Aviation Company, Tulsa OK	1.6.48
				Leonard Burns, San Francisco CA	22.7.48
				American Airmotive Corporation, Miami FL	4.4.49/51
				(noted as executive conv., Miami FL 55)	
				(to FA Nicaragua as FAN 50)	c56
				displ. in park, Carretera del Sur,	
				Managua, Nicaragua	75/77
			N99385	Military Aircraft Restoration Corp, Chino CA	14.3.77/92
				(open storage, MARC yard, Chino ("50") 80/91)	
				lease: Air Heritage Inc, Beaver Falls PA	.91/92
				(trucked from Chino to Beaver Falls PA .91,	
				stored dism. Beaver Falls, planned rest. to fly)	
23762 •	A-20K	44-539		(to FA Braziliera as FAB 5159)	
				Museu Aerospacial da Forca Area Braziliera	79/88
	A-20	-		(to FA Braziliera as FAB 6085)	
				displ. Quaratingueta AB, Sao Paulo	68/88

COLOUR PAGE CAPTIONS

Page 19: Top - *Battle of Britain Memorial Flight* Lancaster B.Mk. 1 PA474 in the summer of 1992. The aircraft is based at RAF Coningsby (John Dibbs) Lower - *The Lone Star Flight Museum's* B-17 *Thunderbird* - 44-85718/N900RW It spent some time in the UK before being flown back to the USA where it was completely stripped down and rebuilt. (Thierry Thomassin).

Page 20 Top:*Sanders Aircraft* of Chino, California, rebuilt this immaculate Boomerang as one of a pair. The other aircraft is now with Guido Zuccoli in Australia (Thierry Thomassin).Lower - *The Lone Star Flight Museum's* P-40M serial 43-5795 once belonged to the *Harrah's Auto Collection* in Nevada before being acquired by Bill Destefani. (Thierry Thomassin)

Page 21 Top - *British Aerospace's* Mosquito RR299 following its complete refurbishment by BAe technicians at Chester. The new fabric was applied and the aircraft painted by Clive Denney and team from Historic Flying at Audley End, Essex. (John Dibbs)Lower- Yet another *Lone Star Flight Museum* machine, this time Grumman F7F Tigercat Bu 80503/N800RW which was rebuilt by Darrell Skurich at *Vintage Aircraft,* Fort Collins, Colorado (Thierry Thomassin).

Page 22 Top and Lower: Elmer and Brett Ward run *Pioneer Aero Service* from Chino, California; as well as rebuilding several top quality P-51s, mainly for *Warbirds of Great Britain* they have rebuilt this unique (now two-place) Grumman F8F. Shown here during rebuild and upon completion (Top by Joe Cupido, lower by Thierry Thomassin)

Page 71 - Top - Douglas AD Skyraider F-AZHK now resident in France, is Bu No 127002 (Thierry Thomassin) Lower - For many years this North American P-51A (a rare machine indeed) has been on rebuild with the *Yankee Air Corps*, also based at Chino. 43-6274 is registered N90358 to Charles F. Nichols. (Thierry Thomassin)

Page 72: *Scandinavian Historic Flight* Invader N167B (44-34602) overshadows North American P-51D Mustang N167F from the same organisation which also has a DH Vampire. The flight is very active at airshows in Europe (Christer Sidelov)

Page 106 -Top - Fiat G-59 I-MRSV is one of two airworthy G-59s, the other aircraft is in Australia with Guido Zuccoli and was rebuilt by *Sanders Aircraft*. (Maurizio Torcolli) Lower- Douglas Skyraider F-AZFN is an ex Gabonese airframe now based in france. Bu number is 125718 (Thierry Thomassin).

Page 174 - Top - *The Fighter Collection's* Hawker Hurricane which was omitted from the last edition of the Directory. Rebuilt by the 'Collection, chief engineer on the project was Paul Mercer who also undertook the majority of the rebuild on the ex Charles Church Hurricane G-ORGI, now based in the United States with the *Museum of Flying* (Thierry Thomassin). Lower - Howard Pardue's Breckenridge based ex Iraqi Fury N666HP which was rebuilt by Nelson Ezell at *Ezell Aviation* at the same base. The aircraft is re-engined with a Wright R-3350 powerplant and is a regular competitor at Reno (Thierry Thomassin).

Page 191- Top - David Tallichet's *Military Aircraft Restoration Corp* is the owner of this B-25J, serial 44-30210/N9455Z ex Paul Mantz and Jeff Hawke. The aircraft was abandoned for a while in France but is now at Chino where it was photographed in 1992 by Thierry Thomassin. Lower- The Dutch based *Duke of Brabant Squadron* own this B-25 which has visited airshows in France and the UK on a regular basis. Shown here at La Ferte Alais (Thierry Thomassin).

Page 192 - Top - The North American T-28 Trojan has become an enormously popular warbird , particularly over the past five years. When we omitted this and the T-6 from the last edition of the *Warbirds Directory* we were bombarded with letters of protest. The aircraft shown here is a T-28C, registered N128FS (Thierry Thomassin). Lower - Al Grant's T-28C seen at Chino; it is Bu No. 140511 .

Page 193 - Top a 1949 model T-6G, this time based in France, F-AZGS is one of the remnants of a significant number of Texans that served with the French Air Force. Lower - Another T-6G, this time 51-14456 alias F-AZCV.

Page 194 - Shown here in pristene condition at Dubendorf is Swiss Air Force P-51D Mustang 44-73349, J-2113, the sole survivor of the Swiss contingent of the type. The rest were brutally butchered and ended up as scrap! (Christophe Donnet) Now based with *Flying Legends* in France is this CAC Mustang, ex N286JB (A68-198) now registered as F-AZIE.

Page 243 - Tom Friedkin at *Cinema Air* added this TF-51D, an ex Bolivian Air Force Cavalier Mustang to his collection recently. Recovered from Bolivia by several Canadians along others it has since been repainted but essentially retains its FAB camouflage colours. The TFs have remained high value Mustangs and are still much sought after by collectors (Thierry Thomassin).Lower: This F-86 Sabre, N105BH is an ex Argentine airframe, one of several recovered by Texan Rick Sharpe. (Thierry Thomassin)

Page 244- *World Jet* rebuilt this immaculate Grumman F9F which also came from Argentina. Regrettably the aircraft was lost in the Gulf of Mexico during a transit flight at high level and was never recovered (Thierry Thomassin). Lower - In spectacular *Golden Hawks* colours, this T-33 is seen at the *Museum of Flying's* aircraft auctions in 1991.

Page 296- Top - Ed Coventry's Yak 11 G-OYAK is an ex Egyptian airframe recovered by Jean Salis. The type has soared in value and is a high performance machine.(John Dibbs) F-AZNN was one of the first Yak-11s to fly in western civilian hands and was rebuilt by the late Pierre Dague and Gerry Marchadier into a single seat configuration. It is based at La Ferte Alais (Thierry Thomassin)

Page 297- Californian Joe Halley had this beautiful Yak-11 rebuilt by *Sanders Aviation* at Chino; re-engined for air racing with an American powerplant (an R-2000 rebuilt by JRS Enterprises) it was based, again on an ex Egyptian airframe from France. Lower; The real McCoy! This genuine Yak-3 was imported into the USA by the Santa Monica based *Museum of Flying* (both Thierry Thomassin).

Page 298- No warbirds book would be complete without mention of Robert Lamplough, one of the original warbird collectors in the UK. Seen here is Rob's Yak-18, G-BMTY. Lower: Back to the Yak 11, one of the most attractive recent Yak rebuilds is F-AZPA which is based with *Capel Aviation* at La Ferte Alais (Both Thierry Thomassin).

Page 411- *The Old Flying Machine Company* own one of the most original Spitfires with combat history, MH434, a Mk IX. It has appeared in so many different paint schemes and films/television the OFMC are still creating history with it in its own right. Lower: rebuilt for Rudy Frasca by *Historic Flying* at Audley End, Mk XVIII TP280 is shown in company with Merlin engined Mk XVII RW382 which was also rebuilt for an overseas customer (both John Dibbs)

Page 412- Top: Spitfire XVI G-OXVI/TD248, doing engine runs at Audley End with *Historic Flying* The stunning paint scheme is a welcome move away from traditional camouflaged aircraft. Owner is Eddie Coventry of *BAC Windows*.(Richard Paver) Lower: Messerschmitt Bf109G Black 6, based at Duxford (John Dibbs).

Page 429- Top: Ray Hanna at the controls of the *Old Flying Machine Company's* FG-1D *Big Hog* (John Dibbs) Lower: Richard Bertea's Corsair, Bu No. 124486.with Steve Hinton at the controls (Frank Mormillo).

Page 430- Top; with *Jet Heritage* at Bournemouth is the unique Swift G-SWIF on rebuild (Aviation Photographs International/J. Flack) Lower: a number of ex RAF Gnats have been imported to the USA including this unidentified airframe marked U.S.Navy (Thierry Thomassin)

Page 296- MiG-15UTI (actually an LiM-3 VH-XIG (s/n 612782)one of a growing number of MiGs in Australia. (P.Hastie).

6874 •	A-26B	41-39161	N317V	Humphrey's Gold Corp, FL	.56
	On Mark			Humphrey's Engineering Co, Denver CO	63/66
			N317W	Metropolitan State College, Denver CO	69
				Air Mayo Inc, Lakewood CO	72
				Slaco Inc, Fort Lauderdale FL	77
			N26RP	Robert P. Lammerts, Oklahoma City OK	9.81/84
				ADA Aircraft Museum, Oklahoma City OK	86/90
				Colonel Aircraft Sales, Oklahoma City OK	5.91/92
				(flies as "436874/L")	
6875	A-26B	41-39162	N72Y	Texas Railroad Equipment Co, Houston TX	54
	RB-26B			(to Armee de L'Air as 4139162)	
				gate guard, Blois-Le Breuil ("CAEM/Z")	71
				Musee de l'Air: stored Blois-Le Breuil	9.78
				Musee de l'Air: stored Paris-Le Bourget	90
				destroyed, hangar fire, Le Bourget	17.5.90
6903	A-26B	41-39190	N9404Z	Moseley Aviation Inc, Tolleson AZ	66/72
				Donaire Sales Inc, Phoenix AZ	73
				Conair Ltd, Abbotsford BC : for parts only	
				sale rep., USCR	78/92
6928 •	A-26B	41-39215	N5292V	Recta Air Enterprises	
	On Mark			On Mark Engineering Co, Van Nuys CA	63
			N4000M	L. B. Maytag Jr, Miami FL	66
			N200M		
			N142ER	Embry Riddle Institute, Daytona Beach FL	69/74
				Milt Stollak, Burbank CA	77
				Gold Coast Classic Cars, Fort Lauderdale FL	5.82
				Courtesy Aircraft Inc, Rockford IL	2.84
				ADA Aircraft Museum, Oklahoma City OK	2.85
				crashed during del. flight, Lawton OK	17.3.85
				Aero Nostalgia Inc, Stockton CA (static rest.)	86/89
				USNAM, NAS Pensacola FL	90/92
				(displ. as "JD-1 USN/Bu77141")	
6934 •	A-26B	41-39221	N9636C	Farrah Manufacturing Co Inc	
	Marksman		N3035S (1	Southern Natural Gas Co, Birmingham AL	63/66
			N256H (2	Mapco Inc, Tulsa OK	69
				Bancroft Manufacturing Co, McComb MS	72
				Park Meadow Inc/ Ligon Air Inc, Ligonier IN	77
				Garrett Corp, Phoenix AZ	c79
				(mod. for testing turbine engine in nose)	
			N26GT	Garrett Corp, Phoenix AZ	4.83/88
				Allied Signal Inc, Phoenix AZ	12.88/90
				struck-off USCR	1.92
6936 •	A-26B	41-39223	N74Y	Texas Railroad Equipment Co, Houston TX	54
	B-28B			(to Armee de L'Air as 4139223/Z-009)	
				wfu Mont de Marsan	c72
				stored at Santes-Thernac, France	.78
6943 •	A-26B	41-39230	N9682C	H. R. Wells	
				Flight Inc, Dallas TX	63/66
				D & D Aero Spraying Inc, Rantoul KS	69/77
				(tanker #105)	
				Confederate Air Force, Harlingen TX	21.8.82/91
				American Airpower Heritage Flying Museum, Midland TX	9.91/92
6990	A-26B	41-39277	N74834	Madden Smith Aircraft Corp, Miami FL	66/69
				sale rep., USCR	78/92
7001 •	A-26B	41-39288		(to FA Brasiliera as 5159)	
				Museu Aerospacial da FAB, Rio de Janeiro	82/85

7016 •	A-26B	41-39303	N5589A	W. C. Powell, Tereboro NJ	58
				Charles Woods Homes Inc, Dothan AL	66
				Alabama Inst. of Aviation Tech., Ozark AL	69
				Paramount Inc, Atlanta GA	70
				John M. Sliker, Wadley GA	72
				John J. Stokes/Central Texas Aviation,	
				San Marcos TX (dism.)	77
				Lynch Air Tankers, Billings MT (dism.)	.78/92
7072 •	A-26B	41-39359	N91281	Aero Union Corp, Chico CA	66/69
	B-26C		CF-BMR	Conair Aviation Ltd, Abbotsford BC	3.70
				(tanker #321)	
			C-FBMR	Conair Aviation Ltd, Abbotsford BC	79/86
				Jerry C. Janes, Rockford IL	.87
			N26BP	Planes of Fame East, Minneapolis MN	11.87/92
				(flies as "39359/21")	
7091 •	A-26B	41-39378		retired to MASDC: arr. Davis Monthan AFB AZ	11.1.70
	B-26K	64-17653		USAFM, Pima County Air Museum, Tucson AZ	4.1.74/90
	A-26A				
7111	A-26B	41-39398	N91317	Allied Aircraft Sales, Phoenix AZ	66
	B-26C			Flight Enterprises Inc, Prescott AZ	69
			CF-DFC	Conair Aviation Ltd, Abbotsford BC	5.71
				(tanker #324)	
				crashed, landing Prince George BC	10.8.71
				crashed, dest., Stoyoma Mountain BC	11.8.74
7114 •	A-26B	41-39401	N3457G	John R. Moore, Los Angeles CA	.59/69
				retired Van Nuys CA: "Whistler's Mother"	59/82
				Challenge Publications Inc, Canoga Park CA	11.82
			N39401	Challenge Publications Inc, Van Nuys CA	5.83
				(rebuilt Van Nuys CA: ff 18.8.83)	
				American Aeronautical Foundation, Van Nuys	1.85/87
				Weeks Air Museum, Tamiami FL	7.87/92
				(flies as "139401/Whistler's Mother")	
7136 •	A-26B	41-39423		(to GN Nicaragua as GN602)	
			N99422	Military Aircraft Restoration Corp, Chino CA	28.3.77/92
				stored Managua-Mercedes as N99422	77/79
				(FAA quote id. "423")	
7140 •	A-26B	41-39427	N75Y	Texas Railroad Equipment Co, Houston TX	54
				Brown & Root Inc	59
				Barnwell Drilling Co, Shreveport LA	63/66
			N240P	William V. Wright, Long Beach CA	69/72
				Aircraft Holdings, Miami FL	76
				Confederate Air Force, Harlingen TX	10.5.77/91
				American Airpower Heritage Flying Museum,	
				Midland TX	9.91/92
				(flies as "437140/R/Spirit of Waco")	
7181 •	A-26B	41-39468	N91354	Allied Aircraft Sales, Phoenix AZ	66/69
				Reeder Flying Service, Twin Falls ID	72/84
				(tanker #28) : struck-off USCR	5.84
7185 •	A-26B	41-39472	N86482	John P. Wilds, Escalon CA	63
	On Mark			Kimberley Leasing Corp, St Paul MN	66/69
				(to FA El Salvadorena as 60....)	
			N26VC	John V. Crocker, San Mateo CA	4.74/80
				ferried El Salvador - San Diego CA	16-18.4.74
				USAFM, Castle AFB CA	10.80/92
				(arr. on del. 26.10.80, displ. as "24-6093",	
				later "435648/Lil' Sal")	
7199	A-26B	41-39486	N9432Z	Transport Aircraft Inc, Sacramento CA	

				John A. Thompson, Santa Clara CA	c63
			N90711	John A. Thompson, Santa Clara CA	72/92
				retired, derelict at Fresno CA: still N9432Z	68/77
				trucked ex Fresno by Thompson	.77
7210 •	A-26B	41-39497	N71Y	Standard Oil Co, Chicago IL	54/63
				Ralph D. Tait, Greensburg PA	66
				Aviation Inc, Charleston WV	69/72
				impounded Bogota-El Dorado, Colombia	75/89
				Robert Kelley, Inglewood CA	77
				Jeremiah S. Boehmer, Grants Pass OR	2.85/92
7228	A-26B	41-39515	N67805	Standard Oil & Gas Co OK	54
				Pan American Petroleum Corp, Tulsa OK	61/63
				noted in scrapyard, Tulsa OK	4.73
7229 •	A-26B	41-39516	N237Y	Standard Oil Co, Chicago IL	54/63
	On Mark			Alsam Inc, Youngstown OH	66/69
				PBF Enterprises, Akron OH	72
				Calspan Corp, Buffalo NY/Edwards AFB CA	77/90
				sale rep., Geneseo NY	92
7230 •	A-26B	41-39517	N91349	reg. res.	.78/92
7225	A-26B	41-39512	N68Y	Eastern Aircraft Sales, New York NY	54
7309 •	A-26B	41-39596		(USAF 603rd SOS/1st SOW "IF") del. MASDC	10.69
	B-26K	64-17676	N268G	State of Georgia Forestry Comm., Macon GA	.71
	A-26A			stored unconv., Macon GA	72/78
			C-GXTF	Air Spray Ltd, Edmonton ALTA : not del.	.77
			N29939	Arthur W. McDonnell, Mojave CA	7.78/80
				noted unconv., camo., 'C-GXTF", Mojave CA	10.78
				(flew in Mojave races, "The Mojave Kid" 6.79	)
				USAFM, Wright-Patterson AFB, Dayton OH	81/88
18428	A-26B	43-22281	N61B	Parker Pen Co, Janesville WI	61/63
				Kwiki Systems Inc, Leawood KS	66
				On Mark Engineering Corp, Van Nuys CA	69
				North American Rockwell Corp, El Segundo CA	72/77
				sale rep., Miami FL	84/92
18504 •	A-26B	43-22357	N91348	Hamilton Aircraft Co Inc, Tucson AZ	66/69
			CF-BMS	Conair Aviation Ltd, Abbotsford BC	4.70
				(tanker #322)	
			C-FBMS	Conair Aviation Ltd, Abbotsford BC	86/89
				B. C. Aviation Museum, Sidney BC : del.	29.8.89/90
18521 •	A-26B	43-22374	N6843D	Rock Island Oil & Refining Co, Wichita KS	66
				Consolidated Aero Export, Los Angeles CA	69/72
				Military Aircraft Restoration Corp, Chino CA	.73/92
				(ferried to Chino .74, ex storage Hutchinson KS; open storage MARC compound, Chino 86/91)	
18641 •	A-26C	43-22494		displ. gate, Davis Monthan AFB, Tucson AZ	64/65
	DB-26C			Pima County Air Museum, Tuscon AZ	.69/90
				(displ. as "0-3494/BC-494")	
18646 •	A-26C	43-22499	N86481	John P. Wilds, Escalon CA	63
				Consolidated Aircraft Sales Inc, Fairfield NJ	66/69
				Bradley Air Museum, Windsor Locks CT	9.71/84
				New England Air Museum, Windsor Locks CT	84/90
				(outdoor display, unrest.)	
18670 •	A-26C	43-22523	N4050A	Korda Leasing Corp, New York NY	63
				DEC Aviation Corp, Madison WI	66
				May Air Inc, Boulder CO	69
				I. N. Burchinall Jr, Paris TX	76
				Ronald Bryant, Springfield MO	.77

				derelict at Fort Lauderdale FL by	10.79/81
				Hill Air Company Inc, Fort Lauderdale FL	84/92
18706	A-26C	43-22559	N91359	Flight Enterprises Inc, Prescott AZ	66/69
				derelict, unconv., Tucson AZ	69/75
18749 •	A-26C	43-22602	N9990Z	Kimberley Leasing Corp, St Paul MN	66/69
	On Mark			Cutless Aviation	
				Carlton B. Baker, Simsbury CT	72
				(open storage, Springfield VT 68/74)	
				Military Aircraft Restoration Corp, Chino CA	74/92
				u/c collapsed Orlando FL, on del. to MARG	.75
				displ. Wings & Wheels Museum, Orlando FL	75/81
				museum closed	.81
				noted West Palm Beach FL, as "3-2260"	84/92
18753	A-26C	43-22606		rep. displ. Boise ID	c73
18759	A-26C	43-22612	N3710G	Reading Aviation Service, Reading PA	61/63
				Photo File Surveys Inc, Philadelphia PA	66
				Aero Service Corp, Washington DC	69/72
				Duane Egli, Fabens TX	77/80
				Euroworld, Biggin Hill UK : del.	12.5.78/80
				op. by Cavalier Air Force, Biggin Hill	
				crashed and dest., Biggin Hill Airshow	21.9.80
18796 •	B-26	43-22649		(USAF 603rd SOS / 1st SOW "IF")	
	B-26K	64-17657	N62104	Arthur W. McDonnell, Mojave CA	25.7.74
	A-26A		N99218	Arthur W. McDonnell, Mojave CA	5.12.74/76
				crashed Chino CA	2.78
				wreck noted Maloney's Yard, Chino CA	10.78
				Rod & Rex Cadman, Canterbury, Kent UK	.86
				cockpit section shipped to UK for spares use	7.86
				nose section displ. Booker Aircraft museum	4.88
18799 •	A-26C	43-22652	N8018E	L. B. Smith Aircraft Aircraft Corp, Miami FL	
				Aerojet General Corp, Azusa CA	61/72
			C-GHCE	Conair Aviation Ltd, Abbotsford BC	6.74/88
				(tanker #3)	
				USAFM, Travis AFB CA : del.	18.7.88/91
				(displ. as "43-5440")	
18800 •	A-26C	43-22653	N9402Z	Idaho Air Tankers Inc, Boise ID	63
				Reeder Flying Service, Twin Falls ID	66/72
				(tanker #26)	
			C-GPTW	Air Spray Ltd, Red Deer ALTA (tanker #26)	5.81/92
18807 •	A-26C	43-22660	N3711G	D & O Equipment Co, Charlotte NC	63
				John M. Sliker, Wadley GA	66
				Kem Air Inc, Worland WY	69
			CF-EZX	Air Spray Ltd, Edmonton ALTA (tanker #3)	.72/86
			C-FEZX	Air Spray Ltd, Red Deer ALTA (tanker #3)	89/92
18820	A-26C	43-22673	N9159Z	Blue Mountain Air Service, La Grande OR	
				Hillcrest Aircraft Co, La Grande OR	63
				Butler Aircraft Co, Redmond OR	66/72
				(tanker #18)	
			C-GHLM	Conair Aviation Ltd, Abbotsford BC	4.75
				(tanker #324)	
				crashed fire bombing, Gates Lake BC	2.7.75
18826	A-26C	43-22679		(to R. Saudi AF as ...)	
	B-26B			noted derelict, scrapyard, Riyadh	75/80
18876	A-26C	43-22729	N9424Z	Richard H. Steves, Miami FL	63
				F. A. Conner, Miami FL	66/69

Continued on Page 107

I-MRSV
125716
22-DC
F-AZFN

Continued from Page 104

c/n	Type	Serial	Reg.	History	Date
				noted F. A. Conner scrap compound, Miami FL	10.78
18877	A-26C	43-22730	N8027E	L. B. Smith Aircraft Aircraft Corp, Miami FL	
				Consolidated Air Parts Corp, Los Angeles CA	66/72
				derelict, unconv., Tucson AZ	69/72
27381	A-26B	44-34102	N4060A	noted USAF black sc., Teterboro NJ	8.59
				John M. Sliker, Wadley GA	66
				Kem Air Inc, Worland WY	69
				Lynch Air Tankers, Billings MT (tanker #01)	72/83
				crashed fire bombing, Hubbards Fork KY	5.3.83
27383 •	A-26B	44-34104	N9484Z		
				(to GN Nicaraguana as GN604)	
			N99420	Military Aircraft Restoration Corp, Chino CA	3.77/92
				Combat Air Museum, Topeka KS : loan	85/90
				(note: FAA changed id. from 41-39507)	
27393	A-26B	44-34114		(to R. Saudi AF as 305)	
				stored derelict, Jeddah Airport	75/80
27400 •	A-26B	44-34121	N4805E	Rock Island Oil & Refining Co, Wichita KS	66/69
	Monarch			Koch Industries Inc, Wichita KS	72
				Lynch Air Tankers, Billings MT (tanker #58) 75/92	
27413 •	A-26B	44-34134	N115RG	R. G. Letourneau Inc, Longview TX	63/66
				Sam Seaton, Fort Smith AR (still on USCR)	69
				impounded, drug smuggling, Brasilia, Brazil	21.6.66
				(to FA Brasileira as FAB C-26B-5176)	
				Museu de Armas e Veiculos Motorizados Antigos,	
				Sao Paulo, Brazil.	1.75/85
27415 •	A-26B	44-34136	N8017E	L. B. Smith Aircraft Aircraft Corp, Miami FL	
				Donaire Inc, Phoenix AZ	66/69
				T. W. Hammon	
			CF-KBM	Kenting Aircraft Ltd, Toronto ONT	8.72
				Conair Aviation Ltd, Abbotsford BC	8.73
				(tanker #320)	
			C-FKBM	Air Spray Ltd, Red Deer ALTA (tanker #20)	.85/92
27423 •	A-26B	44-34144		(to R Saudi AF as 308)	
				stored derelict, Jeddah Airport	75
27425	A-26B	44-34146	N5426E	Rock Island Oil & Refining Co, Wichita KS	
				Don A. Goodman, Missoula MT	69/72
				crashed, Idaho Falls ID	10.7.73
				crashed and dest., Grand Valley CO	16.7.76
27432	A-26B	44-34153	N8022E	L. B. Smith Aircraft Aircraft Corp, Miami FL	
				Consolidated Air Parts Corp, Los Angeles CA	66/69
				derelict, unconv., Tucson AZ	69/72
27435 •	A-26B	44-34156	XB-COM	Altos Hornos de Mexico	
	TB-26B		XC-CAZ	Petroleos Mexicanos - PEMEX	60/67
			N190M	JRT Aero Service Co, Wichita Falls TX	69
				Antonio Ortiz, Santee CA	76
				Joseph Morgan, Leucadia CA	77
				Toni Widham	81
				I. N. Burchinall Jr, Paris TX	84
				Aero Nostalgia Inc, Stockton CA	8.85/88
				crashed on del., Pattonville TX (rebuilt)	17.8.85
				USAFM, Vance AFB OK	.88/90
27444 •	A-26B	44-34165	N9146H	Cornell Aero Laboratory Inc, Buffalo NY	.63/72
	TB-26B			Calspan Corp, Buffalo NY/Edwards AFB CA	.72/86
				Flight Test Historical Museum, Edwards AFB	86/91

27451 •	A-26B B-26C	44-34172	N4806E	Rock Island Oil & Refining Co, Wichita KS Consolidated Aero Export Corp, Los Angeles Dennis W. Childers, Claremore OK Courtesy Aircraft Inc, Rockford IL (stored unconv. 60/85, no civil conversion) Rod & Rex Cadman, Canterbury, Kent UK shipped to UK for rebuild: arr. Southend A-26 Europe Inc, Rockford IL (rebuild to fly, Southend UK)	66 69/72 4.83/84 85 .86/91 17.7.86 6.88/91
27592 •	A-26B	44-34313	N5457V C-GHLK	Aero Atlas Inc, Red Bluff CA Wilson Aviation Industries, Lewiston ID Butler Aircraft, Redmond OR (tanker #A20; #16) Conair Aviation Ltd, Abbotsford BC (tanker #323) Reynolds Aviation Museum, Wetaskiwin ALTA (flies as "French AF 434313/K/BC-313")	 63 66/69 4.75/88 1.88/91
27623	A-26B	44-34344	N91356	Ames Applicator Corp, Ames IA Aero Union Corp, Chico CA damaged, nose wheel collapse, Ames IA broken up, Ames IA	66/69 72 .72 c74
27669	A-26B	44-34390	N6836D	Rock Island Oil & Refining Co, Wichita KS Wells Aircraft Inc, Hutchinson KS Edron Co, Las Vegas NV sale reported	66/69 .70/72 77 78
27702	A-26B On Mark	44-34423	N9594Z C-GHLI	Stahmann Farms Inc, Las Cruces NM Victor W. Newman Conair Aviation Ltd, Abbotsford BC (tanker #329) : struck-off reg.	63/72 73 1.75 6.86
27762 •	A-26B B-26K A-26A	44-35483 64-17666		stored MASDC, Davis Monthan AFB AZ USAFM, Hurlburt Field FL (displ. on pole)	71 .72/91
27787 •	A-26B	44-34508	N74874	Kreitzberg Aviation, Salem OR Rosenbalm Aviation, Medford OR William Dempsay, East Wenatchee WA (tanker #107) Bruce Kinney, Richey MT (tanker #107)	63/66 69/72 77 84/92
27799 •	A-26B	44-34520	N9420Z C-GHCF N94207 N126HP	A. S. Wilstrom Inc, New York NY Conair Aviation Ltd, Abbotsford BC (tanker #328) USAFM: for trade Hawkins & Powers Aviation, Greybull WY Hawkins & Powers Aviation, Greybull WY (tanker #28)	63/72 4.74/88 .88 11.88 7.89/92
27802 •	A-26B	44-34523	N9174Z C-GTOX	On Mark Engineering Co, Van Nuys CA Garrett Corp, Los Angeles CA & Phoenix AZ (mod. for turboprop engine in nose position) Air Spray Ltd, Red Deer ALTA (tanker #14)	63 66/77 1.82/92
27805 •	A-26B Marksman	44-34526	N827W N551EH N400V N7977 N26AB	A. M. Wheaton Glass Corp E. T. S. Hokin Corp, San Francisco CA CWC Air Inc, Flushing MI Twin Cities Aviation Inc, Edina MN Dennis M. Sherman, West Palm Beach FL Oklahoma Aircraft Sales, Yukon OK Continental Jet Inc, Clarksville TN Charles Bella, El Paso TX/ Chaparral NM	 66 69 72 76/78 4.81/86 3.87 88/92

27817 •	A-26B	44-34538	N6839D	Rock Island Oil & Refining Co, Wichita KS	
				Hughes Aircraft Co, Culver City CA	66/87
				Gower Lebel Inc, Seattle WA	88
				A & T Productions Inc, Pacific Palisades CA	5.90
			N34538	A & T Productions Inc, Pacific Palisades CA	9.90/92
				(flies in USAF back sc., "434538/BC-538")	
27829	A-26B	44-34550	N7769C	On Mark Engineering Co, Van Nuys CA	
	On Mark		CF-CCR	Canadian Comstock Racing Team	.62/63
			N355Q	Orange County Airways Inc, Montgomery NY	69
			HK-1247W	J. R. Acosta & L. C. H. Lizcano	
			HK-1247P	J. R. Acosta & L. C. H. Lizcano	
				crashed on take-off, Bogota-El Dorado	21.9.88
27834 •	A-26B	44-34555		(to l'Armee de l'Air as 44-34555) ret. USAF	.55
	On Mark		N84W	E. G. Rodman, Odessa TX	63
				Rodman Supply Co, Odessa TX	66/69
			N841W	Carl W. Swan, Oklahoma City OK	.71/72
			N5BP	rereg.	.73
			N550	Rojo Inc, Hilton Head Island SC	77
				Bank of Beaufort, Hilton Head Island SC	.78
				Larry S. Jeter, Lubbock TX	84/89
				Southwest Aviation Inc, Fairacres NM	8.89
			N26HK	Hal Kaden/Southwest Aviation, Fairacres NM	9.90/92
				(open storage, Opa Locka FL 84/91)	
27838 •	A-26B	44-34559		USAFM, Jackson ANGB, Jackson MS	73/88
				(displ. on pole in USAF black sc.)	
27846 •	A-26B	44-34567	N9412Z	On Mark Engineering Co, Van Nuys CA	
	Marksman		ZS-CVD	South African Iron & Steel Industrial Corp,	
				Wonderboom, South Africa	2.62/71
				damaged, belly landing, Omaruru	13.1.71
				SAAF Museum, Ysterplaat	.77/83
27847 •	A-26B	44-34568		(to l'Armee de l'Air as 44-34568) ret. USAF	.55
			N202PP	Purolator Products, New York NY	59/63
				J. P. O'Connor, Fort Lauderdale FL	66/69
				rep. gun-running in Pakistan	.65
			AP-AVV	M. Anwar Khan, Karachi	.70
				wfu Karachi, open storage	81
27860	A-26B	44-34581	N8038E	L. B. Smith Aircraft Corp, Miami FL	
	B-26C			Consolidated Air Parts Corp,	
				Los Angeles CA	66/72
				derelict, unconv., Tucson AZ	69/72
27871	A-26B	44-34592	N8631E	Rock Island Oil & Refining Co, Wichita KS	66
	TB-26B			Consolidated Air Parts Corp, Los Angeles CA	69
				Da Pro Rubber Inc, Van Nuys CA	72
			CF-FJG	Mercury Flights, Edmonton ALTA	4.73
			C-FFJG	Conair Aviation Ltd, Abbotsford BC	6.74
				(tanker #329)	
				crashed, dest., Mercury ALTA	29.9.74
27881 •	A-26B	44-34602	N8392H	Stahmann Farms Inc, Las Cruces NM	66/87
	Monarch			RLS 51 Ltd, San Francisco CA	87/88
				(del. Oslo as "434602/BC-602: 8 gun nose)	5.88
			N167B	RLS 51 Ltd, San Francisco CA	2.89/92
				op. Scandinavian Historical Flight, Oslo	
				(flies as "434602/BC-602 Sugarland Express')	
27886	A-26B	44-34607	N8395H	Stahmann Farms Inc, Las Cruces NM	66/69
	TB-26B			noted Tucson AZ, unconv. USAF sc.	4.68
			CF-FBV	Conair Aviation Ltd, Abbotsford BC	5.71
				(tanker #323)	
				crashed , dest.	3.12.74

27888 •	A-26B	44-34609	N4819E	Rock Island Oil & Refining Co, Wichita KS	
				John Hamacher, San Francisco CA	63/69
				stored for proposed Global Air Museum,	
				Litchfield Park AZ	72
				noted stored, Buckeye AZ (ex tanker)	10.78/79
				Donaire Inc, Phoenix AZ	84/92
27889 •	A-26B	44-34610		(ANG Bureau: last operational USAF B-26)	VB-26B
				NASM, Silver Hill MD	.72/87
				handed over to NASM at Andrews AFB MD	17.9.72
27903	A-26B	44-34624	N6101C	Farah Manufacturing Co, El Paso TX	63
				Rogers Brothers, Beaumont TX	66/69
				Texas State Optical Corp	69
				Confederate Air Force, Harlingen TX	1.70/77
				(flew as "RG-A")	
27921	A-26B	44-34642	N8626E	Rock Island Oil & Refing Co, Wichita KS	66
	TB-26B			Allied Aircraft Sales Corp, Tucson AZ	69
				derelict, unconv., Tucson AZ	69/72
27932	A-26B	44-34653	N9417H	Cornell Aeronautical Laboratories, Buffalo NY	63/72
				Calspan Corp, Buffalo NY	77
				wing failed, crashed near Edwards AFB CA	3.3.81
27938	A-26B	44-34659	N9163Z	National Flight Services Inc, Toledo OH	63
				David Voltz, Phoenix AZ	66
				Aircraft Specialties Inc, Mesa AZ	69/72
				struck-off USCR	30.5.74
				(displ. on roof, Oshawa ONT as N9163Z)	c74
27944 •	A-26B	44-34665		ANG Bureau, Washington DC	
	VB-26B			USAFM, Offutt AFB NE	74/91
27950 •	A-26B	44-34671		(to R Saudi AF as 301)	
				stored derelict , Jeddah Airport	76/80
27976 •	A-26B	44-34697	N4807E	Rock Island Oil & Refining Co, Wichita KS	66
				Consolidated Aero Export Corp, Los Angeles	69/72
				Military Aircraft Restoration Corp, Chino CA	.74/92
27992 •	A-26B	44-34713	N706ME	Star Flite Inc	61
	B-26C			On Mark Engineering Co, Van Nuys CA	63
	Marksman		N36BB (2	W. R. Bailard, Ventura CA	66/72
			N26MR	Micky Rupp, Mansfield OH	74
				Sherman Aircraft Sales, West Palm Beach FL	1.75
			N26WB	Don Whittington, Fort Lauderdale FL	.75
				A. S. Barber Inc, Kirksville MO	77
				sale rep., Danville IL	84/86
				Mid South Aircraft Sales Inc, Memphis TN	3.87
				Wayne County Sheriff Dept, Detroit MI	7.88
				National Warplane Museum, Geneseo NY	88/92
28001 •	A-26B	44-34722	N3222T	Wilson C. Edwards, San Angelo TX	63/69
				John J. Stokes, San Marcos TX	4.81/92
				(flies as "443472")	
28003	A-26B	44-34724	N7662C	The Robert Dollar Company	61
				Pacific Flight Services Inc, Angwin CA	63/66
				Kem Air Inc, Worland WY	69
			CF-BVH	Dontuss Industries, Edmonton ALTA	8.70/74
				Air Spray Ltd, Edmonton ALTA	76/80
				(tanker #6)	
			C-FBVH	Air Spray Ltd, Red Deer ALTA	80
				crashed while firebombing, Slave Lake ALTA	24.4.80

28004	A-26B	44-34725	N4824E	Rock Island Oil & Refining Co, Wichita KS	
				Manuel S. Jovenich, New York NY	66/69
				stripped, derelict hulk, Homer AK	73
28005 •	A-26B	44-34726	N3152G	RALCO, Cheyenne WY	66/69
				sale rep., USCR	78/92
28015	A-26B	44-34736	N4821E	Rock Island Oil & Refining Co, Wichita KS	66
	B-26C			Allied Aircraft Sales Corp, Tucson AZ	69/72
				derelict unconv. ("MATS/Cont.") Tucson AZ	69/72
28017 •	A-26B	44-34738	N600D	Dean Milk Co, Franklin Park IL	66/72
	On Mark		N808D		
			C-GWLU	Air Spray Ltd, Red Deer ALTA	5.75/92
				(tanker #8/"Old Yella")	
28025	A-26B	44-34746		displ. VFW Post 382, El Reno OK	73
28028 •	A-26B	44-34749	N4823E	Rock Island Oil & Refining Co, Wichita KS	66
	B-26K			(conv.to B-26K standard, Hamilton Aircraft)	.69
				(to FA Brasiliera as B-26C -5174)	.69
				wfu , to instructional airframe, derelict	
			N4959K	Tired Iron Inc, Casper WY	9.84
				(ferried Brazil-US: rebuilt as "Puss in Boots")	
				Guarantee Federal Bank, Casper WY	.87
				Airplane Sales Intnl., Beverly Hills CA	8.87/88
				Abrams Airborne Manufacturing, Tucson AZ	10.89/92
28034	A-26B	44-34755	N67839	Superior Oil Co Inc, Chicago IL	54
				Ken McGee Oil Industries Inc	
			N256H (1	Flint Steel Corp, Tulsa OK	63
				Mid America Pipeline Co, Tulsa OK	66
			N3035S(2	John Rourke, Bartlesville OK	69
				Intercontinental Mining, New York NY	72
				Rebel Aviation Inc, Atlanta GA	77
				struck-off USCR	.78
28037	A-26B	44-34758	N67908	Ford Motor Co, Detroit MI	54
				(to l'Armee de l'Air as 44-34758)	
				wfu Chateaudun AB, France	c72
28038 •	A-26B	44-34759	NX67834	Milton Reynolds ("Reynolds Bombshell")	.47
			N67834	Bill Odom ("Reynolds Bombshell")	48
				(around World flight)	
				(exec. conv Southwest Airmotive, Dallas TX)	10.49
				Phillips Drilling Corp, San Antonio TX	.49/54
				(advertised for sale, Jack Davis NC)	12.55
			N28W		
			N956	Colorado Interstate Gas, Colorado Springs CO	59/63
			N956R	Colorado Oil & Gas Corp, Denver CO	66
				Northrop Corp, Newbury Park CA	69/72
				abandoned Tehran, Iran	76
				Jerry Cornell, Tehran, Iran	77
				Bell Helicopter International Inc, Tehran	78
				sale rep., USCR	78/92
				derelict Tehran, Iran	86
28040 •	A-26B	44-34761	N67158	Superior Oil Co LA	54
	Marksman		N400E	Colorado Interstate Gas, Colorado Springs CO	61/63
				Occidental Leasing Corp, Los Angeles CA	66/69
			N60XY	Occidental Chemical Corp, Los Angeles CA	71/72
			N60XX	sale rep., USCR	76/92
28041 •	A-26B	44-34762	N4000	Swiftlite Aircraft Corp, New York NY	54
			N4000K	Slick Airways, San Antonio TX	
				Aero Service Corp, Philadelphia PA	63/66
				Aero Service Corp, Manila, Philippines	69/72
				abandoned, Dili, Timor	75/86

28044 •	A-26B	44-34765	N67160	Sperry Gyroscope Co, Great Neck NY	54/63
				R. C. Johnson, Las Vegas NV	66
				Intnl. Commercial Aviation Serv. Kennedy NY	69
				(delivered via Shannon to Europe)	10.7.69
				lsd: Antwerpse Kreesten Central, Antwerp	69
			D-CAFY	W. Rall	8.70
			N67160	reg. pending	72
				impounded, parked in open Antwerp, Belgium	72/74
				Musee Royal de l'Armee, Brussels, Belgium	76/91
28045 •	A-26B	44-34766	N67807	Bendix racer #91	48/49
				Stanolind Oil & Gas Co, Tulsa OK	54
			N1243	Pan American Petroleum Corp, Tulsa OK	61/63
			N910G	Nine Ten Corp, Chicago IL	66
			N9150	Paramount Trading Co, Vero Beach CA	68/69
				Miami Aircraft Ventures Inc, Miami FL	72
				Vicky Miller, Burbank CA	77
				USAFM, Castle AFB CA	83
				(displ. as USN JD-1 "34766" port side;	
				and USAF "34766/Mary Jo" starbd.)	
				noted at Stockton CA, camouflaged	7.84
				V. Mark Johnson, Lakewood CO	12.84/87
				Donald Douglas Museum, Santa Monica CA	.87/90
				(displ. as "434766/Pretty Patti/J")	
				Larry Leaf, Williston FL	90/91
				David Brady, Cartersville GA	91/92
				dam. in midair collision with Brady's T-37,	
				landed safely Cartersville GA	7.6.91
				Reva J. Brady, Cartersville GA	2.92
28048 •	A-26B	44-34769	N67162	Superior Oil Co Inc, Chicago IL	50/54
	On Mark		N500M	Fletcher Oil & Gas	
				H. B. Zachry Co, San Antonio TX	66
				George J. Rivera, Milton CA	69
				Lloyd A. Hamilton, Santa Rosa CA	71/72
				(racer #16)	
			N29711	John J. Mark, Hales Corner WI	77
				George J. Rivera, San Jose CA	12.81
			N500MR	George J. Rivera, San Jose CA	3.82/89
				William M. Farrell, Cincinatti OH	5.90/92
				(flies camouflaged "434769/K/Gator Invader")	
28052 •	A-26B	44-34773	N67944	Stevens & Co LA	54
				(to l'Armee de l'Air as 44-34773)	c58
				Musee de l'Air et l'Espace, Paris-Le Bourget	75/88
28053 •	A-26B	44-34774	N67163	Standard Oil Co, Chicago IL	49/54
			N163Y	Standard Oil Co, Chicago IL	61/63
			N917Y	Greenacres Farm Inc, Lexington KY	66/72
				Joel McNeal, San Diego CA	77/84
				Courtesy Aircraft Inc, Rockford IL	.85
				Collings Foundation, Stowe MA	3.85/90
				Warbird & Vehicles Inc, Seattle WA	11.90/92
28056 •	A-26B	44-34777	N66661	Stanolind Oil & Gas Co, Tulsa OK	54
	Marksman		N1242	Pan American Petroleum Corp, Tulsa OK	61/63
			N910F	Nine Ten Corp, Chicago IL	66
			N919P	Republic National Bank of Tulsa, Tulsa OK	69
				ditched in Lake Michigan (later salvaged)	c.71
				Walter Soplata Collection, Newbury OH	83/85
28057 •	A-26B	44-34778	N67943	Raytheon Manufacturing Co, Bedford MA	54/72
			C-GWLT	Air Spray Ltd, Red Deer ALTA	5.75/92
				(tanker #7; later #98)	
28480	A-26C	44-35201	N8025E	L. B. Smith Aircraft Corp, Miami FL	

			N137WG	Woodward Governor Co, Rockford IL	63/66
			N437W	Supreme Machine Products, Rockford IL	69
				Stan Burnstein, Tulsa OK	72
				Lester Risley, Anchorage AK	77
28483 •	A-26C	44-35204		USAFM, Chanute AFB, Rantoul IL	65/91
				(displ. as "434314")	
28496	A-26C	44-35217	N4820E	Rock Island Oil & Refining Co, Wichita KS	
				Flight Enterprises Inc, Prescott AZ	63/72
				(tanker #C29)	
			CF-FIM	Air Spray Ltd, Edmonton ALTA	5.73
			C-FFIM	Air Spray Ltd, Red Deer ALTA	84
				(tanker #5") crashed near Calgary ALTA	13.7.84
28503 •	A-26C	44-35224	N9421Z	Belcher Aircraft Corporation	
				Fred M. Strozer, Beverley Hills CA	63
				John Moore, Toluca Lake CA	66
				I. N. Burchinall Jr, Brookston & Paris TX	69/77
			N6240D	Milt Stollak, Burbank CA	4.78
				USAFM, March AFB CA: del.	4.78/90
				(displ. as "44-35224/Sweet Miss Lillian")	
28511	A-26C	44-35232		USAF/Inter-American Air Forces Academy,	
	GB-26			Howard AFB, Panama Canal Zone	74
				(ground inst. airframe, marked "G-5")	
28517	A-26C	44-35238	N3477G	L. B. Smith Aircraft Corp, Miami FL	66/69
				derelict, unconv. Miami FL	68/72
28519	A-26C	44-35240	N122Y	Ayer Associates Automobile Inc	
			N1221	Trathan Drilling, Shreveport LA	63/66
				W. L. Bostwick, Palm Beach FL	69
				John P. Coate, Miami FL	72
28546	A-26C	44-35267	N8034E	L. B. Smith Aircraft Corp, Miami FL	
	B-26B			Consolidated Air Parts Corp, Los Angeles CA	66/72
				derelict, unconv., Tucson AZ	69/72
28602 •	A-26C	44-35323	N8026E	L. B. Smith Aircraft Corp, Miami FL	
	RB-26C			Kreitzberg Aviation Inc, Salem OR	66
				Aeroflight Inc, Troutdale OR	69
				Aero Union Corp, Chico CA	.69
			CF-CDD	Conair Aviation Ltd, Abbotsford BC	5.70
			N8026E	Aero Union Corp, Chico CA (tanker #C55)	9.70/72
				William Dempsay, East Wenatchee WA	77
				(tanker #55)	
				Don A. Goodman, Missoula MT	.77
				Lester Risley, Anchorage AK	c78
				Dr Don Rogers	c79
				The Air Museum, Chino CA	7.80/92
				(del. ex Alaska 7.80, flies as "435323/Ginny Sue")	
28605 •	A-26C	44-35326	N401Y	Boothe Leasing Corp, San Francisco CA	63/66
				Business Aircraft Lessors, Elyria OH	69
				Active Air Inc, Wakeman OH	77
				George J. Rivera, San Jose CA	.81/84
				Endless Turn Inc, Leoti KS	87/88
				Stallion Aircraft, Bensenville IL	5.90/92
28642 •	A-26C	44-35363	N91347	off USCR by	63
				re-added USCR: sale rep.	.78/92
28644	A-26C	44-35365	N91353	Flight Enterprises Inc, Prescott AZ	66/69
				derelict,unconv. ("MT ANG") Tucson AZ	69/72
28650 •	A-26C	44-35371	N4818E	Rock Island Oil & Refining Co, Wichita, KS	66
	TB-26C			Consolidated Air Parts Corp, Los Angeles CA	69

c/n	Type	USAAF	Reg.	Owner / History	Date
				Lynch Air Tankers, Billings MT (tanker #59) .67/92	
28651 •	A-26C	44-35372	N8028E	L. B. Smith Aircraft Corp, Miami FL	
B-26B				Consolidated Air Parts Corp, Los Angeles CA	66/90
				derelict, unconv., Tucson AZ	69/72
				Pima County Air Museum, Tucson AZ	76/90
28664	A-26C	44-35385	N91352	Flight Enterprises Inc, Prescott AZ	66/69
	RB-26C			derelict, unconv., Tucson AZ	69/75
	TB-26C				
28704	A-26C	44-35425	N3427G	Aero Enterprises Inc	
				Pacific Flight Service Inc, Angwin CA	63
				James L. Shipley/Kem-air, Worland WY (tanker #B27)	66/69
				Lynch Air Tankers, Billings MT (tanker #59)	73/76
				crashed fire bombing, Grand Junction CO	8.8.76
28718 •	A-26C	44-35439	N74833	JPR Corp. c/o Madden-Smith Aircraft Corp., Miami FL	.63/69
				John M. Sliker, Wadley GA	72
				John J. Stokes, San Marcos TX	77
				Lynch Air Tankers, Billings MT	4.5.79/90
				Evergreen Ventures Inc, McMinville OR	3.90/92
				(flies as USAF "435439")	
28719 •	A-26C	44-35440	N6838D	Rock Island Oil & Refining Co, Wichita KS	66/72
				Aero Union Corp, Chico CA	71
			CF-MSB	Conair Aviation Ltd, Abbotsford BC (tanker #325)	6.71
			C-FMSB	Conair Aviation Ltd, Abbotsford BC	77/88
				USAFM, Travis AFB : del.	.88/90
				(displ. as "435440/BG-O")	
28723 •	A-26C	44-35444	N7656C	Vance Roberts, Seattle WA	63/69
	RB-26C		CF-TFB	Air Spray Ltd, Edmonton ALTA	71
			C-FTFB	Air Spray Ltd, Red Deer ALTA (tanker #4)	6.73/92
28735 •	A-26C	44-35456	N330WC	Western Contracting Corp, Sioux City IA	63/69
	RB-26C			Aero Union Corp, Chico CA	72
			CF-AGO	Conair Aviation Ltd, Abbotsford BC (tanker #326)	7.72/80
				u/c collapsed landing, Fort St John BC	14.5.80
			C-FAGO	Air Spray Ltd, Edmonton ALTA (tanker #36/"Dragon Lady")	.83/92
28745	A-26C	44-35466	N8019E	L. B. Smith Aircraft Corp, Miami FL	
	TB-26B			Consolidated Air Parts Corp, Los Angeles CA	66/72
				derelict, unconv., Tucson AZ	69/71
28772 •	A-26C	44-35493	N2852G	Dollar Lines Inc, San Francisco CA	
	RB-26C			Pacific Flight Service Inc, Angwin CA	66/69
				Arthur W. McDonnell, Lancaster CA	70/72
				Stencel Aero Engineering, Ashville NC	77
				Oklahoma Aircraft Sales, Yukon OK	84
				John MacGuire, El Paso TX	86/87
			N576JB	War Eagles Air Museum, Santa Teresa NM	17.2.87/92
				(see N94445: id. unknown at end of listing)	
28774	A-26C	44-35495	N507WB	Williams Bothers Co	61
				Tradewinds Aircraft Supply, San Antonio TX	66/69
				Milt Stollak, Burbank CA	77
28776 •	A-26C	44-35497	N3426G	Johnson Flying Service, Missoula MT (tanker #A17)	63/69
	RB-26C			Evergreen Air, Missoula MT (tanker #A17)	.75
				Lynch Air Tankers, Billings MT (tanker #56)	.77/92

28783 •	A-26C	44-34504		(to l'Armee de l'Air as 44-34504)	
				gate guard, Chateaudun AB, France	72/77
28784 •	A-26C	44-35505	N4815E	Rock Island Oil & Refining Co, Wichita KS	
				Tallmantz Aviation Inc, Orange County CA	63/76
				Albert Redick, Chino CA	77
				On Mark Aviation, Knoxville TN	.78
				sale rep., Chino CA	84/92
28802 •	A-26C	44-35523	N3428G	Aero Atlas Inc, Red Bluff CA	
				Rosenbalm Aviation Inc, Medford OR	63/72
				(tanker #F29; #29)	
				William Dempsay, East Wenatchee WA	c72/77
				(tanker #108)	
				Kinney Air Tankers, Richey MT (tanker #108)	c81
				Custom Farm Service of Montana, Richey MT	84
				William A. Dempsay, East Wenatchee WA	7.85
				Central Air Service, East Wenatchee WA	86/88
28803 •	A-26C	44-35524	N9401Z	Donaire Inc, Phoenix AZ	66/69
				Thomas W. Hammon, Phoenix AZ	72
			CF-CUI		72
			C-FCUI	Air Spray Ltd, Red Deer ALTA (tanker #12)	81/92
28820	A-26C	44-35541	N8032E	L. B. Smith Aircraft Corp, Miami FL	
				Consolidated Air Parts Corp, Los Angeles CA	66/92
				derelict, unconv., Tucson AZ	69/72
28831 •	A-26C	44-35552	N5544V	Rosenbalm Aviation, Medford OR	63/72
				William Dempsay, East Wenatchee WA	c72/77
				(tanker #104)	
				Kinney Air Tankers, Richey MT	6.81
				(tanker #104)	
				Duane D. Sly, Platte SD	3.85/92
28841 •	A-26C	44-35562	N707TG	Texas Gas Transmission Corp, Owensboro KY	61/66
	On Mark		N7079G	Natrona Service Inc, Casper WY	69/88
				Conrad Yelvington, South Daytona FL	8.89/92
				op: Lady Barbel Abela & Len Perry, London UK	.91/92
				(flies as, "Bar-Belle Bomber")	
28859	A-26C	44-35580	N74831	Madden-Smith Aircraft Corp, Miami FL	66/69
				sale rep., USCR	78/92
28860	A-26C	44-35581	N3485G	Stahmann Farms Inc, Las Cruces NM	63
				M. S. Jovenich, New York NY	66
				Hamilton Aircraft Co, Tucson AZ	69
				Aircraft Surplus Co, Tucson AZ	72
			C-GWJG	Air Spray Ltd, Red Deer ALTA	6.76/82
				(tanker #9)	
				crashed near Watson Lake, Yukon Territory	1.7.82
28869 •	A-26C	44-35590	N3248G	E. J. Quick	
	RB-26C			Ray Karrels, Port Washington WI	63/69
				Earl Reinert/Victory Air Museum,	
				Mundelein IL : displ. as 3rd BG "Nightmare"	76/79
				Earl Reinert, Arlington Heights IL	9.87/92
28875 •	A-26C	44-35596	N5636V	Hawaii Public Trade & Instructional School,	
	RB-26C			Honolulu International Airport, Honolulu HI	66/79
				USAFM, Hickam AFB HI	82/89
28880 •	A-26C	44-35601	N202R	B. S. Hagill	
				Metropolitan Paving Co, Oklahoma City OK	63
				Harry Mallory, Oklahoma City OK	66
				Aero Industries Inc, Addison TX	69
				Texas Instruments Inc, Dallas TX	72/77

				Edward Counselman, Topeka KS	.78
				Rodney G. Huskey, Grand Junction CO	84/92
28896 •	A-26C	44-35617	N600WB	Ridge Associates Inc, Flint MI	61/63
	RB-26C			Mid America Air Transport, Chicago IL	66
	Marksman			Red Dodge Aviation Inc, Anchorage AK	69/72
				John Steinmetz, Griffin GA	77
				Oklahoma Aircraft Corp, Yukon OK	84/87
				impnd. alleged drug smuggling, US Customs	c85
				USAFM, Travis AFB CA	87/90
28906 •	A-26C	44-35627		displ. on pylon Dodge City Airport KS	73/88
28916	A-26C	44-35637	N8040E	L. B. Smith Aircraft Corp, Miami FL	
				Consolidated Air Parts Corp, Los Angeles CA	66/92
				derelict, unconv., Tucson AZ	69/72
28919	A-26C	44-35640	N4204A	L. B. Smith Aircraft Corp, Miami FL	60
	Smith			Pinellas Aircraft Inc, St Petersburg FL	63
	Tempo			Appliance Buyers Credit Corp, St Joseph MI	66
				Newton A. Ball, Dillingham AK	69
				University of Nevada, Reno NV	.69/80
				crashed Nevada, on weather research flight	2.80
28922 •	A-26C	44-35643		(to l'Armee de l'Air as 44-35643)	4.54
	RB-26C			returned to USAF	.55
	Monarch		N6841D	Rock Island Oil & Refining Co, Wichita KS	63/69
				William K. Mayfield, Halstead KS	72
				Robert Diemert, Carman, Manitoba : del.	14.10.73
			C-GCES	Robert Diemert, Carman, Manitoba	10.74/79
			N8015H	reg.	6.79
				Confederate Air Force, Harlingen TX	3.10.79/84
			N226RW	Confederate Air Force, Pine Bluff AR	2.84/91
				American Airpower Heritage Flying Museum, Midland TX	9.91/92
				(flies as "4435643/Daisy Mae/A")	
28940 •	A-26C	44-35661	N9996Z	Donaire Inc, Phoenix AZ (tanker #C11)	63
				George H. Stell, Phoenix AZ (tanker #C11)	66/72
			CF-CBK	O. Huitikka, Fort Francis ONT	11.72
			C-FCBK	Air Spray Ltd, Red Deer ALTA	79/92
				(tanker #11)	
28950	A-26C	44-35671	N8033E	L. B. Smith Aircraft Corp, Miami FL	
	B-26B			Consolidated Air Parts Corp, Los Angeles	66/92
				derelict, unconv., Tucson AZ	69/72
28960	A-26C	44-35681	N60Y	Mechanical Products Inc, Jackson MI	54
				Philips Petroleum	
			N168Y	Amerada Petroleum Corp, Tulsa OK	66
			CF-VPR	Survair Ltd, Ottawa	.67/70
28961 •	A-26C	44-35682	N5181V	R. F. Todd	
	RB-26C			(conv. to exec. Monarch 26 abandoned)	
	Monarch			John M. Sliker, Wadley GA (dism.)	63
				John J. Stokes, San Marcos TX (dism.)	
				Lynch Air Tankers, Billings MT (dism.)	80/92
28975 •	A-26C	44-35696	N8036E	L. B. Smith Aircraft Corp., Miami FL	
				William E. Strader, Fresno CA	63/77
				Dwight Reimer Shafter CA	78/79
				(race #26/"Cotton Jenny")	
				Courtesy Aircraft Inc, Rockford IL	84
				Collings Foundation, Stowe MA	86/92
28987 •	A-26C	44-35708	N5530V	On Mark Engineering Co, Van Nuys CA	63/66
				Raytheon Co, Bedford MA	69/72

			C-GXGY	Air Spray Ltd, Red Deer ALTA (tanker #10)	12.76/92
28989 •	A-26C	44-35710	N7705C	Mayhew Supply Inc, Gulfport MS	63
				Appliance Buyers Credit Corp, St Joseph MI	66/69
				Rusk Aviation, Kankakee IL	72
				Eugene H. Akers, San Diego CA	77/87
				Eugene H. Akers, Georgetown SC	88
				sale rep., Chino CA: open storage Chino	89/92
29000 •	A-26C	44-35721	N9425Z	Central Oregon Airial Co Inc, Bend OR	63
				Lynch Air Tankers, Billings MT (tanker #57)	66/92
29003 •	A-26C	44-35724	N7954C	J. E. Gardner	
				Rosenbalm Aviation, Medford OR	63
				Flick Aviation, La Grande OR (tanker #83)	66/69
				Rosenbalm Aviation, Medford OR	72
				William A. Dempsay, East Wenatchee WA	73
				(tanker #83; later #106)	
				Central Air Service, East Wenatchee WA	83
				USAFM, Beale AFB CA	.83/88
				(displ. as "434517/Monnie")	
29004	A-26C	44-35725	N800W	James M. Cook, Jacksboro TX	63
				U.S. Dept of Commerce, Washington DC	64/69
				MASDC, Davis-Monthan AFB, Tucson AZ by	11.69
				(stored as "N800W/35725")	
				Allied Aircraft Inc, Tucson AZ: del. ex MASDC	2.4.76
29012 •	A-26C	44-35733		USAFM, Wright-Patterson AFB, Dayton OH	9.57/90
				(displ. as "435733/BC-733/Dream Girl")	
29031 •	A-26C	44-35752	N8627E	Rock Island Oil & Refining Co, Wichita KS	66
				Donaire Inc, Phoenix AZ	69
				Thomas W. Hammon, Phoenix AZ	c71
			CF-KBZ	Kenting Aircraft Ltd, Toronto ONT	6.72
				Conair Aviation Ltd, Abbotsford BC	8.73
				(tanker #327)	
			C-FKBZ	Conair Aviation Ltd, Abbotsford BC	79/86
				Canadian Warplane Heritage, Mount Hope ONT	18.1.88
			N81797	Courtesy Aircraft Inc, Rockford IL	6.89/92
				(flies as "435752/Rude Invader")	
29038	A-26C	44-35759	N5588A	R. A. Firestone, Teterboro NJ	
				William C. Powell, Dallas TX	63
				derelict, Miami FL	68/71
29059 •	A-26C	44-35780	N8021E	L. B. Smith Aircraft Corp., Miami FL	
	TB-26B			Madden-Smith Aircraft Corp, Miami FL	63
				Consolidated Air Parts Corp, Los Angeles CA	66/72
				Allied Aircraft Sales, Tucson AZ	74/92
				derelict unconv, Tucson AZ	69/92
29067 •	A-26C	44-35788	N8058E	L. B. Smith Aircraft Corp., Miami FL	
				open storage, Charlotte SC	62/72
				John J. Stokes, San Marcos TX	77/78
				Joe Mabee, Midland TX	c81
				EAA Aviation Foundation, Oshkosh WI	.83/84
				Sanders Lead Co Inc, Troy AL	.87/92
				(flies in USAAF sc.)	
29087	A-26C	44-35808	N8041E	L. B. Smith Aircraft Corp., Miami FL	
	RB-26C			Consolidated Air Parts Corp, Los Angeles CA	66/72
				derelict unconv., ("AR ANG") Tucson AZ	69/72
29089 •	A-26C	44-35810	N9403Z	Clifton H. Troxell, Arden NV	66/69
				Reeder Flying Service, Twin Falls ID	72/77
				(tanker #27)	
			C-GPUC	Air Spray Ltd, Red Deer ALTA (tanker #27)	4.81/92

29136 •	A-26C	44-35857	N9300R	L. B. Smith Aircraft Corp., Miami FL	
				Consolidated Air Parts Corp, Los Angeles CA	66/69
			CF-ZTC	Forest Patrol Ltd	7.71
			C-FZTC	J. D. Irving	79
				Air Spray Ltd, Red Deer ALTA	8.79/92
				(tanker #14, later #13/"Lucky Jack")	
29137	A-26C	44-35858	N8039E	L. B. Smith Aircraft Corp., Miami FL	
	RB-26C			Consolidated Air Parts Corp, Los Angeles CA	66/72
				derelict unconv., Tucson AZ	69/72
29138	A-26C	44-35859		(to Armee de L'Air as 44-35859)	
				stored Bordeaux Merignac	78
29139	A-26C	44-35860	N8049E	L. B. Smith Aircraft Corp., Miami FL	
	B-26B			Consolidated Air Parts Corp, Los Angeles CA	66/72
				derelict unconv.,Tucson AZ	69/72
29146	A-26C	44-35867	N8035E	L. B. Smith Aircraft Corp., Miami FL	
				Consolidated Air Parts Corp, Los Angeles CA	66/72
				derelict unconv., ("MO ANG") Tucson AZ	69/72
29149 •	A-26C	44-35870	N320	Maytag Aircraft Corp, Miami FL	
	Marksman			L. B. Maytag Jnr, Miami FL	63
				National Bank, Tulsa OK	66/69
				Trinity Industries Inc	69
				Confederate Air Force, Harlingen TX	.70/72
				struck-off USCR: rep. sold to South America	c75
			N99426	noted in ferry marks, Opa Locka FL	7.81
				F. J. Luytjes, Dalton PA	84
				T. K. Edenfield, Albuquerque NM	5.85
				C. H. Midkiff, San Antonio TX	9.86
				Outlaw Aircraft Sales Inc, Clarksville TN	4.87
				Wayne County Sheriff Dept, Detroit MI	7.88/90
				sale rep., Brooksville FL	92
29154 •	A-26C	44-35875	N4816E	Rock Island Oil & Refining Co, Wichita KS	
			CF-PGF	DM Air Enterprises Ltd, Vancouver BC	.63/65
				Air Spray Ltd, Edmonton ALTA (tanker #1)	.70/78
			C-FPGF	Air Spray Ltd, Red Deer ALTA (tanker #1)	79/92
29159	A-26C	44-35880	N8048E	L. B. Smith Aircraft Corp., Miami FL	
				Consolidated Air Parts Corp, Los Angeles CA	66/72
				derelict unconv., Tucson AZ	69/72
29167 •	A-26C	44-35888	N4810E	Rock Island Oil & Refining Co, Wichita KS	66
				Consolidated Aero Export Corp, Los Angeles	69/72
				Military Aircraft Restoration Corp, Chino CA	.74/92
29171 •	A-26C	44-35892	N4811E	Rock Island Oil & Refining Co, Wichita KS	66
				Consolidated Aero Export Corp, Los Angeles	69/72
				Pueblo Memorial Aircraft Museum, Pueblo CO	.72/79
				Frank E.Weisbrod Aircraft Museum, Peublo CO	88
29172 •	A-26C	44-35893	N4812E	Rock Island Oil & Refining Co, Wichita KS	66
				Consolidated Aero Export Corp, Los Angeles	69/72
			C-GHCC	Conair Aviation Ltd, Abbotsford BC	6.74
				(tanker #331)	
				Air Spray Ltd, Red Deer ALTA (tanker #31)	.82/92
29177 •	A-26C	44-35898	N3328G	Lear Inc, Santa Monica CA	61/63
				Lear Siegler Inc, Santa Monica CA	66
				Aerospace Modifications, Coatsville PA	69
			CF-PGP	Air Spray Ltd, Edmonton ALTA (tanker #2)	7.71/76
			C-FPGP	Air Spray Ltd, Red Deer ALTA (tanker #2)	76/92

29180 •	A-26C	44-35901	N91351	Flight Enterprises Inc, Prescott AZ	66/69
	TB-26C			derelict unconv., Tucson AZ	69/92
				sale rep., USCR	.78/92
29190 •	A-26C	44-35911		(to l'Armee de l'Air as 44-35911) ret. USAF	.55
	Monarch		N6840D	Rock Island Oil & Refining Co, Wichita KS	63
				Magnolia Homes Manuf. Corp, Vicksburg MS	66
				Aero Specialities Inc, Long Beach CA	69
				Westinghouse Credit Corp, Brynmawr PA	72
				Milt Slollak, Burbank CA	77
				Stephen L. Miles, Carmel Valley & Salinas CA	10.83/88
				Courtesy Aircraft Inc, Rockford IL	1.89/90
				Coleman Warbird Museum, Coleman TX	92
				(flies camouflaged as "435911/Bandido")	
29192 •	A-26C	44-35913	N303W	On Mark Engineering Co, Van Nuys CA	
	On Mark		N303WC	Western Contracting Corp, Lincoln NE	63/69
				Texas Instruments Inc, Dallas TX	72/77
				Guy E. Counselman, Topeka KS	84
				USAFM, Dyess AFB TX	84
29197 •	A-26C	44-35918	N7953C	Beech Aircraft Corp, Wichita KS	60/61
				(used for air-to-air refuelling trials)	
			TI-1040L	Frank Marshall , Costa Rica	
			TI-1040P		
			HR-276		5.70
				(to FA Hondurena as FAH276 later FAH510)	.5.71
			N2781G	David Zeuschel, Van Nuys CA	12.82/83
				ferried Tegucigalpa AB, Honduras - Kelly AFB	.83
				USAFM, Kelly AFB TX	.83
				USAFM, Lackland AFB TX	87/92
				(displ. as "435918/BC-918/Versatile Lady")	
29202	A-26C	44-35923		Aircraft Industries Museum, Louisville KY	73
29216	A-26C	44-35937		(to FA Chile as FAC 846)	
				Confederate Air Force, Harlingen TX	3.80
				(rep. presented to CAF) : no further info.	
				(also rep. as FAC 842/43-22728)	
29217	A-26C	44-35938	N4203A	G. C. Murphy Co, McKeesport PA	59/61
	RB-26C		N510X	G. C. Murphy Co, McKeesport PA	6.63/67
	On Mark		N510A		
			N516X	Ralph Tait	67/69
				Twin Cities Aviation Inc, Minneapolis MN	69
			D-BACA	Friederich Stetzler/Transport Dienst GmbH,	
				Dusseldorf	8.69/73
				wheels up landing, Stuttgart West Germany	11.8.70
				crashed landing, Zurich, Switzerland	23.2.73
				burnt for fire practice, Zurich	5.7.73
29224	A-26C	44-35945		rep. at King County Airport, Seattle WA	74
				(marked as "HL-NG")	
29227 •	A-26C	44-35948	N67164	Stanolind Oil & Gas Co OK	54
			N1244	Pan American Petroleum Corp, Tulsa OK	61/63
			N910H	Nine Ten Corp, Chicago IL	66
			N161H	Motorola Inc, Scottsdale AZ	69
				Grumman Ecosystems Corp, Bethpage NY	72
			C-GHLX	Conair Aviation Ltd, Abbotsford BC	7.75/86
				(tanker #332)	
				Air Spray Ltd, Red Deer ALTA (tanker #32)	90/92
29234 •	A-26C	44-35955	N8394H	Kenlyn Petroleum Corp, Los Angeles CA	63/69
	TB-26B			Rodney G. Huskey, Grand Junction CO	84/92
29243	A-26C	44-35964	N4813E	Rock Island Oil & Refining Co, Wichita KS	63

				Aim Aviation Inc, Houston TX	66/69
				Environmental Protectection Agency,	
				Las Vegas NV	77
				Combat Air Museum, Topeka KS	84/88
				(flew in camouflage sc.)	
				crashed and destroyed, Cimarron NM	26.6.88
29265 •	A-26C	44-35986	N6382T	Detroit Airport Instructional School MI	66/80
				(instr. airframe, Detroit-Metro Airport MI)	
				USAFM, Selfridge ANGB MI	89
				(displ. as "5986")	
29273 •	A-26C	44-35994	N4822E	Rock Island Oil & Refining Co, Wichita KS	66
	TB-26C			Allied Aircraft Sales Corp, Tucson AZ	69
				stored, derelict (tanker #C32), Buckeye AZ 78/79	
- •	B-26K	64-17640		(USAF 603rd SOS/1st SOW "IF") del. MASDC	10.69
	A-26A		N267G	State of Georgia Forestry Comm., Macon GA	71
				stored unconverted, Macon GA	72/78
			N2294B	Arthur W. McDonnell, Mojave CA	7.78/86
				stored unconv. (camo. "IF/640"), Mojave CA	79
				USAFM, Ellsworth AFB SD	86/88
- •	B-26K	64-17651		(USAF 609th SOS/56th SOW "TA") at MASDC	71
	A-26A			ROKAF Museum, Seoul, South Korea	73/87
- •	B-26K	64-17671		(USAF 609th SOS/56th SOW "TA") at MASDC	71
	A-26A			Florence Air & Missile Museum, Florence SC	73/90
				(displ. as "64671/TA")	
- •	B-26K	64-17679		(USAF 603rd SOS/1st SOW) del. MASDC	11.69 A-26A
			N269G	State of Georgia Forestry Comm., Macon GA	.71
				stored unconv., Macon GA	72/78
			C-GXTG	Air Spray Ltd, Edmonton ALTA : not del.	.77
				dam. on landing during test flight, Macon GA	.77
			N4988N	Lynch Air Service, Billings MT	10.78/92
				(rebuilt, flies in camouflage as USAF "IF-679")	
-	A-26	-	N1144		
			XB-PEX	reported at Mexico City	c72
- •	A-26	-		(to FA Mexicana as 1302)	
	LAS Super 26		N5052N	Mesta Machine Co, Pittsburgh PA	54/66
				(rebuilt Ontario CA .60 by Lockheed Aircraft	
				Service as prototype LAS Super 26)	60
			N52NM	Westernair of Albuquerque, Albuquerque NM	69
				Bruce Irwin, Scottsdale AZ	72
			XB-SIJ	"Koba Wiki"	c75
				wfu San Antonio TX: spar and legal problems 6.79/80	
			C-GQPZ	Air Spray Ltd, Red Deer ALTA (for spares)	81/92
				del. San Antonio-Red Deer ALTA, then dism.	81/92
				(orig. mainplane XB-SIJ with Aero Nostalgia Inc,	
				Stockton CA, for USAFM A-26 static rebuild 91)	
				(note: FAA quote id. 1302)	
-	A-26	-	N62289	reg. reserved	.74
				John J. Stokes, San Marcos TX	77/ 84
				(FAA quote id. "1125"): struck-off reg.	7.84
-	A-26	-	N62290	reg. reserved	.74
				(FAA quote id. "3890")	
- •	A-26B	-		(to GN Nicaraguana as GN.......)	
			N99425	David C. Tallichet/ MARC, Chino CA	3.77/92
				(FAA quote id. "162"; also rep. as c/n 6875)	
- •	A-26	-	N36B		
			N36BB (1	B.B. Branch, Ventura CA	63
			N94445	Hughes Aircraft Corp, Culver City CA	66/69

					(FAA quote id."7": prob. On Mark conv. c/n)	
					USAFM, Grand Forks AFB ND	85/88
					(displ. as "434220": id. quoted by USAFM as	
					c/n 28772, viz 44-35493/N2852G: que se) - •	A-26 -
					USAFM, Robins AFB GA	91
					(displ. as "435732")	
-		A-26	-	YV-E-IPV	noted, Caracas, Venezuela	1.74
-	•	A-26	-		(to FA Brasiliera as C-26B-5156)	
					FAB Academy Museum, Pirassunga, Sa Paulo	85
-	•	A-26C	-		(to FA Chile as FAC 848)	
					displ. Municipal Park, Mejillones, Chile	82
-	•	A-26C	-		(to FA Chile as FAC 8...)	
					displ. El Bosque, Chile	82
					(displ. as "FAC 848")	
-	•	A-26C	-		(to FA Chile as FAC 8...)	
					displ. Cerro Moreno AB, Chile	82
					(displ. as "FAC 863")	
-	•	A-26	-		(to FA Colombiana as 2519)	
					Museo FAC, Catam AB, El Dorado, Bogota	72/79
-	•	A-26	-		(to Indonesian AF/AURI as M-265)	
					Indonesian Air Force Museum, Jogjakarta	89
-	•	A-26	-		(to FA Mexicana as FAM 1300)	
					Museo de la FAM, stored Mexico City	71/79
-	•	A-26	-		(to FA Portuguesa as 7104)	
					Museo do Ar, Alverca AB, Portugal	79/85
-	•	A-26	-		(to FA Revolucionaria, Cuba as ....)	
					displ. Havana, Cuba as "FAR 933"	90
-	•	A-26	-		(to R Saudi AF as 309)	
					stored derelict, Jeddah Airport	76/80
-	•	A-26	-		(to R Saudi AF as 3....)	
					stored derelict, Jeddah Airport with one other	76/80

DOUGLAS SBD DAUNTLESS

-	•	SBD-3	Bu06508		crashed off USS Wolverine, Lake Michigan	.43
					recov. from Lake Michigan by USNAM	.90
					USNAM, NAS Pensacola FL	90/92
1708	•	SBD-4	Bu06833		(USN "B8"): ditched, Lake Michigan	16.9.44
					recov. from Lake Michigan by USNAM	.91
					Kevin Hooey, Corning NY	91
2350	•	A-24A	42-60817	N9142H	City of Portland Mosquito Control, OR	58/65
					op. Aero Flight Inc, Troutdale OR : sprayer	
				N15749	USMC Museum, MCAS Quantico VA	.65
					USNAM, NAS Pensacola FL	.66/91
					(del. by road, Portland - Pensacola .66)	
					(displ. as SBD-3 "2-S-12")	
2478	•	SBD-4	Bu10518		MGM Studios, Culver City CA	
					(fuselage only, rigged as wind machine)	
					The Air Museum, Ontario CA	c68
					Admiral Nimitz Museum, Fredericksburg TX	
					Bruce D. Roberts, New London Airport PA	75
					loan: Bradley Air Museum, Windor Locks CT	
				N4864J	Yankee Air Corps, Chino CA	4.84/92
					(airworthy rest. Chino, but not flown,	

c/n		Type	Serial	Reg'n	History	Date
					using wings recov. from Guadalcanal by YAC)	
-	•	SBD-4	Bu10575		ditched in Lake Michigan, off Chicago IL	14.9.44
					recov. from Lake Michigan by USNAM	.91
-	•	SBD-4	Bu10715		recov. from Lake Michigan by Ed Marshall	c81
					Yankee Air Corps, Chino CA	86
					(rest. project, using wings recov. from Guadalcanal, South Pacific by YAC)	
					Military Aircraft Restoration Corp, Chino CA	.87/91
					Museum of Flying, Santa Monica CA	.91
					(arr. Santa Monica dism. 7.91, rest. project)	
3883	•	SBD-5	Bu28536		(to RNZAF as NZ5062)	
					returned to USMC, Russell Field, South Pacific	10.5.44
					MGM Studios, Culver City CA (wind machine)	
					The Air Museum, Ontario CA	c68/87
				N670AM	The Air Museum, Chino CA	.87/92
					(rebuilt Chino, using wings recov. from Guadalcanal, South Pacific: ff 2.7.87)	
4812	•	SBD-5	Bu36173		(USN "B21"): ditched, Lake Washington WA	
					recov. from Lake Washington, WA	.88
					Patriots Point Naval & Maritime Museum/ USS Yorktown Museum, Mount Pleasant SC	.88/92
					(static rest., displ. on USS "Yorktown")	
6119	•	SBD-6	Bu54605		Smithsonian Institute	.48/70
					stored Weeksville NC	5.48/61
					USMC Museum, MCAS Quantico VA	.70
					NASM, Washington DC	75/92
					(displ. as "VS-51/54605/109")	
17371	•	A-24B	42-54532	NL94513	Seaboard & Western Airlines, San Francisco CA	.47
					(to F A Mexicana as .....)	
				XB-QUC	Compania Mexicana Aerophoto, Mexico City	60/63
					Tallmantz Collection, Orange County CA	.64
					The Air Museum, Ontario CA	.65/67
				N54532	Robert L. Griffin/CAF, San Antonio TX	.70/72
					Confederate Air Force, Harlingen TX	10.78/91
					American Airpower Heritage Flying Museum, Midland TX	9.91/92
					(flies as SBD-3, "54532/2-B-4/B14")	
17421	•	A-24B	42-54582	N4488N	Marsh Aviation, Litchfield AZ	54
					City of Portland Mosquito Control, OR	60/69
					op. Aero Flight Inc, Troutdale OR : sprayer	
					Pacific Aeronautical Corp, Lake Oswego OR	.71/74
				N17421	Doug Champlin/Windward Aviation, Enid OK	3.74/75
					USMC Museum, MCAS Quantico VA	3.75/87
					(displ. as "SBD-5/USMC/S6")	
17432	•	A-24B RA-24B	42-54593		MGM Studios, Culver City CA (wind machine)	
					Admiral Nimitz Museum, Fredericksburg TX	
					Trade Tech. School, Waco TX : to scrapyard	
					Nick Pocock, China Springs TX	75/91
					Kevin R. Smith, Fredericksburg VA	.91
					(fuse only, planned rest. to fly)	
17482	•	A-24B	42-54643		MGM Studios, Culver City CA (wind machine)	
					Admiral Nimitz Museum, Fredericksburg TX	72/74
					Bradley Air Museum, Windsor Locks CT: arr.	4.12.74/88
					Bruce Roberts, New London PA	.88
				N51382	Weeks Air Museum, Tamiami FL	.88/90
					(rest. project)	

17493 •	A-24B	42-54654		MGM Studios, Culver City CA (wind machine)	
				Military Aircraft Restoration Corp, Chino CA	79/91
				(rest. Akron-Canton Airport OH, for MARC 91)	
17521 •	A-24B	42-54682		(to F A Mexicana as .....)	
			XB-ZAH	Compania Mexicana Aerophoto, Mexico City	63
				(noted wfu, engineless, Mexico City 12.63)	
				Tallmantz Aviation/Movieland of the Air,	
				Orange County CA (displ. as 'USN/SBD')	4.64
			N74133	Rosen-Novak Auto Co, Omaha NE	66/68
				remained on displ. Orange County : auctioned 29.5.68	
				John McGregor, San Fernando CA	69
				Admiral Nimitz Foundation, Fredericksburg TX	.72/91
				(rest. by Trade School, Waco TX)	
				(displ. Admiral Nimitz Museum as SBD-3 "5-B-1")	
17621	A-24B	42-54782	NL9449H	noted in civil scheme, New York NY	.46
			N9449H	Seaboard & Western Airlines Inc, NY : USCR	63/69
17651	A-24B	42-54812	NX46472	Sperry Gyroscope Co, New York NY	47
	RA-24B		N46472	City of Portland Mosquito Control OR	56/65
				Aero Flight Inc, Kent WA	1.7.65
				Confederate Air Force, Mercedes TX	10.65
				crashed on del. flight, Brownwood TX	10.10.65
				rear fuselage noted on dump. Harlingen TX	76
- •	SBD	-		ditched, Lake Michigan, near Chicago IL	c43
				recov. from Lake Michigan by USNAM	c90
- •	SBD	-		rep. recov. from Lake Michigan	
				Kermit A. Weeks/Weeks Air Museum,	
				Tamiami FL	90/91
- •	SBD	-		hulk recov. from Vanuatu, South Pacific	c87
				RNZAF Museum, Wigram AB NZ	87/91
				(static rest. project)	
- •	SBD	-		rep. hulk, recov. ex crash sites FL	
				Harry S. Doan, New Smyrna Beach FL	87/90
- •	SBD	-		rep. hulk, recov. ex crash sites FL	
				Harry S. Doan, New Smyrna Beach FL	87/90
- •	SBD	-		rep. hulk, recov. ex crash sites FL	
				Harry S. Doan, New Smyrna Beach FL	87/90

1930 •	XBT2D-1	Bu09102		Naval Historical Centre,	
	XAD-1			Washington Navy Yard, Washington DC	79
				USMCM, Quantico MCAS VA	
				displ. Oceana NAS, Virginia Beach VA	87/92
				(displ. as "F501", later "09102/AE500"	
1931 •	XBT2D-1	Bu09103		dism. in junkyard, Fairless Hills PA	65
	XAD-1			Walter Soplata Collection, Newbury OH	85
2085 •	AD-1	Bu09257		stored trucking yard, Oklahoma City OK	60/70
	AD-2		N2AD	Douglas W. Wood, Dallas TX	4.81/92
6933 •	AD-3	Bu122811		NATTC, NAS Memphis TN	
	A-1E			EAA Museum, Oshkosh WI	78/90
7133 •	AD-4	Bu123827		gate guard, DeKalb-Peachtree Airport GA	59/66
			N54162	David M. Forrest, Avondale Estates GA	.66/69
			N23827	David M. Forrest, Avondale Estates GA	78/87
				(ff 5.12.78 as "168B/Navy Atlanta")	
				James McMillan/FOAG Inc, Breckenridge TX	2.87/88
				Wiley C. Sanders, Troy AL	90/92
7392 •	AD-4W	Bu124086		(to RN Fleet Air Arm as WV106)	
	AEW.1			FAA Museum: stored RNAS Culdrose	70
				Cornwall Aero Park, Helston	78/90
				(displ. as "WV106/C-427")	
7427 •	AD-4W	Bu124121		(to RN Fleet Air Arm as WT121)	
	AEW.1			FAA Museum, RNAS Yeovilton UK	6.72/92
				(displ. as "WT121/CU-415")	
7449 •	AD-4N	Bu124143		(to l'Armee de l'Air as No.14)	10.6.60
	A-1D			(to F.A. Gabonaise as TR-KFP)	72/84
			N91909	ntu: Jack Spanich, Detroit MI	76
			F-WZDP	Aero Retro, St Rambert d'Albion: del.	20.7.84
			F-AZDP	Jean Baptiste Salis, La Ferte-Alais	7.84/91
				(flies as "24143/RM-205/USS Saratoga")	
7462 •	AD-4N	Bu124156		(to l'Armee de l'Air as No.30)	.60
	A-1D			(to F.A. Gabonaise as ....)	c68/76
				recov. from Gabon by Gyra France	.76
			N91935	Jack Spanich, Detroit MI	1.77
				del. Chateaudun AB to USA, via Dublin	9.3.77
				Jimmy McMillan/Breckenridge Tank Truck Inc	3.83/87
				William E. Harrison, Tulsa OK	.87/88
				Wiley C. Sanders/West Indies Investments Ltd, Troy AL	11.88/92
				(flies as "24156/AK-404/USS Intrepid")	
7609 •	AD-4N	Bu125716		(to l'Armee de l'Air as No.11)	
				(to F.A. Chad as ....)	15.2.77
			F-AZFN	Didier Chable, Melun/Etampes	8.88/91
				arr. Melun, France on del. ex N'djamena, Chad	9.11.88
				(flies as "125716/22-DC")	
7632 •	AD-4N	Bu125739		Bradley Air Museum, Windsor Locks CT	11.70/81
				New England Air Museum, Windsor Locks CT	.81/90
				(to be rest. with parts of Bu122312/122818, both recov. from crash burial sites NALF Charlestown RI)	
7677	AD-4NA	Bu126877		(to l'Armee de l'Air as No.21)	.61/77
	A-1D			noted in store, Chateaudun AB, France	6.77
				rep. scrapped	
7680	AD-4NA	Bu126880		(to L'Armee de L'Air as No.34)	.61/77
	A-1D			(to F.A. Chad as ......)	15.2.77

c/n	Type	Military id	Reg.	History	Date
			F-AZGA	Didier Chable, Melun/Etampes	8.88/90
				Escadrille Pegase, Aix-les-Milles	92
				(ferry permit: N'djamena, Chad to France 2.92)	
				crashed on del., in sandstorm, Agades, Niger	16.4.92
				(id. also quoted as Bu126934)	
7682 •	AD-4NA	Bu126882		(to l'Armee de l'Air as No.85)	.61
	A-1D			(to F.A. Gabonaise as ....)	c68/76
				recov. from Gabon by Gyra France	.76
			N91945	Jack Spanich, Detroit MI	1.77/84
				del. Chateaudun AB to USA, via Dublin	9.3.77
				badly damaged, landing accident	c82
				Doan Helicopters Inc, New Smyrna Beach FL	85/92
				(rebuilt, flew as "37543/AK-409/USS Intrepid")	
				crashed, Titusville FL (Doan k.)	4.4.92
7712 •	AD-4NA	Bu126912		(to l'Armee de l'Air as No.41)	.60
A-1D				(to F.A. Gabonaise as No.41) del.	8.2.76/85
				recov. by Jean Salis, La Ferte Alais, France	4.85
				Robs Lamplough, North Weald : arr. by sea	3.88
				Pacific Fighters, Chino CA : shipped ex UK	17.9.90/91
			N4277P	Erickson Air Crane, Central Point OR	5.91/92
7722 •	AD-4NA	Bu126922		(to l'Armee de l'Air as No.42)	60
	A-1D			(to F.A. Gabonaise as No.42) del.	8.2.76/85
				recov. by Aero Retro, St Rambert d'Albion	.85
				Aero Retro : arr. by ship, Le Havre	17.4.85
			F-AZED	Amicale Jean Baptiste Salis/Jean Francois	
				Perrin & Partners, Le Havre	27.8.86/91
				The Fighter Collection, Duxford UK : del.	24.12.91
				(flies as "26922/JS-937/USS Hornet)	
7724 •	AD-4NA	Bu126924		(to l'Armee de l'Air as No.19)	.60
	A-1D			(to F.A. Gabonaise as No.19) del.	8.2.76/85
				recov. by Jean Salis, La Ferte Alais, France	.85/88
				Salis Collection : arr. by ship, Le Havre "RM"	17.4.85
				M. Etchetto, Le Havre	87/88
			N2096P	Jeffrey G. Thomas, Anchorage AK	11.89
			N924JT	Vintage Wings, Anchorage AK	2.90/92
7735 •	AD-4NA	Bu126935		(to l'Armee de l'Air as No.56)	11.1.61
	A-1D			(to F.A. Chad as ......)	7.4.76
			F-AZFO	Didier Chable, Melun/Etampes	8.88/89
				arr. France on del. ex N'djamena, Chad	7.2.89
			N2088G	Richard & Hyla Bertea, Corona del Mar CA	9.89/92
				(shipped Long Beach CA, del. to Chino 9.9.89)	
7756 •	AD-4NA	Bu126956		(to l'Armee de l'Air as No.45)	4.11.60
	A-1D		TR-KMP	(to F.A. Gabonaise as No.45) del.	8.2.76/84
			F-WZDQ	Aero Retro, St Rambert d'Albion	84
			F-AZDQ	Amicale Jean Baptiste Salis, Le Ferte Alais	7.84/85
				J. Bourret/Aero Retro, St Rambert d'Albion	5.9.85/91
				(flies as "VMC-1/126956/RM-3)	
7759 •	AD-4NA	Bu126959		(to l'Armee de l'Air as No.50)	7.12.60
	A-1D			(to F.A. Chad as ......)	7.4.76
			F-AZFP	Didier Chable, Melun/Etampes	8.88
				arr. France on del. ex N'djamena, Chad	20.3.89
			N2088V	Don Hanna/Chancellor Air, Costa Mesa CA	9.89/92
				(shipped Long Beach CA, del. to Chino 9.9.89)	
7765 •	AD-4NA	Bu126965		(to l'Armee de l'Air as No.54)	.61
	A-1D			(to F.A. Chad as ......)	7.4.76
				returned to French AF, stored Chateaudun	79/83
				Musee de l'Air, Le Bourget (stored)	84/85
			F-ZVMM	reg.	.85
			OO-FOR	Eric Vormezeele, Brasschaat, Belgium	27.6.85/90
				(flies as French AF "126965")	

7770	AD-4NA	Bu126970		(to l'Armee de l'Air as No.79)	.61
	A-1D		N91954	Jack Spanich, Detroit MI	1.77/84
				(del. Chateaudun AB to Detroit 26-28.5.77)	
				(flew in camouflage "AF 26-970/TC")	
				cr. mountain nr Culpepper VA (Spanich k.)	4.11.84
7779 •	AD-4NA	Bu126979		(to l'Armee de l'Air as No.53)	.61
	A-1D			Musee de l'Air, Le Bourget : displ. as "MK"	78/88
7796	AD-4NA	Bu126996		(to l'Armee de l'Air as No.38)	.60
	A-1D		N92023	ntu: Jack Spanich, Detroit MI	1.77
				noted in storage, Chateaudun AB, France	6.77
7797 •	AD-4NA	Bu126997		(to l'Armee de l'Air as No.78)	.61
	A-1D		N92053	Jack Spanich, Detroit MI	1.77
				(del. Chateaudun AB to Detroit 26-28.5.77)	
				Preston Parish, Kalamazoo MI	77/78
				Spanich Corp, Livonia MI	9.85
			N409Z	Landon J. Cullum, Dallas TX	7.86/91
				Cinema Air, Carlsbad CA	92
				(flies as "JC-409/USS Intrepid")	
7798 •	AD-4NA	Bu126998		(to l'Armee de l'Air as No.37)	.61/77
	A-1D			(to F.A. Chad as ......)	15.2.77
			F-AZKY	Didier Chable, Melun/Etampes	8.88/91
				(del. to France ex N'djamena, Chad .88,	
				flies as USN "Bu126937")	
7802 •	AD-4NA	Bu127002		(to l'Armee de l'Air as No.61)	.61
	A-1D			awaiting del. to USA, Chateaudun AB, France	76
			N91989	ntu : Jack Spanich, Detroit MI	1.77
			TR-LQE	(to F.A. Gabonais as ....)	.77
				(recov. ex Gabon by Michelle Gineste 1.92)	
			F-AZHK	Michele Gineste/Maurice Etchetto, Le Havre	1.92
7832	AD-4W	Bu126849		(to RN Fleet Air Arm as WT849)	.55
	AEW.1		SE-EBN	Svensk Flygtjanst AB, Bromma	9.69/71
				crashed Sundsvall	5.71
7850 •	AD-4W	Bu126867		(to RN Fleet Air Arm as WV181)	.55
	AEW.1		SE-EBK	Svensk Flygtjanst AB, Bromma : del.	15.5.63/84
				Aces High Ltd, North Weald	.85
			G-BMFB	Robs Lamplough/Coys of Kensington Ltd,	
				North Weald (shipped to UK 85, stored)	16.9.85/89
				Pacific Fighters, Chino CA : shipped ex UK	17.9.90/91
			N4277N	Erickson Air Crane Co, Central Point OR	5.91/92
7903 •	AD-4NA	Bu127888		(to l'Armee de l'Air as No.65)	.61
	A-1D		N92034	Jack Spanich, Detroit MI	1.77
				(del. Chateaudun AB to Detroit 26-28.5.77)	
				Preston Parish, Kalamazoo MI	28.4.77/88
				US Army TT contract, based Kalamazoo MI	78
				Southern Packing & Storage, Greenville TN	8.82
				Preston Parish/Kalamazoo Aviation History	
				Museum, Kalamazoo MI	84/92
				(flies as " USN 127888/B")	
7909 •	AD-4NA	Bu127894		(to l'Armee de l'Air as No.68) SOC	6.8.76
				(to F.A. Gabonaise as TR-KFQ)	
			N92072	ntu : Jack Spanich, Detroit MI	1.77
				not del., stored France	77/85
				SAAF Museum, Ysterplaat: shipped ex France	11.85/92
				(stored unrest., Capetown- D.F.Malan 92)	
7937 •	AD-4W	Bu127922		(to RN Fleet Air Arm as WT987)	
	AEW.1		SE-EBL	Svensk Flygtjanst AB, Bromma : del	19.6.63/84
				Military Aircraft Restoration Corp, Chino CA	.84
				(del. as SE-EBL, arr. Linden NJ 7.6.84)	

			N5469Y	Military Aircraft Restoration Corp, Chino CA	8.84
				(open storage, Linden NJ as SE-EBL 6.84/89)	
				National Warplane Museum, Geneseo NY	8.89/91
7946 •	AD-4W	Bu127931		(to RN Fleet Air Arm as WT951)	.53
	AEW.1		SE-EBM	Svensk Flygtjanst AB, Bromma : del.	9.7.63/84
				Aces High Ltd, North Weald	.85
			G-BMFC	Robs Lamplough/Coys of Kensington Ltd,	
				North Weald (shipped to UK 85)	16.9.85/89
				Pacific Fighters, Chino CA : shipped ex UK	17.9.90/91
			N4277L	Erickson Air Crane Co, Central Point OR	5.91
				Cham S. Grill, Medford OR	92
				(also rep. as c/n 7964; plate confirms 7946)	
7957	AD-4W	Bu127942		(to RN Fleet Air Arm as WT944)	
	AEW.1		SE-EBG	Svensk Flygtjanst AB, Bromma : del.	26.3.63/74
				retired, later broken-up Malmo	4.10.74
7960 •	AD-4W	Bu127945		(to RN Fleet Air Arm as WT947)	
	AEW.1		SE-EBI	Svensk Flygtjanst AB, Bromma : del.	26.4.63/73
				retired, stored for museum	15.8.73/84
				Flygvapen Museum, Malmslatt, Sweden	84/88
				(also rep. as Bu124777; plate confirms c/n 7960)	
7962 •	AD-4W	Bu127947		(to RN Fleet Air Arm as WT949)	
	AEW.1		SE-EBB	Svensk Flygtjanst AB, Bromma : del.	10.62/74
				retired, stored for museum	29.8.74
				Luftfarmuseet, Arlanda, Stockholm	79/85
7963	AD-4W	Bu127948		(to RN Fleet Air Arm as WT950)	
	AEW.1		SE-EBD	Svensk Flygtjanst AB, Bromma : del.	15.1.63/74
				retired, later broken-up Malmo	28.9.74
7965	AD-4W	Bu127950		(to RN Fleet Air Arm as WT952)	
	AEW.1		SE-EBA	Svensk Flygtjanst AB, Bromma : del.	14.9.62/74
				retired, later broken-up Malmo	13.1.74
7969	AD-4W	Bu127954		(to RN Fleet Air Arm as WT956)	
	AEW.1		SE-EBE	Svensk Flygtjanst AB, Bromma : del.	25.1.63/74
				retired, later broken-up Malmo	4.9.74
7970	AD-4W	Bu127955		(to RN Fleet Air Arm as WT957)	
	AEW.1		SE-EBF	Svensk Flygtjanst AB, Bromma : del.	1.3.63/76
				crashed, landing Lulea-Kallax	25.2.76
7975 •	AD-4W	Bu127960		(to RN Fleet Air Arm as WT962)	
	AEW.1		SE-EBC	Svensk Flygtjanst AB, Bromma : del.	11.62/74
				retired, stored for museum	27.5.74
				Svedino's Bil Och Flygmuseum, Halmstad	79/85
8369 •	AD-4B	Bu132261		displ. Camp Barrett, nr MCAS Quantico VA	76
				USMC Museum, MCAS Quantico VA	88
8927 •	AD-5Q	Bu132532		USNAM, stored NAS Pensacola FL	76/88
	EA-1F				
8929 •	AD-5Q	Bu132534		stored NAS Quonset Point RI	70
	EA-1F			displ. Pawtucket Boys Club, Pawtucket RI	.72/78
				Gordon Newell, New Hartford NY	c80
				(stored derelict, Utica-Riverside Airport NY)	
				Wayne Jordan, Binghamton NY	.85
				Harry S. Doan, New Smyrna Beach FL	90/92
				(stored derelict, "USS Independence": for rest.)	
8993 •	AD-5N	Bu132598		(to SVNAF as 132598)	
	A-1G			(to USAF as 51-598: 1st SOW)	
				USAFM, Hurlburt Field FL	73/91
				(displ. as "USAF 51-598")	

9385 •	AD-5W EA-1E	Bu132789		EAA Museum, Oshkosh WI	76/90
9460 •	AD-5 NA-1E	Bu132443		USAFM, Confederate Air Force, Harlingen TX Military Marine Academy, Harlingen TX	72/79 82/85
9480 •	AD-5 A-1E	Bu132463		NASM, stored NAF Washington DC USAFM, McClellen AFB CA (del. by C-5A 29.10.85; displ. as"USAF 32463/EC")	.74/85 .85/88
9506 •	AD-5 A-1E	Bu132649		(to USAF as 32649/IZ) USAFM, Wright-Patterson AFB, Dayton OH (displ. as "32649/IZ")	 .67/90
9540 •	AD-5 A-1E	Bu132683	 N39147	(to SVNAF as 132683) recov. ex Thailand by Yesterdays Air Force, stored unconv., Long Beach CA Military Aircraft Restoration Corp, Chino CA	 1.80/85 4.83/92
9701 •	AD-6 A-1H	Bu134472		(to SVNAF as 134472) Royal Thai AF Museum, Don Muang, Bangkok (displ. as "USAF/The Proud American")	 85/90
9917 •	AD-6 A-1H	Bu135273		Walter Soplata Collection, Newbury OH (incomplete, fire damaged)	65/85
9944 •	AD-6 A-1H	Bu135300		USNAM, NAS Pensacola FL	76/91
9976 •	AD-6 A-1H	Bu135332	 N32612 N39148	(to SVNAF as 135332) recov. ex Thailand by Yesterdays Air Force, stored unconv., Long Beach CA ntu: Yesterdays Air Force, Chino CA Military Aircraft Restoration Corp, Chino CA	 1.80/88 9.82/86 4.83/92
10095 •	AD-5Q EA-1F	Bu135018		USAFM, Pima County Air Museum, Tucson AZ (displ. as "VAQ-33/GD-703")	.69/88
10229 •	AD-5W EA-1E	Bu135152		stored NAS Memphis TN ("NATTC Memphis") Harry S. Doan, New Smyrna Beach FL (recov. derelict ex Memphis, rest. to fly)	75 89/92
10255 •	AD-5W EA-1E	Bu135178	 N62466	Naval Aerospace Medical Institute USMC Museum, MCAS Quantico VA, del. Doug Champlin Collection, Enid OK John Downing Don Hendrick SC Airlift Inc Paul O'Connell, Donna TX Peter W. Thelen, Fort Lauderdale FL Lone Star Flight Museum, Houston TX Peter W. Thelen, Fort Lauderdale FL Taylor Energy Co, New Orleans LA (flies as "135178/MR")	 18.6.71/74 74 75 76/81 83 7.83 1.84/85 4.86/87 88/89 90/92
10265 •	AD-5W EA-1E	Bu135188	 N188BP	Thomas Stafford (recov. ex NAS China Lake CA to Chino CA 5.89) Planes of Fame East, Plymouth MN (rebuilt Chino CA, ff 8.7.91 as "Marines 21/BP")	.89 3.90/92
10678 •	AD-6 A-1H	Bu137602		NAS Lemoore CA (displ. on pole)	65/79
10838 •	AD-6 A-1H	Bu139606		(to SVNAF as 139606) recov. ex Thailand by Yesterdays Air Force, stored unconv., Long Beach CA	 1.80/87

			N3915B	Military Aircraft Restoration Corp, Chino CA	4.83/86
			N39606	Donald Douglas Museum, Santa Monica CA	7.88/90
				The Museum of Flying, Santa Monica CA	90/92
				(rebuilt Chino .89, flies as "USN/D-606")	
10897 •	AD-6 A-1H	Bu139665		(to SVNAF as 139665)	
				recov. ex Thailand by Yesterdays Air Force,	
				stored unconv., Long Beach CA	1.80/88
			N39149	Military Aircraft Restoration Corp, Chino CA	4.83/91
				stored unconv., MARC compound, Chino CA	.88/91

DOUGLAS SKYSHARK

7596 •	XA2D-1	Bu125485		recov. by Ed Maloney from LAX fire dump	
				The Air Museum, Ontario CA	65/76
				Military Aircraft Restoration Corp, Chino CA	78/87
				Pacific Fighters, Chino CA : stored	88/91

FAIREY ALBACORE

F.3538 •	Mk. I	N4172		recov. Whiten Head, Glen Cova, Norway	
				Fleet Air Arm Museum, RNAS Yeovilton	83/92
				(fuse. static rest. St Just, Lands End .84/87)	
				(fuse arr. Yeovilton 16.4.87, wings to be rest.)	
				completed, displ. Yeovilton .91 as "N4389/4M")	

FAIREY BATTLE

- •	Mk. I	L5340		(to RCAF as L5340)	
				recov., derelict, from farm Canada	
				Sir W. J. D. Roberts/Strathallan Aircraft	
				Collection, Auchterader, Scotland	.72
				RAF Museum Store, RAF Henlow	73/83
				RAF Museum, RAF St.Athan	83/87
				(parts used in rest. of L5343)	
- •	Mk. I	L5343		forced landing, aband. Kaldadaranes, Iceland	13.9.40
				recov. from Iceland by RAF Museum	8.73
				RAF Museum Store, RAF Henlow	73
				(rest. begun RAF Leeming, then RAF Cardington)	
				RAF Museum, RAF St.Athan	83/90
				(static rest. completed St.Athan 3.90)	
				RAF Museum, Hendon	.90/92
				(displ. as "L5343/VO-S")	
-	Mk. I	P2183		(to RCAF as P2183)	
				recov., derelict, from farm Canada	
				RAF Museum, parts used in rebuild of L5343	
F.4139 •	Mk. I	P2234		(to RCAF as 1317)	
				Tex LaVallee/LaVallee Cultural & Aeronautical	
				Collection, St Chrysostome QUE	88
- •	Mk. I	R3950		(to RCAF as 1899) BOC 7.4.41 SOC	16.2.45
				sold to farmer, MacDonald ALTA	.45/69
				Tom Voll, Michigan (planned rest. to fly)	70/72
				Sir W. J. D. Roberts/Strathallan Aircraft	
				Collection, Auchterader, Scotland	11.72/87
				Charles Church, Winchester	.87/89
				loaned: Imperial War Museum, Duxford	.88
				Historic Aircraft Collection,	.89/90
				Musee Royal de l'Armee, Brussels, Belgium	.90/91
				(del. by C130 3.5.90; displ. as "HA-L")	
F.4848 •	Mk. I (T)	R7384		(to RCAF as R7384)	
				Canadian National Aviation Museum,	
				Rockcliffe ONT (displ. as "R7384/35")	65/90

Fairey Battle

c/n	Mark	Serial	Reg	History	Dates
- •	Mk. I	RCAF2139		Tex LaVallee/LaVallee Cultural & Aeronautical	
				Collection, St Chrysostome QUE	80
				Canadian Museum of Flight & Transportation,	
				Vancouver BC	.80/92
				(incomplete, poor condition)	
- •	Mk. I (T)	RCAF3947		Western Canada Aviation Museum,	
				Winnipeg MAN	79/88
				(parts recov. from various aircraft)	

FAIREY FIREFLY

c/n	Mark	Serial	Reg	History	Dates
F.5607 •	TT Mk. 1	Z2033	SE-BRD	Svensk Flygtjanst AB, Bromma	3.49/64
	F Mk. 1		G-ASTL	Peter F. M. Thomas/Skyfame Aircraft Museum,	
				Staverton : del.	5.5.64/78
				Imperial War Museum, Duxford	.78/91
				(displ. as "Z2033/275/Evelyn Tentions")	
F.6071 •	TT Mk. 1	DT989	SE-BRG	Svensk Flygtjanst AB, Bromma	.50/69
				Technical Museum, Arlanda, Stockholm	.69/85
				wfu, stored Stockholm-Arlanda	66/69
				Bjorn Lowgren, Stockholm (rest. project)	.85/90
F.6121 •	TT Mk. 1	PP392	SE-CAW	Svensk Flygtjanst AB, Bromma	.56/64
				Malmo Technical Museum, Malmo	.65/80
				Swedish Air Force Museum, Malmslatt	.80/90
F.6180 •	TT Mk. 1	PP469	SE-CAU	Svensk Flygtjanst AB, Bromma	.56/64
				in fire training area, Midlanda Airport	.64/85
				Bjorn Lowgren, Stockholm (rest. project)	.85/90
				(also rep del as SE-CBZ)	
F.7402 •	Mk. 1	MB410		(to R Thai AF as SF11) : del.	21.1.52
				RTAF Museum, Don Muang AB, Bangkok	66/90
F.8026 •	TT Mk. 4	VH127		Fleet Air Arm Museum, RNAS Yeovilton	73/92
				(displ. as "VH127/E-209")	
F.8309 •	AS Mk. 5	VT409		Unimetal Ltd, Droysden : scrapyard	60/80
				E. Nick Grace, St.Merryn, Cornwall	82
				(hulk stored St.Merryn, with WD833)	
				North East Aircraft Museum, Sunderland	84/87
				(composite rest. project, with WD899)	
F.8420 •	AS Mk. 6	VX388		(to RAN as VX388)	3.53/65
	TT Mk. 6			del. Bankstown NSW for disposal	3.3.65
				M. D. N. Fisher/Historical Aircraft	
				Preservation Society, UK: not collected	1.67
				Camden Museum of Aviation, Camden NSW	
				later Narellan NSW	.69/92
F.8497 •	AS Mk. 5	WB271		(to RAN as WB271)	3.53/65
	TT Mk. 5			del. Bankstown NSW for disposal	3.3.65
				RN Fleet Air Arm Museum, RNAS Yeovilton	8.2.66/72
				(shipped to UK on carrier HMS Victorious 4.67)	
				FAA Historic Flight, RNAS Yeovilton : ff.	21.9.72/92
F.8637 •	AS Mk. 6	WB440		Unimetal Ltd, Droysden	60/83
				Manchester Air and Space Museum	.83/87
				(rebuilt, fuselage only)	
F.8646 •	AS Mk. 6	WB518		(to RAN as WB518)	12.50/65
	TT Mk. 6			del. Bankstown NSW for disposal	3.3.65
				Returned Services League, Griffith NSW : del.	2.67/91
				(displ. on pole as "WB518/903NW")	
				Classic Aviation Pty Ltd, Bankstown NSW	.91/92
				(rest. to fly Bankstown, using parts WD828)	

F.8654 •	AS Mk. 5 TT Mk. 5	WD826		(to RAN as WD826)	12.50
				NAS Schofields NSW : inst. airframe	64/74
				Naval Aviation Museum, NAS Nowra NSW	12.74/86
			VH-NVU	RAN Historic Flight, NAS Nowra NSW	30.9.86/92
				(rest. Nowra,ff 4.10.86 as "RAN WD826/245K")	
F.8655 •	AS Mk. 6	WD827		(to RAN as WD827)	12.50/56
				Australian Air League, Blacktown NSW	11.56/73
				Moorabbin Air Museum, Moorabbin VIC	5.73/91
				(shipped Sydney-Melbourne, arr 6.5.73, displ. as "WD827/911NW")	
F.8656 •	AS Mk. 6 TT Mk. 6	WD828		(to RAN as WD828)	12.50/65
				del. Bankstown NSW for disposal: TT 913	3.3.65
				Moorabbin Air Museum, Melbourne VIC: del.	18.2.67/82
				(trucked to Essendon VIC 21.7.73, rebuild to fly)	
			VH-HMW	Michael B. Wansey, Newcastle NSW	.82/89
				(rebuild completed at Ballarat VIC, ff 28.9.84 as "WD828/271K/Mickey's Mouse")	
				crashed, forced landing, near Camden NSW	4.12.87
				Classic Aviation Pty Ltd, Bankstown NSW	2.89/92
				(arr. Bankstown 1.90, for rebuild using WB518; airframe WD828 rest. for static displ.)	
				Returned Services League, Griffith NSW	.91/92
				(displ. on pole, Griffith NSW)	
F.8661 •	AS Mk. 6	WD833		(to RAN as WD833)	12.50
				RAN Base Hastings VIC : gate guard	60
				R. H. Grant Scrap Metals, Melbourne VIC	64/67
				Tom B. King, Melbourne VIC	68/70
				Berwick Museum of Transport, Berwick VIC	72/74
				Sir W. J. D. Roberts/Strathallan Aircraft Collection, Scotland : stored, unrest.	12.74/81
				E. Nick Grace, St Merryn, Cornwall	.81/84
				(stored St.Merryn, with parts VT409, 81/84)	
				Ward Wilkins, Fort Collins CO	8.84/88
				(shipped ex Southampton to USA 16.4.86)	
				Henry J. Schroeder III, Danville IL	.88/89
			N833WD	Henry J. Schroeder III, Danville IL	11.89/92
				(rebuild to fly, Danville IL)	
F.8668 •	AS Mk. 6 TT Mk. 6	WD840		(to RAN as WD840)	6.53/65
				del. Bankstown NSW for disposal	3.3.65
				Jarman Aircraft Engine Overhaul Services, Sydney NSW : del. Camden	1.67
				Ed Fleming/Skyservice Aviation,Camden NSW	.67/69
				Robert Diermert, Carman MAN	.69/72
			CF-CBH	Robert Diermert, Carman MAN	.72/75
				(ff Carman 17.9.72, Merlin 500 ex Avro York, cockpit fitted out as 8-seater!)	
			N810J	Jerry Barg, South Easton MA	.75
			N1840	Gene Fisher/Mid Atlantic Air Museum, Middletown PA	5.82/84
				Don Knapp/DK Precision, Fort Lauderdale FL	89/90
				Lone Star Flight Museum, Galveston TX	.90/92
				(stored pending rest.)	
F.8722 •	AS Mk. 6	WD899		North East Aircraft Museum, Sunderland	.84/89
				(hulk recov. ex Unimetal Ltd, Droysden .84)	
				(composite rest. project WD899/VT409)	
F.8724	AS Mk. 6 TT Mk. 6	WD901		(to RAN as WD901)	6.53/65
				del. Bankstown NSW for disposal	3.3.65
				Casula Auto Wreckers, Casula NSW : displ.	1.67
				William F. G. Gambella, Charleston SC	.67
				(shipped to USA on SS African Crescent .67)	
			N7469	John M. Sliker, Wadley GA	.68/71
			CF-BDH	Dennis Bradley & Alan Ness/Canadian Warplane	

c/n	Mark	Serial	Civil reg	History	Date
				Heritage, Hamilton ONT	9.71/77
				(del. GA-Toronto 9.71; flew as "RCN BD-H")	
				crashed into Lake Ontario (Ness k.)	2.9.77
F.8755 •	AS Mk. 6	WH632		(to RAN as WH632) BOC 6.53 SOC	29.5.60
				Australian Air League, Marrickville, NSW	5.60/66
				Camden Museum of Aviation, Camden NSW	17.6.66/78
				Canadian Warplane Heritage, Hamilton ONT	6.78
				(shipped ex Sydney to Canada 6.78)	
			C-GBDG	Canadian Warplane Heritage, Hamilton ONT	88/92
				(rebuild to fly, Hamilton ONT & Victoria BC, ff 4.92 Victoria BC)	
				cr. on takeoff Victoria BC	7.5.92
F.8813 •	AS Mk. 6	WJ109		(to RAN as WJ109)	
	TT Mk. 6			NAS Nowra, NSW : gate guard	65/72
				Naval Aviation Museum, Nowra NAS, NSW	12.74/91
				(displ. as "WJ109/207K")	
- •	Mk. I	-		(to RCAF as ....; to Ethiopian AF as ....)	
				stored in open Asmara, Ethiopia	85
- •	Mk. I	-		(to RCAF as ....; to Ethiopian AF as ....)	
				stored in open Asmara, Ethiopia	85
-	Mk. I	-		(to MLD as ....)	
				displ., Biak Naval HQ, Irian Jaya	70

FAIREY FULMAR

c/n	Mark	Serial	Civil reg	History	Date
F.3707 •	Mk. I	N1854		first production aircraft : ff Ringway	4.1.40
	Mk. II		G-AIBE	Fairey Aviation Ltd, White Waltham	26.2.47/59
				(ret. to Royal Navy as N1854)	30.4.59
				RN Lossiemouth, (last flight 18.12.62)	.62/72
				Fleet Air Arm Museum, RNAS Yeovilton	9.72/92

FAIREY SWORDFISH

c/n	Mark	Serial	Civil reg	History	Date
- •	Mk. II	W5856		Ernie Simmons, Tillsonburg ONT	46/70
	Mk.IV			farm auction, sold to Alabama USA	3.9.70
				Sir W. J. D. Roberts/Strathallan Aircraft Collection, Auchterader, Scotland	8.77/85
			G-BMGC	Strathallan Aircraft Collection, Auchterader	10.85/90
				FAA Historic Flight, RNAS Yeovilton	.90/92
				(rebuild at BAe Brough)	
- •	Mk. II	HS503		Ernie Simmons, Tillsonburg ONT	46/70 Mk.IV
				farm auction, sold to CNAC, Rockcliffe ONT	3.9.70/90
				RAF Museum Store, RAF Henlow: airfreighted	10.70/90
-	Mk. II	HS517		Ernie Simmons, Tillsonburg ONT	46/70
				farm auction, sold to:	
				Grattons Weldwood Farm Museum, London ONT	3.9.70/79
- •	Mk. II	HS554		Ernie Simmons, Tillsonburg ONT	46/70
	MK.IV			farm auction, sold to:	
				Bob Spence & E. Sharpe, Muirkirk ONT	3.9.70/91
			C-GEVS	Robert Spence, Muirkirk ONT	30.8.91/92
				(rebuilt Muirkirk, ff. due 5.92 as "RN HS554")	
- •	Mk. II	HS618		Fleet Air Arm Museum, RNAS Yeovilton	.65/92
				(displ. as "W5984", later "P4139")	
- •	Mk. II	LS326	G-AJVH	Fairey Aviation Co Ltd, White Waltham	28.5.47/59
				(returned to RN as LS326)	30.4.59
				Fleet Air Arm Historic Flight, RNAS Yeovilton	10.60/92

- •	Mk. III	NF370		Imperial War Museum, London	80
				Imperial War Museum, Duxford	86/92
- •	Mk. III	NF389		FAA Museum, RNAS Lee on Solent	60/91
- •	Mk. II	-		Ernie Simmons, Tillsonburg ONT	46/3.9.70
	Mk.IV			sold at farm auction, Tillsonburg ONT	3.9.70
			N2235R	Mira J. Slovak, Santa Paula/Ojai CA	2.83/92
				Donald Douglas Museum, Santa Monica CA	90/91
				(fuselage displ. as "HS164")	
				(FAA quote id. "A14250B15564")	
- •	Mk. III	-		Ernie Simmons, Tillsonburg ONT	c46/65
	Mk.IV			Canadian National Aeronautical Collection	.65
				National Aviation Museum, Rockcliffe ONT	.65/90
				(displ. as "NS122/TH-M")	
- •	Mk. II	-		Ernie Simmons, Tillsonburg ONT	46/70
	Mk.IV			farm auction, sold to:	
				Bob Spence & E. Sharpe, Muirkirk ONT	3.9.70/88
- •	Mk. II	-		Ernie Simmons, Tillsonburg ONT	46/70
	Mk.IV			sold at farm auction, Tillsonburg ONT	3.9.70
				private owner, Waco TX	88
- •	Mk. III	-		Ernie Simmons, Tillsonburg ONT	46/70
	Mk.IV			sold at farm auction, Tillsonburg ONT	3.9.70
				Shearwater Aviation Museum,	
				CFB Shearwater NS	88/90
				(rebuild to fly, Toronto ONT)	
- •	Mk. II	-		Ernie Simmons, Tillsonburg ONT	46/70
	Mk.IV			sold at farm auction, Tillsonburg ONT	3.9.70
				Spruce Goose Memorial, Long Beach CA	88
-	Mk. III	-		Ernie Simmons, Tillsonburg ONT	c46/70
	Mk.IV			farm auction: Jack Arnold, Brantford ONT	3.9.70
				Luther A Young, Lakeland FL	c73
-	Mk. III	-		Ernie Simmons, Tillsonburg ONT	c46/70
	Mk.IV			farm auction: Jack Arnold, Brantford ONT	3.9.70
				Luther A Young, Lakeland FL	c73
-	MK.IV	-		Ernie Simmons, Tillsonburg ONT	46/65
				Age of Flight Museum, Niagara Falls ONT	68/70
				stored dism., unrest., Oshawa ONT	70

FIAT CR.42

•	CR-42	MM5701		forced landing on beach Orford Ness UK	11.11.40
				(to RAF as BT474)	
				stored crated 43/64; displ. Biggin Hill	.64
				RAF Museum, RAF St.Athan : static rest.	.68/78
				RAF Museum, Hendon	.78/92
				(displ. as "MM5701/13-95")	
- •	CR-42			(to Swedish Air Force as Fv2543)	
	J-11			Flygvapenmuseum Malmen, Linkoping, Sweden	84

14		G.46	MM52781	I-AEHN	Ministero di Fesa Aeronautica	5.59/72
43		G.46-3B	MM52800	I-AEHI	Ministero di Fesa Aeronautica	10.58/76
					CofA expired 19.5.80, retired at Urbe	80/87
44		G.46-3B	MM52801	I-AEHU	Ministero di Fesa Aeronautica	9.59/72
				G-BBII	Hon. Patrick Lindsay, Booker	13.9.73/76
					(flew in desert camouflage sc.)	
					The Aircraft Restoration Co.	
					Duxford	9.92
46		G.46-3B	MM52803	I-ADRO	Ministero di Fesa Aeronautica	10.58/76
91		G.46-3A	MM52817	I-AEKF		
					crashed Bolognia	16.7.69
136		G.46-3B	MM53086	I-AEKK	Ministero di Fesa Aeronautica	10.59/76
140	•	G.46-3B	MM53090	I-AEKM		
				I-AEHF		
					Museo Storico dell'Aeronautica Militaire	
					Italiana, Vigna di Valle	84
141	•	G.46	MM53091	I-	Italian AF Flying Club	
					(crated ex Padova to USA c70)	
				N46FM	Frank M. Marici, Roslyn NY	72/92
142		G.46-3B	MM53092	I-BIBY	reg.	2.61
					P.Bosio, Brescia	72/76
					CofA suspended Breschia	17.1.85
					struck-off reg.	.91
143	•	G.46-4A	MM53093	I-AEHO		
					Eric Vormezeele, Brasschaat AB	84
152		G.46	MM53102	I-AEKG	Ministero di Fesa Aeronautica	2.60/76
164		G.46-4B	MM53404	I-AEHJ		
					gateguard Bresso, Italy	78
165		G.46	MM53405	I-AEHW	Ministero di Fesa Aeronautica	9.59/72
179		G.46	MM53303	I-AEHR	Ministero di Fesa Aeronautica	11.59/72
180	•	G.46-4B	MM53304	I-AEKA	Ministero di Fesa Aeronautica	12.59/76
				I-LSBA		
				I-AEKA	G.Sorini, Montegaldella	1.8.90
189	•	G.46-4A	MM53283		Museo Storico dell'Aeronautica Militaire	
					Italiana, Vigna di Valle	84
192	•	G.46-4A	MM53286	I-AELM		
					Museo Storico dell'Aeronautica Militaire	
					Italiana, Vigna di Valle	84
198	•	G.46-4A	MM53292		Museo Storico dell'Aeronautica Militaire	
					Italiana, Vigna di Valle	84
199	•	G.46-4A	MM53293	OO-VOR	Eric Vormezeele, Brasschaat AB	8.77/84
					(ff after rest. 6.79)	
216		G.46	MM53491	I-AEKT	Ministero di Fesa Aeronautica	9.68/72
					Aero Club Roma	76
219		G.46-4A		I-ARYA	Aero Club di Firenz	67
					crashed Petriolo, nr Florence	14.5.67

222		G.46	MM53497	I-AEKZ	Aero Club Roma	9.60/72
					Ministero di Fesa Aeronautica	76
-		G.46-4	MM53211		arr. RAF Northolt by IAF C-119	.70
					stored Shoreham	70
					Historic Aircraft Museum, Southend	.71/83
					(displ. as IAF "FHE")	
					Jeff Hawke/Visionair, Coventry	10.5.83
					Patrick Luscombe/British Air Reserve, Lympne	84/85

FIAT G-59

61	•	G.59-4B	MM53276		Museo Storico dell'Aeronautica Militaire Italiana, Vigna di Valle	84
74	•	G.59-2A	MM53265		Museo Storico dell'Aeronautica Militaire Italiana, Vigna di Valle	84
					(rep. to be rebuilt as a G.55)	
131	•	G.59-4A	MM53526		Spagnolia, Museo Storico	70/82
179	•	G.59-4B	MM53772		stored Practica di Mare AB, Italy	70/82
					Pino Valenti, Italy	
					Guido Zuccoli, Darwin, NT Australia	.82
					(shipped Italy-USA for rebuild Chino CA .84)	
				N59B	Guido Zuccoli, Darwin Australia	7.87
					(ff Chino 2.9.87, flew as "Ciao Bella")	
					(shipped CA-Australia 8.88)	
				VH-LIX	Guido Zuccoli, Darwin NT	5.9.89/91
181	•	G.59B-4B	MM53774		Pino Valenti, Italy	.84
				I-MRSV	Pino Valenti, Venice	.91
					(rebuild to fly Venice, ff May .92)	

FIAT G-60

-	•	G.60bis			(to Yugoslav AF as 3505)	
					Yugoslav Aviation Museum, Belgrade: stored	88/92

Pino Valenti's Fiat G-59-4B MM53774, registered I-MRSV was the second of the type to fly; Guido Zuccoli's aircraft (VH-LIX) flew in September 1987. (Maurizio Torcoli)

FOCKE WULF Fw189

Nr0112100	Fw 189A-1	Nr2100		shot down, Louhki eastern Finland (hulk recov. from crash site, Russia 1.92)	4.5.43
				Jim Pearce/Sussex Spraying Services UK (shipped to Hull from Russia, arr. 2.92)	2.92

FOCKE WULF Fw190

Nr1227 •	Fw 190A-5	Nr1227		("DG+HO") crashed near Leningrad USSR	.44
				recov.	.90
				arr. crated, Booker UK : rest. project	7.6.91
				Warbirds of GB Ltd, Biggin Hill	91
				arr. Biggin Hill (rest. project)	30.8.91
Nr350177•	Fw 190A-8	Nr350177		recov. ex wartime crash site, Norway	
			N4247L	Texas Air Museum, Rio Hondo TX	5.91/92
Nr550214•	Fw 190A-6 /R6	Nr550214		(I/NJ Gr.10)	
				(to RAF, Farnborough for trials as AM.10)	.45/46
				delivered Schleswig - Farnborough	16.6.45
				arr. by sea Capetown, South Africa	6.11.46
				Fort Klapperkop Military Museum SA	46
				South African National Museum of Military History, Saxonwold, Johannesburg	82/92
Nr550470•	Fw 190A-6	Nr550470	N126JG	Malcolm B. Laing, Lubbock TX	3.92
Nr584219•	Fw 190A-8 /U-1	Nr584219		(JG Schule 103)	
				(to RAF for trials as AM.29 : to PN999 del. Schleswig - Farnborough 22.9.45)	.45/46
				RAF Museum Store, RAF Henlow	64
				RAF Museum, RAF St. Athan	75/89
				RAF Museum, Hendon	90/91
Nr601088•	Fw 190D-9	Nr601088		IV/JG3	
				shipped to USA on HMS Reaper	7.45
				(USAAF trials as FE-120)	
				Smithsonian Institute, stored Park Ridge IL	.46
				NASM, Silver Hill MD	65/91
				loan: USAFM ,Wright-Patterson AFB, OH	68/91
Nr732183•	Fw 190A-3	Nr732183		(Black 3)	
				Kongelige Norsk Luftforssvaret Collection, Bergen, Norway	84/91
			N90FW	John W. Houston/Texas Air Museum (rest. by Texas Air Museum, Rio Hondo TX for KNL Collection 88/91; rest. fuselage returned to Gardermoen AB, Norway .91)	90
Nr733682•	Fw 190A-8 /R6	Nr733682		(II KG/200)	
				(to RAF, Farnborough for trials as AM.75)	.45
				Imperial War Museum, Lambeth, London (rest. at Duxford .86/90)	64/92
- •	Fw 190A-8	-		Zemun, Yugoslavia	88
- •	Fw 190D-9	-		JG26 : crashed into Lake Schwerin	17.4.45
				Luftwaffen Museum, Uetersen AB WG	11.90/92
				salvaged ex Lake Schwerin, East Germany (static rest. project)	11.90
Nr836017•	Fw 190D-13	Nr836017		3/JG26	
				shipped to USA on HMS Reaper	7.45
				(USAAF trials as FE-118)	
				Georgia Institute of Technology	c48
				Nazi Museum, Santa Barbara CA (hulk)	71
			N190D	Doug Champlin/Windward Aviation Inc, Enid OK	.72/77

				(shipped to Germany for rebuild .72/76)	
				Champlin Fighter Museum, Mesa AZ	81/92
				(FAA quotes type TA152, Nr174013:	
				rep. rebuilt from Fw190A Nr174013)	
Nr930838•	Fw 190F-8	Nr930838		captured Zagreb - Pleso	.44
				(to Yugoslav AF as 43)	
				Yugoslav Aeronautical Museum, Belgrade	70/92
Nr931862•	Fw 190F-8	Nr931862		5/JG9 : shot down over Norway	9.2.45
				(recov from fjord for KNL Collection c84)	
				Kongelige Norsk Luftforssvaret Collection,	
				Bergen , Norway	84/88
				John W. Houston/Texas Air Museum	.88/91
			N91FW	Texas Air Museum, Rio Hondo TX	4.90/91
				(rest. to fly at Rio Hondo TX, using parts from	
				four other Fw190 wrecks recov. ex Norway)	
				(FAA quote type as Fw190A-4)	
Nr931884•	Fw 190F-8 /R1	Nr931884		SG2, Yellow 10; captured near Munich	
				shipped to USA on HMS Reaper	7.45
				(USAAF trials as FE-117; T2-117)	
				Smithsonian Institute, stored Park Ridge IL	.46
				NASM, Silver Hill MD	65/89
				(rep. rebuilt from Fw190A-7 Nr649969)	
Nr150003•	Ta 152H-1	Nr150003		Stab /JG301, captured by British	
				shipped to USA on HMS Reaper	7.45
				(USAAF trials as FE-112; T2-112)	
				Smithsonian Institute, stored Park Ridge IL	.46
				NASM, stored Silver Hill MD	72/91
No.62 •	NC.900 (Fw190A-8)	No.62		Musee de l'Air et de l'Espace, Le Bourget	80/89
				(displ. as "7298")	

GENERAL MOTORS P-75 EAGLE

•	P-75A	44-44553		NASM, Silver Hill MD	
				USAFM, Wright-Patterson AFB, Dayton OH	.77/90

GLOSTER GLADIATOR

- •	Mk. I	K8042		RAF Museum, Hendon	73/92
- •	Mk. I	L8032		Gloster Aircraft Ltd	23.2.48/50
				(stored Hucclecote .44/11.50)	
				Air Service Training Ltd, Hamble	11.50
				del. by road, instructional airframe	11.50
				Vivian Bellamy/Flightways Ltd, Eastleigh	12.51/53
			G-AMRK	Vivian Bellamy/Flightways Ltd, Eastleigh: ff	13.6.52
				GlosterAircraft Ltd, Hucclecote	8.53/60
				(flown as "K8032" and "L8032" during 50s)	
				Shuttleworth Trust, Old Warden	11.60/91
				(flies as "N2308/HP-B")	
- •	Sea Gladiator I	N5519		Palace Armoury Museum, Valetta, Malta	9.43/73
				National War Museum, Fort St.Elmo, Valetta	73/92
				(fuse. only, displ. as "Faith")	
- •	Mk. II	N5579		recov. from Lake Lesjaskogsvatn, Norway	
				stored at Dovre, Norway	72/88
				(planned rest. for Armed Forces Museum, Oslo)	
- •	Mk. II	N5589		recov. from Lake Lesjaskogsvatn, Norway	
				stored at RAF Wildenrath, West Germany	72/88
- •	Mk. II	N5628		recov. from Lake Lesjaskogsvatn, Norway	
				RAF Museum, Hendon (fuselage only)	.72/91
- •	Mk. II	N5641		fcd landing near Lake Lesjaskogsvatn, Norway	25.4.40

			stored in shed near Lake by Mr Hope	40/77
			Norwegian Defence Museum, Rygge AFB	.77/80
			Royal Norwegian Airforce Museum,	
			Gardermoen AB (displ. as "N5641/HE-G")	90
- •	Mk. II	N5903	Gloster Aircraft Ltd, Hucclecote (stored)	.48
			Air Service Training, Ansty : del. dism.	11.50
			Air Service Training, Hamble (inst. airframe)	.51
			Vivian Bellamy, Eastleigh	12.51
			Shuttleworth Trust, Old Warden	60/91
			loan: Fleet Air Arm Museum, RNAS Yeovilton	.78/91
			(rest. for displ. as Sea Gladiator "N2276")	
- •	J8A		(to Finnish AF as 278)	
			R Swedish AF Historical Collection, Linkoping	77/84
			Flygvapen Museum, Linkoping	.84/90

Grumman F8F-2 N800H alias Bu121752 arrived with Warbirds of Great Britain in December 1990. Douglas Arnold was one of the first large scale warbird collectors and over the years he has handled more warbirds than any other single individual. Son David Arnold is just as enthusiastic and this is just one of what is now considered by many to be one of the best private warbird collections in the world. The aircraft shown here was formerly raced as 'Precious Bear' and 'Bearcat Bill'.(Jeremy Flack/Aviation Photographs International)

D.10 •	XF8F-1	Bu90446		NASM: stored dism., Silver Hill MD	52/76
	F8F-1			Darryl G. Greenamyer, Van Nuys CA	
	F8F-1D			(exchanged NASM for D.1020/ N1111L)	.76
			N99279	Wolcott Air Service, Wolcott CT	3.77/82
			N14HP	Howard E. Purdue, Breckenridge TX	3.83/92
				(flies as USN "14P")	
D.18 •	F8F-1	Bu90454	N6624C		
				E. D. Weiner, Los Angeles CA	.59
			N3351	E. D. Weiner, Los Angeles CA	.59/63
				Vernon D. Jarvis, Decatur IL	.63
				R. E. Schreder, Bryan OH	65/66
			N9G	Gunther W. Balz, Kalamazoo MI	.68/78
				(race #1; later #7)	
				Preston Parish/Kalamazoo Aviation History	
				Museum, Kalamazoo MI	.78/92
				(flew as "RTAF/G", later "USN 3F8")	
D.205 •	F8F-1	Bu94956		(to R. Thai AF 15-178/98)	
				R Thai AF Museum, Don Muang, Bangkok	68/89
D.527 •	F8F-1	Bu95255		(to Armee de l'Air as 95255)	
				(to SVNAF as 95255)	
				displ. Tan Son Nhut AB, South Vietnam	67/87
D.610 •	F8F-1	Bu95338		(to Armee de l'Air as 95338)	
				(to SVNAF as 95338)	
				displ. Tan Son Nhut AB, South Vietnam	67/87
D.614 •	F8F-1	Bu95342		(to R. Thai AF as ......)	
				displ. Nakorn-Sawan AB, Thailand	87
D.628 •	F8F-1	Bu95356	N7247C	Vernon D. Jarvis, Decatur IL	63
				Ernest J. Saviano, Lombard IL	66/69
				John J. Mark, Hales Corners WI	69
				crashed Madison WI	.69
				Joe Tobul, Wexford PA (wreck)	82
			N4752Y	John J. Dowd Jr, Syracuse KS	6.84/92
				(rebuild to fly, using parts from Bu95089 &	
				Bu121470 recov. by NEAM from burial site	
				after crashes at NLAF Charlestown RI)	
D.641 •	F8F-1	Bu95369		(to Armee de l'Air as 95369)	
				(to SVNAF as 95369)	
				displ. Nha Trang AB, South Vietnam	67/87
D.779 •	F8F-1B	Bu122095		(to R. Thai AF as ......)	
				displ. outside Govt. offices, Bangkok	65/80
				Jean Salis Collection, La Ferte Alais, France	.86/87
				(shipped to France ex Thailand .87)	
				The Fighter Collection, Duxford	.87/92
				(arr. Duxford for long-term rebuild to fly 6.88)	
			G-BUCF	The Fighter Collection, Duxford	18.2.92
				(arr. for rebuild to fly, Chino CA 4.92)	
D.832 •	F8F-1B	Bu121488		(to Armee de l'Air as 121488)	
				(to SVNAF as 121488)	
				displ. Tan Son Nhut AB, South Vietnam: "484"	71
D.854 •	F8F-1B	Bu121510		(to Armee de l'Air as 121510)	
				(to SVNAF as G1510)	
				displ. Bien Hoa AB, South Vietnam: "G1510"	67/87
D.963	F8F-2	Bu121589	N5171V	Norwood R. Hanson, Bloomington IN	.61/63
				(flew as "Last of The Red Hot Cats")	
			N5555H	Norwood R. Hanson, New Haven CT	65/69

				crashed into mountain, dest., Scott NY	c70
D.982	F8F-2P	Bu121608	N7700C	J. W. (Bill) Fornof, Houma LA	c60/71
				(purchased San Antonio TX, stored after frustrated sale to Cuba)	
				crashed, NAS Quonset Point RI (Fornof k.)	5.6.71
D.988 •	F8F-2	Bu121614	N7957C	Bearcat & Co/CAF, Mercedes TX	.58/69
				Confederate Air Force, Harlingen TX	73/74
				crashed	5.74
				(wreck stored dism., Chino CA)	.87/91
				Steve Hinton, John Maloney & Kevin Eldridge, Chino CA (rebuild to fly, Chino)	92
D.1020 •	F8F-2	Bu121646	N7699C	Antelope Valley Aerial Surveys, Palmdale CA	.59
			N1111L	Darryl G. Greenamyer, Mojave CA	.61/76
				(race #1/"Conquest")	
				(piston eng. air speed record 483.041mph 16.8.69)	
				NASM, Silver Hill MD	.76/90
				(displ. as N1111L/"Buff")	
D.1053 •	F8F-2	Bu121679	N4992V	Bud Marquis, Marysville CA	c59/63
				Michael E. Coutches, Hayward CA	6.64
			N818F	Michael E. Coutches, Hayward CA	.66/92
D.1081 •	F8F-2	Bu121707	N1027B	Kaman Aircraft Corp, CT	c59/70
				(unconv., used as cross-wind machine)	
				USMC Museum, MCAS Quantico VA	.70/78
				(trucked to Mojave c78 for rebuild by McDonnell Enterprises, for USMC Museum)	
				A. Wally McDonnell, Mojave CA	16.4.80
				Elmer F.Ward/Pioneer Aero, Chino CA: dism.	82/92
				(rebuild Chino CA 85/92, using parts D.1261)	
D.1084 •	F8F-2	Bu121710		Naval Training Station, Bainbridge MD	
				USNAM, NAS Pensacola FL	.64/91
D.1088 •	F8F-2P	Bu121714	N4995V	The Air Museum, Claremont CA	.57/60
				The Air Museum, Ontario & Chino	60/72
			N1YY	Harold 'Bubba' Beal & Charles 'Chubb' Smith/ B & S Advertising Inc, Knoxville TN	.72
			N700H	B & S Advertising Inc, Knoxville TN	.77
			N700HL	B & S Advertising Inc, Knoxville TN	1.81/92
				The Fighter Collection, Duxford UK	
				del. US to Geneva, arr.	3.6.81/92
				(flies as "VF-11/S-100")	
D.1105	F8F-2	Bu121731	N1028B	New Jersey Air Co, Hackensack NJ	c59/64
				Sky Service Inc, Linden NJ	.64
			N500B	Chester F. Christopher, New Shewsbury NJ	.66/68
			N5005	Judsen S. Smith, Lebanon NJ	.69
				Mike Geren, Kansas City MO	.70/71
				(race #14; #66; #44)	
				crashed, dest., San Diego CA (Geren k)	18.7.71
D.1122 •	F8F-2	Bu121748	N1029B	New Jersey Air Co, Hackensack NJ	c59/64
				Michael E. Coutches, Hayward CA	.64/66
			N618F	Stanley M. Krazet, Covina CA (race #7)	.69/75
			N200N	John Gury, St Louis MO	.75/79
				Harold Beal & Charles Smith, Knoxville TN	.79/92
				lsd: World Jet Inc, Fort Lauderdale FL	.82/87
D.1125	F8F-2	Bu121751	N9885C	William M. Stead, Reno NV	63/66
				(race #80/"Smirnoff")	
				Moseley Aviation Inc, Tolleson AZ	66/68
				I. N. Burchinall Jr, Paris TX	69/72

				Mike Smith, Johnson KS : del.	11.72/77
				(race #41/"Lois Jean")	
				Harold Beal & Charles Smith, Knoxville TN	.77/80
				(flew as USN "VF-11/S-200")	
				crashed and dest., Commerce GA (Smith k.)	18.6.80
D.1126 •	F8F-2	Bu121752	N7827C	John W. Dorr, Orinda CA	.58/64
				Thomas P. Mathews, Monterey CA	.64/68
				(race #10/"Tom's Cat")	
				Walter E. Ohlrich, Norfolk VA	.68/72
				(race #10/"Miss Priss")	
				John Herlihy, Montara CA	.72/73
				(race #8/"Sweet Pea")	
			N2YY	Harold Beal, Knoxville TN	.73
			N800H	Harold Beal & Charles Smith/B & S Advertising	
				Knoxville TN (race #8/"Precious Bear")	.75/77
				World Jet Inc, West Palm Beach FL	.77/90
				(race #8/"Bearcat Bill")	
				Warbirds of GB Ltd, Biggin Hill	.90/91
				(shipped to UK, arr 30.12.90)	
D.1148 •	F8F-2	Bu122619		stored at NAS Litchfield Park AZ until	63
			N7958C	T. A. Underwood, Buckeye AZ	.63
				Frank Williams, Port Arthur TX	.63
				Hamilton Aircraft, Sonoma CA	.64/65
				Aviation Amazement-Amusement Inc/	
				Confederate Air Force, Oklahoma City OK	.66/67
				Gardner Flyers/CAF, Brownwood TX	.68/72
				Max Hoffman	c72
				Ken Boomhower	c72
				Harold Beal & Charles Smith, Knoxville TN	.73/75
			N700F	Harold Beal, Knoxville TN	.75/78
				Whittington Brothers Inc, West Palm Beach FL	.78
			N14WB	Whittington Brothers Inc, West Palm Beach FL	9.79
				EAA Aviation Foundation, Oshkosh WI	.80/91
				(displ. as USN "122619/Denver/P-14")	
D.1162 •	F8F-2	Bu121776	N1030B	off USCR by	63
				USMC Museum, MCAS Quantico VA (stored)	76/88
D.1170 •	F8F-2	Bu122629	N1031B	crashed at Valparaiso IN	.62
				(wreck stored Valparaiso IN .62/68)	
			N777L	Lyle T. Shelton, Granada Hills CA	.68/92
				(rebuilt Long Beach CA, Wright R-3350, ff 9.69;	
				flew as mod. racer #77/"Able Cat","Rare Bear";	
				world piston eng. speed record 528 mph 21.8.89)	
D.1181	F8F-2P	Bu121787	N6821D	M. W. Fairbrothers, Rosemount MN	.63/66
			N148F	New Jersey Air Co, Hackensack NJ	.66/68
				(race #11)	
				John Church, Carmel CA	.68
				Walter (Budd) Fountain/Hawke Dusters,	
				Modesto CA (race #99; #24)	.68/73
				crashed and dest., Mojave (Fountain k.)	20.10.73
D.1190 •	F8F-2	Bu122637	N1033B	William Johnson, Miami FL	.63/65
				New Jersey Air Co, Hackensack NJ	.66/68
				Sherman Cooper, Merced CA	.68/71
				John Church, Hackensack NJ	.71/73
			N198F	John Gury, St Louis MO	.73/80
				(flew as USN "G-98"; race #99; #11; #98)	
				John Herlihy, Montara CA	.80
				Cecil H. Harp, Canby OR	.81/84
				Cinema Air Inc, Houston TX/Carlsbad CA	5.84/92
				(flies as USN "122637/C98")	
D.1227 •	F8F-2P	Bu122674	N7825C	E. D. Weiner, Los Angeles CA	.58
				Leo J. Demers, Aurora OR	63

				Richard S. Tobey, Newport Beach CA	66
				Paul D. Finefrock, Hobart OK	69
				Gary R. Levitz, Long Beach CA/Avalon TX	.69/72
				Confederate Air Force, Harlingen TX	8.2.72/91
				(rebuild Chino CA 89/91, ff Chino 17.12.91)	
D.1261 •	F8F-2	Bu122708	N7701C	Michael J. Devanny, Cincinatti OH	66
				Ronald E. Reynolds , Norwalk CT	69/72
				Jack M. Sliker, Wadley GA	73/75
				(race #4/"Escape II")	
				crashed, Flagstaff AZ (Sliker killed)	16.9.75
				Elmer F. Ward, Chino CA (wreck)	85/92
				(parts used in rebuild of D.1081, Chino CA)	
D.1262 •	G-58B Gulfhawk		N700A	Grumman Aircraft Eng. Corp, Bethpage NY	3.49/59
				(op. by Roger Wolfe Kahn, Grumman President)	
				Cornell Aeronautical Lab., Buffalo NY	.59/66
				William Ross, Elk Grove Village IL	
				J. W. (Bill) Fornof, Houma LA	69/77
				Champlin Fighter Museum, Mesa AZ	.81/84
				Planes of Fame East, Plymouth MN	86/92
- •	F8F-1	-		(to Armee de l'Air as ....)	
				(to SVNAF as ....)	
				displ. SVNAF Base	60/75
				Museum of Flying, Santa Monica CA	.90
			N65135	Liberty Aero Corp, Santa Monica CA	9.90/92
				rep. impounded by US Customs	.91
				(FAA quote id. "001": rest. to fly, Santa Monica)	
- •	F8F-1	-		(to R Thai AF as '342')	
				displ. Nakorn-Sawan AB, Thailand	85
- •	F8F-1	-		(to R Thai AF as '4000')	
				displ. Takhli AB, Thailand	67/85
- •	F8F-1	-		(to R Thai AF as 15-43/93)	
				displ. outside Govt. offices, Bangkok	85
				(additional aircraft to D.779)	

GRUMMAN F3F

0972 •	F3F-2			rebuilt by Texas Airplane Factory	
			N20RW	Lone Star Flight Musdeum	.9.92
1028 •	F3F-2			rebuilt by Texas Airplane Factory	
			N19FG	Cinema Air, Carlsbad, CA	.9.92
1033 •	F3F-2			rebuilt by Texas Airplane Factory	
			N20FG	Cinema Air, Carlsbad, CA	.9.92

GRUMMAN F6F HELLCAT

A-212 •	F6F-3	Bu08825	N4965V	Michael E. Coutches, Hayward CA	c62
				Wayne B. Fowler, Shaw Island WA	65/66
				Charles F. Willis/Willisco Inc, New York NY,	
				op. c/o Alaska Airlines, Seattle WA	69/72
				(flew as "Little Nugget")	
				Willard Compton, Canby OR	75/91
				crashed and badly dam., Canby OR	12.6.77
				(long-term rebuild project)	
A-218	F6F-3	Bu08831		(VF-6 /USS Intrepid) : BOC	5.11.43
				Chicago Vocational School, Chicago IL	47/69
				Earl Reinert/Victory Air Museum,	
				Mundelein IL : stored, incomplete	.69/79

				Planes of Fame Museum, Chino CA	.79
				(rear fus. used in rebuild of N4964W)	
				(centre-section to Charles F. Nichols/YAC,	
				Chino CA : used in rebuild of N100TF)	.80
				(previously rep. as Alex Vraciu's Bu40467)	
A-1257 •	F6F-5	Bu66237		ditched, Pacific Ocean, near San Diego CA	12.1.44
				recovered from depth 3400ft, by USN	9.10.70
				San Diego Air & Space Museum, San Diego CA	72
				Pima County Air Museum, Tucson AZ	74/92
				(displ. as recov. "Z11")	
				(under rest., Roy Stafford, Jacksonville FL)	
A-2742 •	F6F-3	Bu41476		Walter E. Ohlrich, Norfolk VA	
			N41476	USMC Museum, MCAS Quantico VA	72/92
A-3100 •	F6F-3K	Bu41834		NASM Store, Silver Hill MD	75/83
				NASM loan: Yorktown Assoc., Charleston SC	10.76/81
				(displ. on USS "Yorktown", Mt.Pleasant SC)	
				NASM Store, Silver Hill MD	.81
				rest. for displ. Grumman Corp, Bethpage NY	.83
				NASM, Washington DC	.87/88
				NASM Store, Silver Hill MD	89/92
				(displ. as "41834/37")	
A-3196 •	F6F-3	Bu41930	N6096C	Wayne B. Fowler, Shaw Island WA	63/64
				John Church, Monterey CA	.64/65
			N103V	Peter Brucia, Garden City NY	.65/69
				William Ross, Elk Grove Village IL	72
				Doug Champlin/Windward Aviation, Enid OK	.72/78
				Champlin Fighter Museum,Mesa AZ	81/90
				Cinema Air, Houston TX	.90
			N30FG	Cinema Air, Carslbad CA	7.91/92
				(flies as "41930/5K")	
A-4140 •	F6F-3	Bu42874		USNAM, NAS Pensacola FL	79
				(recov. ex ocean ditching)	
				San Diego Aerospace Museum, San Diego CA	79/92
A-4280 •	F6F-3	Bu43014		recov. from Boy Scout campground	
			N7537U	John R. Sandberg, Minneapolis MN	69
				David B. Robinson, Miami Springs FL	72/84
				(rest. project, Miami Airport 74/84)	
				Weeks Air Museum, Tamiami FL	.84/92
				(id. prev. incorrectly rep. as Bu80167)	
A-5634 •	F6F-5	Bu70222		derelict, Fergus Falls Airport MN	62
			N1078Z	John R. Sandberg, Minneapolis MN	.62/72
				Lloyd P. Nolan/CAF, Harlingen TX	.72/73
				Ed Messick/Confederate AF, Harlingen TX	9.4.73/90
				(id. prev. incorrectly rep. as Bu80166)	
A-8867 •	F6F-5K	Bu77722		US Naval Reserve Base,Andrews AFB MD: del.	.65/88
				(displ. on pole as USN "22")	
A-9790 •	F6F-5	Bu78645	N9265A	Yankee Air Corps, Chino CA	3.78/92
				(flies as USN "45")	
A-10337•	F6F-5K	Bu79192		Bradley Air Museum, Windsor Locks CT : arr.	25.10.73
				(recov. from NAS China Lake CA .73)	
				New England Air Museum, Windsor Locks CT	83/92
				(displ. in VBF-11 sc.)	
A-10738•	F6F-5K	Bu79593		Bradley Air Museum, Windsor Locks CT	.73
				(recov. from NAS China Lake CA .73)	
				USS Alabama Memorial, Mobile AL	76/91
				(displ. as F6F-3, "41476")	

A-10814	F6F-5N	Bu79669		NAS Moffett Field CA	65/72
				(displ. as "1158")	
A-10828•	F6F-5K	Bu79683	N7896C	John A. Ortseifen, Fort Lauderdale FL	63/77
				(retired, Chicagoland Airport IL 66/77)	
				Preston Parish, Kalamazoo MI	.79/81
			N4PP	Kalamazoo Aviation History Museum, Kalamazoo MI	7.81/92
				(rebuilt Kalamazoo, ff .81: flies as USN "4")	
A-10924•	F6F-5 Mk. II	Bu79779		(to Royal Navy FAA as KE209)	
				RNAS Lossiemouth : stored for FAA museum	
				Fleet Air Arm Museum, RNAS Yeovilton	65/92
A-11008•	F6F-5K	Bu79863		Grumman Aircraft Co, Bethpage NY	56/57
				USNAM, NAS Pensacola FL	.57/72
			N79863	Aerial Classics, Atlanta GA	.72/84
				Patriots Point Development Authority/ USS Yorktown Museum, Mount Pleasant SC	86/91
				(displ. on USS "Yorktown")	
				rep: Doug Arnold/Warbirds of GB Ltd	.91/92
A-11286•	F6F-5K	Bu80141	N80142	USMC Museum, MCAS Quantico VA	65/69
				W. C. Yarbrough, Marietta GA	72
			N100TF	Thomas H. Friedkin, Rancho Santa Fe CA	1.77/79
				crashed, forced landing, San Marcos CA	3.4.79
			N10CN	ntu: Yankee Air Corps, Chino CA	.81/88
				(reb. Chino 85/88, using center-section Bu08831)	
			N100TF	Military Aircraft Restoration Corp, Chino CA	.88/89
				The Fighter Collection, Duxford	.89/91
				(ff Chino 7.89; shipped to UK, arr. 1.8.90)	
			G-BTCC	The Fighter Collection, Duxford	12.90/92
				(flies as USN "40467/19")	
A-11631•	F6F-5	Bu93879	N4994V	The Air Museum, Claremont CA	58/62
				The Air Museum, Ontario & Chino CA	62/92
				dam. landing, Elsinore Dry Lake CA (repaired)	.72
A-11955•	F6F-5	Bu94203	N7865C	Nicholas Parks, Hayward CA	66/70
				Aerial Classics, Atlanta GA	.70/72
				USNAM, NAS Pensacola FL	73/91
				(displ. as USN "Minsi III")	
A-11956•	F6F-5N	Bu94204		Normandie Iron and Metal Company	59
			N4998V	Eddie Fisher, Hollywood CA	
				The Air Mus., Ontario & Chino CA	67/70
				(unconv. "94204/FASRON 4/The Beguine")	
				Michael E. Coutches, Hayward CA	5.70/86
				loan: Wagons to Wings Museum, San Jose CA	10.74/86
				Lone Star Flight Museum, Houston	.86/87
				Lone Star Flight Museum, Galveston TX	90/92
				(rebuilt Hayward CA, ff 4.5.89 as "USN 32")	
A-12015•	F6F-5K	Bu94263		NAS Norfolk VA (stored)	65/70
				USMC Museum, MCAS Quantico VA	76/90
				rest. static displ., MCAS Cherry Point NC	78
				loan: Cradle of Aviation Museum NY	83/92
				(displ. as "94263/VMF-511/IM")	
A-12137•	F6F-5	Bu94385	N7861C	Michael E. Coutches, Hayward CA	61
				Tom O'Connor/CAF, Victoria TX	9.61/66
				Henry L. Gardner/CAF, Victoria TX	69
				crashed, Victoria TX	7.69
				Michael E. Coutches, Hayward CA (wreck)	72/92

A-12225•	F6F-5K	Bu94473		The Air Museum, Ontario CA	67/70
				(displ. in red drone sc. "473"; then stored)	
				The Air Museum, Chino CA	70/84
				(rebuilt Chino 83/84, with parts Bu08831)	
			N4964W	Planes of Fame East, Minneapolis MN	.84/92
				crashed landing, Chino CA (repaired)	19.3.84
				(flies as USN "58644/36")	
•	F6F	-		Sea-Air-Space Museum, New York NY	91
				(displ. as VF-18 "24803/39" on USS Intrepid)	
- •	F6F-3K	-		(to Uraguayan Navy as ....)	
				rep. stored awaiting displ., Montevideo	77
- •	F6F-5	-		(to Uraguayan Navy as ....)	
				rep. stored	82
- •	F6F-5	-		(to Uraguayan Navy as ....)	
				rep. stored	82

GRUMMAN F7F TIGERCAT

C.115 •	F7F-3	Bu80373	N7654C	Calvin J. Butler/Butler Farm Air Service,	
				Redmond OR (tanker #F18; later #18)	63/66
				TBM Inc, Tulare CA (tanker #E63)	69/80
				USNAM, NAS Pensacola FL	.80/91
				(displ. as "80373/12")	
C.116 •	F7F-3N	Bu80374	N7629C	Cal-Nat Airways Inc, Grass Valley CA	66/69
				(tanker #E62; later #E41)	
				Sis Q Flying Service, Santa Rosa CA	.69/81
				(tanker #E41)	
				USMC Museum, MCAS Quantico VA	.81/91
				Darryl Greenamyer, Ocala FL	.91
C.117 •	F7F-3E	Bu80375		NAS Anacostia	
	F7F-3N			USMC Museum, MCAS Quantico VA	76
				Pima County Air Museum, Tucson AZ	10.87/88
				(stored derelict unconv., "Marines")	
C.124 •	F7F-3N	Bu80382		NAS Anacostia	
				USMC Museum, MCAS Quantico VA	75
				(trucked to USNAM via Norfolk VA .75)	
				USNAM, NAS Pensacola FL	.75/85
				Yankee Air Force Museum, Willow Run MI	88/89
				Planes of Fame Museum, Chino CA	.90/92
				(displ. in orig. sc "Marines/382")	
C.132 •	F7F-3N	Bu80390	N6129C	Kreitzberg Aviation, Salem OR	.
	F7F-3P			Johnson Flying Service, Missoula MT	63
				Calvin J. Butler/Butler Farm Air Service,	
				Redmond OR (tanker #F16; later #16)	63/66
				TBM Inc, Tulare CA (tanker #E62)	69/78
				Harold Beal/On Mark Aviation, Knoxville TN	11.78
			N700F	Preston Parish/Kalamazoo Aviation History	
				Museum, Kalamazoo MI	3.80
			N700FM	ntu : Air Training Inc, Knoxville TN	1.81
			N700F	Kalamazoo Aviation History Museum,	
				Kalamazoo MI	81/92
				(del. ex Knoxville 3.85, flies as "80390/D3")	
C.139	F7F-3	Bu80397	N6177C	S. V. Flying Service, Montague CA	63
				Sis Q Flying Service, Montague/	
				Santa Rosa CA (tanker #E31)	63/74
				crashed and dest., Ukiah CA	31.8.74
C.146 •	F7F-3	Bu80404	N7626C	Aero Ads Inc (sky-writing)	58
				Cal-Nat Airways Inc, Grass Valley CA	63/69

				(tanker #E42)	
				Sis Q Flying Service, Santa Rosa CA	.69/84
				Macavia International Corp, Santa Rosa CA	6.85/86
				(tanker #E42)	
				Weeks Air Museum, Tamiami FL	.86/92
				(displ. in USN blue scheme)	
C.152 •	F7F-3	Bu80410	N7627C	Cal-Nat Airways Inc, Grass Valley CA	62/69
				gear folded landing, Grass Valley CA	31.8.62
				Sis-Q Flying Service, Santa Rosa CA (wreck)	.69/72
				Weeks Air Museum, Tamiami FL	88/90
				(stored dism., Borrego Springs CA 88/89)	
				Pima County Air Museum, Tucson AZ	.91
				(rebuilt Rialto CA, as "Marines/80410")	
C.154 •	F7F-3	Bu80412	N7628C	Cal-Nat Airways Inc, Grass Valley CA	62/69
				(tanker #E59)	
				crashed landing, Ukiah CA	7.66
				Sis-Q Flying Service, Santa Rosa CA	.69/72
				bought as wreck, stored Santa Rosa CA	72
				Weeks Air Museum, Tamiami FL	88/90
				(stored dism., Borrego Springs CA 88/89)	
				Planes of Fame East, Eden Prairie MN	91/92
				(rest. Chino CA 92)	91/92
C.167 •	F7F-3P	Bu80425	N7235C	Calvin J. Butler/Butler Farm Air Service,	
				Redmond OR (tanker #F17; later #17)	63/66
				TBM Inc, Tulare CA (tanker #E64)	69/79
				Military Aircraft Restoration Corp, Chino CA	.82/92
				(flies as "Marines/VMFN-513")	
C.225 •	F7F-3	Bu80483	N6178C	Cal-Nat Airways, Grass Valley CA	.64/66
				(tanker #E43)	
				Sis-Q Flying Service, Santa Rosa CA	69/85
				Macavia International Corp, Santa Rosa CA	6.85/86
				(tanker #E43)	
				Weeks Air Museum, Tamiami FL	
				stored Santa Rosa CA	87/88
				Lea Aviation (US) Inc, Tampa FL/Duxford UK	.88/92
				(arr. Duxford on del. 13.11.88, op. by Plane	
				Sailing Air Displays, flies as "USN JW/483")	
C.236	F7F-3	Bu80494	N6179C	Fred J. Arnberg Inc, Yreka CA	63
				Sis-Q Flying Service, Montague/	
				Santa Rosa CA (tanker #E23)	.63/74
				crashed Rohnerville CA	26.9.74
C.245 •	F7F-3N	Bu80503		TBM Inc, Sequoia CA	60/80
				(stored dism., unconv. in hut, Sequoia CA 73)	
			N800RW	Lone Star Flight Museum, Galveston TX	1.89/92
				(rebuilt Fort Collins CO .88/89 ; flies as	
				"Marines 80503/RW/Big Bossman"	
C.261	F7F-3	Bu80525	N7238C	Dick Gordon, Santa Rosa CA	63
				Cal-Nat Airways, Grass Valley CA	.63
				(tanker #E41)	
				Sis-Q Flying Service, Santa Rosa CA	66/74
				(tanker #E22)	
				crashed Rohnerville CA	21.10.74
C.268 •	F7F-3	Bu80532	N7195C	George F. Kreitzberg, Salem OR	63
				Sis-Q Flying Service, Santa Rosa CA	63/79
				(tanker#E32", later#E40)	
				Gary H. Flanders & Mike Bogue, Oakland CA	8.79/92
				(flies as "Marines/VMP-254/80532")	

Grumman FM-2 Bu 46867/N909WJ is owned by Warbirds of Great Britain. Rebuilt by Darrell Skurich of Vintage Aircraft, Fort Collins, Colorado for Doug Arnold this aircraft was formerly owned by Earl Reinert of the Victory Air Museum, Mundelin, Illinois. Seen here at Cranfield in 1991 at a special air racing event organised by Air Displays International. (Jeremy Flack/Aviation Photographs International)

Shown here with Dick Melton Aviation at Micheldever, Hants, Hawker Hurricane ex RCAF5481 was acquired by Charles Church in Canada before Dick was contracted to rebuild it. Hurricane specialist Paul Mercer, (now Chief Engineer at Historic Flying) provided his expert assistance in the restoration of the aircraft, registered G-ORGI in the UK. The aircraft was sold to the Museum of Flying at Santa Monica, arriving there in March 1992 where it was registered N678DP. (Jeremy Flack/Aviation Photographs Int'l).

Grumman TBM-3E Bu85869 (c/n2688) is based in France with Didier Chable as F-AZJA. The aircraft formerly flew as a tanker with Aircraft Specialities, Mesa, Arizona before being sold to Globe Air and then Justus O. Jackson of Comstock, Texas. It was delivered to France on 30th September 1989. (Thierry Thomassin)

Another Warbirds of Great Britain machine, this time Vought F4U-5 Corsair Bu 122179 was rebuilt in Florida for Peter Thelen. The aircraft was sold to Warbirds of Great Britain where it joined two others at Biggin Hill in Kent. (Gary R. Brown)

c/n		Type	Serial	Reg.	History	Date
-	•	F4F-3 Martlet 1	AL246		(for French Navy/Aeronavale: not del.)	
					(diverted to RN Fleet Air Arm as AL246)	
					Loughborough College, Loughborough UK	.45/61
					RNAS Lossiemouth; stored for future mus.	.61/63
					Fleet AirArm Museum, RNAS Yeovilton	65/92
-	•	F4F-3	Bu3872		Lake Michigan, near Chicago IL	21.7.43
					recov. from Lake Michigan by USNAM	.91
					USNAM, NAS Pensacola FL	.91
838	•	F4F-3A	Bu3956		recov. from Lake Michigan	c87
					Patriots Point Naval Museum, Mt. Pleasant SC	87/90
					(static rest. by Grumman, NY : to be displ. on board "USS Yorktown", Charleston SC)	
-	•	F4F-3	Bu4039		ditched Lake Michigan, near Chicago IL	21.7.43
					recov. from Lake Michigan by USNAM	.91
					USNAM, NAS Pensacola FL	.91
3763	•	F4F-4	Bu12068		VMF-214, cr. Henderson Field, Guadalcanal	21.1.43
					War Museum, Honiara, Solomon Islands	.73/91
					(barged to Honiara .73, displ. as unrest. hulk)	
3809	•	F4F-4	Bu12114		trade school, White Centre, Seattle WA	55/65
					USMC Museum, MCAS Quantico VA	69/87
					(displ. as "12114/2")	
5920	•	F4F-3	Bu12260	N12260	National Museum of Naval Aviation	2.92
					Jim Porter, Batavia IL	.92
5956	•	F4F-3	Bu12296	N3210D	National Museum of Naval Aviation	2.92
					Warbirds Aircraft Restoration & Salvage Inc, Waterford MI	.92
-	•	F4F-4 Mk. V	-		(to RN Fleet Air Arm as JV482)	
					ditched Portmore Lough, Ireland	24.12.44
					Ulster Aviation Society, Castlereagh: recov.	4.84/86
401	•	FM-1	Bu15392		instruct. airframe Tech School, Norman OK	c47/c49
					NASM, stored Silver Hill MD	c49/73
					restored for display, Grumman Bethpage NY	74/75
					NASM, Washington DC	75/87
-	•	FM-2	Bu16278		ditched Lake Michigan, near Chicago IL	26.6.45
					recov. from Lake Michigan by USNAM	.91
					USNAM, NAS Pensacola FL	.91
2020	•	FM-2	Bu46867		displ. service station, Palwaukee IL	61/65
					Victory Air Museum, Mundelein IL	68/76
					stored dism. Chino CA	
					World Jet Inc, Fort Lauderdale FL	89
					Warbirds of GB Ltd, Biggin Hill	.89/91
				N909WJ	(rebuild to fly, Ft.Collins CO 89/90)	
					flown to Chino CA, shipped to UK : arr.	30.12.90
					(note: FAA & N909WJ plate quotes id. Bu16023)	
2183	•	FM-2	Bu47030	N315E	Alexis I. Dupont, Wilmington DE	69/72
					Alexis I. Dupont/Colonial Flying Field Museum, Toughkenamon PA	73/92
					(flies as "USN F-13")	
2313	•	FM-2	Bu47160	N2876D	Western Aerial Contractors, Eugene OR	63
					R. J. Hartlaub, Summit NJ	66/69
					Keith J. Mackey, Miami FL	72
					Wings of Yesterday Flying Air Museum, Santa Fe NM	77/84

			N551TC	John C. Hooper/Intracoastal Terminal Inc, Harvey LA	5.84/91
				Lone Star Flight Museum, Galveston TX	8.91/92
				(flies as "USN 7/Old Fang")	
3226 •	FM-2	Bu55585	N681S	Joe Speidel, Miami FL	61
				Lloyd P. Nolan/Confederate Air Force, Mercedes TX	5.61/63
				Gerald Martin/CAF, Hereford TX	66/72
				(flew as "N6815" 66/70)	
				Confederate Air Force, Harlingen TX	2.2.72/91
				American Airpower Heritage Flying Museum, Midland TX (flies as "USN 55585")	9.91/92
3268 •	FM-2	Bu55627	N7906C	The Air Museum, Ontario CA	59/72
			N47201	James Nunn, Ontario CA	.76/77
				The Fighter Collection, Duxford UK	.82/86
				(del. USA to France, arr. 11.6.82)	
				John V. Crocker, San Mateo CA	84
				Planes of Fame East, Spring Park MN	6.85/92
				(id. also quoted as Bu03455)	
4312 •	FM-2	Bu74120		park war memorial, Windsor Locks CT	50/67
				Bradley Air Museum, Windsor Locks CT	25.5.67/80
				New England Air Museum, Windsor Locks CT	83/92
4704 •	FM-2	Bu74512		Edison Technical School, Seattle WA	50/60
				park playground, White Centre, Seattle WA	65/69
				Pacific Northwest Aviation History Museum, Boeing Field WA	.69/83
				(static rest., Fairchild AFB WA 83)	
				Museum of Flight, Boeing Field, Seattle WA	.83/91
				(rest. for static displ.)	
4752 •	FM-2	Bu74560	N90523	Air Service Kontrol Inc, West Bend WI	c50/60
				Frank G. Tallman, Orange County CA	60
				Wade R. Porter, Columbus IN	63
				Yankee Air Club Inc, Sunderland MA	66
				Damn Yankee Air Force, Turner Falls MA	66/69
				William C. Whitesell, Medford NJ	.69
				Doug Champlin/Windward Aviation, Enid OK	.71/79
				Champlin Fighter Museum, Mesa AZ	78/90
			N16TF	Tom Friedkin/Cinema Air, Houston TX	12.90
			N29FG	Tom Friedkin/Cinema Air, Carlsbad CA	7.91/92
4955	FM-2	Bu74763	N29B	noted as sprayer, Safford AZ	7.58
				Sonora Air Service, Columbia CA	63/69
				(FAA quoted id. 4955: Buno assumed)	
5618 •	FM-2	Bu86564	N4629V	Tallmantz Aviation/Movieland of the Air Museum, Orange County CA	58/63
				Rosen Novak Auto Co, Omaha NB	66
				(remained at Tallmantz Aviation until auction)	29.5.68
				F. R. Davis, Beaverton OR	69
				Yankee Air Corps, Chino CA	6.83/92
5626 •	FM-2	Bu86572	N35MK	reg.	.54
				Lyman Rice, Laconia NH	59
				Hamilton Aircraft Co, Tucson AZ	63
				New London Airport, New London PA	66/69
				Jaques R. Dupont, Newcastle DE	72
			N35M	sale rep.	84/88
				struck-off USCR	4.90
5635 •	FM-2	Bu86581	N86581	Gunther W. Balz, Kalamazoo MI	72
				Preston Parish, Kalamazoo Air Zoo MI	73

			N1PP	Kalamazoo Aviation History Museum, Kalamazoo MI (flies as "86581/1")	83/92
5734	•	FM-2	Bu86680	NX55558		
			N777A	(modified to carry 4 passengers!)	55
			YV-T-OTO		1.62
			YV-T-HTJ	struck-off reg.	10.2.69
			N11FE	Frederick W. Edison, Kalamazoo MI	5.70/74
				crashed into Lake Michigan (salvaged)	29.6.75
				Richard Foote, Summerland Key FL	76/84
				Richard Foote/Professional Aircraft Sales, New Smyrna Beach FL	86/92
				(flies as "Bu5134 USS Tulagi")	
				(note: id. confusion with c/n 5835 which see: FAA quote id. 5734; also quoted as Bu86870)	
5744	•	FM-2	Bu86690	N20HA	Don Underwood, Phoenix AZ (sprayer)	56/58
				S. S. Steele, Safford AZ	63
				James R. Freese, Fremont & Modesto CA	66/72
				Jack Lenhardt/Lenhardt Airpark, Hubbard OR	77/79
				(flew as "Marines/2")	
				USNAM, NAS Pensacola FL	.79/90
				(displ. as "86690/2")	
				(FAA quote id. "51-235")	
5765	•	FM-2	Bu86711	N4845V	Dale P. Newton, Medford OR	66/69
				Eric G. Mingledorff, Monroe LA	77/92
				displ. Chennault Air Museum, Monroe LA	
5795	•	FM-2	Bu86741	N19K	Alexis I. Dupont, Wilmington DE	66/84
				Alexis I. Dupont, Toughkenamon PA	86/88
				Weeks Air Museum, Tamiami FL	.88/90
			N222FM	Weeks Air Museum, Tamiami FL	8.90/92
				(rest. to fly)	
5804	•	FM-2	Bu86746	N6290C	Michael G. Rattke, Atlanta GA	66
				Michael G. Rattke, Merritt Island FL	69
				Rudy Frasca/Antiques & Classics Inc, Champaign IL (flies as "USN/5")	72/92
				(id. also quoted as Bu86940)	
5805	•	FM-2	Bu86747	N68843	Charlie T. Jensen, Reno NV (sprayer)	66/72
				Kenneth Spiva, Lovelock NV	77
				USNAM, NAS Pensacola FL	81/91
				(displ. as "86747")	
5808	•	FM-2	Bu86750	N12371	Robert L. Younkin, Fayetteville AR	69/77
				crashed, Houston-Lakeside Airport TX	14.10.83
				Jack B. Barnett, Arabi TX	84/92
5812	•	FM-2	Bu86754	N58918	sprayer	.55/58
				Ron Zerbel, Nyssa OR	63
				Spray Rite Inc, Oakley ID	66/69
				Don H. Novas, Blackfoot ID	77/90
				Erickson Air Crane, Central Point OR	.90/92
5831	•	FM-2	Bu86773	N1352N	sprayer	56
				Medford Air Service, Medford OR	63/69
				Robert L. Younkin, Fayetteville AR	77/92
5832	•	FM-2	Bu86774	N7835C	The Air Museum, Claremont CA	66/69
				Planes of Fame Museum, Chino CA	11.86/88
5835	•	FM-2	Bu86777	N90541	I. N. Burchinall Jr, Paris TX	12.74
			N5HP	Howard E. Pardue, Breckenridge TX	2.81/92
				(flies as "USN 5/Kimberly Brooke"	
				(id. confused with c/n 5734)	

5877	•	FM-2	Bu86819	N.........	Butler Aviation, Redmond OR (sprayer)	c52
					crashed while spraying	c55
					various owners under rebuild	
					Eugene Mahlon OR	73
					Yankee Air Corps, Chino CA	.81
				N5833	Yankee Air Corps, Chino CA	8.83/88
					Air Group One, Ramona CA	.86
					(trucked Chino-Ramona : rebuilt ff 24.4.87)	
					Military Aircraft Restoration Corp, Chino CA	.88
					Confederate Air Force, Harlingen TX	1.89/91
					American Airpower Heritage Flying Museum, Midland TX	9.91/92
					(FAA quote id. 5833, flies as USN "86819")	
6014	•	FM-2	Bu86956	N18PK	E. J. Saviano, La Grange IL	63
				N18P	William D. Ross, Chicago IL	66/67
					Louis V. Gallo, Hillside IL	69/77
					Joseph G. Mabee, Midland TX	84/89
					Weeks Air Museum, Tamiami FL	
					(stored dism. as N18PK)	89
-	•	FM-2	-	N6699K	American Aviation Inc, Walnut Ridge AR	90/92
					(rebuild by Yankee Air Corps, Chino CA)	
					(FAA quote id. "428B")	
-	•	F4F-3	-		Cradle of Aviation Museum, Garden City NY	88
-	•	F4F-3	-		ditched Lake Michigan, near Chicago IL	17.8.43
					recov. from Lake Michigan by USNAM	.90
					USNAM, NAS Pensacola FL	.90
-	•	FM-1	-		ditched Lake Washington, near Seattle WA	
					Bruce D. Roberts, New London PA : recov.	c85/90
-	•	FM-2	-		ditched Lake Washington, near Seattle WA	
					Bruce D. Roberts, New London PA : recov.	c85/90

GRUMMAN OV-1 MOHAWK

2	•	OV-1A	59-2604	N4235Z	Lortz & Son Manufacturing Co Inc	17.3.81
					Thunderbird Aviation Inc, Deer Valley AZ	84/88
					Lone Star Flight Museum, Galveston TX	6.90/92
4	•	OV-1A	59-2606	N72606	Richard A. Boulais, Glendale AZ	10.89/92
6	•	OV-1A	59-2608	N2608	reg. res.	90/92
15	•	OV-1A	59-2617	N75207	reg. res.	84/92
21	•	OV-1A	60-3722	N2623Q	Moseley Aviation Inc, Phoenix AZ	29.11.82
					reg. pending	88/92
34		OV-1A	60-3735	N75213	Thunderbird Aviation Inc, Deer Valley AZ	77/83
-	•	OV-1C	61-2692	N4376D	reg. res.	92
-	•	OV-1C	62-5856	N6744	struck-off USCR	1.90
					National Warplane Museum, Geneseo NY	2.90/92
					(rebuild project)	
-		OV-1B	62-5866	N171	US Geological Survey Department, Panama	.71/74
-		OV-1B	62-5880	N512NA	NASA, Langley Research Center, Hampton VA	84
48A	•	OV-1A OV-1B	63-13118	N75205	reg. res.	84/92

49A •	OV-1A	63-13119		(to USN as 63-13119)	
	OV-1B		N90788	noted NAS Patuxant River MD	4.74
			reg. res.	84/88	
58A •	OV-1A	63-13128	N87864	Pittsburgh Institute of Aeronautics,	
				Allegheny County Airport, Pittsburgh PA	78/92
-	OV-1B	64-14244	N637NA	NASA, Lewis Research Center, Cleveland OH	74/77
-	OV-1C	67-18915	N928NA	NASA	

GRUMMAN TBF/TBM AVENGER

- •	TBF-1C	Bu01747		ditched Lake Michigan, near Chicago IL	11.6.43
				recov. from Lake Michigan by USNAM	.91
				USNAM, NAS Pensacola FL (static rest.)	.91
- •	TBF-1C	Bu05954	N5954A	reg. res.	92
4045 •	TBF-1C	Bu05997		MGM Studios, Culver City CA	70
				The Air Museum, Chino CA	.70/72
				Military Aircraft Restoration Corp, Chino CA	.72/82
				Yankee Air Corps, Chino CA	83/91
				(stored unconv. in orig. scheme, Chino CA)	
4968 •	TBF-1C	Bu24085		NASM, stored Silver Hill MD	65/91
5219 •	TBF-1C	Bu24336		(to RNZAF as NZ2504)	
				Te Rapa AB NZ : displ.	7.59/69
				RNZAF Museum, Wigram AB	79/91
5220 •	TBF-1C	Bu24337		(to RNZAF as NZ2505)	
				in playground, Opunake, Taranaki NZ	69
				rep. with preservation group, Wellington NZ	73
5625 •	TBF-1C	Bu47859		(to RN as JZ321; RNZAF as NZ2527) del.	1.44
				ZK-CBO	reg. 3.62
				crop sprayer conv. abandoned : struck-off	3.64
				in playground, Kuirau Park, Rotorua	69
				Museum of Transport & Technology, Auckland	74/91
				(displ. Dairy Flat airfield, Auckland NZ)	
5782 •	TBF-1C	Bu48016		(to RNZAF as NZ2539)	
				in playground, Havelock North NZ	69/73
5746 •	TBM-3	Bu23602		NAS Mustim Field, Philadelphia PA : stored	47/75
				USNAM: displ. USS "Intrepid", Philadelphia	.76
				Bradley Air Museum, Windsor Locks CT	18.9.76/79
				badly damaged by tornado, Windsor Locks CT	3.10.79
				New England Air Museum, Windsor Locks CT	89/90
				(static rest., using parts from hulks of Bu53100	
				& Bu53527, recov. by NEAM from burial site	
				after crashes at NALF Charlestown RI)	
2062 •	TBM-3	Bu69323	N7961C	Daro Inc, San Clemente CA	63/69
				(tanker #E92; later #24)	
				Sis-Q Flying Service, Santa Rosa CA	.70
			C-GLEJ	Evergreen Air Service, Roxboro QUE	12.74
				Forest Protection Ltd, Fredericton NB	81/92
				(tanker #24)	
2064 •	TBM-3U	Bu69325	N104Z	U. S. Forestry Service, Davis CA	.56/61
			N1044	Aero Insect Control Inc, Rio Grande NJ	63/66
			CF-XOM	Maritime Air Service Ltd, Moncton	6.69/70
				Hicks & Lawrence Ltd, St Thomas ONT	79
				(tanker #18)	
			N325GT	Syracuse Flying Service, Syracuse KS	10.85/88

				Stallion Aircraft Inc, Bensenville IL	89/92
				(note: CCAR quoted id. as "69324")	
2066 •	TBM-3E	Bu69327		(to RCN as 326) BOC 27.9.50: SOC	5.7.60
			CF-KCG	Skyway Air Services, Langley BC	61/65
				Conair Aviation Ltd, Abbotsford BC	.69/76
				(tanker #615)	
				Forest Protection Ltd, Fredericton NB	
				Warbirds of GB Ltd, Blackbushe	
				Imperial War Museum, Duxford UK	.77/92
				(long-term rest., Duxford)	
2068 •	TBM-3E	Bu69329	N73642	Reeder Flying Service, Twin Falls ID	63/84
				(tanker #D23; later #23)	
				noted derelict, Twin Falls ID	80/84
				Gary Wolverton, Twin Falls ID	84
			N700RW	Waltrip/Lone Star Flight Museum,	
				Houston/Galveston TX	10.86/92
				(flies as USN "329")	
2083 •	TBM-3E	Bu69344	N66475	Ball Ralston Flying Service, Hillsboro OR	63
				AV Aircraft Co, Deming NM	66/69
				Hemet Valley Flying Service, Hemet CA	c71
				stored Stockton CA	74
				sale reported : USCR	84/92
				(FAA quote id. 2083: BuAer serial assumed)	
2094 •	TBM-3E	Bu69355	N7850C	reg.	.59
				Cisco Aircraft Inc, Lancaster CA	63
				Aircraft Specialties, Mesa AZ	66
				Ag Air Inc, Dos Palos CA	69
				Marom Ltd, Herzelia, Israel	.69
				derelict at Herzelia as N7850C	74
				Israeli Air Force Museum, Hazerim AB	89/91
				(rest., displ. in RAF scheme)	
2100 •	TBM-3E	Bu69361	N9596C	P & B Aviation, Oroville CA (tanker #E19)	63
				Aero Union Corp, Chico CA	63
				Air Tankers Inc, Newcastle WY/ Casper WY	66/72
			C-GOEG	Norfolk Aerial Spraying, Fredericton NB	5.75
				Reynolds Aviation Museum, Wetaskiwin ALTA	88/92
				(stored whole, nat. metal sc.: no marks)	
2113 •	TBM-3E	Bu69374	N9650C	Bill Wood, Imperial Beach CA	63/72
				Military Aircraft Restoration Corp, Chino CA	79/91
2114	TBM-3	Bu69375	N3965A	Nevadair, Tonopah NV	63/69
				Charlie T. Jensen, Tonopah NV	72/78
2198 •	TBM-3E	Bu69459	N8397H	Cisco Aircraft Inc, Lancaster CA	63
				Aerial Applicators Inc, Salt Lake City UT	66/72
				Hillcrest Aircraft, Lewiston ID	77
				Paramount Leasing Corp, Bakersfield CA	84
				Northwest Warbirds Inc, Kimberly ID	86/87
				War Eagles Air Museum, Santa Teresa NM	88/92
2211 •	TBM-3	Bu69472	N9593C	Frontier Airways, Visalia CA	63
				Clayton V. Curtis, Boise ID (tanker #D5)	63
				Loening Air Inc, Boise ID	66
				Clayton V. Curtis, Boise ID	69
				Bill Dempsay/D & D Aero Spray, Rantoul KS	72
				James Levrett, Reno NV	77
				Pima County Air Museum, Tucson AZ	83/91
				(displ. as USN "69472")	
2241 •	TBM-3E	Bu69502		(to Royal Navy FAA as XB446)	

	AS.4			Fleet Air Arm Museum, RNAS Yeovilton	72/92
				(displ. as "XB446/C-992")	
2270	TBM-3	Bu69531	N179Z	U. S. Forestry Service	63
			N17930	Seeley Flying Serv., Newcastle & Casper WY	66/69
				Air Tankers Inc, Casper WY	72
			C-GOBK	Norfolk Aerial Spraying, Fredericton NB	5.74
				crashed while spraying, Minto NB	30.5.78
2273 •	TBM-3	Bu85454		rep. Wings of History Museum, Santa Fe NM	91
2279 •	TBM-3	Bu85460		(to RCN as 346) BOC 22.7.50: SOC	5.7.60
			N7032C	crashed on take-off, Idaho City ID	9.7.61
				Richardson Aviation, Yakima WA	63/72
				leased Marom Ltd, Herzelia, Israel	67
				(noted spraying in Greece 68)	
			C-GFPS	Evergreen Air Service, Roxboro QUE	5.76
				Forest Protection Ltd, Fredericton NB	81/92
				(tanker #3)	
2318	TBM-3	Bu85499	N9597C	Calvin J. Butler, Redmond OR	63
				Johnson Flying Service, Missoula MT	66/72
				(tanker #A6)	
			C-GLEM	Evergreen Air Service, Roxboro QUE	4.75
				Forest Protection Ltd, Fredericton NB	
				reg. cancelled	6.80
2325 •	TBM-3	Bu85506		(to RCN as 385) BOC 16.6.52: SOC	30.1.58
			N6582D	Simsbury Flying Service, Simsbury CT	63/66
				Ag Air International, Dos Palos CA	.67
				Marom Ltd, Herzelia, Israel	.67/91
				(noted based Athens, spraying contract 7.68)	
				stored derelict, Herzelia, Israel as N6582D	74/91
2379	TBM-3	Bu85560	N6830C	Nevadair, Tonopah NV	63/69
				Charlie T. Jensen, Tonopah NV	72/77
2413	TBM-3	Bu85594	N1366N	TBM Inc, Bakersfield later Tulare CA	59/74
				(tanker #E66 ; later #E60)	
				lsd: Aero Union Corp, Chico CA	73
				(tanker #E60)	
				crashed Placerville CA	18.8.73
2416 •	TBM-3	Bu85597		(to RCN as 381) BOC 23.6.52: SOC	17.1.58
			CF-IMK	Skyway Air Services, Langley BC	61/65
				Conair Aviation Ltd, Abbotsford BC	.69/76
				(tanker #602)	
			C-FIMK	Forest Protection Ltd, Fredericton NB	81/90
				(tanker #2)	
2442	TBM-3	Bu85623		(to MLD as 1-29; 037)	.55
				displ. De Kooy NAS, Holland	70
2451 •	TBM-3E	Bu85632	N7002C	Plains Aero Service, Dalhart TX	63
				Air Tankers Inc, Newcastle WY	66/72
			C-GOBJ	Norfolk Aerial Spraying, Fredericton NB	5.74
				Forest Protection Ltd, Fredericton NB	85/89
				(tanker #B15)	
			N81865	Northwest Warbirds Inc, Kimberly ID : del.	28.6.89
				Wayne G. Rudd, Carbondale CO	.89/92
				(FAA quote id. as "5632")	
2469 •	TBM-3	Bu85650		(to MLD as 16-102; 045)	
	TBM-3W2			Netherlands Luchtvaart Museum, Den Haag	70/72
				Strathallan Collection, Auchterader, Scotland	5.76
			G-BTBM	Strathallan Collection, Auchterader, Scotland	23.12.77
				Warbirds of GB Ltd, Blackbushe	14.7.81/85
				stored Blackbushe : struck-off reg.	20.4.82
				Aces High Ltd, Duxford	7.6.85

				sold in US	22.7.85
			N61BD	Andrew E. Deeds, Charlotte VA	4.86/89
			N452HA	Andrew E. Deeds, Charlotte VA	7.89
				Herbert H. Avery, Morganton NC	90/92
2484	TBM-3	Bu85665		(to RCN as 322) BOC 8.6.50: SOC	30.1.58
			CF-IMV	Wheeler Airlines, St Jean QUE	58/65
				Wheeler Northland Airways Ltd, St Jean QUE	70
				Evergreen Air Service, Roxboro QUE	72
				crashed	9.6.77
2534 •	TBM-3	Bu85715	N1369N	TBM Inc, Bakersfield/Tulare CA	63/69
				(tanker #E36)	
				Sis-Q Flying Service, Santa Rosa CA	72
				(tanker #E36; later #E27)	
			C-GLEF	Evergreen Air Service, Roxboro QUE	4.75
				Forest Protection Ltd, Fredericton NB	81/92
				(tanker #8)	
2536	TBM-3E	Bu85717		displ. on pole, NAS Memphis TN	65/73
				rep. scrapped	
2552 •	TBM-3E	Bu85733	N6824C	Wilson Aviation Industries, Lewiston ID	63
				Johnson Flying Service, Missoula MT	66/72
				(tanker #A12)	
			C-GLEK	Evergreen Air Service, Roxboro QUE	4.75
				Forest Protection Ltd, Fredericton NB	81/92
				(tanker #14)	
2613 •	TBM-3E	Bu85794	N7001C	Central Air Service, Lewistown MT	.57/77
				Gordon Plaskett, King City CA	.80
				Flytex Inc, Dallas TX	.83/84
				Fighting Air Command, Dallas TX	86/87
				Coke V. Stuart, Valdosta GA	.88/92
				(flies as "USN X2")	
2648	TBM-3	Bu85829		(to RCN as 369) BOC 19.10.50: SOC	30.1.58
			N6584D	Simsbury Flying Service, Simsbury CT	66
			CF-XON	Maritime Air Service Ltd, Moncton NB	6.69/72
				reg. cancelled	5.75
2652	TBM-3	Bu85833		(to RCN as 364) BOC 30.6.50: SOC	26.3.58
			CF-IMO	Forest Patrol Ltd, St John NB	65/70
				retired	5.71
2655	TBM-3E	Bu85836	N7014C	Johnson Flying Service, Missoula MT	63/72
				(tanker #A11)	
			C-GLEP	Evergreen Air Service, Roxboro QUE	4.75
				Forest Protection Ltd, Fredericton NB	81/84
				crashed St Croix NB	10.6.84
2663	TBM-3U	Bu85844	N106Z	U. S. Forestry Service, Davis CA	.56/59
				registration cancelled	8.59
			N3356G	Hemet Valley Flying Service, Hemet CA	63/69
				(tanker #E75) crashed and dest.	28.7.70
2673	TBM-3E	Bu85854	N7015C	Johnson Flying Service, Missoula MT	63/72
				(tanker #A7)	
			C-GLEQ	Evergreen Air Service, Roxboro QUE	4.75
				crashed	23.6.77
2680 •	TBM-3E	Bu85861		crashed in Bedford Bay, nr HMCS Shearwater	6.8.53
				recov. from sea, displ. CFB Shearwater NS	.73/91
2688 •	TBM-3E	Bu85869	N9927Z	Aircraft Specialties Inc, Mesa AZ	63/77
				(tanker #C3; #E39; #C39)	

				Globe Air Inc, Mesa AZ	4.81/84
				Justus O. Jackson, Comstock TX	86/88
			F-AZJE	Didier Chable/AMPAA, Etampes : del.	30.9.89/91
				(flies as "USN/SK-401")	
2701 •	TBM-3E	Bu85882	N9584Z	reg.	.60
				Cisco Aircraft Inc, Lancaster CA	63
				Loening Air Inc, Boise ID	66/69
				Ralph M. Ponte, Cedar Ridge CA	77
				Joseph G. Mabee, Midland TX	84/92
2702	TBM-3E	Bu85883	N6825C	Ralph M. Ponte, Visalia CA	63/66
				op. by Cal-Nat Airways, Grass Valley CA	63/67
				(tanker #E37)	
				Hemet Valley Flying Service, Hemet CA	69/72
				(tanker #E37)	
				crashed, Columbia CA	4.9.71
2705 •	TBM-3E	Bu85886	N9586Z	Cisco Aircraft Inc, Lancaster CA	63
				Loening Air Inc, Boise ID	66
				Hillcrest Aircraft, Lewiston ID	69
				G & M Investments, Lewiston ID	72
				Craig Aero Service, Buttonwillow CA	77
				Ralph M. Ponte, Grass Valley CA	.78
				Joe Dulvick	81
				Jack L. Kelley, Dallas TX	83/88
				TBF Inc, Tenafly NJ	90/92
				(flies as USN "85886/SL-401")	
2709 •	TBM-3E	Bu85890	N1952M	Georgia Forestry Commission, Macon GA	63/72
				USMC Museum, MCAS Quantico VA	74/91
				(rest. Cherry Point MCAS NC .74, del. Quantico under helicopter .76; displ. as "85890/19")	
2747	TBM-3	Bu85928		(to RCN as 338) BOC 30.6.50: SOC	6.3.58
			CF-IMW	Wheeler Airlines, St Jean QUE	65
				Wheeler Northland Airways Ltd, St Jean QUE	70
				Evergreen Air Service, Roxboro QUE	72
				crashed	10.6.75
2757 •	TBM-3E	Bu85938	N7226C	Sierra Avaition, Porterville CA	63
				(tanker #E44)	
				Wen Inc, Porterville CA	63
				Whirly Birds Inc, Porterville CA	66/69
				Capitol Aire Inc, Carson City NV	72
				Craig Aero Service, Buttonwillow CA	77
				Stewart Aviation Inc, Moses Lake WA	84/88
				Summers Farm & Ranch Inc, Sugar City ID	5.90/92
2776 •	TBM-3E	Bu85957	N9547Z	Aero Crop Service Inc, Tolleson AZ	63
				(tanker #E80)	
				Reeder Flying Service, Twin Falls ID	66/84
				(tanker #E80)	
				Gary W. Wolverton, Kimberly ID	84
				Northwest Warbirds Inc, Twin Falls ID	87/92
2802 •	TBM-3E	Bu85983		(to RCN as 374) BOC 29.5.52: SOC	26.3.58
			N4039A	Simsbury Flying Service, Simsbury CT	
				(reported at Simsbury c72)	
			CF-BEG	Miramichi Air Service	5.74/79
				Hicks & Lawrence Ltd, St Thomas ONT	
				(tanker #1/"Yogi Bear")	
			N28SF	Syracuse Flying Service, Syracuse KS	11.85/86
				Chuck Wentworth/C & C Air Corp, Rialto CA	.87/92
2839 •	TBM-3E	Bu86020		(to RCN as 327) BOC 5.10.50: SOC	22.4.58
			N7157C	Donald A. Goodman, Missoula MT	63/69
				(tanker #63)	

			C-GFPL	Evergreen Air Service, Roxboro QUE	5.76
				Forest Protection Ltd, Fredericton NB	81/92
				(tanker #22)	
2883	TBM-3E	Bu86064	N7161C	Jim Routh/Routh Aircraft, Paso Robles CA	63
				(tanker #E97; #C97)	
				Multiple Management Corp, Long Beach CA	63
				Hemet Valley Flying Service, Hemet CA	66/72
				(tanker #E97)	
			C-GFPO	Evergreen Air Service, Roxboro QUE	5.76
				Forest Protection Ltd, Fredericton NB	81
				reg. cancelled	1.85
2909	TBM-3	Bu86090	N9434Z	F. H. Haradon, Goleta CA (tanker #E52)	63
				Sonora Flying Service, Columbia CA	63
				Fire Flyers Inc, Reno NV	66
				Hemet Valley Flying Service, Hemet CA	69/72
				(tanker #E52)	
			C-GFPP	Evergreen Air Service, Roxboro QUE	5.76
				crashed	17.6.77
2910	TBM-3	Bu86091	N9307Z	Cisco Aircraft Inc, Lancaster CA	62/63
				(tanker#E82)	
				D & D Aero Spraying, Rantoul KS	66/69
			CF-AYL	Norfolk Aerial Spraying, Nixon ONT	70
				crashed	17.6.73
2917	TBM-3	Bu86098		(to RCN as 366) BOC 8.7.50: SOC	30.1.58
			CF-IMX	Wheeler Airlines, St Jean QUE	6.3.58/65
				Wheeler Northland Airways Ltd, St Jean QUE	70
				Evergreen Air Service, Roxboro QUE	72
2937	TBM-3	Bu86118	N9860C	Jim Routh/Routh Aircraft, Paso Robles CA	63
				(tanker #E95)	
				Hemet Valley Flying Service, Hemet CA	66/70
				(tanker #E95)	
				crashed near Ramona CA	4.9.70
2942 •	TBM-3	Bu86123	N6831C	Charlie T. Jensen, Sacramento CA	62/63
				(tanker #E22)	
				Charlie T. Jensen/Nevadair, Tonopah NV	63/77
				Richard J. Dieter, South Bend IN	82/83
				Tom A. Thomas, Oklahoma City OK	84
				Ada Aircraft Museum, Frederick OK	86/92
				(flies as "86123/RB-123")	
2999 •	TBM-3	Bu86180		(to RCN as 324) BOC 19.10.50: SOC	5.7.60
			CF-MUD	Skyway Air Services, Langley BC	61/65
				(tanker #12)	
				Conair Aviation Ltd, Abbotsford BC	.69/71
				(tanker #612)	
				ditched while spraying, Lake Nigault QUE	11.6.71
				Forest Protection Ltd, Fredericton NB	78/92
				(tanker #12)	
3014	TBM-3E	Bu86195	N7229C	Hemet Valley Flying Service, Hemet CA	59/71
				(tanker #E71)	
				crashed and destroyed, Lake Piru CA	30.8.71
3063	TBM-3E	Bu86244	N6826C	Sonora Flying Service, Columbia CA	63
				(tanker #C53)	
				John P. Lippott, Salmon ID	66
				Idaho Aircraft Co, Boise ID	69/72
			CF-AGN	Conair Aviation Ltd, Abbotsford BC	4.72/76
				(tanker #607)	
			C-FAGN	Forest Protection Ltd, Fredericton NB	81/84

				reg. cancelled	11.87
3099 •	TBM-3E	Bu86280	N7219C	Christopher G. Davis, Kansas City KS	63
				Thurman E. Yates, Gila NM (tanker #C50)	.63/66
				P. F. Flickinger, Bayard NM (tanker #C50)	69
				Maples Aviation Co, Vichy MO	72
			N86280	Thomas L. Wofford, Weiner AR	12.76/88
				Ronson Machine & Mfg Co., Independence MO	89/90
				displ. Combat Air Museum, Topeka KS	90
				Jim A. Cavanaugh, Dallas TX	92
3134	TBM-3	Bu53072		(to RCAF as 53072) BOC 19.8.52: SOC	5.7.60
			CF-KCH	Skyway Air Services, Langley BC	c60/65
				Conair Aviation Ltd, Abbotsford BC	.69/74
				(tanker #606)	
				crashed : struck-off reg.	24.7.74
3140	TBM-3	Bu53078		(to RCN as 420) BOC 29.5.52: SOC	14.5.58
			CF-JJC	reg.	.58
			N68683		64
				Ivan Gustin, Lewiston ID	66
				Hillcrest Aircraft Co, Lewiston ID	69
				G & M Investments, Lewiston ID	72
			CF-BEF	crashed	20.5.75
				(id. also quoted as "6125")	
3181 •	TBM-3E	Bu53119		(to RCN as 378) BOC 29.5.52: SOC	9.5.58
				Simsbury Flying Service, Simsbury CT	
			N33BM	Baron Volkmer	71/73
				Wilson C. Edwards, Big Spring TX	74/92
3201 •	TBM-3E	Bu53139		(to RCN as 361) BOC 27.9.50: SOC	30.1.58
			CF-IMN	Skyway Air Services, Langley BC	61/65
				Conair Aviation Ltd, Abbotsford BC	.69/76
				(tanker #605)	
				Forest Protection Ltd, Fredericton NB	81/92
				(tanker #5)	
3262 •	TBM-3	Bu53200		(to RCN as 377) BOC 29.5.52: SOC	17.1.58
			N9010C	Hillcrest Aircraft, Lewiston ID	63/66
				(tanker #D6)	
				Johnson Flying Service, Missoula MT	69/72
				(tanker #A13)	
			C-GLEL	Evergreen Air Service, Roxboro QUE	4.75
				Forest Protection Ltd, Fredericton NB	81/92
				(tanker #13)	
3271	TBM-3	Bu53209	N7960C	Major Oil Corp, Tucson AZ	63
				Sonora Aviation Inc, Tucson/ Carson City NV	66/69
			CF-AXS	Norfolk Aerial Spraying, Fredericton NB	6.71
				crashed nr Serogle NB	15.6.79
3291 •	TBM-3	Bu53229	N7236C	Georgia Forestry Commission, Macon GA	.63/69
				David C. Tallichet/MARC, Chino CA	87/91
				stored Tallichet compound, Chino CA	87
3303	TBM-3	Bu53241		(to RCN as 307) BOC 15.7.50: SOC	10.1.58
			CF-IMM	Skyway Air Services, Langley BC	61/65
				Conair Aviation Ltd, Abbotsford BC	.69/73
				(tanker #604)	
				crashed spraying, Sussex NB	14.5.73
3318	TBM-3	Bu53256	N9592C	Aerial Applicators ,Salt Lake City UT	63/69
				(tanker #D19)	
			CF-ZYB	Hicks & Lawrence Ltd, St Thomas ONT	6.71
				crashed	1.6.71
3369	TBM-3	Bu53307	N9078Z	Daro Inc, San Clemente CA	63/69
				(tanker #E98)	

				Sis-Q Flying Service, Santa Rosa CA	.70/72
				(tanker #E26)	
			C-GLEI	Evergreen Air Service, Roxboro QUE	4.75
				crashed	8.5.75
3381 •	TBM-3R	Bu53319	N3966A	Nevadair, Tonopah NV	58/69
				Charlie T. Jensen, Tonopah NV	72/77
				stored unconv. ("RB-319"), Sacramento CA	58/80
				Aero Union, Chico CA	.80/87
				(flown to Chico .81, stored unconv.)	
				TBM Aircraft Inc, Holmdell NJ	88/90
				Anthony Haig-Thomas, North Weald UK:	.88/91
				(shipped to UK 1.89, ff Ipswich 25.1.89)	
			G-BTDP	Anthony Haig-Thomas, Ipswich	5.2.91
3396	TBM-3	Bu53334		(to RCN as 349) BOC 17.10.50: SOC	22.4.58
			CF-KPJ		
			N68663	Klamath Aircraft Inc, Klamath Falls OR	66
				Sis-Q Flying Service, Santa Rosa CA	69/72
				(tanker #E25)	
			C-GLEG	Evergreen Air Service, Roxboro QUE	4.75
				crashed	4.7.75
3399 •	TBM-3	Bu53337		(to RCN as 390) BOC 29.5.52: SOC	10.1.58
			CF-IMI	Skyway Air Services, Langley BC	61/65
				Conair Aviation Ltd, Abbotsford BC	.69/76
				(tanker #601)	
				Forest Protection Ltd, Fredericton NB	81/92
				(tanker #1)	
3413	TBM-3	Bu53351	N7411C	Harold Parkhurst, Managua, Nicaragua	63/69
			CF-ZTA	Miramichi Air Service Ltd	6.71
				crashed	21.7.74
3415 •	TBM-3	Bu53353	N5264V	Georgia Forestry Commission, Macon GA	.63/69
				off USCR	72/78
				Harry S. Doan, Daytona Beach FL	84/88
				Wiley C. Sanders, Troy AL	89/92
				(flies as "USN WS53")	
3454	TBM-3	Bu53392		(to RCN as 306) BOC 16.6.50: SOC	5.7.60
			CF-KCK	Skyway Air Services, Langley BC	61/65
3465 •	TBM-3E	Bu53403		NAS Norfolk VA (stored)	65
				USNAM, NAS Pensacola FL	.68/91
3482 •	TBM-3	Bu53420		(to RCN as 343) BOC 19.10.50: SOC	5.7.60
			CF-KCM	Skyway Air Services, Langley BC	61/65
				Conair Aviation Ltd, Abbotsford BC	.69/76
				(tanker #616)	
			C-FKCM	Forest Protection Ltd, Fredericton NB	78/92
				(tanker #16)	
3516 •	TBM-3E	Bu53454	N7030C	Tom White/Idaho Air Tankers Inc, Boise ID	63
				(tanker #D13)	
				Reeder Flying Service, Twin Falls ID	66/84
				(tanker #13)	
				Gary Wolverton, Twin Falls ID	84
				Southeastern Aircraft Inc, Live Oak FL	86/87
				Military Aircraft Restoration Corp, Chino CA	90
				USNAM, NAS Corpus Christi TX	.87/92
				(displ. as "53454/Gipsy III", later "X-2")	
3541 •	TBM-3E	Bu53479	N9595C	reg.	.57
				Cisco Aircraft Inc, Lancaster CA	62/63
				(tanker #E67)	
				D & D Aero Spray, Rantoul KS	66/77

				sale rep.	84/90
3551 •	TBM-3	Bu53489		(to RCN as 304) BOC 28.7.50: SOC	30.1.58
			N6580D	Simsbury Flying Service, Simsbury CT	
				derelict, still in RCN scheme, Simsbury CT	72/75
				Leonard Tanner, Barre MA	88/89
				Corwin H. Meyer Aviation Assoc, Ocala FL	.89/90
				(hulk moved to FL .89 for rebuild to fly)	
3554	TBM-3	Bu53492	N9083Z	Riverside Aircraft Co, Riverside CA	62/63
				(tanker #E63)	
				Aero Union Corp, Chico CA	66/72
				(tanker #E28)	
				crashed, Chester CA	2.8.73
3565 •	TBM-3E	Bu53503		(to RCN as 315) BOC 30.6.50: SOC	1.1.58
			N6583D	Simsbury Flying Service, Simsbury CT	63/70
				Joe E. Jones/ CAF, Harlingen TX	.70/72
			N53503	Confederate Air Force, Harlingen TX	13.1.72/90
				Confederate Air Force, Grand Junction CO	90/91
				American Airpower Heritage Flying Museum,	
				Grand Junction CO (flies as USN "82")	9.91/92
3584 •	TBM-3E	Bu53522	N7410C	Stencel Aero Engineering, Ashville NC	63/72
				John J. Stokes, San Marcos TX	77/79
				Howard E. Pardue, Breckenridge TX	.79
			N88HP	Howard E. Pardue, Breckenridge TX	10.80/88
				Flying Dutchman Marine Corp, Wilmington DE	90/92
				(flies as USN "88")	
3616	TBM-3	Bu53554		(to RCAF as 53554) BOC 19.8.52: SOC	5.7.60
			CF-KCF	Skyway Air Services, Langley BC	61/65
				Conair Aviation Ltd, Abbotsford BC	.69/71
				(tanker #603)	
				crashed Winfield BC	8.8.71
3637 •	TBM-3E	Bu53575	N6447C	Sonora Av. Inc, Tucson AZ/Carson City NV	63/69
				(tanker #C47)	
				Capitol Aire Inc, Carson City NV	72
				Craig Aero Service, Buttonwillow CA	77
				Stewart Aviation Inc, Moses Lake WA	84
				Northwest Warbirds Inc, Kimberley ID	86/87
				Jack A. Erickson, Central Point OR	88/92
3654	TBM-3E	Bu53592	N5168V	Hemet Valley Flying Service, Hemet CA	63/72
				(tanker #E68)	
			C-GFPQ	Evergreen Air Service, Roxboro, QUE	6.76
				Forest Protection Ltd, Fredericton NB	81/82
				crashed near Edmunston NB	8.6.82
3655 •	TBM-3E	Bu53593	N6822C	TBM Inc, Tulare CA	.58/82
			N5567A	stored unconv. "USN/New York/141/N5567A",	
				Sequoia CA	70/82
			N6822C	USNAM, NAS Pensacola FL : del. ex Sequoia	9.82/91
				(listed under both registrations: USCR 66/84)	
3669	TBM-3	Bu53607	N8398H	Cisco Aircraft Inc, Lancaster CA	63
				Aerial Applicators , Salt Lake City UT	66/69
				(tanker #D20)	
			CF-ZYC	Hicks & Lawrence Ltd, St Thomas ONT	5.71
				crashed	20.5.75
3672 •	TBM-3E	Bu53610		(to RCN as 303) BOC 22.7.50: SOC	30.1.58
			CF-IMR	Wheeler Airlines, St Jean QUE	6.3.58/65
				Wheeler Northland Airways Ltd, St Jean QUE	70
			C-FIMR	Forest Protection Ltd, Fredericton NB	81/92
				(tanker #23)	

3694	TBM-3	Bu53632		(to RCN as 309) BOC 25.7.50: SOC	5.7.60
			CF-MXN	Skyway Air Services, Langley BC	61
				Canadian Collieries, Vancouver BC	65
				Conair Aviation Ltd, Abbotsford BC (tanker #619)	.69/73
				crashed into river, Kamloops BC	31.7.71
				crashed, while fire bombing Moyie Lake BC	18.8.73
3700 •	TBM-3	Bu53638		(to RCAF as 53638) BOC 19.8.52: SOC	5.7.60
			CF-KCL	Skyway Air Services, Langley BC	61/65
				Conair Aviation Ltd, Abbotsford BC (tanker #609)	.69/76
				crashed, Oromcoto Lake NB	29.5.78
				Allan Rubin/International Vintage Aircraft, Hamilton ONT	86/92
				(under rest. to fly, Markham ONT)	
3759	TBM-3E	Bu53697		(to RCAF as 53697) BOC 25.7.52: SOC	5.7.60
			N9711Z	Sierra Aviation, Porterville CA (tanker #E46)	.62/63
				Wen Inc, Porterville CA (tanker #E46)	63
				P & B Aviation, Red Bluff CA	66
				Sis-Q Flying Service, Montague CA (tanker #33)	69
			C-GLEH	Evergreen Air Service, Roxboro QUE	4.75
				Forest Protection Ltd, Fredericton NB (tanker #11)	81/86
				crashed landing, Brockway NB	18.5.84
3788 •	TBM-3E	Bu53726	N7076C	Marsh Aviation Co, Litchfield Park AZ	63
				Reeder Flying Service, Twin Falls ID (tanker #56)	66/84
				Gary Wolverton, Twin Falls ID	84
				Northwest Warbirds Inc, Twin Falls ID	87/88
				USMC Museum, MCAS El Toro CA	88/91
3789	TBM-3	Bu53727	N9082Z	Hemet Valley Flying Service, Hemet CA (tanker #E73)	63/72
				crashed firebombing, Bear Mountain CA	28.7.70
3794	TBM-3	Bu53732		(to RCN as 316) BOC 8.6.50: SOC	5.7.60
			CF-KCN	Skyway Air Services, Langley BC	61/65
				Conair Aviation Ltd, Abbotsford BC (tanker #617)	.69/72
				crashed Angus Home Lake BC	27.8.72
3822	TBM-3E	Bu53760		(to RCN as 392) BOC 16.6.52: SOC	30.1.58
			N6581D	Simsbury Flying Service, Simsbury CT	63/77
				Richard Foote/Professional Aircraft Sales Co, Willimantic CT & New Smyrna Beach FL	84/88
				crashed and dest., nr Danielson CT	6.88
3830 •	TBM-3U	Bu53768	N103Z	U. S. Forestry Service, Davis CA	.56/62
			N10361	Seeley Flying Service, Newcastle WY (tanker #B18)	66/69
				Air Tankers Inc, Casper WY	71
			C-GLDX	Norfolk Aerial Spraying, Fredericton NB	5.75
			N683G	Odegaard Aviation, Kindred ND (flies as "53768/63")	9.85/92
3837	TBM-3E	Bu53775		(to RCAF as 53775)	
			N7028C	Hillcrest Aircraft Co, Lewiston ID (tanker #D7)	63/72
			CF-ZTR	reg.	.71
3846	TBM-3	Bu53784	N9590C	Dennis G. Smilanich/Idaho Aircraft, Boise ID	63/72

				(tanker #D1)	
			CF-AGL	Conair Aviation Ltd, Abbotsford BC	72
				(not put into service by Conair)	
3847 •	TBM-3E	Bu53785	N7075C	Marsh Aviation Co, Litchfield Park AZ	63
				Reeder Flying Service, Twin Falls ID	66/77
				(tanker #55)	
				Dwight Reimer, Shafter CA	79/80
				(flew as "My Assam Dragon")	
				Gordon Plaskett, King City CA	82
				(remained in USA)	
				Planes of Fame East, Spring Park MN	83/92
				(flies in RN/FAA scheme as "JR456/RP")	
3849 •	TBM-3E	Bu53787	N3969A	Edgar L. Thorsrud, Missoula MT	63/72
				Johnson Flying Service, Missoula MT	72
				(tanker #A21)	
			C-GFPT	Evergreen Air Service, Roxboro QUE	5.76
				Forest Protection Ltd, Fredericton NB	81/92
				(tanker #10)	
3866 •	TBM-3E	Bu53804		(to RCAF as 53804) BOC 19.8.52: SOC	5.7.60
			N9710Z	Columbia Flying Service, Hollister CA	63
				(tanker #E79)	
				George C. Abell, Topanga CA (tanker #E79) 66/69	
				Military Aircraft Restoration Corp, Chino CA	.72/90
				displ. NAS Corpus Christi TX as "53804/X2"	90
3880 •	TBM-3E	Bu53818		(to RCN as 386) BOC 16.6.52: SOC	10.1.58
			N9187Z	Columbia Flying Service, Hollister CA	63
				(tanker #E89)	
				Ewing Aviation Co, Sepulveda CA	63
				George C. Abell, Topanga CA	66/69
				Ralph M. Ponte, Grass Valley CA	75
				Leo Conavan, Fort Worth TX	77
			N93818	Leo Conavan, Fort Worth TX	4.79
				Wilbert R. Porter, Sacramento CA	84/92
				(flies as USN "17")	
3890 •	TBM-3	Bu53828		(to RCN as 388) BOC 16.6.52: SOC	17.1.58
			N9014C	Vincent S. Buraas, Northwood ND	63/69
				derelict hulk, Northwood ID	74
				Minnesota Air & Space Museum, St Paul MN	87
			N28FB	Edwin E. Forsberg, Wilmington CA	1.89/92
3891 •	TBM-3E	Bu53829	N9591C	Pete Fountain, Moscow ID	63
				Sonora Aviation, Carson City NV	66/69
				(tanker #55)	
			CF-AYG	Norfolk Aerial Spraying, Fredericton NB	7.71
			N293E	Odegaard Aviation, Kindred ND	9.85/88
				Tri State Aviation Inc, Wahpeton ND	90/92
3897 •	TBM-3	Bu53835	N3967A	Nevadair, Tonopah NV	63/69
	TBM-3U			Charlie T. Jensen, Tonopah NV	72
				Maynard Lund, Ritzville WA	.78
				Skarda Flying Service, Hazen AR	84/92
				(flies as "53835/GS-41")	
3904 •	TBM-3E	Bu53842	N7025C	Chris D. Stoltzfus & Assoc, Coatesville PA	63
			N603	New York Conservation Dept, Albany NY	66/72
			N60393	State of New York, Albany NY	75/87
				Patriots Point Naval & Maritime Museum,	
				Mt Pleasant SC	87/91
				(displ. on USS Yorktown as "USN X-2")	
3919 •	TBM-3E	Bu53857	N7017C	Central Air Service, Lewistown MT	63/72
			C-GFPM	Evergreen Air Services, Roxboro QUE	5.76
				Forest Protection Ltd, Fredericton NB	81/92
				(tanker #21)	

3920 •	TBM-3E	Bu53858	N3357G	Hemet Valley Flying Service, Hemet CA	63/72
				(tanker #E72)	
			C-GFPR	Evergreen Air Service, Roxboro QUE	5.76
				Forest Protection Ltd, Fredericton NB	81/92
				(tanker #4)	
3976 •	TBM-3E	Bu53914	N7029C	John E. Orahood, Rocky Ford CO	63
				Aerial Applicators, Salt Lake City UT	66/72
				(tanker #D16)	
			CF-BQS	Hicks & Lawrence Ltd, St. Thomas ONT	.72
				crashed, Maine : abandoned at site	19.5.72
				Rhode Island Aviation Heritage Assn., RI	.90/92
				(recov. to NAS Quonset Point RI by helicopter 11.91, planned rest. to fly)	
				(note: c/n also quoted as 6961)	
4015 •	TBM-3E	Bu91110	N6827C	TBM Inc, Tulare CA (tanker #E58)	63/72
				Hillcrest Aircraft, Lewiston ID	77
				Paramount Leasing Corp, Bakersfield CA	84
				Gro Pro Corp, Oklahoma City OK	86/88
				Merlin Aire Ltd, King City CA	88/92
				op: Old Flying Machine Co, Duxford	.88/92
				(shipped to UK, arr. 12.5.88; flies as "USN/X-2")	
4064	TBM-3	Bu91159	N3249G	Johnson Flying Service, Missoula MT	63/69
				(tanker #A14)	
			C-GLEN	Evergreen Air Service, Roxboro QUE	4.75
4076	TBM-3U	Bu91171	N107Z	U. S. Forestry Service, Davis CA	.56/59
			N7858C		8.59
				Parsons Airpark Inc, Carpinteria CA	63
				T. A. Underwood, Buckeye AZ	64
				Aerial Applicators , Salt Lake City UT	66/72
				(tanker #D17)	
			CF-BQT	Ag Air Inc, Dawson Creek BC	5.72
4093 •	TBM-3U	Bu91188	N108Z	U. S. Forestry Service, Davis CA	.56/63
				(tanker #08)	
			N108Q	Georgia Forestry Commission, Macon GA	66/69
				(tanker #2)	
				Dale F. Carter, Elsa TX	72
				George W. Clapp, Allegany NY	84
				Lance Aircraft Supply Inc, Dallas TX	86/88
				Georgia Historical Aviation Museum, Stone Mountain GA (displ. in USN sc.)	89/91
4100 •	TBM-3R	Bu91195		(to JMSDF as 23...)	
				rep. Tateyama, Japan	c80/91
4169 •	TBM-3E	Bu91264	N7835C	The Air Museum, Claremont CA	.58/69
				later Ontario CA: static displ., derelict by	73
				Planes of Fame Inc, Chino CA	77/92
				(rest. Chino CA, flies as "USN Bu7154")	
				(FAA quotes id. as 7154)	
4194 •	TBM-3	Bu91289	N7833C	Hemet Valley Flying Service, Hemet CA	60/72
				(tanker #E56, #E74)	
			C-GFPN	Evergreen Air Service, Roxboro QUE	5.76
				Forest Protection Ltd, Fredericton NB	81/92
				(tanker #17)	
4293 •	TBM-3E	Bu91388	N9564Z	Cisco Aircraft Inc, Lancaster CA	63
				Aircraft Specialties Inc, Mesa AZ	.63
				(tanker #C34)	
				Desert Aviation Service, Phoenix AZ	66
				Ontario Flight Service, Ontario OR	69

				crashed nr John Day OR: wreck abandoned	c71
				derelict hulk , Ironside OR	73/78
				Ralph M. Ponte, Grass Valley CA	12.83/88
				Taylor Energy Co, New Orleans LA	90/92
4331 •	TBM-3E	Bu91426		(to RCAF as 91426) BOC 19.8.52: SOC	5.7.60
			CF-MUE	Skyway Air Services, Langley BC	61/65
				Conair Aviation Ltd, Abbotsford BC (tanker #618)	.69/70
				Forest Protection Ltd, Fredericton NB (tanker #618)	78/92
4341	TBM-3	Bu91436	N9569Z	Cisco Aircraft Inc, Lancaster CA	63
				Desert Aviation Service, Phoenix AZ	66/69
				Aircraft Specialties Inc, Mesa AZ : hulk	81
				stored dism. Kissimmee FL, pending rest.	90
4355 •	TBM-3	Bu91450	N7239C	Riverside Aircraft Co, Riverside CA	63
				Aero Union Corp, Chico CA	66/69
				David C. Tallichet/Yesterdays Air Force, Chino CA	.72
			C-GCWG	Canadian Warplane Heritage, Mount Hope ONT (flies as "RCN 91450/VG-ABG") (FAA & DoT quote id. as 7340)	6.78/91
4358 •	TBM-3E	Bu91453	N4170A	Reeder Flying Service, Twin Falls ID (tanker #D10; later #10)	63/77
				Gary M. Wolverton, Kimberly ID	84
				James R. Williams, O'Brien OR/Berkeley CA (flies as "Marines/91453/15")	86/92
4379	TBM-3	Bu91474	N9926Z	Aircraft Specialties Inc, Mesa AZ (tanker #E38)	63/69
4426 •	TBM-3E	Bu91521	N4171A	Reeder Flying Service, Twin Falls ID (tanker #D11; later #11)	63/72
				Louis Deterding, Havre MT	77
				Donald J. von Siegel, Parkin AR	84/87
				Corwin H. Meyer Aviation Assoc., Ocala FL	88/92
				rep. dest. by fire: only wings saved	.89
4470	TBM-3	Bu91565	N4168A	Reeder Flying Service, Twin Falls ID (tanker #D8; later #8)	63/72
4491 •	TBM-3E	Bu91586	N9433Z	reg.	.57
				Sonora Flying Service, Columbia CA (tanker #C56)	63
				Sonora Aviation Inc, Tucson/Carson City NV	66/69
				Capitol Aire Inc, Carson City NV (tanker #56)	72
				Craig Aero Service, Buttonwillow CA	77
				Stewart Aviation, Moses Lake WA	84
				Northwest Warbirds Inc, Kimberly ID	86
				Friends for Long Is. Heritage, Muttontown NY (static rest. by Grumman, Bethpage NY 88/90)	87/92
				Cradle of Aviation Museum, Garden City NY (displ. as VMTB-624 "113")	91
4503 •	TBM-3E	Bu91598	N9548Z	Rector Air Service, Pacific Palisades CA (tanker #E76)	62/66
				Hemet Valley Flying Service, Hemet CA (tanker #E76)	69
				crashed Tuolomne CA	18.8.73
				stored damaged, Stockton CA	74
				Ralph M. Ponte, Cedar Ridge CA, rebuilt	.76/84
				Weeks Air Museum, Tamiami FL (flies as USN "X-2")	5.84/92
4542	TBM-3	Bu91637	N10164	Chris D. Stoltzfus & Assoc, Coatesville PA	59/69

				sale rep., USCR	72/92
4619 •	TBM-3E	Bu91714	N9429Z	Reeder Flying Service, Twin Falls ID	62/84
				(tanker #E51, later #D12 ,#57,#12)	
				Charles T. Reeder, Twin Falls ID	88/91
				Jack S. Miller, Buchanan TN	92
4631 •	TBM-3E	Bu91726	N5260V	reg.	.58
				Riverside Aircraft Co, Riverside CA	62/63
				(tanker #E65)	
				Aero Union Corp, Chico CA	66/69
				Capitol Aire Inc, Carson City NV	72
				Bernard Hinman, Liberal KS	77
				Henry Oliver III, Santa Fe NM	84/86
				Ridge Grande Contract Furnishing,	
				Albuquerque NM	87/88
				Evergreen Ventures Inc, McMinnville OR	89/92
				(flies as "USN 91726/32NE")	
4638 •	TBM-3E	Bu91733	N9590Z	Cisco Aircraft Inc, Lancaster CA	62/63
				(tanker #E81)	
				Aircraft Specialties Inc, Mesa AZ	66/77
				(tanker #C25)	
				Globe Air, Mesa AZ	4.81/84
				Collings Foundation, Stowe MA	87/92
				(stored, then rest. to fly, Kissimmee FL 88/91)	
4646 •	TBM-3U	Bu91741	N6829C	TBM Inc, Tulare CA	63
				Ag Air International, Dos Palos CA	66/69
				Marom Ltd, Herzelia, Israel	12.64
				(del. via Prestwick UK 15.12.64)	
				derelict, Herzelia, Israel	74
				Israeli AF Museum, Hazerim AB : stored	89/91
- •	TBM-3E	-	N4169A	Reeder Flying Service, Twin Falls ID	63/77
				(tanker # 63; later #9)	
				Gary M. Wolverton, Kimberly ID	84/92
				(id. quoted as 5653)	
- •	TBM-3E	-	N4172A	Aerial Applicators, Salt Lake City UT	63/72
				(tanker #D18)	
				Louis Deterding, Havre MT	77
				stored derelict, Salt Lake City UT	77
				Tom Reilly Vintage Aircraft, Kissimmee FL	84/92
				(stored dism., Kissimmee FL)	
				(id. quoted as 6810)	
-	TBM-3	-	N4173A	Hillcrest Aircraft Co, Lewiston ID	63/72
				(id. quoted as 5708)	
-	TBM-1C	-	N5635N	Idaho Aircraft Co, Boise ID	63/69
				(tanker #D3) : reg. pending	72
				(id. quoted as "A20260")	
- •	TBM-3S2	-		(to JMSDF as 2344)	
				Kure AB, Hiroshima, Japan: rep. preserved	72
- •	TBM-3S2	-		(to JMSDF as 2347)	
				Shimofusa AB, Japan : rep. preserved	72
- •	TBF-1	-		recov. from Lake Michigan	c77
				Indiana Museum of Military History,	
				Indianapolis IN	88/90

HANDLEY PAGE HALIFAX

- •	Mk. II	W1048	crashed Lake Hoklingen, Norway	28.4.42
			(lost during attack on "Tirpitz")	
			recov. from lake by RAF Museum team	6.73
			RAF Museum, Hendon	83/92
			(remains displ. as recov., "W1048/TL-S")	
- •	Mk. II	HR792	crashed takeoff, Stornoway	13.1.45
			(fuse. to farm, Isle of Lewis, as chicken coop)	
			Yorkshire Air Museum, Elvington, Yorks	5.84/91
			fuselage recov. from farm, Isle of Lewis	5.84
			(rebuild with parts LW687 & JP158, using mainplane from Hastings TG556)	
-	Mk. VII	PN323	Handley Page Aircraft, Radlett	50/60
			(ground inst. airframe for radio trials)	
			scrapped, Radlett	.61
			nose section to Graham Trant	.62
			Peter Thomas/Skyfame Museum, Staverton	66
			Imperial War Museum, Duxford : nose	87
			Imperial War Museum, London : nose only	90

HANDLEY PAGE HAMPDEN

EEP/ 22522 •	Mk. I	P1344	forced landing Petsamo, Finland	4.9.42
			recov. ex USSR by Jeet Mahal, Canada	.90
			hulk shipped to UK, arr.	4.9.91
			(static rest. project)	
FAL/ • CA/80	Mk. I	P5436	(to RCAF as P5436) BOC	6.1.42
			ditched, Patricia Bay, Vancouver Island BC	15.11.42
			Canadian Museum of Flight & Transportation, Vancouver BC: recov.from 600 ft. depth	.85/92
			(static rest., using parts recov. from AN132 & AN136 at BC crash sites: almost complete by 92)	
- •	Mk. I	AE436	recov. from Tsatsa Mountains, Sweden	.76
			RAF Museum Store, RAF Henlow	.76/87
			Brian Nicholls/Lincolnshire Aviation Heritage Centre, East Kirkby: rest. project	.87

W/0 5422 •	Mk. I	L1592		RAF Air Historical Branch, Stanmore	54
				Science Museum, London	62/87
- •	Mk. I	N2394		(to Finnish AF as HU-452, later HC-452)	
				Aviation Museum of Central Finland, Luonetjarvi AB,Tikkakoski	72/85
- •	Mk. I	P2617		RAF Kenley, for movie "Reach For The Sky"	.55
				RAF Air Historical Branch, Stanmore	.55
				RAF Rufforth : stored,	58
				RAF Bicester	65/71
				RAF Museum, Hendon	11.72/92
				(displ. as "P2617/AF-F")	
- •	Mk. I	P3175		RAF Museum, Hendon	79/92
				(displ. as remains only)	
- •	Mk. I	V6846		(to Indian AF as V6846)	6.44
				displ.derelict Patna AB, India	66/73
CCF/41H 4013 •	Sea Hurr. Mk. 1b	Z7015		Loughborough Training College (inst. airframe)	46/61
				Shuttleworth Trust, Old Warden, Beds	.61/83
				(taxy scenes in movie "Battle of Britain" .68)	
			G-BKTH	Shuttleworth Trust/IWM, Duxford	24.5.83
				(under rest. Duxford)	92
CCF/ R30019 •	Sea Hurr. Mk. XIIA	BW853		(to RCAF as BW853)	
				AJD Engineering, Suffolk UK	88
			G-BRKE	AJD Engineering, Milden UK (rest. project)	6.10.89
CCF/ R30028 •	Sea Hurr. Mk. XIIA	BW862		(to RCAF as BW862) BOC	30.12.41
				crashed forced ldg., Lac St. Jean QUE	6.7.44
				Tex LaVallee/LaVallee Cultural & Aeronautical Collection, St Chrysostome QUE	80
				(incomplete hulk recov. ex junkyard QUE)	
				Ed Zalesky/Canadian Museum of Flight & Transportation, Vancouver BC	.80/91
- •	Sea Hurr. Mk. XIIA	BW873		(to RCAF as BW873)	
				Jack Arnold Aviation Museum, Brantford ONT	88
CCF/ R32007 •	Sea Hurr. Mk. XIIA	BW881		(to RCAF as BW881)	
				Jack Arnold, Brantford ONT: recov. ex farm	
				Matt Sattler, Carp ONT	88
				A. J. Ditheridge, Suffolk UK	12.88/89
- •	Mk.IV	KX829		Loughborough Training College (inst. airframe)	.45/61
				Birmingham Museum of Science & Industry	.62/89
- •	Mk. IV	KZ191	-	(to IDFAF as ....)	
				Robs Lamplough, Duxford UK	.83/89
				(hulk recov. from kibbutz, Israel)	
				(rest. project, stored North Weald 89/92)	
- •	Mk. IV	KZ321		(to Yugoslav AF as ....)	
				(to IDFAF as ....)	
				Warbirds of GB Ltd, Blackbushe	83/89
				(hulk recov. from kibbutz, Jaffa, Israel)	
			G-HURY	Warbirds of GB, Biggin Hill	31.3.89/91
				(rest. project, stored Biggin Hill 89)	
				The Fighter Collection, Duxford	.91
				(rebuild to fly, Duxford)	
- •	Mk. IIc	LD619		(to SAAF as 5285)	
				S. African National War Museum, Saxonwold	60/89

41H	Mk. IV	LD975		(to Yugoslav AF as 9539)	
368368 •				Yugoslavian Aviation Museum, Belgrade	79/92
				(displ. as "LD975")	
- •	Mk. IIc	LF345		(to RBAF as ML-B)	
				Musee Royal de l'Armee, Brussels, Belgium	70/91
				(displ. as "LF658/ZA-P")	
41H	Mk. IIc	LF363		RAF Air Historical Branch, Stanmore	54
469290 •				RAF Kenley: for movie "Reach for the Sky"	.55
				RAF Battle of Britain Memorial Flight	6.57/91
				(flew in movie "Battle of Britain" .68)	
				forced landing, burned, RAF Wittering	11.9.91
				(flew as "LF363/GN-A")	
				To be rebuilt for flight	10.92
- •	Mk. IIc	LF686		RAF Bridgenorth	62
				RAF Museum, RAF Colerne	65/70
				NASM Silver Hill MD	74/92
- •	Mk. IIc	LF738		RAF Biggin Hill, Memorial Chapel	58/84
				(stored Rochester, pending rest. by RAeS 85/92)	
- •	Mk. IIc	LF751		RAF Waterbeach	
				RAF Bently Priory	54/85
				(static rest. by RAeS, Rochester 3.85/88)	
				RAF Manston : displ. as "BN230/FT-A"	4.88/92
- •	Mk. IIc	PZ865		last Hurricane built : ff. Langley	27.7.44
				Hawker Aircraft Ltd, Langley: trials use	8.44/50
			G-AMAU	Hawker Aircraft Ltd, Dunsfold	1.5.50/72
				(flew in movie "Battle of Britain" .68)	
				RAF Battle of Britain Flight	29.3.72/91
				(flies as "PZ865/RF-U/ Last Of The Many")	
42012 •	Mk. XII	RCAF5377		Jim Roy, Portage la Prairie (derelict on farm)	46/64
				Robert E. Diemert, Carman, MAN	.64
			CF-SMI	Robert E. Diemert, Carman, MAN	.66
				(rebuilt, flew as "RCAF 5585")	
			G-AWLW	Spitfire Productions Ltd, Elstree	10.7.68
				(flew in movie "Battle of Britain" .68)	
				N. A. W. Samuelson, Elstree	.68/69
				Sir W. J. D. Roberts, Shoreham	12.69
				Sir William Roberts/Strathallan Collection,	
				Auchterader, Scotland	3.72/84
				(flew as "P3308/UP-A")	
			C-GCWH	Canadian Warplane Heritage, Hamilton ONT	5.84/91
				(del. to Hamilton by RCAF C-130: ff 4.6.84)	
				(flies as "P3069/YO-A")	
42015 •	Mk. XII	RCAF5380		rep. under rest., Ontario, Canada	88
42024 •	Mk. XII	RCAF5389		Centennial Planetarium, Calgary ALTA	c73
				Aero Space Museum of Calgary ALTA	88
				Calgary International Airport Museum ALTA	91/92
				(displ. during static rest.)	
42025 •	Mk. XII	RCAF5390		Bob Schneider/RRS Aviation, Hawkins TX	88
				USAFM, Wright Patterson AFB OH : arr.	9.90
				(static rest., displ. as RAF "Z3174")	
- •	Mk. XII	RCAF5400		Don Bradshaw, Saskatoon	85
				Kermit A. Weeks/Weeks Air Museum,	
				Tamiami FL (rest. project)	.85/89
- •	Mk. XII	RCAF5409		Neil M. Rose, Vancouver WA	89
44013 •	Mk. IIb	RCAF5418		Reynolds Pioneer Museum, Wetaskiwin ALTA c73/86	

				Reynolds Aviation Museum,Wetaskiwin ALTA (rest., engine runs 12.88 as "RCAF 5418")	87/89
44019	Mk. IIb	RCAF5424		Centennial Planetarium, Calgary ALTA loaned out for rest., Regina SASK incorporated into another rebuild project	70 .70/82 87
46002 •	Mk. XII	RCAF5447		Harry Whereatt, Assiniboia SASK	88/89
-	Mk. XII	RCAF5455		derelict on farm Stewart Valley, SASK Harry Whereatt, Assiniboia SASK	 72
- •	Mk. XII	RCAF5461		Commonwealth Air Training Plan Museum, Brandon MAN	 88/89
60372 •	Mk. IIb	RCAF5481	 G-ORGI N678DP	Jack Arnold Aviation Museum, Brantford ONT Charles Church (Spitfires) Ltd, Sandown UK arr. crated ex Davidstown, Canada Charles Church Displays Ltd, Micheldever Dick Melton Aviation, Micheldever (rebuilt Micheldever, ff 8.9.91) David G. Price/Museum of Flying, Santa Monica CA: shipped to Chino CA, arr. (ff Chino CA 17.4.92 as "US-X")	84 .86/89 6.86 20.11.89 90/91 1.3.92
52019 •	Mk. XII	RCAF5584		National Aviation Museum, Rockcliffe ONT (displ. as "5584/A")	.64/90
52024 •	Mk. XII	RCAF5589	 G-HURR	Harry Whereatt, Assiniboia SASK (recov. ex farm, Saskatoon SASK) Brian Angliss/Autokraft Ltd, Brooklands Brian Angliss/Autokraft Ltd, Brooklands (rebuild Brooklands, due to fly .93 as "BE417")	 88/90 30.7.90/92
52025 •	Mk. XII	RCAF5590		rest. project, Ontario, Canada	89
- •	Mk. XII	RCAF5627		rest. project, Ontario, Canada	89
56021 •	Mk. IIb	RCAF5666		crashed, forced ldg. Moosehead Lake ME Tex LaVallee/LaVallee Cultural & Aeronautical Collection, St Chrysostome QUE (incomplete hulk recov. ex scrapyard QUE) Canadian Museum of Flight & Transportation, Vancouver BC	29.10.44 80 .80/91
56022 •	Mk. IIb	RCAF5667	N2549	Neil M. Rose, Vancouver WA (rest. complete, due to fly .93)	65/92
72036 •	Mk. XIIa	RCAF5711	 G-HURI	Centennial Planetarium, Calgary ALTA B. J. S. Grey, Duxford : shipped ex Canada The Fighter Collection, Duxford (rebuilt Coventry, Coningsby & Duxford, ff Duxford 1.9.89 as "Z7381/XR-T")	 12.82 9.6.83/92
- •	Mk. I	-		Composite airframe Anthony L. Dyer UK Static rebuild using parts from several aircraft	 88/92
- •	Mk. XII	-		The Kap Aeronautical Collection, Kapuskasing ONT	 88
- •	Mk. XII	-		The Kap Aeronautical Collection, Kapuskasing ONT	 88
- •	Mk. IIB	-		Duane Egli, Fabens TX	72

Continued on Page 175

U.S. AIR FORCE

XR
T

Continued from Page 172

Hawker Hurricane

					(recov. swamp near Gander, trucked TX .72)	
					Len Tanner, New Baintree CT : rest. to fly	88/91
					Lone Star Flight Museum, Galveston TX	8.91/92
					(rest. Fort Collins CO,)	
					id. quoted as "CCF-96")	
-	•	Mk. IIB	-		(to Indian AF as ....)	
					Indian AF Museum, Palam AB, New Dehli	75/91
					(displ. as "AP832")	
-	•	Mk.IIB			(to Soviet AF as.......)	
					Recovered from Russia for Fighter Collection, Duxford	6.92
-	•	Mk.IIB			(to Soviet AF as.......)	
					Recovered from Russia for Fighter Collection, Duxford	6.92
					trade to Imperial War Museum	8.92
-	•	Mk. XII	-		(to RCAF as ....)	
					Bob Schneider/RRS Aviation, Hawkins TX	89
					(Five derelict airframes recov. ex farms, Canada)	
-	•	Mk.II	-		(to Soviet AF as ......)	
					recov. ex crash site near Revda USSR	c80
					displ. on plinth, Revda USSR: dedicated	3.9.89 -
-	•	Mk.II	-		(to Soviet AF as ......)	
					recov. ex crash site Russia	
					rep. to Californian dealer: stored Moscow	91

HAWKER TEMPEST

-	•	Mk. II	LA607		College of Aeronautics, Cranfield	55/63
					Skyfame Museum, Staverton & Duxford	67/83
					Kermit A. Weeks, Tamiami FL	14.4.83
				N607LA	Weeks Air Museum, Tamiami FL	11.83/92
-	•	Mk. II	MW376		(to Indian AF as HA564)	.47
					recov. by Warbirds of GB Ltd, Blackbushe	.79
					Tangmere Flight, Tangmere, Sussex, UK	.80
					C. P. Horsley	.88
					Windmill Aviation, Spannhoe (rest. to fly)	90
				G-BSHW	Badsaddle Stables Ltd, Spanhoe	21.3.91
1181	•	Mk. II	MW401		(to Indian AF as HA604)	.47
					recov. by Warbirds of GB Ltd, Blackbushe	.79
					E. Nick Grace/Tangmere Flight	.80
					Brian Angliss/Autokraft Ltd, Brooklands	.88
				G-PEST	Autokraft Limited, Brooklands	9.10.89/92
					(rest. to fly, Brooklands)	
-	•	Mk. II	MW404		(to Indian AF as HA557)	.47
					recov. by Warbirds of GB Ltd, Blackbushe	.79
					Tangmere Flight, Sussex, UK	.80
					C. P. Horsley	.88
-	•	Mk. II	MW741		(to Indian AF as HA622)	.47
					rep. still stored in India	88
-	•	Mk. II	MW758		(to Indian AF as HA580)	.47
					airfield decoy, Poona AB, India	69
					recov. by Warbirds of GB Ltd, Blackbushe	.79
					Tangmere Flight, Sussex, UK	80
420	•	Mk. II	MW763		(to Indian AF as HA586)	.47
					recov. by Warbirds of GB Ltd, Blackbushe	.79
					E. Nick Grace/Tangmere Flight	.80

			G-TEMT	Brian Angliss/Autokraft Ltd, Brooklands Autokraft Ltd, Brooklands (rest. to fly, Brooklands)	88 9.10.89/92
- •	Mk. II	MW810		(to Indian AF as HA591) recov. by Warbirds of GB Ltd, Blackbushe E. Nick Grace/Tangmere Flight New England Air Museum, Windsor Locks CT sold	.47 .79 c79 1.7.86/90 .90
- •	Mk. II	MW848		(to Indian AF as HA623) IAF Museum, Palam AB, New Dehli	.48 69/91
- •	Mk. V	NV778		RAF Proof & Experimental Establishment, Shroeburyness, Essex RAF Middleton St. George (displ. as "SN219") RAF Museum, RAF Cosford RAF Museum, Hendon RAF Museum Store, RAF Cardington	 58 61/62 67 .72/91 11.91/92
- •	Mk. II	PR538		(to Indian AF as HA457) airfield decoy, Poona AB, India recov. by Warbirds of GB Ltd, Blackbushe E. Nick Grace/Tangmere Flight RAF Museum Store, Cardington (static rest. Duxford for RAF Museum 90/91) RAF Museum, Hendon : arr. (also quoted as PR536, displ. as "PR536/OQ-H")	 69 .79 87 .87 10.11.91
- •	Mk. V	EJ693		Technical High School, Delft, Netherlands RAF Museum Store Nick Grace/Tangmere Flight Weeks Air Museum (composite)	63 68/88 89/92 9.92

HAWKER TYPHOON

- •	Mk. IB	MN235	(to USAF for eval., Wright Field as T2-491) Smithsonian Institute (stored) loan: Museum of Science & Industry, Chicago RAF Museum, Hendon	.44 65 4.68/92
- •	Mk. IB	-	Friends of Biggin Hill, Biggin Hill UK (rest. project)	87
- •		-	Phil Earthy/Classic Warbirds, Norfolk UK (rest. project, using components ex scrapyard)	91

-	FB Mk.11	TF956		Hawker-Siddeley Aircraft Ltd, Langley	.63/71
				FAA Historic Flight, RNAS Yeovilton	.71/89
				(ff Yeovilton 21.1.72: flew as "TF956/123/T")	
				cr. into sea off Prestwick, Scotland	10.6.89
41H/	FB Mk.11	TG114		(to RCN as TG114) BOC	5.47
609972 •			CF-OYF	Brian Baird, Toronto ONT	c11.62
			N54M	J. W. Fornof, Houma LA	66/69
				crashed Houma LA, stored dam. Mesa AZ	c67
				(rebuild Phoenix AZ using parts VR918 & VR919)	
			N232J	Frank C. Sanders, Chino CA	71/76
				(conv. 2 seater, flew as "N232/232/0")	
				Lloyd A. Hamilton, Santa Rosa CA	80
				William E. Sims, Charleston IL	.82/87
				Ronald M. Runyan, Springdale OH	5.88/92
				Robert J. Lamplough, North Weald UK: leased	.88/92
				(del. by air: arr North Weald 24.4.90)	
41H/	FB Mk.11	TG119		(to RCN as TG119) BOC	24.5.48
609977 •				Bancroft Industries	63
				Canadian National Aeronautical Collection	.63
				National Aviation Museum, Rockcliffe ONT	.63/91
				(displ. as "TG119/110")	
- •	FB Mk.11	VR930		RAF Museum, RAF Colerne	65/75
				FAA Museum, RNAS Wroughton & Yeovilton	.75/92
- •	FB Mk.11	VW232		(to RAN as VW232) BOC	5.49
				Museum of Applied Sciences, Sydney NSW	3.59/74
				(stored, Sydney Technical College, Ultimo NSW,	
				painted as "RAN VX730")	
				Camden Museum of Aviation NSW : loan	11.74
				Australian War Memorial, Canberra ACT	82/87
				Naval Aviation Museum, Nowra NAS, NSW	.87/91
				(displ. as "RAN VX730")	
- •	FB Mk.11	VW623		(to RAN as VW623) BOC	5.49
				Nowra NAS, NSW : displ. "102/K"	65/72
				Naval Aviation Museum, Nowra NAS, NSW	12.74/91
				(under rest. to fly Nowra, "102/K")	
- •	FB Mk.11	VW647		(to RAN as VW647) BOC 3.49 SOC	15.11.59
				Experimental Building Station, Ryde, Sydney	11.59/69
				(wind machine to test building materials)	
				Ed Fleming/Skyservice Aviation, Camden NSW	.69
				Camden Museum of Aviation, Camden later	
				Narellan NSW	10.69/92
				(rest. as "VW647/127K", first engine runs 10.76)	
ES.3615 •	T Mk.20S	VX281		Hawker-Siddeley Aircraft Ltd, Langley	.57
			D-CACO	Deutsche Luftfahrt-Beratungsdienst, Bonn	10.6.63/74
			G-BCOW	Warbirds of GB Ltd : del.	11.10.74
				Spencer Flack, Elstree	.77/80
			N8476W	Dale Clarke, Gardena CA	7.80/84
				(race #40/Nuthin Special")	
				Liberty Aero Corp, Gardena CA	6.84/88
			N281L	Liberty Aero Corp, Santa Monica CA	3.88/92
				(flies as RN "281/Dragon of Cymru")	
ES.8502 •	T Mk.20S	VX300		Hawker-Siddeley Aircraft Ltd, Langley	.57
			D-FAMI	Deutsche Luftfahrt-Beratungsdienst : del	29.8.58
			D-CAMI	Deutsche Luftfahrt-Beratungsdienst, Bonn	4.59/74
			G-BCKH	Warbirds of GB Ltd ; del.	9.8.74
			N62147	John J. Stokes, San Marcos TX	9.74
				(del. to USA, via Prestwick 20.10.74)	
			N924G	Sanders Aircraft, Chino CA	78/92

				(race #88; flies as "Royal Navy 924")	
ES.3613 •	T Mk.20S	VX302		Hawker-Siddeley Aircraft Ltd, Langley	.57
			D-CACE	Deutsche Luftfahrt-Beratungsdienst, Bonn	5.4.63/74
			G-BCOV	Warbirds of GB Ltd, Blackbushe	10.74/80
				(del. Germany - Blackbushe 11.10.74)	
				Mike Stow, Blackbushe	78/85
			N613RD	Richard S. Drury, Goleta CA : del to USA	6.85/87
				(flew as RN "VX302/43D/Iron Angel")	
			N51SF	Jerry C. Janes & Assoc. Inc, Rockford IL	8.87/92
				(Wright R3350, race #20/"Cottonmouth")	
ES.8501 •	T Mk.20S	VX309		Hawker-Siddeley Aircraft Ltd, Langley	.57
			D-FIBO	Deutsche Luftfahrt-Beratungsdienst, Bonn	29.8.58
			D-CIBO	Deutsche Luftfahrt-Beratungsdienst, Bonn	70/72
				FAA Museum Historic Flight, RNAS Yeovilton	.76
				for spares use, RNAS Wroughton, Yeovilton	80/92
- •	FB Mk.11	VX653		stored RNAS Anthorn, RNAS Lossiemouth	
				RAF Museum, Hendon	.72/91
				The Fighter Collection, Duxford	11.91/92
				(arr. Duxford by road 24.11.91, rest. to fly)	
			G-BUCM	The Fighter Collection, Duxford	26.2.92
-	FB Mk.11	VX715		(to Kon Marine as 6-14)	
				inst. airframe Gilze-Riijen AB (stored)	74
				Lloyd A. Hamilton, Santa Rosa CA	4.74
				shipped to USA, stored Santa Rosa CA	.74/83
				(rebuilt with parts of WH589 and adopted that id.)	
ES.8503 •	T Mk.20S	VZ345		Hawker-Siddeley Aircraft Ltd, Langley	.57
			D-FATA	Deutsche Luftfahrt-Beratungsdienst, Bonn	16.9.58
			D-CATA	Deutsche Luftfahrt-Beratungsdienst, Bonn	70/74
				(to RAF as VZ345) : del. 10.74	
				RAF/A &AEE, RAF Boscombe Down UK	10.74/92
				(del. 15.10.74, flew as "VZ345 CH/272")	
				crashed, RAF Boscombe Down	10.4.85
				(rebuild to fly, RAF Boscombe Down)	
ES.9505	T Mk.20S	VZ350		Hawker-Siddeley Aircraft Ltd, Langley	.57
			D-COCO	Deutsche Luftfahrt-Beratungsdienst, Bonn	11.8.59/72
				John J. Stokes, San Marcos TX	78
			N20SF (1	Dr William Harrison, Tulsa OK	.78
				(flew as FAA "52")	
				Robert Z. Friedman/Everco Industries, IL	12.78
				crashed on take-off Waukegan IL (Friedman k.)	16.12.78
				wreckage to Frank Sanders, Chino CA	79
				Sanders Aircraft, Chino, CA	92
				(id. transferred to VZ368 for rebuild of N20SF(2)	
ES.9506 •	T Mk.20S	VZ351		Hawker-Siddeley Aircraft Ltd, Langley	.57
			D-CEDO	Deutsche Luftfahrt-Beratungsdienst, Bonn	11.8.59/72
			OO-SFY	Eric Vormezeele, Antwerp, Belgium	.75/85
				Jimmie Hunt, Memphis TN	10.85/87
				George H. Baker/American Aero Service,	
				New Smyrna Beach FL	.87/90
ES.3612	T Mk.20S	VZ365		Hawker-Siddeley Aircraft Ltd, Langley	.57
			D-CACA	Deutsche Luftfahrt-Beratungsdienst, Bonn	28.3.63/72
				noted derelict, Cologne	4.74
				Eric Vormezeele, Antwerp, Belgium (hulk)	75/85
				Jimmie Hunt, Memphis TN	10.85
				George H. Baker/American Aero Service,	
				(hulk only: used in rebuild to Skyfury racer	
				of IAF 325/N30SF: which see)	87

- •	T Mk.20	VZ368		Hawker-Siddeley Aircraft Ltd, Langley	.57
				(to Burmese AF as UB-451)	
				Frank C. Sanders, Chino CA : stored dism.	.79/82
			N20SF (2	Sanders Aircraft, Chino CA	7.83/92
				(rebuilt Chino, ff 6.8.83 as P&W R4360 Skyfury,	
				race #8/"Dreadnought" : adopted id. VZ350)	
ES.8504 •	T Mk.20S	WE820		Hawker-Siddeley Aircraft Ltd, Langley	.57
			D-FOTE	Deutsche Luftfahrt-Beratungsdienst, Bonn	9.58
			D-COTE	Deutsche Luftfahrt-Beratungsdienst, Bonn	70/72
			N85SF	John J. Stokes , San Marcos TX	80
				Eric Lorentzen, Caldwell NJ	84/87
				(rebuilt as modified racer with Wright R-3350,	
				race #88/"Blind Man's Bluff")	
				Eric Lorentzen/Window Magic of Arizona Inc,	
				Scottsdale AZ	8.87/88
				Steven A. Bolan, Scottsdale AZ	1.88/89
				Western Wings Aircraft Sales Co, Oakland OR	10.89/90
				crashed landing Reno NV (race #90)	9.90
				Tom A. Dwelle, Auburn CA (rebuild to fly)	91/92
ES.3611	T Mk.20S	WE824		Hawker-Siddeley Aircraft Ltd, Langley	.57
			D-CABY	Deutsche Luftfahrt-Beratungsdienst, Bonn	7.3.63/70
				written-off	3.3.70
-	T Mk.20	WE825		Star Avia Metals Ltd, Church Crookham UK	63
				Star Avia Metals Ltd, Lasham UK	72
41H/	FB Mk.11	WG565		(to RCN as WG565)	
636292 •				Southern Alberta Inst of Technology, Calgary	4.57/66
				CFB Tecumseh, Calgary : gate guard	5.66/84
				Aero Space Museum of Calgary ALTA	84
				Naval Museum of ALTA: stored CFB Tecumseh	.88/91
41H/	FB Mk.11	WG567		(to RCN as WG567)	
636294 •			CF-VAN	Robert P. Vanderveken, Pierrefords QUE	9.61/65
			N878M	Michael D. Carroll, Long Beach CA	.65/69
				Sherman Cooper, Merced CA	70/72
				(race #87/"Miss Merced")	
				crashed,forced landing near Mojave CA	11.71
				Frank C. Sanders, Chino CA (wreck)	80/81
				James A. Mott, South Gate CA	84/92
				(rebuilt Chino CA 84/88: race #42/"Super Chief")	
ES.3617 •	FB Mk.11	WG599		(to RNAF as ....)	c54
	FB Mk.50		D-CACY	Deutsche Luftfahrt-Beratungsdienst, Bonn	12.64/72
				Luftwaffenmuseum, Uetersen AB, WG	78/90
- •	FB Mk.11	WG630		(to RAN as WG630) BOC 3.52 SOC	15.11.59
				Experimental Building Station, Ryde NSW	11.59/86
				(wind machine to test building materials)	
				Australian War Memorial, Canberra ACT	8.86
				Naval Aviation Museum, Nowra NAS, NSW	.87/91
				(rebuild to fly, Nowra NAS)	
ES.8509	T Mk.20	WG652		Hawker-Siddeley Aviation Ltd, Langley	.57
			D-CAFO	Deutsche Luftfahrt-Beratungsdienst, Bonn	23.5.60/74
			G-BCKG	Warbirds of GB Ltd, Blackbushe	30.7.74
			N46990	ntu: John J. Stokes, San Marcos TX	.74
			N62143	Dr Merryl D. Schulke, Orlando FL	9.74
				(departed UK on delivery flight by Schulke)	13.10.74
				John J. Stokes, San Marcos TX	.74/77
				Lloyd A. Hamilton, Santa Rosa CA	5.77
				(conv. to single-seater .79)	
				Jimmy R. McMillan, Breckenridge TX	84
				Arthur W. McDonnell, Mojave CA	5.84/88
				(race #106/JR-106")	
				dest. in hangar fire, Shafter CA	7.88

c/n	Model	Serial	Reg.	History	Date
ES.3616• 41H/ 636070	T Mk.20S	WG655		Hawker-Siddeley Aviation Ltd, Langley	7.57/63
			D-CACU	Deutsche Luftfahrt-Beratungsdienst, Bonn: del	7.8.63/70
				(ret. to RN/FAA as WG655)	6.76
				FAA Historic Flight, RNAS Yeovilton : del.	23.6.76/90
				forced landing, crashed near Yeovilton	14.7.90
41H/ 636334 •	FB Mk.11	WH587		(to RAN as WH587) BOC	3.52
				Lord Trefgarne, Sydney, NSW	.64
			N260X	Grant Weaver, San Jose CA (race #33)	5.65/67
				Stan Booker, Fresno CA (race #33)	67
				James R. Fugate, Aurora OR	69
				Sherman Cooper, Merced CA	.71/72
				Westernair of Albuquerque, Albuquerque NM	.72
				Ellsworth Getchell, San Jose CA	77/92
				(flies as RAN "WH587/105")	
41H 636335 •	FB Mk.11	WH588		(to RAN as WH588) BOC 3.52 SOC	23.9.63
				Fawcett Aviation, Bankstown, NSW	.63
			VH-BOU	Fawcett Aviation, Bankstown, NSW	11.65/69
				Arnold J. Glass, Sydney NSW	71/72
			N588	Lloyd A. Hamilton, Santa Rosa CA : shipped	4.72/91
				dam., fcd. landing nr Santa Rosa (repaired)	5.5.74
				(race #16/"RAN WH588/16K/Baby Gorilla")	
41H 636336 •	FB Mk.11	WH589		(to RAN as WH589) BOC	3.52
				Fawcett Aviation, Bankstown NSW	.63/69
				Ormond Haydon-Baillie, Vancouver BC	.69
				(shipped Sydney - USA on USS "Coral Sea" .69)	
			CF-CHB	Ormond Haydon-Baillie, Vancouver BC	.70
				(del. Vancouver - Southend: arr. 23.11.73)	
			G-AGHB	Ormond Haydon-Baillie, Southend	9.5.74/78
				Spencer Flack, Elstree	79
				crashed Munster, West Germany	24.6.79
				Angus McVitie, Cranfield UK (wreck)	80/83
				Craig Charleston, Colchester UK (wreck)	90
			N4434P	Lloyd A. Hamilton, Santa Rosa CA	10.83/92
				(rebuilt as modified racer with P&W R-4360, race #15/"Furias": composite rebuild of VX715 & WJ290, using parts of WH589: adopted id. WH589)	
- •	FB Mk.11	WJ231		RNAS Anthorn : displ. as "WE726"	8.65
				Fleet Air Arm Museum, RNAS Yeovilton	72/92
				(stripped for spares for FAA Historic Flight)	
-	FB Mk.11	WJ244		Malcolm D. N. Fisher/Historic Aircraft Preservation Society, Biggin Hill	.66
				Historic Aircraft Museum, Southend (dism.)	71/72
			G-FURY	Spencer Flack, Elstree (dism.)	5.7.78/81
				crashed and dest., near Waddington	2.8.81
41H/ 696792 •	FB Mk.11	WJ288		RNAS Lossiemouth (into storage)	9.5.61/63
				Hawker Siddeley Aircraft Ltd, Dunsfold : del.	12.3.63/66
				Malcolm D. N. Fisher/Historic Aircraft Preservation Society, Biggin Hill : arr.	2.9.66
				Historic Aircraft Museum, Southend : arr.	6.5.67/83
				Patrick Luscombe : museum auction	10.5.83
			G-SALY	Patrick Luscombe/British Air Reserve, Lympne/Duxford	12.7.83/88
				Warbirds of GB Ltd, Biggin Hill	.88/89
				Ed Stanley, Portland OR: shipped to Chino CA	.90
			N15S	Edwin Stanley, Portland OR	6.91/92
				Maria F. Stanley	10.92
- •	FB Mk.11	WJ290		Hawker Siddeley Aircraft Ltd, Langley	.57
				Delft Technical School, Holland	

				Lloyd A. Hamilton, Santa Rosa CA (used in rebuild of VX715 as N4434P)	80
37514 • (ISS20)	Fury FB.10		N21SF	(to Iraqi AF as 250) Ed Jurist & David C. Tallichet, Orlando FL (recov. ex Iraq, stored dism. Orlando FL) Michael H. Mock & Robert del Valle/ International Ship Repair Service, Tampa FL Russ Francis, Wallingford VT Sanders Truck Lines, Troy AL (flew as "RAN DM/369") crashed landing Troy AL (rebuild with P&W R3350, Breckenridge TX)	 .79 81/85 7.86/88 10.88/92 7.7.90
37517 •	Fury FB.10		N24SF	(to Iraqi AF as .....) Ed Jurist & David C. Tallichet, Orlando FL (recov. ex Iraq, stored dism. Orlando FL) Ed Jurist/Vintage Aircraft Intnl., Nyack NY Sonoma Valley Aircraft Inc, Vineburg CA Milton C. Leshe, Chandler AZ	 .79/82 84/88 7.88 7.89/92
37522 •	FB Mk.11	WJ298	N26SF	(to Iraqi AF as 303) : del. ex Langley Ed Jurist & David C. Tallichet, Orlando FL (recov. ex Iraq, stored dism. Orlando FL) Ed Jurist/Vintage Aircraft Intnl., Nyack NY John J. Dowd, Syracuse NY	9.7.52 .79/82 84 88/92
37525 • 41H/ 656823	Fury FB.10		N30SF	(to Iraqi AF as 325) Ed Jurist & David C. Tallichet, Orlando FL (recov. ex Iraq, stored dism. Orlando FL) Ed Jurist/Vintage Aircraft Intnl., Nyack NY George H. Baker/American Aero Services,	 .79/82 84

				New Smyrna Beach FL	87/89
				(rebuild as "Sky Fury" with P&W R-3350, using	
				parts of VZ365/D-CACA : ff .90, race #71)	
			N71GB	George H. Baker, New Smyrna Beach FL	9.89/92
				dam. Oshkosh WI (under repair)	8.91
37534 •	Fury FB.10			(to Iraqi AF as 243) : del. ex Langley	23.9.49
(ISS13)			N28SF	Ed Jurist & David C. Tallichet, Orlando FL	.79/81
				(recov. ex Iraq, stored dism. Orlando FL)	
				Guido Zuccoli, Darwin NT : shipped	1.82
			VH-HFX	Guido Zuccoli, Darwin NT	22.4.85
				Bruce Andrews, Melbourne VIC	11.85/91
				(flew as RAN "WH589")	
			G-BTTA	The Old Flying Machine Company, Duxford	
				shipped, arr. Duxford	25.7.91/92
37536 •	Fury FB.10			(to Iraqi AF as 255)	
(ISS25)			N34SF	Ed Jurist & David C. Tallichet, Orlando FL	.79/82
				(recov. ex Iraq, stored dism. Orlando FL)	
				Ed Jurist/ Vintage Aircraft Intnl., Nyack NY	84
				Howard Pardue/Breckenridge Aviation Museum,	
				Breckenridge TX	87
			N666HP	Breckenridge Aviation Museum TX	2.88/92
				(rebuilt with Wright R3350, race #66/"HP")	
37537 •	Fury FB.10			(to Iraqi AF as 254)	
(ISS24)			N35SF	Ed Jurist & David C. Tallichet, Orlando FL	.79/82
				(recov. ex Iraq, stored dism. Orlando FL)	
				Ed Jurist/Vintage Aircraft Intnl., Nyack NY	84/92
37539 •	Fury FB.10			(to Iraqi AF as 315)	
			N36SF	Ed Jurist & David C. Tallichet, Orlando FL	.79/82
				(recov. ex Iraq, stored dism. Orlando FL)	
				Ed Jurist/Vintage Aircraft Intnl., Nyack NY	84/88
				W. R. Laws, Coleman TX	7.89/91
				John Bradshaw, Wroughton UK : arr. by sea	9.91/92
				Barbara A. Bradshaw	10.92
				(flies as Netherlands Navy "361")	
37541 •	Fury FB.10			(to Iraqi AF as 314)	
			N38SF	Ed Jurist & David C. Tallichet, Orlando FL	.79/82
				(recov. ex Iraq, stored dism. Orlando FL)	
				Ed Jurist/Vintage Aircraft Intnl., Nyack NY	84/92
37542 •	FB Mk.11	WJ293		(to Iraqi AF as 302)	
			N39SF	Ed Jurist & David C. Tallichet, Orlando FL	.79
				(recov. ex Iraq, stored dism. Orlando FL)	
				Henry Haigh/Haigh Industries, Howell MI	84/92
				(rebuilt Breckenridge TX with Wright R3350,	
				ff .90 as camouflaged "HH")	
37703 •	Fury FB.10			(to Iraqi AF as 253) : del. ex Langley	21.11.49
(ISS23)			N40SF	Ed Jurist & David C. Tallichet, Orlando FL	.79/81
				(recov. ex Iraq, stored dism. Orlando FL)	
				Guido Zuccoli, Darwin NT : shipped	1.82
			VH-HFA	Ted Allen, Proserpine QLD	25.1.84/88
				(incorrect id. "WJ231" quoted,	
				flew as RAN "253/K/Magnificent Obsession")	
				John MacGuire, Abilene TX	
				shipped ex Darwin	11.88
			N57JB	John MacGuire/War Eagles Air Museum,	
				Santa Teresa NM	11.88/92
37721 •	FB Mk.11	WM483		(to Iraqi AF as 304)	
			N42SF	Ed Jurist & David C. Tallichet, Orlando FL	.79/82
				(recov. ex Iraq, stored dism. Orlando FL)	

c/n	Type	Serial	Reg'n	History	Date
				Ed Jurist/Vintage Aircraft Intnl., Nyack NY	84/90
				Richard Bertea, Irivine CA	92
37723 • 41H/ 643827	Fury FB.10			(to Iraqi AF as 326)	
			N43SF	Ed Jurist & David C. Tallichet, Orlando FL	.79/86
				(recov. ex Iraq, stored dism. Orlando FL)	
				Ed Jurist/Vintage Aircraft Intnl, Nyack NY	84
			ZK-SFR	New Zealand Sea Fury Syndicate, Ardmore	11.2.87/90
				(airfreighted to NZ by RNZAF C130, rebuilt Ardmore, ff 12.3.88: flies as "WJ232/O")	
				Flightwatch Services Ltd, Ardmore	91/92
				(fitted wing-folding mechanism ex WG655 .91)	
37724 •	Fury FB.10			(to Iraqi AF as 312)	
			N45SF	Ed Jurist & David C. Tallichet, Orlando FL	.79
				(recov. ex Iraq, stored dism. Orlando FL)	
				Sonoma Valley Aircraft Inc, Glen Ellen CA	6.83/92
				(rebuilt: flying by 89)	
37726 •	Fury FB.10			(to Iraqi AF as 318)	
			N46SF	Ed Jurist & David C. Tallichet, Orlando FL	.79/82
				(recov. ex Iraq, stored dism. Orlando FL)	
				Ed Jurist/Vintage Aircraft Intl., Nyack NY	84/92
37727 • (ISS22)	Fury FB.10			(to Iraqi AF as 252)	
			N48SF	Ed Jurist & David C. Tallichet, Orlando FL	.79
				(recov. ex Iraq, stored dism. Orlando FL)	
				Ed Jurist/Vintage Aircraft Intnl., Nyack NY	84/87
37729 • 41H/ 65802	FB Mk.11			(to Iraqi AF as 308)	
			N..SF	Ed Jurist & David C. Tallichet, Orlando FL	.79/81
				(recov. ex Iraq, stored dism. Orlando FL)	
				Guido Zuccoli, Darwin NT : shipped	1.82
			VH-HFG	Guido Zuccoli, Darwin NT	9.11.83/92
				(rest. Darwin, ff 14.11.83 as "RAN 308")	
				dam.,fcd. ldg. nr. Toowoomba, QLD (repaired)	24.3.84
				(id. orig. quoted as c/n 37522/N26SF: which see)	
37731 • (ISS19)	Fury FB.10			(to Iraqi AF as 249) : del. ex Langley	23.9.49
			N54SF	Ed Jurist & David C. Tallichet, Orlando FL	.79/81
				(recov. ex Iraq, stored dism. Orlando FL)	
			VH-HFR	Rob Poynton, Toodyay WA : shipped	1.82
			VH-ISS	Rob Poynton, Perth WA	85/92
				(rest. to fly, Toodyay/Cunderdin WA as "IAF 249")	
37733 •	Fury FB.10			(to Iraqi AF as 316)	
			N56SF	Ed Jurist & David C. Tallichet, Orlando FL	.79
				(recov. ex Iraq, stored dism. Orlando FL)	
				John D. Rodgers, St Charles IL	84/92
37734 41H/ 623271	Fury FB.10 (2 seat)			(to Iraqi AF as 324)	
			N58SF	Ed Jurist & David C. Tallichet, Orlando FL	.79
				(recov. ex Iraq, stored dism. Orlando FL)	
				Weeks Air Museum, Tamiami FL	.80/92
				dam. in hangar fire, Rockford IL	19.7.89
37755 •	FB Mk.11	WM484		(to Iraqi AF as 305)	
			N59SF	Ed Jurist & David C. Tallichet, Orlando FL	.79/82
				(recov. ex Iraq, stored dism. Orlando FL)	
				Ed Jurist/Vintage Aircraft Intnl., Nyack NY	84/87
				Tom Reilly, Kissimmee FL	2.88/92
37757 • 41H/ 65816	FB Mk.11	WN480		(to Iraqi AF as ...)	
			N60SF	Ed Jurist & David C. Tallichet, Orlando FL	.79
				(recov. ex Iraq, stored dism. Orlando FL)	
				John D. Rodgers, St Charles IL	82/91
				Crew Concepts Inc, Boise ID	92

				(flies as FAA "757/JR")	
-	FB Mk.11	WN482		(to Iraqi AF as 310)	
			N19SF	Ed Jurist & David C. Tallichet, Orlando FL	.79
				(recov. ex Iraq, stored dism. Orlando FL)	
				Tom Crevasse, Live Oak FL	.79/80
				(rebuilt: ff 13.7.79: flew as "RCN 121")	
				John Williams	81
				crashed and dest., Harlingen TX (Williams k.)	9.10.81
87953 •	Fury			(to Iraqi AF : poss. as spare airframe)	
			N62SF	Ed Jurist & David C. Tallichet, Orlando FL	.79/82
				(recov. ex Iraq, stored dism. Orlando FL)	
				Ed Jurist/Vintage Aircraft Intnl., Nyack NY	84/92
87954 •	Fury			(to Iraqi AF : poss. as spare airframe)	
			N63SF	Ed Jurist & David C. Tallichet, Orlando FL	.79/82
				(recov. ex Iraq, stored dism. Orlando FL)	
				Ed Jurist/Vintage Aircraft Intnl., Nyack NY	84/92
(ISS4)	Fury FB.10			(to Iraqi AF as 234)	
				(to Moroccan AF as.....)	
				stored, Rabat, Morocco	.78
				rep. via French broker to USA	
(ISS11) •	Fury FB.10			(to Iraqi AF as 241)	
			N64SF	Ed Jurist & David C. Tallichet, Orlando FL	.79/82
				(recov. ex Iraq, stored dism. Orlando FL)	
				Ed Jurist/Vintage Aircraft Intnl., Nyack NY	87
	-		N1324	Utilco Inc, Tifton GA	7.90/92
62382 (ISS29)	Fury FB.10			(to Iraqi AF as 259)	
				(to Moroccan AF as .....)	
				stored, Rabat, Morocco	.78
				rep. via French broker to USA	
- •		FB Mk. 11	-	(to FA Cubana as 541)	.58
				Bay of Pigs Museum, Playa Giron, Cuba	76/88
	- •	FB Mk. 11	-	(to FA Cubana as 542)	.58
				Museum of the Revolution, Havana, Cuba	80/88
-		Fury		(to Iraqi AF as .....)	
				(to Moroccan AF as .....)	
				stored, Rabat, Morocco	.78
				rep. via French broker to USA	
-		Fury		(to Iraqi AF as .....)	
				(to Moroccan AF as .....)	
				stored, Rabat, Morocco	.78
				rep. via French broker to USA	
6310 • (Fokker)	FB Mk.5	06-43		(Kon Marine)	
				Delft Technical School, Delft, Netherlands	
				Aviodome Museum, Schipol, Amsterdam	70/90
				(id. also quoted as c/n 6289)	

HEINKEL He46

Nr846 •	He 46D	Nr846		Musee de l'Air et de l'Espace, Villacoublay	79/84
				Musee de l'Air , Paris-Le Bourget : stored	90
				dest. by fire, museum hangar Le Bourget	17.5.90

Nr1526	•	He 111P-1	Nr1526		(Luftwaffe 33+C25; later 5J+CN)	
					crashed near Lesjaskog, Norway	4.40
					recov. for restoration to static display	7.76
					Kongelige Norsk Luftforssvaret Collection,	
					Gardermoen AB, Norway: displ. as "5J+CN"	78/92
Nr2940	•	He 111E-1	Nr2940		(to Legion Condor, Spain) del.	3.38
					(to Ejercito del Aire as B.2-82) wfu	.56
					Museo del Aire, Cuatro Vientos AB, Madrid	65/86
					(displ. as "B.2-82/14-16")	
Nr701152	•	He 111H-23	Nr701152		Air Historical Branch Museum	54
					stored Stanmore, Middlesex	54
					stored RAF Biggin Hill	60
					RAF Museum, RAF St.Athan	70/77
					RAF Museum, Hendon	.78/92
					(displ. as "701152/NT+5L")	
		CASA-2.111D	BR2.1-10	N99260	Dolph Overton, Kenley NC	2.77
				G-BFFS	Warbirds of GB Ltd, Blackbushe	4.11.77
					crashed on del., near Escorial, Spain	11.12.77
535	•	CASA-2.111D	BR2.1-14		Air Classik, Frankfurt-Rhein Main	84
-	•	CASA-2.111D	BR2.1-129		Musee de l'Air et de l'Espace, Le Bourget	75/85
	•	CASA-2.111E	B.21-27	N99230	Dolph Overton, Kenley NC	2.77/83
					(del. to USA,via Prestwick, Scotland 11.10.77)	
					displ. Wings & Wheels Museum, Orlando FL	81
					Military Aircraft Restoration Corp, Chino CA	7.83/92
					loan: Combat Air Museum, Topeka KS	90
					(flies as "Luftwaffe 9K+EZ")	
167	•	CASA-2.111D	B.21-37		T. G. "Hamish" Mahaddie, Tablada, Spain	.67
				G-AWHB	Hamish Mahaddie/Spitfire Productions Ltd,	
					Duxford (for movie "Battle of Britain") del.	21.5.68/69
					stored West Malling	70/72
					Historic Aircraft Museum, Southend	
					(displ. as "6J+PR")	3.72/83
					Paul Raymond/ Whitehall Theatre of War	10.5.83/85
					Kermit A. Weeks, Tamiami FL (not del.)	5.6.85
					remained stored dism., Royston, Herts	83/87
					Aces High Ltd, North Weald	.88/90
					(also rep. as B.21-57, c/n 049)	_
025	•	CASA-2.111D	B.21-77		T. G. "Hamish" Mahaddie, Tablada, Spain	.67
				G-AWHA	Hamish Mahaddie/Spitfire Productions Ltd,	
					Duxford (for movie "Battle of Britain")	14.5.68/69
					displ. in West Germany for movie promotion	.69/70
				D-CAGI	reg.	8.70
					Deutsches Museum, Munich ("6J+PR")	72/85
					(also rep. as B.21-166)	_
108	•	CASA-2.111E	B.21-97			
		CASA-2.111B	T.8B-97		Museo del Aire, Cuatro Vientos AB, Madrid	.72/86
					(displ. as "T.8B-97/462-04")	_
	•	CASA-2.111B	B.21-103		Ejercito del Aire, Tablada AB, Spain	75/86
	•	CASA-2.111E	B.21-117		Luftwaffen Museum, Uetersen AB, Hamburg	73/85
					(displ. as "GI+AD") _	
	•	CASA-2.111E	T.8B-124	G-BDYA	Doug Arnold/Warbirds of GB Ltd, Blackbushe	21.5.76
					(del Madrid-Blackbushe 18.6.76)	

Heinkel He 111/CASA 2.111

		N72615	Confederate Air Force, Harlingen TX (delivered to USA via Prestwick 24.9.77) dam. landing, Harlingen TX (repaired) American Airpower Heritage Flying Museum, Midland TX (flies as "Luftwaffe 1H+GS")	8.77/91 10.89 9.91/92
- •	CASA-2.111D	-	USAFM Wright-Patterson AFB, Dayton OH (under rest. for static displ. 89)	73/89

HEINKEL He51

- •	He 51B	-	recovered from Lake Biscarosse, France Association de Protection des Epaves du Lac du Biscarosse, Biscarosse	c81 .81/89

HENSCHEL Hs293

Nr21816 •	Hs 293	Nr21816	Kongelige Norsk Luftforssvaret Collection, Gardermoen AB, Norway loan:Forsvarsmuseet, Akershus Castle, Oslo	 78/84 84
Nr242886•	Hs 293A-1	-	Vojenske Muzeum, Kbely AB, Czechoslovakia	84
- •	Hs 293	-	Luftwaffen Museum, Uetersen AB, Hamburg	84

HORTON Ho229 GOTHA

V3 •	Ho 229		captured, Friedrichscrode Werks Royal Aircraft Establishment,Farnborough (to USA for trials as FE-490; T2-490) Smithsonian Institute, stored Park Ridge IL NASM, stored Silver Hill MD	 45 .46 66/90

ILYUSHIN IL-10 STORMOVIK

- •	Il-10		Beijing Aeronautical Institute, Beijing China	87
- •	Il-10 (Avia)		(to Polish AF as "4") Army Museum, Krakow, Poland Aviation & Space Museum, Krakow	 68/74 92
B33-502•	Il-10 (Avia)		Letecka Expozice Vojenskeho Muzea, Prague-Kbely, Czechoslovakia	 74

JUNKERS Ju388

Nr560049 •	Ju388L-1	Nr560049	captured at Merseburg Werks shipped to USA on HMS Reaper (US trials as FE-4010, T2-4010) Smithsonian Institute, stored Park Ridge IL NASM, Silver Hill MD	.45 7.45 45 .46 72/90

Notes

Nr4043 •	Ju 52	Nr4043	D-ABIS	Deutsche Lufthansa "Kurt Wolfe"	
	/3mGe		PP-CAX	Syndicicato Condor "Gurupira"	
			LV-ZBD		
			LQ-ZBD	Museo Nacional de Aeronautica, Buenos Aires	67/91
				(displ. as "FA Argentina T-149", later	
				"T-158/LADE, Rio Negro") _	
Nr4145 •	Ju-52	Nr4145		(to Ejercito del Aire/Spanish AF as T.2B-108)	
	/3mGe			Verkehrsmuseum, Munich WG : del.	.65
				(displ. Munich as "D-2201")	7.65
				stored RAF Gatow, West Germany	.67/84
				(rest. for static display .74 as "D-2201")	
				Berlin Senat Transport Museum	74
				Museum fur Verkehr und Technik, Berlin	84/91
Nr5489 •	Ju 52	Nr5489	D-AQUI	Lufthansa (ff 6.4.36): del.	10.4.36
	/3mG2e			"Fritz Simon", operated on floats	
			LN-DAH	DNL-Norwegian Airlines "Falken"	1.7.36/40
				confiscated by German Army in Norway	4.40
			D-AQUI	Lufthansa "Kurt Wintgens"	10.40/45
				(to Norwegian Air Force as ...)	.45
			LN-KAF	DNL-Norwegian Airlines : floatplane	18.5.46
				(rebuild .47, used fuselage ex Luftwaffe	
				Ju52/3mG8e Nr 130714)	
				Scandinavian Airlines System: floatplane	.47/56
				Kapitan Christian Drexel, Ecuador	.56
				wfu 10.56 Oslo Harbour, sunk in harbour	.56
				salvaged, rest. as landplane: shipped Ecuador	7.57
			HC-ABS	Transportes Aereos Orientales, Quito	.57/63
				(landplane "Amazonas")	
				wfu .63 Quito, parked for 7 years	
			N130LW	Lester F. Weaver, Polo IL	5.69
				rest. Quito, ff 10.11.70; del. Dixon IL, arr.	22.11.70
				Cannon Aircraft	74
			N52JU	Martin Caidin Productions, Cocoa Beach FL	.74/84
				(del. Tico FL 5.3.75, rebuild 11.76, BMW radials	
				replaced by P&W R1340's : flew as "Iron Annie")	
				dam. accident, Gainesville FL (repaired)	17.7.80
			D-CDLH	Lufthansa Traditionsflug, Hamburg	12.84/92
				(del. USA-Hamburg 13/28.12.84, rest.	
				Hamburg, ff 1.4.86 as "Lufthansa D-AQUI")	
				(airfreighted to USA for flying tour 6.90-2.91)	
-	Ju 52	-		(to FA Portuguesa as 103, later 6303)	.37
	/3mG3e			childrens playground Evora, Portugal	69/85
Nr5596	Ju 52	Nr5596		(G6+OM) : crashed Kirkenes, Lapland	19.10.44
	/3mG3e			wreck located Lapland	73
				planned recov. by Finnish Air Force _	
Nr5661 •	Ju 52	Nr5661		(to FA Portuguesa as 104, later 6304)	.37
	/3mG3e			Portugal dos Pequeninos, childrens playground,	
				Coimbra, Portugal	69/82
				Museu do Ar, Alverca AB, Lisbon	87/92
				(open storage, dism.) _	
Nr5664 •	Ju 52	Nr5664		(to FA Portuguesa as 106, later 6306)	.37
	/3mG3e			Museu do Ar, Alverca AB, Lisbon	72/91
				(open storage, dism.)	
-	Ju 52	-		(to FA Portuguesa as 6300)	.37
	/3mG3e			Portuguese Air Force Museum, Alverca AB	73/91
				(open storage, dism.)	
-	Ju 52	-		(to FA Portuguesa as 101, later 6301)	.37
	/3mG3e			Portuguese Air Force Museum, Alverca AB	73/91

					(open storage, forward section badly damaged)	
Nr5670	•	Ju 52	Nr5670		(to FA Portuguesa as 109, later 6309)	.37
		/3mG7e			Portuguese Air Force Museum, Alverca AB	.72/85
					Musee Royal de l'Armee, Brussels	.85/91
				OO-AGU	SABENA Old Timers, Brussels	25.8.87/91
					(shipped to Brussels ; arr. 24.4.85)	
					(rebuild to fly Zaventem: fitted tailplane FAP 6310)	
-	•	Ju 52	-		(to FA Portuguesa as 6320)	.37
		/3mG3e			displ. Hohn AB, West Germany	.75/85
					(airfreighted to Hohn by Luftwaffe C-160 .75)	
					(note: id also rep. as 6306)	
Nr6580	•	Ju 52	-		(to Swiss AF as A-701)	.39
		/3mG4e		HB-HOS	reg. for international flights	13.9.48
					(returned to Swiss AF as A-701)	9.59/82
				HB-HOS	Friends of Dubendorf Museum/Ju-Air,	
					Dubendorf AB	8.82/92
					(flies as "A-701")	
Nr6595	•	Ju 52	-		(to Swiss AF as A-702)	.39
		/3mG4e		HB-HOT	reg. for international flights	27.3.51
					(returned to Swiss AF as A-702)	9.59/85
				HB-HOT	Friends of Dubendorf Museum/Ju-Air,	
					Dubendorf AB	7.85/92
					(flies as "A-702")	
Nr6610	•	Ju 52	-		(to Swiss AF as A-703)	.39
		/3mG4e		HB-HOP	reg. for international flights	9.5.47
					(returned to Swiss AF as A-703)	9.59/82
				HB-HOP	Friends of Dubendorf Museum/Ju-Air,	
					Dubendorf AB	10.82/92
					(flies as "A-703")	
Nr6134	•	Ju 52	Nr6134		(CO+EI)	.39
		/3mG4e			landed on ice, Lake Hartvikvann, Norway	13.4.40
					sank Lake Hartvikvann	5.40
					recov. from Lake Hartvikvann by KNL	.86
					Kongelige Norsk Luftforssvaret Collection,	
					Gardermoen AB, Oslo Norway : stored	88/91
Nr6657	•	Ju 52	Nr6657		(III/KGzbV 102: CA+JY)	30.8.39
		/3mG4e			landed on ice, Lake Hartvikvann, Norway	13.4.40
					sank Lake Hartvikvann	5.40
					recov. from Lake Hartvikvann by KNL	10.6.83
					Kongelige Norsk Luftforssvaret Collection,	
					Gardermoen AB, Oslo Norway	.84
					displ. Oslo-Fornebu Airport as "CA+JY"	84
Nr6693	•	Ju 52	Nr6693		(DB+RD)	.39
		/3mG4e			landed on ice, Lake Hartvikvann, Norway	13.4.40
					sank Lake Hartvikvann	5.40
					recov. from Lake Hartvikvann by KNL	.86
					Kongelige Norsk Luftforssvaret Collection,	
					Gardermoen AB, Oslo Norway	.86/89
					Luftwaffe Museum : rest. Wunstorf AB	91/92
Nr6791	•	Ju 52	Nr6791		(VB+UB)	.39
		/3mG4e			landed on ice, Lake Hartvikvann, Norway	13.4.40
					sank Lake Hartvikvann	5.40
					recov. from Lake Hartvikvann by KNL	.86
					Kongelige Norsk Luftforssvaret Collection,	
					Gardermoen AB, Oslo Norway : stored	.86/91
					to West Germany	89

Nr55657 •	Ju 52 /3mG4e	Nr55657		(IZ+BY) landed on ice, Lake Hartvikvann, Norway sank Lake Hartvikvann recov. from Lake Hartvikvann by KNL Kongelige Norsk Luftforssvaret Collection, Gardermoen AB, Oslo Norway rep. to West Germany	.39 13.4.40 5.40 .86 .86/87 89
Nr501196•	Ju 52 /3mG7e	Nr501196		(to Royal Norwegian AF as Y-AC) (to FA Portuguesa as 111: later 6311) displ. Aero Clube de Viseu, Viseu Portugal Museu do Ar, Alverca AB (open storage)	.45/50 9.50 77/82 83/92
Nr501219•	Ju 52 /3mG7e	Nr501219		(to Royal Norwegian AF) (to FA Portuguesa as 110: later 6310) Museu do Ar, Alverca AB	 9.50 73/92
- •	Ju 52 /3mGe	-		(to FA Colombiana as FAC 625) Colombian Air Force Museum, Bogota	.34 67/88
- •	Ju 52 /3m	-		(to Czech AF as ....) Vojenske Aviation Museum, Kbely AB Czechoslavakia (fuse. only)	 85
No.053 •	Amiot AAC.1	No.053		(to FA Portuguesa as 6320) displ. FAP BA2, Ota AB, Portugal Hugo Junkers Kaserne, Hohn WG (displ. as Luftwaffe "IZ+IK")	26.11.60 72/75 76/92
No.205 •	Amiot AAC.1	No.205		(to FA Portuguesa as 6315) Portuguese Air Force Museum, Alverca AB (open storage)	2.12.60 69/91
No.216 •	Amiot AAC.1	No.216		(to French Navy as DK-2, 55S.32, No216) retired, stored Villacoublay AB Musee de l'Air, Paris-Le Bourget (rest., displ. from 5.78 as "334/DG") Musee de Tradition de l'Aeronautique Navale, Rochefort/Soubbbise	 c65/75 .75/91 .91
No.222 •	Amiot AAC.1	-	F-BBYB	Societe Transatlantique Aerienne (to JRV/Yugoslav AF as 7208) Yugoslav Aeronautical Museum, Belgrade (open storage Belgrade Airport 69/80, then displ.)	26.8.46/48 .50/60 7.69/92
No.363 •	Amiot AAC.1	No.363		Deutsches Museum, Munich	26.3.58/91
- •	Amiot AAC.1	-		(to FA Portuguesa as 6316) Imperial War Museum, Duxford: arr. dism. (displ. as "1Z+NK")	11.60 6.9.73/92
50 •	CASA 352L	T.2B-140	N9012P	Military Aircraft restoration Corp, Chino CA (stored Cuatro Vientos AB, Madrid, del. via France and WG to Stansted UK, arr. 27.8.83) op. Keith May/Ju52 Flight Ltd, Rochester UK (flew as Luftwaffe "IZ+EK") dep. Rochester to West Germany	11.78/92 83/85 .85
- •	CASA 352L	T.2B-142	N9012N	Military Aircraft restoration Corp, Chino CA (operated by Jeff Hawke, Biggin Hill 79/82) (dep. Biggin Hill for USA 19.11.82 but grounded Dublin 25.11.82, stored Dublin 82/86) Auto und Technik Museum, Sinsheim WG	11.78/92 .86/91
127 •	CASA 352L	T.2B-144	N88927 D-CIAS	reg. Kurfiss Aviation/Air Classik, Stuttgart: del.	 4.74

					Air Classik, Frankfurt : del. for display	14.9.74/85
					Frankfurt Rhein-Mein Airport Authority	.85/92
					(also rep. as c/n 54, displ. as "D-CIAS")	
-	•	CASA 352L	T.2B-148	N99234	Dolph Overton, Kenly NC	2.77/82
					(del. to USA, arr. Strathallen, Scotland 14.7.78, continued via Reykjavik 20.6.79)	
					displ. Wings & Wheels Museum, Orlando FL	.79/82
				C-GARM	Western Canada Avn. Mus. Winnipeg MAN	25.1.82/91
					(dep. Orlando on del. flight to Canada 11.5.82)	
					(conv. to Ju-52cao/ce at Winnipeg, rolled-out 1.4.85, displ. as " Canadian Airways CF-ARM")	
-		CASA 352L	T.2B-163		stored derelict, Cuatro Vientos AB	74
					childrens playground, Cuatro Vientos	77
121	•	CASA 352L	T.2B-165	D-CIAK	Air Classik: displ. Bonn-Wahn : del.	26.4.75/76
					Air Classik: displ. Dusseldorf : del.	19.5.76/85
					(displ. Dusseldorf Airport in Lufthansa scheme)	
					Ikarus Flugverkehsmuseum, Marl WG	87
					(displ. as "Lufthansa D-ADAM")	
					moved to Bochum WG, for displ.	.89/92
67	•	CASA 352L	T.2B-176	N99059	Confederate Air Force, Harlingen TX	.77/80
					(del. to USA via Biggin Hill 9.79/9.7.80)	
				N352JU	Confederate Air Force, Harlingen TX	10.80/91
					(del. Harlingen 19.7.80, flies as "1Z+AR")	
					American Airpower Heritage Flying Museum, Midland TX	9.91/92
-	•	CASA 352L	T.2B-181		displ. Murcia-Alcantrilla AB, Spain	83/91
					(displ. as "T.2B-181/721-10")	
-	•	CASA 352L	T.2B-209		displ. El Avion restaurant, Plasencia Spain	84
					rep. sold to West Germany by	88
					rep. to Auto & Technik Museum, Sinsheim WG	
					displ. as "5J+CN")	
102	•	CASA 352L	T.2B-211		Museo del Aire, Cuatro Vientos AB, Madrid	.73/91
					(rest. Cuatro Vientos, ff 19.4.88; flies as "T.2B-211/911-16")	
103	•	CASA 352L	T.2B-212	G-BECL	Warbirds of GB Ltd, Blackbushe	27.6.76/85
					(del. Blackbushe 30.7.76. flew as "N9+AA")	
					Keith May/Ju52 Flight Ltd, Rochester	24.5.85
					(stored Blackbushe 81/85, ferried to Coventry 8.10.85 for open storage 85/90	
				F-AZJU	Amicale J-B Salis, La Ferte Alais : del.	1.6.90/91
					(flies as Luftwaffe "N9+AA")	
					(under complete rebuild 10.92)	
128	•	CASA 352L	T.2B-237		noted stored Cuatro Vientos AB, "461-4"	10.77
				D-CIAD	Air Classik, Dusseldorf	10.80/82
					(del. from Barcelona to Dusseldorf 18.2.81)	
					Luftfahrtausstellung Museum, Hermeskeil WG	8.82/90
					(del. Saarbrucken 23.8.82, by road to museum)	
					(also rep. as T.2B-127, c/n 37)	
135	•	CASA 352L	T.2B-244		USAFM, Wright-Patterson AFB, Dayton OH	.71/92
					(displ. in Spanish AF sc. "901-20", later displ. in Luftwaffe camouflage scheme)	
137	•	CASA 352L	T.2B-246		displ. Torrejon AB, Madrid	77/91
					(displ. as "T.2B-246/792-20"	
145	•	CASA 352L	T.2B-254		Museo del Aire, Cuatro Vientos AB, Madrid	.73/91

Continued on Page 195

02344
Lorys II

711
RESCUE
NAVY
VT-27
N128PS
T-28C
146270
711

AL GRANT
BOBBIE
RESCUE
NAVY
T-28C
140511
NX140AG
AG

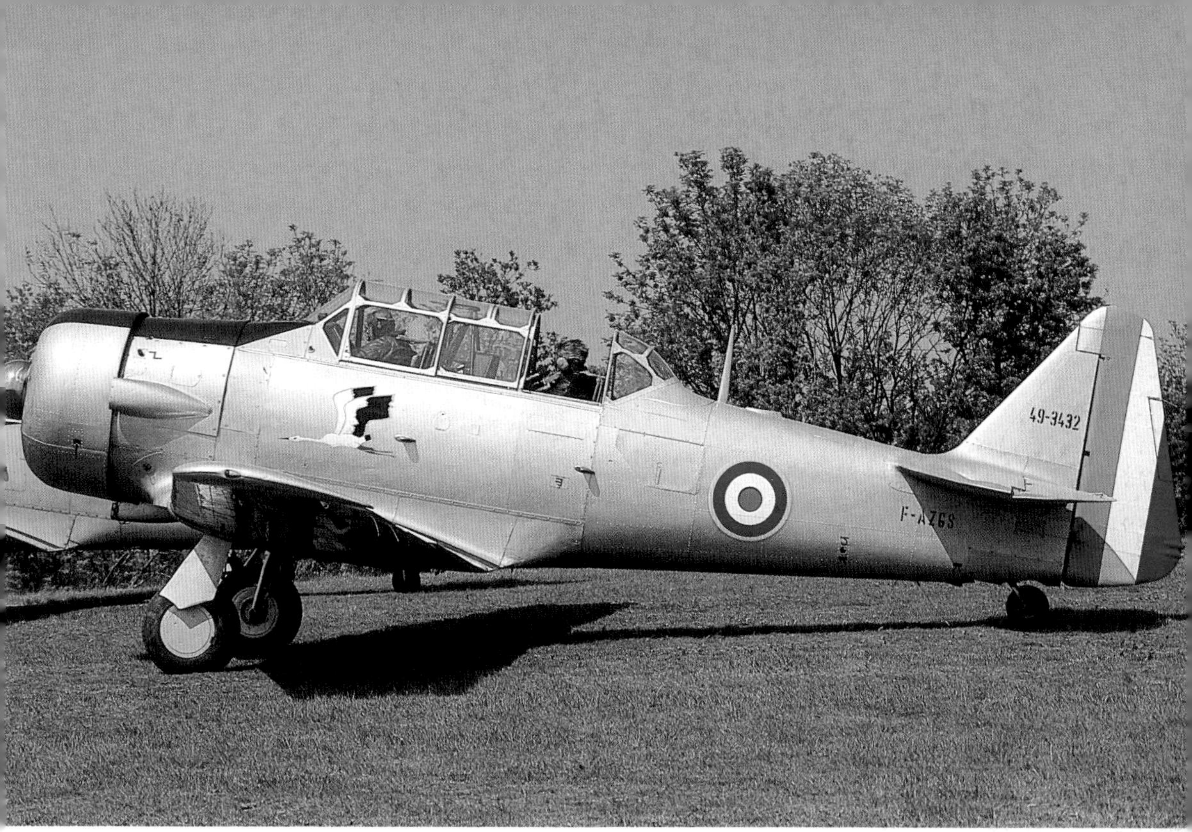
49-3432
F-AZGS

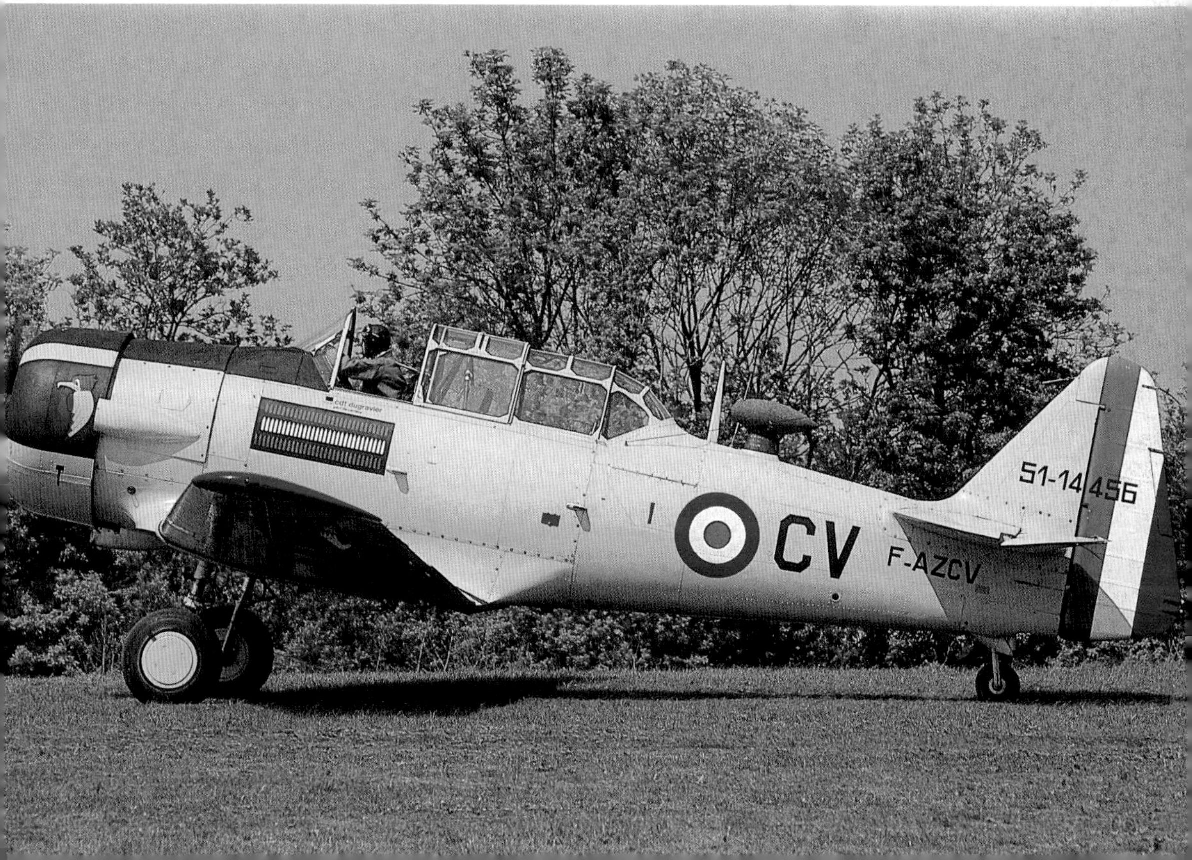
cdt dugravier
51-14456
CV
F-AZCV

Continued from Page 190

Junkers Ju52/CASA 352

					(displ. as "T.2B-254/721-14")	
146	•	CASA 352L	T.2B-255	G-BFHD	Warbirds of GB Ltd, Blackbushe	11.77/82
					(del. Blackbushe 4.7.78, flew as "N9+AA")	
					Brian Woodford/Wessex Aviation & Transport Ltd	7.3.85/87
					(arr. dism. Bournemouth 9.85 : stored)	
					Aces High Ltd, North Weald	25.6.87
					NASM, stored Washington-Dulles Airport MD	.87/91
					(displ. as "D-ODLH/Deutsche Luft Hansa") _	
148	•	CASA 352L	T.2B-257	D-CIAL	Air Classik: displ. Stuttgart Airport: del.	7.4.75/85
					(displ. as "Lufthansa D-ADAM")	
					(moved to Malsheim airfield for storage 2.9.85)	
					Auto und Technik Museum, Sinsheim WG	.86/91
					(displ. on pole as "D-2527")	
155	•	CASA 352L	T.2B-262	G-BFHG	Warbirds of GB Ltd, Blackbushe	11.77/84
					(arr. Blackbushe on del. ex Spain 6.78)	
					Aces High Ltd, Duxford/North Weald	12.84/92
					(flew as Luftwaffe "D2+600", later "VK+AZ")	
					Weeks Air Museum, Tamiami FL	.92
					(c/n also quoted as 153, plate shows 155)	
163	•	CASA 352L	T.2B-272		RAF Museum, RAF Cosford	5.78/91
					(del. ex Spain, arr. Biggin Hill 18.5.78)	
					(displ. as "British Airways G-AFAP")	
164	•	CASA 352L	T.2B-273	G-BFHE	Warbirds of GB Ltd, Blackbushe	11.77/81
					dam. in gales Cuatro Vientos AB, Madrid	.77
					(arr. Blackbushe on del. ex Spain 4.7.80)	
					South African Airways, Johannesburg	.81/83
					(del. Blackbushe-Bremen WG 12.5.81, then shipped to Johannesburg)	
				ZS-UYU	South African Airways	11.8.83
					(rebuilt Johannesburg, ff 14.1.84 as "ZS-AFA")	
				ZS-AFA	SAA "Jan van Riebeeck"	10.86/91
166	•	CASA 352L	T.2B-275	G-BFHF	Warbirds of GB Ltd, Blackbushe	11.77/85
					(del. Blackbushe 6.78, flew as "N7+AA")	
					Keith May/Ju52 Flight Ltd, Rochester	24.5.85
					(arr. by road Coventry ex Blackbushe 9.85, stored dism.; dep. for WG 30.1.86)	
					Auto und Technik Museum, Sinsheim WG	1.86/91
					(displ. as Luftwaffe "RJ+NP")	

JUNKERS Ju86

0860412	•	Ju86K-5 Tp-73			(to Swedish AF Fv155)	
					Flygvapenmuseum Malmen, Linkoping	70/88

JUNKERS Ju87

Nr2883	•	Ju 87G-2	Nr494085	(R1+JK): to RAF for trials as AM.37	
				RAF Museum, RAF St. Athan	60/78
				RAF Museum, Hendon	.78/92
				(displ. as "494085/R1+JK") _	
Nr5954	•	Ju 87R-2	Nr5954	(1/St. G.2 : A5+HL) : captured in Libya	
				Museum of Science & Industry,Chicago IL	65
				loaned: EAA Air Museum, Oshkosh WI	73/76
				Chicago Museum of Science & Industry,	
				Chicago IL (displayed as "A5+HL")	88/89
Nr16970	•	Ju 87	Nr16970	recov. from Mediterranean, nr Malta	
				National War Museum, Valetta, Malta	85/92
				(parts only)	
-	•	Ju 87B-2	-	Yugoslavian Aviation Museum, Belgrade	88/92
				(stored : incomplete fuselage)	

JUNKERS Ju88

Nr0881033	•	Ju 88	-	(4D-5H) : recov. by RNoAF	.89
				Kongelige Norsk Luftforssvaret Collection,	
				Gardermoen AB, Norway	.89
Nr0881478	•	Ju 88	-	(...+BH) : recov. by RNoAF	.89
				Kongelige Norsk Luftforssvaret Collection,	
				Gardermoen AB, Norway	.89
Nr360043	•	Ju 88R-1	Nr360043	flown to RAF Dyce by defecting crew	9.5.43
				(to RAF for trials as PJ876)	
				Air Historical Branch Museum	54
				stored Stanmore, Middlesex	54
				RAF Museum Store, RAF Henlow	73
				RAF Museum, RAF St.Athan	77/78
				RAF Museum, Hendon	.78/92
				(displ. as "360043/D5+EV")	
Nr430650	•	Ju 88D-1/ Trop	Nr430650	(to Rumanian AF as ....)	
				defected to RAF Cyprus, impounded	22.7.43
				(to RAF as HK959; ferried Cairo-USA .43)	
				(to USAAF for trials as FE-1598)	9.43
				stored Davis-Monthan AFB AZ	.46/60
				USAFM Wright-Patterson AFB, Dayton OH	1.60/91
				(displ. as "F6+AL", later "Rumanian AF 105")	
-	•	Ju 88	-	Kongelige Norsk Luftforssvaret Collection,	
				Gardermoen AB, Norway	79/84
				(under rest. from several airframes 84)	
-		Ju 88A-5	-	wreck located Lappland	73
				planned recov. by Finnish Air Force _	
-	•	Ju 88	-	planned recov. by RNoAF for	
				Kongelige Norsk Luftforssvaret Collection,	
				Gardermoen AB, Norway	90
-	•	Ju 88	-	planned recov. by RNoAF for	
				Kongelige Norsk Luftforssvaret Collection,	
				Gardermoen AB, Norway	90
-	•	Ju 88	-	planned recov. by RNoAF for	
				Kongelige Norsk Luftforssvaret Collection,	
				Gardermoen AB, Norway	90

KAWANISHI H8K "Emily"

- •	H8K1	426	to US by ship for evaluation as "T-31"	.44
			stored, NAS Norfolk VA	45/79
			Museum of Maritime Science, Tokyo, Japan	.79/91
			(arr. by ship ex NAS Norfolk 12.7.79)	

KAWANISHI Ki45

4268 •	Ki-45	4268	NASM, Silver Hill MD	66/92

KAWANISHI N1K KYOFU "Rex"

- •	N1K1 Floatplane	44	NAS Willow Grove PA	58/91
			(displ. as "44")	
- •	N1K1 Floatplane	514	NASM, Silver Hill MD	60/91
			loan: Admiral Nimitz State Historical Park, Fredericksburg TX (loan)	85/86
			(displ. complete, good condition)	

KAWANISHI N1K SHIDEN-KAI "George"

514 •	N1K2-J		NASM, Silver Hill MD	87/91
			(displ. as "A/3-15")	
5128 •	N1K2-J		Naval Research Laboratory,Washington DC	57
			(derelict in childrens playground)	
			USNAM	
			loan Bradley AIr Museum, Windsor Locks CT	.75/81
			(trucked via NAS Norfolk,arr. Bradley 4.12.75)	
			New England Air Museum, Windsor Locks CT	81/90
5312 •	N1K2-J	62387	City of San Diego CA	
			USAFM, Wright Patterson AFB OH	.59/91
			(displ. as "343-A-II")	
-	N1K2-J		NAS Willow Grove PA	65/73

KAWASAKI Ki 61 "Tony"

195	Ki-61		crashed Borpop Strip, New Ireland	c42
			recov .74 : rep. still on New Ireland	79
379 •	Ki-61-IIb		Roy Worcester, Wewak PNG	72/74
			recov. ex Cape Wom strip, near Wewak	c70
			Frank Taylor, Bakersfield CA	
			Kermit A. Weeks/Weeks Air Museum, Tamiami FL (crated ex Chino .86)	.86/91
			(displ. dism. in museum, tailplane ex 640)	
640 •	Ki-61		Air Museum of PNG : salvage rights	75
			National Museum, Port Moresby PNG	.84/90
			(recov. from crash site .84, arr. dism.	
- •	Ki-61		Bruce Fenstermaker CA	
			recov. from Indonesian island	c90
			Museum of Flying, Santa Monica CA	.91
			(hulk arr. Santa Monica 6.91, for rest.)	
- •	Ki-61		Kimikaze Museum, Chiran, Kyushu, Japan	87/91
- •	Ki-61		Kawaguchiko Motor Museum, Yamanashi Prefecture, Japan	91

KYUSHU J7W SHINDEN

•	J7W1		(to USAF for trails as T2-326)	
			NASM, Silver Hill MD	66/91

KAWASAKI Ki-100

c/n		Type	Serial	Reg.	History	Dates
	•	Ki-100			USAFM, Wright Patterson AFB OH	.58/90
-	•	Ki-100-1b			RAF Museum, RAF Cosford	77/85
					RAF Museum, RAF St. Athan	86/90
					(displ. as "V24")	

LAVOCHKIN La-9

c/n		Type	Serial	Reg.	History	Dates
-	•	LA-9			Beijing Aeronautical Institute, Beijing China	87
					(displ. as "7504")	

LAVOCHKIN La-11

c/n		Type	Serial	Reg.	History	Dates
-	•	LA-11	-		Beijing Aeronautical Institute, Beijing China	87
					(displ. as "7505")	

LOCKHEED P-38 LIGHTNING

c/n		Type	Serial	Reg.	History	Dates
7081	•	P-38F	42-12647		National Museum, Port Moresby PNG	11.78/92
					recov. from swamp, nr. Port Moresby PNG	11.78
					under rest. for static displ.	
7518		P-38F	42-13084		National Museum, Port Moresby PNG	11.78/92
					(recov. ex swamp, nr. Port Moresby PNG 11.78)	
					derelict hulk : parts for rest. of 42-12647	
7539		P-38F	42-13105		National Museum, Port Moresby PNG	.69/92
		F-5			(orig. recov. abandoned .69, finally recov.	
					from swamp, near Port Moresby 7.79)	
					derelict hulk: parts for rest. of 42-12647	
7834	•	P-38G	42-13400		wartime crash: purchased in-situ from USAF	9.8.84
				N55929	US Historic Aircraft Preservation Museum,	
					Anchorage AK	8.84/88
					American Vets Memorial Museum, Denver CO	88/92
1417	•	P-38H	42-66905		National Museum, Port Moresby PNG	79/88
					(recov. ex crash site as "Jap Sandman")	
2054	•	P-38J	42-67543		Marvin L. Gardner, Mercedes TX	.64/87
					(derelict hulk recov. ex Austin TX,	
					stored Mercedes TX 64/87)	
					The Fighter Collection, Duxford UK	.87/92
					(hulk trucked to Chino CA .87 for rebuild)	
				N3145X	The Fighter Collection, Duxford UK	1.92
					(rebuilt Chino, ff 11.1.92; shipped to UK 3.92)	
2273	•	P-38J	42-67762		US Air Force Collection, Park Ridge IL	16.8.46/60
					NASM, Silver Hill MD	.60/90
2922	•	P-38J	42-104088	N5260N	Page Airmotive, Yukon OK (hulk)	70/73
					Gary R. Levitz, Dallas TX	c73
					Confederate Air Force : stored dism.	75
				N38LL (2	Confederate Air Force, Harlingen TX	18.2.76/91
					American Airpower Heritage Flying Museum,	
					Midland TX	9.91/92
					(rebuild to fly, San Marcos TX: ff 28.2.92)	
-		P-38L	43-50281	NX33638	Fairchild Camera & Instrmt. Co, Van Nuys CA	47
		F-5G			(to FA Boliviana as FAB....)	.49
					not del. : stored Washington DC	49/50
					Jack P. Hardwick, El Monte CA	.50
				N33638	Fairchild Camera & Instrument Co	c52/63
					(noted with camera nose, Van Nuys CA)	7.64
					Darryl G. Greenamyer, Burbank CA	65/66
				N138X	Darryl G. Greenamyer, Burbank CA	67
					(race #1 "Yippie")	

				Coastal Chemical Co, Abbeville LA	69
			N38LL (1	Revis Sirmon, Abbeville LA	.69/74
				(race #1, later #38 "Scatterbrain Kid")	
				crashed Lafayette LA (Sirmon killed)	19.10.74
4318 •	P-38J	44-23314		Hancock Field School of Aeronautics,	
				Santa Maria CA	c50
			N29Q	Jack P. Hardwick, El Monte CA	.54/60
				The Air Museum, Ontario CA	.60/72
				Planes of Fame, Chino CA	76/88
				(static displ. 60/87, rest. Chino ff 22.7.88)	
				Planes of Fame East MN	88/89
			N38BP	Robert J. Pond, Spring Park MN	10.89/92
				(flies as "423314/Joltin Josie")	
5747	P-38L	44-24743	N34933		
	F-5G		CF-NMW	Bradley Air Services, Carp ONT	60/61
				(flew last Canadian P-38 survey mission 9.61)	
				Age of Flight Museum, Niagara Falls ONT	.61/65
			N3005	Colonial Flying Corps Museum, New Garden	
				Flying Field, Toughkenamon PA	72/76
			N38PS	Peter S. Sherman, Maitland FL	22.7.78
				crashed (Sherman killed)	8.78
6790 •	P-38L	44-25786		Yugoslavian Aviation Museum, Belgrade	89/92
				(stored : incomplete airframe)	
7765 •	P-38L	44-26761	N6190C	Castler Air Surveys, Tulsa OK	c50
			CF-GKE	Spartan Air Services Ltd, Ottawa ONT	55/56
			N6190C	Hycon Aerial Surveys, Pasadena CA	5.56
				dam. Ascuncion, Paraguay: abandoned.	c63
				I. N. Burchinall Jr, Paris TX (USCR)	69
				William E. Padden, Los Angeles CA (USCR)	72
				recov. at Ascuncion by Bob Diemert,	
				Carman MAN c71: shipped to Richmond VA	.72
				Dick Lambert, Plainfield IL (stored dism.)	75/82
			N2897S	Kermit A. Weeks/Weeks Air Museum,	
				Tamiami FL (displ. dism.)	3.82/92
7965 •	P-38L	44-26961		(to FA Hondurena as FAH504)	.48/60
			N74883	Bob Bean Aircraft, Blythe CA	31.3.60
				The Air Museum, Ontario CA	65/67
				(displayed as "FAH504")	
				G. E. Blumer, Puyellup WA	69
				Air Maintenance Inc, Puyellup WA	72
				(race #59/"Scrap Iron IV")	
			N38DH	Don Hull, Houston TX	76
				Friends of Harbor Island Inc, San Diego CA	.77
			N6961	John G. Deahl, Denver CO	77/81
				cr. dest. Salt Lake City UT (Deahl k.)	3.81
				Lester Friend, Palomar CA (wreck)	.88
7973 •	P-38L	44-26969	NX53753	Aero Exploration Co Inc, Tulsa OK	.46/48
	F-5G		N53753	Mark Hurd Aerial Surveys, Minneapolis MN	58
			N503MH	Mark Hurd Aerial Surveys, Minneapolis MN	3.58/66
				Bruce L. Pruett, Livermore CA	6.12.68/90
				(long-term rebuild to fly 68/90: 8-gun nose)	
				(FAA quotes id. 8006: ie 44-27022)	
7985 •	P-38L	44-26981		Aero Exploration Co, Tulsa OK	22.3.46
	F-5G		NX53752	Aero Exploration Co Inc, Tulsa OK	10.5.46/48
			NL53752	Aero Exploration Co Inc, Tulsa OK	.48/49
				wfu, Tulsa OK by	7.49/51
			CF-GCH	Spartan Air Services Ltd, Ottawa ONT	.51/56
			N5596V	Hycon Aerial Surveys, Pasadena CA	8.11.56/62
				Don E. May, Phoenix AZ	25.6.62/63
				Ben W. Widtfeldt/Desert Aviation Inc,	
				Phoenix AZ	19.6.63

				Aero Enterprises, La Porte IN	9.9.63
				Laurel Walsh, Birmingham MI	11.11.63
				J. W. Bohmier/New London Airport,	
				New London PA	6.12.63/64
				Jim Cullen/Westair Co, Westminster CO	2.11.64/65
				Troy G. Hawkins, Wichita Falls TX	9.9.65/67
				J. L. Ausland/Sports Air, Seattle WA	20.4.67/68
				William E. Padden, Los Angeles CA	20.4.68/70
				I. N. Burchinall Jr, Paris TX	19.8.70/73
				crashed & badly damaged, Paris TX	.72
				David M. Boyd, Tulsa OK (rebuild)	2.4.73/79
				Eagle Aviation, Tulsa OK	3.1.79
				John P. Silberman, Key West FL	4.1.79/85
				(rebuild Live Oaks FL, ff 9.85: camoufl. "985")	
				John P. Silberman, Albermarle NC	.85/89
				Donald Douglas Museum, Santa Monica CA	11.10.89
				Museum of Flying, Santa Monica CA	12.89/90
				William Lyons, Orange County CA	19.5.90
				Martin Aviation, Santa Ana CA	92
				(FAA also quote id. 7985/44-26996)	
8057 •	P-38L	44-27053	NX65485		46
	F-5G		NX345	Russell C. Reeves, Tulsa OK	4.46/50
			N345	Tennessee Valley Authority TN	11.50/53
				Aero Service Corp, Philadelphia PA	7.53/57
				James M. Cook, Jacksboro TX	1.57/69
				Gary R. Levitz, Dallas TX	6.69/72
				(race #55; #38/"Double Trouble Too")	
				Confederate Air Force, Harlingen TX	8.2.72/83
				(damaged, u/c collapsed Reno NV 9.83)	
			N345DN	Gary R. Levitz/Invader Aviation, Dallas TX	11.83/84
			N577JB	John MacGuire, El Paso TX	4.87/90
				War Eagles Air Museum, Santa Teresa NM	90/91
8087 •	P-38L	44-27083		Russell C. Reeves, Tulsa OK	8.4.46
	F-5G			Raymond H. Miller, Tulsa OK	11.4.46/47
			NX75551	Raymond H. Miller, Wenatchee WA	9.1.47/48
			N75551	Mark Hurd Mapping Co, Minneapolis MN	7.2.48/56
				Mark Hurd Aerial Surveys, Minneapolis MN	8.56/57
			N502MH	Mark Hurd Aerial Surveys,Santa Barbara CA	30.1.57/68
				noted derelict, Santa Barbara CA	68
				Bruce L. Pruett, Livermore CA	6.12.68/90
				(stored, awaiting restoration)	
				(FAA quote id. 8273: ie 44-53018)	
8187 •	P-38L	44-27183		Kargl Aerial Surveys, Midland TX	13.5.46
	F-5G		NC62441	Kargl Aerial Surveys, Midland TX	17.5.46/47
				Aero Exploration Co, Tulsa OK	12.47/53
			N62441	Mark Hurd Aerial Surveys, Minneapolis MN	2.1.53/58
			N501MH	Mark Hurd Aerial Surveys, Minneapolis MN	3.58/65
				Pacific Aerial Surveys, Seattle WA	24.5.65
			N517PA	Pacific Aerial Surveys, Seattle WA	12.65/69
				Wally D. Peterson, Manson WA	21.5.69/71
				I. N. Burchinall Jr, Paris TX	27.8.71/73
				David M. Boyd, Tulsa OK	3.4.73/81
				(rebuild Tulsa .73/75)	
			N517PA	N. Merrill Wien & Richard A. Wien,	
				Fairbanks AK (based Chino CA)	28.2.81/90
			N718	Yankee Air Corps, Chino CA	13.3.90/92
8235 •	P-38J	44-27231	NX79123	J. L. Harp, Aurora IL (Bendix racer #95)	7.46
	F-5G			Jack P. Hardwick, El Monte CA	.55
				stored Brackett Field, CA & Hardwick's yard	55/76
			N79123	Joseph P. Jacobson, Stilwell KS (not del.)	66/69
				Earl Reinert/Victory Air Museum,	
				Mundelein IL (not del.)	

				Military Aircraft Restoration Corp, Chino CA	3.77/87
				(rebuild Tulsa OK & Chino CA 84/91)	
				Military Aircraft Restoration Corp, Chino CA	10.87/91
8270 •	P-38L F-5G	44-53015	NX57492	MacMillan Oil Co	46
				(Bendix racer #55/"MacMillan Meteor")	
				Rex H. Mayes CA	47
			N9957F	Hycon Aerial Surveys, Pasadena CA	11.55/64
				Tallmanz Collection, Orange County CA	1.64/65
				Rosen Novak Auto Co, Omaha NE	c65/66
				(remained displ., Tallmantz CA)	
				W. H. Erikson, Minneapolis MN	69
				Military Aircraft Restoration Corp, Chino CA	72/80
				(fighter nose; flew as "453015/KI-W")	
				Gary R. Larkins/RMP Aviation, Colfax CA	.80/81
				USAFM, McGuire AFB NJ	.81/92
				del. by air by Tallichet, arr. McGuire AFB	4.5.81
				(displ. as "Pudgy (V) / 131")	
8342 •	P-38L P-38M	44-53087		Forrest M. Bird/Bird Airways, Long Beach CA	25.3.46
			NX62887	David A. Bishop, Green Bay WI	13.6.46
				Ralph B. Lenz, De Pere WI	14.8.46/47
				R. C. Allwon, Wichita KS	26.5.47/48
				George L. Harte, Denton TX	25.6.48
			CF-GDS	Spartan Air Services Ltd, Ottawa ONT	56
			N1107V	Hycon Aerial Surveys Inc, Pasadena CA	23.5.56/58
				Vern W. Cartwright/ Cartwright Aerial Surveys, Sacramento CA	12.5.58/59
			YV-C-BAR	Cartwright Aerial Surveys, Caracas	9.59
			N1107V	Cartwright Aerial Surveys,Sacramento CA	61
				Marvin L. Gardner & Lloyd P. Nolan/ Lightning & Co, Mercedes TX	12.9.61/64
				Robert H. Kucera/Kucera & Associates Inc, Cleveland OH (survey in South America)	3.4.64/67
				A. G. Wilson/Wilson Flight Training Center, Kansas City KS	12.1.67
				Mark Hurd Aerial Surveys, Santa Barbara CA	22.3.67/68
				(noted retired, stored Santa Barbara CA 1.68)	
				Wilson Flight Training Center, Kansas City KS	23.2.68/69
				Peter W. Kahn/Corporate Air Motive, San Jose CA	3.7.69/70
			N3800L	Peter W. Kahn, Danville IL	7.70/73
				Jack Flaherty/Flaherty Factors, Monterey CA	27.3.73
				Wilson C. Edwards, Big Spring TX	4.9.73/81
				EAA Aviation Foundation, Oshkosh WI	7.12.81/92
				(airworthy: fitted P-38E nose ex MGM Studio CA, displ. as Richard Bong's "2103993/Marge")	
8350 •	P-38L	44-53095		(to FA Hondurena as FAH506)	.48
			N9005R	Bob Bean Aircraft, Blythe CA	2.2.60/70
				(stored unconv., Blythe CA 60/70)	
				William Ross, Elk Grove Village IL	.70/86
				(flew as "453095/Der Gabelschwanz Teufel")	
				Lone Star Flight Museum, Houston/ Galveston TX	11.86/92
				(flies as "Putt Putt Maru/100")	
8352 •	P-38L P-38M	44-53097	NX67861	(to FA Cubana as ....)	
				(to FA Hondurena as FAH503)	
			N9011R	Bob Bean Aircraft, Blythe CA	2.2.60/68
				(stored unconv., Blythe CA 60/71)	
				Aviation Service Co, Atlanta GA	69
				Herbert L. Sander, Atlanta GA	71
			N7TF	Tom Friedkin, Carlsblad CA	.71/74
				(arr. Van Nuys CA ex Blythe storage .71 for certification, ff after rebuild Van Nuys 9.72)	
			N3JB	John P. Bolton, Orlando FL	.74/76
				John J. Stokes, San Marcos TX	.76/77

				Cecil Harp & Robert Ennis, Modesto CA	.78/83
				Champlin Fighter Museum, Mesa AZ	12.83/92
				(conv. to P-38L, flies as "53097/4-JS")	
8441 •	P-38L	44-53186	NL62350	Kargl Aerial Surveys, Midland TX	22.3.46/47
	F-5G			Aero Exploration Co, Tulsa OK	12.47/52
			N62350	Mark Hurd Aerial Mapping Co, Minneapolis MN	11.52/58
				(noted at Prestwick & Naples 10.57-6.58)	
			N505MH	Mark Hurd Aerial Surveys, Minneapolis MN	3.58/67
				(stored Santa Barbara CA 63/67)	
				Harrah's Automobile Collection, Reno NV	4.1.67/82
				(static displ. as "453186")	
				John D. Pearl/Rudulphs Flying Circus, Chino CA	11.6.82/85
				Military Aircraft Restoration Corp, Chino CA	10.1.85/87
				(rebuilt Reno NV, Casper WY & Chino CA)	
				Warbirds of GB Ltd, Biggin Hill	10.87/90
				(del. Biggin Hill 16.5.89, flew as "Miss Behavin")	
				Evergreen Ventures Inc, McMinville OR	8.2.90/92
				(dep. Biggin Hill on del. Marana AZ 9.7.90)	
			N38EV	reg. res: 747 Inc, McMinnville OR	92
				(FAA quotes id. "197425-501")	
8487 •	P-38L	44-53232		(to FA Hondurena as FAH505)	
				Bob Bean Aircraft, Blythe CA	31.3.60
				USAFM, Wright-Patterson AFB, Dayton OH	5.61/90
				(displ. as P-38J "267855/KI-W")	
8491 •	P-38L	44-53236		Richard I. Bong Memorial, Poplar WI	5.55/90
				displ. as Richard Bong's "2103993/Marge",	
				later "423964/Marge"	
8497 •	P-38L	44-53242	NX57496	Bendix racer #47	c47
	F-5G		N57496	Weather Modification Co, Redlands CA	c55/69
				crashed, forced landing CA	c60
				Museum of Flying, Santa Monica CA	.90/91
				(badly damaged wreck, recov. ex crash site)	
				Tom Reilly Vintage Aircraft, Kissimmee FL	10.91
8502	P-38L	44-53247	NX90813		
	F-5G		N90813	Aero Service Corp, Philadelphia PA	5.51/60
				Virgil Kaufman Foundation, Philadelphia PA	12.60/61
				Bob Bean Aircraft, Blythe CA	5.61/70
				(stored Blythe CA 61/70)	
				USAFM, Pima County Museum, Tucson AZ	73/88
				(displ. as "453247")	
				Musee de l'Air, Paris-Le Bourget, France	26.5.89/90
				dest. in museum hangar fire, Le Bourget	17.5.90
8509 •	P-38L	44-53254	NX25Y	J. D. Reed, Houston TX	.47/49
				(Bendix racer #14/"Sky Ranger")	
			N25Y	Sylvan Lair & Vernon Thorpe, Yukon OK	63
				Marvin L. Gardner& Lloyd Nolan/ Confederate Air Force, Mercedes TX	.64/69
				Joe Henderson, Brownwood TX	72
				Marvin L. Gardner, Harlingen TX	77/92
				(race #25 ; later #13/ "White Lightnin")	
				(id. also quoted as c/n 5339/44-24335)	

MACCHI MC202 FOLGORE

	Type	Serial	Reg	History	Date
•	MC.202	MM9476		(to USAAF as FE-300) NASM, Washington DC (also rep. as FE-498)	 74/92
- •	MC.202	MM9546		Italian Air Force Museum, Vigna di Valle (displ. as MC.205V Veltro "MM9345")	84
- •	MC.202	MM9667		Italian Air Force Museum, Vigna di Valle (displ. as "MM7844")	

MACCHI MC200 SAETTA

	Type	Serial	Reg	History	Date
•	MC.200	MM8146		("372-5") captured Benghazi, North Africa (shipped to USA for war bonds tours) to childrens playground, USA Bradley Air Museum, Windsor Locks CT (hulk) New England Air Museum, Windsor Locks CT Jeet Mahal, Canada shipped to Italy for rest. by Aermacchi : arr. (static rest. Venegono as "MM8146/372-5", rolled out 12.12.91) USAFM, Wright Patterson AFB, Dayton OH	11.42 50/65 11.65/80 83/89 .89/92 4.12.89/91 .92
- •	MC.200	MM8307		Museo Aeronautico Caproni di Taliedo, Milan Italian Air Force Museum, Vigna di Valle (displ. as "MM7707")	75 84/92

MACCHI MC205V VELTRO

	Type	Serial	Reg	History	Date
- •	MC.205V	MM91818	 I-MCVE	Malignani Technical Institute, Udine rest. to fly Venegono by Aermacchi Aeronautica Macchi (ff Venegono 9.12.80, flew as "MM92214" later "MM9327") damaged taxy accident, Venegono rebuilt by Aermacchi for static displ. National Museum of Science & Technology, Milan, Italy (displ. as "MM92215")	60/79 .79/80 .80 23.7.82 82/87 87/90
- •	MC.205V	MM92166		(to Egyptian AF as 1243) National Museum of Science & Technology, Milan, Italy Aeronautica Macchi, Venegono (rebuild to fly, using parts of MM91818)	 77/82 .82/91

MANSYU Ki79 OTSU

	Type	Serial	Reg	History	Date
•	Ki-79			abandoned by Japanese, Maguwo NEI (rebuilt by AURI; ff Maguwo 27.10.45) Armed Forces Museum, Jakarta Indonesia (displ. as AURI "01")	44 75/88

-	B-26	40-1426		rep. recov. from Trobriand Island SWPA	c74
- •	B-26	40-1451		forced landing Smith River BC	15.1.42
				Military Aircraft Restoration Corp, Chino CA	.71/91
				(recov. ex Smith River 9-11.71)	
				(stored dism., MARC yard, Chino CA 72/87)	
				lease: Air Heritage Inc, Beaver Falls PA	91/92
				(stored Beaver Falls PA, planned rest. to fly)	
- •	B-26	40-1459		forced landing Smith River BC	15.1.42
				Military Aircraft Restoration Corp, Chino CA	.71/91
				(recov. ex Smith River 9-11.71)	
			N4299K	Military Aircraft Restoration Corp, Chino CA	4.91/92
				stored dism., MARC yard, Chino CA	72/91
- •	B-26	40-1464		forced landing Smith River BC	15.1.42
				Military Aircraft Restoration Corp, Chino CA	.71/91
				(recov. ex Smith River 9-11.71)	
			N4297J	Military Aircraft Restoration Corp, Chino CA	4.91/92
				(long-term rest. Chino CA, ff 18.4.92)	
- •	B-26	40-1501	N4299S	Military Aircraft Restoration Corp, Chino CA	4.91/92
- •	B-26B	41-31773		(322nd BG/ 449th BS/ PN-O/"Flak Bait")	
				Smithsonian Institution	.49
				NASM, Silver Hill MD & Washington DC	60/90
				(nose displ. Washington DC: remainder stored)	
-	B-26B	41-31856		Mr. Patterson, Pacific Palisades CA	c49/c75
				(stored at house, planned conv. to camper van)	
				Military Aircraft Restoration Corp, Chino CA	c75
				(nose section only)	
				(from same source: nose of "42-35075")	
2253 •	B-26C	41-35071	N5546N	United Airlines	9.9.46
	TB-26C			Leland H. Cameron/Allied Aircraft Co,	
				North Hollywood CA	29.3.48
				Leland H. Cameron/Advance Industries,	
				North Hollywood CA	1.6.49
				(Bendix racer #24/"Valley Turtle")	
				S. Murray, Oakland CA	5.4.50
				Tennessee Gas Transmission Co, Houston TX	29.8.51
	B-26C-T			(converted B-26C-T executive model by	
				AiResearch Aviation Service,	
				Los Angeles CA c53: official date 5.6.58)	
			N500T	Tennessee Gas Transmission Co, Houston TX	28.3.57
			N5546N	Tennessee Gas Transmission Co, Houston TX	22.7.57
				William C. Wold & Assoc, New York NY	23.9.59
				California Airmotive Corp, Van Nuys CA	15.4.61
				Bacon Aircraft Co, Santa Monica CA	7.9.61
			XB-LOX	Ing. Jorge Mendez/PEMEX Corp, Mexico	11.9.61
				Ace Norris, Chatanooga TN	10.65
			N5546N	Ace Norris/Aero Carpet, Chatanooga TN	17.11.65
				Carolina Aircraft Corp, Fort Lauderdale FL	24.2.66
				Westernair of Albuquerque, Albuquerque NM	2.3.66
				W. Meller Associates (for engine testing)	11.9.66
				State Bank of Greeley, Greeley CO	10.11.67
				Confederate Air Force, Harlingen TX	11.67/91
				u/c collapsed during engine run Harlingen	.69
				(rebuild began 10.75, first flight 11.9.84)	
				nose gear u/c collapsed Harlingen (repaired)	12.10.85
				American Airpower Heritage Flying Museum,	
				Midland TX	9.91/92
				(flies as "135071/N/Carolyn")	

- •	B-26G	43-34581		(to l'Armee de l'Air as 334581) Air France Apprentices School, Vilgenis USAFM, Wright-Patterson AFB, Dayton OH (airfreighted by C-124 ex Chateauroux AB France 6.65; rest., displ. as "334581/TZ-G" later "295857/FW-K/Shootin-in")	 .51/65 6.65/92
-	B-26G	44-68219		(to l'Armee de l'Air as 468219) Air France Apprentices School, Vilgenis Musee de l'Air: stored dism. Villacoublay Musee de l'Air: stored dism. Paris-Le Bourget (note: id. prev. rep. as 42-85857)	 .51/65 .65/90 5.90/91
- •	B-26	-		Military Aircraft Restoration Corp, Chino CA (nose section only, recov. ex movie studio) Carl Scholl/Aero Trader, Chino CA (nose section planned rest., for static displ.)	c76/90 .90/91

MESSERSCHMITT Bf109/HA-1112 M1L

Nr790	•	Bf-109E-3		(to Condor Legion as "6•106"2/J88) (to Spanish AF as 6-106) Deutsches Museum, Munich (displ. as "Nr2804 AJ+YM")	c37 c39 c55/87
Nr1185	•	Bf-109E-6 'Me209V1'	D-INJR	Messerschmitt Werke GmbH World speed record breaker Muzeum Lotnictwa I Astronautyki, Krokov (fuselage and major components)	 c39 79
Nr1190	•	Bf-109E-6		(JG/26): forced landing Eastdown, Sussex to RAE: displ. Canada & USA Canadian Civil Defence College, Arnprior ONT Peter Foote, Hurn UK (stored)	 65 .66/89
Nr1289	•	Bf-109E-3		(Black 2/ JG26: SH+FA) crashed in sea off Rye war loan tours South Africa South African National Museum of Military History, Saxonwold, Johannesburg	 28.11.40 43/44 .44/91
Nr2242	•	Bf-109E-3		(to Swiss AF as J-355) Swiss Air Force Museum, Dubendorf AB	.40 68/89
Nr4101	•	Bf-109E-3		(2/JG51) forced landing Manston, Kent (to RAF/RAE as DG200) Rolls Royce Ltd, Hucknall/A&AEE Imperial War Museum Store, Biggin Hill RAF Museum, RAF St.Athan : rest. RAF Museum, Hendon (displ. as "4101/12")	27.11.40 43/69 .69/76 .78/92
-	•	Bf-109E		(to Legion Condor as 6•88) (to Spanish AF as C.4E-88) Robert J. Lamplough, Duxford UK (recov. ex fire dump Leon AB, Spain .83) loaned: Tangmere Aviation Museum UK	c37 c39 1.83/85 87/89
	•	Bf-109F-2Trop		(believed 1/JG27): captured North Africa by 7 Squadron, South African Air Force South African National Museum of Military History, Saxonwold	 .43 47/87
Nr10639	•	Bf-109G-2Trop		(Black 6 3/JG77): captured Gambut airfield, Libya by 3 Squadron, RAAF flown as RAAF "CV-V"; ferried Egypt shipped to RAF in UK for trials as RN228	 11.42 .43 12.43

				RAF Air Historical Branch : display use	47/54
				stored Stanmore, Middlesex	54
				RAF Wattisham	.61/72
				(rest. to fly RAF Lyneham, Northolt & Benson with DB605A engine 72/90)	
			G-USTV	Imperial War Museum, Duxford	10.90/92
				(ff RAF Benson 17.3.91; flies as "Black 6")	
Nr14792 •	Bf-109G-6	14792		(to Yugoslav Air Force as 9663)	
				Yugoslavian Aviation Museum, Belgrade	70/90
				(note: see Nr610824 below)	
Nr160163 •	Bf-109G-6	160163		captured, shipped to USA	.44
				(to USAAF for trials as FE-496)	
				Smithsonian Institute, stored Park Ridge OH	.46
				NASM, Washington DC	65/90
Nr163824 •	Bf-109G-6/ U-2			to RAAF Laverton VIC, for trials	
				Australian War Museum, Canberra ACT	50/63
				(stored Duntroon ACT)	
				Brian Wetless, Sydney NSW	.63
				Sid Marshall Collection, Bankstown NSW	64/75
				Jack P. Davidson, Bankstown NSW	75/79
			G-SMIT	ntu Fairoaks Aviation Services, Blackbushe	10.12.79
				frustrated export: seized Customs, Sydney	20.12.79
				(stored RAAF Stores Depot, Sydney 79/87)	
				Australian War Memorial, Canberra ACT	87/92
				(stored dism., Duntroon ACT)	
Nr165227 •	Bf-109G-6			(to Finnish AF as MT-452)	
				displ. Santa Hamina	c65/70
				Suomen Ilmailumuseo, Utti AB	.70/87
Nr167271 •	Bf-109G-6			(to Finnish AF as MT-507) : last flight	13.3.54
				displ. Utti AB	57/70
				restored for engine runs Rissala AB	.70/71
				Suomen Ilmailumuseo, Luonetjarvi AB	72/87
Nr610824 •	Bf-109G-6			(to Bulgarian AF as ....)	
				(to Yugoslav AF as 9664)	
				Yugoslav Aeronautical Museum, Belgrade	84
				Warbird of GB Ltd, Bitteswell	.85/88
				Warbirds of GB Ltd, Biggin Hill	.89/90
			N109MS	Evergreen Ventures Inc, McMinnville OR	5.90/92
				(rebuild to fly, Fort Collins C0)	
				(id. also rep. as ex YAF 9663: see Nr14792)	
Nr610937 •	Bf-109G-10/ U-4			(USAF trials as FE-124 & T2-124)	
				Georgia Institute of Technology	
				John M. Caler CA	
				Warbirds of GB Ltd, Blackbushe	79/88
				Warbirds of GB Ltd, Biggin Hill	.89/90
			N109EV	Evergreen Ventures Inc, McMinnville OR	5.90/92
				(rebuild to fly, Fort Collins C0)	
Nr611943 •	Bf-109G-10/ U-4		Yellow 13		
				shipped to USA on HMS Reaper	7.45
				(USAAF trials as FE-122; T2-122)	
				displ. at University USA	
				The Air Museum, Claremont/Ontario CA	58/70
				Planes of Fame Museum, Chino	74/91
				(displ. as "611943/13")	
- •	HA-1112K-1L	C.4J-10		Museo del Aire, Cuatro Vientos AB, Madrid	.65/86
				(displ. as "94-28")	

67	•	HA-1112M-1L	C4K-31		T. G. "Hamish" Mahaddie, Tablada, Spain	7.66
				G-AWHE	Hamish Mahaddie/Spitfire Productions Ltd,	
					Duxford (for movie "Battle of Britain")	14.5.68
				N109ME	Wilson C. Edwards, Big Spring TX	20.2.69
					Confederate Air Force, Harlingen TX	17.2.71/91
					American Airpower Heritage Flight Museum,	
					Midland TX	9.91/92
-	•	HA-1112M-1L	C4K-64		USAFM Wright-Patterson AFB, Dayton OH	.67/90
					(rest. as Bf-109G-5 with DB.605 engine .82)	
137		HA-1112M-1L	-	N6109	Jack Hardwick, El Monte CA	70
					Robert Murphy, Quantico VA	78/84
					(FAA quote id. as "8-109-116-137")	
139	•	HA-1112M-1L	C4K-75		T. G. "Hamish" Mahaddie, Tablada, Spain	7.66
				G-AWHG	Hamish Mahaddie/Spitfire Productions Ltd,	
					Duxford (for movie "Battle of Britain")	14.5.68
					20th Century Fox Films (for "Patton")	1.69
					dam. on take off Le Havre, France	
					en route UK to Spain for filming	1.69
					Hamish Mahaddie, London	2.69
					Paul Jameson, Betchworth UK : arr dism.	7.70
					Fairoaks Aviation Services, Blackbushe	21.2.73/74
				N3109G	Merryl D. Schulke, Orlando FL	8.74
					Military Aircraft Rest. Corp, Chino CA	25.10.74
				N3109	Military Aircraft Rest. Corp, Chino CA	5.86/92
					(rebuilt Casper WY 84/86; crashed Casper .86)	
					(FAA quote id. as "8-109-116-40")	
187	•	HA-1112M-1L	C4K-99		T. G. "Hamish" Mahaddie, Tablada, Spain	7.66
				G-AWHM	Hamish Mahaddie/Spitfire Productions Ltd,	
					Duxford (for movie "Battle of Britain")	14.5.68
				N90604	Wilson C. Edwards, Big Spring TX	20.2.69/92
					(stored dism. Big Spring TX)	
171	•	HA-1112M-1L	C4K-100		T. G. "Hamish" Mahaddie, Tablada, Spain	7.66
				G-AWHJ	Hamish Mahaddie/Spitfire Productions Ltd,	
					Duxford (for movie "Battle of Britain")	14.5.68
				N90605	Wilson C. Edwards, Big Spring TX	20.2.69/80
					(stored Big Spring TX)	
					Kalamazoo Aviation History Museum,	
					Kalamazoo MI	83/87
				N76GE	Kalamazoo Aviation History Museum	.87/92
					(flies as "C.4K-19")	
172	•	HA-1112M-1L	C4K-102		T. G. "Hamish" Mahaddie, Tablada, Spain	7.66
				G-AWHK	Hamish Mahaddie/Spitfire Productions Ltd,	
					Duxford (for movie "Battle of Britain")	14.5.68
				N9938	Wilson C. Edwards, Big Spring TX	10.68
					Confederate Air Force, Harlingen TX	71/91
					CAF, Detroit MI : static displ.	87
					American Airpower Heritage Flying Museum,	
					Midland TX	9.91/92
145	•	HA-1112M-1L	C4K-105		T. G. "Hamish" Mahaddie, Tablada, Spain	7.66
				G-AWHH	Hamish/Mahaddie/Spitfire Productions Ltd,	
					Duxford (for movie "Battle of Britain")	14.5.68
				N6036	Wilson C. Edwards, Big Spring TX	10.68/92
					(stored dism. Big Spring TX)	
					(FAA quote id. "149")	
166	•	HA-1112M-1L	C4K-106		T. G. "Hamish" Mahaddie, Tablada, Spain	7.66
				G-AWHI	Hamish Mahaddie/Spitfire Productions Ltd,	
					Duxford (for movie "Battle of Britain")	14.5.68
				N90607	Wilson C. Edwards, Big Spring TX	20.2.69/92
					(stored dism. Big Spring TX)	

170	•	HA-1112M-1L	C4K-107		T. G. "Hamish" Mahaddie, Tablada, Spain (taxiing scenes at Tablada, for movie "Battle of Britain" .68)	7.66/68
					Victory Air Museum, Mundelein IL by	70/76
				N170BG	BG Aero Inc, King City CA	84/86
					E. Nick Grace: shipped to UK	.86/88
				G-BOML	E. Nick Grace/Tangmere Flight	15.4.88
					Old Flying Machine Co, Duxford	11.88/92
40/2	•	HA-1110K-1L (2 seat)	C4K-112		T. G. "Hamish" Mahaddie, Tablada, Spain	7.66
				G-AWHC	Hamish Mahaddie/Spitfire Productions Ltd, Duxford (for movie "Battle of Britain")	14.5.68
				N1109G	Wilson C. Edwards, Big Spring TX (stored dism. Big Spring TX)	20.2.69/92
183	•	HA-1112M-1L	C4K-114		T. G. "Hamish" Mahaddie, Tablada, Spain	7.66
					Hamish Mahaddie/Spitfire Productions Ltd, RAF Henlow, as spares source by (static views in movie "Battle of Britain" 68)	9.67/68
					Canadian National Aeronautical Collection	.68
					National Aviation Museum, Rockcliffe ONT	.68/90
178	•	HA-1112M-1L	C4K-121		T. G. "Hamish" Mahaddie, Tablada, Spain (taxiing scenes at Tablada, for movie "Battle of Britain" .68)	7.66/68
					Victory Air Museum, Mundelein IL	70/76
					Don Knapp, Fort Lauderdale FL	87/90
					William C. Anderson, New York NY (rebuild to fly, Geneseo NY: DB.605 engine)	.90/92
186	•	HA-1112M-1L	C4K-122		T. G. "Hamish" Mahaddie, Tablada, Spain	7.66
				G-AWHL	Hamish Mahaddie /Spitfire Productions Ltd, Duxford (for movie "Battle of Britain")	14.5.68
					20th Century Fox Films (for "Patton") (flew UK-Spain as "P-51B 714112" 1.69)	1.69
					Hamish Mahaddie, London	2.69/70
					displ. West Germany for movie promotion	69/70
					Luftsportverein, Hellertal WG (displ. Siegerland airfield, JG54 scheme 70/73)	9.70
				N109J	Doug Champlin, Enid OK (conv. to Bf109E standard with DB.601 engine at Augsburg WG .73/76 : shipped to US)	.73/81
					Champlin Fighter Museum, Mesa AZ (FAA quote id. "392")	81/92
190	•	HA-1112M-1L	C4K-126		T. G. "Hamish" Mahaddie, Tablada, Spain	7.66
				G-AWHD	Hamish Mahaddie /Spitfire Productions Ltd, Duxford (for movie "Battle of Britain")	14.5.68
				N90603	Wilson C. Edwards, Big Spring TX (stored dism. Big Spring TX)	20.2.69/92
199	•	HA-1112M-1L	C4K-127		T. G. "Hamish" Mahaddie, Tablada, Spain	7.66
				G-AWHO	Hamish Mahaddie /Spitfire Productions Ltd, Duxford (for movie "Battle of Britain")	14.5.68
				N90601	Wilson C. Edwards, Big Spring TX	20.2.69/83
				N109BF	EAA Aviation Museum, Oshkosh WI	2.83/92
193	•	HA-1112M-1L	C4K-130		T. G. "Hamish" Mahaddie, Tablada, Spain	7.66
				G-AWHN	Hamish Mahaddie /Spitfire Productions Ltd, Duxford (for movie "Battle of Britain")	14.5.68
				N90602	Wilson C. Edwards, Big Spring TX	20.2.69/88
					Jack A. Erickson/Erickson Air Crane, Central Point OR	89/92
201	•	HA-1112M-1L	C4K-131		T. G. "Hamish" Mahaddie, Tablada, Spain (taxiing scenes at Tablada, for movie	7.66/68

					"Battle of Britain" .68)	
					Victory Air Museum, Mundelein IL	70/76
					Jimmie Hunt, Memphis TN	85
					Eric Vormezeele, Braaschaat, Belgium	3.10.85
				OO-MAF	Eric Vormezeele, Braaschaat	21.5.91/92
					(rest., due to fly .92)	
194	•	HA-1112M-1L	C4K-134		T. G. "Hamish" Mahaddie, Tablada, Spain	7.66/68
					(taxiing scenes at Tablada, for movie	
					"Battle of Britain" .68)	
					Victory Air Museum, Mundelein IL	70/76
					JG71, Wittmundhafen AB, West Germany	88
195	•	HA-1112M-1L	C4K-135		T. G. "Hamish" Mahaddie, Tablada, Spain	7.66/68
					(taxiing scenes at Tablada, for movie	
					"Battle of Britain" .68)	
					Victory Air Museum, Mundelein IL	75
					MBB Aircraft, Manching West Germany	.75/91
					(rebuilt with DB.605 engine, as Bf109G-6;	
					ff Manching 23.4.82 as "FM+BB")	
				D-FMBB	MBB Aircraft/Flugzeug-Union Sud GmbH	4.82/91
					crashed Neuburg AB, WG	3.6.83
					(rebuilt .86 using HA1112 fuselage c/n 156)	
					dam. groundloop, Manching, WG (repaired)	27.10.86
208		HA-1112M-1L	C4K-144		T. G. "Hamish" Mahaddie, Tablada, Spain	7.66
				G-AWHP	Hamish Mahaddie /Spitfire Productions Ltd,	
					Duxford (for movie "Battle of Britain")	14.5.68
				N8575	Wilson C. Edwards, Big Spring TX	20.2.69
					Confederate Air Force, Harlingen TX	28.4.70/87
					crashed Harlingen TX	19.12.87
213	•	HA-1112M-1L	C4K-40?		Ejercito del Aire, Tablada AB	
				D-FEHD	Hans Dittes, Speyer near Mannheim WG	.80/91
					(rest. Mannheim, ff .86 in Luftwaffe scheme)	
					(rebuild to Bf109G standard with DB.605 .91)	
220	•	HA-1112M-1L	C4K-152		T. G. "Hamish" Mahaddie, Tablada, Spain	7.66
				G-AWHR	Hamish Mahaddie /Spitfire Productions Ltd,	
					Duxford (for movie "Battle of Britain")	14.5.68
				N4109G	Wilson C. Edwards, Big Spring TX	10.68/92
					(stored dism. Big Spring TX)	
-	•	HA-1112M-1L	C4K-156		Musee de l'Air et de l'Espace, Le Bourget	73/90
					(displ. as "C4K-156/471-28")	
226	•	HA-1112M-1L	C4K-158		Museo del Aire, Cuatro Vientos AB, Madrid	.65/86
					(displ. as "471-23")	
-	•	HA-1112M-1L	C4K-162		Ejercito del Aire, Tablada AB	84
					Jean-Michel Goyat & Rene Meyer, Paris	7.85
					Aeronautique Provencale Victor Tatin	85/89
					(to be restored with DB.605 engine 90)	
234	•	HA-1112M-1L	C4K-169		T. G. "Hamish" Mahaddie, Tablada, Spain	7.66
				G-AWHT	Hamish Mahaddie /Spitfire Productions Ltd,	
					Duxford (for movie "Battle of Britain")	14.5.68
				N9939	Confederate Air Force, Harlingen TX	10.68/88
					dam. in groundloop	
					Confederate Air Force, Dallas TX : rebuild	87
					Harold E. Kindsvater, Clovis CA	.88
				N109W	Harold E. Kindsvater, Clovis CA	3.90/92
					(rebuild to fly, Clovis CA .90)	
228	•	HA-1112M-1L	C4K-170		T. G. "Hamish" Mahaddie, Tablada, Spain	7.66
				G-AWHS	Hamish Mahaddie /Spitfire Productions Ltd,	
					Duxford (for movie "Battle of Britain")	14.5.68
					20th Century Fox Films (for "Patton")	1.69

c/n	Type	Id	Reg	History	Date
				(dep. UK for Spain as "P-51B 743652" 1.69)	
				Hamish Mahaddie, London	2.69
				displ. West Germany for movie promotion	69/70
				Andre Weise/Technical University,	
				Aachen, West Germany: arr. dism.	7.10.71/83
				(rest. as Bf109G, with DB.605D engine)	
				Auto & Tecknik Museum, Sinsheim WG	87/91
				(displ. as Luftwaffe Bf109G of JG53/6)	
235 •	HA-1112M-1L	C4K-172		T. G. "Hamish" Mahaddie, Tablada, Spain	7.66/68
				(taxiing scenes at Tablada, for movie	
				"Battle of Britain" .68)	
				Victory Air Museum, Mundelein IL	76
			N48157	William E. Harrison, Tulsa OK	77/78
				crashed, groundloop, Tulsa OK	10.77
				Robs Lamplough, Duxford: arr dism.	7.78
			G-BJZZ	Robert Lamplough, Duxford	30.3.82/83
				(rebuilt Duxford, ff. 3.4.82 as "Luftwaffe 14")	
				dam. landing, Biggin Hill	15.5.82
				Paul Raymond/Whitehall Theatre of War,	
				London	.83/85
				Robs Lamplough, Duxford	5.6.85
				Charles Church, Micheldever	.86
			G-HUNN	Charles Church (Spitfires) Ltd, Sandown	29.4.87/90
				(rebuilt Sandown, ff. 15.8.87 as red "14")	
				op: Dick Melton Aviation, Winchester	90/91
			N109GU	Dennis M. Sherman/Sherman Aircraft Sales,	
				West Palm Beach FL : shipped ex UK	10.91/92
- •	HA-1112M-1L	C4K-....	N700E	On Mark Aviation, Knoxville TN	
			N109DW	Harold Beale, Knoxville TN	80/81
				(race #109; #5): crashed Reno NV	18.9.81
			N700E	The Air Museum, Chino CA	9.81/92
				(trucked Reno-Chino 9.81; rebuilt, ff 19.5.89)	
				(FAA quote id. "577")	
-	HA-1112M-1L	C4K-....		Bradley Air Museum, Windsor Locks CT	78/80
				New England Air Museum, Windsor Locks CT	82
- •	HA-1112-M1L	C4K-....		Luftwaffen Museum, Ueterson AB, Hamburg	72/85
				(displ. in Luftwaffe sc.)	
199565 •	Avia CS-199	UC-26		Vojenske Muzeum, Kbely AB,	
				Czechoslovakia	84/87
- •	Avia S-199	-		Vojenske Muzeum, Kbely AB,	
				Czechoslovakia (rest. project)	84/87
- •	Avia CS-199	-		(to IDFAF as ....)	
				Be'er Sheva AB, Israel : displ.	81
				IDFAF Museum, Hazerim AB, Israel	87/90
				(displ. as "112-T"	

MESSERSCHMITT Bf110

c/n	Type	History	Date
Nr3084	Bf110C-1	dam. Memmingen, Germany	8.41
Nr4502 •	Bf110E-2	(rebuilt as Bf110E-2 Wk.Nr. 4502)	.41
		"M8-ZE" : crashed Ond Ozero, Russia	11.3.42
		(recov. from crash site by helicopter .91)	
		Jim Pearce/Sussex Spraying Service UK	2.92
		(shipped from Russia, arr. Hull 2.92)	
Nr730301 •	Bf110G-4 /R-3	NJG/3: captured at Knokke, Belgium	.44
		(to RAF for trials as AM.34 : AX772)	
		RAF Museum Store, RAF Henlow	69
		RAF Museum, RAF St.Athan	77/78
		RAF Museum, Hendon	.78/92

				(displ. as "730301/D5+RL")	
-	•	Bf110G-2		shot down by P-38 over Austria recov. from Neusiedlersee Lake, Austria Amt der Burgenlandischen Landesregierung, Eisenstadt, Austria : rest. for static displ.	23.4.44 c79 79/84

MESSERSCHMITT Me410

Nr420430 •	Me 410A-1 /U-2	Nr420430		captured Vaerlose, Norway (to RAF as AM.72) : del Farnborough RAF Museum, RAF Cosford RAF Museum, RAF St. Athan RAF Museum, RAF Cosford	4.44 13.10.45 .61/82 86 90/91
Nr018 •	Me 410A-3			2(F)/FAG122 "F6+WK" captured, Sicily shipped USA for trials as EB-103 (USAAF trials as FE-499; T2-499) Smithsonian Institute, stored Park Ridge IL NASM, Silver Hill MD	.43 .44 .46 65/90

MITSUBISHI A6M ZERO

•	A6M2-21	11593		USAFM, Wright-Patterson AFB OH (stored dism., awaiting rest. 88)	74/91
- •	A6M2-21			US War Bond tour sold for scrap Atlanta Museum Antique Store, Atlanta GA (open storage, derelict)	c44 .45 .45/91
- •	A6M5			JSDF Museum, Hamamatsu City Japan recov. ex Guam	88/91
3618 •	A6M2			W. G. Chapman/Air Museum of PNG (recov. from Buin, Bougainville .68) Australian War Memorial, Canberra ACT arr. RAAF Wagga NSW for rest.	.68/72 .72/90 10.82/92
3869 •	A6M2		N6582L	reg. res.	92
4043 •	A6M5			N. M. Armstrong, Auckland NZ (salvage rights: Jacquinot Bay, New Britain) RAAF Museum, RAAF Point Cook VIC (recov. ex Jacquinot Bay .77) RAAF Point Cook ; arr. for storage Australian War Memorial, Canberra ACT (arr. RAAF Wagga 10.82, stored unrest. 88)	 .77 6.77/82 .82/92
4461 •	A6M5		N62175	Keat E. Griggers, Tucson AZ	76
5349 •	A6M2			Darwin Aviation Museum, Darwin NT ("BII-124", hulk only, first enemy aircraft shot down over Australia 2.42)	90/91
5357 •	A6M5-52	61-120	 N46770	captured Asilito airfield, Saipan shipped to US for evaluation, arr. San Diego test-flew 190hrs NAS Patuxent River MD Ed Maloney/The Air Museum, Claremont CA (displ. complete as "V101") The Air Museum, Ontario & Chino CA Ed Maloney/Planes of Fame Museum, Chino (rebuilt Chino, original Sakae engine, ff. 28.6.78 as "61-120"; tour of Japan 78/79) (FAA quote id. "82020": see below) (id. also rep. as 5347)	18.6.44 16.7.44 44/45 c50 64/78 78/92
5358 •	A6M5-52			Bob Diemert, Carman MAN recov. ex Ballale Island, Solomons	.69/85 .69

c/n		Type	Id	Reg	History	Date
					rebuilt Carman MAN, using parts of several	
					wrecks recov.ex Pacific:fitted P&W R1830	70/85
				N58245	Confederate Air Force, Harlingen TX	.85/91
					(ff Carman 12.8.85, del. to Texas)	
					American Airpower Heritage Flying Museum,	
					Midland TX (flies as "EII-102")	9.91/92
					(FAA quote id. "807";	
					type also rep. as A6M2-21, id. "842")	
5359	•	A6M5-52			Bob Diemert, Carman MAN	.69/85
					recov. ex Ballale Island, Solomons	.69
					ff Carman MAN, crashed on landing	20.9.73
					(fitted B-25 QEC, F-86 drop tanks)	
					USMC Museum, MCAS Quantico VA	82/91
					(displ. as "136"; type also rep. as A6M2-21)	
					loaned Liberal Air Museum, Liberal KS	89/91
5784	•	A6M2			Admiral Nimitz Foundation, Texas	.73
					recov. from Gasmata, New Britain: not del.	.73
					export refused: stored Port Moresby PNG	.74
					Australian War Memorial, Canberra ACT	.77/92
					recov. Gasmata, stored RAAF Point Cook VIC.77	
					(arr. RAAF Wagga NSW for static rebuild 10.82)	
					completed, displ. as "V-173"	.88/92
					stored AWM Mitchell Storage Facility ACT	
-	•	A6M5-52	4340		captured Saipan	6.44
					shipped to US for evaluation as "FE-310"	.44
					NAS Willow Grove PA: displ. as "31"	58
					NASM, Silver Hill MD	65
					USMC Museum, MCAS Quantico VA	66/71
					NASM, Washington DC: displ. as "61-131"	78/91
82020	•	A6M5	HK-102		captured Truk, shipped US for evaluation	.44
					sold for scrap, wings cut off	
					Ed Maloney/The Air Museum, Claremont CA	c50
					Ed Maloney/The Air Museum, Ontario CA	64/70
					Ed Maloney/Planes of Fame Museum, Chino	75/90
					(shipped to Japan for display 2.80, ret. 5.80)	
-	•	A6M7			NASM, Silver Hill MD	65/91
					loan: San Diego Aerospace Museum, CA	.81/91
-	•	A6M		N72584	reg. res.	87/92
					(FAA quote id. 4306)	
-	•	A6M2-21			Geoff Pentland & Barry Coran, Melbourne	.72
		2 seater			recov. from sea near Rabaul, New Britain	8.72
					restored Essendon Airport VIC: arr. by sea	23.9.72/75
					National Science Museum, Tokyo Japan	.75/91
-	•	A6M2-21			Papua New Guinea War Memorial Trust	
					Tom B. King, Melbourne VIC	68/70
					("13", recov. from Kavieng, New Britain)	
					USAFM, Wright Patterson AFB, Dayton OH	.70/85
					(crated RAAF Pt.Cook VIC .71, shipped to US)	
-	•	A6M3-22			Domain War Museum, Auckland, NZ	88/91
-	•	A6M5-21			Malmaluan Coastwatchers Memorial Lookout,	
					Rabaul, New Britain : displ. on pole	68/72
					(recov. ex Tobera strip, New Britain)	
					War Memorial, Rabaul New Britain	88/91
-	•	A6M5			Indonesian Air Force Museum,	
					Adisucipo AB, Yogyakarta	88/91

				(displ. as "30-1153")	
-	•	A6M5-52		Military Museum of the Chinese People's Revolution, Beijing	87/91
-	•	A6M5		displ. Ueno Park, Tokyo Japan	91
-	•	A6M5-52		Air & Space Museum, Aichi Japan	91
-	•	A6M7-63		Kyoto-Arashiyama Museum, Kyoto Japan	91
-	•	A6M5-52		Gifu AB, Gifu Prefecture Japan	91
-	•	A6M5-52		Hamamatsu AB, Shizuoka Prefecture Japan	91
-	•	A6M5		Nobuo Harada, Tokyo Japan	91
-	•	A6M5		Nobuo Harada, Tokyo Japan 2nd airframe	91
-	•	A6M		Japanese surrender aircraft, Jacquinot Bay, New Britain shipped to NZ, arr. RNZAF Hobsonville (to RNZAF as NZ6000: for evaluation) Auckland War Memorial Museum, Auckland	 8.45 10.45 .59/92
-	•	A6M2-21		John Sterling : shipped to USA (hulk recov. ex Pacific Island) Caldwell Air Museum, Caldwell ID	2.91 91
-	•	A6M2-32		John Sterling : shipped to USA (hulk recov. ex Pacific Island)	2.91
-	•	A6M2-32		John Sterling : shipped to USA (hulk recov. ex Pacific Island)	2.91
-	•	A6M2-33		Bruce Fenstermaker CA (recov. ex Indonesian island) Museum of Flying, Santa Monica CA (under rebuild to fly, Santa Monica)	 .91
-	•	A6M2-52		shot down, crash in sea, New Britain American War Aces Assoc., San Diego CA (recov. from sea, Rabaul, New Britain .71) USAFM: loan San Diego Aerospace Museum (displ. unrest. as recov. 71/72)	11.11.43 .71 71/72

MITSUBISHI G4m "Betty"

3041	•	G4M3	3041	(to USA for evaluation as T2-2205) NASM, Silver Hill MD (fuselage sections only)	 87/91
-	•	G4M1	-	Bruce Fenstermaker CA (recov. ex Indonesian island c90) Museum of Flying, Santa Monica CA hulk arr. Santa Monica, for static rest.	 .91 6.91
-	•	G4M	-	Military Museum of the Chinese People's Revolution, Beijing	87/91
-	•	G4M	-	Kawaguchiko Motor Museum, Yamanashi Prefecture, Japan	91

MITSUBISHI J8M

403	•	J8M1		captured at Yokusuka shipped to USA for evaluation Ed Maloney/The Air Museum, Claremont CA (recov. ex scrapyard)	.45 .45 c50

				Ed Maloney/The Air Museum, Ontario CA	64/70
				Ed Maloney/Planes of Fame Museum, Chino	75/90

MITSUBISHI G4J2M RAIDEN "Jack"

-	J2M1			NASM, Silver Hill MD	65
3014 •	J2M			captured Atsugi airfield, Japan	.45
				shipped to USA for evaluation	.45
				Frank Wiggins Trade Tech. College CA	
				Travel Town, Los Angeles : displ. as "Zero"	
				Ed Maloney/The Air Museum, Claremont CA	c58
				Ed Maloney/The Air Museum, Ontario CA	64/70
				Ed Maloney/Planes of Fame Museum, Chino	80/91
				(displ. as "ED-1158")	

MITSUBISHI Ki 46 "Dinah"

5439 •	Ki-46-III			RAF Museum, RAF Cosford	65
				RAF Museum Store, RAF Henlow	69
				RAF Museum, RAF St Athan	82/88

MITSUBISHI Ki51 "Sonia"

- •	Ki-51	-		Indonesian Air Force Museum,	
				Adisucipo AB, Yogyakarta	88/91

NORTH AMERICAN O-47

25-222 •	O-47A	37-279		NASM Silver Hill MD	65/88
25-554	O-47A	38-284	XB-QEU		
			XB-KEU		
			N4725V	Lou Stolp & Curley Adams, Tulare CA	c58
				Ed Maloney/The Air Museum, Ontario CA	.61/82
				(flew as 'Phoenix' in film "Flight of Phoenix" 65)	
				static display, Ontario, later Chino CA	65/76
				(rest., flew as USAAF "5 15NG")	
				crashed and dest., Porterville CA	13.6.82
25-565 •	O-47A	38-295		forced landing in swamp, nr Hollyridge NC	.41
				salvaged in good cond. by US Army CH-53	24.8.78
				stored by US Army for static restoration	
				USMC Museum, MCAS Quantico VA: stored by	82
			N1047P	Leonard O. Bening, Carbondale IL	.84/88
				Minnesota ANG Historical Museum, Minneapolis -	
				St Paul IAP MN (loaned - unrestored)	87/88
				Planes of Fame, Chino CA	.89
				(for rebuild to fly, with parts of c/n 25-554)	
51-1011 •	O-47B	39-098	NC73716	Aero Exploration Co, Tulsa OK	47
			N73716	General Aerial Surveys Inc, Tulsa OK	63/65
				William A. Dempsey/D & D Aero Inc,	
				Rantoul KS	.65/82
				Combat Air Museum, Topeka KS	.82/90
				trucked Rantoul - Forbes Fld, Topeka KS	c.8.82
				stored pending rebuild	82/90
51-1025 •	O-47B	39-112	NC73722	Aero Exploration Co, Tulsa OK	.47
			XB-YUW	noted, airworthy, Mexico City	4.66
				noted as N73722/XB-YUW, Topeka KS	4.68
			N73722	Johan M. Larsen, Minneapolis MN	69/78
				Loren Florey, Eden Prairie MN	.78
				USAFM, Wright-Patterson AFB, Dayton OH	.78/89
				(rest., displ. as O-47A "37-328")	

62-	B-25	40-2168		(17th BG) BOC	2.41
2837 •	RB-25			Gen. Hap Arnold's RB-25 VIP transport	43/44
			N75831	Charles R. Bates, Chatanooga TN	22.1.47
				Bankers Life & Casualty Co, Chicago IL	4.11.48
				Hughes Tool Co, Houston TX	28.6.51/62
				Hughes/Acme Aircraft Co	.62
			XB-GOG		.62
			N2825B	JRT Aero Service, Wichita Falls TX	19.1.67
				John P. Silberman, Savannah GA	25.8.71
				SST Aviation Museum, Kissimmee FL	8.10.74/79
				Mustang Productions Inc	.75
				Samuel Pool, Lake Wales FL	.77
				Dewey Miller, Mobile AL	28.8.77/83
				(del. Kissimmee FL to Mobile AL 12.12.78,	
				rest. as "Proud Mary")	
				Fighting Air Command, Dallas TX	
				(flew as "02168/The General")	.83/87
				Jeff Clyman/TBF Inc, Tenafly NY	.89/92
62-	B-25B	40-2347		fus. recov., Ed Maloney, Hollywood studio	c66
3016 •				The Air Museum, Ontario CA	66/67
				fuselage noted, Ontario CA "Lemon Queen"	67
				Admiral Nimitz Found., Fredericksburg TX	
				Aero Trader, Chino CA	
				fus. stored Borrego Springs CA	88/90
80-	B-25C	41-12442		(499th BS/"Feather Merchant")	
5077 •				recov. and displ. Tadji, PNG	74/90
				rebuilt with tail section 41-30074/"Tin Liz"	
82-	B-25C	41-13251	N75635		
5886 •			N3968C	Hughes Tool Co, Culver City CA	54/72
				Antelope Valley Air Museum, Lancaster CA	.74/81
				Milestones of Flight Museum, Lancaster CA	87/92
				(stored dism., Lancaster-Fox Field 74/91)	
87-	B-25D	41-29784	NL5078N	Timken Roller Bearing Co, Canton OH	54
7949 •	TB-25D		N122B	Timken Roller Bearing Co, Canton OH	.54/63
				Fred Clausen, Minneapolis MN	66
				Westernair of Albuquerque, Albuquerque NM	69
				Lucille N. Ekmpton, Mesa AZ	72
			N2DD	Richard DuPont, Greenville DE	78
			N2XD	Patriots Point Naval & Maritime Museum,	
				Mt Pleasant SC	84/90
				(displ. on USS Yorktown, as "Fertile Myrtle")	
87-	B-25D	41-30163		(38 BG/"Butch": 345th BG)	
8328				crashed, Pt Moresby PNG	8.43
				National Museum, Port Moresby PNG	79/88
87-	B-25D	41-30222		(380 BG/" Hawg-mouth ")	
8387 •				forced landed 75m E of Tennant Creek NT	25.1.45
				(recov. by Darwin Aviation Historical Society	
				Darwin NT 6.74: towed out of desert)	
				East Point Artilliary Museum, Darwin NT	74/76
				Darwin Aviation Museum, Darwin NT	.76/92
				(rest., displ. as "Hawg-mouth")	
87-	B-25D	41-30792		(to RAF FR193: 320 (Dutch) Sqdn)	23.4.44
8957 •				(to MLD as A-17; M-6; B-6; 2-6) BOC	7.47
				SOC	8.7.54
				Deelen Technical School	.55/59
				National Orlogs en Verzetsmuseum,	
				Overloon, Holland	.59/90
				(displ. as "2-6"; later "FR193/NO-L")	

94-12762 •	B-25C	42-32354		used as movie studio prop	
				Jack Hardwick, El Monte CA	
				stored dismantled in Hardwick's yard	
				Aero Trader, Chino CA	
				rebuild to fly Borrego Springs & Chino CA	88/90
100-20634 •	B-25D Mk.II	43-3308		(to RCAF as KL156) BOC 5.1.45: SOC	22.11.61
			N8011	noted Opa Locka FL	5.66
			HP-428	Aerovias Internacional Alianza	.66
			CP-915	Transportes Aeros Benianos, La Paz	4.70
				Sudamericana, La Paz	
				J.S.Angueza, La Paz	
				noted La Paz, "Bolivian Airways" titles	12.72
				wfu La Paz, derelict by	76
				Roy M. Stafford, Jacksonville FL	.87
				(shipped to USA, rest. Chino CA as PBJ-1D .87)	
				USMC Museum, Quantico VA (listed)	88/90
				USMC Museum, MCAS El Toro CA	91/92
				(disp. as PBJ-1D in grey sc.)	
100-20644 •	B-25D Mk.II	43-3318		(to RCAF as KL161) BOC 19.1.45: SOC	12.2.62
			CF-OGQ	Joe E. Goldney, Vancouver BC	2.62
			N88972	San Juan Agencies Inc, Seattle WA	.67
				North Star Aviation Corp, Fairbanks AK	69
				Colco Aviation Inc, Fairbanks AK	6.69/72
				stored Fairbanks AK , ex fire bomber	77/81
				Noel Merrill Wien, Anchorage AK/Kent WA	.83/87
				The Fighter Collection, Duxford UK: del.	8.11.87/92
				Robert J. Pond, Plymouth MN: op. TFC	90/92
				(flies as "KL161/VO/Grumpy")	
100-20700 •	B-25D RB-25D	43-3374		stored Davis-Monthan AFB AZ	50/57
				USAFM, Wright-Patterson AFB, Dayton OH	.57/90
				(rest. as B-25B by NAA; del. to USAFM 4.58)	
				(displ. as Gen. Jimmy Doolittle's "02344")	
100-23460 •	B-25D Mk.II	43-3634		(to RCAF as KL148) BOC 18.10.44: SOC	18.6.62
			CF-NWV	Hicks & Lawrence Ltd, St Thomas ONT	6.63
			N3774	Glenn H. Lamont, Detroit MI	66/87
				Yankee Air Force Museum, Ypsilanti MI	.87/92
				(flies as "Gallant Warrior")	
108-24356 •	B-25J VB-25J	43-4030		(Gen. Dwight D. Eisenhower's VIP trans.)	5.43/44
			N3339G	Eldorado Corp, Dallas TX	63
				Joseph C. Frazier, El Paso TX	66/69
				The Air Museum, Chino CA	78
				USAFM, March AFB CA	84/85
				(displ. as "34030 Blonde Bomber")	
				USAFM, Ellsworth AFB SD	87/90
				(displ. as "34030")	
98-21107 •	B-25H	43-4106	N5548N	Bendix Corp Aviation Corp, Detroit MI	54
				Bendix Corp, Towson MD	61/69
				Richard D. Lambert, Plainfield IL	72/78
				Heritage In Flight Museum, Springfield IL	c72
				Walter Wild & Louis A. Fulgaro/Weary Warriors Squadron, Rockford IL	.80/92
				(recov. ex farm, Plainfield IL c81, rest. with 75mm cannon nose, ff .91 "34380/Barbie III")	
98-21109 •	B-25H	43-4108	N58HA	US Historical Aircraft Preservation Museum, Anchorage AK: reg. res.	3.85
98-21337	B-25H	43-4336	N67998	Grand Central Aircraft Co, Glendale CA	9.11.50/54
			N96GC	Grand Central Aircraft Co, Glendale CA	59
				Bert Wheeler, Fort Worth TX	63

				Aero Industries, Addison TX	66/72
				Ben Kerr, Dallas TX	c72
				I. N. Burchinall Jr, Paris TX	.73
				Charles V. Moody, Tampa FL	.74
				crashed into mountain and dest.,	
				Dawsonville GA	3.6.75
98-	B-25H	43-4432	N90399	Barbara Hutton, New York NY	
21433 •			N10V	Porifio Rubirosa, Washington DC	54
				Mechanical Productions Inc, Jackson MI	54
				Husky Oil Co, Cody WY	58
				Long Island Airways, New York NY	63/66
				Filmways Inc, Hollywood CA	68/72
				(flew in movie "Catch 22": "Berlin Express")	
				Sherman Cooper, Merced CA	.72
				EAA Aviation Foundation, Oshkosh WI	.72/92
				(flies as "34030/City of Burlington")	
98-	B-25H	43-4643		ex War Assets Corp, Seacy Field OK	19.2.46
21644	TB-25H		N1203	Paul Mantz, Glendale CA	19.2.46/61
				("The Bug Smasher")	
				Tallmantz Aviation, Santa Ana CA	.61/72
				(flew in movie "Catch 22" 68/69)	
				Vicki Meller, Burbank CA	.78
				crashed in Columbia	c78
98-	B-25H	43-4899		State Teachers College, Dickinson ND	
21900 •	TB-25H			SAX Aviation Co, Dickinson ND	7.5.50
	RB-25H			Theodore X. Fabian, East Orange NJ	17.3.52
			N66572	William L. Rausch, Teterboro NJ	18.3.52
				Rausch Aviation, Teterboro NJ	17.7.52
			N1582V	Rausch Aviation, Teterboro NJ	14.1.55
				(FAA quote id. "BD-895")	
			N37L	Le Franc Corp, San Francisco CA	12.8.55/59
				(exec. conversion: tip tanks, airstair,	
				Jato units; fitted mod. wings ex N5865V)	
				Oakland Airmotive Co, Oakland CA	3.6.59
				Carrier Services Corp, Flint MI	16.9.59/63
				Grimes Manufacturing Co, Urbana OH	7.5.63
				Air International, Columbus OH	24.9.64/70
				dam., drug run: impounded Glynn County GA	c69
				Golden Isles Aviation Inc, St Simons Is. GA	7.7.70/72
				John Hanson, Manistee MI	14.3.77/80
				(trucked dism. GA-Manistee for museum)	
				Kalamazoo Aviation History Museum,	
				Kalamazoo MI (displ. as "4899")	2.2.80/92
98-	B-25H	43-4999	N3970C	Babb Co Inc, Newark NJ	53/54
22200 •				(advertised for sale in full military config.,	
				including guns)	6.53
				(to FA Dominicana as FAD 2502)	
				Bradley Air Museum, Windsor Locks CT	4.70/84
				damaged by tornado at museum	3.10.79
				New England Air Museum, Windsor Locks CT	86/90
				(under rest. for static display)	
108-	B-25J	43-27596	N9865C	E. D. Weiner, Los Angeles CA (tanker #30)	63
32109 •	TB-25N			Peter Coward, Opa Locka FL	72
				James Hazlitt, Galveston TX	78
				Historical Aircraft Preservation Group,	
				Borrego Springs CA	84/86
				Gerald S. Beck, Wahpeton ND	87/88
				USAFM, Grand Forks AFB ND	89
				(FAA quote id. as 44-28834)	
108-	B-25J	43-27712		displ. main gate, Davis Monthan AFB AZ	65/69
32235 •	TB-25N			USAFM, Pima County Museum Tucson AZ	10.69/91
				(displ. as "0-32712/BD-712")	

108-	B-25J	43-27868	N9077Z	Dothan Aviation Corp, Dothan AL	63/72
32381 •	TB-25N			Charles Skipper, Boerne TX	78
				Confederate Air Force, Harlingen TX	19.9.79
			N25YR	Confederate Air Force, Harlingen TX	8.81/91
				American Airpower Heritage Flying Museum, Midland TX	9.91/92
				(flies as "327868/Yellow Rose/AW")	
108-	B-25J	43-28059	N9857C	Earl Dodge, Anchorage AK	63/69
32572 •	TB-25N			reg. pending	72
				Edgar Thorsrud, Missoula MT	78
			C-GTIM		
			N26795	Kermit A. Weeks, New Tamiami FL	11.81
			N1943J	Kermit A. Weeks, New Tamiami FL	3.84/92
				(rebuild to fly Aero Trader, Chino CA)	
108-	B-25J	43-28096		(to FA Venezuela as FAV 5B40)	.48
32609 •				Museo Aeronautico FAV, Maracay AB	79/91
108-	B-25J	43-28204	N9856C	Idaho Aircraft Inc, Boise ID (tanker)	63
32717 •	TB-25N			Dennis G. Smilanich, Boise ID	63/66
				Filmways Inc, Hollywood CA	68/72
				(flew in movie "Catch 22" 68/69)	
				Ted Itano/Aero Trader, Chino CA	.72/92
				(flies as "43-28204/Pacific Princess")	
108-	B-25J	43-28222	N5256V	Zack C. Monroe, Burbank CA	63
32735 •	TB-25N			Les Bowman, Los Angeles CA	66/69
				derelict, engineless, Grass Valley CA	78
				Ralph M. Ponte, Grass Valley CA	c78/80
				USAFM, Beale AFB CA: del.	8.80/89
				(displ. as "328222")	
108-	B-25J	43-35972	N9552Z	Dothan Aviation, Dothan AL	63/72
32762 •	TB-25N			John J. Stokes, San Marcos TX	78
				Confederate Air Force, Harlingen TX	13.1.82/91
				American Airpower Heritage Flying Museum, Midland TX	9.91/92
108-	B-25J	43-36074	N9079Z	Donaire Inc, Phoenix AZ (tanker #32)	63
35059 •	TB-25N			Hubert H. Clements, Indiantown FL	66
				Clements & Howe Aviation, Indiantown FL	69/72
				SST Aviation Museum, Kissimmee FL	73/82
				(displ. as "430734")	
				BOM Corporation, Wichita Falls TX	.82/90
				(rebuilt Kissimmee FL; ff 3.86 as "430734/Panchito")	
				dam. landing Wichita Falls TX (repaired)	18.9.88
				Richard F. Korff, Lewiston NY	91/92
				(note: FAA changed id. from 43-36074 to 44-30734 in 72: see N9080Z)	
108-	B-25J	44-28738	N3441G	United Aerial Applicators Inc, Papillion NE	66
33065 •	TB-25N			Midwest Seafoods Inc, Denver CO	69
				derelict, unconv., Omaha NE "BD-738"	73
				USAFM, Offutt AFB NE	.75/91
				(disp. as sectioned fuselage)	
108-	B-25J	44-28765	N9443Z	Dothan Aviation Corp, Dothan AL	63/72
33092 •	TB-25N			sale rep., Ozark AL USCR	78/90
	VB-25J			Heritage of Flight Museum IL	c78
				(displ. as "Piece of Cake")	
				Carl Scholl/Aero Trader, Chino CA	c80/89
				stored dism., Borrego Springs CA	88/89
108-	B-25J	44-28866	N5277V	Wenatchee Air Service Inc, Wenatchee WA	63

33191 •			CF-OND(2	Wenairco of Canada Ltd, Vancouver BC	65
				Northwestern Air Lease, Edmonton ALTA	70/90
				(tanker #90)	
108- 33200 •	B-25J TB-25J	44-28875		displ. Servicemens Centre, San Angelo TX	65
				USAFM, Goodfellow AFB, San Angelo TX	88
108- 33250 •	B-25J TB-25N	44-28925	N7687C	Parsons Air Park, Carpenteria CA	63
				Aerial Applicators Inc, Salt Lake City UT	66
				Trans West Air Service, Salt Lake City UT	68
				Tallmantz Aviation Inc, Orange County CA	.68/70
				(flew in movie "Catch 22": "Tokyo Express")	
				Veterans Cemetery, Pittsburg PA	.71/84
				(displ. on pole as "428925/Daisy Jean")	
				Valiant Air Command, Titusville FL	.84
				Harry Doan, Daytona Beach FL	.84
				(trucked to Florida for rebuild 10.84)	
				stored, dism., Kissimmee FL	84/90
				(FAA quote id. 108-32200/43-27687)	
108- 33257 •	B-25J TB-25N	44-28932	N3476G	Earl Dodge, Anchorage AK	63
				Robert P. Schlaefli, Port Orchard WA	66/84
				Collings Foundation, Stowe MA	.85/92
				(flew as "428932/7A/Hoosier Honey")	
				crashed, Minute Man Field, Stowe MA	10.6.87
				(under rebuild)	
108- 33263 •	B-25J TB-25N	44-28938	N7946C	Wenatchee Air Service Inc, Wenatchee WA	63
				Red Dodge Aviation Inc, Anchorage AK	69/72
				Yolanda Rodriguez, Tucson AZ	78
				Jim Ricketts/Aero Nostalgia Inc, Stockton CA	82/88
				sale rep., Stockton CA	88/92
				(flies as "428938/9C/Dream Lover")	
108- 33270	B-25J	44-28945	N3184G	Edwards Petroleum Co, Fort Worth TX	
				Wilson C. Edwards, San Angelo TX	63
				Bendix Corp, Towson MD	10.63/66
				Double A Leasing, Miami FL	3.68/69
				Perez Santiago, Miami FL	70
			CP-970	Transaereos Beni, La Paz, Bolivia	.72
				crashed	7.6.76
108- 33357 •	B-25J	44-29032		(to NEIAF/KNIL as N5-239; later M-439)	
				(to AURI/Indonesian AF as M-439)	
				Indonesian Air Force Museum, Jogjakarta	80/89
108- 33446 •	B-25J TB-25N	44-29121	N86427	Compass Aviation Inc, San Francisco CA	63/69
				(flew as "02344": Doolittle raid 25th anniversary, NAS Alameda CA)	10.67
				American Air Museum, Oakland CA	71/72
				Lee Schaller, Las Vegas NV	78
				Visionair International Inc, Miami FL	78/88
				arr. Luton UK for movie "Hanover Street"	11.5.78
				(flew as "151724/Brenda's Boys", later "151451/Miami Clipper")	
				abandoned, Malaga, Spain (movie "Cuba")	.79/85
				Museo del Aire, Cuatro Vientos, Madrid	88
				(displ. as "Ejertico del Aire/41-30338")	
108- 33452 •	B-25J TB-25N	44-29127	N9899C	Constatine Zaharoff, Arlington TX	66/69
				Anthony J. Martella, Grand Prairie TX	72
				I. N. Burchinall Jr, Paris TX	78/84
				Colvin Aircraft Inc, Big Cabin OK	86/92
108- 33453 •	B-25J	44-29128		(to RCAF as 5236) BOC 24.1.52: SOC	23.5.62
			N92872	Columbus L. Woods, Lewistown MT	.61
				Roy M. Egeland, Missoula MT	63

				Lebate Corp, Los Angeles CA	66/69
				Technical Museum, Mexico City	72/89
				(displ. on pole, Chapultepec Park, Mexico City)	
108-33524 •	B-25J	44-29199	N9117Z	A. B. Sellards/Abe's Aerial Service, Safford AZ	63
				Aircraft Specialties Inc, Mesa AZ	66/72
				(tanker #C35)	
				wfu derelict, Mesa AZ	69/76
				John J. Stokes, San Marcos TX	77
				Robert A. Lumbard, Diamond Bar CA	78
				Air Force of The Potomac/Yankee Air Mus.	79
				William P. Muszala, Rialto & Fontana CA	84/86
				Robert A. Lumbard, Fontana CA	.86/92
				(flies as "429199/ In The Mood")	
108-33691 •	B-25J TB-25N	44-29366	N9115Z	Sonora Flying Service, Columbia CA	63/66
				Filmways Inc, Hollywood CA	68/72
				(flew in movie "Catch 22" 68/69)	
				Military Aircraft Resoration Corp, Chino CA	.72
				displ. Tampa FL, "Toujours-au-Danger"	77
				arr. Luton UK for movie "Hannover Street"	16.5.78
				(flew as "151645/Marvellous Miriam")	
				Warbirds of GB Ltd, Blackbushe	.79/82
				RAF Museum, Hendon : arr. dism.	10.82/92
				(displ. as "34037")	
108-33790 •	B-25J TB-25N	44-29465	N3523G	Ernest Beckman, Battle Creek MI	63/69
				Glenn H. Lamont, Detroit MI	.77/84
			N25GL	Glenn H. Lamont, Detroit MI	2.86/92
				(flies as "429465/Guardian of Freedom")	
108-33832 •	B-25J TB-25N VB-25N	44-29507	N3698G	Verco Tropical Fisheries, Columbus OH	63
				Robert R. Johnson, Fort Lauderdale FL	66
				Austin Williams, West Palm Beach FL	69/72
				sale rep.	78
				Aero Solutions Inc, Baton Rouge LA (flew as "Cochise")	84/89
			N320SQ	Amho Corp, Wilmington DE	1.90/92
				op: Duke of Brabant Air Force, Eindhoven, Netherlands: arr. Eindhoven on del.	25.5.90/91
				(flies as "HD346/ND-V")	
108-34003	B-25J VB-25J	44-29678	N9958F	Babb Co Inc, Newark NJ	53/54
				adv. for sale flyaway unconv. Newark NJ	6.53
				Bob Bean Aircraft, Blythe CA	63/66
				Glen W. Dunn, Lawndale CA	69
			XB-DOF	displ. Mexico City: scrapped	.89
108-34133	B-25J TB-25N	44-29808	N5248V	Jasper Oil Tool Corp, Long Beach CA	3.1.58
				Les-Calco, Long Beach CA	15.1.58/62
				Los Angeles Board of Education CA	29.1.62
				instr.airframe: LA Trade Tech. School, LAX	62/76
				broken-up for scrap	.76
108-34137 •	B-25J TB-25N	44-29812	N2854G	off USCR	63/72
				Paul Bunyan Amusement Park, Brainard MN	73/84
				(displ. as "BD-812")	
108-34160 •	B-25J TB-25N	44-29835	N3676G	Jerome A. Eddy, San Antonio TX	63
				Rowsey Development Inc, Kerrville TX	66
				Confederate Air Force, Harlingen TX	69/87
				USAFM, Lackland AFB TX	88/92
108-	B-25J	44-29839	N7669C	United Aerial Applicators Inc, Pappilion NE	66/69

Continued on Page 222

Historic Flying Limited

At Historic Flying we have a team of experienced and skilled engineers working to the highest standards. We ensure a first class rebuild to the strictest modern safety standards whilst preserving the historical flavour of the original airframe. Successful rebuilds have included four Spitfires, (two for overseas customers), and we are currently undertaking a number of other warbird projects including a rare Yak-1 fighter. We have also recently undertaken the complete refurbishment (fabric) of British Aerospace's famous Mosquito. Historic Flying will undertake anything from a complete rebuild to repairs and maintenance of your warbird or vintage aircraft. Metal and fabric work are undertaken to the highest standard. Painting and finishing to your specifications can be undertaken in our Spraybake unit at our Audley End facility. If you have any questions relating to work you would like us to undertake for you please telephone.

Historic Flying, Mitchell Hangar, Audley End Airport, Audley End, Saffron Walden, ESSEX CB11 4JG UK

Tel: (0799) 528084 (Int'l +44 799 528084)
Fax: (0799) 524699 (Int'l +44 799 524699)

Continued from Page 220

North American B-25 Mitchell

34164 •	TB-25N			sale rep.	78/90
108-34194 •	B-25J	44-29869	N3160G	off USCR	63/72
				Harvard Corp, Minneapolis MN	78
				Confederate Air Force, Harlingen TX	13.8.79/91
			N27493	Confederate Air Force, Midland TX	6.91
				American Airpower Heritage Flying Museum, Midland TX	9.91/92
				(flies as "Miss Mitchell")	
108-34212 •	B-25J TB-25N	44-29887	N10564	US Forestry Service CA (tanker #E91)	.59/61
				Parsons Air Park, Carpinteria CA (tanker #E91)	63
				Hemet Valley Flying Service, Hemet CA	65/68
				stored engineless, Hemet CA	65/68
				Tallmantz Avn, Santa Ana CA	.68/71
				(flew in movie "Catch 22" 68/69)	
				David Allen/Davu Aviation Inc, Sarasota FL	72/73
				Wings of Yesterday Museum, Santa Fe NM	75/78
				Warbirds of the World, Dunnellon FL	82/85
				(flew as "429887/Carol Jean/6M")	
				NASM: stored Washington-Dulles Airport	.85/92
				(FAA quotes c/n 108-33162 ie 44-28837)	
108-34264 •	B-25J TB-25N	44-29939	N9456Z	Tallmantz Aviation, Santa Ana CA	63/69
				(flew in movie "Catch 22" 68/69)	
				Donald Buchele, Columbia Station OH	3.71/78
				Gene Fisher, Harrisburg PA	.78/81
				Mid Atlantic Air Museum, Middletown PA	12.81/92
				(flies as "327638/Briefing Time/9D")	
108-34268 •	B-25J TB-25J	44-29943	N9444Z	Colco Aviation, Anchorage AK	63/69
				derelict on fire dump, Fairbanks AK	76/79
				Richard A. Benner, Wasilla AK	86/87
				(hulk airlifted by helicopter ex Fairbanks .86)	
			N943	Southwest Aviation Inc, Fairacres NM	8.87/92
				(rebuild to fly, Wasalla AK)	
108-34335 •	B-25J	44-30010	N9641C	Arrow Sales Co, Hollywood CA	63/69
				Aero Trader, Chino CA (stored dism.)	89
108-34394 •	B-25J	44-30069		(to FA Braziliera as 5127)	
				Museu Aerospacial da Forca Area Braziliera Rio de Janeiro	79/90
108-34402 •	B-25J TB-25N	44-30077	N2849G	Avery Aviation, Greybull WY	63/66
				Filmways Inc, Hollywood CA	68/72
				(flew in movie "Catch 22": "Mouthy Mitchell")	
				Richard Sawyer, Vlarence IA	78
				GA Historical Av. Mus, Stone Mountain GA	.81/84
				Tom Reilly, Kissimmee FL	86/92
				(stored dism. Kissimmee,"Mouthy Mitchell")	
108-34415 •	B-25J TB-25N	44-30090	N9633C	Rockdale Flying Service, Rockdale TX	c60
				(stored unconv., Rockdale TX c60/83)	
				Aero Trader, Chino CA	10.83/90
				stored dism., Borrego Springs & Chino CA	
108-34454 •	B-25J TB-25N	44-30129	N7947C	C. C. Wilson, San Diego CA	63
				Walter Soplata Collection, Newbury OH	65/83
				Steven A. Detch, Alpharetta GA	12.90/92
				(id. also quoted as 44-30121)	
108-34535 •	B-25J TB-25N	44-30210		surplused at MASDC, Davis-Monthan AFB	31.12.59
			N9455Z	Paul Mantz Air Service, Santa Ana CA	61

				(tanker: based Caracas, Venezuela 61)	
				Les Bowman Engineering Co, Long Beach CA	66/69
				(tanker #82)	
				Daryl M. Jackson, Moses Lake WA	72
				Military Aircraft Resoration Corp, Chino CA	78/92
				arr. Luton UK for movie "Hanover Street"	11.5.78
				(flew as "151863/Big Bad Bonnie")	
				(stored Blackbushe & Dublin 78/81)	
				Mitchell Flight, Cranfield: del.	5.81/83
				abandoned Avignon, France	83
				Warplane Flying Grp,Wellsbourne Mountford	.83
				dep. UK on ferry to Chino CA	1.8.86
				USAFM, March AFB CA : loan	87/90
				(displ. as "30210/Big Bad Bonnie/8U")	
				open storage Chino CA	91
108- 34568 •	B-25J TB-25N	44-30243	N9622C	Clyde C. Werner, Elkhart IN	63
				Jerry Christenson, Tacoma WA	66
			N17666	Aero Dix, New Albany OH	69/72
				Victory Air Museum, Mundelein IL	.71/79
				(displ. as "Tokyo Express")	
				sale rep. USCR	78/92
108- 34579 •	B-25J	44-30254		(to RCAF as 5211) BOC 25.10.51: SOC	7.11.61
			CF-MWC		11.61
				Cascade Drilling Co, Calgary ALTA	65
				Northwestern Air Lease, Edmonton ALTA	70
				G & M Aircraft Ltd, St Albert ALTA	82/92
				(tanker #2: #337)	
				(DoT quote c/n 108-33529 viz 44-29204)	
108- 34649 •	B-25J TB-25N	44-30324	CF-OND (1		
			N3161G	Aviation Rental Service, St Paul MN	66/69
				Lynn L. Florey, New Brighton MN	12.69
				Archaeopteryx Corp, Minneapolis MN	72/78
				Military Aircraft Restoration Corp, Chino CA	84/92
108- 34688 •	B-25J TB-25J	44-30363		USAFM, Offutt AFB NE	65/91
				(displ. as "0-43363/Desert Boom")	
108- 34703	B-25J	44-30378		Aircraft Industries Museum, Louisville KY	73
108- 34724 •	B-25J	44-30399		(to NEIAF/KNIL as N5-258; later M-458)	
				(to AURI/Indonesian AF as M-458)	
				Armed Forces Museum, Jakarta	79/89
108- 34746 •	B-25J	44-30421		(to RCAF as 5272) BOC 20.8.53: SOC	16.2.62
			CF-OVN		
			N7674	Robert Sturges, Troutdale OR	69/78
				sale rep., Burlington NC	84/92
108- 34748 •	B-25J	44-30423	N3675G	The Air Museum, Ontario CA	65/72
				Planes of Fame, Chino CA	78/92
				(flies as "Shangri-la Lil", "Photo Fanny")	
108- 34769 •	B-25J TB-25M	44-30444		General Mitchell Airport, Milwaukee WI	71/89
				(displ. as "0-30444/WISC ANG")	
108- 34781 •	B-25J TB-25N	44-30456	N3512G	R. H. Hickish, Pico-Riviera CA	63
				Airstream Aviation, Carlsbad CA	66
				A. C. Ellis, Galveston TX	69
			C-GTTS	Robert Diemert, Carman, MAN del.	17.4.73
				Air Spray Ltd, Edmonton ALTA	.81
			N43BA	William G. Arnot, Breckenridge TX	.82/92
				(flies as "Silver Lady/BA")	
108-	B-25J	44-30470	N3443G	Henry E. Huntington III, Carmel CA	63

34795				Westair Co, Westminster CO	66
				Yankee Air Club Inc, Sunderland MA	69
				crashed, landing Turners Falls, Orange MA	8.9.70
108-34809	B-25J	44-30484		(to RCAF as 5250) BOC 9.5.52: SOC	22.11.61
			N92882	Columbus L. Woods, Lewistown MT	.61
				H. D. Anderson & T.A. Tiegen, Bozeman MT	1.9.64
				noted impounded Port-au-Prince, Haiti	3.74
				derelict, Port-au-Prince, Haiti	76
108-34818 •	B-25J TB-25J TB-25N	44-30493	N9451Z	National Metals Inc, Phoenix AZ	15.1.60
				Spring Aviation, Tucson AZ	24.8.60/67
				Tallmantz Aviation, Santa Ana CA	13.7.68
				Filmways Inc, Hollywood CA	11.9.68/71
				(flew in movie "Catch 22" 68/69: "Dumbo")	
				Tallmantz Aviation, Santa Ana CA	18.8.71/85
				Sherman Aircraft Sales, W. Palm Beach FL	.85
				USAFM, Malmstrom AFB MT	86/90
108-34860 •	B-25J TB-25N	44-30535	N9462Z	Dothan Aviation Corp, Dothan AL	63/72
				Edward George, Minster OH	78
				Kenneth R. Cunningham, Lawton OK	84
				Ada Aircraft Museum, Oklahoma City OK	6.84/92
				(flies as "0535/Iron Laiden Maiden")	
108-34931 •	B-25J TB-25N	44-30606	N5249V		
			N201L	C. M. Jasper, Reno NV	
				Union Bank, Los Angeles CA	63
				Jack Davis, La Jolle CA	66/69
				Warbirds Inc, Hobbs NM	72/87
				Ted R. Melsheimer, Carson City NV	.89/92
				(flies as "430606A/Tootsie")	
108-34932 •	B-25J TB-25N	44-30607	N9582Z	Avery Aviation, Greybull WY	63/69
				sale rep., Jeanerette LA	78/92
108-34960 •	B-25J TB-25N	44-30635		USAFM, Chanute AFB, Rantoul IL	65/91
				(displ. as "02344"; later"2279/Whiskey Pete")	
108-34974 •	B-25J TB-25N	44-30649	N9452Z	Filmways Inc, Hollywood CA	.68/72
				(del. Orange County CA .68 in unconv. USAF scheme for use in movie "Catch 22" .68)	
				USAFM, Wright-Patterson AFB, Dayton OH 74	
				USAFM, Tuskegee AL	86
				USAFM, Maxwell AFB AL	.87/90
				(displ. as "42-53373 & 44-34974/Poopsie")	
108-35062	B-25J	44-30737	N9446Z	Richard B. Flint, Tucson AZ	63
				Donald Aircraft Corp, Tucson AZ	66
				Darryl Berg, Los Angeles & San Diego CA	69/72
				I. N. Burchinal Jnr, Paris TX	73/74
				Air Chicago Freight Lines, Chicago IL	18.7.74/75
				War Aero Inc, Chicago IL	1.4.75
				crashed, Midway Airport, Chicago IL	6.8.76
108-35073 •	B-25J TB-25N	44-30748	N3447G		
			N8195H	Avery Aviation, Greybull WY	63/66
				Filmways Inc, Hollywood CA	68/72
				(flew in movie "Catch 22" 68/69)	
				Milan S. Pupich, Van Nuys CA	78/92
				(flies as "430748/Heavenly Body")	
108-35081 •	B-25J TB-25N	44-30756	N9936Z	Colco Aviation Inc, Anchorage AK	63/69
				derelict & stripped, Fairbanks AK	76/79
				John C. Morgan, La Canada CA	84
				Southwest Aviation Inc, Fairacres NM	86/92

				(stored dism., Alaska 88)	
108-	B-25J	44-30761	N3398G	The Air Museum, Ontario CA	65/72
35086 •				Planes of Fame, Chino CA	78/92
				(flies as "Betty Grable")	
108-	B-25J	44-30772	N9076Z	Aero Insect Control Inc, Rio Grand NJ	63
35097 •				Nico Inc, Miami FL	66/69
				noted impounded at Ascuncion, Paraguay	3.72
				derelict, Ascuncion, Paraguay	83
108-	B-25J	44-30779		rep. displ. in park, Odessa TX	73
35104					
108-	B-25J	44-30801	N3699G	Avery Aviation, Greybull WY	63/66
35126 •	TB-25N			Filmways Inc, Hollywood CA	.68/72
				(flew in movie "Catch 22" 68/69)	
				Challenge Publications, Van Nuys CA	.72
			N30801	Challenge Publications, Van Nuys CA	78/84
				American Aeronautical Foundation,	
				Van Nuys CA	86/92
				(flies as "430801/Executive Sweet")	
108-	B-25J	44-30823	N1042B	Ralph Richardson, Yakima WA	.58
35148 •	TB-25J			Earnest Lee & Arb Osen, Yakima WA	10.58V
	B-25J			Wenatchee Air Service Inc, Wenatchee WA	12.58/62
	VB-25N			Tallmantz Aviation, Santa Ana CA	17.5.62/85
				(used in movie "Catch 22" 68/69)	
				Sherman Aircraft Sales, W. Palm Beach FL	.85/87
				Consolidated Aviation Enterprises,	
				Burlington VT	11.87/89
				Universal Aviation Corp, Dover DE	3.89/92
				op. by Aces High Ltd, North Weald, UK: del.	9.4.88/92
				(flies as "430823/69/Dolly")	
108-	B-25J	44-30832	N3155G	J. J. Rivituso, West Covino CA	63
35157 •	TB-25N			Joanne M. Mahr, San Clemente CA	66/72
				Carl Scholl, Borrego Springs CA	78
				Donald C. Davis, Casper WY	.80/86
				First National Bank, Evanston WY	87
				Southwest Aviation Inc, Fairacres NM	11.87
				(flew as "Bronco Bustin Bomber/0832")	
				Showplanes & Aircraft Co, Arvada CO	89/92
				(flies as "Can Do")	
108-	B-25J	44-30854		Doolittle Memorial, Valparaiso FL	c73
35179 •	JB-25J			USAFM, Eglin AFB FL (displ. as "02344")	79/91
108-	B-25J	44-30861	N9089Z	Aero American Corp, Cincinatti OH	61/63
35186 •	TB-25J			del. to UK for movie "633 Squadron",	
				flew as "N908"	.61/63
				Aero Associates Inc, Tucson AZ	66/69
				abandoned Biggin Hill UK after filming	.64/66
				Historical Aircraft Preservation Society,	
				Biggin Hill	.66/67
				Historic Aircraft Museum, Southend	7.67/83
				(arr. by road 7.67, displ. as "HD368/VO-A")	
				Visionair International, London	10.5.83
			G-BKXW	ntu: Aces High Ltd, Duxford	.84
				(displ. as "HD368/VO-A")	
				Aces High Ltd, North Weald : arr. dism.	10.87/89
				(static displ. as "430861/Bedsheet Bomber")	
				The Fighter Collection, Duxford	.89/91
				(still stored, North Weald: last flown 64)	
108-	B-25J	44-30925	N9494Z	National Metals Co, Phoenix AZ	.60
35250 •	TB-25N			John C. Estes, Beaumont TX	66
				Filmways Inc, Hollywood CA	.68/69

				(used in movie "Catch 22" 68/69)	
				Confederate Air Force, Harlingen TX	72
				John J. Stokes, San Marcos TX	78
				(flew as "Laden Maiden")	
				Visionair International Inc, Miami FL	.78/88
				arr. Luton UK for movie "Hanover Street"	11.5.78
				(flew as "151632/Gorgeous George-Ann",	
				later "Thar She Blows")	
				stored Blackbushe after filming	78/82
				trucked Blackbushe-Wellesbourne Mountford	10.82
				trucked to Coventry for rebuild by Visionair	9.85/90
108-35301 •	B-25J	44-30976	N8193H	Oscar S. Wyatt, Corpus Christi TX	63/66
				United Traffic Corp, Miami FL	69
				noted abandoned, Ascuncion, Paraguay	3.72
				derelict, Ascuncion, Paraguay	83
108-35304 •	B-25J TB-25N	44-30979		The Air Museum, Ontario & Chino CA	67/76
108-35313 •	B-25J	44-30988	N5865V	Robert Gure, Chicago IL	63
				Air Services, Addison TX	64
				Aero Industries, Addison TX	66/69
				Robert A. Mathews, Jacksonville NC	71/72
				derelict at Fort Lauderdale FL	72/79
				Tom Reilly, Orlando FL	.78
				Craig Tims, Conifer CO & Roanoke TX	.81/88
				(ff 11.82 : reg. 8.83)	
				(flew as "Big Ole Brew'n Little Ole You")	
				Confederate Air Force, Harlingen TX	6.88/91
				American Airpower Heritage Flying Museum, Midland TX	9.91/92
				(FAA quote id. 108-34263 viz 44-29938)	
108-35321	B-25J TB-25N	44-30996	N9991Z	James J. Wright, Cleveland OH	63
				Freddy Van Dux, Chicago IL	66
			PI-C905	Aero Service Corp, Manila PI	
				dest. by cyclone, Virac Island airstrip PI	14.10.70
108-35329 •	B-25J TB-25N	44-31004	N9463Z	Dothan Aviation Corp, Dothan AL	63/72
				USS Alabama Battleship Memorial Park, Mobile AL	74/91
				(displ. as "431004", later "02344")	
108-35357 •	B-25J TB-25N	44-31032	N3174G	Walston Aviation Inc, East Alton IL	66
				Filmways Inc, Hollywood CA	.68/72
				(used in movie "Catch 22" 68/69)	
				Military Aircraft Resoration Corp, Chino CA	.72/92
				loan: USAFM, March AFB CA	82/90
108-35429 •	B-25J	44-31104	N39E	General Electric Corp, Schenectady NY	58
				Irving Reingold, Hackensack NJ	63/69
				derelict Teterboro NJ	70
				stored derelict, Pawling NY	74/83
				(FAA quotes id. 108-34379)	
108-35436 •	B-25J	44-31121		Walter Soplata Collection, Newbury OH	85
108-35496 •	B-25J JTB-25J	44-31171	N7614C	Radio Corporation of America, New York NY	59/63
				Flying W Productions, Medford OR	66/69
				based Luton UK, for filming then stored	.70/71
				impounded Dublin, Prestwick and Shoreham	
				Imperial War Museum, Duxford: by road	10.76/91
				(under rest. Duxford, for static displ.)	
108-	B-25J	44-31172	LV-GXH	Enrique Denwert	19.6.61

35497 •	TB-25N			Empresa Provincial de Aviacion	
				static display, Santiago del Estero Airport	76/83
108-37233 •	B-25J	44-31258		(to KLu as N5-264)	
				del. to RAAF 18 (NEI) Sqdn	25.6.45
				(to KNLI as M-464: later to AURI as M-464)	
				shipped Indonesia - Holland, arrived	12.5.71
				Militaire Luchtvaart Museum, Soesterberg	71/91
				(displ. as RNAF "M-464")	
108-37360 •	B-25J	44-31385	N3481G	Grafton Insurance Inc, Grafton WI	63
	TB-25J			John C. Lowe, Riverside IL	66
				Jack Rhoades, Seymour IL	69
				Northwest Development Corp, Kohler WI	.79
				Jack L.Rhoades Aircraft Sales, Columbus IN	81/83
				Air Classics Inc, St Charles MO	3.83/84
				Confederate Air Force, Harlingen TX	10.85/91
				American Airpower Heritage Flying Museum, Midland TX	9.91/92
				(flies as "Show Me/1361")	
108-37374	B-25J	44-31399		(to RCAF as 5234) BOC 15.1.52: SOC	26.4.62
			CF-NTV	ferried to Kamloops BC	c62
				derelict, unconverted, Kamloops BC	71
108-37468	B-25J	44-31493		(to RCAF as 5249) BOC 3.4.52: SOC	26.4.62
			CF-NTX	ferried to Kamloops BC	c62
				derelict, unconverted, Kamloops BC	71
108-37479 •	B-25J	44-31504		(to RCAF as 5218) BOC 21.11.51: SOC	16.2.62
	TB-25N		N9753Z	A. J. Warlick, Seattle WA	63
				Flair Inc, Kauai HI	66/69
				Technical Trade School, Honolulu Airport HI	71/74
				USAFM, Hickam AFB HI	77/90
				(displ. as "1504")	
108-37483 •	B-25J	44-31508	N6578D	Trans Calypso Inc, Miami FL	63
				Leon H. Patin, Miami FL	66
				Euramerica Air Inc, Miami FL	67/69
				(del. Bovington UK 15.12.67: camera ship for "Battle of Britain" movie, Spain & UK 67/68)	
				Airspeed International Inc, Ft Lauderdale FL	72
				derelict Caldwell-Wright Field NJ	74/77
				Tom Reilly, Kissimmee FL	.78
				(ferried Caldwell to FL for rebuild 3.2.79)	
				B-25 Bomber Group Inc, Ocala FL	.83/92
				(flies as "431508/Chapter XI")	
108-37492 •	B-25J	44-86698		(to RCAF as 5248) BOC 15.1.52: SOC	30.11.61
	TB-25N		CF-NWU		12.61
			N543VT	I. N. Burchinall Jr, Paris TX	69/72
				Daniel Jackson, Seymour TX	78
				displ. SST Aviation Mus., Kissimmee FL	78
			C-GUNO	G & M Aircraft Ltd, St Albert ALTA	5.83/92
				(tanker #3: #338)	
				(FAA/DoT quote "108-47452" ie 44-86798)	
108-37493 •	B-25J	44-86699		(to RCAF as 5244) BOC	25.1.52
	TB-25J			National Aviation Museum, Rockcliffe ONT .64/91	
				(displ. as RAF 98 Sqdn 'D')	
108-37495	B-25J	44-86701	N7681C	Filmways Inc., Hollywood CA	.68/72
	TB-25N			(arr. Orange County CA 10.68 for "Catch 22" movie, unconv. USAF scheme)	
				David C. Tallichet/MARC, Chino CA	72/79
				(arr. Luton UK 11.5.78 for movie "Hanover Street", flew as "151790/Amazing Andrea")	
				abandoned France after film work	.78

				Musee de l'Air, Paris-Le Bourget (stored)	.79/90
				dest. by museum hangar fire, Le Bourget	17.5.90
108-37509 •	B-25J TB-25N	44-86715	N3442G	United Aerial Applicators Inc, Papillion NE	66
				Midwest Seafoods Inc, Denver CO	69
				derelict South Omaha Airport NE	79
				Joseph L. Davis, Clovis CA	.79/84
				William R. Klaers, Apple Valley CA	87/92
108-37518 •	B-25J	44-86724		(to RCAF as 5203) BOC 6.7.51: SOC	26.4.62
				Avaco Service	
			CF-NTU	ferried to Kamloops BC	c62
				derelict, unconv., Kamloops BC	71
				CAFB Winnipeg MAN (displ. at gate)	74/87
108-37519 •	B-25J	44-86725		(assigned to RCAF as 5224: ntu)	28.11.51
				(to RCAF as 5243) BOC 25.1.52: SOC	12.11.63
				(to FA Venezuela as 5880)	
				(to FA Boliviana as TAM541)	
				displ. La Paz, Bolivia	83
			N25NA	C. A. Bird : reg. reserved	5.85
				ferried La Paz - Florida	.86
				Doan Helicopter Inc, Daytona Beach FL	86/92
				forced landing in swamp, Cocoa Beach FL	2.4.87
				under rebuild, New Smyrna Beach FL	88/91
108-37520 •	B-25J	44-86726		(to RCAF as 5237) BOC 24.1.52: SOC	19.2.62
			N92880	Columbus L. Woods, Lewistown MT	.61
			CF-NTP	Belmore H. Schultz/Belmore's Altamont Museum, Coutts ALTA	88
				Reynolds Air Museum, Wetaskiwin ALTA	92
				(also rep. as CF-NTS/44-30641: but noted in outside storage as '5237' prob. unconv.)	
108-37521 •	B-25J	44-86727		(to RCAF as 5230) BOC 15.1.52: SOC	23.5.62
			N92875	Columbus L. Woods, Lewistown MT	.61
				South West Air Contractors, Deming NM	66
				Met. Operations Inc, Hollister CA	69/72
				Arthur W. McDonnell, Mojave CA	75
				USMC Museum, MCAS Quantico VA	76/90
				(flew as "328217")	
108-37522	B-25J	44-86728		(to RCAF as 5247) BOC 15.1.52: SOC	26.4.62
			CF-NTW	ferried to Kamloops BC	c.62
				derelict, unconv., Kamloops BC	71
108-37528 •	B-25J	44-86734	N9090Z	Commercial Eng. & Control, Falls Church VA	63
				Peninsula Piling Co, Williamsburg VA	66/69
				Douglas Hazel, Broad Run	78
			N600DM	Dean Martin, East Middlesburg VT	.79/84
				Air Service Inc, Houston TX	
			N333RW	Air Service Inc, Houston TX	1.86/87
				Lone Star Flight Museum, Houston, later Galveston TX	11.87/92
				(flies as USN PBJ-1J "Special Delivery")	
108-37541 •	B-25J TB-25N	44-86747	N8163H	Frontier Flying Service, Fairbanks AK	63
				RJD Corp, Fairbanks AK	66
				Donald Gilbertson, Fairbanks AK	69/72
				(tanker #7)	
				Noel M.Wien, Anchorage AK	78
				The Air Museum, Chino CA	.79/86
				Robert J. Pond, Spring Park MN	.86/92
				(flies as "287293/Mitch The Witch")	
108-	B-25J	44-86749	N8194H	H. M. Trussel, Houston TX	63

37543 •				Hugh E. Wandel, Longview TX	66/69
				noted abandoned Ascuncion, Paraguay	3.72
				derelict Ascuncion, Paraguay	83
108-37552 •	B-25J	44-86758	N9643C	Rockdale Flying Service, Rockdale TX	63/74
				Three Point Aviation, Belton MO	78
				Confederate Air Force, Harlingen TX	5.11.80/91
				American Airpower Heritage Flying Museum, Midland TX	9.91/92
				(flies as USMC PBJ-1J "Devil Dog")	
108-37566	B-25J TB-25N	44-86772	N9333Z	David W. Brown, Miami FL	63
				abandoned, Teodolina, Santa Fe, Argentina	62
				displ. Villa Canas Aero Club	63
				derelict at Villa Canas Airfield	83
108-37567 •	B-25J	44-86773		(to RCAF as 5282) BOC 8.10.53: SOC	22.11.61
			N8010		12.61
			YV-E-IPU		7.65
			YV-19CP		c.75
				crashed	11.8.77
				derelict at Caracas- Maiquetia	83
108-37571 •	B-25J TB-25N	44-86777	N9167Z	Fike Plumbing Inc, Phoenix AZ	63/66
				James E. Landon, Phoenix AZ	69
				Allan R. Crosby, Wauwatosa WI	72
				Crosby Enterprises Inc, Wauwatosa WI	78
				Richard T. Crosby, Wauwatosa WI	84/86
				(flew as "486777/BD-777")	
				Vintage Aircraft Inc, Kissimmee FL	87
				Mid South Lumber Co, Cropwell AL	6.88/92
				(flies as "Martha Jean")	
108-37579 •	B-25J TB-25N	44-86785	N5262V	Charlie T. Jensen, Tonopah Air Service NV	c58/76
				(stored in hangar, Tonopah NV c58/76)	
				Mid Pacific International Inc, Eugene OR	78
				Gary Flanders, Oakland CA	82/83
				Wiley Sanders Truck Lines Inc, Troy AL	6.83/92
				(flies as "486785/Georgia Mae")	
108-37585 •	B-25J TB-25J	44-86791	N8196H	Ace Smelting Inc, Phoenix AZ	18.5.59
				Merrill & Richard Wien, Fairbanks AK	19.5.59
				Merric Inc, Fairbanks AK	8.6.61
				Frontier Flying Service, Fairbanks AK	19.5.62
				RJD Company, Fairbanks AK	3.2.63
				Aero Retardent, Fairbanks AK	4.4.67
				Pacific Alaska Airlines, Fairbanks AK	13.6.77
				Donald Gilbertson, Fairbanks AK	28.8.79
				Aero Heritage Inc, Melbourne, Australia	4.6.82/85
				arrived Brisbane on ferry flight from USA	20.12.83
			VH-XXV	Australian War Memorial, Canberra ACT	85/91
				(flew as "A47-31/KO-P")	
				long term storage Canberra: last flown	30.11.87
108-37591 •	B-25J TB-25J	44-86797	N3438G	Caribbean Enterprises Int., Gulfport MS	66
				Herbert G. Ransom, Brentwood CA	69/72
				Aero Trader, Chino CA	.73/84
				Richard Skadsheim	84
				Wiley Sanders Truck Lines Inc, Troy AL	.84/92
				(flew as "Samantha"; "Old Grey Mare"; later "USN 486797/WS")	
108-47474	B-25J	44-86820		(to RCAF as 5204) BOC 6.7.51: SOC	23.5.62
			N92874	Columbus L. Woods, Lewistown MT	.61
			N232S	Quick Freeze Corp, St Thomas USVI	63/65
				Curtiss National Bank, Miami FL	66
			CP-808	F. Garcia, La Paz	4.67
				crashed at Itagua, Bolivia	19.4.67
				Bolivariana, La Paz	72
				crashed	21.11.77

108-47497	B-25J TB-25N	44-86843	N3507G	Major Air Corp, Tucson AZ (tanker #05C)	63/66
				Filmways Inc, Hollywood CA	.68/69
				(used in movie "Catch 22" 68/69)	
				USAFM, Grissom AFB IN	74/90
				(displ. as "486843/Passionate Paulette")	
108-47498	B-25J	44-86844	N3453G	Art Jones, Slidell LA	63/69
				derelict New Orleans-Lakefront AP LA	73/77
108-47520 •	B-25J	44-86866	N9069Z	Amazon Trading Co, Miami FL	63
				Donald E. Lynch, Miami FL	66/69
				impounded Quito, Ecuador	
				Museo Aero de La FAE, Quito AFB	78/89
				(displ. in FAE sc. as "B-N9069Z")	
108-47526 •	B-25J	44-86872	N2888G	Dennis G. Smilanich, Boise ID	66/69
				noted derelict & stripped, Boise ID	83
				Aero Nostalgia Inc, Stockton CA (rebuilt)	87
				USAFM, Robins AFB GA	.87/91
				(displ. as "486872")	
108-47527	B-25J TB-25K	44-86873	N9639C N87Z	California Aircraft Engine Co,	
				San Lorenzo CA	63/66
				Midwest Seafoods Inc, Denver CO	69
				(off USCR 72/78: parked Tamiami FL 80/82)	
				Marcelo R. Ortiz, Miami FL	82
				crashed, Long Island, Bahamas	2.8.82
108-47534 •	B-25J TB-25N	44-86880		displ. on pole Reese AFB, Lubbock TX	65/73
				USAFM, Reese AFB, Lubbock TX	87/90
				(displ. as "44-6880")	
108-47545 •	B-25J	44-86891	N3337G		.59
				L. K. Roser, Phoenix AZ	63
				Aero Industries, Addison TX	66/69
				The Payne Company, Pecos TX	72
				J. K. West, Corpus Christi TX	c72
				John J. Stokes, San Marcos TX	.73
				Dwight Reimer, Shafter CA	78
				L. W. Richards, Chico CA	11.79
				USAFM, Castle AFB CA: del.	14.1.80/92
				(displ. as "02344")	
108-47547 •	B-25J	44-86893	N6123C	A. B. Sellards/Abe's Aerial Service,	
				Safford AZ	63
				Aircraft Specialties Inc, Mesa AZ	66/72
				(tanker #C34)	
				wfu, derelict Mesa AZ, by	69/76
				John J. Stokes, San Marcos TX	77
				Kansas City Warbirds Inc, Kansas City MO	78/92
				(flies as "486893/Fairfax Ghost")	
108-47562 •	B-25J	45-8811	N9621C	Air Traders Inc, Miami FL	63
				C. M. Stephenson, Miami FL	66/69
				Richard Lloyd, Miami FL	12.69
				Antonio Rodriguez, San Juan PR	72
				Seagull Enterprises, Christiansted USVI	78
				Doan Helicopter Inc, Daytona Beach FL	.80/91
				(ferried St Croix to Daytona Beach FL .80,	
				rest., ff 2.82: flew camouflaged as "HD")	
				Apache Aviation, Dijon, France	5.91/92
				op by Flying Legends, Dijon	
				(del. via St.Johns-Lisbon 21.5.91)	
108-	B-25J	45-8835	N69345	Bendix Aviation Corp, Teterboro NJ	48/66

c/n	Type	Serial	Reg	Owner	Date
47586 •				Bendix Field Engineering Corp, Columbia MD	69/72
			CF-DKU	Aurora Aviation Ltd, Edmonton ALTA	12.72
			C-FDKU	G & M Aircraft Ltd, St Albert ALTA	82/92
				(tanker #1:#336)	
108-47633	B-25J	45-8882	N75754	Albert Trostel & Son, Milwaukee WI	50s
			N32T	Albert Trostel & Son, Milwaukee WI	54
				New Jersey Air Co, Hackensack NJ	66/69
				derelict, Teterboro NJ	70/72
				broken-up, Teterboro NJ (to rebuild N34E)	.74
				Carl Scholl/Aero Trader, Chino CA	89
				(forward fuselage section only)	
108-47634 •	B-25J	45-8883	N75755		c47
				Northern Pump Co, Minneapolis MN	54
				Bendix Corp, Teterboro NJ	
				Perter Volid, Chicago IL	63
				crashed, damaged, Northbrook IL	16.8.65
				Jack Adams Aircraft Sales, Walls MS	66
				R. H. Wood, Laurel MD	69
				Wilbert Vault Service Inc, Laurel MD	72
			C-GCWA	ntu: Canadian Warplane Heritage, Sidney BC	.75
			C-GCWM	Canadian Warplane Heritage, Sidney BC	5.75/91
				(flies as "HD372/VO-D")	
108-47635 •	B-25J	45-8884	N3156G	Aviation Rental Service, St Paul MN	66
				Johan M. Larsen, Minneapolis MN	69/78
				Minnesota Aircraft Mus., Minneapolis MN	.72
				Jerry C Janes, Vancouver BC	79
			C-GCWJ	Canadian Warplane Heritage, Sidney BC	8.80
				(flew as "Death Wish"; "City of Edmonton")	
			N5833B	David Brady, Cartersville GA	26.8.85
				Harry S. Doan/Doan Helicopter Inc, Daytona Beach FL	9.85
				David Brady, Cartersville GA	86
				Randall Porter, Woodstock GA	87/92
				(flies as "458884/Georgia Girl")	
108-47638 •	B-25J TB-25N	45-8887	N3680G	H. H. Coffield, Rockdale TX	63/69
				Rockdale Flying Service, Rockdale TX	72
				I. N. Burchinall Jr, Paris TX	c75
				Frederick Bates, Austin TX	78
				u/c collapsed landing, Vega TX	c78
				Mark Thompson	c80
				Historic Aircraft Preservation Group, Borrego Springs/Chino CA	84/92
				(trucked from TX: stored dism. Borrego Springs, later by Aero Trader, Chino CA)	
108-47649 •	B-25J TB-25N	45-8898	N898BW	Binary Warriors Inc, Weston MA	12.85/92
				(flies in RAF camouflage scheme)	
-	B-25J	-	CF-NWJ	reported at Toronto-Malton ONT	72
- •	B-25J	-		(to FA Boliviana as FAB 542)	
				displ. on pylons, Cochabamba AB, Bolivia	83/90
- •	B-25J	-		(to FA Brasileira as 5075)	
				displ. Sao Paulo AFB, Brazil	67/75
- •	B-25J CB-25J	-		(to FA Brasileira as 5097)	
				Museu de Armas e Vehiculos Motor, Antigos	79
				Eduardo Andrea Matarazzo War Museum, Bebeduoro, Brazil	83
- •	B-25J	-		(to FA Brasileira as 5133)	
				Air Force Academy Museum,	

				Pirassununga, Sao Paulo, Brazil	85
-	B-25H	-		(to Chinese AF as 120) rep. displ. occasionally, Beijing present status unknown	 c73
-	B-25H	-		(to Chinese AF as 329) rep. displ. occasionally, Beijing present status unknown	 c73
- •	B-25J	-		(to FA Uruguaya as G3-158) Museo Nacional de Aviacion, Montevideo (displ. as "160")	6.50 79/91

NORTH AMERICAN F-82 TWIN MUSTANG

120- 43743 •	XP-82 ZXF-82	44-82887		Walter Soplata Collection, Newbury OH (incomplete airframe)	65/85
123- 43748 •	F-82B	44-65162		USAFM, Lackland AFB TX Confederate Air Force, Mercedes TX (ferried Lackland AFB to Mercedes TX .66)	.56/65 .66
			N12102	Confederate AF, Mercedes/Harlingen TX ground accident, Harlingen TX (repaired) American Airpower Heritage Flying Museum, Midland TX (flies as"465162/PQ-162")	31.1.68/91 10.10.87 9.91/92
123- 43754 •	F-82B	44-65168		USAFM, Wright-Patterson AFB, Dayton OH (displ. as "465168/PQ-168/Betty-Jo")	21.6.57/92
144- 38141 •	F-82E	46-255		Walter Soplata Collection, Newbury OH	65/85
144- 38148 •	F-82E	46-262		USAFM, Lackland AFB TX (displ. as USAF "6262/FQ-262")	.56/92

73-101 •	XP-51	41-38		(allotted to RAF as AG348: not del.)	
				NASM, stored Park Ridge IL/Silver Hill MD	50/75
			N51NA	EAA Foundation, Hales Corner/Oshkosh WI.	75/92
				(rebuilt Fort Collins CO, ff .76;	
				retired to EAA Museum after last flight 1.8.82)	
97-15883 •	A-36A	42-83665	N39502	Essex Wire Corp, (Bendix racer #44; #2)	.46
				(Bendix racer #15 "City of Lynchburg")	.47
				crashed during race, Cleveland OH	1.9.47
				Hanby Enterprises	
				Charles P. Doyle, Rosemount MN	66/69
				USAFM, Wright-Patterson AFB, Dayton OH .71/91	
				(displ. as "83665/BF Margie H")	
97-15949 •	A-36A	42-83731		Jack P. Hardwick, El Monte CA (stored)	50/75
				Thomas L. Camp, Livermore CA : for rebuild	.75
			N50452	Dick Martin, Carlsbad CA	8.80
			N251A	Cinema Air Inc, Carslbad CA	83/92
				displ. Champlin Fighter Museum, Mesa AZ	91
97-15956 •	A-36A	42-83738	N4607V	Sidney Smith, Sheridan IL & Bradenton FL	63/72
				(rep. ex storage, Jack Hardwick, El Monte CA)	
				Wings of Yesterday Air Museum, Santa Fe NM	75/79
				John R. Paul, Hamilton MT & Boise ID	82/92
				(under rebuild Caldwell ID, as P-51B)	
99-22109 •	P-51A	43-6006		forced landing Fairbanks-Anchorage AK	24.2.44
				wreck recov. by W.Spillers	10.77
			N51Z	Waldon D. ("Moon") Spillers, Versailles OH	.77/92
				(rebuilt Versailles, using P-51D fus. components	
				and ex-AURI mainplane: ff 7.85 as "36006")	
99-22281 •	P-51A	43-6178		trade school, Freeman Field, Seymour IN	50/60
			N8647E	Walter Erickson, Rosemount MN	66/78
				Kermit A. Weeks, Tamiami FL	81/84
			N51KW	Weeks Air Museum,Tamiami FL	1.85/92
				(stored awaiting restoration)	
99-22354 •	P-51A	43-6251		Cal Aero Technical Institute, Glendale CA	.46/53
				The Air Museum, Claremont CA	.53/79
			N4235Y	Planes of Fame, Chino CA	2.81/92
				(rebuilt Chino ex static displ., ff 19.8.81)	
99-22377 •	P-51A	43-6274	N73630		
			N90358	Yankee Air Corps, Chino CA	81/92
				(rest. to fly, Chino CA)	
104-25789 •	P-51B	43-24760	NX28388	Jacqui Cochrane, Los Angeles CA	.46
				(Bendix racer #13) : crashed	9.48
				reported stored, Indio CA	73
105-25931 •	XP-51G	43-43335		used as cockpit (Link) trainer	c55
				rediscovered,en route scrap dealer	.75
				John Morgan, La Canada CA (for rebuild)	c76/89
103-26199 •	P-51C	42-103645		static display, Billings MT; recov. by CAF	c65
				Confederate Air Force, Mercedes TX: stored	c65
			N9288	Confederate Air Force, Omaha NE : rebuild	73/85
			N215CA	Confederate Air Force, St. Paul MN : rebuild	85/89
103-26385 •	P-51C	42-103831		Paul Mantz, Glendale CA	19.2.46
				(USAAF disposal ex Stillwater AFB OK 19.2.46)	
			NX1204	Paul Mantz, Los Angeles CA	.46
				Bendix racer #60/"Latin America"; later #46)	
			N1204	Tallmantz / Movieland of the Air Museum,	
				Orange County CA	c48/84

				Frank G. Tallman, Orange County CA	84
				Weeks Air Museum, Tamiami FL	.85/92
				(rebuild to fly)	
103-26778 •	P-51C	43-25147	N51PR	Peter Regina, Van Nuys CA	3.81/86
				(rebuilt Van Nuys: composite using P-51B mainplane & P-51D fuselage ex IDFAF "13" both recov. ex Israel; ff 11.6.81)	
				Joseph Kasparoff, Montebello CA	87/92
				(flies as "36913/The Believer")	
				(id also reported as 43-25171)	
109-26890 •	P-51D	44-13257		(to NACA as NACA 108)	
	EF-51D		N4222A	Cavalier Aircraft Corp, Sarasota FL	
	Cavalier			Trans Florida Aviation, Sarasota FL	.59/69
(c/n 11)			N51DL	David B. Lindsay/Lindair Inc, Sarasota FL	72/92
109-26911 •	P-51D	44-13278		Yugoslavian Aviation Museum, Belgrade	84/92
				(stored, incomplete airframe)	
109-27024 •	P-51D	44-13571		USAFM, Armament Museum, Eglin AFB FL	79/87
	Cavalier Mk. 2	68-15796		(also rep. as 44-13574)	
109-27924 •	P-51D	44-14291		Musee de l'Air, Paris-Le Bourget	84/91
				(displ. as recov. ex beach forced landing)	
109-28207 •	P-51D	44-14574		(479th FG/436th FS, Wattisham "Little Zipper")	
				ditched off Clacton Pier	13.1.45
				East Essex Aviation Museum, Essex : recov.	16.8.87/90
109-28459	P-51D	44-14826		Trottner Iron & Metal Co, San Antonio TX	.49
				(destined RNZAF: still in original packing case)	.51
			N1740B	Dal-Air, Dallas TX	.51
				(to FA Haiti as 14826: later FAH 826)	10.7.51
				(to FA Dominicana for disposal)	
			N551D (3	Bruce Morehouse, San Antonio TX : USCR	78/84
				Gordon Plaskett, King City CA	c73
				Cavalier Aircraft Corp, Opa Locka FL	c73/74
				(id. transferred to CA-17 c/n 1364: que se)	
109-28549	P-51D	44-14916		Trottner Iron & Metal Co, San Antonio TX	.49
				(destined RNZAF: still in original packing case)	.51
			N1736B	Dal-Air, Dallas TX	.51
				(to FA Haiti as 14916: later FAH 916)	18.5.51
				(to FA Dominicana for disposal)	
				rep. to Gordon Plaskett, King City CA	c73
				rep. to Cavalier Aircraft Corp, Opa Locka FL	c73/74
111-29080 •	P-51C	44-10947		Paul Mantz, Glendale CA	19.2.46
				(USAAF disposal ex Stillwater AFB OK 19.2.46)	
			NX1202	Paul Mantz, Los Angeles CA	.46/48
				(Bendix racer #46/"Excalibur"; later #60)	
			N1202	Paul Mantz, Orange County CA	
				NASM, Silver Hill MD	74/87
				loan: California Museum of Science & Industry, Los Angeles CA	88/90
111-29286 •	P-51K	44-11153		(to FA Salvadorena as FAS-401)	9.68
			N34FF	Flaherty Factors Inc, Monterey CA	1.11.74
				(adopted id. 44-11153 when registered: also reported to be 45-11559/FAS-409)	
				Scott Smith	
				William Clark/Clark Motor Co, PA	83/85
			N51WE	Clark Motor Co, State College PA	9.85/88
				crashed near State College PA (Clark killed)	7.3.88

111-29940 •	P-51K	44-11807		USAFM, McEntire ANGB, Florence SC	73/90
111-30249 •	P-51K	44-12116	NX79161	Robert Swanson	.46
				(Bendix racer #80/"Second Fiddle")	
				Thompson Products Museum, Cleveland OH	58
				Frederick Crawford Museum, Cleveland OH	79/87
				(displ. as NX79161/#80/"Second Fiddle")	
111-30258 •	P-51K	44-12125		(to RNAF as H-307)	
				Militaire Luchtvaart Museum, Soesterberg AB	69/91
111-30259 •	P-51K	44-12126	N9140H	(to IDFAF as ....)	50s
				rep. Israeli Air Force Museum	84
111-30272 •	P-51K	44-12139		(to FA Dominicana as FAD....)	
				Brian O'Farrell/Johnson Aviation, Miami FL	.84
			N90613	Brian O'Farrell Inc, Miami FL	7.89
				(note: id. confused with 44-12852: que se)	
111-30273 •	P-51K	44-12140	NX66111	Bendix racer	.46
				crashed Cleveland OH	.46
			N66111	Glenn Hussey, Carmichael CA	66/69
				Aadu Karemaa, San Diego CA (rebuild)	86
			N119AK	Aadu Karemaa, San Diego CA	10.89/92
				(id. also rep. as 44-12119)	
			N119VF	re-reg.Type quoted as Aero Classics P-51D by FAA	4.92
111-30591 •	P-51K	44-12458		(to ROKAF as ....)	
				(captured by CNAF as ....)	
				displ. Beijing Institute, Beijing, China	88
111-36135 •	P-51K F-6K Cavalier	44-12852	NX40055	Bendix racer #65	
				Jack P. Hardwick, El Monte CA	
				(rebuilt by Hardwick .54 with dual controls)	
			N90613	Intercontinental Airways, Canastota NY	54
				B. L. Tractman/Aviation Corp of America	15.3.54
				(to FA Dominicana as FAD 1900)	26.4.54/84
				Brian O'Farrell/Johnson Aviation, Miami FL	.84/88
			N21023	James E. Beasley, Philadelphia PA	.88/92
				flies as "413318/C5-N/Frenesi")	
				(id. confused with P-51K 44-12139: que se)	
122-31076 •	P-51D	44-63350	N2870D	Clarence A. Head, Eglin IL	63
				Mark R. Foutch, Champaign IL	66/84
				Tom Kelly & John Dilly/Ft Wayne Air Services, Fort Wayne IN (rebuilt as TF-51D)	.84
			N51TK (2	Fort Wayne Air Services, Fort Wayne IN	5.86/88
				International Aircraft Ltd, Hockessin DE	4.89/92
				crashed on takeoff, Ft. Wayne IN	11.4.89
122-31133 •	P-51D	44-63407		(to FA Guatamalteca as FAG 324)	
			N63407	Wilson C. Edwards, Big Spring TX	84/87
122-31207	P-51D Cavalier	44-63481		(to RCAF as 9553) BOC 7.6.47 SOC	27.12.57
			N6303T	James H. Defuria & Fred J. Ritts/ Intercontinental Airways, Canastota NY	11.56/60
				Aero Enterprises, Elkhart IN	10.5.60/61
				Century Mutual Insurance, Des Moines IA	18.3.61
				Aero Enterprises, Elkhart IN	12.7.61/62
				Bernard Little/Pinellas Aircraft Inc, St. Petersburg FL	7.2.62
				The Brane Corp, Largo FL	25.4.62
				Bernard Little/Agels Inc, Tampa FL	23.8.63/64
				Richard K. Kestle/Pizza On Call Franchise Inc, Columbus GA	15.2.64/72

				(race #13/"Miss Diet Rite","Miss Gatorade Cola")	
				(mod. to tall fin Cavalier by TFA 66/67)	
				crashed, minor damage, Atlanta GA	12.5.67
				crashed, dest., Griffin GA (Kestle k.)	3.6.72
122-31233	P-51D	44-63507		(to RCAF as 9554) BOC 7.6.47 SOC	20.9.60
			N6345T	James H. Defuria & Fred J. Ritts/	
				Intercontinental Airways, Canastota NY	25.2.57/60
				(stored unconv., Carberry MAN 57/61)	
				Aero Enterprises, Elkhart IN	10.5.60/63
				Harold R. Hacker, Noblesville IN	12.63/64
				crashed, minor dam., La Porte IN	22.2.64
				Aero Enterprises, La Porte IN	7.3.64
				Hammonton Investment Co, Hammonton NJ	1.9.64
				John Dilley, Elkhart IN	10.64/65
				Gardner Flyers Inc, Brownwood TX	16.9.65/72
				crashed, badly dam., Brownwood TX	c68
			N12073	ntu	
				(rep. used in rebuild of 44-72483/N13410)	.78
			N6345T	Marvin L. Gardner, Mercedes TX : hulk	4.85/90
				Pioneer Aero Service, Chino CA :	90/92
122-31268 •	P-51D	44-63542		sold surplus McClellan AFB CA	11.12.57
			N5450V	David L. (Homer) Rountree, Marysville CA	18.2.58/79
				(open storage, Marysville CA 58/81)	
				Ted E. Contri, Reno NV	.79
			N51HR	Ted Contri & Homer Rountree, Reno NV	6.82
				Contri Contstruction Co, Yuba City CA	90/92
122-31302 •	P-51D	44-63576	NX37492	(Bendix racer #37/"Wraith"; "Jay Dee")	.46/49
				stored	c47/74
			N37492	Max I. Ramsay, Johnson KS	77
			N51DH	Consolidated Airways, Fort Wayne IN	2.81/84
				(rebuilt Chino CA 77/85)	
				Frank Strickler/Fox 51 Limited, Denton TX	1.85/87
				Evergreen Ventures Inc, McMinnville OR	88/92
122-31303 •	P-51D	44-63577		(to FA Uraguaya as FAU 265)	4.4.49
				Museo Aeronautica, Montevideo	60/85
				(displ. as "FAU 285")	
				Dante Heredia, Montevideo, Uruguay	1.85
			N51TE	Tyrone Elias, Tulsa OK	2.85/92
				(long-term rebuild to fly)	
122-31339 •	P-51D	44-63613		(to FA Uraguaya as FAU 270) BOC .50 SOC	6.60
				displ. Carrasco AB, Montevideo, Uruguay	65/84
				Joseph Kasparoff, Montebello CA	.86/90
				(static rebuild, Van Nuys CA 86/87)	
				displ. Tuskegee Foundation, Tuskegee AL	89
				(note: id. also rep as 44-63615)	
122-31360	P-51D	44-63634		(to R Swedish AF as Fv26121)	
				(to FA d'L GN Nicaragua as GN....)	17.1.55
			N6149U	MACO Sales Financial Corp, Chicago IL	9.63
			N2114	Guglielmo Silini, Springfield IL	66/68
				crashed, Springfield IL	21.4.68
				(see 44-84634)	
122-31381 •	P-51D	44-63655		(to R Swedish AF as Fv26.....)	
				(to FA d'L GN Nicaragua as GN 84)	17.1.55
			N6153U	MACO Sales Financial Corp, Chicago IL	2.9.63
				crashed on delivery flight to USA	1.5.65
			N5500S	Will Martin/Wings & Wheels Inc,	
				Palos Park IL	1.85/92
122-	P-51D	44-63663		Trans Florida Aviation, Saragosa FL	c58

31389 •				(to FA Guatemalteca as FAG 354)	.62
			N41749	Don Hull, Sugarland TX	8.72
				Wilson C. Edwards, Big Spring TX	78/92
122-31401 •	P-51D	44-63675		(370th FG/402nd FS/9th AF "Sierra Sue/E6-D")	
				(to R Swedish AF as Fv26152)	
				(to FA d'L GN Nicaragua as GN.....)	
				displ. Officers Mess , FAN Base	
				MACO Sales Financial Corp, Chicago IL	9.63
			N5452V(2	Dave Allender	73
				(rebuilt: ff 11.9.73; race #19)	
				Roger A. Christgau, Edina MN	78
			N1751D	Roger A. Christgau, Edina MN	84/92
				(flies "463675/Sierra Sue/Fv26152")	
122-31427 •	P-51D Cavalier	44-63701		(to Swedish AF as Fv26015)	23.4.45
				(to FA Dominicana as FAD 1904)	10.52/84
				Brian O'Farrell/Johnson Aviation, Miami FL	19.5.84/87
				Vincent Tirado, Miami FL : rebuild	87/91
			N51VT	Vincent Tirado, Miami FL	92
122-31501	P-51D Cavalier	44-63775		(to Swedish AF as Fv26......)	
				(to FA d'L GN Nicaragua as GN 100)	
		Turbo	N6167U	MACO Sales Financial Corp, Chicago IL	2.9.63
				T. J. Black Co, Atlanta GA	66
				Cavalier Aircraft, Opa Locka FL	69/73
				(RR Dart turboprop conv."Turbo Mustang III")	
			N201PE	Piper Aircraft, Lockhaven PA	
				(Enforcer programme development aircraft)	
				(id. suspect: 44-63775 dest. Hawaii 27.11.45)	
122-31514 •	P-51D	44-63788	N6171C	Haber Aircraft Inc, Burbank CA	20.9.57
				E. D. Weiner, Los Angeles CA	30.11.57
			N335J (1	E. D. Weiner, Los Angeles CA	13.1.58
			N3350	E. D. Weiner, Los Angeles CA	24.2.58
				Jim Morton Co Inc, Cheyenne WY	4.9.58
				Robert A. Mitchem, Broomfield CO	16.3.59
				William D. Roosevelt, Englewood CO	6.11.59/67
				George A. Whipple, New York NY	28.11.67
			N166G	George A. Whipple, New York NY	28.10.68
				Bruce D. DeJager & Peter P. Hoffman, Minneapolis MN	14.8.72
				Bruce D. DeJager, Minneapolis MN	9.2.73
				A. R. Buckner, Albuquerque NM	13.8.73
				Westernair Of Albuquerque, Albuquerque NM	6.5.74
				Mike Smith, Johnson KS	14.6.74
				Mike Smith & Ronald K. Kendrick, Johnson KS	1.12.75
				Sylmar Aviation, Sylmar CA	.78
				Doug Arnold/Warbirds of GB Ltd, Blackbushe	2.79
				(arr. Blackbushe on del. ex USA 11.11.79)	
			G-PSID	Fairoaks Aviation Services, Blackbushe	27.7.81/87
				The Fighter Collection, Duxford	1.87/88
			F-AZFI	Jean Salis, La Ferte-Alais, France	2.88/91
122-31533 •	P-51D Cavalier	44-63807		(to FA Uraguaya as FAU 272)	4.12.50
				(to FA Boliviana as FAB 506)	19.3.60
				recov. Arny Carnegie, Edmonton ALTA	12.77
			C-GXUO	Bill Bailey/Bailey Aviation Service ALTA	7.78/84
			N20MS	Ed L. Stringfellow/Mid South Lumber Company, Birmingham AL	6.85/92
122-31536 •	P-51D	44-63810		displ. Norton AFB CA as "463810"	63
				The Air Museum, Ontario CA	65/72
				(rebuild to fly Chino .72: adopted id. 45-11367)	
			N63810	The Air Museum, Chino CA	72
				Robin Collard, Weslaco TX	78
				Jerry Hayes, Henderson CO	82/88

				dam. belly landing, Denver CO (repaired)	6.84
				Bernard H. Raouls, Zephyr Cove NV	.88/92
				Joseph K. Newsome, Cheraw, SC	10.92
122-31590 •	P-51D	44-63864		(78th FG/83th FS "Twighlight Tear/HL-W")	
				(to R Swedish AF as Fv26158)	17.6.49
				(to IDFAF as 38)	9.2.53
				Israeli Air Force Museum	
				rep. open storage, Herzlia, Israel	78
				Israel Yitzhaki, Sde-Dov, Israel	3.78
				(rest. Herzlia 78/84, ff Herzlia 5.2.84, fuse. also rep. ex IDFAF 42/44-13228)	
			4X-AIM	Israel Yitzhaki, Herzlia	2.84/86
			SE-BKG	Novida AB / Flygexpo, Malmo	12.86/90
				(del. to Malmo 23.12.86, flew as "Fv26158")	
			N42805	Cham S. Gill, Central Point OR	5.91
				Kenneth A. Hake, Tipton KS	92
				(note: id. as quoted by FAA, true id. uncertain. FAA also quotes 44-63864 as id. for N251L: William R. Pearce, Fullerton CA 63/69, rep. ex IDFAF: but a P-51D N251L crashed Iceland during del. from USA to Israel 6.6.53!)	
122-31591 •	P-51D	44-63865		(354th FG / 353rd FS "FT-M")	
				(to R Swedish AF as Fv26018)	
				(to FA d'L GN Nicaragua as GN 90)	17.1.55
			N6163U	MACO Sales Financial Corp, Chicago IL	23.9.63
				PAAL Inc, East Point GA	66
				O. J. Kistler, Long Valley NJ	69/72
			N51JK	O. J. Kistler, Long Valley NJ	73/92
122-31597 •	P-51D	44-63871		(to R Swedish AF as Fv26039)	
				(To IDFAF as ......)	
			N9772F	Robert D. Turner/Marom Air Service, Tel Aviv, Israel	65/69
				noted, minor damage, Cannes, France	9.65
				Musee de l'Air, Paris-Le Bourget	75/89
				(displ. as "466318/MO-C")	
				(FAA quote id. 44-63821)	
122-31598	P-51D	44-63872		(to RCAF as 9552) BOC 10.7.47 SOC	27.12.57
			N6519D (1	James H. Defuria & Fred J. Ritts/ Intercontinental Airways, Canastota NY	11.56/60
				Aero Enterprises, Elkhart IN	10.5.60
				Gerald L. Walbrun, Chicago IL	28.12.60
				(N6518D/19D painted on incorrect airframes!)	
			N6518D (2	Gerald L. Walbrun, Chicago IL	3.4.61/66
				Robert R. Runte, Greendale WI	20.8.66/67
				David M. Halla, Minneapolis MN	2.10.67
				James Fugata/Air Carrier Inc, Aurora OR	27.12.68
				John Gale, Minneapolis MN	8.1.69
				May Air Inc, Boulder CO	19.4.69
				Courtesy Aircraft Ltd, Loves Park IL	4.4.69
				Tom J. Kuchinsky, Milwaukee WI (race #18)	17.7.69/70
				crashed, dest., Harlingen TX (Kuchinsky k.)	27.6.70
122-31615 •	P-51D	44-63889	N7710C	Harold Reavis, Fayetteville NC	66/69
				Dan Furtrell, Nashville TN	8.69
				W. R. Rodgers, Rolling Fork MS	72
			CF-FUZ	Gary D. McCann, Stratford ONT	12.73
			C-FFUZ	Gary D. McCann, Stratford ONT	84/89

c/n	Type	Serial	Reg.	History	Date
122-31619 •	P-51D	44-63893		(to RCAF as 9560) BOC 7.6.47 SOC	9.60
				stored unconv., Carberry MAN	57/60
				Aero Enterprises Inc, Elkhart IN	60/62
				RCAF Lincoln Park, ALTA : gate guard	.60/62
				Ed Fleming, Calgary ALTA : rebuilt	.63
			CF-PIO	Helmsworth Construction, Wetaskiwin ALTA	65
				Keir Air Transport, Edmonton ALTA	
			N3333E	Specialty Restaurants Inc, Long Beach CA	69/75
				Military Aircraft Restoration Corp, Chino CA	75/92
				USAFM: March AFB CA (loan)	80/90
				(FAA quote id. 122-51619)	
122-31718 •	P-51D	44-63992		(to R Swedish AF as Fv26020)	
				(to IDFAF as 58)	
				Flygvapenmuseum Malmen, Linkoping, Sweden	79/84
				(id. as quoted: true original id. uncertain:	
				also rep. as ex IDFAF 54)	
122-31731 •	P-51D	44-64005		(361st FG / 376th FS/"Mary Mine / E9-Z")	
				(to RCAF as 9561) BOC	7.6.47
			N6339T	James H. Defuria & Fred J. Ritts/	
				Intercontinental Airways, Canastota NY	12.58/60
				(stored unconv., Carberry MAN 57/61)	
				Aero Enterprises, Elkhart IN	10.5.60/62
				(del. Carberry-Winnipeg-Elkhart .62)	
				Lewis C. Buell, Springfield OH	27.9.62/65
				Sherman Aircraft Sales, Baer Field IN	8.5.65
				G. S. Vincent, Winchester MA	30.7.65
				Robert Bleeg, Seattle WA	10.67/73
			N51WB (1	Wayne Brown, Port Gibson MS	.73
				Joe Arnold, Eudora/Mulberry AR	4.10.75
			N51CK	Charles S. Kemp, Jackson/Hazlehurst MS	20.7.78/92
				cr. landing King City CA (rebuilt)	.81
				(flies as "464005/E9-Z/Mary Mine")	
122-31848 •	P-51D	44-64122		(to Swedish AF as Fv26130)	
				(to FA d'L GN Nicaragua as GN 80)	17.1.55
			N6151U	MACO Sales Financial Corp, Chicago IL	23.9.63
			N150U	John Lowe, Chicago IL	
				Gardner Flyers Inc, Brownwood TX	66
				Wilson C. Edwards, Big Spring TX	69/92
122-31887 •	P-51D	44-72028	N22B	reg.	.48
				(to IDFAF as 41)	18.7.48
				hulk recov. ex Palmahim kibbutz playground,	
				Israel by Robs Lamplough, Duxford UK	.76
				Noel Robinson & David Laight, North Yorks	82/92
				at Tees-side Airport UK)	
122-31894 •	P-51D	44-72035	N5411V	Whiteman Enterprises, Pacoima CA	63/78
			HK-2812P	H. Escobar V, Columbia SA	5.82/87
			HK-2812X		
			N5306M	reg.	12.88
			F-AZMU	Jacques Bouret/Aero Retro, St. Rambert	9.89/92
				(flies as 472035/Jumpin' Jacques"	
122-31910 •	P-51D Cavalier	44-72051		(to R Swedish AF as Fv26026)	21.5.45
				(to FA Dominicana as FAD 1912)	10.52/84
				Brian O'Farrell/Johnson Aviation, Miami FL	19.5.84/85
				John R. Sandberg, Minneapolis MN	.85
			N68JR	John R. Sandberg, Minneapolis MN	4.88/91
				(rebuild Chino CA, ff 21.3.91 as "Platinum Plus")	
				Janet Bjornstad Trustee	92
122-31945 •	P-51D Cavalier	44-72086		(to Swedish AF as Fv26009) del.	21.4.46
				(to FA Dominicana as FAD 1936)	20.5.53/84
				Brian O'Farrell/Johnson Aviation, Miami FL	19.5.84
				(conv. to TF-51 dual controls by FAD .84)	

			N789DH	Brian O'Farrell/Johnson Aviation, Miami FL	4.86
				Joseph E. Scogna/Vintage Air, Yardley PA	.87/92
				(flies as "415137/Baby Duck/LH-R")	
122-31982 •	P-51D	44-72123		(55th FG/ 343rd FS "The Millie G")	
				(to R Swedish AF as Fv26092)	21.8.47
				(to FA Dominicana as FAD 1914)	31.10.52
				displ. on pole, San Isidro AB, Dominican Rep.	.84/90
109-35934 •	P-51D	44-15651	NX79111	Steve Beville & Bruce Raymond IL	.46/49
				(Bendix racer #77/"The Galloping Ghost")	47/49
			N79111	Clifford D. Cummins, Riverside CA	63/79
				(race #69/"Miss Candace")	
				Dave Zeuschel, Van Nuys CA	.79
				Sanders Truck Lines, Troy AL	.80/81
				(race #69/"Jeannie")	
				Jimmy Leeward/Bahia Oaks Inc,	
				Ocala FL (race #10/"Spectre"; later #9)	.81/92
109-35958	P-51D	44-15655		Trottner Iron & Metal Co, San Antonio TX	.49
				(dest. for RNZAF: still in orig. packing case 51)	
			N1738B	Dal-Air, Dallas TX	.51
				(to FA Haiti as 15655: later FAH 655)	10.7.51
				(to FA Dominicana : for disposal)	
				rep. Gordon Plaskett, King City CA	c73
				rep. Cavalier Aircraft Corp, Sarasota FL	c73/74
111-36100 •	F-6K Cavalier	44-12817	N4963V		
			N85BW		
			N5151T	Bob Abrams (flew as "N5151")	65
				cr. racing Las Vegas NV (Abrams k.)	.65
				Cavalier Aircraft Corp, Sarasota FL	66/69
				Lindsay Newspapers, Sarasota FL	72/84
				David B. Lindsay, King City CA	87
				David B. Lindsay/Lindair Inc, Sarasota FL	90/92
111-36123 •	F-6K FP-51K	44-12840		Victory Air Museum, Mundelein IL	76
				Bill Conner	82
				Joseph Kasparoff, Montebello CA	87/90
				(under rebuild, Chino CA 82/87)	
111-36135 •	F-6K FP-51K	44-12852	NX66111	(Bendix racer #80 /"Full House")	46
				crashed during race, Cleveland OH	.46
				Jack P. Hardwick, El Monte CA	
				(rebuilt, conv. to TF-51 dual controls)	
			N90613	Intercontinental Airways, Canastota NY	.54
				B. Lawrence Tractman/Aviation Corporation of America	15.3.54
				(to FA Dominicana as FAD 1900 (2))	26.4.54
				Brian O'Farrell/Johnson Aviation, Miami FL	.84/90
111-36292 •	P-51D	44-13009		(to RAAF as A68-687) BOC 21.7.45: SOC	22.12.47
				(to AURI/TNI-AU as ....)	
				Stephen Johnson/Vanpac Carriers,	
				Oakland CA : recov. ex Indonesia	.78
			N31RK	Richard E. Knowlton, Portland ME	85/90
				(rest. project: fuselage still marked "A68-687")	
111-36299 •	P-51D	44-13016		(to RAAF as A68-674) BOC 7.45: SOC	12.48
				Pearce Dunn/Warbirds Aviation Museum,	
				Mildura, VIC	.66/82
				(recov. ex farm Benalla VIC .66: stored dism.)	
			VH-CVA	reg. res.: Vince Thomas, Albury, NSW : dism.	82/87
				(shipped to Shafter CA, for rebuild .84/87)	
			N9002N	Steve Willman/King City Aviation Inc,	
				King City CA	12.87

			N9200N	King City Aviation Inc, King City CA (rebuild King City CA, due to fly .92)	12.87/92
111- 36388 •	P-51D	44-13105		(to RAAF as A68-679) BOC 7.45: SOC Pearce Dunn/Warbirds Aviation Museum, Mildura, VIC (recov. from farm Benalla VIC .66, static rest., displ. as "A68-679") David Zeuschel, Van Nuys CA (shipped to USA, rebuilt as mod. racer, race #7/"Strega")	12.48 .66/80 c80
			N71FT	Bill Destefani, Shafter CA John R. Sandberg, Scottsdale AZ Bill Destefani, Bakersfield CA	12.83/89 90 92
111- 36389 •	P-51D	44-13106		(to RAAF as A68-648) BOC Royal Melbourne Institute of Technology Australian War Memorial, Canberra ACT (static rest., RAAF Point Cook VIC 86/92)	6.45/50 30.6.50/83 .83/92
111- 36533 •	P-51D	44-13250		(to FA Salvadorena as FAS.....) Flaherty Factors, Monterey CA	 10.74
			N151DM	Daniel Martin, San Jose CA (race #7/"472308/WD-A/Ridge Runner")	78/92
126- 37691 •	P-51H	44-64265		USAFM, Chanute AFB, Rantoul IL	65/90
126- 37740 •	P-51H	44-64314	N1108H	Michael E. Coutches, Hayward (rebuild: composite of parts ex scrap dealers and wreck recov. ex crash site Utah c62)	66
			N551H	Michael E. Coutches, Hayward CA (race #51/" 464551")	69/92
126- 37801 •	P-51H	44-64375		wreck salvaged from Alaska	
			N67149	Paul Shoemaker, Orting WA (long-term rebuild project) James R. Parks, Bend OR	78/90 90/92
126- 37802 •	P-51H	44-64376		USAFM, Lackland AFB, TX (displ. as "464376/HO-M")	65/92
126- 37841 •	P-51H	44-64415		(to NACA as NACA130)	
			N313H	William E. Hogan, Hamilton OH (race #3)	66/78
			N49WB	Bill & Don Whittington, Fort Lauderdale FL (race #08)	83/92
122- 38604 •	P-51D	44-72145	N6169C		
				N311G John C. Seidel, Sugar Grove IL Waldo Klabo, Pleasanton CA (race #85/"Fat Cat") Peter McManus, Fort Lauderdale FL	63/69 78/83 84
			N51PT	Peter McManus/Castlewood Realty,Miami FL Castlewood Airmotive, Baltimore MD (flies as "472145/HO-M/Petie 3rd") damaged Hurricane Andrew	1.85/90 90/92 24.8.92
122- 38651 •	P-51D	44-72192	N5460V	James H. Bohlander, Roselle IL William S. Cochran III, Houston TX John V. Crocker, San Mateo CA California Warbirds, San Jose CA (flies as "414111/"Straw Boss 2/PE-X")	63 66 69/72 78/92
122- 38661 •	P-51D Cavalier	44-72202		(to R Swedish AF as Fv26112) del. (to FA Dominicana as FAD 1917) Brian O'Farrell/Johnson Aviation, Miami FL SAAF Museum, Saxonwald, South Africa	13.6.47 12.52/84 19.5.84/87 88

122-38675 •	P-51D	44-72216		(352nd FG/487th FS, "Silver Dollar/HO-L" : later "Miss Nita/HO-M")	
				(to R Swedish AF as Fv26116)	25.2.48
				(to IDFAF as 43)	19.3.53
				hulk recov. from Ein Geddie kibbutz, Israel by Robs Lamplough, Duxford UK	.78
			G-BIXL	Robs Lamplough, Duxford/North Weald	3.7.81/92
				(rebuilt with mainplane 44-72770 ex Dutch technical school: ff North Weald 5.5.87, flies as "472216/HO-L & HO-M")	
122-38798 •	P-51D Cavalier	44-72339		(to R Swedish AF as Fv26115)	13.6.47
				(to FA Dominicana as FAD 1918)	10.52/84
				Brian O'Farrell/Johnson Aviation, Miami FL	19.5.84
				Elmo Hahn, Muskegon MI	.84
			N51EH	Elmo Hahn/ Hahn Inc, Muskegon MI	11.85/90
				(shipped ex FAD 9.84, ff Ft.Wayne IN 15.10.85)	
			N251JC	James A. Cavanaugh, Dallas TX	12.91/92
122-38823 •	P-51D Cavalier	44-72364		(353rd FG/352nd FS "Upopa Epops/SX-L")	
				(to R Swedish AF as Fv26061) del.	25.4.47
				(to FA Dominicana as FAD 1916)	10.52/84
				Brian O'Farrell/Johnson Aviation, Miami FL	19.5.84/87
122-38859 •	P-51D	44-72400	NX69406	Woody Edmondson, Lynchburg VA	
				(Bendix racer #42/"City of Lynchburg VA")	1.7.46
			NX13Y	Woody Edmondson, Lynchburg VA	5.12.46
				DiPonti Aviation, Minneapolis MN	21.12.46
				Anson Johnson, Miami FL: (race #45)	21.7.47/59
				(attempt on piston airspeed record .52)	
			N502	Robert Bean, Danville IL	28.9.59
				John Juneau & George Nesmith, Opa Locka FL	5.62
				John Juneau, Opa Locka FL	11.62
				Robert D'Orsay, Opa Locka FL	c12.62
				Frank Lloyd, Miami FL	
				Walter E. Ohlrich, Tulsa OK	2.65
			N913Y	Richard Vartanian, Pasedena CA	3.66/72
				Leonard Tanner, Granby CT	19.7.72
			N13Y	Bradley Air Museum, Windsor Locks CT	16.8.72/88
				New England Air Museum, Windsor Locks CT	.88/90
				(stored, pending static rest.)	
122 38860	P-51D Cavalier	44-72401	NX65453	Bendix racer #2; later #21)	
			N71LN	Cavalier Aircraft Corp, Sarasota FL	66/69
				Lindsay Newspapers Inc, Sarasota FL	72
				David B. Lindsay, King City CA (stored)	84/87
				struck-off USCR	10.83
				(NX65453 also reported to Cuba: see 44-73978, NX65453 also rep. as 44-73401)	
122-38897 •	P-51D Cavalier	44-72438		(to Swedish AF as Fv26131) del.	24.4.48
				(to FA Dominicana as FAD 1920)	10.52/84
				Brian O'Farrell/Johnson Aviation, Hialeah FL	19.5.84/87
				Selby R. Burch, Kissimmee FL	.87/91
				(on rebuild Kissimmee FL 87/91)	
122-38905 •	P-51D	44-72446		(to Swedish AF as Fv26139)	
				(to FA d'L GN Nicaragua as GN 76)	17.1.55/63
			N6164U	MACO Sales Finance Corp, Chicago IL	2.9.63
				(stored in Mexico 63/71)	
			N12700	W. W. Martin, Palos Park IL	78/81
				(flew as "F.A. Costa Rica/El Gato Rapido")	
				DK Precision, Fort Lauderdale FL	84/90
				crashed Dyess AFB TX (Knapp k.)	23.6.90
				(FAA quote id. "44-26139")	

Continued on Page 244

GOLDEN HAWKS
ROYAL CANADIAN AIR FORCE
RCAF
21557

turbopower

Continued from Page 242

122-38942 •	P-51D	44-72483		(355th FG/ 354th FS "WR-P")	
				(to Swedish AF as Fv26087)	
				(to FA d'L GN Nicaragua as GN 85)	17.1.55
			N6160U	MACO Sales Finance Corp, Chicago IL	23.9.63
				David M. Forrest, Avondale CA	66/69
				(id. changed from 44-63769 to 44-72483)	
			N13410	David M. Forrest, Avondale CA	69/72
				(to FA Salvadorena as ....)	
				Flaherty Factors Inc, Monterey CA	10.74
			N36DD	ntu: Flaherty Factors Inc, Monterey CA	1.11.74
			N38FF	ntu: Marvin L. Gardner, Brownwood TX	
			N13410	Ray Stutsman, Elkhart IN	78/81
				(rebuild, rep. using 44-63507/N6345T, flew as "414303/SX-B/Double Trouble two")	
			N51EA	Don C. Davidson, Nashua NH (race #27)	4.82/90
				Max Vogelsang/Swiss Warbirds, Basel : del.	26.8.90/91
				(flies as "463684/Double Trouble two/SX-B")	
122-39198 •	P-51D	44-72739		Universal Studios, Hollywood CA, open storage	
				recov. by Ascher Ward, Van Nuys CA	8.70
			N44727	Ascher Ward, Van Nuys CA	71/73
				Elmer F. Ward Chino CA	.75/92
				(flies as "414292/QP-A/"Man O'War")	
122-39226 •	P-51D Cavalier	44-72767	N6836C	Walter Oaks, Ida Grove IA	63
				O. K. Airways Inc, Chicago IL	66
				Cavalier Aircraft Corp, Sarasota FL	69
				Lindsay Newspapers Inc, Sarasota FL	72
				struck-off USCR	12.83
				David B. Lindsay, King City CA (stored)	84/87
122-39232 •	P-51D	44-72773		(to FA d'L GN Nicaragua as GN 120)	17.1.55
			N12066	Will Martin/MACO Sales Finance Corp, Chicago IL	8.7.63
				I. N. Burchinall Jr , Honey Grove & Paris TX	66/84
				Robert L. Ferguson, Wellesley MA	86
				Charles Church (Spitfires) Ltd, Winchester	.86/87
				(del. by air, arr. UK 26.6.87)	
			G-SUSY	Charles Church (Spitfires) Ltd, Winchester	6.87/90
				Paul Morgan, North Weald	91
				(flies as "47773/Susy")	
122-39236 •	P-51D Cavalier Mk. 2	44-72777 72-1537		(52nd FG/ 5th FS (15th AF) "Doc Watson/MX-F")	
				Cavalier Aircraft, Opa Locka FL	28.8.59/67
				(to TNI-AU as F-344)	.67
				Stephen Johnson/Vanpac Carriers,Oakland CA	.78
				Al Letcher, Mojave CA	16.7.79
			N8064V	Al Letcher, Mojave CA	4.81
				(rebuild Mojave, ff 22.4.81)	
			N151D	Steve Seghetti, Vacaville CA/Farmer City IL	14.4.84/92
				(rebuilt, ff 23.4.87)	
122-39270 •	P-51D	44-72811		(to IDFAF as 13)	
				reg. candidate: Holtz Technical School, Israel	.80
				Angelo Regina & Ascher Ward, Van Nuys CA	80
				(rebuilt Van Nuys .82 as TF-51D dual control, using ex CA ANG airframe recov. ex movie prop)	
			N268BD	Phil "Buck" Dear, Terry MS	83/84
				Bob Byrne, Bloomfield MI	.87/88
			N215RC	Robert Converse, Sisters OR	.88
			N471R	Cascade Warbirds Co, Sisters OR	5.89/92
				(race #71, flies as "472276/Huntress III")	
				(note: FAA quote id. 44-26060)	
122-39285 •	P-51D	44-72826		(to RCAF as 9563) BOC 7.6.47 SOC	20.9.60
			N6344T	James H. Defuria & Fred J. Ritts/ Intercontinental Airways, Canastota NY	25.2.57/60
				(stored unconv., Carberry MAN 57/62)	

				Aero Enterprises Inc, Elkhart IN	10.5.60/62
				(ferried Carberry-Winnipeg-Elkhart 7.62)	
				John Milton, Edwardsville IL	4.5.64/73
				Max & Danny Ramsay, Johnson KS	31.3.73/78
				Thomas J. Watson, Stowe VT	4.1.78/84
			C-FBAU(2	Dennis J. Bradley/Canadian Warplane Heritage,	
				Hamilton ONT	3.85/91
			N51YS	Steve C. Collins, Dunwoody GA	11.91/92
				(flies as "472826/Old Boy/TJ-W")	
122-39299 •	P-51D	44-72840	N7718C (2	David B. Lindsay, King City CA (stored)	84/88
122-39303 •	P-51D Cavalier	44-72844		sold surplus McClellan AFB CA	17.2.58
			N5076K	Trans Florida Aviation, Sarasota FL	59
			N156C	Trans Florida Aviation, Sarasota FL	59
				Chamberlain Engineering Corp, Akron OH	63/66
			N764C	Edward C. Kellermeyer, Haileah FL	9.9.66
				Cavalier Aircraft Corp, Sarasota FL	8.5.68/69
			N7406	David B. Lindsay, King City CA (stored)	10.69/87
				struck-off USCR	12.83
122-39361 •	P-51D	44-72902		(to RCAF as 9564) BOC 7.6.47 SOC	20.9.60
			N6343T	James H. Defuria & Fred J. Ritts/	
				Intercontinental Airways, Canastota NY	25.2.57/60
				(stored unconv., Carberry MAN 57/61)	
				Aero Enterprises Inc, Elkhart IN	10.5.60/64
				(ferried Carberry-Elkhart .61)	
			N335	E. D. Weiner, Santa Monica CA (race #14)	17.4.64/73
				Violet M. Bonzer, Los Angeles CA	8.5.73/92
122-39366 •	P-51D Cavalier	44-72907		(to FA Guatamalteca as FAG 357)	c58
			N41748	Don Hull, Sugarland TX	8.72
				Wilson C. Edwards, Big Spring TX	78/92
122-39381 •	P-51D Cavalier	44-72922		(479th FG/ 434th FS "Scat VII/L2-W")	
			N7718C (1	Robert H. Fee, San Antonio TX	17.2.58
			N18Y	Larry Sheerin, San Antonio TX	c5.58
				Robin Eschauzier, Lackland AFB TX	20.11.58
			N6803T	Robin Eschauzier, Lackland AFB TX	3.2.61
				William D. Owens, Hondo TX	25.10.62
			N577W	William D. Ownes, Hondo TX	28.1.63
				Appliance Buyers Credit Corp	.63
			Space Systems	Laboratory Inc, Melbourne FL	63/66
				David B. Lindsay/Trans Florida Aviation,	
				Sarasota FL	24.3.67
			N577WD	Cavalier Aircraft Corp., Sarasota FL	9.9.71
				David B. Lindsay/Lindsay Newspapers, FL	10.9.71/84
				(rep. stored King City CA 71/80)	
				Gordon W. Plaskett, King City CA	.84
				John Dilley/Fort Wayne Air Service,	
				Fort Wayne IN (rebuild)	87/92
122-39393 •	P-51D	44-72934	N513PA	Pioneer Aero Service, Chino CA	4.91
				Warbirds of GB Ltd, Biggin Hill	.91/92
				shipped to UK; ff Biggin Hill 3.3.92)	
122-39395 •	P-51D	44-72936	N7711C	Arthur J. Stasney, Altadena CA	63/66
				Solomon J. Pasey, Coatesville PA	6.69
				Warren G. Schulden, Elizabeth NJ	72/78
				crashed, Eufala AL	16.12.79
				Marvin L. Crouch, Encino CA (rebuild)	3.83/92
122-39407 •	P-51D	44-72948		WV ANG: Kanawha Co Airport, Charleston WV	71/90
				(displ. as "Wham Bang")	

122-39448 •	P-51D	44-72989		WI ANG: Volk Field ANGB WI	84/90
122-39449 •	P-51D	44-72990		(to RCAF as 9283) BOC 23.1.51 SOC	29.4.58
			N6322T	James H. Defuria & Fred J. Ritts/	
				Intercontinental Airways, Canastota NY	25.2.58/60
				Aero Enterprises, Elkhart IN	10.5.60/62
				Eastern Truck Rentals, Lowell MA	17.4.62/63
				Aero Enterprises, Elkhart IN	0.6.62
				James W. Vandeveer, Dallas TX	24.1.64/65
				John Peters, Norwood CO	5.5.65/66
				crashed, Grand Junction CO (rebuilt)	21.8.65
				Stanley W. Kurzet, Covina CA	2.2.66/67
				(accident 21.8.65 at Grand Junction CO,	
				US Army, Edwards AFB CA	27.4.67/78
				(chase plane, flew as "US Army 0-72990")	
				US Army Aviation Museum, Fort Rucker AL	7.2.78/90
				(displ. as "US Army 0-72990")	
122-39486	P-51D Cavalier	44-73027		(to RCAF as 9250) BOC 6.12.50 SOC	15.10.59
			N9146R	Trans Florida Aviation, Sarasota FL	20.5.59/60
				E. D. Weiner, Los Angeles CA	8.11.60/61
				Mario Villareal, El Paso TX	11.61
				El Paso Airmotive Inc, El Paso TX	7.12.61/65
				Southwest Air Rangers, El Paso TX	25.3.65
				Harold Barlow, Los Angeles CA	27.3.65
				Haynes McLellan & John Percival, Tracy CA	10.66/70
				Roger Wolfe, Fallon NV (race #12)	11.70/72
			N5747	Robert E. Guildford/Mustang Pilots Club,	
				Beverley Hills CA	7.9.72/77
				dam. landing wheels-up, Mojave CA	10.74
				(arr. Duxford for UK visit 15.6.77)	
				crashed, wheels-up landing due in-flight fire,	
				Bakersfield Air Park, Bakersfield CA	9.10.77
				(rebuilt Chino, Philippine AF mainplane, ff .80)	
			N51MP	Mustang Pilots Club, Los Angeles CA	79/80
				crashed and dest., Lancaster CA	4.10.80
				William A. Speer, La Mesa CA	7.91/92
				(rep. rebuild based on AURI airframe)	
122-39488 •	P-51D	44-73029		(to FA d'L GN Nicaragua as GN 122)	31.5.58
			N7999A	MACO Sales Finance Corp, Chicago IL	13.7.63
				Jerald L. Baker, Angleton TX	66
			N51JB	Jessie A. Baker, Houston TX (race #51)	6.69/78
				James E. Beasley, Philadelphia PA	.79/92
				(flies as "473029/B7-E/Bald Eagle")	
122-39504 •	P-51D	44-73053		(to TNI-AU as F-3.....)	
				Fighter Rebuilders, Chino CA	84
122-39538 •	P-51D	44-73079	N7716C	Joseph P. Dangelo, Campbell CA	63
			N576GF	Growers Frozen Foods, Salinas CA	.63/66
				Jerry G. Brassfield, San Jose CA	6.69/71
				Experimental Aircraft Assn., Franklin WI	78
				Robert Love, Oakland CA	82/84
				Russell R. Francis, San Francisco CA	88
			N151BL	Russell R. Francis, South Lake Tahoe CA	7.89/90
				Bill Dause, Wellington UT	92
122-39540 •	P-51D	44-73081	N5074K	Michael E. Coutches, Hayward CA	66/92
122-39588 •	P-51D	44-73129		Tony Randozza, Oakland CA	.58
			N5480V	J. M. Jackson, Long Beach CA	63
				Stans Aircraft Sales, Fresno CA	66
				Frank A. Barrena, San Luis Obispo CA	69
				(to FA Haiti as FAH 15650)	7.69
				dam. mid-air collision another FAH P-51	c70

				recov ex FAH, stored dism., Miami FL	72
			N51SL	Dixon J. Smith, Seattle WA	72
				Rodney Barnes, Oconomowoc WI	78/87
				Stuart Eberhardt, Danville CA	.87/92
				(race #22/"Merlin's Magic")	
122-39599 •	P-51D	44-73140		(to RCAF as 9567) BOC 7.6.47 SOC	20.9.60
			N6337T	James H. Defuria & Fred J. Ritts/	
				Intercontinental Airways, Canastota NY	25.2.57/60
				(stored unconv., Carberry MAN 57/62)	
				Aero Enterprises, Elkhart IN	10.5.60/64
				(ferried Carberry-Winnipeg-Elkhart 7.62)	
				J. D. Kent, Des Moines IN	13.4.64/67
				N169MD(2 Dr. Burns M. Byram, Marengo IA (race #71)	8.11.67/78
			N51N	Charles Ventors/Aerodyne Sales, El Reno OK	10.78/82
			C-FBAU (1	D J. Bradley/Canadian Warplane Heritage ONT	1.82
				crashed, burned, fcd. landing, Massey ONT	7.7.84
				(id. transferred to rest. project: source unknown):	
				Marvin L. Gardner, Mercedes TX	4.86
			N314BG	Gordon Plaskett/BG Aero, King City CA	9.86
				Brett Ward/Pioneer Aero Service, Chino CA	1.87/88
				(rebuild Chino CA: ff 25.7.88; del. to UK)	
				Warbirds of GB Ltd, Biggin Hill	.88/91
				(flies as "414151/HO-M/Petie 2nd")	
122-39601	P-51D	44-73142	N6173C	Michael T. Loening, Salmon ID	63
				Westair Co,	
				Westminster CO	66
				Vernon S. Peterson, Bensenville IL	69
				Vernon S. Peterson, Valley View TX	72/78
			N51PW		
			N51VP	Universal Life Church TX	84
				J. Bradford Enterprises, Prescott AZ	87/89
				crashed on takeoff, Denton TX (Peterson k.)	6.9.89
			N51BK	Bruce C. Morehouse, Denton TX	7.91/92
122-39608 •	P-51D	44-73149		(to RCAF as 9568) BOC 7.6.47 SOC	20.9.60
			N6340T	James H. Defuria & Fred J. Ritts/	
				Intercontinental Airways, Canastota NY	25.2.57/60
				(stored unconv., Carberry MAN 57/61)	
				Aero Enterprises, Elkhart IN	10.5.60/62
				(trucked dism. Carberry-Elkhart 6.62)	
				Ernest W. Beehler, West Covina CA	30.7.62/74
				Charles E. Beck & Edward J. Modes,	
				Burbank CA (race #7 "Candy Man")	19.8.74/76
				Robert E. MacFarlane, Placerville CA	4.8.76/80
				Stephen Grey/The Fighter Collection, Duxford	5.80/86
				(del. Geneva ex USA 5.80, arr. Biggin Hill 2.5.81)	
			N51JJ	John V. Crocker, San Mateo CA	5.86/91
				The Fighter Collection, Duxford	86/91
			G-BTCD	The Fighter Collection, Duxford	11.1.91/92
				(flies as "463221/Candyman/Moose G4-S")	
122-39622 •	P-51D	44-73163		(to RCAF as 9285) BOC 8.2.51 SOC	29.4.58
			N6300T	James H. Defuria & Fred J. Ritts/	
				Intercontinental Airways, Canastota NY	5.2.57/60
				Aero Enterprises, Elkhart IN	10.5.60/61
				Suncoast Aviation, St. Petersburg FL	8.7.61
				Valair Aircraft Inc, Cincinatti OH	28.9.61/63
				Farnum Brown, Michigan City MI	4.3.64
				Robert A. Mitchem, Broomfield CO	12.3.64
				James D. Morton/Aero Enterprises,Elkhart IN	14.4.64
				D. K. Fesenmyer, Mount Pleasant MI	25.4.64
				Robert H. Pollock, Abbotstown PA	21.5.65/66
			N5151M	Herbert E. (Mickey) Rupp, Mansfield OH	17.11.66
			N5151R	Rupp Industries, Mansfield OH	69

			N51MR	Rupp Industries Inc, Mansfield OH	72
				Edward O. Messick, San Antonio TX	2.3.74/78
				(flew as "473656/TX ANG/Minute Man")	
				Charles Knapp, Los Angeles CA	84/89
				Jackson McGoon Aircraft, Los Angeles CA	89/92
				crashed on takeoff, Santa Monica CA	2.9.89
				on rebuild	8.92
122-39655 •	P-51D	44-73196	N5449V	Fred H. Johnson, Summitville OH	63
				Walter H. Hackett, Smithville OH	66/69
				Charles Milam, Layfayette LA	78
				Don C. Davis, Casper WY (race #81 "Habu")	81/84
				crashed, dest. nr Aspen CO (Earl Ketchen k.)	15.7.84
122-39665 •	P-51D	44-73206		sold surplus at McClellan AFB CA	.58
			N7724C	reg.	.58
			N3751D	Cavalier Aircraft Corp, Sarasota FL	63
			F-AZAG	Jean-Francois Lejeune, Faaa, Tahiti	.75/83
			N3751D	Jean-Francois Lejeune, Chino CA	4.83
				Clyde Logan Neill, Indian Wells CA	4.83
				(rest. Chino .83 as "Hurry Home Honey")	
				Charles A. Osborne/ Blue Sky Aviation, Louisville KY	85/92
122-39669 •	P-51D Cavalier 2000	44-73210	N5461V	Flying W Inc, Medford NJ	63
				Edward G. Fisher Jr, Kansas City KS	66/69
				Gardner Flyers Inc, Brownwood TX	72
				Kenneth Boomhower KS	73
				crashed, Fort Collins CO (Boomhower k.)	17.5.73
				(rebuilt by Regina bros using fus. ex IDFAF)	
			N1040N	Angelo Regina, Van Nuys CA	81/87
				Joseph Kasparoff, Montebello CA	88/92
122-39675	P-51D	44-73216		(to RCAF as 9569) BOC 7.6.47 SOC	12.6.58
			N6302T	James H. Defuria/Intercontinental Airways, Canastota NY	20.5.58/60
				Aero Enterprises, Elklhart IN	15.8.60/61
				Richard B. Dillard, Laredo TX	7.5.61/62
				crashed, Cape Girardeau MS	7.5.61
				Barrett Investment Co, San Antonio TX	4.5.62/64
				Stan E. Shaw, Saratoga CA	28.8.64/67
				Jack R. Urich, Hacienda Heights CA	1.3.67
				Joe H. Garrett, Tulsa OK	15.9.67/69
				Dan Futrell, Nashville TN	8.10.69/71
				crashed, dest., Hot Springs AR	24.3.71
				(id. transferred to P-51D rebuild, origin unknown):	
				Rick Brickert, Manhattan Beach CA	81
			N3278D	Jerry D. Owens, Scottsdale AZ	9.82/87
				Wayne Meylan, Elkhorn NE	.87
				crashed, dest., Manistee MI (Meylan k.)	26.6.87
				Still registered Meylan Enterprises Inc, Omaha NE	90/92
122-39699	P-51D	44-73240	N7721C		
			N469P	Douglas W. Wood, Fresno CA (race #7)	66
				Kent W. Jones, Dallas, Addison Airport TX	69
				Roger W. Dennington, Atlanta GA	72
				crashed, dest.	8.4.73
122-39713 •	P-51D	44-73254		(to RCAF as 9571) BOC 7.6.47 SOC	20.9.60
			N6328T	James H. Defuria & Fred J. Ritts/ Intercontinental Airways, Canastota NY	27.2.57/60
				(stored unconv., Carberry MAN 57/61)	
				Aero Enterprises Inc, Elkhart IN	10.5.60/61
				(ferried Carberry-Elkhart .61)	
				Clifford C. Pettit, Ligonier IN	3.10.61/63
				crashed, dest., Crumstown IN	31.5.63
				(id. transferred to rebuild, source unknown):	
				A. C. Lofgren, Battle Creek MI	6.6.72

				Donald R. Weber, Baton Rouge LA	15.8.74/89
				(rebuilt, ff. 1.78 after 3 year rest.)	
122-39719	P-51D Cavalier	44-73260	N5075K		
			N451D	Joseph E. Anzelon, Whitestone NY	63
				Howard Olsen, Midland TX	66
				Trans Florida Aviation, Sarasota FL	69
				Cavalier Aircraft Corp, Sarasota FL	8.69
				(to TNI-AU as F-360) : crashed Java	24.6.75
				rep. recov. by Stephen Johnson, Oakland CA	.79
122-39723 •	P-51D	44-73264	N5428V	Mathew P. Kibler, Luray VA	63
				John M. Sliker, Wadley GA	66
				William Ross Enterprises Inc, Chicago IL	69
				Confederate Air Force, Harlingen TX	70
				George F. Williams, Hobbs NM	72
				Confederate Air Force, Harlingen TX	3.11.77/91
				crashed Omaha NE (repaired)	17.6.81
				American Airpower Heritage Flying Museum, Midland TX	9.91/92
				(flies as "Gunfighter II/CY-U")	
122-39732 •	P-51D	44-73273		(to FA Salvadorena as FAS......)	7.69
			N34DD	reg. res.	76
			N200DD	Donald R. Anderson, Saugus CA	78
				John G. Deahl Estate, Denver CO: USCR	84/92
			N210DD	Charles Mothon, Gallway NY	89
122-39734 •	P-51D	44-73275		sold surplus McClellan AFB CA	16.9.57
			N2868D	Richard E. Blakemore, Tonopah NV	63
			N119H	Vernon E. Thorpe, Oklahoma City OK	.66
				Paul D. Finefrock, Hobart OK	69
				Richard L. Wood, Houston & Refugio TX	6.69/72
				Jack Flaherty, Monterey CA (race #9)	73
				Wilson C. Edwards, Big Spring TX	78/83
				Fay Midkiff, Houston TX	84
				Alan S. Kelly, Middlebury CT	88
				Kelco Aircraft, Wilmington DE	89/90
				Aviation Sales Inc, Englewood CO	92
122-39746 •	P-51D	44-73287		disposal ex McClellan AFB CA	.58
			N5445V	William Kelbaugh, Chico CA	3.58/63
				William S. Cooper, Merced CA	.64/72
				James Francis, Medina OH	.74
				Courtesy Aircraft, Rockford IL	.78
			N51DF	James S. Francis, Medina OH	8.80
				Jack A. Rose, Spangle WA	6.82/87
			N751JC	C & C Vintage Aircraft, Rockford IL	.88
			N5445V	John J. Castrogiovanni, Rockford Il	.88
				Michael J. George, Springfield IL	90/92
122-39779	P-51D Cavalier	44-73320	N5463V	Cavalier Aircraft Corp, Sarasota FL	66/69
				Lindsay Newspapers Inc, Sarasota FL	72
				David B. Lindsay, King City CA (stored)	78/88
				struck-off USCR	3.84
122-39782 •	P-51D	44-73323	N6167C	Aero Service Inc, Nogales AZ	63
				Darryl G. Greenamyer, Van Nuys CA	66
				Michael A. Geren, Kansas City MO	69
			N4270P	Marvin L. Crouch, Encino CA	1.81
			N151MD	Marvin L. Crouch, Encino CA (rebuild)	4.81/92
122-39798 •	P-51D	44-73339		(to TNI-AU as F-3..)	
				recov. by Stephen Johnson, Oakland CA	.79
				Ronald M. Runyan, Fairfield OH	82/84
				(rebuilt Chino CA 82/84: adopted id. 44-74008,	

				ff Chino .84 as "Dallas Doll")	
			N151MC	ntu: Ronald M. Runyan, Fairfield OH	2.84
			N51RR	Ronald M. Runyan, Fairfield OH : del.	12.84/89
				Robs Lamplough, North Weald UK	.89/91
				Dave Gilmour, North Weald UK	.91/92
				(del. ex USA 14.2.91, flies as "474008/VF-R")	
122-39802 •	P-51D	44-73343	N5482V	Ben W. Hall, Seattle WA	63/66
				(race #2 "Seattle Miss")	
				Chance Enterprises Inc, Half Moon Bay CA	69
				Michael T. Loening, Boise ID, (race #2)	6.69/72
				crashed, badly damaged Reno NV	9.71
				Bruce Morehouse, San Antonio TX	84/87
				struck-off USCR	6.87
122-39806 •	P-51D	44-73347		(to RCAF as 9298) BOC	16.3.51
				Canadian War Museum	9.8.61
				Canadian National Aviation Museum, Rockcliffe ONT (displ. as "9298/Y2-E")	65/92
122-39808 •	P-51D	44-73349		(to Swiss AF as J-2113)	
				Swiss Air Force Museum, Dubendorf	60/90
				loan: Swiss Transport Museum, Lucerne	80/90
122-39809 •	P-51D Cavalier	44-73350	N6176C		
			YS-210C	Archie A. Baldocchi, Illopango, El Salvador	.65
				(to FA Salvadorena as FAS 402	7.69
			N33FF	Flaherty Factors Inc, Monterey CA	1.11.74
				Wilson C. Edwards, Big Spring TX	78/88
				Robert H. Nottke, Barrington Hills IL	.88/92
122-39874 •	P-51D	44-73415		(to RCAF as 9289) BOC 8.2.51 SOC	14.8.59
			N6526D	James H. Defuria/Intercontinental Airways, Canastota NY	21.7.58/60
				R. Ferrer, Patchoque NY	21.3.60/66
				crashed, major damage, Richmond VA	15.2.62
				Frederick Walter Wild, Averne NY	6.1.66
				Airlease Inc, Chicago IL	10.1.66
				Frank Guzman, Massapequa PA	10.1.66/68
				Don Bateman, Las Vegas NV	9.3.68/69
				Michael E. Coutches, Hayward CA	17.6.69/74
				H. Matteri, State Line NV	15.1.74/75
				William Veatch, Olympia WA	1.9.75
				crashed on takeoff, Olympia WA	19.3.77
				William A. Speer, La Mesa CA	87/92
				(rebuilt Chino CA, ff .88 race #45 "Pegasus"; during rebuild Chino, parts also used for P-51D static rest. for RAF Museum: see end of listing)	
122-39879 •	P-51D	44-73420		disposal ex McClellan AFB CA	.58
			N7722C	Michael E. Coutches/American Aircraft Sales Co, Hayward CA	17.2.58
				Ronald E. West/ West Foods Inc, Soquel CA	.58
				Richard B. McFarlane	21.7.58
				Donald G. Bell, Livermore CA	25.8.58/63
				Robert G. Bixler, San Jose CA	10.65/69
				Robert H. Phillips, Phoenix AZ	3.71/78
				Robb Satterfield, Aaron F. Giebel & Dallas L. Smith, Midland TX	9.9.78
				Robb Satterfield & Dallas Smith, Midland TX	83/89
				Dallas L. Smith, Midland TX	90/92
122-39894 •	P-51D	44-73435		(to RCAF as 9290) BOC 8.2.51 SOC	1.11.60
			CF-MWN	James H. Defuria/Intercontinental Airways, Canastota NY	12.58/60
			N6311T	Aero Enterprises, Elkhart IN	10.5.60/61
				Suncoast Aviation, St. Petersburg FL	10.61/62
				James G. Shaw, Columbia SC	27.2.62/63

				Angels Aviation, Zephyrhills FA	3.5.63
				Selby R. Burch, Wintergarden FL	3.5.63/69
				crashed Daytona Beach FL	6.7.68
				Marvin L. Gardner/Gardner Flyers, Mercedes TX (wreck)	84
				Pioneer Aero, Chino CA	87/89
122-39895 •	P-51D	44-73436		(to RCAF as 9300) BOC 16.3.51 SOC	1.11.60
			N6313T	James H. Defuria/Intercontinental Airways, Canastota NY	12.58/60
				Aero Enterprises, Elkhart IN	.60
				Ralph Rensink, Lewiston ID	10.1.62
				Walter D. Peterson, Manson WA	26.6.62/77
			N51TK (1	Tom Kelly & John Dilley/Consolidated Airways, Fort Wayne IN (race #19/"Lou IV")	17.8.77/86
			N51KD	American Horizons Inc, Fort Wayne IN	3.86/92
				(flies as "413926/E2-S/Cutters Capers")	
122-39913 •	P-51D Cavalier 2000	44-73454	N6172C	Ligonier Flying Service Inc, Ligonier IN	63
				Champion Developers Inc, Jacksonville FL	66
				crashed Jacksonville FL	14.5.67
				Cavalier Aircraft Corp, Sarasota FL	69
			N2051D	Trans Florida Aviation, Sarasota FL	
				Rufus A. Applegarth, Plymouth Meeting PA	.69/72
				John J. Schafhausen, Spokane WA	5.72
				Richard Bach	.73
				crashed on landing, Midland TX	24.9.73
				John Herlihy, Montara CA	78/81
				Richard A. Bjelland, Dairy OR	84/92
				(flies as "414911/This is It")	
122-39917 •	P-51D	44-73458		(to RCAF as 9294) BOC 16.3.51 SOC	14.8.59
			N6525D	James H. Defuria/Intercontinental Airways, Canastota NY	21.7.58
			N6347T	James H. Defuria, Canastota NY	60
			N554T	Ray A. Alexander, Memphis TN	63
				W. R. Rodgers, Rolling Fork MS	66
				(to FA Salvadorena as FAS 404)	.69
				(mod. to TF-51D by FAS, crashed in FAS service)	
			N36FF	Flaherty Factors Inc, Monterey CA: wreck	28.10.74
				John Herlihy/C-Vu Airmotive, Half Moon Bay CA : wreck	12.3.75
			N4151D	Gordon W. Plaskett, King City CA	24.6.75/78
				(rebuilt Chino CA, using wing 44-74012/N6519D as TF-51D, ff 22.11.77 as "484660/TF-660")	
				Ben R. Bradley, Fort Lauderdale FL	81
				Basil C. Deuschle, Pompano Beach FL	.81/82
				World Jet Inc, Fort Lauderdale FL	.83/85
				Air SRV Inc/Lone Star Flight Museum, Houston TX	87/88
				Warbirds of GB Ltd, (did not leave USA)	88
				William L. Hane, Mesa AZ	91/92
				(flies as "484660/TF-660")	
				(displ. Champlin Fighter Museum, Mesa AZ)	
122-39922 •	P-51D	44-73463		(to RCAF as 9575) BOC 7.6.47 SOC	20.9.60
				James H. Defuria & Fred J. Ritts/ Intercontinental Airways, Cabnastota NY	27.2.57/60
				(stored unconv., Carberry MAN 57/61)	
				Aero Enterprises Inc, Elkhart IN	.60/62
				(stripped, trucked Carberry-Elkhart 6.62)	
				sold as scrap metal	
				Len Tanner, North Granby CT	
				(rep. recov. ex scrapyard, Decatur IL)	
				Duane Egli, Fabens TX	

				Richard Ransopher, Grapevine TX	77
				Richard Ransopher, Kernersville NC/Tampa FL	82/89
				(rest. project: fuse. section RCAF 9575, wings and other parts from N1335, N6175C, N5478V)	
122-39942	P-51D	44-73483	N351D	Graubart Aviation Inc, Valparaiso IN	63
				Jack Shaver/Maryland Airmotive MD	64
				Chance Enterprises Inc, Half Moon Bay CA	66
				Elaine Loening, San Francisco CA	69
				Waldon Spillers, Versailles OH (hulk only)	84
122-39953 •	P-51D	44-73494		(to Rep. of Korea AF as 205)	
				displ. Yongdungpo AB, Seoul, South Korea	67/89
122-39977 •	P-51D	44-73518	N5483V (1	Edward G. Fisher Jr, Kansas City KS	63/72
				Don Whittington, Fort Lauderdale FL	78/92
				(mod. Merlin racer #09/"Precious Metal")	
				ditched in sea near Galveston TX (salvaged)	24.1.90
				(see N5483V (2 Griffon racer: id. unknown, at end of listing)	
122-40002 •	P-51D	44-73543	N5458V	Trans Florida Aviation, Opa Locka FL	.58
				(to TNI-AU as F-3......)	
				recov. by Stephen Johnson, Oakland CA	.78
				Chris Warrilow, Woburn Green, Bucks UK	.80/85
				(rest. project, shipped to UK : arr 2.81)	
			G-BLYW	Chris Warrilow, High Wycombe	3.6.85
				D. K. Precision Inc, Fort Lauderdale FL	3.6.85/86
			N800DK	D. K. Precision Inc, Fort Lauderdale FL	4.86/87
				Whittington Bros., Fort Lauderdale FL	88
				sale rep., Fort Lauderdale FL	90/92
122-40033	P-51D	44-73574	N5478V	Marvin L. Gardner, Mercedes TX	63
				Gardner Flyers Inc, Brownwood TX	66
				Beth Allen Truck Rental Inc, Stowe PA	69
				off USCR by	72
				Richard Ransopher, Kernersville NC (hulk)	84/87
122-40043 •	P-51D Cavalier	44-73584	N5447V		
			N51Q	Cavalier Aircraft Corp, Sarasota FL	66/69
				Lindsay Newspapers Inc, Sarasota FL	72
				David B. Lindsay, King City CA (stored)	78/88
				struck-off USCR	10.83
122-40045	P-51D	44-73586	N5412V	Tri State Aviation Service, Huntington WV	63
				Thomas P. Luck, Lancaster CA	66
				Garden State Aviation Inc, Neptune NJ	69/74
				crashed, destroyed	10.74
122-40196 •	P-51D Cavalier	44-73656	N5073K	disposal ex McClellan AFB CA	.58
				Delta A & E	
				Parts Inc, NC	2.58
				Michael E. Coutches/American Aircraft Sales, Hayward CA	5.58
				Trans Florida Aviation, Sarasota FL	.58/63
				Stanley Dunbar Studios, Charlotte NC	.63
				Howard Olsen, Midland TX (race #1)	66
				Duncan Airmotive Inc, Galveston TX	.68
				(to FA Salvadorena as FAS 406)	c12.68
			N32FF	Flaherty Factors Inc, Monterey CA	1.11.74
				(adopted id. 44-12473 on return to USA)	
				Gordon W. Plaskett, King City CA	.75
			N2151D	Gordon W. Plaskett, King City CA	81
				Chris Williams, Ellensburg WA	.81/87
				Vlado Lenoch, La Grange IL	4.88/92
				(flies as "414237/Moonbeam McSwine/HO-W")	
122-	P-51D	44-73683		(to FA d'L GN Nicaragua as FAN GN119)	23.5.58

40223 •			N12064	MACO Sales Financial Corp, Chicago IL	.63
				George W. Drucker Jr, Los Angeles CA	66
				George A. Brown, Canoga Park CA	69
				Meteorological Operations Inc, Hollister CA	69
				John S. Steinmetz, Londonerry NH	72
			N5551D	Tri-T Aviation, Griffin GA	78
				Heritage Aircraft Inc, Fayetteville GA	84/90
				sale rep., San Diego CA	92
				(flies as "414251/WZ-I/Contrary Mary")	
122-	P-51D	44-73693		(to FA d'L GN Nicaragua as FAN GN116)	23.5.58
40233 •			N6357T	MACO Sales Financial Corp, Chicago IL	9.63
				Ronald L. Bryant, Jacksonville Beach FL	66
				Alvin T. George, Atlanta GA	69
				(to FA Salvadorena as FAS 408)	7.69
			N35FF	Flaherty Factors Inc, Monterey CA	1.11.74
				(adopted id. 44-13253 on return to USA)	
				Wilson C. Edwards, Big Spring TX	78/87
				(race #45/"Risky Business")	
				Richard L. Pack/Mustang 4 Inc, Chino CA	88/90
122-	P-51D	44-73704	N6168C	Plauche Electric Inc, Lake Charles LA	63/69
40244 •				Marvin L. Gardner/Gardner Flyers Inc,	
				Brownwood & Mercedes TX	72/92
				(race #25/"Thunderbird")	
122-	P-51D	44-73751	N5444V	Robert Mitchum, Broomfield CO	63
40291 •				Keith Larkin, Watsonville CA	66/69
				Ron Van Kretgan/PTI Inc, San Jose CA	8.69/92
122-	P-51D	44-73832	N2873D		
40372 •			N117E	Frank C. Sanders, Phoenix AZ	66
				David Webster, Glendo WY	69/72
				Scott Smith, Orlando FL	78
				crashed Ellisville MS	15.2.78
				Gary McCann FL	84
				Clarke Aviation Corp, Daytona Beach	
				Bob Byrne Aviation, Bloomfield MI	89
				H.E. Hunewill Construction Co, Wellington NV	89/92
122-	P-51D	44-73843		(to RCAF as 9271) BOC 11.1.51 SOC	4.12.56
40383 •			N10601	Stinson Field Aircraft, San Antonio TX	10.56/57
				Lloyd P. Nolen/Mustang & Co, Mercedes TX	10.57/77
				Confederate Air Force, Harlingen TX	12.77/91
				American Airpower Heritage Flying Museum,	
				Midland TX	9.91/92
122-	P-51D	44-73849		(to RCAF as 9247) BOC 6.12.50 SOC	27.12.57
40389			N6516D	James H. Defuria & Fred J. Ritts/	
				Intercontinental Airways, Canastota NY	26.11.56
				Aero Enterprises Inc, Elkhart IN	10.5.60
			N335J (1	Ed Weiner, Los Angeles CA	10.60/62
			N835J	Aero Enterprises, Elkhart IN	21.6.62/63
				Joseph A. Truhill, Addison TX	2.11.64/65
				Jim Vandeveer, Dallas TX	1.10.65/71
				Gerald A. Swayze, Mesquite TX	13.1.71
				Robert Walker, Tulsa OK	11.71/73
			N51WH	William E. Harrison, Tulsa OK	19.4.73/74
			N51JL	Jack N. Levine, Livonia MI	10.74/84
				crashed and dest., Ray MI (Levine k.)	18.11.84
122-	P-51D	44-73856	N5077K	Jim Jeffers, Stateline NV (race #83)	63
40396 •				Fowler Aeronautical Services, Burbank CA	66
				Air Carriers Inc, Aurora OR	69
			N711UP	Gale Air Corp, Minneapolis MN (race #0)	8.69
			N7TF	Tom Friedkin/Cinema Air Inc, Houston TX/	

				Carlsbad CA (flies as "HO-W")	76/92
122-40397	P-51D	44-73857		(to RCAF as 9244) BOC 6.12.50 SOC	1.11.60
			N6315T	James H. Defuria/Intercontinental Airways, Canastota NY	30.12.58
				Aero Enterprises, Elkhart IN	20.10.60
			N651D	Richard G. Snyder, Tucson AZ	11.61/66
				(mod. wet-wing racer, #45/"Miss Phoebe II")	
				Michael R. Cuddy, Klamath Falls OR	13.2.66/69
				Bill Kemp Pontiac & Cadillac, Dover DE	30.3.69/71
				Bill Kemp/Kemp Aircraft Corp, Potomac MD	5.4.71/75
				Don Plumb/Spitfire Inc, Windsor ONT	23.1.75
				John Boulton, Sanford FL	21.2.75
				crashed & dest., Big Spring TX (Boulton k.)	15.10.75
122-40411	P-51D	44-73871		(to RCAF as 9245) BOC 6.12.50 SOC	2.5.56
				crated at Whiteman Air Park CA for Israel	.59
				(to IDFAF as ....)	.59
				Israel Aircraft Industries	64
			N7098V	Pioneer Aero Service, Burbank CA	22.6.64/70
				Cavalier Aircraft, Sarasota FL	8.9.70/78
				Albert McKinley, Hillsboro OH	14.8.78
				Elmer Ward/Pioneer Aero Service, Chino CA	90/91
				(rest. Chino CA as TF-51D, ff .91 as "473871/TF-871")	
				Warbirds of GB Ltd, Biggin Hill	.91/92
				(shipped to UK, ff Biggin Hill 19.3.92)	
122-40417 •	P-51D	44-73877		(to RCAF as 9279) BOC 23.1.51 SOC	29.4.58
			N6320T (1	James H. Defuria & Fred J. Ritts/ Intercontinental Airways, Canastota NY	25.2.57/60
				Aero Enterprises, Elkhart IN	.60
			CF-PCZ	Neil McClain, Strathmore ALTA	.60/68
			N167F	Paul D. Finefrock, Hobart OK	29.4.68
				crashed Euless TX (rebuilt)	1.9.69
				Paul D. Finefrock, Brownwood TX	10.70/80
				Anders Saether/RLS 51 Ltd., Oslo Norway	8.80/92
				(rebuilt Ft.Collins CO 80/85; del. Oslo 27.6.86)	
				(flies as "473877/Old Crow/B6-S")	
122-40442 •	P-51D Cavalier	44-73902		(to FA Guatemalteca as FAG 315)	16.12.54
			N38227	Don Hull, Sugarland TX	8.72
				Wilson C. Edwards, Big Spring TX	78/92
				(FAA quote id. 44-77902)	
122-40460 •	P-51D	44-73920		(to Chinese Nationalist AF as ....)	15.3.46
				(taken over by Chinese Comm. AF as "03")	1.10.49
				Chinese People's Revolutionary Military Museum, Beijing, China	87
				Air Force Museum, Xi Jiao, China	88
122-40512 •	P-51D	44-73972		USAFM: Fresno ANGB, Fresno CA	65/91
122-40513 •	P-51D	44-73973		(to RCAF as 9281) BOC 23.1.51 SOC	29.4.58
			N6325T (2	James H. Defuria & Fred J. Ritts/ Intercontinental Airway, Canastota NY	25.2.57/60
				Aero Enterprises, Elkhart IN	10.5.60/62
				Peter Rosi, Notre Dame IN	10.62/63
				Aero Enterprises, Elkhart IN	3.4.63/64
				Farnum Brown, Michigan City IN	4.3.64
				Joseph D. Wade, Houston TX	6.3.64/65
				A. E. Lee, Atlanta GA	10.65/66
				James W. Gentle, Birmingham AL	16.6.66/67
				Wendell K. Trogden, Fort Lauderdale FL	10.8.67/69
				(to FA Salvadorena as FAS......)	7.69
			N35DD	ntu: Flaherty Factors Inc, Monterey CA	1.11.74
			N37FF	Flaherty Factors Inc, Monterey CA	6.3.75
				(adopted id. 44-10755 on return to USA)	

			N51JC	Jerry C. Janes, Vancouver BC	14.8.75
				(composite: parts of various ex FAS aircraft;	
				rebuilt Chelan WA 76/77, del. Vancouver 1.78)	
			C-GJCJ (1	Jerry C. Janes/Grabber Screw Products,	
				Vancouver BC	11.79
			N51JC	David G. Price, Los Angeles CA	11.83
			N151DP	David G. Price, Santa Monica CA	1.84/92
				(race #49) crashed Reno NV (rebuilt)	17.9.88
122-	P-51D	44-73978		(to RCAF as 9241) BOC 6.12.50 SOC	4.12.56
40518 •			N89E	Stinson Field Aircraft, San Antonio TX	26.10.56
				Don O. Thayer & Mark Shaw, Forest Hills NY	1.5.57
				op: Exec-Air, mod. for cloud-seeding	57
				Allen McDonald, Miami Springs FL	.58
				(FA Rebelde/Revolucionia (Cuba) as FAR-401)	12.58
				displ. Museum de la Revolucionaia, Havana	63/90
				(also quoted as 44-72401: que se)	
122-	P-51D	44-73979		(to RCAF as 9246) BOC 6.12.50 SOC	16.5.51
40519 •				accident, grounded in RCAF service	16.5.51
				conv. to Instructional Airframe A-612	10.5.55
				College Militaire Royale, St Jean QUE	.55
				Imperial War Museum, Duxford UK	.68/87
				Imperial War Museum, London UK	89/92
				(displ. as "472258/WZ-I/Big Beautiful Doll")	
122-	P-51D	44-73990		(to RCAF as 9282) BOC 23.1.51 SOC	14.5.59
40530 •			N8674E	James H. Defuria/Intercontinental Airways,	
				Canastota NY	27.2.59/60
				Aero Enterprises, Elkhart IN	18.6.60
				Kieran Aviation Sales, Birmingham AL	14.8.60/62
				Jack Adams Aircraft Sales, Walls MS	3.2.62
				T. E. Guillot/Jackson Dental, Jackson MS	5.62
				Robert Graf, Tarkio MO	13.8.62/65
				Leonard A.Tanner/Tan Air Industries Inc,	
				North Granby CT	19.1.65/69
			N51LT	Len Tanner, North Granby CT	72/73
			N2116 (2	ntu: John P. Silberman, Sherborn MA	8.4.73
				crashed, struck car landing, Yanceyville NC	6.9.73
			N51LT	Len Tanner, North Granby CT	18.3.75/79
				(rebuilt, using parts from A68-175/N64824)	
			N51TH	Tom W. Henley, Emelle AL	8.1.79/92
122-	P-51D	44-74008		(to RCAF as 9274) BOC 11.1.51 SOC	14.5.59
40548			N8676E	James H. Defuria/Intercontinental Airways,	
				Canastota NY	27.2.59/60
				M. N. Bostick, Waco TX	24.6.60/66
				Courtesy Aircraft, Loves Park IL	16.12.69
				Richard W. Foote/Automatic Business	
				Products Inc, Hartford CT (race #51, #71)	20.1.69/73
			N76AF	C. G. Kreuger/ North American Flyers,	
				Brookfield CT,	12.73/74
				John Crumlish, Southbury CT	74/75
				crashed, Marthas Vineyard CT (Crumlish k.)	8.6.75
			N151MC	Mark Clark, State College PA : wreck	11.78/84
				Ronald M. Runyan, Fairfield OH : wreck	2.84
				(id. tfd. to 44-73339/N51RR: que se)	
122-	P-51D	44-74009		(to RCAF as 9275) BOC 11.1.51 SOC	17.9.57
40549 •			N6323T (1	James H. Defuria & Fred J. Ritts/	
				Intercontinental Airways, Canastota NY	25.2.57/60
			N988C	Aero Enterprises, Elkhart IN	1.5.60/61
				SuncoastAviation, St. Petersburg FL	8.7.61/62
				A. Fasken, Midland TX	29.9.62/63
				Houston Aircraft Sales, Houston TX	1.5.63/65
				William Fiore, Clairton PA	30.4.65/68

				Frank Cannavo Jr, Lester PA	3.2.68/69
				Robert J. Shaver, Brigantine & Linwood NJ	26.6.69/78
				Robert L. Ferguson, Wellesley MA	79/92
				(flies as "Ain't Misbehavin/RL-F")	
122-40552 •	P-51D	44-74012		(to RCAF as 9243) BOC 6.12.50 SOC	17.8.59
			N6518D (1	James H. Defuria/Intercontinental Airways, Canastota NY	21.7.58/60
				Aero Enterprises, Elkhart IN	15.8.60
				(N6518D/19D painted on incorrect airframes!)	
			N6519D (2	Jerry McCutchin, Dallas TX	10.63/64
				Gordon Travis/River Oaks Aircraft & Engine Brokers, Fort Worth TX	9.12.64/66
				Robert R. Redding, Houston TX	13.6.66
				Leroy B. Penhall, Anaheim CA (race #81)	4.11.68/75
				crashed, forced landing, Hudson WI	4.8.74
				Gordon W. Plaskett, King City CA : wreck	30.9.75
			C-GPSI (1	Robert H. Jens/Executive Air Craft Ltd, Vancouver BC (rebuild, not completed)	27.9.76/84
			N6519D	Duane Williams, Kellogg ID : rebuild	2.84/87
				James E. Smith, Fortine MT	.87/92
122-40742 •	P-51D	44-74202	N5420V	Michael E. Coutches, Hayward CA	66/78
				Mike Bogue, Oakland CA	84/87
				Michael E. Coutches, Hayward CA	90/92
122-40744	P-51D	44-74204	N5451V	Robert F. Deweese, Newport Beach CA	63
				David S. Salerno, Santa Ana CA	66/69
			N51U	David S. Salerno, Santa Ana CA	72
				Wolcott Air Services, Wolcott CT	78/90
				(flew as "413691/Passion Waggon")	
				crashed & dest., Cape Cod MA (Enhorning k.)	29.9.90
122-40756 •	P-51D	44-74216		USAFM:	
				USS Alabama Battleship Memorial, Mobile AL	74/88
122-40770 •	P-51D	44-74230	N5466V	Robert G. Bixler, San Jose CA	63
				C. L. Caprioglio, Fresno CA	66
				Frank R. Davis, Beaverton OR	69
				United States National Bank, Beaverton OR	72
				David Norland, Denver CO	78/89
				James F. Norland, Wasilla AK	90/92
122-40851 •	P-51D	44-74311		(to RCAF as 9577) BOC 7.6.47 SOC	27.12.57
				James H. Defuria & Fred J. Ritts/ Intercontinental Airways, Canastota NY	11.56/60
				Aero Enterprises, Elkhart IN	.60
				Louis Hecklesberg, Bartlesville OK	c62/84
				(recov. ex LaPorte IN, stored in RCAF crates)	
			C-GPSI (2	Ritchie Rasmussen/Trans-Am Helicopters, Edmonton ALTA	2.85/91
				(stored Edmonton ALTA)	
122-40931 •	P-51D Cavalier	44-74391		(to FA Guatelmateca as FAG 351)	
			N38229	Don Hull, Sugarland TX	8.72
				Wilson C. Edwards, Big Spring TX	78/92
122-40944 •	P-51D	44-74404		(to RCAF as 9276) BOC 11.1.51 SOC	27.12.57
			N4132A(1	James H. Defuria & Fred J. Ritts/ Intercontinental Airways, Canastota NY	11.56/60
				M. L. Alson/Aero Enterprises, Elkhart IN	60
				crashed landing, Elkhart IN	
				Gary Harris, Half Moon Bay CA : fuse. only	74/88
				William A. Spear, San Diego CA : rest. project	
				Gerald S. Beck/Tri-State Aviation, Wahpeton : rest. project	90
			N7129E	Robert E. Odegaard, Kindred ND: rest. project	9.90/92
				(id. quoted as 122-41064, ie. 44-74524)	

122-40947 •	P-51D	44-74407		USAFM: Hector Field ANGB, Fargo ND	65/89
122-40949 •	P-51D	44-74409		(to RCAF as 9235) BOC 6.12.50 SOC	1.11.60
			N6319T	James H. Defuria & Fred J. Ritts/	
				Intercontinental Airways, Canastota NY	12.58/60
				Aero Enterprises, Elkhart IN	20.10.60
				J. H. Cunningham, Lexington NC	2.12.61/62
				Dean J. Ortner, Wakeman OH	19.8.62/68
				Joe Bruce, Palm Springs CA	15.5.68
				Cavalier Aircraft Corp, Opa Locka FL	3.6.68/69
				Clint R. Hackney, Friendswood TX	11.4.69/71
				Frank D. Strickler, Grapevine TX	2.11.71/77
			N4409	Frank D. Strickler, Grapevine TX	30.12.77
				Peter Bottome, Caracas, Venezuela	.81
			N555BM	Gordon W. Plaskett, King City CA	1.81
				(rebuild by Plaskett at King City CA 81/84	
				for Bottome, flew as "Barbara M 4th")	
			YV-508CP	Peter Bottome, Caracas, Venezuala	.82/89
			N555BM	Group 44 Inc, Winchester VA	3.91
			N51RT	Group 44 Inc, Winchester VA	4.91/92
122-40957 •	P-51D	44-74417		(to RCAF as 9586) BOC 2.11.50 SOC	1.11.60
			CF-MWB	James H. Defuria/Intercontinental Airways,	
				Canastota NY	12.58/60
			N6327T	Aero Enterprises, Elkhart IN	10.5.60/63
				Garland R. Brown, Freeland MI/Ft.Wayne IN	16.2.63/87
				crashed, major damage, Fort Wayne IN	4.8.66
				Robert Byrne, Bloomfield MI	.87/89
				Richard P. James, Fennimore WI	90/92
				(flies as "472197/ FF-197")	
122-40963 •	P-51D	44-74423		(to RCAF as 9595) BOC 8.11.50 SOC	14.8.59
			N6517D	James H. Defuria/Intercontinental Airways,	
				Canastota NY	21.7.58/59
				Madison Aviation Corp, Canastota NY	11.11.59
				Naylor Aviation Inc, Clinton MD	12.11.59
			N182XF	North American Maritime Corp,Cambridge MA	11.59/62
				Hamilton Aircraft Co, Tucson AZ	2.10.62
				Hillcrest Aviation Industries, Lewiston ID	1.11.62/64
			N182X	California Airmotive Corp, Burbank CA	1.5.64/70
				(op. by Clay Lacy, race #64)	
				H. Clay Lacy, Burbank CA (race #64)	11.67/70
			N64CL	H. Clay Lacy, Van Nuys CA (race #64)	70/92
				(note: FAA changed id. to "10216" .67;	
				poss. rebuilt using 44-10216 recov. ex	
				FA Nicaragua by MACO Sales, Chicago IL .63)	
122-40965 •	P-51D	44-74425		(to RCAF as 9591) BOC 8.11.50 SOC	29.4.58
			N6522D	James H. Defuria & Fred J. Ritts/	
				Intercontinental Airways, Canastota NY	25.2.57/59
				Madison Aviation Corp, Canastota NY	20.10.59
				Naylor Aviation Inc, Clinton MD	10.59/63
				Frank J. Capone/Bonanza Inc, Broomall PA	3.1.63/64
				Eli Graubart/Graubart Aviation, Valparaiso IN	25.6.64
				Joseph W. Bohmeir/New London Airport,	
				New London PA	27.7.64
				James Fugate, Oswego OR	30.9.64
				R. A. Hanson Co, Palouse WA	8.12.64/66
				Charles P. Harral/Superstition Air Service,	
				Mesa-Falcon Field AZ	6.1.66/68
				Larry N. Mitchell, Hopkinsville KY	10.68/71
			N51HB	ntu: Harold F. Beal, Concord TN	18.6.71
			N6522D	Jack W. Flaherty/Flaherty Factors Inc,	
				Monterey CA	1.9.71

				Harold F. Beal, Concord TN	72
				dam. landing, Knoxville TN	10.72
			N11T	John Herlihy, Half Moon Bay CA (race #8)	.73
				ground collision, Half Moon Bay CA	10.11.74
				Johnny Bolton Ford Inc, Maitland FL	3.9.75
				Pete Sherman Exotic Cars, Maitland FL	2.3.76/78
				Ben R. Bradley, Oakland Park FL	11.1.78
				Gordon W. Plaskett, King City CA	.81/82
				Robert Byrne, Bloomfield MI	84
				WW II Enterprises Inc, Scotch Plains NJ	87/88
				Western Wings Aircraft Sales Co, Oakland OR	89
				Robert J. Pond/Planes of Fame East, Plymouth MN	90/92
122-40967 •	P-51D	44-74427		(to RCAF as 9592) BOC 8.11.50 SOC	15.10.59
			N9148R	Trans Florida Aviation, Sarasota FL	20.5.59/62
			N2251D	Robert A. Hoover/North American Aviation, El Segundo CA	19.3.62/67
				dam. accident, Myrtle Beach FL (repaired)	20.1.65
				North American Rockwell Corp, Los Angles CA	10.67/70
				badly damaged, ground explosion, Oshkosh WI	9.8.70
				Steve Shulke & John B. Bolton, Maitland FL	.70/75
				(rebuilt Chattanooga TN, using components of N130JT/44-74435, flew as "Doc's Doll")	
				John J. Stokes, San Marcos TX	6.8.75/78
				John T. Baugh/Baugh Aviation, Nashville TN	10.1.78/89
				Paul Romine/Aero Charter Inc, Indianapolis IN	90/92
122-40970	P-51D	44-74430		(to RCAF as 9588) BOC 8.11.50 SOC	14.5.59
			N8673E	James H. Defuria/Intercontinental Airways, Canastota NY	27.2.59/60
				Aero Enterprises, Elkhart IN	18.6.60/61
				John Hibbard, Corcoran CA	3.3.61/62
				Gerald T. Smith, Bakersfield CA	13.4.62/63
				Ronald A. Hevle, Bakersfield CA	23.1.63/64
				Glenn Johnson Realty, Sacramento CA	16.9.64/65
				Leland F. Spalding, Sacramento CA	13.2.65
				Robert J. Love, San Jose CA	11.5.65
			YS-149P	Robert J. Love, El Salvador	.65/67
				(erroneously rep. to YS-210P, FA Salvadorena as FAS 410, later to FA Guatamalteca)	
			TG-REI	Roberto & Enrique Ibarguen, Quezaltenango	.67/78
			N2265P	William Harrison & Terry Randall/ HarRan Aircraft Sales, Muskogee OK	5.78
			N52HA	Lynn Florey, Eden Prairie MN	5.6.78
				crashed Tuxtla Gutierrez, Mexico on del. flight to USA (pilot Burns Byram k.)	5.6.78
122-40975 •	P-51D	44-74435		(to RCAF as 9221) BOC 15.11.50 SOC	29.4.58
				James H. Defuria & Fred J. Ritts/ Intercontinental Airways, Canastota NY	29.4.58
				Aero Enterprises, Elkhart IN	60
			CF-LOQ	Lynn Garrison, Calgary ALTA	26.9.61/63
				Gerald W. Wolton, Calgary ALTA	13.3.63/66
			N130JT	John W. Temple, Signal Mountain TN	26.4.66/70
				crashed, minor dam., Calgary ALTA (rebuilt)	29.4.66
				crashed, badly dam.	23.10.70
				(parts used in rebuild N2251D/44-74427 .70)	
				James J. Chernich, Lake Zurich IL	20.2.76/92
122-40981	P-51D Cavalier 2000	44-74441		(to RCAF as 9593) BOC 8.11.50 SOC	15.10.59
			N9149R	Trans Florida Aviation, Sarasota FL	20.5.59/62
				J. W. (Bill) Fornof/Fornof Motor Co, Houma LA	4.8.62/72
				G. R. Dunagan/Crawford & Co, Atlanta GA	14.3.72
				crashed, dest., Gainesville FL	30.12.72
122-	P-51D	44-74445		(to RCAF as 9594) BOC 8.11.50 SOC	4.12.56

40985 •			N4143A	Stinson Field Aircraft, San Antonio TX	10.56/57
				Truman E. Miley/Big Piney Aviation, Roy UT	3.5.57/59
			N4132A(2	M. L. Alson/Aero Enterprises Inc, Elkhart IN	1.10.59/61
				George E. Monea & Mario I. Corbi, Alliance OH	5.8.61/62
				Harold J. Shelton, Belle Fourche SD	28.3.622
				Grazing Inc, Alzada MT (cloud seeding mods)	9.5.62
				M. L. Alson/Aero Enterprises, Elkhart IN	10.62
				Richardson Construction Co, Sterling VA	2.11.62
				Harold L. Barkman, Indianapolis IN	15.1.63/67
				John E. Dilley, Auburn IN	11.67/69
				Bill H. Hubbs, Pecos TX (race #71)	5.5.69/92
122-40986 •	P-51D	44-74446		(to RCAF as 9223) BOC 15.11.50 SOC	1.11.60
				James H. Defuria/Intercontinental Airways, Canastota NY	30.12.58
				Aero Enterprises, Elkhart IN	.60
			CF-LOR	Milt Harradance, Calgary ALTA	.60/61
				Gary L. Oates, Weston ONT	.65/66
				Mike Malagies, Toronto ONT	.68/69
				Froates Aviation, Toronto ONT	.69/70
				Howard A. Sloan	20.8.70
				John W. Temple & R. L. Robertson TN	6.11.70
			N1451D(2	John W. Temple, Signal Mountain TN	14.3.75
				John J. Stokes/Cen-Tex Aviation, San Marcos TX	13.11.75
				Cecil H. Harp, Lodi CA	12.1.76/78
				Michael Clarke, Phoenix AZ/Prescott AZ	26.3.78/92
				(on rebuild Chino as "Unrulie Julie/ MX-C")	
122-40992 •	P-51D	44-74452		(to RCAF as 9225) BOC 15.11.50 SOC	29.4.58
				James H. Defuria & Fred J. Ritts/ Intercontinental Airways, Canastota NY	29.4.58/59
				(noted stored unconv., Canastota NY 7.59)	
				(to FA Guatemalteca as FAG 366)	3.62/72
			N74190	Don Hull, Sugarland TX	8.72/76
				Wilson C. Edwards, Big Spring TX	.76/92
				(note: id."44-75452" quoted on recov. ex FAG)	
122-40993 •	P-51D Cavalier	44-74453		(to RCAF as 9597) BOC 8.11.50 SOC	15.10.59
			N9150R	Trans Florida Aviation, Sarasota FL	20.5.59/60
			N1335	E. D. Weiner, Los Angles CA	29.7.60/61
				Margaret & Frank Woodside, Lubbock TX	10.61/62
				Aero Enterprises, Elkhart IN	12.3.62/63
				John M. Barker, Indianapolis IN	25.2.63/69
				crashed landing, Indianapolis IN (Barker k.)	17.3.63
				Bill Destafani, Shafter CA : wreck	81/84
				(rebuild Shafter, rep. using TNI-AU airframe, adopted id. 44-13903 : race #102/"312102")	
			C-GJCJ (2	Jerry C. Janes, Vancouver BC	87/89
			N151JP	James R. Priebe, Findlay OH	88/91
				(flies as "Glamorous Jan")	
122-40998 •	P-51D Cavalier	44-74458		(to RCAF as 9226) BOC 15.11.50 SOC	15.10.59
			N9145R	Trans Florida Aviation, Sarasota FL	20.5.59/61
				Marine Maintenance Co, Galveston TX	10.1.61
				Lorraine P. Bodine, Texas City TX	28.2.61/62
				Aero Enterprises Inc, Elkhart IN	21.8.62
				crashed in cornfield, near Elkhart IN	9.3.63
				Dave Zeuschel & Mike Geren CA: wreck	
				Aerospace Modifications, Van Nuys CA	.70
				(rebuild Van Nuys CA to TF-51 config. 70)	
				John Marlin, Los Angeles CA	71
			N65206	John Marlin (FAA: "assembled from parts")	.73/87
				(rebuild completed Compton CA 71/77, race #17 "Green Machine"; later #102 "Daydreamer")	
			N351DM	David Marco/Barnstormers Aviation,	

				Jacksonville FL	2.88/91
				(dism. Chino, trucked to Ft. Lauderdale FL .88, rest. 88/91 as "415326/QP-H/Sizzlin' Liz")	
122-41006 •	P-51D	44-74466		(to RCAF as 9227) BOC 15.11.50 SOC	4.1.56
			N10607	Stinson Field Aircraft, San Antonio TX	26.10.56
				George D. Hanby, Evanston IL	27.2.57
				Thermal Belt Air Service, Tryon NC	12.5.57
				Northrop Carolina Inc, Ashville NC	3.8.57
				George D. Hanby, Philadephia PA	63/69
				John M. Sliker, Wadley GA	19.3.69/76
				(race #17 "Escape")	
				Madelaine H. Sliker, Wadley GA	24.3.76/84
				Wiley Sanders, Troy AL	85/92
				crashed Reno NV (rebuilt)	14.9.85
				(flies as race #69/"Georgia Mae")	
122-41009 •	P-51D Cavalier Mk. 2	44-74469	N7723C	Trans Florida Aviation, Sarasota FL	.58/60
				(to FA Dominicana as FAD 1919)	.60/84
				recov. by Brian O'Farrell/Johnson Aviation, Miami FL	19.5.84
			N7723C	Jerry Miles/Fighterbirds West, Riverbend AZ	.86/90
				(rebuilt Chino CA, ff 13.9.87)	
				Classic Air Parts, Miami FL	92
122-41012	P-51D	44-74472		(to RCAF as 9277) BOC 11.1.51 SOC	17.9.57
			N6323T (2	James H. Defuria & Fred J. Ritts/ Intercontinental Airways, Canastota NY	25.2.57/60
				Aero Enterprises, Elkhart IN	1.5.60
				(rep. to FA Guatelmateca)	
122-41023 •	P-51D	44-74483		(to RCAF as 9228) BOC 15.11.50 SOC	17.8.59
			N6523D	James H. Defuria/Intercontinental Airways, Canastota NY	21.7.58
				minor damage, Basking Ridge NJ	4.2.60
				Robert J. Hartland/Dogwood Inc, Summit NJ	7.7.60/61
				Stencel Aero Engineering Corp, Ashville NC	17.2.61
				W. R. Lowdermilk, Greenville SC	25.9.62/64
				Airplanes Inc, Fort Worth TX	31.10.64
				John H. Herlihy, San Meteo CA	11.65/66
				George Perez, Daly City CA (race #8)	5.12.66/72
			N51GP	George Perez, Sonoma CA/Anchorage AK	77/92
122-41034 •	P-51D	44-74494		(to RCAF as 9237) BOC 6.12.50 SOC	1.11.60
			N6313T	ntu: James H. Defuria/Intercontinental Airways, Canastota NY	12.58/60
				(ferried to USA as N6313T but not reg.)	
			N6356T	Aero Enterprises, Elkhart IN	10.5.60/63
				Capital Steel, Baton Rouge LA	13.6.63/64
				Aero Enterprises, Elkart IN	20.3.64
				Benjamin B. Peck/Interocean Airways, Luxembourg & Munich WG	20.2.64/66
				(del. US to Luxembourg, arr. 28.7.64)	
				Charles Masefield, Shoreham UK	8.66/70
				(dep. Shoreham for Spain 15.1.69, for movie "Patton", painted as USAAF "643147")	
				Ed A. Jurist/Vintage Car Store, Nyack NY	15.3.70/72
				(shipped to USA 1.71, flew as "415271/OC-E")	
				Ed A. Jurist/Vintage Aircraft International, Brownwood TX	27.2.72/75
				David C. Tallichet/ MARC, Chino CA	3.75/79
				Wally McDonnell, Mojave CA	.79
				Bill Destefani, Bakersfield CA	.79/81
			N72FT	Bill Destefani, Shafter CA	1.81/87
				(race #72 "Mangia Pane/474494/LH-D")	
				Vintage Aircraft Inc, Mountain View CA	88/92
				(flies as "411661/Iron Ass")	

122-41037 •	P-51D	44-74497		(to RCAF as 9230) BOC 15.11.50 SOC	1.11.60
			N6320T(2	James H. Defuria/Intercontinental Airways, Canastota NY	30.12.58
				Aero Enterprises, Elkhart IN	60
				Ralph W. Rensink, Lewiston ID	10.1.62/66
				Kenneth W. Neal, Medford OR	26.3.66/69
				crashed Lancaster CA	2.8.69
				Glenn Cook, Seattle WA	26.1.70
				Mike Smith, Johnson KS	.70/72
				(trucked Seattle-Johnson KS, rebuilt: ff 3.71)	
				I. N. ("Junior") Burchinall, Paris TX	14.11.72
				Kent Jones, Dallas TX	3.1.73/75
				John Rutherford, Fort Worth TX	11.75/79
				Jim Hunt, Atlanta GA	.79/80
				Hess Bomberger/Heritage Aircraft Inc, Fayetteville GA	.80/92
				(flies as "415080/Vergeltungswaffe")	
122-41042 •	P-51D	44-74502		(to RCAF as 9232) BOC 6.12.50 SOC	1.11.60
			CF-MWC	James H. Defuria/Intercontinetal Airways, Canastota NY	30.12.58
			N6321T	Aero Enterprises, Elkhart IN	60
				rep. seized en route to Cuba	.62
				Otha D. Aishman, Salina KS	20.7.62/64
				Edward Fisher Flying Service, Kansas City KS	2.7.64/73
				Leroy Penhall, Balboa CA	21.8.73
				Military Aircraft International Inc, Miami FL	2.11.73
			N70QF	Ken Burnstine (race #34 "Miss Foxy Lady")	76
				M. D. Pruitt Furniture Co, Phoenix AZ	5.3.76
				Gary Levitz/Western Aircraft Leasing, Scottsdale AZ	4.6.76
			N51VC	John V. Crocker, Oakland CA	3.8.76/92
				(race #6/"Sumthin Else")	
				crashed landing, Seattle WA	7.90
122-41046 •	P-51D	44-74506		(to RCAF as 9231) BOC 6.12.50 SOC	1.12.60
			CF-MWM	James H. Defuria & Fred J. Ritts/ Intercontinental Airways, Canastota NY	30.12.58
			N6325T	ntu: Aero Enterprises, Elkhart IN	60
				(ferried to Elkhart as N6325T, but not reg.)	
			N6317T	Aero Enterprises, Elkhart IN	60
			N335J (3	Ed Weiner, Los Angeles CA (race #14, #49)	24.3.63/73
				Violet M. Bonzer, Los Angeles CA	8.5.73/79
				EAA Museum, Hales Corner WI : loan	73/79
				Max Hoffman, Fort Collins CO	79
				Wolcott Air Services, Wolcott CT	80
				Gary Norton/Norton Aero, Athol ID	82/90
				Sierra Aviation, Boardman OH	92
				(flies as "474832/GA-N")	
122-41076 •	P-51D	44-74536	N5452V (1	Donald G. Singleton, Van Nuys CA (race #19)	63
				David S. Allender Jr, San Aario CA	66
			N991RC	Robert N. Cleaves	69
				Keefe Corp, Pacific Palisades CA	6.69
			N991R	Keefe Corp, Pacific Palisades CA (race #11)	72/78
				Ron & Janette Smythe, Everett WA	.83/84
				RGS Incorporated, Edmonds WA	87/88
				Hanover Aero Inc, Nashua NH	6.89/92
122-41083	P-51D	44-74543		(to RCAF as 9252) BOC 6.12.50 SOC	17.9.57
				James H. Defuria & Fred J. Ritts/ Intercontinental Airways, Canastota NY	25.2.57
				(ferried to Canastota NY .57, open storage)	
				Ray O. Denman, Brewerton NY : as scrap	28.6.61/65
				Richard M. Vartanian, Pasadena CA	30.6.65
				(trucked from Canastota 6.74, stored dism.	

				Brewerton & Johnstown NY 80/82)	
			N4543	Richard M. Vartanian, Los Angeles CA	78/92
				(rep. used in rebuild Chicago IL .90, adopting id. 44-63655/N5500S)	
122-41122 •	P-51D	44-74582		(to RCAF as 9253) BOC 6.12.50 SOC	19.8.59
			N6524D	James H. Defuria/Intercontinental Airways, Canastota NY	21.7.58
			N6329T	Aero Enterprises, Elkhart IN	11.60/61
				A. G. Ainsworth/A-Mack Co, Luling TX	10.61/63
				Landon Cullum, Wichita Falls TX	14.3.63/84
				John C. Hooper, Harvey LA	.84/87
				Robert Byrne/Byrne Aviation Inc, Bloomfield Hills MI	88/90
				Joseph H. Thibodeau, Denver CO	92
122-41140	P-51D	44-74600		Trottner Iron & Metal Co, San Antonio TX	.49
				(dest. RNZAF: still in original packing case 51)	
			N1739B	Dal-Air, Dallas TX	.51
				(to FA Haiti as 74600, later FAH 600)	18.5.51
				to FA Dominicana)	
				rep. to Cavalier Aircraft Corp, Sarasota FL	
				rep. to Gordon Plaskett, King City CA	c73
			N512ED	Robert J. Bleeg, Mercer Island WA	85/89
				(rest., ff 7.10.87 as "474600/E2-D")	
				Robert J. Pond, Plymouth MN	5.90
				crashed near Flying Cloud MN	18.6.90
122-41142 •	P-51D	44-74602		(to RCAF as 9255) BOC 6.12.50 SOC	1.11.60
			N6318T	James H. Defuria/Intercontinental Airways, Canastota NY	30.12.58
				Aero Enterprises, Elkhart IN	19.8.61
				Robert E. King, South Bend IN	11.61/63
				Aero Enterprises, Elkhart IN	27.3.63
			N35N	C. E. Crosby, Bellingham WA	20.5.63/67
				(race #3; "Mr Choppers")	
			N3580	Jack Hovey/Hovey Machine Products, Walnut Creek/Oakland CA	10.7.67/92
				(race #2; camouflage RAF sc,"HM-P")	
122-41167 •	P-51D	44-74627		(to Philippines AF as 3373/001)	
				displ. Basa AB PI: "The Shark of Zimbales"	77/87
122-41234	P-51D Cavalier 2000	44-74694		sold surplus at McClellan AFB CA	15.8.58
			N7720C	Marshall H. Ratliffe, Battle Creek MI	63
				Samuel Whatley, Mt Clemens MI	64
			N16S	Louis H. Long, Aberdeen SD	66
			N6851D	Jerry Tyler, Ellenton FL	
				Cavalier Aircraft Corp, Sarasota FL	
				(del. to Italy via Shannon 8.12.68)	
			I-BILL	Ditta Billi & Co, Florence, Italy	5.69/77
				Ormond Haydon-Baillie, Duxford, UK	6.77
				cr. Mainz-Finthen, Germany(Haydon-Baillie k)	3.7.77
122-41279 •	P-51D Cavalier	44-74739		(to RCAF as 9297) BOC 16.3.51 SOC	14.5.59
			N8672E	James H. Defuria/Intercontinental Airways, Canastota NY	27.2.59/60
				Aero Enterprises, Elkhart IN	18.6.60/61
				Midwest Airways, Cincinatti OH	10.5.61/62
				(Cavalier conv. by Trans Florida Aviation 4.62)	
			N151Q	Aerial Services Inc, London OH	10.62/63
				Valair Aircraft, Cincinatti OH	23.5.63
				E. R. Cantrell/Angels Aviation, Zephyrhills FL	30.5.63/64
				Space Systems Laboratory Inc, Melbourne FL	3.7.64/67
				Trans Florida Aviation Inc, Sarasota FL	28.3.67
				Cavalier Aircraft Corp, Sarasota FL	4.8.67/71
				(remanufactured as Cavalier .71)	
			N51RH	Robert A. Hoover/North American Rockwell	

				Corp, El Segundo CA	8.5.71
				Robert A. Hoover/Rockwell International, El Segundo CA	74/85
				dam., wing fire, Marysville OH (repaired)	8.9.84
				Robert A. Hoover/Evergreen International, Los Angeles CA	87/92
122-41296	P-51D	44-74756	N5443V	Elmo C. Johnson, Hunsville AL	63
			N2112	J. J. Tururek Manufacturing Co, Chicago IL	66
				William D. Ross, Chicago IL	67
				Leasing Consultants Inc, Forest Hills NY	69
			N69QF	Ken Burnstine (race #33)	73/76
				crashed, dest., Mojave CA (Burnstine k)	6.76
122-41314 •	P-51D	44-74774		(to RCAF as 9270) BOC 11.1.51 SOC	20.9.60
			N6341T	James H. DeFuria & Fred J. Ritts/ Intercontinental Airways, Canastota NY	11.56/60
				(stored unconv., Carberry MAN 57/61)	
				Aero Enterprises, Elkhart IN	10.5.60/62
				(ferried Carberry-Winnipeg-Elkhart 7.62)	
				Margaret Kahlow, Madisonville KY	27.8.62/65
				William L. Sullivan/Audubon Service Inc, Henderson KY	12.6.65/70
				TAS Flight Services, Granville OH	29.7.70/71
				A. C. Lofgren, Hickory Corners MI	3.11.71/81
				Bob Byrne Aviation, Bloomfield Hills MI	.81/92
				(flies as "474774/Rascal")	
				(note: RCAF 9270 also quoted as 44-74474)	
122-41353 •	P-51D	44-74813		(to RCAF as 9261) BOC 10.1.51 SOC	17.8.59
			N6301T	James H. Defuria/Intercontinental Airways, Canastota NY	21.7.58
				rep. crashed and dest., Canastota NY	27.6.60
				Aero Enterprises, Elkhart IN	30.8.60
				D.C. Mullery, Chicago IL	11.62/66
				Richard D. Burns, Hinsdale IL	28.9.66/87
				Jack D. Rodgers, Rockford IL	.87/89
				Richard D. Burns, Hinsdale IL	90/92
122-41367 •	P-51D Cavalier	44-74827 72-1541		Trans Florida Avn, Sarasota FL (stored)	58/66
				Cavalier Aircraft Corporation, Sarasota FL	66
				(to TNI-AU as F-367)	.68/85
				(stored Bandung, Indonesia 76/85)	
				RNZAF Museum, Wigram AB NZ	.85/91
				(displ. as "NZ2410")	
122-41369 •	P-51D	44-74829		(to RCAF as 9265) BOC 10.1.51 SOC	14.5.59
			N8675E	James H. Defuria/Intercontinental Airways, Canastota NY	27.2.59/60
				(stored Winnipeg MAN, ferried to USA .59)	
				Aero Enterprises, Elkhart IN	18.6.60
			N169MD(1	Dr. Burns M. Byram, Marengo IA	18.8.60/66
				crashed, night fcd. ldg. near Des Moines IA: Byram unhurt, passenger bailed out	6.4.67
			N769MD	John E. Dilley, Muncie IN	11.1.68/73
				Max I. Ramsay, Johnson KS	10.1.73/78
				(noted stored dism., Chino CA 77; used in rebuild of 45-11558/N6175C at Chino .79)	
				Fort Wayne Air Service, Fort Wayne IN	81/84
				(rebuilt Ft.Wayne 81/84 as composite, using ex AURI P51D: ff 13.11.84)	
				Tim Wallis/Alpine Helicopters, Wanaka NZ	.84
			ZK-TAF	Tim Wallis/Alpine Deer Group, Wanaka	27.5.86/89
				(shipped to NZ, ff 23.1.85; flies as "NZ2415")	
				NZ Historic Aircraft Trust, Ardmore	89/92

122-41372	P-51D	44-74832		(to RCAF as 9269) BOC 10.1.51 SOC	1.11.60
			CF-MWT	James H. Defuria/Intercontinental Airways, Canastota NY	30.12.58
			N6310T (1	James H. Defuria, Canastota NY	60
				Aero Enterprises, Elkhart IN	10.5.60
				Clyde C. Werner, Elkhart IN	17.6.61/68
				Courtesy Aircraft, Loves Park IL	5.6.68
				William J. Allen, Greensboro NC	13.9.68/69
				Tifton Air Services, Tifton GA	7.6.69/71
				Max R. Hoffman, Fort Collins CO	4.3.71/78
				Gerald Konig/Konig Spraying Svce, Yuma CO	10.76/78
				Max R. Hoffman, Fort Collins CO	1.2.78
				Ward Wilkins, Linden IN	80
				Gary Norton/Norton Aero, Athol ID	81
				(displ. Henley Aerodrome & Museum of Transportation, Athol ID)	
				dest. in hangar fire, Athol ID	.81
				(id. transferred to 45-11453/N551MR)	
122-41376 •	P-51D	44-74836		(to RCAF as 9260) BOC 10.1.51 SOC	4.12.56
			N3991A	Stinson Field Aircraft, San Antonio TX	26.10.56
				Jack Adams Aircraft Sales, Memphis TN	30.5.57/58
			N69X	James E. Hall, Abilene TX	1.4.58/63
				crashed, Dallas-Love Field TX	1.1.59
				wreck to junkyard, Dallas	c60/c80
				Walter Soplata Collection, Newbury OH : hulk	79/86
				Brian O'Farrell/Johnson Aviation, Miami FL	86
122-41390	P-51D	44-74850	N6726C	James E. Hodges, Fort Lauderdale FL	63
			N2116 (1	John M. Sliker, Wadley ID	66
				John P. Silberman, New York NY	69
				Westernair of Albuquerque, Albuquerque NM	71/72
			CF-USA	Don Plumb/Spitfire Inc, Windsor ONT	10.72
				crashed, near Big Spring TX (Plumb k.)	16.10.75
122-41399	P-51D	44-74859		(to RCAF as 9257) BOC 10.1.51 SOC	17.11.51
				crashed Carlton Place ONT	9.11.51
				rep. to Israel with other dam. RCAF P-51Ds (to IDAFAF as 39) : unconf.	
				Sterling Aircraft Supply	64
				Pioneer Aero Service, Burbank CA	2.12.64
			N7097V	ntu: Pioneer Aero Service, Burbank CA	.65
				(id quoted as "44-74839-59")	
				Pioneer Aero	1.92
				Warbirds of Great Britain	7.92
				rebuilt as TF-51D	
122-41405 •	P-51D	44-74865		(to RCAF as 9258) BOC 10.1.51 SOC	14.5.59
			N8677E	James H. Defuria/Intercontinental Airways, Canastota NY	27.2.59
				(stored Winnipeg MAN, ferried to USA .59)	
				Aero Enterprises, Elkhart IN	18.6.60/61
				Walter H. Erickson, Minneapolis MN	11.4.61/65
				crashed on take-off, Minneapolis MN (rebuilt)	.61
				Don H. Novas, Blackfoot ID	5.5.65/92
122-41418 •	P-51D	44-74878		(to RCAF as 9259) BOC 10.1.51 SOC	17.9.57
			N6306T	James H. Defuria & Fred J. Ritts/ Intercontinental Airways, Canastota NY	25.2.57/60
				Aero Enterprises, Elkhart IN	10.5.60/61
				Suncoast Aviation, St. Petersburg FL	8.7.61
				Florida Airmotive Sales, Ft. Lauderdale FL	14.11.61
				Sherman Aircraft Sales, Fort Wayne IN	7.7.62/64
				Howard Olsen Development Co, Midland TX	3.8.64/65
				Huntley Aviation Service, Leland MS	7.1.65/69
				Marvin L. Gardner/Gardner Flyers Inc, Brownfield TX	7.1.69
				Tom Wood Aircraft Co, Kalamazoo MI	6.3.69

				Tom Wood Pontiac, Indianapolis IN	10.71/92
122-41442	P-51D	44-74902		(to FA Guatemalteca as FAG 342)	
				rep. sold to USA	8.72
122-41448 •	P-51D Cavalier	44-74908		(to RCAF as 9273) BOC 11.1.51 SOC	14.5.59
				crashed landing, Winnipeg MAN (stored)	17.6.56
			N1070Z	James H. Defuria/Intercontinental Airways, Canastota NY	27.2.59
				(RCAF disposal: engineless airframe,Winnipeg; open storage Winnipeg 59/62)	
				Aero Enterprises, Elkhart IN	13.5.59/62
				Charles P. Doyle, Minneapolis MN	15.3.62
				(rebuilt Winnipeg, del. by Doyle 18.7.63)	
			N965D	Charles P. Doyle, Apple Valley MN	69/78
			N151BP	Planes of Fame East, Spring Park MN	80/92
122-41450 •	P-51D Cavalier	44-74910		sold surplus at McClellan AFB CA	17.8.59
				Cavalier Aircraft Corp, Sarasota FL	
				(to TNI-AU as F-351)	
				recov. by Stephen Johnson, Oakland CA	.78
			N51SJ	Stephen J. Johnson, Oakland CA	4.81/86
				Yankee Air Corps, Chino CA	.87/88
			N74920	Yankee Air Corps, Chino CA	2.88/92
122-41463 •	P-51D	44-74923	N5438V	J. J. Wolohan, Livingston CA	63
				Walter M. Fountain/Hawke Dusters, Modesto CA	66/69
				(to FA Salvadorena as FAS 410)	7.69
				(adopted id. 44-11353 on return to USA)	
			N132	Donald R. Anderson, Saugus CA	.76
			N100DD	Donald R. Anderson, Saugus CA	78
				(rebuilt by Dave Clinton & Don Anderson 74/81)	
				John R. Sandberg, Robstown TX	.81/84
				(race #28/"Tipsy Too")	
				crashed Reno NV (repaired)	9.83
			N345	Gary R. Levitz, Dallas TX (race #38)	10.84/92
122-41476 •	P-51D	44-74936		USAFM, Wright-Patterson AFB, Dayton OH	.58/90
				(displ. as 15th AF "Shimmy IV")	
122-41479 •	P-51D	44-74939		NASM, Washington DC	65/90
122-41482 •	P-51D	44-74942	N5427V	Robert Fulton Co, Newtown CT	63/83
				Gordon W. Plaskett, King City CA	.83/86
				Anthony A. Buechler, Elm Grove WI	.86/92
				(flies as "414151/Petie 2nd")	
				(FAA quotes 44-72942)	
122-41490 •	P-51D	44-74950	N5464V		
			N511D	Melvyn Paisley, Great Falls MT	63
				Mustang Pilots Club Inc, Van Nuys CA	66/72
				crashed, dest. near Lancaster CA	25.8.71
				(id. transferred to CA-18 c/n 1500: que se)	
			N20JS	John P. Silberman, Key West & Tampa FL	76/84
			N7496W	Selby R. Burch, Winter Garden FL	11.84/92
				(flies as USAF "200")	
122-41502 •	P-51D	44-74962		(to TNI-AU as F-3......)	
				recov. by Stephen Johnson, Oakland CA	.78
			N51DK	Consolidated Airways, Fort Wayne IN	11.80
				Fort Wayne Air Service, Fort Wayne IN	84/92
122-41516 •	P-51D Cavalier	44-74976		(to TNI-AU as F-311)	8.59
				recov. by Stephen Johnson, Oakland CA	.78

				Ralph W. Johnson, Oakland CA	.79
			N98582	Ralph W. Johnson, Oakland CA	13.8.81/84
				Jeffrey R. Michael, Lexington NC	.87/92
				(rest., flies as "Obsession")	
122-41517 •	P-51D	44-74977	N5448V	Earl Dodge, Anchorage AK	63/66
				Michael E. Coutches, Hayward CA	69/92
				(stolen Tonopah NV 5.5.84: found Merced CA 9.84)	
122-41518	P-51D	44-74978		(to F.A.d'L GN Nicaragua as GN...)	
			N6169U	MACO Sales Financial Corp, Chicago IL	31.3.64
				Richard M. Vartanian, Pasadena CA	66/69
			N74978	Richard M. Vartanian, Arcadia/Shafter CA	72/88
				Arthur W. McDonnell, Mojave CA	.88
				dest. in hangar fire, Shafter CA	7.88
122-41536 •	P-51D	44-74996	N5410V	Prevost F. Smith Parachute Co, Santee CA	63/69
				Michael E. Coutches, Hayward CA	78
				Bill Destefani, Bakersfield CA	81/83
				(rebuilt Shafter CA 81/82 as mod. racer, #4/"Dago Red")	
				Frank Taylor, Bakersfield CA	.83
				Frank Sanders, Chino CA	84
				Alan Preston, Dallas TX	87/88
				Sherman Aircraft Sales, West Palm Beach FL	88
				David G. Price, Santa Monica CA	.88/90
				Liberty Aero Corp, Santa Monica CA	.90
				American Golf Development, Santa Monica CA	92
122-41547 •	P-51D Cavalier	44-75007	N5462V		
			N3451D	Trans Florida Aviation Inc, Sarasota FL	66
				Tempress Research Co Corp, Sunnyvale CA	69
				Jerry Brassfield (race #96)	73
				Paul Poberezny/EAA Foundation, Oshkosh WI	78/92
				(flies as "4475007/Paul VI")	
122-41549 •	P-51D	44-75009	N5474V	David L. Rountree, Anderson CA	66/69
				Homer Rountree, Anderson CA	78
				Ted E. Contri, Reno NV	84/87
			N51TC (2	Ted E. Contri, Yuba City CA	3.87/92
				(flies as "Rosalie")	
122-41564 •	P-51D	44-75024		(to TNI-AU as F-3......)	
				John MacGuire, El Paso/Fort Hancock TX	84/89
			N4261U	reg. res. res. cancelled	7.91
124-44246 •	P-51D	44-84390	N2869D	Charles A. Lyford , Belleview WA	63/72
				(race #8/"Bardahl Special")	
				Life Science Church, San Diego CA	78
				Charles Hall, San Diego CA (race #3)	81
				Douglas D. Driscoll, American Falls ID	84/92
				(race #3/"484390")	
124-44345 •	P-51D	44-84489		(to RAAF as A68-750) BOC	8.45
				SOC for target use in Korea	1.4.52
				American Aeronautics Corp., Burbank CA	2.53
			VH-POB	reg. res: Peter N. Anderson, Sydney, NSW	.87/92
				(fuselage stored CA, rest. project)	
124-44471 •	P-51D	44-84615		(to IDFAF as ......)	
			N7099V	Pioneer Aero Service, Burbank CA	66
				Larry R. Strimple, Mansfield OH	69
			N9LR	Larry R. Strimple, Mansfield OH	
			N55JL	Jimmy Leeward/Bahia Oaks Inc, Ocala FL	.74/92
				(race #9/"Cloud Dancer")	
124-44490 •	P-51D	44-84634		(to FA d'L GN Nicaragua as GN96)	
			N6165U	MACO Sales Financial Corp, Chicago IL	2.9.63

				Thomas J. Kuckinsky, Menomonee Falls WI	66/69
				Aviation Business Services Inc	70
				Air Sales Inc, Fort Lauderdale FL	72
				Max I. Ramsay, Johnson KS	78
			N51JV	Firebird Enterprises OH	84/89
				Ohio Associated Enterprises, Painseville OH	90
			N51ES	Edward H. Shipley, Malvern PA	2.92
				(note: FAA quote id. 44-85634,	
				id. also rep. as 44-63634: que se)	
124-44514 •	P-51D TF-51D Cavalier	44-84658 N851D (1		(to FA d'L GN Nicaragua as GN99)	20.2.58
				Trans Florida Aviation Corp, Sarasota FL	63
				Cavalier Aircraft Corp, Sarasota FL	66/69
				(to TNI-AU as F-361)	c68
				recov. by Stephen Johnson, Oakland CA	.78
				John MacGuire, El Paso TX	79/84
				(rebuilt as TF-51D, Fort Collins CO .83/85)	
			N51TF	John MacGuire, Fort Hancock TX : del.	1.85
				John MacGuire/War Eagles Air Museum,	
				Santa Teresa NM	89/92
				(flies as "484658/"The Friendly Ghost")	
124-44516	P-51D TF-51D Cavalier	44-84660		(to FA Guatelmateca as FAG 345)	20.10.57
			N38228	Don Hull, Sugarland TX	8.72/73
				Wilson C. Edwards, Big Spring TX	76
				crashed at Big Spring TX	21.8.76
124-44525 •	P-51D TF-51D	44-84669		(to Rep. of Korea AF as 201)	
				displ. Teague (K-2) AB, South Korea	64/89
124-44601 •	P-51D TF-51D	44-84745	N5439V	Cline Cantarini, Lancaster CA	63
				Stanley M. Kurzet, Covina CA	66/69
				Lindsay Newspapers, Sarasota FL (dism.)	72/82
			N851D (2	David B. Lindsay/Lindair Inc, Sarasota FL	6.82
				Gordon W. Plaskett, King City CA	84
				(rebuilt as TF-51D, King City CA 84)	
				Bob Amyx, Oklahoma City OK	.84/85
				Bob Byrne Aviation, Bloomfield MI	87
				Doug Schultz/Stallion 51 Inc, Nashua NH	4.87
				Stallion 51 Corporation, Kissimmee FL	88/92
				(flies as "484745/Crazy Horse")	
124-44609 •	P-51D	44-84753	N5436V	Robert L. Rodman, Fullerton CA	63
				Les Grant, Santa Barbara CA	66/73
			N51TC (1	Ted E. Contri, Reno NV	81/87
			N51BE	ntu: Ted E. Contri, North Highland CA	11.86
			N251BP	Planes of Fame East, Plymouth MN	2.87/92
124-44642 •	P-51D F-6D	44-84786		sold surplus at McClellan AFB CA	25.11.49
				frustrated export to IDFAF	
				Michael E. Coutches, Hayward CA : stored	c52/61
				Bill Myers, St Louis MO : stored	.61/81
				Henry J. Schroeder/Midwest Aviation	
				Museum, Danville IL	.81
			N51BS	Henry J. Schroeder, Danville IL	1.83/92
				rest. to fly, Danville IL:	
				adopted id. 44-73822/N5484V: que se)	
124-44706 •	P-51D Cavalier	44-84850		(to TNI-AU as F-3.....)	
				recov. by Stephen Johnson, Oakland CA	.78
			N87JB	John MacGuire, El Paso TX	1.82/88
				War Eagles Air Museum, Santa Teresa NM	88/92
				(flies as "484850/Ghost Rider")	
124-44716 •	P-51D	44-84860		(to TNI-AU as F-3......)	
				recov. by Stephen Johnson, Oakland CA	.78

			N55509	John MacGuire, El Paso & Ft Hancock TX	8.84/88
				Aero Classics, Chino CA	6.89
			N327DB	Darryl Bond/Aero Classics, Chino CA	.90/91
				(rebuilt Chino CA as TF-51D: ff 19.5.89;	
				built from spares: CAC mainplane, fuse. ex	
				Enforcer programme: new id. "PAS82087")	
				(flies as "484860/Lady Jo")	
124-	P-51D	44-84864		(to NACA as NACA126)	
44720 •	ETF-51D		N4223A	Kibler Bros	.57
				Sidney A. Franklin, Pacific Palisades CA	63
				Glenn Johnson Realty, Sacramento CA	66/69
				Michael E. Coutches, Hayward CA	.69/92
				loan: Wagons to Wings Mus., Morgan Hill CA	79/89
124-	P-51D	44-84896	N5416V	Lake Air Corp, Michigan City IN	63
44752 •				James C. Keichline, Huntington Park CA	66/69
				Kenneth M. Scholz, Playa del Ray CA	78/92
124-	P-51D	44-84900		(to NACA as NACA127)	
44756 •	ETF-51D			USAFM, Greater Pittsburg ANGB PA	73/89
				(displ. as" PA ANG 48490")	
124-	P-51D	44-84933		disposal ex McClellan AFB CA; $2160	20.9.57
44789 •			N2874D	Earl V. Dakin, Sacramento CA	20.9.57
				Douglas W. Brown/Mustang Aviation,	
				Great Falls MT	11.58/62
				Kathleen C. Murphy, Great Falls MT: dism.	8.10.62/64
				Edward G. Fleming, Calgary ALTA	10.3.64
				(trucked Great Falls to Calgary, rebuilt)	
			CF-RUT	Edward G. Fleming, Calgary ALTA	4.8.65
				Donald F. McGillivray, Nanaimo BC	13.8.65/67
				Charles E. Roberts/Calg-Air Sales, Calgary	4.11.67
			N201F	Futrell Aircraft Sales, Hot Springs AR	12.12.67
				Alexander J. Edelman, Great Neck NY	69
				Suffolk Flight Associates, Huntington NY	6.69/72
				John J. Mark, Milwaukee WI	78/84
				John J. Mark/ MA Inc, Oshkosh WI	84/92
124-	P-51D	44-84952	N6495C		
44808 •			N210D	Contractor Equipment Co, Salem OR	66
				Joseph Hartney, Chino CA	78
				Steve Tognoli CA	84
				Northeast Aircraft Assoc., Wilmington DE	87/92
124-	P-51D	44-84961		disposal ex McClellan AFB CA	.58
44817 •			N7715C	Capitol Airways, Nashville TN	2.58/64
				Charles F. Willis Jr, Frank Lynott &	
				Charles Hall, Seattle WA	7.64/71
				(race #5, "Miss RJ")	
				Gunther W. Balz, Kalamazoo MI	7.71/73
				(race #5, "Roto-Finish")	
				John M. Sliker, Wadley GA	10.10.73
	RB-51			Ed Browning/Brownings Inc, Idaho Falls ID	2.74/79
				(rebuilt Van Nuys CA: mod. racer RB-51 with	
				Griffon 54, contra-rotating props; ff 3.6.75:	
				race #5, "Red Baron")	
				(world piston record 499.018mph -14.8.79)	
				crashed, wrecked, Reno NV	9.79
				Richard Ransopher, Grapevine TX (wreck)	.80
				Steven J. Hinton/Fighter Rebuilders, Chino CA	.85/92
				(id. tfd to rebuild of ex TNI-AU P-51D at Chino,	
				ff Chino 9.85, flies as "413334/G4-U")	
				(hulk of RB-51 to Terry & Bill Rogers, Sherman	
				TX .89 : to be rebuilt as Griffon RB-51 racer .92)	
124-	P-51D	44-84962		(to ROKAF: later TNI-AU as F-312)	
44818 •				recov. by Stephen Johnson, Oakland CA	.78

				Stephen W. Johnson, Oakland CA	.79
			N9857P	Lee W. Schaller, Montville NJ	13.8.81
				Lee W. Schaller, New Athens IL	87/92
				(note: F-312 unconv. MARC hangar, Chino CA 90)	
124-48120	P-51D	45-11367	N2871D	American Aircraft Sales Co, Hayward CA	63
				James L. Ventura, Goleta CA	66/67
				crashed during air race (Ventura k.)	3.9.67
			N4078K	reg. res.	
				(id. transferred to 44-63810/N63810)	.72
124-48124 •	P-51D	45-11371		(to FA d'L GN Nicaragua as GN121)	31.5.58
			N12067	MACO Sales Financial Corp, Chicago IL	8.7.63
				Joe Binder, Fremont OH	63/70
			N1051S	George Sullivan	6.70
				Mustangs Aviation Inc, Miami FL	72/78
				Peter McManus, Fort Lauderdale FL	7.79/84
				Whittington Bros, Fort Lauderdale FL	.84
				Rick E. Sharpe, Rosharon TX	84
			N751CB	Connie Bowlin/Bowlin Enterprises, Griffin GA	5.85
			N1051S	Jimmie R. MacMillan/Breckenridge Air Museum, Breckenridge TX	10.85/87
				Spencer Flack/Myrick Aviation, Miami FL	1.87/91
				(based Southend UK: arr. on del. 22.6.87)	
				Flakair Inc, Fort Collins CO	92
				(flies as "511371/VF-5/Sunny VIII")	
124-48134 •	P-51D	45-11381	N5471V	Vulcan Engineering Co Inc, Little Rock AR	63/66
				Jack Huismann/Mustang Corp, Pewaukee WI	69/72
				Ed Browning/Brownings Inc, Roberts ID	78
				crashed near Casper WY	6.81
			C-GRLR	Ritchie Rasmussen, Edmonton ALTA	9.83/84
				(rebuilt, ff .83 as "The Flying Undertaker")	
			N151MR	Herbert E. Rupp, Port Salerno FL	4.85
			N551CB	Connie Bowlin/Bowlin Enterprises, Griffin GA	9.85/90
				Carrier Aviation, High Point NC	92
				(flies as "414888/Glamorous Glen III")	
124-48144 •	P-51D	45-11391	N6170C	Thomas A. Drummond, Ridgecrest CA	63
				Jeffrey D. Cannon, Los Angeles CA	66
				Arthur R. Tucker, Norwood NJ	69
			N5151N	Arthur R. Tucker, Norwood NJ	70
			N51WT	John I. Watson, Blackwood NJ	78/92
124-48206 •	P-51D	45-11453	N5479V	John A. Colling, Scottsdale AZ	63
				Sanford Aviation, Gardena CA	66
				(to FA Boliviana as FAB 511)	10.6.66
			C-GXUP	Arny Carnegie, Edmonton ALTA (dism.)	12.77
			N59038	George Roberts, FL	
			N6310T(2		.78
				Whittington Bros, Ft. Lauderdale FL	
				(rebuilt Ft.Collins CO, ff 5.85: adopted id. 44-74832)	
			N551MR	Herbert E. Rupp, Port Salerno FL	9.85/92
				(flies as "414450/Old Crow")	
124-48211 •	P-51D	45-11458		(to RAAF as A68-801) BOC	9.45
			N4886V	American Aeronautics Corp, Burbank CA	23.2.53
				(to FA Boliviana as FAB 504)	c2.55
				Museo Aeronautico, Maracay AB, Venezuela	87/91
124-48224 •	P-51D	45-11471	N5481V		
			N332	David Maytag, Colorado Springs CO (race #9)	63/69
				David Zeuschel, Van Nuys CA	73/78
				James Barkley, AZ	79
				crashed, Borrego Springs CA (Barkley k.)	21.8.79

				Alan Preston Air Racing Team, Dallas TX	7.9.84/87
				(rebuilt using fus. of IDFAF 69 & wing of	
				IDFAF 28 as mod. racer #84 "Stiletto")	
				Sherman Aircraft Sales, West Palm Beach FL	.87/89
				Liberty Aero Corp, Santa Monica CA	90/92
124-	P-51D	45-11483		(to RAAF as A68-813) BOC 9.45 : disposal	1.53
48236				American Aeronautics Corp, Burbank CA	23.2.53
			N4674V(1	American Aeronautics Corp, Burbank CA	17.8.54/56
				Dwight Gibson, Los Angeles CA : dism.	5.9.56/58
				Jack Wollom/Sterling Aircraft Supply Co,	
				Hollywood CA : dism.	21.2.58/64
			N7096V	Pioneer Aero Service, Burbank CA	12.64/68
				Leo E. Pike, Bakersfield CA	20.3.68
				(id. tfd. to CA-18 c/n 1523: que se)	
				(also rep. to FA Boliviana as FAB-503 1.2.55)	
124-	P-51D	45-11489	N5421V		
48242	Cavalier		N551D (2	Stan Hoke/Stanley Dunbar Studios,	
				Charlotte NC (race #99)	63/64
				crashed, dest., Lincoln VA	17.4.66
			N5421V	Ed Browning/Brownings Inc, Roberts ID	78
				(id. transferred to CA-17 c/n 1364: que se)	
124-	P-51D	45-11507		(to RNZAF as NZ2417) BOC	6.9.45
48260 •				Ron E. Fechney, Canterbury NZ	4.58
			ZK-CCG	Ron Fechney & Jack MacDonald, Aylesbury	11.64/74
				(flown to Christchurch 4.4.74 for shipping USA)	
			N921	John F. Schafhausen, Spokane WA	10.74/75
				Stocker Chevrolet, State College PA	78
				Von Weeks Flugwerke Inc, Tamiami FL	.78/84
				Weeks Air Museum, Tamiami FL	84/92
				(flies as "413321/HO-P/Cripes a Mighty 3rd")	
				badly damaged Hurricane Andrew	
124-	P-51D	45-11513		(to RNZAF as NZ2423) BOC	6.9.45
48266 •				W. Ruffell, Blenheim NZ	5.58/64
				John Smith, Mapua, Nelson NZ	.64/89
124-	P-51D	45-11518		(to RNZAF as NZ2427) BOC	6.9.45
48271 •				Peter Coleman, Blenheim NZ : stored dism.	5.58/90
				Tim Wallis/Alpine Fighter Group,Wanaka NZ	.90/91
				(rest. to fly)	
124-	P-51D	45-11525		(to TNI-AU as F-3....)	
48278 •	Cavalier			recov. by Stephen Johnson / Vanpac	.78
			N91JB	John MacGuire, El Paso & Ft Hancock TX	3.82/88
				John MacGuire/War Eagles Air Museum,	
				Santa Teresa NM	88/92
				(flies as "511525/Silver Ghost")	
124-	P-51D	45-11540	N5162V	Dennis Schoenfelder, Santa Barbara CA	78
48293 •			N151W	Joe G. Mabee, Midland TX	84/92
124-	P-51D	45-11546	N5470V		
48299			N518M	Northern Air Service, Grand Rapids MI	63
			N518MC	Don Shepherd, Houston TX	66
			N518M	Douglas L. Champlin, Enid OK	69
				Well Aircraft Inc, Hutchinson KS	8.69
			PI-C1046	Enrique Zobel, Manila Philippines	
			RP-C1046	Enrique Zobel, Manila Philippines	
			N51JW	John P. Wright, San Francisco CA	.71/82
				crashed, dest., Elko NV (Wright k.)	9.82
124-	P-51D	45-11553		sold surplus McClellan AFB CA	20.9.57
48306 •			N5414V		
			N713DW	Richard D. Weaver, Van Nuys CA	63/69
				(race #6, later #15)	

			N22DC	Anthony J. Alessandris, Reno NV	72
			N51T (1	Anthony J. Alessandris, Reno NV	
			N51TZ		
			N5415V (2	Richard Smith, Bradbury CA	77/88
				(rebuilt using components 45-11571/N5415V)	
				RWR Development, Las Vegas NV	89
				Unlimited Air Racing Inc, Van Nuys CA	90/92
				(flies as "USAF/511553/FF-553/Miss Fit")	
124-48311 •	P-51D	45-11558	N6175C (1	Aerodynamics Inc, Pontiac MI	63
				James C. Gorman, Mansfield OH	66
				Herbert E. Rupp, Port Salerno FL	.66
				crashed, Georgia	.67
				(rebuilt using parts 44-74829 & 44-73822)	
				John E. Dilley, Auburn IN	69/72
				John Rutherford, Fort Worth TX	78/79
				Courtesy Aircraft, Rockford IL	.82
				Joseph Kasparoff, Montebello CA (race #39)	83/92
				cr. takeoff, Van Nuys CA (repaired)	6.8.85
				(note: fuselage 45-11558 rep. held by M.Gardner Mercedes TX in 84)	
124-48312 •	P-51D Cavalier	45-11559	N5469V	Jim B. Tregoning, Bakersfield CA	63
				Burford Co International Corp, Maysville OK	66
			N6451D	Levitz Furniture Co, Dallas TX	69
				Volkmer Manufacturing Co, Dallas TX	6.69
				(to FA Salvadorena as FAS-409)	7.69
			N30FF	Flaherty Factors Inc, Monterey CA	1.11.74
				(also rep. as 44-11153: to FAS-401 30.9.68)	
				Ward Wilkins, Linden IN	78
				Henry J. Schroeder/Midwest Aviation Museum, Danville IL	82/92
				(flies as "5-11559/ North American Maid")	
124-48324 •	P-51D	45-11571	N5415V (1	Arni L. Sumarlidason, Nice France	63
				Marvin Parker, Shelton CT	66/69
				South Delta Aviation, Rolling Fork MS	8.69
				Anthony J. D'Alessandris, Reno NV	72
				(rebuilt: adopted id. 45-11553)	
			N51T (2	Anthony J. D'Alessandris, Reno NV	78/92
124-48335 •	P-51D	45-11582	N5441V	The Air Museum, Claremont CA	6.11.57
				The Air Museum, Ontario/Chino CA	64/84
				Planes of Fame, Chino CA	84/92
				(flies as "Spam Can")	
124-48339	P-51D	45-11586		disposal ex McClellan AFB CA	1.57
			N5423V	Walter D. Oakes, Chicago IL	63/69
				Albert Shirkey, Tulsa OK	78
			N51HA		
			N13LF	Lynn L. Florey FL	83/84
				Harry E. Tope, Mount Pleasant MI	11.86
			N51HT	Harry E. Tope, Mount Pleasant MI	2.87/90
				(flew as "Death Rattler")	
				crashed, dest., Ottawa ONT (Tope k.)	1.7.90
124-48373	P-51D	45-11620	N2872D	American Aircraft Sales Co, Hayward CA	63
				Kevin D. Derth, Novota CA	66
				Holiday Magic Inc, San Rafael CA	69
				William Penn Patrick/Spectrum Air Inc, Novota CA	12.69/72
				crashed, dest., Lake County CA (Patrick k.)	9.6.73
124-48381 •	P-51D	45-11628	N5446V	Michael E. Coutches, Hayward CA	61
				Thomas P. Mathews, Monterey CA	63
			N151X	Walter E. Stewart, Monterey CA	66/72

c/n	Type	Serial	Reg	History	Date
				John T. Johnson, Rexburg ID	78/81
				W. L. Hane & J. T. Johnson, Rexburg ID	17.9.81
				William L. Hane, Portland OR/Mesa AZ	82/92
				displ. Champlin Fighter Museum, Mesa AZ	
				(flies as "Ho Hun/CY-H")	
124-48386 •	P-51D	45-11633	N5413V	William G. Lacy/Lacy Steel Inc, Honolulu HI	63/92
				damaged, ground accident, Honolulu HI	c72
				Wm. G. Lacy	92
124-48389 •	P-51D	45-11636	N5467V	Tallmantz Aviation Inc, Glenview CA	63
				Rosen Novak Auto Co, Omaha NB	66
				John Dilley, Fort Wayne IN	68
			N11636	Michael W. Bertz, Cheyenne WY/Nashville TN	8.68/78
				Michael W. Bertz, Lakewood CO	78/92
				(flies as "511636/WD-KK/Stang Evil")	
1326 •	CA-17 Mk. 20	A68-1		RAAF BOC 7.45 : ff Fishermans Bend VIC	5.46
				used for Atomic tests, Emu Junction SA	10.53
				Stanley Booker/Stan Air Inc, Fresno CA	8.67
				(dep. Emu on ferry Adelaide 31.10.67, stored)	
			VH-EMQ	ntu: Tony Schwerdt, Adelaide SA	.69
				damaged during shipping Adelaide - USA	6.69
			N7773	Stan Air Inc, Fresno CA	.70
				Ed Jurist/Vintage Aircraft Int'l, Nyack NJ	
				Randy Sohn	
				Gary Levitz, Dallas TX	
			N51WB (2	Bill & Don Whittington, Fort Lauderdale FL	.79/81
				(rebuilt Ft Collins CO, ff 11.80 : adopted id. 44-15757)	
				Wiley Sanders, Troy AL	.81/92
				(race #38/"A68-1001")	
1364 •	CA-17 Mk. 20	A68-39		RAAF BOC 12.45 SOC	12.53
			VH-BOY	Fawcett Aviation/Illawarra Flying School, Bankstown NSW (target-tug)	10.59/79
				crashed on take-off Bankstown (rebuilt)	5.6.76
				Gordon W. Plaskett, King City CA	.79
				Flying Tiger Farms, Bakersfield CA	.81
			N551D	Bill Destefani, Bakersfield CA	83
				(rebuilt, adopted id. 45-11489; ff 5.10.83)	
				(later adopted new id. 44-14826/N551D)	
				Jack Erickson/Erickson Air Crane, Central Point OR (flies as "A68-39/BF-D")	11.83/92
1396 •	CA-17 Mk. 20	A68-71		RAAF BOC 16.4.46: damaged ldg Pearce WA	24.4.49
				to RAAF "Inst. No. 14" at RAAF Pearce: SOC	10.52
				Midland Technical School Aeronautical Annexe, Perth Airport WA : instructional airframe	10.52/72
				Airforce Association Aviation Museum, Perth	3.72/84
			VH-PSI	ntu: Derek A. Macphail, Perth WA	28.6.84
			VH-SID	Derek A. Macphail, Perth WA	88/92
1425 •	CA-18 Mk. 21	A68-100		RAAF BOC 11.47 SOC	4.58
				A. J. R. Oates, Sydney NSW	23.4.58
				Fawcett Aviation, Bankstown NSW	.60
			VH-BOW	Fawcett Aviation, Bankstown NSW	25.8.61/67
				Ed Fleming/Skyservice Aviation, Camden NSW	.67
				James Ausland, Seattle WA	20.11.67
				(shipped to Seattle, rebuilt 68/71: adopted id. 44-14777/N51AB)	
			N51AB	James Ausland/Sports Air, Seattle WA	7.71
				Joe Arnold, Greenville MS	20.2.74
				Robby R. Jones, Minter City MS	25.8.75/89
				Norman V. Lewis, Louisville KY	90/92
				(flies as "414777/J-RR/Miss Escort")	
1429 •	CA-18	A68-104		RAAF BOC 11.47 SOC	4.58

c/n	Type	Serial	Reg	History	Date
	Mk. 21			Tarren Point Non-Ferrous Metals P/L, Sydney	23.9.60
				A. J. R. Oates, Sydney NSW	60
				Adastra Airways Pty Ltd, Mascot NSW	11.62/64
				Edgar Pickles, Barham NSW: del. ex Mascot	2.8.64
				Dr. Tony Fisher, Jerilderie NSW	66/70
			VH-BOB	Robert Eastgate, Melbourne VIC	10.70/92
				(rest. Essendon VIC, ff 26.2.76 as "A68-104")	
1430 •	CA-18	A68-105		RAAF BOC 21.11.47 SOC	23.4.58
	Mk. 21			R. H. Grant Metals, Tocumwal NSW	4.58
				Peter Freason, Laverton VIC	12.60/64
				displ. at Fleetwings Garage, Laverton VIC	60/64
				Moorabbin Air Museum, Melbourne VIC	11.64/69
				Richard E. Hourigan, Melbourne VIC	11.69/92
				loaned: RAAF Museum, RAAF Point Cook VIC	7.77/90
			VH-JUC	Richard E. Hourigan, Melbourne VIC	.90/92
				(moved to Tyabb VIC 24.3.90, rest. to fly)	
1432 •	CA-18	A68-107		RAAF BOC 12.47 SOC	5.58
	Mk. 21			VH-AUB A. J. R. Oates, Bankstown NSW	24.4.58/66
				Ewan McKay, Rosedale Station, Jericho QLD	4.66
				Col Pay, Scone NSW	75/92
				(flies as "A68-107")	
1443 •	CA-18	A68-118		RAAF BOC 10.5.48: SOC	4.58
	Mk. 21			Wilmore Aviation Services, Moorabbin VIC	23.4.58
			VH-WAS	Joe R. Palmer/Wilmore Aviation Services	.60/78
				retired & parked, Bankstown NSW	6.8.60/73
				loan: Camden Museum of Aviation NSW: arr.	7.7.73/78
			VH-AGJ	Jeff Trappett, Morwell VIC	.78/92
				(flies as "A68-118")	
1444	CA-18	A68-119		RAAF BOC 11.6.48: SOC	23.4.58
	Mk. 21			R. H. Grant Trading Co, Tocumwal NSW	4.58
				Ralph H. Capponi, Apollo Bay VIC	.64/67
				(flown on DCA permit as "A68-119")	
				Ed Fleming/Skyservice Aviation,Camden NSW	11.67/68
			N65119	ntu: Stans Airplane Sales, Fresno CA: not del.	68
				Langdon Badger, Adelaide SA	.68
			VH-IVI	Langdon Badger Furnishings, Adelaide SA	20.6.69/70
				Raymond J. Whitbread, Sydney NSW	30.9.70/73
				crashed & dest. Windsor NSW (Whitbread k.)	11.6.73
1462 •	CA-18	A68-137		RAAF BOC 26.11.48: SOC	2.60
	Mk. 23			Aeronautical Research Labs., Melbourne VIC	.60/70
				RAAF Museum, Point Cook VIC (ex fire dump)	74
			VH-PPV	ntu: Vic Perry, RAAF Base Townsville QLD	74/80
				RAAF Museum: RAAF Base Townsville QLD	80/92
				(under rest. to fly, displ. as "KH791/CV-P")	
1495 •	CA-18	A68-170		RAAF BOC	2.50
	Mk. 23			displ. RAAF Stores Depot., Toowoomba, QLD	60/68
				RAAF Museum, RAAF Point Cook VIC	72/92
				(rest. to fly, displ. as"A68-170/Duffy's Delight")	
1500 •	CA-18	A68-175		RAAF BOC 4.50 SOC	1.59
	Mk. 23			Col Pay, Narromine NSW	60/65
				Ed Fleming/Skyservice Aviation,Camden NSW	.65/67
			CF-WWH	John C. Kehler, Plumb Coulee MAN	1.5.67/71
				(shipped to Vancouver, rebuilt Carman MAN by Bob Diemert: conv. 4-seater, CF-100 canopy!)	
			N64824	Frank Martucci, Roslyn Heights NY	18.5.71/73
			N5789	ntu: flew with this unauthorised reg.	
			N64824	Frank Gruzman, West Babylon NY	31.1.73
				John P. Silberman, Sherborn MA	8.11.73/75
				Arthur & Dan Vance, Santa Rosa CA	5.8.75/92

				(rebuilt 75/82, rep. using ex AURI airframe	
				& hulk ex junkyard: ff Shafter CA 5.82;	
				flies as "413678/V-C5"/Million Dollar Baby")	
1512 •	CA-18	A68-187		RAAF BOC 10.50 SOC	4.58
	Mk. 22			A. J. R. Oates, Sydney NSW	23.4.58
				Adastra Airways Pty Ltd, Mascot NSW	.60/61
				Fawcett Aviation/Illawarra Flying Service,	
				Bankstown NSW	.61/67
				Chieftain Aviation Pty Ltd, Bankstown NSW	.67/69
				(advertising displ. on pole, Bankstown Airport)	
				Hockey Treloar, Sydney NSW	7.69/92
			VH-UFO	ntu: Hockey Treloar, Sydney NSW	3.73
				(conv. to RR Dart turboprop, Canberra ACT	
				70/76: not flown, conv. abandoned)	
				(rebuild to fly with Merlin, Toowoomba QLD)	
1517 •	CA-18	A68-192		RAAF BOC 3.51 SOC	4.58
	Mk. 22		VH-FCB	F. Chris Braund, Tamworth NSW	4.58/61
				Jack McDonald, Moorabbin VIC	.61/66
				Ed Fleming/Skyservice Aviation, Camden NSW	10.66/69
			PI-C651	George Scholey/Prontino Inc, Manila	27.2.69
			RP-C651	George Scholey/Prontino Inc, Manila	73/75
				crashed landing, Manila Airport	18.10.73
			VR-HIU	Ray Hanna & Mal Rose/Hong Kong Aeronautical	
				Engineering Co, Kai Tak Airport, Hong Kong	.75/85
				(rebuilt Kai Tak 75/85, ff 2.85)	
			G-HAEC	The Old Flying Machine Company, Duxford	2.82/92
				arr. Gatwick by airfreight 28.2.85	
				(flies as "472917/Ding Hao")	
1518	CA-18	A68-193		RAAF BOC 5.51 SOC	4.58
	Mk. 22			R. H. Grant Trading Co, Tocumwal NSW	.58/63
				Dr. Tony Fisher, Jerilderie NSW	.63/69
			VH-DBB	Don Bushe, Melbourne VIC	4.4.69/70
				crashed, dest., Bendigo VIC (Bushe k.)	15.2.70
1523 •	CA-18	A68-198		RAAF BOC 7.51 SOC	4.58
	Mk. 22			Fawcett Aviation, Bankstown NSW	62/68
				Arnold J. Glass, Sydney NSW	66/68
				Ed Fleming/Skyservice Aviation, Camden NSW	.68
				Stan Booker/Stan's Airplane Sales, Fresno CA	.68
				(shipped to USA, noted at Bakersfield CA 11.68)	
			N65198	Joe Banducci & Elmer Rossi, Bakersfield CA	.68/69
			N4674V(2	Joe Banducci & Elmer Rossi, Bakersfield CA	.70/77
				(adopted id. 45-11483/A68-813/N4674V)	
				(race #86 "Ciuchetton")	
			N607D	ntu:	76
			N86JB	Joe F. Banducci, Bakersfield CA (race #86)	10.77/82
			N286JB	Joe F. Banducci, Bakersfield CA	3.82
				Don Whittington, Fort Lauderdale FL	84
				Frank Strickler/Fox 51 Ltd, Denton TX	85/88
				Janet Spencer Shaw/Fox 51 Ltd, Dallas TX	89/90
				(flew as "511483/FF-483")	
				Victor Haluska/Santa Monica Propeller CA	91
				Flying Eagles Inc, Wilmington DE	91
				Apache Aviation, Dijon France	.91
				(flies as "JD-8/The Best Years of Our Lives")	
1524 •	CA-18	A68-199		RAAF BOC 7.51 SOC	4.58
	Mk. 22			A. J. R. Oates, Bankstown NSW	.60
			VH-BOZ	Fawcett Aviation/Illawarra Flying School,	
				Bankstown NSW (target-tug)	11.60/79
				crashed takeoff, Bankstown NSW (repaired)	6.6.76
			G-MUST	ntu: Douglas W. Arnold/Warbirds of GB Ltd	20.12.79
				HM Customs Australia: impounded	12.79/84
				RAAF Museum, RAAF Point Cook VIC	.84/92
				(stored dism., RAAF Stores Depots, Sydney &	

				Dubbo NSW 79/92; trucked to RAAF Williamtown NSW 15.2.92 for rest. to fly)	
- •	Cavalier Mk. 2	67-14865		(to FA Boliviana as FAB 522)	10.67 T
				rep. stored by FAB for planned museum	85
- •	Cavalier T Mk. 2	67-14866		(to FA Boliviana as FAB 521)	19.1.68
			C-GXUR	recov. by Arny Carnegie, Edmonton ALTA	12.77
				Neil J. McClain/McClain Flight Service, Strathmore ALTA	11.78/91
			N20TF	Tom Friedkin/Cinema Air, Houston TX	10.91/92
- •	Cavalier Mk. 2	67-22579		(to FA Boliviana as FAB 519)	19.10.67
			C-GXRG	recov. by Arny Carnegie, Edmonton ALTA	12.77
				Neil J. McClain/McClain Flight Service, Strathmore ALTA	11.78/84
			N52BH	Robert E. Hester, Bladenboro NC	9.85/92
				(flies as "722579/FF579")	
			N251RM	Change of owner	5.92
- •	Cavalier Mk. 2	67-22580		(to FA Boliviana as FAB 520)	19.1.68
			C-GXUQ	recov. by Arny Carnegie, Edmonton ALTA	12.77
				Neil J. McClain/McClain Flight Service, Strathmore ALTA	8.78/84
			N151RK	Richard F. Korff, Lockport NY	10.86/92
				(flies as "422580/Six Shooter")	
- •	Cavalier Mk. 2	67-22581		(to FA Boliviana as FAB 523)	9.5.68
			C-GMUS	recov. by Arny Carnegie, Edmonton ALTA	12.77
				Ross F. Grady, Edmonton ALTA	8.78/90
				(flies as "FAB 523/Whats up Doc?")	
- •	Cavalier T Mk.2	68-15795		(to US Army as 68-15795)	.67
				RAF Museum : airfreighted to Mildenhall AFB	22.6.76
				(refurbished Upper Heyford AFB 76/77)	
				RAF Museum Store, RAF Henlow: arr.	11.77/80
				USAFM: returned by RAFM as unsuitable	.80
				USAFM, Minnesota ANGB, Minneapolis MN	82/90
- •	Cavalier T Mk.2	68-15796		(to US Army as 68-15796)	.67
				US Army Museum, Fort Rucker AL	
				USAFM, Eglin AFB FL	87/91
				(displ. as "413571")	
- •	P-51D	-	N6WJ	World Jet Inc, Fort Lauderdale FL	90
				(FAA quote id. "44-88")	
- •	Cavalier Mk.2	-		(to FA Salvadorena as FAS 405)	12.68
			N31FF	Flaherty Factors Inc, Monterey CA	1.11.74
				(adopted false id. 44-10753 on return to USA)	
				Wilson C. Edwards, Big Spring TX	78/92
-	P-51D	-	N26BD	reg. res.	90/92
				(FAA quote id. "206060")	
- •	P-51D	-	N31248		
			N51DJ	Diane Dejacomo, Scottsdale AZ	5.80/92
				(race #51, later #100/"41073/Sunshine")	
				(FAA quote id. "44-61449")	
- •	P-51D	-	N51KJ	Jerry D. Owens, Scottsdale AZ	8.82/92
				(FAA quote id. "44-12962")	
- •	P-51D	-	N51RG	Delmer L. Hoagland, Des Plaines IL	2.92
				(FAA quote id. "12150", type Hoagland P-51)	

Continued on Page 279

Continued from Page 276

- •	P-51D	-	N91JD	John Dilley/Fort Wayne Air Service IN (mod. racer, Learjet mainplane &tail; race #19/"Vendetta")	8.87
			N91KD	Fort Wayne Air Service, Fort Wayne IN North American Dilley Inc, Fort Wayne IN Fort Wayne Air Service, Fort Wayne IN crashed struck-off USCR (rebuild by FWAS as stock P-51D) (FAA quote type P-51R, id. "87-1001")	6.88 9.88 3.89/90 4.90
- •	P-51D	-	N5306M	reg. res. ntu: aircraft to French owner (FAA quote id. "44-72035")	90
- •	P-51D	-	N5483V (2	Don Whittington, Fort Lauderdale FL (rebuilt as mod. racer, RR Griffon with contra- rotating props .88, #09/"Precious Metal") crashed, badly dam., Reno NV (see N5483V (1 : 122-39977)	88/90 17.9.88
- •	P-51D	-	N87997	reg. res. (FAA quote id. "45-003661")	90/92
- •	P-51D	-	N87998	reg. res. (FAA quote id. "45-003211")	90/92
- •	P-51D	-	N87999	reg. res. (FAA quote id. "45-003315")	90/92
- •	P-51D	-		Eagle Squadron Association, San Diego CA (static rest. Chino CA based on ex AURI airframe,with parts from 44-73415/N6526D) RAF Museum, Hendon (airfreighted to RAF Lyneham 13.2.89: displ. Hendon as "413573/B6-V/Little Friend")	86/89 .89/92
- •	P-51D	-		(to FA Guatemalteca as FAG 336) displ. La Aurora AB, Guatemala as "FAG 360"	3.56 79/87
- •	P-51D	-		(to IDFAF as 28) hulk recov. ex kibbutz playground, Israel by Robs Lamplough, Duxford/North Weald UK (part rebuild , RAF Watton/North Weald 87/89)	 .78/90
- •	P-51D-			(to IDFAF as 38) IDFAF Museum, Haifa AB, Israel IDFAF Museum, Hazerim AB, Israel (displ. as "IDFAF 008")	 84 87/90
- •	P-51D	-		(to IDFAF as 146) hulk recov. ex kibbutz playground, Israel by Robs Lamplough, Duxford/North Weald UK loan: Rebel Air Museum, Great Saling UK (stored, North Weald 89)	 .78/90 82/87
- •	P-51D	-		(to TNI-AU as F-303) displ. Halim AB, Jakarta, Indonesia	 75/87
- •	P-51D	-		(to TNI-AU as F-338) Indonesian Air Force Museum, Jogjakarta	 87/89
- •	P-51D	-		(to TNI-AU as F-347) Armed Forces Museum, Jakarta, Indonesia	 77/89
- •	P-51D	-		(to TNI-AU as F-363) displ. Kalijanti, Indonesia	 87

- •	P-51D	-		(to Swedish AF as Fv.....)	
				(to IDFAF as 2338)	
				static rest. completed Camiel,Israel "2338"	.89
- •	P-51D	-		(to Italian AF as MM4292)	.47
				to instructional airframe Rome-Ciampino	
				stored dism., Cappenelli, Italy "SM-64"	
				recov. by Robs Lamplough, Duxford UK	c80
				Whitehall Theatre of War, London	.82/85
			G-BMBA	Aces High Ltd, Duxford	5.6.85
				Steve Dill, Orlando FL (shipped ex UK)	.85
				Cougar Helicopters, Daytona Beach FL	87
				(under rebuild to fly)	
- •	P-51D	-		(to Italian AF as MM4323)	
				Italian Air Force Museum, Vigna di Valle AB	84/87
- •	P-51D	-		(to Rep. Philippines AF as ......)	
				PAF Museum, Nichols/Villamor AB, Manila	79/91
- •	P-51D	-		(to Rep. Philippines AF as ......)	
				Kim Rolfe-Smith, Brisbane QLD	90/92
				(rest. project, Fort Wayne IN)	
- •	P-51D	-		USAFM: Barksdale AFB LA	87
				(rep. composite of several airframes)	
- •	P-51B	-		(to Soviet AF as ......)	
				Central Museum of Armed Forces, Moscow	c50
				Zhukovsky Memorial Museum, Moscow	79/92

NORTH AMERICAN P-64

68-3061 •	P-64	41-19085	NX37498	Jack Canary/Phoenix Aviation Inc,Phoenix AZ	48
				(operated with rain-making mods.)	
				Charles Barnes, Phoenix AZ	.49
				Precipitation Control Corp, Phoenix AZ	50
			XB-KUU	Precipitation Control Corp	52/59
				(returned USA, stored Long Beach CA 59/62)	
			N68822	refurbished Flabob Airport CA	.64/65
			N840	EAA Air Museum, Hales Corner/Oshkosh WI	66/92

159-4	T-28A	49-1492	N7492C	noted in CA, civil reg. over USAF scheme	.57
159-5	T-28A	49-1493	N7680C	H. E. Artman, Miami FL	63
				Melody Maid Pizza Co Inc, Columbus GA	66/69
159-6 •	T-28A JT-28A	49-1494		USAFM, Wright-Patterson AFB, Dayton OH	65/90
159-7 •	T-28A	49-1495	N9019V	George J. Rivera, San Jose CA	1.79
			N2800A	George J. Rivera, San Jose CA	6.79
				Glenn A.Ware, Costa Mesa CA/Carson City NV	84/88
159-8 •	T-28A ET-28A JT-28A T-28D	49-1496		(to R Thai AF as ....)	.66
				(to R Lao AF as 34..)	
				Col Pay/Pays Air Service, Scone NSW	.88
				(recov. from Thong Hi Hin AB, Laos: trucked overland to Bangkok, shipped to USA .88)	
				Sanders Aircraft Services, Chino CA	3.88/89
				Brian P. Kenney, Chino CA	5.89
			N1496K	Brian P. Kenney, Myrtle Point OR	5.90
			N2496	Brian P. Kenney, Myrtle Point OR	7.90/92
				(flies in camouflage as "USAF 49496/AD")	
159-15	T-28A	49-1503	N7668C	Larry S. Martin, San Fernando CA	63
				Lyon Laboratories, Royal Oak MI	66/69
				sale rep., USCR	78/92
159-17	T-28A	49-1505	N3707G	Bauer Co, Fort Worth TX	63
				Ridge Road Village Inc, Dallas TX	66/69
159-18	T-28A	49-1506	N9612C	John H. Helms, San Rafael CA	66/69
159-22	T-28A	49-1510	N3670G	Joseph F. Fitzgerald, Glenhan NY	63
				Michael J. Madden, Waterford NY	66/69
159-25 •	T-28A	49-1513	N9879C	Thomas C. Owens, Dallas TX	63
				(to FA Dominicana as 280.)	
			HI-315	reg.	.77
			N300AF	International Jet Transport Inc, Daytona Beach FL	84/87
				Teresa E. Wisdom, Mansfield OH	88/92
159-26 •	T-28A	49-1514	N9669C	E. G. Husband, Hollywood CA	63/69
				Institute of Atmospheric Sciences, Rapid City SD	78
159-27	T-28A	49-1515	N7708C	Joseph M. Nagy, South Pasedena CA	63/69
				sale rep., USCR	78/92
159-28 •	T-28A	49-1516	N7665C	Mark Hurd Aerial Surveys, Minneapolis MN	66
			N510MH	Mark Hurd Aerial Surveys, Minneapolis MN	
				Meteorology Research Inc, Altadena CA	69
				Inst. of Atmospheric Sciences, Rapid City SD	84/92
159-29	T-28A	49-1517	N9898C	Nancy J. Brown, Indianapolis IN	63
				Lee R. Griffiths, Dallas TX	66/69
159-31 •	T-28A T-28D	49-1519	N8098H	Max L. Biegert, Phoenix AZ	63
				Lou Kaufman, Mesa AZ	66
				Sylvia J. Guthrie, Los Angeles CA	69
				(to R Lao AF as 3408)	
				Col Pay/Pays Air Service, Scone NSW	.88
				(recov. from Thong Hi Hin AB, Laos: trucked overland to Bangkok, shipped to Australia .88)	
				John Weymouth, Darwin NT	.89
			VH-AVC	John Weymouth, Darwin NT	.91/92

159-32 •	T-28A	49-1520	C-GTDG	Skywest Airways Inc, Regina SASK	3.86
			N7038U	reg.	8.88
				Kenneth F. McLaughlin, Nashua NH	92
159-37 •	T-28A	49-1525	N76912	Daniel Jackson, Seymour TX	78
				James E. Kaylor, New Port Richey FL	84/86
				Durbano Metals, Malad ID	87/88
				T-28 Inc, Northbrook IL	92
159-41	T-28A	49-1529	N2808G	Edward J. Worton, Miami FL	66/69
159-46 •	T-28A	49-1534	N2814G	Larry R. Matson, Anchorage AK	66
				Michael E. Coutches, Hayward CA	69/92
				cr. Big Bar Creek BC, during del. from AK	7.8.69
159-47 •	T-28A	49-1535	N9687C	Photography Unlimited, El Paso TX	63
				K. E. Pickles, San Jose CA	66/69
				K. E. Pickles, Richland WA	72/78
				K. E. Austin, Richland WA	84
			N91535	K. E. Austin, Richland WA	10.85/92
159-51 •	T-28A	49-1539	N3519G	Puckett Aerial Surveys Inc, Concordia KS	63
				Aerial Sales Survey Co, Tucson AZ	66
				Gloria Burchinall, Brookston TX	69
				Albert Shirkey, Tulsa OK	78
			N1F	Paul H. Poberezny, Oshkosh WI	8.84/89
				William E. Harrison, Tulsa OK	92
159-52 •	T-28A	49-1540	N3708G	Byron A. Susan, Grand Prairie TX	63
	T-28D			(to FA Nicaragua as 217)	
			N99395	David C. Tallichet/MARC, Chino CA	25.3.77/86
				(dep. Managua on del. to USA 26.3.77)	
				M. Diehl, Reno NV	87/92
159-55	T-28A	49-1543		to USAF 606th SOS Laos & Cambodia	60s
	AT-28D			(to FA Dominicana as 280.)	77
			HI-283	reg.	.77
159-56 •	T-28A	49-1544	N6FY	Gregory Flying Service, Tynan TX	12.88/92
159-57	T-28A	49-1545	N6514C	Harry V. Fugguitt Sr, La Puente CA	66/69
	T-28D			(to FA Ecuatoriana as 91545)	
				Museo Aereo de FAC, Quito	77/79
159-59 •	T-28A	49-1547	N200AF	Northeast Excavation Co, Sandusky OH	84/92
159-63	T-28A	49-1551	N3669G	New Jersey Air, Teterboro NJ	63/69
159-65	T-28A	49-1553	N2867G	Executive Aircraft Sales Inc, Portland OR	63
				Merle H. Maine, Ontario OR	66/69
159-66	T-28A	49-1554	N2891G	George F. Kreitzburg, Salem OR	63
				Lincoln City Livestock Co, Roswell NM	66/69
159-69 •	T-28A	49-1557	N3469G	Hamilton Aircraft Co Inc, Tucson AZ	59/69
	T-28R-2			(5 seat civil conversion by Hamilton Aircraft	
	Nomair			in 1959, as T-28R-2 Nomair)	
			N800DM	Dean Martin/Warplanes Inc, Burlington VT	6.77/78
			N1557A	rereg.	1.80
				Peter G. Knox, Mooresville NC	84
				Richard D. Ervin, Indianapolis IN	86/92
				(FAA quote id. N1557A as "1300DM")	
159-73 •	T-28A	49-1561		(to Philippine AF as ....)	
	T-28D			Ken Hawkins/Fighter Imports USA	

				F. W. (Bill) Pike, Sydney NSW (stored pending rest., Cessnock NSW)	.90/92
159-75	T-28A	49-1563	N3750G	George Klein, Madison NJ	66
159-76	T-28A	49-1564	N2824G	W. S. Cooper, Merced CA (to R Thai AF as "0-91564")	66/69
159-77 •	T-28A	49-1565	N7663C	Munsey E. Crost, Allenhurst & Neptune NJ Gibson Air Academy, Farmingdale NJ	63/88 5.90/92
159-78 •	T-28A	49-1566	N3232G	off USCR by reg. pending John H. Batte, Vineburg CA	63/72 78 84/92
159-79	T-28A	49-1567	N1920G	Kiyoshi Hirata, Long Beach CA Richard Neasham, Bakersfield CA	63 69
159-86 •	T-28A	49-1574	N80696 N3742R N28TE N80696	noted Chino CA as "N80696/91574" ntu: Thomas Wright, Eden Prairie MN Roger A. Christgau, Edina MN	80 3.80 8.80 84/90
159-89	T-28A	49-1577	N3662G	Ewell K. Nold, Houston TX	63
159-90	T-28A	49-1578	N2815G	Earl Dodge, Anchorage AK Arctic Air Academy Inc, Anchorage AK	63 66
159-91 •	T-28A	49-1579	 N7055N	(to FA Mexicana as ....) Texas Turbo Jet Inc, Dallas TX Tom Lake, Boise ID	 1.89 92
159-93	T-28A	49-1581	N3154G	Unique Screw Machine Corp, Lindenhurst NJ	63/69
159-96 •	T-28A Nomad AT-28D	49-1584	N8391H	conv. to NA.260 Nomad by California Airmotive, Van Nuys CA Grimes Manufacturing Co, Urbania OH John M. Mount, McLean VA (to R Thai AF as ....) (to R Lao AF as 3410) Col Pay/Pays Air Service, Scone NSW (recov. from Thong Hi Hin AB, Laos; trucked overland to Bangkok, shipped to Australia 12.88) Jack McDonald, Melbourne/Caboolture QLD Bruce Andrews, Melbourne VIC (arr. dism. Caboolture QLD for rebuild 9.2.91)	 c58 63 66/69 .88 89/91 .91/92
159-104•	T-28A	49-1592	 N7055M	(to FA Mexicana as ......) Texas Turbo Jet Inc, Dallas TX Rudy Blakey Inc, Perry FL	 1.89 89/92
159-112	T-28A T-28D	49-1600	N2890G	Robert Marts, Somers Point NJ (to R Lao AF as 49-1600)	63/69
159-113	T-28A	49-1601	N9667C	Rambler Witkin, Los Angeles CA Aircraft Charter Corp, Greenwood SC	63 66/69
159-114	T-28A	49-1602	N9668C	Rambler Witkin, Los Angeles CA	63
159-118	T-28A	49-1606	N3221G	Parsons Airpark Inc, Carpentiria CA	63
159-123•	T-28A	49-1611		USAFM, Lackland AFB TX	79/88
159-124	T-28A	49-1612	N7285C	George O. Turner, Bedford NH Nathaniel Hawthorne College, Antrim NH	63 66/69
159-125	T-28A	49-1613	N7641C	Kenneth Burmeister, Seattle WA Joseph M. Natoli, Lorton VA	63 66

				crashed Hagerstown MD	7.4.66
				Michael Hyrasyn, Hillside NJ	69
				sale rep., USCR	78/92
159-126•	T-28A	49-1614	N3233G	sale reported, Winlock WA	84
				Ronald A. Bobarge, Edmonds WA	87
				Mitchell Zahler, Stillwater MN	88
				Roger A. Christgau, Edina MN	89
			N628AR	Roger A. Christgau, Edina MN	3.90/92
159-128•	T-28A	49-1616	N2882G	Del Thoman, San Raphael CA	63
				Omeddon Inc, Indianapolis IN	66/69
				sold abroad : off USCR by	72
			N400AF	Seagull Enterprises Inc, Daytona Beach FL	11.80
				Deakins Carroll Insurance, Port Salerno FL	84/86
				John L. Moore, Sarasota FL	87/88
				ISRMS Inc, Land-o-Lakes FL	92
159-130 •	T-28A	49-1618		(to FA Mexicana as .....)	
			N7054L	Texas Turbo Jet Inc, Dallas TX	1.89/92
159-131•	T-28A	49-1619	N7491C	William E. Padden, Pasadena CA	63
				Richard B. Hoegh, Los Angeles CA	66/72
				Richard Holland, Fountain Valley CA	78
				August Doppes, Fort Lauderdale FL	83
			N113CA	August Doppes/Colorado Aircraft Brokers, Ft Lauderdale FL	1.84
				Dolphin Aviation Inc, Sarasota FL	86
			N128AF	Walter M. Mayer, Beaumont TX	4.87
				Ernest F. Durbano, Ogden UT	88/92
159-132•	T-28A	49-1620	N23ES	Earl Schafer, Waco TX	9.90/92
159-134	T-28A	49-1622	N3660G	Thomas Z. Winther, Nashua NH	63
159-138•	T-28A	49-1626	N9624C	Edward T. Maloney, Claremont CA	66/69
				Sydney A. Torgerson, Kalispell MT	9.85/92
				(wfu, open storage Kalispell Municiple MT 91)	
159-139	T-28A T-28D	49-1627	N2837G	William Nielson, Edmonds WA	63
				Wayne A. Joslin, Redmond WA	66/69
				(to R Lao AF as 49-1627)	
159-140	T-28A	49-1628	N2800G	George J. Rivera, Sunnyvale CA	66/69
159-142•	T-28A	49-1630		Rick R. Clemens, Sunland CA: del. ex MASDC	19.7.78
			N28NA	Cactus Air Force Inc, Sunland CA	11.84/89
				Jeff Kertes, Sunland CA	90/92
				Cactus Air Force, Carson City NV	92
159-143	T-28A	49-1631	N3186G	Norman M. Hodgkin, Lafayette LA	63
				Melvin Lake, Mill Valley CA	66/69
159-144•	T-28A	49-1632		George J. Rivera, San Jose CA	19.7.78
			N9022A	George J. Rivera, San Jose CA	1.79
				Bernard G. Combos, Simi Valley CA	84/86
				Robert E. Albee, Northridge CA	87/88
				Rick R. Clemens, Carson City NV	92
159-145	T-28A	49-1633	N9617C	Swift Construction Inc, Sherman Oaks CA	63
				James F. Johnson, Palo Alto CA	66/69
159-146•	T-28A T-28D	49-1634	N9878C	George J. Rivera, Sunnyvale CA	66/69
				(to FA Zaire as FG 634)	
			N99160	William Nelson, El Paso TX	12.77/78
				(del. via Biggin Hill UK 16.12.77/7.8.79)	

Continued on Page 286

Darton International, Inc.

"A World of Excellence in Warbird Kits"

Clean Kit ®

The ORIGINAL and the only one guaranteed to work. Join the growing list of T-28 Clean Kit users, which now numbers over 120 worldwide. We are currently designing and expect to install custom Clean Kits on a TBM Avenger and a R-2800 powered Corsair.

NATOPS

To be completely legal and avoid abuse from your friendly FAA Inspector on your next ramp check, you are required to keep a copy of the flight manual in the aircraft and accessible to the pilot. Because of the size of the NATOPS, this is sometimes inconvenient. Darton's reduced-size NATOPS is readable and complies with the requirement to carry the flight manual and allows convenient storage of this valuable document many places in the cockpit. A great idea, and it also saves wear and tear on that precious original NATOPS you have been carrying to be legal.

Pre-Oil

The single most important controllable factor in the preservation and dependability of engine operation is proper lubrication. It is a demonstrated fact that a significant amount of engine wear occurs during the starting sequence, primarily due to lack of lubrication. By military mandate, it is prohibited to operate the 1820-powered T-28 unless within the previous 72 hours the engine has been pre-oiled. Darton's unique on-board pre-oil system for the T-28 and OTHER Warbirds provides for a high-quality, fully engineered system comprised of all new or overhauled parts. Unlike competitor versions, our system includes a pressure side filter and check valve to isolate the pre-oil system except in time of use. Once installed, the system is relatively maintenance-free and pre-lubrication of the engine can then be accomplished PRIOR TO EVERY START.

Auto Canopy Kit®

Canopy Open

Canopy Closed

Flaps Down

Flaps Up

To secure a T-28 in an airshow environment or on a crowded ramp requires the flaps to be up and the canopy closed. With the flaps down, the invitation to climb on the airplane is difficult to overcome. The solution: A DARTON AUTOMATIC CANOPY KIT. This ingenious flexible system allows independent operation of both the canopy and the flaps from multiple spots on the exterior of the airplane through an onboard electric/hydraulic standby system. Usable also as emergency backup for hydraulic pump failure or as an on-board "mule" during the annual inspection for gear swings.

Canopy Lock

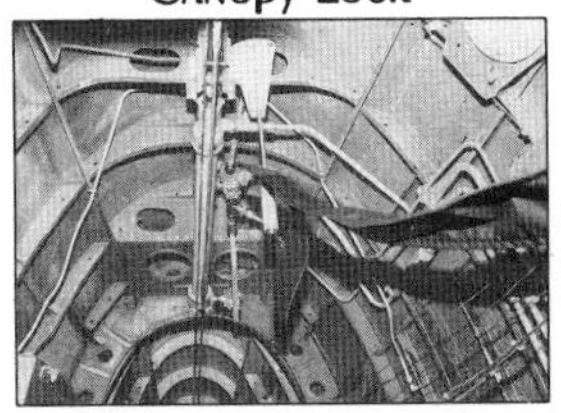

Another Darton first to secure your T-28 simply through a foolproof mechanical design actuated from the inside of the baggage compartment. System incorporates a prevention feature to inhibit the exterior emergency handle from being activated when the canopy is locked. Includes a baggage door lock system and dovetails nicely with our Automatic Canopy Kit.

Annual Inspection Book

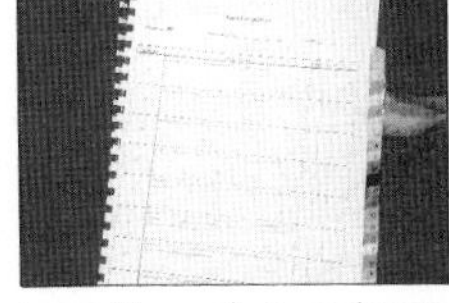

Most T-28 operators know of the frustration in trying to accomplish a comprehensive annual inspection using the military documents. Because the military maintained the airplane in stages, no concise document existed until now of a thorough step-by-step approach to performing a comprehensive annual inspection on the T-28. Darton's new annual inspection book is comprised of 26 sections which leads you through an annual inspection starting with chocking the wheels and ending with a post-inspection test flight. Two separate sections are provided with squawk sheets for the engine and the airframe. Meets all civilian and military requirements for performing annual and periodic inspections. Buy one every year's annual inspection and you will have the finest maintenance library available for your T-28.

New For 1992!

Darton's oil tank measuring quantity measuring system depicted on a 2-1/4" guage with a low-level red light.

Coming in January is our oil tank pre-heater kit which will be thermostatically controlled and ground adjustable. You can throw away those salamanders and heated bear skin rugs and feel assured that with warm oil you can pre-oil and start your engine safely regardless of the outside air temperature.

Call Us Now

Darton International, Inc.
2725 Jefferson Street, #7
Carlsbad, CA 92008
(619) 434-3919 FAX
(619) 434-0701

Continued from Page 284

				Mike Bogue, Oakland CA	81
				Wiley Sanders Truck Lines Inc, Troy AL	84/92
159-147	T-28A	49-1635	N5252V	David S. Salerno, Gardena CA	63/69
159-149	T-28A	49-1637	N98Z	E. D. Weiner, Los Angeles CA	63/66
				Larry Guliher, Oklahoma City OK	69
159-150	T-28A	49-1638	N2868G	Floyd R. Kingston, Zephyr Hills FL	63
				Robert F. Burt, Fort Myers FL	66
				Desert Aerial Photographic Co Corp, Independence MO	69
				sale rep., USCR	78/92
159-154	T-28A	49-1642	N9854C	Richard D. Ward, Sun Valley CA	63
159-155•	T-28A	49-1643	N9674C	Norman B. Dennis Jr, Brookneal VA	66/72
			N28RE	Robert Eggmann, Belleville IL	78/84
			N81643	Edward A. Buerckholtz, Chesterfield MO	10.85/92
159-156	T-28A	49-1644	N9872C	Daco Rubber Inc, Van Nuys CA	63/72
				Air Training Inc, Knoxville TN	78
			N700H	Air Training Inc, Knoxville TN	3.81/84
				cr. dest. Louden County TN	23.6.84
159-157•	T-28A	49-1645	N2851G	Thomas R. Preston, Knoxville TN	63
	T-28D			(to FA Nicaragua as 218)	
			N99394	David C. Tallichet/MARC, Chino CA	3.77/85
				(dep. Managua on del. to USA 26.3.77)	
				loan: USAFM, March AFB CA	85
				Robert W. Nightingale, Ontario CA	86/88
				Banaire Enterprises, Hemet CA	89/92
159-158•	T-28A	49-1646	HI-276	reg.	.77
			N70743	Associated Aircraft, Newton Falls OH	78
				Heritage Aircraft Museum, Fayetteville GA	84
				Richard P. Mouhut, Lantana FL	84/88
				James L. Griffin, Tulsa OK	92
159-159	T-28A	49-1647	N9859C	Larry Hamilton, San Anselmo CA	63
	T-28D			Edward G. Peters, Shafter CA	66
				(to FA Ecuatoriana as 0-91647)	
				Museo Aereo de FAC, Quito	77/79
159-162	T-28A	49-1650	N9677C	Aero Enterprises Inc, Elkhart IN	66/69
159-166•	T-28A	49-1654	N5251V	Kemp Pontiac Cadillac Inc, Newington CT	66
				Metropolitan Air Services Inc, New York NY	69
				Charles Smith, Knoxville TN	74
				Anthony Guirreri, Atlanta GA	78
				Richard I. Williams, Aurora CO	84
				David K. Burnap Advertising Inc, Dayton OH	87/92
159-168•	T-28A	49-1656	N28SV	Henry J. (Butch) Schroeder, Danville IL	1.91/92
159-169	T-28A	49-1657	N6254C	Scruggs & Rucker, Tucson AZ	66/69
159-174	T-28A	49-1662	N9630C	Richard A. Harter, Corona CA	63
				Rusk Aviation Inc, Kankakee IL	66/69
				sale rep., USCR	78/92
159-175•	T-28A	49-1663		USAFM, Hurlburt Field FL	78/91
	AT-28D			(displ. as USAF "41863")	
159-177•	T-28A	49-1665		(to FA Dominicana as 280.)	-77
AT-28D			HI-282	reg.	.77

			N64785	Donald Anklin, Davidson NC	7.77/78
				Robert W. Urbine/Aviation Insurance Unlimited, Greensboro NC	82/86
				Daniel D. Blackwell, Pittsburgh PA	87/89
			N665DB	Daniel D. Blackwell, Pittsburgh PA	9.89
			N665PB	Randal E. Patrick, Gaithersburg MD	1.92
159-178	T-28A	49-1666	N2838G	Peter J. Thurston, San Diego CA	63
				Harry S. Thomas, Lancaster CA	66/69
159-180	T-28A	49-1668	N7277C	Rosario E. Neville, Miami FL	63/69
159-181	T-28A	49-1669	N9867C	John V. McHugh Jr, Bloomfield NJ	63/69
				Benjamin J. Demonstranti, Juno FL	78/85
				cr. dest. Lantana FL	24.11.85
159-182	T-28A	49-1670	N8156Y	Texas Turbo Jet Inc, Dallas TX	4.89/92
159-185	T-28A	49-1673	N9611C	Border Aviation Inc, Yuma AZ	66
				Donald R. Alderson, Van Nuys CA	69/72
				William Blakemore, Midland TX	78
				Confederate Air Force, Harlingen TX	7.7.82/84
				Carsan Charters, Lovington NM	86/87
				crashed New Mexico, two killed	5.87
159-186	T-28A	49-1674	N7289C	Charlotte Aircraft Corp, Charlotte NC	66/69
159-188•	T-28A	49-1676	N2896G	Robert Marts, Somers Point NJ	63/69
				George J. Rivera, Santa Clara CA	78
			N6851D	rereg.	7.78
				Rick R. Clemens, Sunland CA/Carson City NV	84/92
159-189	T-28A	49-1677	N7450C	Donald R. Pittman, Kenosha WI	63
				Jack M. Kruzelock, Des Plaines IL	66/69
159-191•	T-28A	49-1679		USAFM, Reese AFB TX	88
159-194•	T-28A	49-1682		USAFM, Laughlin AFB TX	88
159-195•	T-28A	49-1683			
			N7062K	reg.	12.88
				Paladin Aircraft, San Diego CA	92
159-198	T-28A	49-1686	N7690C	Grafton Insurance Agency Inc, Grafton WI	63/66
				(to F.A. Ecuatoriana as 491686	
159-199	T-28A	49-1687	N7686C	Helvin Flying Service, San Antonio TX	63
				Graham Elliot Associates Inc, Dallas TX	66/69
159-200	T-28A	49-1688	N7498C	A. R. Hoffman, Santa Ana CA	63/66
159-201•	T-28A	49-1689		USAFM, Vance AFB OK	88
159-202•	T-28A	49-1690		(to R Saudi AF as 49-1690)	
				noted open storage, Jeddah	81
			N8156U	Texas Turbo Jet Inc, Dallas TX	4.89/92
				(note: id. quoted as "49-1960")	
159-206•	T-28A	49-1694	N7497C	United Aerial Survey Inc, Tulare CA	63/66
				Rays Aircraft Service, Porterville CA	69/72
				Rolland Kruckow, Minneapolis MN	78
				Todd C. Fruen, Scottsdale AZ	84/92
159-207•	T-28A	49-1695		USAFM, Randolph AFB TX	88
				(displ. as "17882")	
159-209	T-28A	49-1697	N7644C		
			HP-308	no further information	

159-210	T-28A	49-1698	N7480C		58
			N101TZ	Thomas Z. Winther, Nashua NH	63
				Aerial Mapping Inc, Hartford CT	66/69
159-211	T-28A	49-1699	N5253V	Tom L. Johnsen, El Monte CA	63/66
	T-28D			(to Philippine AF as 49-1699)	
159-212•	T-28A	49-1700	N3659G	Robert E. Reynolds, Blue Point NY	63/66
				Margaret J. Yates, Mt Holly NJ	69
				Gordon J. Newell, New Hartford NY	72
			N28JS	Sun Master Awnings Inc, Mishawaka IN	3.77/78
			N28AM	Arthur E. Muth, Darien CT	11.78/84
				Yankee Flyers Museum Inc, Fraser MI	86/87
				Harry S. Purnell, Birmingham AL	88
				Dennis T. Hallman, Lake Wylie SC	92
159-213	T-28A	49-1701	N9665C	Furniture Wholesalers Inc, Pompano Beach FL	66/72
159-214	T-28A	49-1702	N5295V	John J. McMahon, Binghamton NY	63
				6600 Inc, Buffalo NY	66/69
159-215•	T-28A	49-1703	N7642C	Daniel J. Donahoe, San Francisco CA	63
				Art Holst, Eugene OR	66
				Lewis P. Hanke, Sunnyside WA	69
			N28100	Richard J. Dieter, South Bend IN	75/88
				David H. Worthington, Cincinatti OH	92
159-216	T-28A	49-1704	N7198C	Donald D. Randall, Santa Ana CA	63
	T-28D			Ken Guthrie, Santa Monica CA	66
				(to Philippine AF as 49-1704)	
159-218	T-28A	49-1706	N5951V	Darrel G. Dikeman, Syracuse KS	63/69
				sale rep., USCR	78/92
159-225	T-28A	49-1713		(to R Saudi AF as 49-1713)	
				for proposed RSAF Museum, Riyadh	79
				noted derelict in compound, Riyadh Airport	81
159-227	T-28A	49-1715	N7283C	Ace Smelting Inc, San Antonio TX	66/69
159-228	T-28A	49-1716	N5247V	Leslie H. Fleming, Ponce PR	63
	T-28D			Hifly Photos, Wichita KS	66/69
				(to R Lao AF as 91716)	
159-229	T-28A	49-1717	N9165Z	Richard F. Lande, Livermore CA	63
	T-28D			H. L. Hutchings, Seal Beach CA	66/69
				sale rep., USCR	78/92
				(to Philippine AF as T-28D 49-1717)	
159-231•	T-28A	49-1719	N7245C	Robert R. Pitcairn, Bryn Athyn PA	63/72
				George J. Rivera, Santa Clara CA	78
				Cactus Air Force, Sun Valley CA	8.88/92
159-233	T-28A	49-1721	N182U	Hamilton Aviation Co Inc, Tucson AZ	c58
	T-28R-2			(converted to Hamilton T-28R-2 c/n 9)	c58
	Nomair			Electronics Corp of America, Cambridge MA	63
				North America Maritime Corp, Cambridge MA	66/72
				crashed landing, Martinez GA	2.7.83
159-234	T-28A	49-1722	CF-LOI	J. McKervey, Calgary ALTA	65/70
159-235	T-28A	49-1723	N2883G	John W. Hibbard, Corcoran CA	63
159-236•	T-28A	49-1724	N2884G	Munsey E. Crost, Allenhurst NJ	63
	T-28D			G. C. Dewey Corp, New York NY	66/69

				(to R Lao AF as 91724)	
				Col Pay/Pays Air Service, Scone NSW	.88
				(recov. from Thong Hi Hin AB, Laos: trucked overland to Bangkok, shipped to Australia 12.88)	
				Steve Death, Albury NSW	89/92
			VH-MEO	Steve Death, Albury NSW	5.92
				(rebuilt Albury NSW, ff 30.5.92)	
159-239•	T-28A	49-1727	N9862C	Joseph H. Thesing, Sylmar CA	63
				Chain Lightning Aircraft Sales, Burbank CA	66/69
				sale rep.	78
				Merle H. Maine, Ontario OR	84/92
159-243	T-28A	49-1731	N9858C	Vernon D. Jarvis, Decatur IL	63
				Crescent Airways Inc, West Hollywood CA	66/69
159-250•	T-28A	49-1738	N7692C	displ. Victory Air Museum, Mundelein IL	74
				Daniel B. Jackson, Seymour IN	78/92
159-252	T-28A	49-1740	N9096Z	Francis R. Fulton, Sharon Springs KS	66/69
159-254•	T-28A	49-1742	N9442Z	Michael Eisenstadt, Las Angeles CA	78
	T-28D		N1742R	WW2 Rebuilders, Davidson NC	8.82
				Ronald G. Roth Co, Phoenix AZ	84/88
				Bill Rheinschild	90
				Wayne Brooks, Huntington Beach CA	92
159-265	T-28A	49-1753	N9616C	John H. Bell, Northbridge CA	63/69
				reg. pending	72
171-2 •	T-28A	50-0196	N9688C	Robert L. Hill Jr, Naples FL	63/69
				(to FA Haiti as 53)	
			N514FR (1	Summit Aviation, Middletown DE	2.84/87
				Air Armco Inc, Middletown DE	88
				struck-off USCR	1.90
171-7 •	T-28A	50-0201	N9102Z	H. W. Bruce, Dallas TX	66/72
				Marcia Kenyon, Eaton CO	78
				James C. Harris, Oklahoma City OK	3.84/88
				Joseph L. Little, Cleveland TN	89/92
171-8 •	T-28A	50-0202	N9104Z	(conv.to Hamilton T-28R-1 Nomair)	
	T-28R-1			(to Brazilian Navy as N-703)	
	Nomair			(To F.A. Brasileira as 0862)	
				Museu Aerospacial da FAB, Rio de Janiero	78/82
171-15	T-28A	50-0209		USAF/ Inter-American Air Forces Academy,	
	GT-28A			Howard AFB, Panama Canal Zone (as "G-2")	74
171-22	T-28A	50-0216	N9120Z	Hardwick Aire, El Monte CA	66/69
				sale rep., USCR	78/92
171-27 •	T-28A	50-0221	N3336G	Robert W. Trow, Fort Lauderdale FL	63
				Jack H. Mantz, Sarasota FL	66/69
				A. S. Kuchan, Hudson IL	84/88
				Sonic Corporation, Wilmington DE	89
			N221LH	Laurence C. Hofmeister, Milford MI	2.89/92
171-31 •	T-28A	50-0225	N9698B	Rick R. Clemens, Sun Valley CA	84/92
171-32	T-28A	50-0226	N9094Z	Kenneth McLaughlin, Nashua NH	66/69
171-40 •	T-28A	50-0234		(to FA Haiti as 215)	
			N234NA	Courtesy Aircraft Inc, Rockford IL	9.85/88
				Jim E. Uhley, Clawson MI	89
				sale rep., Southfield MI	92
171-46	T-28A	50-0240	N3297G	E. D. Weiner, Los Angeles CA	63/66

171-52	T-28A	50-0246	N9092Z	sale rep., USCR	78/92
171-59	T-28A	50-0253	N1026B	Charlotte Aircraft Corp, Charlotte NC	66/69
171-64	T-28A	50-0258	N9603C	Joseph H. Thesing, Sylmar CA	63
				Robert V. Lewis, Burbank CA	66
171-65	T-28A	50-0259	N3464G	Mehdi Tarafdar, Salerno FL	63
				Ace Smelting Inc, Phoenix AZ	66/69
171-68	T-28A	50-0262	N3299G	Solomon Cohen, San Antonio TX	63
				Alfred Hunter Jr, Lynn MA	66/69
171-70	T-28A	50-0264	N9081Z	E. F. White, Dallas TX	63
				H. J. Hoeppner, San Francisco CA	66/69
171-78 •	T-28A	50-0272		(to FA Haiti as 212)	
			N272NA	Courtesy Aircraft Inc, Rockford IL	9.85/86
				Walter M. Mayer, Beaumont TX	87
				Rick Hegenberger & Assoc., Westport CT	88/92
171-79	T-28A T-28D	50-0273	N7617C	James A. Clark Jr, New York NY	63/66
				(to R. Lao AF as ....)	
171-80	T-28A	50-0274	N3306G	Ace Smelting Inc, Phoenix AZ	66/69
171-81	T-28A	50-0275	N9684C	Jane G. Balsam, Miami FL	63
				Rusk Aviation Inc, Kankakee IL	66
				Jack B. Weidemier, Kansas City MO	69
171-84	T-28A	50-0278	N7452C	Bub Leaders, St Cloud MN	66
				John T. Laney, San Antonio TX	69
171-89 •	T-28A T-28D	50-0283	N7666C	William J. Furlick, Caldwell NJ	63
				Simsbury Flying Service Inc, Simsbury CT	66/69
				(to R Lao AF as ....)	
				Col Pay/Pays Air Service, Scone NSW	.88
				(recov. from Thong Hi Hin AB, Laos: trucked overland to Bangkok, shipped to Australia 12.88)	
			VH-XVT	Randal W. McFarlane, Brisbane QLD	12.88/92
				(ff Bankstown 31.11.90, as "SVNAF 38372")	
				(CAA quote id. as 50-0273)	
171-90 •	T-28A	50-0284	N9692C	Robert A. Mitchem, Broomfield CO	63
				Orville K. Anstaett, Garden City KS	66/72
				Harry Noe, Houston TX	5.81/92
171-95	T-28A	50-0289	N8094H	R. L. Hunt, Naples FL	63
				Nathaniel Hawthorne College, Antrim NH	66/69
171-96 •	T-28A	50-0290	N9640C	Harry G. Thomas, Ogden UT	63
				Bruce & Gunn Inc, Addison TX	66/78
				Paul S. Array, Delray Beach FL	84/88
				Earl J. Schafer, Waco TX	92
171-100	T-28A	50-0294	N3293G	off USCR by	66
171-101	T-28A	50-0295	N6182C	Arkansas Civil Defence Agency, Conway AR	66/69
171-105•	T-28A	50-0299	N9095Z	Mid Atlantic Air Museum, Reading PA	5.90/92
				(prob. ex FA Argentina "63", noted stored dism. at Reading PA 90)	
171-106•	T-28A	50-0300	N3292G	Eagle Sqdn Inc, Sidney MT	66
				Stanley J. Sweetack, Fond Du Lac WI	69

			N213PC	Joseph F. Dulvick, Lake Orion MI	77
			N28JD	Joseph F. Dulvick, Lake Orion MI	4.77
				Conrad Hagle, Kennesaw GA	84
				Centre Equities Corp, Atlanta GA	86/87
				Consolidated Aviation Ent., Burlington VT	88
				ISRMS Inc, Land-o-Lakes FL	92
171-109	T-28A	50-0303	N3338G	Robert A. Kuhn, Morristown NJ	63
	T-28D			James B. Sandberg, Minneapolis MN	66/69
				(to R Lao AF as ....)	
171-110	T-28A	50-0304	N7667C	Charles A. Ohanlon, San Jose CA	63
				W. E. Howell Associates Inc, Lexington MA	66
			N151P	Stephen J. Roberts, Newark DE	69/78
171-125	T-28A	50-0319	N7274C	Rocky Mountain Homes Inc, Cortez CO	63/69
174-17 •	T-28A	51-3479	CF-IWJ	Leonard Kelly, Peterborough ONT	65
			N499KB	Aero Enterprises Inc, Fresno CA	69
				Nation Flight Service, Santa Rosa CA	72
			N699	rereg.	.73
				K. R. Williamson, State College PA	78
				Richard L. Woodruff, Birmingham AL	84/92
174-23	T-28A	51-3485	N7640C	Adolph Witkin, Hollywood CA	63/69
174-33	T-28A	51-3495		(to L'Armee de l'Air as Fennec No. 77)	
	Fennec		N14100	Waco-Pacific Inc, Van Nuys CA	.68
				Winter Wolff & Co, New York NY	69
174-38	T-28A	51-3500	N9686C	Paul E. Davis, Pittsburgh PA	63
				B. H. Glover, Madison WI	66/69
174-43 •	T-28A	51-3505		(toL'Armee de l"Air as Fennec No.47)	
	Fennec			(to Moroccan AF as ....)	
			N9873A	Jeff Hawke & David C. Tallichet/	
				Visionaire International Inc, Miami FL	5.78
				(to FA Nicaragua as ....)	c80
				(to FA Sandanista as ....)	87
				recov. by Victoria Aircraft Maintenance BC	.87
			C-FNAF	Charles J. Money, Calgary ALTA	11.7.88/90
				(flies as "RCN T28F 131228/CJ/On The Prowl")	
				(C-FNAF id. quoted as "436"; also rep. ex 51-3503)	
174-51 •	T-28A	51-3513		(to L'Armee de l'Air as Fennec No.51)	
	Fennec			(to Moroccan AF as ....)	
			N9868A	Jeff Hawke & David C. Tallichet/	
				Visionaire International Inc, Miami FL	5.78/83
				(stored at Fort Lauderdale Executive 79/81)	
				David C. Tallichet/MARC, Chino CA	3.83/87
				Floyd R. Murphy, Walnut CA	88/91
				Frank J. Hoover, Upland CA	92
174-59	T-28A	51-3521	N3663G	Thomas Neal, La Canada CA	63
				George Husband, Costa Mesa CA	66/69
174-66 •	T-28A	51-3528		(to L'Armee de l'Air as Fennec No.52)	
	Fennec		CN-AEK	(to Moroccan AF as 51-3528)	
			HR-231A	(to FA Hondurena as FAH 2....)	.78
				rep. impounded USA ; not del.	.78
				(stored FLL-Exec. 79/81 as HR-231)	
			N8523B	Euroworld Inc : reg. reserved	6.80
				Jeff Hawke & David C. Tallichet/	
				Visionaire International Inc, Miami FL	12.80/84
				Ron Maggard, Independence MO	
			N128RM	Ron Maggard, Independence MO	7.85/88
				struck-off USCR	11.88

174-68 •	T-28A Fennec	51-3530		(to L'Armee de l'Air as Fennec No.49)	
			CN-AEH	(to Moroccan AF as ....)	
			HR-230A	(to FA Hondurena as FAH 2....)	.78
				rep. impounded USA; not del.	.78
				(stored FLL-Executive 79/81 as HR-230A)	
			N8523A	Euroworld Inc: reg. res.	6.80
				Jeff Hawk & David C. Tallichet/	
				Visionaire International Inc, Miami FL	12.80/84
				David C. Tallichet/ MARC, Chino CA	86/92
174-90	T-28A	51-3552	N5205V	W. H. Ostenberg, Morrison CO	63
			N254JB	Mouchet Baugh, Charlotte NC	66
				Valley Aerial Services Inc, Bakersfield CA	69
				sale rep., Bakersfield CA	78/92
174-91 •	T-28A Fennec	51-3553		(to L'Armee de l'Air as Fennec No. 100)	
			N14101	Waco-Pacific Inc, Van Nuys CA	.68
				Winter Wolff & Co, New York NY	69/72
				Stephen Folkman, Philadelphia PA	78
			N991CA	Courtesy Aircraft Inc, Rockford IL	1.80/84
			C-GJCJ	Jerry C. Janes, Vancouver BC	8.84
			N5832X	William G. Bennett, Las Vegas	6.85/86
				Enstrom West Corp, Palos Verdes CA	87/92
174-92 •	T-28A Fennec	51-3554		(to L'Armee de l'Air as Fennec No. 48)	
				(to Moroccan AF as 13554)	
			N54613	Jeff Hawk & David C. Tallichet/	
				Visionaire International Inc, Miami FL	3.78/79
				u/c collapse during del., Dinard, France	18.7.78
				(del. via Blackbushe 18.8.78/3.7.79)	
				(to FA Nicaragua as 165)	c80
				(to FA Sandanista as 165)	87
				recov. by Victoria Aircraft Maintenance, BC	.87
			C-FSAN	322052 BC Ltd, Sidney BC	5.10.88
				Victoria Air Maintenance, Victoria BC	90
				(flies as "FA Nicaragua 165"	
				(note: C-FSAN id. quoted as "485")	
174-95 •	T-28A Fennec	51-3557		(to L'Armee de l'Air as Fennec No.43)	
			CN-AEE	(to Moroccan AF as ....)	
			HR-229A	(to FA Hondurena as FAH 2....)	.78
				rep. impounded USA ; not del.	.78
				(stored FLL-Exec. 79/80 as HR-229)	
			N85228	Euroworld Inc : reg. res.	6.80
				David C. Tallichet/MARC, Chino CA	12.80
				Jeff Hawk & David C. Tallichet/	
				Visionaire International Inc, Miami FL	3.83/87
				Robert W. Nightingale, Ontario CA	88/92
174-96	T-28A	51-3558	N9689C	A. E. Ferguson, Phoenix AZ	63/66
174-100•	T-28A	51-3562		(to FA Mexicana as T28-929)	
			N5206V	reg. pending	78/88
			N128DR	Jack L. Rhoades, Columbus IN	3.91/92
				(FAA quote id. "929")	
174-103• Fennec	T-28A	51-3565		(to L'Armee de l'Air as Fennec No. 56)	
			CN-AEN	(to Moroccan AF as ....)	
			HR-232A	(to FA Hondurena as FAH 2....)	.78
				rep. impounded USA ; not del.	.78
			N8522Z	Euroworld Inc: reg. res.	6.80
				David C. Tallichet/ MARC, Chino CA	12.80/88
174-104	T-28A Fennec	51-3566		(to L'Armee de l'Air as Fennec No. 58)	
			N14102	Waco-Pacific Inc, Van Nuys CA	.68
				Winter Wolff & Co, New York NY	69

174-108•	T-28A	51-3570		(to L'Armee de l'Air as Fennec No. 98)	
	Fennec		N14103	Waco-Pacific Inc, Van Nuys CA	.68
	AT-28D			Winter Wolff & Co, New York NY	69
				Quality Components Inc, Los Angeles CA	72
				(to FA Haiti as ....)	10.73
			N14103	Lan-Dale Co, Reno NV	3.78
				Warbirds Inc, Queens NY	84/87
				Robert W. Urbine, High Point NC	88
				LTA Insurance Brokers, Greensboro NC	92
174-111•	T-28A	51-3573		(to L'Armee de l'Air as Fennec No. 82)	
	Fennec		N14119	Waco-Pacific Inc, Van Nuys CA	.68
				Winter Wolff & Co, New York NY	69/72
				LaSalle Electronics, Galesburg IL	78
				MMB Inc, Thomson GA	84/92
174-112•	T-28A	51-3574		(to F.A.Argentina as E-608)	
				Museo Nacional de Aeronautica,	
				Aeroparque Airport, Buenos Aires	78/90
174-126•	T-28A	51-3588		(to R Lao AF as 3405)	
	T-28D			Col Pay/Pays Air Service, Scone NSW	.88
				(recov. from Thong Hi Hin AB, Laos: trucked	
				overland to Bangkok, shipped to Australia 12.88)	
				F. W. Pike, Sydney NSW	89/92
			VH-WPA	F. W. (Bill) Pike, Sydney NSW	.92
				(rest. Sydney-Bankstown, due to fly .92)	
				(note: aircraft arr. painted as RLAF13388,	
				but NA plate shows 51-3588 !)	
174-128	T-28A	51-3590		(to L'Armee de l'Air as Fennec No.54)	
	Fennec			(to Moroccan AF as ....)	
			N9863A	Euroworld Inc	5.78
				sale rep., Miami FL	84/92
174-131	T-28A	51-3593	N79Z	prototype T-28S/Fennec conv. by	
	Fennec			Pacific Airmotive Corp, Burbank CA	
				Cie. Sud Aviation (Fennec prototype No. 01)	.59
				shipped to France	7.59
				crashed during test flights, France	.60
174-150•	T-28A	51-3612		(to US Army as 51-3612)	
				US Army Aviation Museum, Fort Rucker AL	87/88
174-153	T-28A	51-3615	N260P	Pacific Airmotive Corp, Burbank CA	63
				Sidney J. Freedman, Buffalo NY	66/69
				(FAA quote id. "153") : off USCR by	72
			N2800G	George J. Rivera, Santa Clara CA	1.78
				(id. also quoted as "174-222")	
174-154•	T-28A	51-3616	N1384T		
	T-28D-5		N28TW	844 Squadron Inc, Boulder CO	9.82/83
				crashed, hit mountain, Winter Park CO	12.2.83
174-158•	T-28A	51-3620		(to L'Armee de l'Air as Fennec No. 60)	
	Fennec		N14104	Waco-Pacific Inc, Van Nuys CA	.68
	AT-28D			Winter Wolff & Co, New York NY	69
				Quality Components Inc, Los Angeles CA	72
				(to FA Haiti as 1244)	10.73
			N14104	Lan-Dale Co, Reno NV	3.78
				(arr. Tucson AZ 5.78 as "1244")	
				Gary Flanders, Oakland CA	81
				Lee W. Schaller, New Athens IL	84/92
174-162	T-28A	51-3624		(to L'Armee de l'Air as Fennec No. 27)	
	Fennec		N14120	Waco-Pacific Inc, Van Nuys CA	.68
				Winter Wolff & Co, New York NY	69

174-164•	T-28A Fennec AT-28D	51-3626		(to L'Armee de l'Air as Fennec No. 96)	
			N14121	Waco-Pacific Inc, Van Nuys CA	.68
				Winter Wolff & Co, New York NY	69
				Quality Components Inc, Los Angeles CA	72
				(to FA Haiti as 1238)	10.73
			N14121	Lan-Dale Co, Reno NV	3.78
				(arr. Tucson AZ 5.78 as "1238")	
				Les Crowder & Rick Shanholtzer	83
				Alan Preston, Dallas TX	84
				sale reported, Dallas TX	86
			C-GJMT(1	Aviation Maintenance Ltd,Sault Ste Marie QUE	5.87
				struck off reg.	1.88
174-165•	T-28A Fennec	51-3627		(to L'Armee de l'Air as Fennec No.64)	
			CN-AEY	(to Moroccan AF as ....)	
			HR-233A	(to FA Hondurena as FAH 2....)	.78
				rep. impounded USA ; not del.	.78
				also rep. cr. in FAH service	21.7.78
				(stored FLL-Executive 79/80 as HR-233)	
			N8539A	Euroworld Inc : reg. res.	6.80
				David C. Tallichet/MARC, Chino CA	12.80/88
				WW2 Rebuilders Inc, Mooresville NC	.82
				William F. Smith, Mooresville NC	84/88
				ISRMS Inc, Land-o-Lakes FL	92
174-168•	T-28A Fennec	51-3630		(to L'Armee de l'Air as Fennec No. 73)	
			N14105	Waco-Pacific Inc, Van Nuys CA	.68
				Winter Wolff & Co, New York NY	69/72
				crashed, Lakeside TX	7.1.77
			N289RD (1	Kal-Aero Inc, Kalamazoo MI	8.78
			N500JG	Kal-Aero Inc, Kalamazoo MI	5.79/88
				Maurice J. Hovious, Vicksburg MI	92
174-185•	T-28A Fennec	51-3647		(to L'Armee de l'Air as Fennec No. 29)	
				(to Argentine Navy as ......)	.66
			N992CA	Courtesy Aircraft Inc, Rockford IL	4.83/84
			C-GLPM	Jacques Lacombe, Lavale QUE	7.84/88
			N28FE	Joseph F. Ware, Camarillo CA	7.89/92
174-197	T-28A T-28D	51-3659	N3319G	Thomas P. Mathews, Monterey CA	63
				Paul Robert, Rawlins WY	66
				Bertz Aviation, Cadiz OH	69
				(to Philippine AF as 51-3659)	
174-201•	T-28A Fennec	51-3663		(to L'Armee de l'Air as Fennec No. 68)	
			N14106	Waco-Pacific Inc, Van Nuys CA	.68
				Winter Wolff & Co, New York NY	69/72
			N2800W	Tulsa Piper Inc, Tulsa OK	78
				David L. Clinton, Leucadia CA	84/87
			N280DC	Dalton International Inc, Reno NV	6.87
				David L. Clinton, Leucadia CA	88/92
174-202•	T-28A Fennec	51-3664		(to L'Armee de l'Air as Fennec No. 93)	
			N14107	Waco-Pacific Inc, Van Nuys CA	.68
				Winter Wolff & Co, New York NY	69
				(to Chinese Nationalist AF as T2833)	
				Chung Cheng Aviation Museum, Taipei Airport	92
174-216•	T-28A Fennec	51-3678		(to L'Armee de l'Air as Fennec No. 118)	
			N14122	Waco-Pacific Inc, Van Nuys CA	.68
				Winter Wolff & Co, New York NY	69/72
				John P. Silberman, Key West FL	78
				James A. Atkinson, Newport WA	1.87/92
174-219•	T-28A T-28D	51-3681		(to FA Hondurena as FAH 226)	
			N81NA	Courtesy Aircraft Inc, Rockford IL	9.85/87

Continued on Page 299

27

Defector
NX2124X
От Ферапонта Петровича
Головатого 2ᵍ САМОЛЕТ
НА ОКОНЧАТЕЛЬНЫЙ РАЗГРОМ ВРАГА!

07
Монгольский
Арат
11
F-AZPA

Continued from Page 294

North American T-28 Trojan

			C-GXUO	Bailey Aviation Service, Calgary ALTA	8.88/90
174-220	T-28A	51-3682		(to L'Armee de l'Air as Fennec No. 105)	
	Fennec		N14123	Waco-Pacific Inc, Van Nuys CA	.68
				Winter Wolff & Co, New York NY	69
174-228	T-28A	51-3690		(to L'Armee de l'Air as Fennec No. 42)	
	Fennec			(to Moroccan AF as 51-3690)	65
			N54612	Jeff Hawke & David C. Tallichet/	
				Visionair International Inc, Miami FL	3.78
				(del. via Blackbushe UK 15.8.78/23.6.79)	
				sale reported, Miami FL	84/92
174-231•	T-28A	51-3693		(to L'Armee de l'Air as Fennec No. 90)	
	Fennec		N14124	Waco-Pacific Inc, Van Nuys CA	.68
				Winter Wolff & Co, New York NY	69/72
				Dennis M. Sherman, West Palm Beach FL	78
				Joseph F. Keenan, Sunnyvale CA	83/92
174-238•	T-28A	51-3700		(to R Lao AF as 3406)	
	T-28D			Col Pay/Pays Air Servioce, Scone NSW	.88
				(recov. from Thong Hi Hin AB, Laos: trucked	
				overland to Bangkok, shipped to Australia .88)	
				Noel Vinson, Bankstown Airport, Sydney NSW	90/92
				(stored Bankstown, awaiting rebuild)	
174-243•	T-28A	51-3705	N74193	Palo Alto Unified School District, Palo Alto CA	78
			N3705D	Stephen R. Scott, Foster City CA	8.78/83
			N83705	Stephen R. Scott, Foster City CA	1.83/92
174-245•	T-28A	51-3707	N8156G	Texas Turbo Jet Inc, Dallas TX	4.89/92
174-260•	T-28A	51-3722		(to Philippine AF as ....)	
	AT-28D			Ian Kenny, Brisbane QLD	.90/92
				(stored Brisbane, pending rest.)	
174-263•	T-28A	51-3725		(to NASA Langley AFB as NASA 223)	c60
			N502NA	NASA, Langley AFB VA	73/80
			N302NA	NASA	2.80
				Maryland Avn. Hist. Society, Annapolis MD	84/86
				William G. Bennett, Las Vegas NV	.86/88
				Silver State Aviation, Las Vegas NV	92
174-280•	T-28A	51-3742		(to L'Armee de l'Air as Fennec No. 104)	
	Fennec		N14141	Waco-Pacific Inc, Van Nuys CA	.68
				Winter Wolff & Co, New York NY	69/72
				sale rep.	78
				Ray Karrels, Port Washington WI	84/88
				Caroline Karrels, Port Washington WI	92
174-289•	T-28A	51-3751		(to L'Armee de l'Air as Fennec No. 02)	
	Fennec		N14108	Waco-Pacific Inc, Van Nuys CA	.68
	AT-28D			Winter Wolff & Co, New York NY	69
				Quality Components Inc, Los Angeles CA	72
				(to FA Haiti as 1245)	10.73
			N14108	Lan-Dale Co, Reno NV	3.78
				(noted unconv. Tucson AZ as "1245" 10.78)	
				Harold L. Abrams, Tucson AZ	84/92
174-294•	T-28A	51-3756		(to L'Armee de l'Air as Fennec No. 103)	
	Fennec		N14142	Waco-Pacific Inc, Van Nuys CA	.68
				Winter Wolff & Co, New York NY	69/72
				Grafton Insurance Agency, Grafton WI	78/88
				William M. Claybaugh, West Bend WI	92

174-304•	T-28A	51-3766	N766NA	William B. Sullivan, Verona NJ	12.89
	T-28D			Wide Band Systems, Lafayette NJ	92
174-313	T-28A	51-3775		(to L'Armee de l'Air as Fennec No. 114)	
	Fennec		N14109	Waco-Pacific Inc, Van Nuys CA	.68
				Winter Wolff & Co, New York NY	69
174-320	T-28A	51-3782		(to Philippine AF as 51-3782)	
	T-28D		RP-C280	Jose Mari Roa, Manila Philippines	88
				(note: composite rebuild with PAF 51-3722)	
174-323	T-28A	51-3785		(to L'Armee de l'Air as Fennec No. 111)	
	Fennec		N14143	Waco Pacific Inc, Van Nuys CA	.68
				Winter Wolff & Co, New York NY	69
				(to FA Haiti as 12...)	10.73
174-324	T-28A	51-3786		conv. second YAT-28E turboprop prototype	11.63
	YAT-28E			Merle H. Maine, Ontario OR	
			N2800E	George J. Rivera, Santa Clara CA	1.78
174-326•	T-28A	51-3788		conv. third YAT-28E turboprop prototype	64
	YAT-28E			Merle H. Maine, Ontario OR	
				Pima County Air Museum, Tucson AZ	5.71/74
				no longer on display by	76
174-344•	T-28A	51-7491		(to L'Armee de l'Air as Fennec No.121)	
	Fennec			Musee de l'Air et d'Espace, Le Bourget	84/88
174-346•	T-28A	51-7493		(to R Lao AF as ....)	
	T-28D			Col Pay/Pays Air Service, Scone NSW	.88
				(recov. from Thong Hi Hin AB, Laos: trucked overland to Bangkok, shipped to Australia 12.88)	
				Steve Death, Albury NSW : spares source	.89/91
				Don Brown, Kongwack VIC : rest. project	91/92
174-353•	T-28A	51-7500		(to Philippine AF as 51-7500)	
	T-28D			Philippine Air Force Museum, Fernando AB	78
174-362•	T-28A	51-7509		(to Philippine AF as 51-7509)	
	AT-28D			(to R Lao AF as 3402)	
				Col Pay/Pays Air Service, Scone NSW	.88/92
				(recov. from Thong Hi Hin AB, Laos: trucked overland to Bangkok, shipped to Australia 12.88)	
174-364	T-28A	51-7511		(to L'Armee de l'Air as Fennec No. 120)	
	Fennec		N14110	Waco-Pacific Inc, Van Nuys CA	.68
	AT-28D			Winter Wolff & Co, New York NY	69
				Quality Components Inc, Los Angeles CA	72
				(to FA Haiti as 1240)	10.73
			N14110	Lan-Dale Co, Reno NV	3.78
				(arr. Tucson AZ 5.78 as "1240")	
				crashed, dest., Rialto CA	15.3.84
174-374•	T-28A	51-7521		(to R Lao AF as 3403)	
	T-28D			Col Pay/Pays Air Service, Scone NSW	.88
				(recov. from Thong Hi Hin AB, Laos: trucked overland to Bangkok, shipped to Australia .88)	
				Guido Zuccoli, Darwin NT	.89/92
				Arthur Schmidt, Darwin NT	92
				(rest. to fly, Darwin NT)	
174-383	T-28A	51-7530		(to L'Armee de l'Air as Fennec No. 115)	
	Fennec		N14111	Waco-Pacific Inc, Van Nuys CA	.68
				Winter Wolff & Co, New York NY	69
				off USCR by 72; rest. to USCR	11.78

174-386•	T-28A Fennec AT-28D	51-7533		(to L'Armee de l'Air as Fennec No. 116)	
			N14144	Waco-Pacific Inc, Van Nuys CA	.68
				Winter Wolff & Co, New York NY	69
				Quality Components Inc, Los Angeles CA	72
				(to FA Haiti as 1237)	10.73
			N14144	Lan-Dale Co, Reno NV	3.78
				(arr. Tucson AZ 5.78 as "1237")	
				H. A. Giffen, Phoenix AZ	9.84/88
				Ronald E. Evans, Highland CA	89/92
174-389•	T-28A	51-7536		(to FA Nicaragua as ....)	
			N99393	David C. Tallichet/ MARC, Chino CA	2.78/92
				(FAA quote id. "389")	
174-395•	T-28A Fennec AT-28D	51-7542		(to ;'Armee de l'Air as Fennec No. 124)	
			N14112	Waco-Pacific Inc, Van Nuys CA	.68
				Winter Wolff & Co, New York NY	69
				Quality Components Inc, Los Angeles CA	72
				(to FA Haiti as 1242)	10.73
			N14112	Lan-Dale Co, Reno NV	3.78
				(arr. Tucson AZ 5.78 as "1242")	
				Wiley Sanders Truck Lines, Troy AL	84/92
174-398•	T-28A Fennec AT-28D	51-7545		(to L'Armee de l'Air as Fennec No. 119)	
			N14113	Waco-Pacific Inc, Van Nuys CA	.68
				Winter Wolff & Co, New York NY	69
				(to FA Haiti as 1236)	10.73
			N14113	Lan-Dale Co, Reno NV	3.78
				(arr. Tucson AZ 5.78 as "1236")	
				Jacob S. Kamborian, Nashua NH	84/92
				(FAA quotes id. "81-1")	
174-411•	T-28A	51-7558		George J. Rivera, San Jose : del. ex MASDC	27.9.78
			N90198	George J. Rivera, San Jose CA	1.79/86
				King City Aviation Inc, King City CA	87/88
				Bishop P. King, Pacific Grove CA	89/92
174-429•	T-28A T-28D	51-7576		(to R Lao AF as 3401)	
				Col Pay/Pays Air Service, Scone NSW	.88
				(recov. from Thong Hi Hin AB, Laos: trucked overland to Bangkok, shipped to Australia .88)	
				Guido Zuccoli, Darwin NT	.89/92
				(rest. to fly, Darwin NT)	
174-435•	T-28A	51-7582	N8156L	Texas Turbo Jet Inc, Dallas TX	4.89/92
174-441•	T-28A	51-7588		(to FA Mexicana as T28-944)	
				stored dism. Freeman Field, Seymour IN	90
			N129DR	Rhoades Aviation, Columbus IN	3.91
				Richard A. Benner, Wasilla AK	92
				(FAA quote id. "944")	
174-459•	T-28A Fennec	51-7606		(to L'Armee de l'Air as Fennec No. 136)	
				(to Argentine Navy as ....)	.66
			N9103F	Westair International USA Inc, Monument CO	7.87/88
				Richard D. Janitell, Colorado Springs CO	92
174-471•	T-28A Fennec	51-7618		(to L'Armee de l'Air as Fennec No. 128)	
			N14114	Waco-Pacific Inc, Van Nuys CA	.68
				Winter Wolff & Co, New York NY	69/72
				Dellis W. Dodson, Tustin CA	78/88
				William Ross Enterprises, Incline Village NV	91/92
174-485•	T-28A Fennec	51-7632		(to L'Armee de l'Air as Fennec No. 1)	.59
			CN-AEP	(to Moroccan AF as ....)	
			HR-226A	(to FA Hondurena as FAH 227)	.78
			N632NA	Courtesy Aircraft Inc, Rockford IL	9.85/86
				William S. Sullivan, Verona NJ	87/88

				DMS Management, Manchester NH	89/92
174-508•	T-28A Fennec	51-7655		(to L'Armee de l'Air as Fennec No. 141)	.59
				(to Argentine Navy as ....)	7.66
				William S. Scully, Marina del Rey CA	90
			N141BS	William S. Scully, Marina del Rey CA	5.91/92
174-517	T-28A Fennec	51-7664		(to L'Armee de l'Air as Fennec No. 140)	
			N14115	Waco-Pacific Inc, Van Nuys CA	.68
				Winter Wolff & Co, New York NY	69
174-522•	T-28A Fennec	51-7669		(to L'Armee de l'Air as Fennec No. 2)	
			N9860A	Euroworld California Inc, Long Beach CA	84
				David C. Tallichet/MARC, Chino CA	4.84/92
174-526	T-28A Fennec	51-7673		(to L'Armee de l"Air as Fennec No. 143)	
			N14116	Waco-Pacific Inc, Van Nuys CA	.68
				Winter Wolff & Co, New York NY	69
174-544•	T-28A	51-7691	N3313G	William Fitchen, Capistrano Beach CA	63
				Lycoming Division of Avco, Stratford CT	66
				Delbert L. Aurey, Southport CT	69/72
				Wolcott Air Service, Wolcott CT	78
				David S. Schlingman, Kansas City MO and Tampa FL	83/92
174-545•	T-28A Fennec	51-7692		(to L'Armee de l"Air as Fennec No. 142)	
				displ. on roof Villeneuve, France	
			F-AZFV	Amicale Ailes Tremontaises, Tremons-Millac	11.88/90
				(rebuilt Dijon/Longevic, ff 16.11.88)	
174-548•	T-28A	51-7695	N8089H	Avia Union, Santa Ana CA	63
				C. O. Hammerwold, Long Beach CA	66
				Richard S. Tobey, Newport Beach CA	69
				Steve Tognoli, Oakland CA	78
				Alan Preston/Fighting Air Command Inc, Dallas TX	8.84/86
				K. F. McLaughton, Nashua NH	1.87/92
174-549	T-28A	51-7696	N8079H	Bob Robinson, Laguna Beach CA	63/69
174-553•	T-28A	51-7700	N8088H	Daniel Ninburg, Anaheim CA	63/66
			Nomad	(rebuilt as NA-260 Nomad)	
				Waco-Pacific Inc, Van Nuys CA	69
				Richard M. Vartanian, Arcadia CA	72
			N100JE	Kal-Aero Inc, Kalamazoo MI	78/84
				Kalamazoo Aviation History Museum, Kalamazoo MI	86/92
174-563	T-28A	51-7710	N3312G	Elwood C. Martin, Newport Beach CA	63
174-583	T-28A Fennec	51-7730		(to L'Armee de l'Air as Fennec No. 4)	
				(to Moroccan AF as 517730)	
			N9857A	Jeff Hawke & David C. Tallichet/ Visionair International, Miami FL	5.78
				(del. via Blackbushe 14.8.78/25.6.79)	
				sale rep., Miami FL	84/92
174-602•	T-28A Fennec	51-7749		(to L'Armee de l"Air as Fennec No. 135)	
				Dijon Air Base, France : displ.	87/88
			F-AZHR	Amicale Ailes Tremontaises, Tremons-Millac	.91
174-613•	T-28A	51-7760		(to Philippine AF as 7760)	
				gate guard, San Fernando AB, Lipa Town	82/90
174-614	T-28A	51-7761		(to L'Armee de l"Air as Fennec No. 129)	

	Fennec		N14117	Waco-Pacific Inc, Van Nuys CA	.68
				Winter Wolff & Co, New York NY	69
174-634	T-28A	51-7781		(to L'Armee de l'Air as Fennec No. 122)	
	Fennec		N14118	Waco-Pacific Inc, Van Nuys CA	.68
				Winter Wolff & Co, New York NY	69
174-635•	T-28A	51-7782		(to L'Armee de l'Air as Fennec No. 113)	
	Fennec			(to Argentine Navy as ......)	.66
			N993CA	Courtesy Aircraft Inc, Rockford IL	4.83/87
				B. Z. Corp, Santa Clara CA	88
				John Castelluci, Los Angeles CA	89/91
				crashed nr. Hollister CA (Castelluci baled out)	8.7.91
174-642•	T-28A	51-7789	N3320G	Ray Karrels, Port Washington WI	63/72
				North American Aerial, Richmond VA	78
			N28EG	North American Aerial, Mesa AZ	84/88
				Richard D. Ervin, Indianapolis IN	92
174-645•	T-28A	51-7792	N8166H	Cherokee Corp, Bedford OH	63
			N96329	John Arbet Co, Chicago IL	5.77/78
				Byrne Aviation Co, Bloomfield Hills MI	82/83
				James E. Neundorfer, Houston TX	84
				Byrne Aviation Co, Bloomfield Hills MI	86/87
				John Hooper, Harvey LA	88
			N28GW	George W. Westmoreland, Rogers AR	12.89/92
174-646	T-28A	51-7793	N9635C	Robert Marts, Somers Point NJ	66/69
174-652•	T-28A	51-7799		(to L'Armee de l'Air as Fennec No. 26)	
	Fennec			(to Argentine Navy as ....)	.66
				(prob. to F.A. Uraguay as ......)	
			N91020	Westair International USA Inc, Monument CO	7.87
				Richard D. Janitell, Colorado Springs CO	88
				Philip J. Godlewski, New Castle DE	92
174-654	T-28A	51-7801	N3201G	GHS Aircraft Group, Phoenix AZ	63
				Richard S. Tubey, Newport Beach CA	66
174-656•	T-28A	51-7803	N8087H	American Aerial Surveys Inc, San Antonio TX	63/69
				John A. Ortseifen, Chicago IL	72/92
174-687•	T-28A	51-7834		(to L'Armee de l'Air as Fennec No. 25)	
	Fennec			(to Argentine Navy as .....)	.66
			N994CA	Courtesy Aircraft Inc, Rockford IL	4.83/88
				sale rep., Lee MA	92
174-688•	T-28A	51-7835		(to L'Armee de l'Air as Fennec No. 24)	
			N14145	Waco-Pacific Inc, Van Nuys CA	.68
				Winter Wolff & Co, New York NY	69/72
				Tom Austin, Greenville TN	78
				Kal Aero Inc, Kalamazoo MI	84/92
174-697	T-28A	51-7844		(to L'Armee de l'Air as Fennec No. 8)	
	Fennec		CN-AEB	(to Moroccan AF as ....)	
			HR-227A	(to FA Hondurena as FAH 2....)	
189-2 •	T-28A	52-1187	N8009G	Courtesy Aircraft Inc, Rockford IL	4.89
				Marion Recovery Inc, Kalamazoo MI	92
				(FAA orig. quoted id. "50-2187")	
189-41 •	T-28A	52-1226		(to L'Armee de l'Air as Fennec No. 23)	
	Fennec		CN-AEC	(to Moroccan AF as ....)	
			HR-228A	(to FA Hondurena as FAH 2....)	
				rep. impounded USA; not del.	.78
				(stored FLL-Exec. 79/81 as HR-228A)	
			N8522X	Euroworld Inc : reg. res.	1.81
				David C. Tallichet/MARC, Chino CA	81/88

189-53 •	T-28A Fennec	52-1238		(to L'Armee de l'Air as Fennec No. 15)	
				(to Argentine Navy as ......)	.66
			N995CA	Courtesy Aircraft Inc, Rockford IL	4.83/86
				Enrique R. Vazquez, San Fernando CA	87/88
			N238V	J. E. Pistons Inc, Huntington Beach CA	1.92
200-3 •	T-28B	Bu137640	N2206G	World Wide Aeronautical Industries, Moorpark CA	12.89
				George L. Gayler, Thermal CA	92
200-6	T-28B	Bu137643	N80473	reg.	8.79
200-8	T-28B	Bu137645	N132Z	US Forestry Service, Albuquerque NM	66/72
				del. MASDC for storage	5.5.76/81
200-15 •	T-28B	Bu137652	N652AS	Airplane Sales International, Beverly Hills CA	7.86/87
				Mona Benson, Suisun CA	88/92
200-20 •	T-28B	Bu137657		Pima Air Museum, Tucson AZ: del. ex MASDC	17.1.82
			N3250D	reg. res.	10.82
				Courtesy Aircraft Inc, Rockford IL	8.85/87
				(noted stored, Pima Air Museum 86)	
				Ronald O'Beirne, Angola IN	88/92
200-24 •	T-28B T-28D	Bu137661		(to R. Thai AF as 0-37661)	
				R. Thai AF Museum, Don Muang Bangkok	.88
200-25 •	T-28B	Bu137662	N662WW	World Wide Aeronautical Industries, Moorpark CA	12.89/92
200-26 •	T-28B QT-28B T-28B	Bu137663	N137NA	Airplane Sales International, Beverly Hills CA	10.85
				King City Aviation Inc, King City CA	86/88
				John F. Strehl, Minden NV	92
200-32 •	T-28B	Bu137669	N669RR	Al Redick, Reno NV	1.86
				Les S. Salz, Reno NV	87/90
			N137LS	Les S. Salz, Reno NV	4.90/92
200-55 •	T-28B	Bu137692	N1184N	Time Aviation, Tucson AZ : del. ex MASDC	24.8.81
				Arlie P. Kelly, Willowick OH	84/86
				Courtesy Aircraft Inc, Rockford IL	87
			N237JB	James Brothers, Fennimore WI	88
				Sharlow R. James, Fennimore WI	92
200-59 •	T-28B	Bu137696		Pima Air Museum, Tucson AZ: del. ex MASDC	17.1.82
			N27556	Lynn C. Hunt, Santa Rosa CA	7.82
			N428B	Lynn C. Hunt, Santa Rosa CA	3.83/92
200-60 •	T-28B T-28D	Bu137697		(to R Lao AF as 54-137697)	
				Col Pay/Pays Air Service, Scone NSW	.88
				(recov. from Thong Hi Hin AB, Laos: trucked overland to Bangkok, shipped to Australia 12.88)	
				(stored dism., Nowra NAS NSW .89)	
200-61 •	T-28B AT-28D	Bu137698		(to Philippines AF as 54-137698)	
			N2067A	Business Air Charter, Portland OR	3.8.89/92
200-63 •	T-28B AT-28D	Bu137700		(to Philippines AF as 54-137700)	
			N20681	Business Air Charter, Portland OR	3.8.89/92
200-65 •	T-28B	Bu137702		USAFM: Edwards AFB CA	88/91
200-69 •	T-28B	Bu137706		(to SVNAF as ....)	
			N4698S	Dennis M. Sherman, West Palm Beach FL	4.84
				Donald Clemmons, Ocala FL	86/89

				Flying Legends Inc, Saulte Ste Marie MI	92
200-79 •	T-28B	Bu137716		(to Philippines AF as 54-137716)	
	AT-28D		N2060V	Business Air Charter, Portland OR	3.8.89
			N514FR(2	Air Armco Inc, Middletown DE	3.90/92
200-86 •	T-28B	Bu137723	N47797	State of Alaska Division of Forestry AK	8.84
			N215SF	State of Alaska, Anchorage AK	1.85/92
200-97 •	T-28B	Bu137734		(to Philippines AF as 54-137734)	
	AT-28D		N20677	Business Air Charter, Portland OR	3.8.89/92
200-99 •	T-28B	Bu137736	N28TP	Ted R. Pieper, Aurora CO	7.89
				sale rep., Englewood CO	92
200-104 •	T-28B	Bu137741		(to Philippines AF as 54-137741)	
	AT-28D		N20677	Business Air Charter, Portland OR	3.8.89/92
200-99 •	T-28B	Bu137736	N28TP	Ted R. Pieper, Aurora CO	7.89
				sale rep., Englewood CO	92
200-104 •	T-28B	Bu137741		(to Philippines AF as 54-137741)	
	AT-28D		N2052H	Business Air Charter, Portland OR	3.8.89/92
200-106 •	T-28B	Bu137743	N5439X	Courtesy Aircraft Inc, Rockford IL	8.84
				Rockingham Aviation Inc, Bridgewater VA	86/92
200-108 •	T-28B	Bu137745	N9038L	David C. Tallichet/MARC, Chino CA	3.87/88
				William R. Montague, Oakland CA	
				sale rep., Oakland CA	92
200-110 •	T-28B	Bu137747		(to US Army as 37747)	
				US Army Aviation Museum, Fort Rucker AL	88/89
200-112 •	T-28B	Bu137749		USAFM, Hill AFB UT	90
				(displ. as "137749/ZD003")	
200-113 •	T-28B	Bu137750	N578HT	R. Stevenson, Jenks OK	9.86
			N750RL	Ronald J. Lee, Lone Beach CA	12.86/88
			N300PT	Robert A. Vermeulen, Franklin MI	9.90/92
200-115 •	T-28B	Bu137752	N752WW	World Wide Aeronautical Industries, Moorpark CA	12.89/92
200-122 •	T-28B	Bu137759	N49914	reg.	5.84/88
			N759T	Combat Air Museum, Topeka KS	5.89/92
200-123 •	T-28B	Bu137760	N128KA	Allan B. Krosner, Santa Ana CA	2.90/9
200-127 •	T-28B	Bu137764	N2207Y	reg.	12.89
				John R. Murphy, Chesterfield MO	92
200-128 •	T-28B	Bu137765		San Diego Aerospace Museum CA	88/91
			N3178U	Jim Price Aircraft Inc, Memphis TN	11.91/92
200-136 •	T-28B	Bu137773		(to R. Thai AF as 5437773)	
	T-28D			(to R Lao AF as 3411)	
200-145 •	T-28B	Bu137782	N9039Z	David C. Tallichet/MARC, Chino CA	3.87/88
				(open storage, unconv., Chandler AZ 88/89)	
				William R. Montague, Oakland CA	
				sale rep., Oakland CA	92
200-150 •	T-28B	Bu137787	N787AS	Airplane Sales International, Beverly Hills CA	7.86/88
				sale rep., Ione CA	92
200-152 •	T-28B	Bu137789	N52424	B. W. Orbiss, Inglewood CA	5.84
				Peter A. Triolo, Garden City KS	86/87

				Robert J. Beranger, Rochester NH	88/92
200-153	T-28B	Bu137790	N4779N	State of Alaska Division of Forestry AK	3.84
			N104SF	State of Alaska, Anchorage AK	1.85/88
				struck-off USCR	8.88
200-156 •	T-28B	Bu137793	N815SH	John C. Harrison, Sacramento CA	8.85/92
200-159 •	T-28B	Bu137796		(to USAF as 47796)	
				displ. on pole, NAS Anacostia DC	88
200-162 •	T-28B	Bu137799	N28YF	Ronald J. Kitchen, Carson City NV	3.92
	T-28D			(FAA quote type as "NA-Weaver T-28D")	
200-164 •	T-28B	Bu137801	N57973	Aero Nostagia, Portland OR	11.84
				Vincent L. Murphy, Portland OR	86/87
				Walter E. Strow, Brookings OR	88
				Charles W. McCoy, Brookings OR	92
200-166 •	T-28B	Bu137803	N68803	Northwest Warbirds Inc, Twin Falls ID	1.87
				Raymond J. St. Germain, Pearland TX	.87
				Western Wings Aircraft Sales Co, Oakland OR	88
				John J. Mason, Washington DC	89
				Bengt L. Kuller, Rockford IL	92
200-171 •	T-28B	Bu137808	N303NA	Maryland Aviation Hist. Soc., Annapolis MD	9.86/88
				Michael E. Keenum, Palos Park IL	89/92
200-174 •	T-28B	Bu138103	N130AS	Airplane Sales International, Beverly Hills CA	7.86/87
				Mona Benson, Suisun CA	88/92
200-181 •	T-28	Bu138110		(to Philippines AF as 54-138110)	
	AT-28D		N2054K	Business Air Charter, Portland OR	3.8.89/92
200-188 •	T-28B	Bu138117	N88AW	GWB Inc, Canby OR	9.85/88
				Arthur Grabowski, Manchester NH	89
				Peter Sideris, Jupiter FL	92
200-190 •	T-28B	Bu138119	N119DB	Dennis G. Buehn, Reno NV	8.86
				Alvin R. Eatinger, Belmont CA	87/92
200-193 •	T-28B	Bu138122		(tfd. to USAF as 138122)	
			N28RF	Richard C. Fernalld, Anchorage AK	11.85
				Richard C. Fernalld, Pendleton OR	86/92
200-196 •	T-28B	Bu138125	N653Z	Maryland Aviation Hist. Soc., Annapolis MD	11.91/92
200-200 •	T-28B	Bu138129	N32257	World Aircraft Museum Inc, Calhoun GA	10.82/88
				sale rep., Tucson AZ	92
200-201 •	T-28B	Bu138130	N944RJ	Robby R. Jones, Minter City MS	1.87
				D. R. Webber	1.87
				reg. pending	88
				Maryland Warbird Museum, White Marsh MD	92
200-206 •	T-28B	Bu138135		(to Philippines AF as 53-138135)	
	AT-28D		N2061W	Business Air Charter, Portland OR	3.8.89
				Conrad H. Hagle, Portland OR	92
200-207 •	T-28B	Bu138136	N7044W	William E. Strickler, Rolla MO	11.88/90
			N27WS	William E. Strickler, Rolla MO	6.90/92
200-211 •	T-28B	Bu138140	N504GH	Glen Hyde, Dallas TX	4.86
				David M. Forrest, Dunwoody GA	87
				Randall O. Porter, Woodstock GA	88
				Tan Air Ltd, Manchester NH	92

200-213	T-28B	Bu138142	N54912	reg. res.	9.84/92
200-215 •	T-28B	Bu138144		displ. NAS Whiting Field FL	88
200-220 •	T-28B	Bu138149	N391NA	Maryland Aviation Hist. Soc., Annapolis MD	2.86/87
				struck-off USCR	8.88
200-221 •	T-28B	Bu138150	N138WW	World Wide Aeronautical Industries, Moorpark CA	12.89/92
200-229 •	T-28B	Bu138158	N138RR	Classics In American Aviation, Reno NV	7.86/88
				Cecil H. Harp, Canby OR	92
200-235 •	T-28B	Bu138164	N9060F	Charles A. Osborn, Louisville KY	7.87
				Charles A. Osborn/Blue Sky Aviation, Sellersburg IN	88/92
200-242 •	T-28B	Bu138171	N8064H	Bill Walker & Associates, St. Simmons Is. GA	4.89
			N171BA	Byron H. Alperstein, Los Angeles CA	10.90/92
200-243 •	T-28B	Bu138172	N82AW	Apex Associates Inc, Canby OR	1.86
				Neale C. Ducharme, Phoenix AZ	87/88
				QRD Equipment Corp, Long Island City NY	89/92
200-246 •	T-28B	Bu138175	N28EP	Eric C. Paul, Charlotte NC	11.88/92
200-249 •	T-28B	Bu138178	N28TY	Lan-Dale Co, Reno NV	1.85
				Roger R. Babb, Saranac MI	86/92
200-250 •	T-28B	Bu138179		Time Aviation, Tucson AZ : del. ex MASDC	31.3.82
			N3905H	Dennis G. Buehn, Long Beach CA	4.83/84
				William E. Harrison, Tulsa OK (race #33)	84
				GWB Inc, Canby OR	86/87
			OE-ESA	Sigi Angerer, Innsbruck	1.88
				Paul Doblinger, Innsbruck	.89/91
200-252 •	T-28B	Bu138181		(to Philippines AF as 53-138181)	
	AT-28D		N2063T	Business Air Charter, Portland OR	3.8.89/92
200-255 •	T-28B	Bu138184	N251NA	Maryland Aviation Hist. Soc., Annapolis MD	11.88/92
200-258 •	T-28B	Bu138187	N187GH	Charles G. Hyde, Roanoke TX	12.90
				Dreamships Inc, Roanoke TX	92
200-262 •	T-28B	Bu138191	N54913	reg. reserved	9.84/87
			N107NA	Maryland Aviation Hist. Soc., Annapolis MD	5.88
				Robert C. Hansen, Delauan WI	92
200-263 •	T-28B	Bu138192		(to Philippines AF as 53-138192)	
	AT-28D		N2065F	Business Air Charter, Portland OR	3.8.89/92
200-265 •	T-28B	Bu138194	N194RR	Leeward Aeronautical Sales, Ocala FL	6.86
				Leeward Racing Inc, Ocala FL	11.86
				Microprose Software Inc, Hunt Valley MD	87/92
200-274 •	T-28B	Bu138203	N131Z	US Forestry Service, Albuquerque NM	66/72
				del. to MASDC for storage	6.5.76
			N950N	US Narcotics Force,Tucson AZ : ex MASDC	27.12.78
				Sunair Inc	
				Westair International Inc, Monument CO	7.82
			N372C	Dapro Rubber Inc, Van Nuys CA	9.83/92
200-277	T-28B	Bu138206	N5493G	reg. res.	9.84/92
200-280 •	T-28B	Bu138209	N209WW	World Wide Aeronautical Industries, Moorpark CA	12.89/92
				(noted stored, Wilmot Metals, Tucson AZ 11.91)	

200-284 •	T-28B	Bu138213	N312AS	Airplane Sales International, Beverly Hills CA	7.86/88
				sale rep., Ione CA	92
200-286 •	T-28B	Bu138215	N7044L	Curly Brehm Leasing, Devine TX	12.88/89
				Tiger Aviation Enterprises, Wilmington DE	5.90
				Sigtronics Corp, Covina CA	92
200-287 •	T-28B	Bu138216	N285MS	M. W. Stevenson Ltd, Pasadena MD	10.85/92
200-289 •	T-28B	Bu138218	N283JR	Coke V. Stuart, Valdosta GA	7.85/87
			N283V	Nav Air Ltd, Fort Salonga NY	11.87/88
			N1283	Nav Air Ltd, Fort Salonga NY	12.91/92
200-291 •	T-28B	Bu138220		Armoflex Inc, Santa Maria CA	
			N220NA	Dannie Nault, Muskogee OK	3.86/92
200-292 •	T-28B	Bu138221	N221MS	M. W. Stevenson Ltd, Pasadena MD	8.85/88
				Richard B. Woodward, Charlotte SC	92
200-294 •	T-28B	Bu138223		USNAM, NAS Pensacola FL	90
200-295 •	T-28B	Bu138224	N628B	L. K. Parker, Orland GA	5.86/87
				Milton C. Leshe, Chandler AZ	88/89
				Gregory Weber, Redmond WA	92
200-303 •	T-28B	Bu138232		(to R Thai AF as 55-138232)	
	T-28D			(to R Lao AF as 3416)	
				Col Pay/Pays Air Service, Scone NSW	.88
				(recov. from Thong Hi Hin AB, Laos: trucked overland to Bangkok, shipped to Australia 12.88)	
				Arthur Schmidt, Darwin NT	91
				Ian Sylvester, Darwin NT	92
				(under rest., Darwin NT)	
200-309 •	T-28B	Bu138238	N238WW	World Wide Aeronautical Industries, Moorpark CA	12.89/92
200-310 •	T-28B	Bu138239	N239GH	Charles G. Hyde, Roanoke TX	5.89
			N726A	James I. Arbogast, Hamilton OH	9.90/92
200-311 •	T-28B	Bu138240	N240WW	World Wide Aeronautical Industries, Moorpark CA	12.89/92
200-312 •	T-28B	Bu138241		(to Philippines AF as 55-138241)	AT-28D
			N2067K	Business Air Charter, Portland OR	3.8.89/92
200-313 •	T-28B	Bu138242		Anthony J. d'Alessandris, Reno NV	
			N242J	Lan-Dale Co, Reno NV	1.86/87
				Brunetto Enterprises Inc, Dover DE	88/92
200-316 •	T-28B	Bu138245	N65491	reg.	11.90
				Randall Porter, Cartersville GA	92
200-318 •	T-28B	Bu138247	N54911	reg.	12.84
				John MacGuire, El Paso TX	86
			N572JB	John MacGuire/War Eagles Air Museum, Santa Teresa NM	4.87/92
200-330 •	T-28B	Bu138259	N86AW	Apex Associates Inc, Canby OR	2.86
				K. D. Kuhlman, Huntington Beach CA	87/88
			VH-SHT	Kim Rolfe-Smith, Brisbane QLD	28.6.90/92
200-334 •	T-28B	Bu138263		Lester Industries,San Antonio TX: ex MASDC	31.3.80
				(to FA Hondurena as FAH 231)	
			N63NA	Courtesy Aircraft Inc, Rockford IL	9.85/86
				Duane Knotts, Alexandria IN	87/92

200-336 •	T-28B	Bu138265	N7139J	Western Wings Aircraft Sales, Oakland OR	5.90/92
200-337 •	T-28B	Bu138266	N391W	Westair International USA Inc, Monument CO	7.86
				Loran Development Corp, Manuh CT	87/92
200-342 •	T-28B	Bu138271		USNAM, NAS Pensacola FL	88
200-346 •	T-28B	Bu138275	N75AF	Doris E. Elkins, Bend OR	11.86
			N28DE	Armoflex Inc, Bend OR	12.86
				Doris E. Elkins, Bend OR	87/88
				Janet L. Mitchell, Klamath Falls OR	92
200-349 •	T-28B	Bu138278	N138NA	Arthur W. McDonnell, Mojave CA	10.85
				Ron Amiran, Portland OR & Encino CA	10.85/87
				(shipped to Australia, assembled Tyabb VIC 2.88)	
			VH-NAW	Judy Pay, Melbourne VIC	5.88/92
200-351 •	T-28B	Bu138280	N4781P	State of Alaska Division of Forestry AK	8.84
			N218SF	State of Alaska, Anchorage AK	1.85/92
200-357 •	T-28B	Bu138286	N5492X	Maryland Aviation Hist. Soc., Annapolis MD	6.85
			N351NA	Maryland Aviation Hist. Soc., Annapolis MD	7.85/88
				Courtesy Aircraft Inc, Rockford IL	92
200-358 •	T-28B	Bu138287		(to Philippines AF as 53-138287)	
	AT-28D		N2065S	Business Air Charter, Portland OR	3.8.89
			N28NB	rereg.	9.91
				Neil R. Anderson, Fort Worth TX	92
200-360 •	T-28B	Bu138289	N80701	John K. Bachmann, Oldwick NJ	4.89
			N828B	John K. Bachmann, Fort Lauderdale FL	9.89/92
200-362 •	T-28B	Bu138291	N8574	Northwest Warbirds Inc, Twin Falls ID	10.86
				Peter A. Triolo, Garden City KS	1.87
				Buddy Bryan/Utilco, Tifton GA	87/88
				Carrier Aviation, High Point NC	92
200-363 •	T-28B	Bu138292	N28FL	Lincoln A. Dexter, Fort Myers FL	10.85/87
				Austin J. Gibbons, Elgin IL	88/92
200-365 •	T-28B	Bu138294	N5440F	Courtesy Aircraft Inc, Rockford IL	8.84
				Southern Cal. Aviation Inc, Newport Beach CA	86/88
				Sasan Farms Inc, Grimes CA	92
200-370 •	T-28B	Bu138299	N54936	reg. res.	9.84/92
200-374 •	T-28B	Bu138303	N9671N	Arthur W. McDonnell, Mojave CA	10.85/87
				Myles S. Douglas, Orlando FL	.87/88
				Estrella Flying Club, Paso Robles CA	92
200-377 •	T-28B	Bu138306	N306WW	World Wide Aeronautical Industries, Moorpark CA	12.89/92
200-379 •	T-28B	Bu138308	N284MS	M. W. Stevenson Ltd, Pasadena MD	10.85/88
				Williston Aircraft Associates, Williston FL	5.89
				Museum of Flying, Santa Monica CA	90/92
200-381 •	T-28B	Bu138310	N393W	Westair International USA Inc, Monument CO	7.86
				Forrest B. Fenn, Santa Fe NM	87/88
				Apache Aviation, Dijon, France : del. ex USA	25.7.90/91
				Lafayette Classic Air, Wilmington DE : USCR	92
200-382 •	T-28B	Bu138311	N4781E	State of Alaska Division of Forestry AK	3.84
			N214SF	State of Alaska, Anchorage AK	1.85/92
200-384 •	T-28B	Bu138313	N128TD	Lan-Dale Co, Reno NV	12.85/92
200-385 •	T-28B	Bu138314	N392W	Westair International USA Inc, Monument CO	7.86

				Mystic Marketing Co, Mystic CT	87/88
				Munro J. Agnelneri, Indianapolis IN	89/92
200-385 •	T-28B	Bu138317		(to Philippines AF as 55-138317)	
	AT-28D		N20551	Business Air Charter, Portland OR	3.8.89/92
200-390 •	T-28B	Bu138319	N93AW	APEXX Co Inc, Canby OR	6.86
				Duncan R. Miller, Suisun CA	87/92
200-391 •	T-28B	Bu138320		(to R. Thai AF as 55-138320)	
	T-28D			(to R Lao AF as ....)	
				Col Pay/Pays Air Service, Scone NSW	.88
				(recov. from Thong Hi Hin AB, Laos: trucked overland to Bangkok, shipped to Australia 12.88)	
				Ray Delaney & Geoff Milne, Melbourne VIC	89/90
			VH-LAO	John Raynor & Jack McDonald, Essendon VIC	91/92
				(rebuilt Essendon VIC, ff 16.4.92 as "0-38320")	
				forced landing, crashed, Wangaratta VIC	13.6.92
200-392 •	T-28B	Bu138321	N52897	Armoflex Inc, Santa Maria CA	6.84
			N28AF	Armoflex Inc, Santa Maria CA	11.84/86
				Edward J. Elkins, Bend OR	87/88
				Michael S. Mitchell, Klamath Falls OR	92
200-396 •	T-28B	Bu138325		(to Philippines AF as 53-138325)	
	AT-28D		N2061Q	Business Air Charter, Portland OR	3.8.89/92
200-397 •	T-28B	Bu138326		USNAM, NAS Pensacola FL	90
200-398 •	T-28B	Bu138327		(to US Army as 138327)	73
				USAFM, McClellan AFB CA	88/89
				(displ. as "US Army 138327")	
200-400 •	T-28B	Bu138329	N5440W	Courtesy Aircraft Inc, Rockford IL	8.84
				Cunningham Aviation Inc, Lawton OK	86
				Colonel Aircraft Sales Inc, Oklahoma City OK	87/92
200-401 •	T-28B	Bu138330	N54419	ntu:	
			N4781K	Courtesy Aircraft Sales Inc, Rockford IL	7.84
				State of Alaska Division of Forestry	8.84
			N217SF	State of Alaska, Anchorage AK	1.85/92
200-402 •	T-28B	Bu138331	N5442X	Courtesy Aircraft Inc, Rockford IL	8.84
			N8331R	John M. Ware, Atlanta GA	6.85/92
200-405 •	T-28B	Bu138334		(tfd. to USAF as 138334)	
			N394W	Westair International USA Inc, Monument CO	6.86
				Mystic Marketing Co Inc, Mystic CT	87/88
				Evergreen Ventures Inc, McMinnville OR	89/92
200-410 •	T-28B	Bu138339	N8065E	Bill Walker & Associates, St. Simmons Is. GA	4.89
			N28XT	rereg.	11.89
				Ralph Glasser, Springfield IL	92
200-411 •	T-28B	Bu138340	N5524L	reg. res.	10.84
				J. A. Carter, Alameda CA	3.87/88
				Howard S. Roberts, Grants Pass OR	92
200-412 •	T-28B	Bu138341	N47801	State of Alaska Division of Forestry AK	8.84
			N105SF	State of Alaska, Anchorage AK	10.84/92
200-414 •	T-28B	Bu138343		Lester Industries,San Antonio TX: ex MASDC	31.3.80
				(to FA Hondurena as FAH 229)	
			N343NA	Courtesy Aircraft Inc, Rockford IL	9.85
			C-FRZQ	Walter Davidson Corp, Fort Langley BC	3.86
			N343NA	Courtesy Aircraft Inc, Rockford IL	12.87

				John Mitchell, Norwalk CT	89/92
200-418 •	T-28B	Bu138347	N83AW	Apex Associates Inc, Canby OR	2.86
				Robert E. Buschmann, Costa Mesa CA	87/88
				TCC Aviation, Roseville CA	92
200-422 •	T-28B	Bu138351		(to R. Lao AF as 0-38351)	
	AT-28D			(to Philippine AF as 55-138351)	
			N20580	Business Air Charter, Portland OR	3.8.89/92
200-423 •	T-28B	Bu138352		(to R. Lao AF as 0-38352)	
	AT-28D			(to Philippine AF as 53-138352)	
			N20523	Business Air Charter, Portland OR	3.8.89/92
200-424 •	T-28B	Bu138353		displ. on pole, Milton FL	91
				(displ. as "136000/E-701")	
200-425 •	T-28B	Bu138354	N1328B	Ralph E. Davis, Daytona Beach FL	7.89/92
200-427 •	T-28B	Bu138356	N91AW	Apex Associates, Canby OR	1.86
				APEXX Co Inc, Canby OR	6.86
				Symbolic Warriors Inc, Weston MA	87/92
200-428 •	T-28B	Bu138357	N114DH	Harry S. Doan/Doan Helicopter Inc,	
				Daytona Beach FL	7.87/88
				Robert L. Dixon, Winston Salem NC	89/92
200-435 •	T-28B	Bu138364		(to USAF as 38364)	
	T-28D			(to SVNAF as 38364)	
			N4698P	Dennis M. Sherman, West Palm Beach FL	4.84/86
				Michael D. Hynek, Rhinelander WI	87/92
200-437 •	T-28B	Bu138366		(to Philippines AF as 55-138366)	
	AT-28D		N2053C	Business Air Charter, Portland OR	3.8.89
				Duane S. Doyle, Castro Valley CA	92
218-1	RT-28B	-		(to JASDF as 63-0581)	.54
	JA3096				
219-4 •	T-28B	Bu140005		(to Philippines AF as 55-140005)	
	AT-28D		N20517	Business Air Charter, Portland OR	3.8.89/92
219-6	T-28B	Bu140007	N5443E	Courtesy Aircraft Inc, Rockford IL	8.84
				Randall Porter , Woodstock GA	86/87
				struck-off USCR	4.88
219-8 •	T-28B	Bu140009	N300JH	John V. Holden, Houston TX	11.85/86
				Menton Aircraft Inc, Bandera TX	87
				Carrier Aviation Inc, Hich Point NC	88
				Aero Dynamics Inc, Wilmington DE	92
219-11 •	T-28B	Bu140012	N283MS	M. W. Stevenson Ltd, Pasadena MD	10.85/88
				Bryan Bumgarner, Marana AZ	92
219-14 •	T-28B	Bu140015	N5827T	reg. res.	10.84/87
			N108NA	Maryland Aviation Hist. Soc., Annapolis MD	6.88/92
219-15 •	T-28B	Bu140016		(to SVNAF as ....)	
			N46984	Dennis M. Sherman, West Palm Beach FL	4.84
				Stewart Dawson, McKinney TX	86/92
219-19 •	T-28B	Bu140020	N8046D	Robert Nottke, Carson City NV	6.89
				Cermac Corp, Houston TX	92
219-24	T-28B	Bu140025		Lester Industries,San Antonio TX: ex MASDC	31.3.80
				(to FA Hondurena as FAH 233)	
			N125NA	Courtesy Aircraft Inc, Rockford IL	9.85/86
			C-FJVW	J. Johnston, Edmonton ALTA	1.87
				Don Crowe/Nahanni Helicopters	89

				crashed Lindell BC	20.8.90
			N228AC	Stallion Aircraft Inc, Bensenville IL	10.91/92
219-28	T-28B	Bu140029	N54916	reg. res.	9.84/92
219-29 •	T-28B	Bu140030		Anthony J. d'Alessandris, Reno NV	
			N130TD	Lan-Dale Co, Reno NV	1.86/87
				Victor Schilleci, Metairie LA	88/92
219-30 •	T-28B	Bu140031		Lester Industries,San Antonio TX: ex MASDC	31.3.80
				(to FA Hondurena as FAH 232)	
			N31NA	Courtesy Aircraft Inc, Rockford IL	9.85/86
			C-FMGI	R. A. Yri, Surrey BC	1.87
			N31NA	reg.	12.89
				A & T Recovery Inc, Berwyn IL	92
219-34 •	T-28B	Bu140035	N281MS	M. W. Stevenson Ltd, Pasadena MD	10.85/86
				Christopher O. Miller, Carson City NV	89/92
219-40 •	T-28B	Bu140041	N28BP	Robert J. Pond, Eden Prairie MN	5.90/92
219-43 •	T-28B	Bu140044		(to Philippines AF as 54-140044)	
	AT-28D		N2052D	Business Air Charter, Portland OR	3.8.89/92
219-45 •	T-28B	Bu140046		USNAM, NAS Corpus Christi TX	91
219-46 •	T-28B	Bu140047	N5443U	Courtesy Aircraft Inc, Rockford IL	8.84
				Southern Cal. Aviation Inc, Newport Beach CA	86/88
				sale rep., Mojave CA	89
				Robert F. Yancey, Klamath Falls OR	92
219-47 •	T-28B	Bu140048		(to US Army as 140048)	
				USAFM: Wright-Patterson AFB, Dayton OH	88
219-48 •	T-28B	Bu140049	N87AW	Apex Associates, Canby OR	1.86
				APEXX Co Inc, Canby OR	6.86
			N228DF	David M. Forrest, Dunwoody/Marietta GA	2.87/92
219-49 •	T-28B	Bu140050	N89AW	Apex Associates, Canby OR	1.86
				APEXX Co Inc, Canby OR	6.86
				Classic Aviation International, Rosharon TX	87/88
				sale rep., Southfield MI	92
226-1 •	T-28C	Bu140053	N51841	County City Defense, Laurel MS: ex MASDC	19.1.78/87
			N111TN	California Coast University, Santa Ana CA	4.88/91
			N28TN (2	California Coast University, Santa Ana CA	7.91/92
226-4 •	T-28C	Bu140056		USNAM, NAS Corpus Christi TX	82/91
226-8 •	T-28C	Bu140060	N28LD	reg. res.	92
226-9 •	T-28C	Bu140061	N9036B	reg. res.	2.87
226-10 •	T-28C	Bu140062	N9719G	Jet Dynamic Co	3.85
				Jones Flying Service, Minter City MS	4.85/86
			N128RH	Eagle Aviation Inc, Jonesboro AR	5.86
			N9719G	David K. Brady, Cartersville GA	87/92
226-11 •	T-28C	Bu140063		Bradley Air Museum, Windsor Locks CT : del.	16.1.78/81
				New England Air Museum, Windsor Locks CT	81/88
			N31431	reg. res.	92
226-12 •	T-28C	Bu140064	N55534	reg. res.	9.84/88
				Fred E. Weisbrod Aircraft Museum,Pueblo CO	88/90
226-16 •	T-28C	Bu140068	N621JT	James R. Tobul, Bamberg SC	2.92

226-19 •	T-28C	Bu140071	N28ZZ	C.E. Brehm Aircraft Sales, Devine TX	5.89
				Taylor Energy Co, New Orleans LA	.89/92
226-24 •	T-28C	Bu140076	N176RR	Classics in American Aviation Inc, Reno NV	11.85/87
				Robert M. Lanyon, Renfrew CA	88/92
226-31 •	T-28C	Bu140454		fire dump NAS South Weymouth MA	
				USS Massachusetts Memorial, Fall River MA	86/88
				(displ. as USN "137765")	
226-33 •	T-28C	Bu140456		(to SVNAF as 140456)	
	AT-28D			(to Philippines AF as 54-140456)	
			N2065J	Business Air Charter, Portland OR	3.8.89/92
226-34 •	T-28C	Bu140457		(to SVNAF as 140457)	
	AT-28D			(to Philippines AF as 54-140457)	
			N2065R	Business Air Charter, Portland OR	3.8.89/92
226-35	T-28C	Bu140458	N256X	no further information	
226-38 •	T-28C	Bu140461	N9025T	Georgia Historical Aviation Museum,	
				Stone Mountain GA: del ex MASDC	11.78/87
				(del. ex MASDC 22.11.78)	
			N404DK	Ghost Aircraft Rest. Inc, Stone Mountain GA	10.88/92
226-41 •	T-28C	Bu140464	N2800J	reg.	6.79
				Weber Mary & Pinrod Inc, Baton Rouge LA	84/87
				Mustang Aviation Inc, Fairfield NJ	88
				Stuart M. Lamb, Amesbury MA	92
226-50 •	T-28C	Bu140473	N31425	Michael D. Vadeboncoeur, Danville IL	3.92
226-52 •	T-28C	Bu140475	N9025Y	Georgia Historical Aviation Museum,	
				Stone Mountain GA : del. ex MASDC	11.78/92
226-57 •	T-28C	Bu140480	N2800N	George J. Rivera, Pensacola FL	84
				sale rep., Auburn CA	86/92
226-58 •	T-28C	Bu140481		Pima Air Museum, Tucson AZ: del ex MASDC	10.3.77/88
226-65 •	T-28C	Bu140488	N28CX	reg.	1.91
				Eric C. Paul, Charlotte NC	92
226-66 •	T-28C	Bu140489	N9019L	Civil Defence Council, Waynesboro MS	.78/88
				(del. ex MASDC 9.11.78)	
				Wayne Rescue Unit, Waynesboro MS	92
226-69 •	T-28C	Bu140492		IN Museum of Natural History,Indianapolis IN	88
			N4168H	Courtesy Aircraft Inc, Rockford IL	3.91/92
226-78 •	T-28C	Bu140501	N9749N	Mystic Marketing Co Inc, Mystic CT	1.87
			N900BW	William W. Whorley, Greensboro GA	12.88/92
226-86 •	T-28C	Bu140509	N280BJ	AMCEP Inc, Tucson AZ	9.91
				John Noble, Upper Lake CA	92
226-88 •	T-28C	Bu140511	N140NA	Airplane Sales International, Beverly Hills CA	10.85
				King City Aviation Inc, King City CA	86
				Alvin P. Grant, Fountain Valley CA	87/89
			N140AG	Alvin P. Grant, Fountain Valley CA	12.89/92
226-91 •	T-28C	Bu140514	N2141D	Dennis G. Buehn, Long Beach CA	3.83
				Frank G. Crompton, Torrance CA	84
				Byron M. Tarnutzer, Costa Mesa CA	86/87
				Ray D. Fulwiler, Green Bay WI	88/92
226-93 •	T-28C	Bu140516		(to FA Zaire as FG 516)	

			N99141	Euroworld Ltd	2.77
				William Nelson, El Paso TX	12.77/78
				(del. via Biggin Hill UK 16.12.77 / 17.4.78)	
			N99153(2	R. J. Enterprises, Robstown TX	84
				Raymond F. Mabrey, McAllen TX	86/87
				William R. Montague, Oakland CA	88/92
				(note: id. confused with 226-153: que se)	
226-96 •	T-28C	Bu140519	N9019N	County Civil Defense, Jackson MS: ex MASDC	9.11.78
				Civil Defense Council, Waynesboro MS	84/88
				Laurel Flying Service, Laurel MS	92
226-100 •	T-28C	Bu140523	N470	reg.	7.90
				James L. Maroney, Fargo ND	92
226-101 •	T-28C	Bu140524		sold as scap ex NAS Corpus Christi TX	
				Ken Hilderbrant/Warrior Aviation,	
				Burlington CO (rebuild to fly)	86
226-102 •	T-28C	Bu140525	C-GTTE	Helair Enterprises Ltd, Delta BC	5.12.91
226-103 •	T-28C	Bu140526	N7160B	reg.	6.90
			N526D	Brian G. Cole, Tucson AZ	12.91/92
226-105 •	T-28C	Bu140528	N71546	Trojan Aircraft Inc, Matthews MD	2.90
				Koenig Farms Inc, Yuma CO	92
226-108 •	T-28C	Bu140531	N91550	Courtesy Aircraft Inc, Rockford IL	11.87/88
			N944SD	Stuart W. Dingman, Belleville MI	9.89/92
				(note: Bu140531 listed with Indiana Museum	
				of Military History, Indianapolis IN 88)	
226-110 •	T-28C	Bu140533		(to Philippine AF as 40533)	
				displ. Villamor AB, Manila	89/91
226-113 •	T-28C	Bu140536	N31428	William T. Ingram, Catlin IL	3.92
226-114 •	T-28C	Bu140537	N7164Z	Steve J. Masket, Los Angeles CA	9.90
			N537Z	Steve J. Masket, Los Angeles CA	10.90/92
226-116 •	T-28C	Bu140539	N4993Y	Confederate Air Force, Harlingen TX	10.78/84
				(del. ex MASDC 18.12.78)	
			N28TN (1	California Coast University, Santa Ana CA	5.85/88
			N166ER	Cinema Air Inc, Houston TX/Carlsbad CA	5.90
226-119 •	T-28C	Bu140542	N5321X	Courtesy Aircraft Inc, Rockford IL	1.88
				sale rep., San Jose CA	92
226-120 •	T-28C	Bu140543	N80269	Harry Doan/Doan Helicopters, Daytona Beach	7.89
				Maruna Airplane Co, Akron OH	2.90/92
226-124 •	T-28C	Bu140547	N2800Q	reg.	6.79
				Tifton Contractors Inc, Tifton GA	84
				H. C. Dodson Farms Inc, Tifton GA	86
				Bardolph Limited, New York NY	86/90
				op: Scandinavian Historic Flight	86/91
				(arr. UK for airshows 23.6.86, based Norway)	
				J. Sporrer, Toulous Blagnac, France	.91
			F-AZHN	J. Sporrer/Sport Air, Tolous Blagnac	.91/92
226-125 •	T-28C	Bu140548	N548NA	Airplane Sales International, Beverly Hills CA	10.85
				King City Aviation Inc, King City CA	86/92
226-126 •	T-28C	Bu140549	N34BJ	(to SVNAF as 140549)	
	T-28D			Aircraft Cylinder & Turbine, Sun Valley CA	1.91

				Telesite Corp, Healdsburg CA	92
226-128 •	T-28C	Bu140551	N9748Y	Westair International USA Inc, Monument CO	11.86
				John H. Batto, Rohnert Park CA	87/92
226-130 •	T-28C	Bu140553		USAFM: Robins AFB GA	87/89
226-134 •	T-28C	Bu140557		USMC Museum, MCAS Quantico VA	88
226-140 •	T-28C	Bu140563	N563GH	Charles G. Hyde, Roanoke TX	5.89
				John Gasho, Phoenix AZ	89
			ZK-JGS	John I. Greenstreet, Auckland	11.89/90
				Trojan Syndicate, Ardmore	91/92
226-143 •	T-28C	Bu140566	N556EB	Emil F. Blomberg, Reno NV	12.85/86
				Sonoma Valley Aircraft Limited, Sonoma CA	87
				Robert D.Marshall, San Rafael CA	88/92
226-147 •	T-28C	Bu140570		Pima County Air Museum, Tucson AZ	88
226-152 •	T-28C	Bu140575		Pima County Air Museum, Tucson AZ	86/88
226-153 •	T-28C	Bu140576		(to FA Zaire as FG576)	
			N99153(3	Euroworld Ltd	
				William Nelson, El Paso TX	78
			N289RD(2	Ronald L. Doney, North Attleboro MA	6.79/84
				Alan Preston/Flytex Inc, Dallas TX	86/87
				Alan Preston/Fighting Air Command,Dallas TX	88
				Kenneth W. Stowe, North Little Rock AR	89
				Joseph M. Rieger, Snohomish WA	92
				(note: id. confused with 226-93: que se)	
226-155 •	T-28C	Bu140578	N8039S	Bert J. Zwaagstra, Mesquite NM	12.88/92
226-158 •	T-28C	Bu140581	N581JS	Maryland Warbird Museum, White Marsh MD	1.91/92
226-163 •	T-28C	Bu140586	N2800R		6.79
				George J. Rivera, Pensacola FL	84
				sale rep., Mojave CA	86/87
				Courtesy Aircraft Inc, Rockford IL	88/91
			N128CT	Jerry C. Janes & Associates, Rockford IL	7.91/92
226-166 •	T-28C	Bu140589	G-USAF	Barry Walker, Sheffield	28.6.82
				(stored dism. Marlow UK 82/89; Booker 89/90)	
				Tom Rogers BC : shipped to Canada ex UK	23.1.91
			C-FPTR	415150 BC Ltd, Boundary Bay BC	23.3.92
226-170 •	T-28C	Bu140593	N9022Y	County Civil Defense, Jefferson City MO	11.78
				(del. ex MASDC 17.11.78)	
				Civil Defense Council, Greenwood MO	84
				Southwest Aviation Inc, Fairacres NM	86
				Ronald S. Miller, Woodland Hills CA	87
				crashed on takeoff, Van Nuys CA	1.1.87
				Courtesy Aircraft Inc, Rockford IL	88
200-179 •	T-28C	Bu140602	N3948B	James P. MacIvor, Miami FL	2.84
			N602JM	James P. MacIvor, Miami FL	4.84/92
200-184 •	T-28C	Bu140607	N70447	Harry S. Doan/Doan Helicopters,	
				Daytona Beach FL	12.88/92
200-187 •	T-28C	Bu140610	N8084V	Baron Aviation Services Ltd, Vichy MO	2.89/92
200-202 •	T-28C	Bu140625	N30625	Raymond J. Germain, Houston TX	7.90/92
226-214 •	T-28C	Bu140637	N65647	Bert J. Zwaagstra, Mesquite NM	12.90
			N28BZ	Bert J. Zwaagstra, Mesquite NM	7.91/92

226-216 •	T-28C	Bu140639	N775CH	Avtec Leasing & Sales Inc, Titusville FL	8.86/88
				crashed, dest., Tico FL	10.3.89
226-222 •	T-28C	Bu140645	N9016R	reg.	11.78
				Delhi Richland Parish Civil Defense, Delhi LA	84/86
				Steve Martin, Delhi LA	87/92
226-226 •	T-28C	Bu140649		USAFM: Robins AFB GA	87
			N649JS	Maryland Warbird Museum, White Marsh MD	92
226-227 •	T-28C	Bu140650	N51928	County City Defense, Laurel MS : ex MASDC	28.2.78/87
				Robby R. Jones, Minter City MS	88/92
226-229 •	T-28C	Bu140652	N652T	Lan-Dale Co, Reno NV	10.85/87
			N28LC	Lud J. Corrao, Reno NV	10.88/92
226-230 •	T-28C	Bu140653	N10260	reg.	4.79
				Warbirds Inc, Miami FL	84
				Vincent Tirado, Miami FL	86
			N653DB	Donald F. Bellek, Zephyr Cove NV	4.87/92
226-234 •	T-28C	Bu140654	N75947	Jeff J. Bumgarner, Tucson AZ	9.91/92
226-235 •	T-28C	Bu140658	N5094J	Courtesy Aircraft Inc, Rockford IL	11.87/88
				Fulwiler Air Inc, Green Bay WI	92
226-236 •	T-28C	Bu140659	N75ES	rep. displ. Pate Museum of Transportation, Ft. Worth TX	88
226-238 •	T-28C	Bu140661	N661NA	Airplane Sales International, Beverly Hills CA	10.85
				King City Aviation Inc, King City CA	88/92
226-239 •	T-28C	Bu140662	N22134	reg.	3.90
				Gary L. Fritzler, Denver CO	92
226-243 •	T-28C	Bu140666	N9022N	County Civil Defense, Jefferson City MO (del. ex MASDC 17.11.78)	11.78
				Civil Defense Council, Greenwood MO	84
				Robert L. Waltrip/Lone Star Flight Museum, Houston TX	86/88
				Louis E. Fischer, Kissimmee FL	89
				Sherman Aircraft Sales,West Palm Beach FL	5.89
				Joel C. Hilgenberg, New Orleans LA	92
252-2 •	T-28C	Bu146239		IN Museum of Military History,Indianapolis IN	88
			N4168E	Courtesy Aircraft Inc, Rockford IL	3.91
				Kipnis Inc, Dover DE	92
252-3 •	T-28C	Bu146240	N240CJ	Gerald A. Smith, Long Beach CA	7.86/87
				Coke V. Stuart, Valdosta GA	88
				Jeffrey S. Gorman, Mansfield OH	89/91
			N240CG	Jeffrey S. Gorman, Mansfield OH	7.91/92
252-5 •	T-28C	Bu146242	N1188C	Fast Corporation, Wilmington DE	7.86/92
252-9 •	T-28C	Bu146246	N2800M	reg.	6.79
				M.A. Inc, Oshkosh WI	84/92
252-12 •	T-28C	Bu146249	N6535K	Richard G. Sugden, Wilson WY	11.90
			N28CV	Richard G. Sugden, Wilson WY	1.91/92
252-13 •	T-28C	Bu146250		World Aircraft Museum, Calhoun GA	88
252-16 •	T-28C	Bu146253	N912KK	Southern California Avn., Corona del Mar CA	1.86
				Daniel W. Lawson, Las Vegas NV	88/92

			N311LK	reg res.	1.92
252-17 •	T-28C	Bu146254	N910KK	Southern California Avn, Corona del Mar CA	1.86/87
				John F. Hulls, St Cloud MN	.87
			N254PJ	John F. Hulls, St Cloud MN	7.88
				Seahorse Aviation, Rye NY	922
252-18 •	T-28C	Bu146255		(to FA Zaire as FG 255)	
			N49308	reg. pending	12.77/78
				(del. via Biggin Hill UK 16.12.77/17.4.78)	
			N39408	rereg.	4.79
				Sunmaster Awnings Inc, Mishawaka IN	84/87
			C-GJMT(2	Aviation Maintenance Ltd, Ste Marie ONT	1.88
252-20 •	T-28C	Bu146257		USAFM, Robbins AFB GA	88
252-23 •	T-28C	Bu146260	N260AN	Aero Nostalgia Inc, Stockton CA	8.86
				Cecil H. Harp, Canby OR	87
				Richard S. Drury, Goleta CA	88/92
252-24 •	T-28C	Bu146261	N728C	Hooked On Trojans, Sebastopol CA	3.91/92
252-25 •	T-28C	Bu146262	N7160C	reg.	6.90
				Dennis A. Smith, Salem OR	92
252-29	T-28C	Bu146266		(to FA Zaire as ....)	
	T-28D		N99163	William Nelson, El Paso TX	78
				(del. via Biggin Hill UK 23.1.78/20.6.78)	
				sale rep., Tulsa OK	84/92
				(FAA quotes id. as "252-295")	
252-33 •	T-28C	Bu146270	N9746Z	Westair International USA Inc, Monument CO	11.86
				Mystic Marketing Co Inc, Mystic CT	87
			N128PS	Wayne A. Sutton, Brooks GA	5.88
				T Bird Inc, Hollywood CA	2.91
				Pierre Dague, Saint Rambert d'Albion, France	.91
				air to air collision Saint Rambert d'Albion (Dague k.)	8.9.91
252-36 •	T-28C	Bu146273	N14NW	Northwest Warbirds Inc, Twin Falls ID	2.87
		N46273		Gary M. Boutz, San Jose CA & Reno NV	6.87/92
252-44 •	T-28C	Bu146281	N2215D	reg.	3.90
				Gene S. Nunn, Elkhart KS	92
252-46 •	T-28C	Bu146283	N1184T	Time Aviation, Tucson AZ : del. ex MASDC	24.8.81
				Roland S. Bond, Jean NV	84
				Robby R. Jones, Minter City MS	86
				Airplane Services Inc, Benoit MS	87
				Richard C. Slaney, Eugene OR	88
				William A. Schiro, Okemos MI	92
252-49 •	T-28C	Bu146286	N146GB	Gerald S. Beck, Wahpeton ND	12.85/88
				Gregory A. Fieber, St Paul MN	89
			N146GF	Gregory A. Fieber, St Paul MN	3.90/92
252-50 •	T-28C	Bu146287	N2304K	Peter Knox/City Blue Print, Allentown PA	75/92
252-51 •	T-28C	Bu146289		(to Republic of Congo AF as ....)	
	T-28D			(to FA Zaire as FA-289, later FG-289)	.64
			N99153 (1	Euroworld Ltd	2.77
				cr. during del. flight, Limoges, France	14.12.77
				Norfolk & Suffolk Aviation Museum,	
				Flixton UK (displ. as "146289/2W")	81/9
- •	T-28A	-		(to FA Sandanista as ....)	
	Fennec			recov. by Victoria Aircraft Maintenance BC	.87
			C-FXRD	R. B. Diaper, Calgary ALTA	11.7.88
				(id. quoted as "521": probably 174-521)	

-	•	T-28A Fennec	-	 C-GMWN	(to FA Sandanista as ....) recov. by Victoria Aircraft Maintenance BC M. Langford, Vancouver BC (id. quoted as "621")	 .87 27.9.89
-	•	T-28A Fennec	-		(to FA Sandanista as 162) recov. by Victoria Aircraft Maintenance BC	 .87
-		T-28	-	EP-CMT	no further information	61
-	•	T-28A T-28R-2 Nomair	-	N28DS	Dwight Reimer, Shafter CA (Hamilton Nomair c/n 10) (flew as USN "150099/DR206") John B. Wallace, Grants Pass OR	78/83 92
-	•	T-28A	-		(to FA Mexicana as T28-957) stored dism. Santa Rosa Air Centre CA (poor condition, with two other FAM T-28s)	 90
-	•	T-28A	-	 N367NA	(to FA Haiti as ....) Courtesy Aircraft Inc, Rockford IL David Huff, Schuylkill Haven PA (id. quoted as "367")	 9.85/87 88/92
-		T-28B	-	N4614	reg. res. (id. quoted as "52-9263")	9.86/92
-	•	T-28B T-28D	-	N5015L	Courtesy Aircraft Inc, Rockford IL sale rep., Van Nuys CA (id. quoted as "557": prob. 174-557)	1.88 92
-		T-28D	-	N39408	William Nelson, El Paso TX (id. quoted as "H750")	78
-	•	T-28	-	N80401	Courtesy Aircraft, Rockford IL (id. quoted as "53-7673")	3.89/92
-		T-28D	-	 N99412	(to FA Zaire as ....) David C. Tallichet/MARC, Chino CA (id. quoted as "122")	 78/92
-		T-28D	-	 N99414	(to FA Zaire as ....) David C. Tallichet/MARC, Chino CA (del. to USA via Biggin Hill/Stornoway 4.78) (id. quoted as "222")	 4.78/92
-	•	T-28A Fennec	-		(to Argentine Navy as ....) displ. on pole, Punta Indio AB, Argentina (displ. as "1-A-251")	 91
-	•	T-28D	-		(to R. Lao AF as 3402) recov. Thong Hi Hin by Col Pay, Scone NSW	 .88
-	•	T-28A	-	HI-276	Seagull Enterprises Inc	.77
-	•	T-28A	-		USAFM, Keesler AFB TX displ. as "13389"	88
-	•	T-28A	-		(to FA Mexicana as T28-957) stored dism. Santa Rosa Air Centre CA (poor condition, with two other FAM T-28s)	 90

64-2206	NA-64	RCAF3350		Ernie Simmons, Tillsonburg ONT	c46/3.9.70
			C-GCWY	Canadian Warplane Hertiage, Mount Hope ONT	88/89
				(rebuilt Hamilton)	
-	NA-64	RCAF3362		Ernie Simmons, Tillsonburg ONT	c46/3.9.70
-	NA-64	RCAF3369		Ernie Simmons, Tillsonburg ONT	c46/3.9.70
				Canadian Warplane Hertiage	88
-	NA-64	RCAF3381		Ernie Simmons, Tillsonburg ONT	c46/3.9.70
				Confederate Air Force, Hobbs NM	88
64-2161	NA-64	RCAF3396		Ernie Simmons, Tillsonburg ONT	c46/3.9.70
				Canadian Warplane Heritage, Mount Hope ONT	
				to US owner	81
64-2150	NA-64	RCAF3397		Ernie Simmons, Tillsonburg ONT	c46/3.9.70
			N4735G	Pima County Air Museum, Tucson AZ	88
64-2419	NA-64	RCAF3400		Ernie Simmons, Tillsonburg ONT	c46/3.9.70
				Indiana Museum of Military History, Indianapolis IN 88	
64-2157	NA-64	RCAF3404		Ernie Simmons, Tillsonburg ONT	c46/3.9.70
				Reynolds Aviation Museum, Wetaskiwin ALTA	88
-	NA-64	RCAF3406		Ernie Simmons, Tillsonburg ONT	c46/3.9.70
				Tom Crevasse FL (restored to fly)	
			N3406	Dave Keller, Toledo OH	88
-	NA-64	RCAF3411		Ernie Simmons, Tillsonburg ONT	c46/3.9.70
				noted mounted on Saloon roof	
-	NA-64	RCAF3415		Ernie Simmons, Tillsonburg ONT	c46/3.9.70
			N3415C	Musee de L'Air et L'Espace, Paris-Le Bourget	30.9.87/90
				destroyed in Museum hangar fire, Le Bourget	17.5.90
-	NA-64	RCAF3425		Ernie Simmons, Tillsonburg ONT	c46/3.9.70
				Danny Linkous, Sumter SC	88
64-2223	NA-64	RCAF3430		Ernie Simmons, Tillsonburg ONT	c46/3.9.70
				Western Canada Aviation Museum,	
				Winnipeg MAN	88
-	NA-64	RCAF3445		Ernie Simmons, Tillsonburg ONT	c46/3.9.70
				Bob Radcliffe ONT (flies)	88
-	NA-64	RCAF3448		Ernie Simmons, Tillsonburg ONT	c46/3.9.70
64-2214	NA-64	RCAF3450		Ernie Simmons, Tillsonburg ONT	c46/3.9.70
			N4574Y	Confederate Air Force, Hobbs NM	88
-	NA-64	RCAF3452		Ernie Simmons, Tillsonburg ONT	c46/3.9.70
-	NA-64	RCAF3454		Ernie Simmons, Tillsonburg ONT	c46/3.9.70
				Tom Dietrich, Guelph ONT (rest.87)	
				crashed and destroyed	10.87
64-3024	NA-64	RCAF3458		Ernie Simmons, Tillsonburg ONT	c46/3.9.70
				Reynolds Aviation Museum, Wetaskiwin ALTA	88
-	NA-64	RCAF3459		Ernie Simmons, Tillsonburg ONT	c46/3.9.70
64-3040	NA-64	RCAF3414		Ernie Simmons, Tillsonburg ONT	c46/3.9.70
				Whereatt's Warbirds, Assiniboia SASK	88

14-143	AT-16 Mk. IIB	42-606	 PH-UEK OO-GDD	(to RAF as FE409) Rijksluchtvaartdienst, Scheveningen COGEA Nouvelle, Ostende cancelled as sold in Congo (rep. possibly to Katanga AF)	 26.10.60 29.10.62
14-186 •	AT-16 Mk. IIB	42-649	 4X-ARI	(to RCAF as FE452) Avitor Ltd, Tel Aviv	 .63/72
14-190 •	AT-16 Mk. IIB	42-653	 PH-UEI OO-JBW	(to RAF as FE456) Rijksluchtvaartdienst, Scheveningen COGEA Nouvelle, Ostende J. Theil, Wevelgem; later Monchengladbach Mr Honkoop, Veen, Netherlands displ. bicycle shop, Boxmeer, Netherlands	 .8.65 15.2.66 7.70 71-
14-201 •	AT-16 Mk. IIB	42-664		(to RAF as FE467) (to Swiss AF as U-332) Museum de Schweizerischen Fliergertruppe, Dubendorf	 79/85
14-205	AT-16 Mk. IIB	42-668	 VT-CQN	(to RAF as FE471) F. J. Mobsby Baroda Rayon Corp, Juhu written-off nr Boisar	 12.47 3.9.77
14-245 •	AT-16 Mk. IIB	42-708		(to RAF as FE511) (to RSwAF/Flyvapnet as Fv16128) Luftfartmuseet, Stockholm-Bromma, Sweden	 79
14-299 •	AT-16 Mk. IIB	42-762		(to RAF as FE565) to Flygvapnet as Fv Nr16030 High Chapparall theme park Hillerstorp Sweden	 82/92
14-324 •	AT-16 Mk. IIB	42-787	 G-AXCR D-FHGK	(to RAF as FE590) (to Swiss AF as U-322) reg. G. Roth, Neckarelz	 27.3.69 10.69/72 87
14-355 •	AT-16 Mk IIB	42-818		(to RAF as FE621) RCAF as 'BE-M' Sola Air Base, Stavanger incomplete	 89
14-366 •	AT-16 Mk. IIB	42-829		(to RAF as FE632) (to RSwAF/Flyvapnet as Fv16109) Flyvapnets Museum, Malmslatt, Sweden	 79/85
14-429 •	AT-16 Mk. IIB	42-892	 G-BTXI	(to RAF as FE695) To Flygvapnet as Fv16105 Fighter Collection Duxford	 .46 25.10.91/92
14-543 •	AT-16 Mk. IIB	42-12296		(to RAF as FE809) (to RNAF as B-181) : reported preserved Gilze Rijen	 77 81
14-545 •	AT-16 Mk. IIB	42-12298		(to RAF as FE876) (to Swiss AF as U-328) Museum de Schweizerischen Fliergertruppe, Dubendorf	 79/85

14-565 •	AT-16	42-12318		(to RAF as FE831)	
	Mk. IIB			(to RSwAF/Flyvapnet as Fv16010)	
				Luftfartmuseet, Stockholm-Arlanda, Sweden	79/85
14-639 •	AT-16	42-12392		(to RAF as FE905)	
	Mk. IIB			(to RDAF as 329)	
			LN-BNM	Fjellfly S. Kjetilson, Skien	5.11.61
				C o A exp. 31.12.68: canc.	29.1.73
				Historic Aircraft Museum, Southend	72
				London Bridge War Museum	7.83
				RAF Museum (on loan to Newark Air Mus.)	92
14-641 •	AT-16	42-12394		(to RAF as FE907)	
	Mk. IIB			(to RNAF as B-64)	
			PH-FAR		
				Militaire Luchtvaart Museum, Soersterberg	79/85
				(mocked-up as Fokker D.XXI "219")	
14-664 •	AT-16	42-12417		(to RAF as FE930)	
	Mk. IIB			(to RNAF as B-163)	
				Myverdal	66
				to Gordon King, Windsor, Berks	87
14-706	AT-16	42-12459		(to RAF as FE972)	
	Mk. IIB		VT-CQD		11.47
				A. Zamplino, Bangalore	2.12.49
				R. S. Cambata, Bombay	
14-710 •	AT-16	42-12463		(to RAF as FE976)	
	Mk. IIB		N1284	Robert H. Hawk,	
				Westfield, IN.	10.92
14-718	AT-16	42-12471		(to RAF as FH150)	
	Mk. IIB			(to RNAF as B-168)	
				Myverdal	85
				to North Weald spares use, Harvard Team	87
14-719	AT-16	42-12472		(to RAF as FE985)	
	Mk. IIB			(to RNAF as B-176)	
			PH-NID	ret. to RNAF as B-176: preserved	77
14-720 •	AT-16	42-12473		(to RAF as FE986)	
	Mk. IIB			(to RNAF as B-174): reported preserved	.66/77
14-724	AT-16	42-12477		(to RAF as FE990)	
	Mk. IIB		PH-NIB	crashed	17.8.59
				(major components used in rebuild of OO-GDQ)	
14-725 •	AT-16	42-12478		(to RAF as FE991)	
	Mk. IIB			(to RSwAF/Flyvapnet as Fv16028)	
				Svedinos Bil Och Flygmuseum, Ugglarp, Sweden	75/88
14-726 •	AT-16	42-12479		(to RAF as FE992: RCAF FE992)	
	Mk. IIB			(to R Swedeish AF as Fv16047/LMA)	
			LN-MAA	J. Murer, Oslo	12.9.72
			G-BDAM	D. G. Jones	1.4.75
				Norman Lees & Euan English, North Weald	87/92
14-730	AT-16	42-12483		(to RAF as FE996)	
	Mk. IIB			(to RNAF as B-186)	
			PH-NIC	ret. to RNAF as B-186: wfu	.64
14-733 •	AT-16	42-12486		(to RAF as FE999)	
	Mk. IIB			(to RNAF as B-177)	
				Militaire Luchtvaart Museum, Gilze-Rijen	77/85

14-739 •	AT-16 Mk. IIB	42-12492		(to RAF as FH105)	
				(to RNAF as B-178)	
				Soesterburg	70
				Atop pylon Maasbracht	72/89
14-748 •	AT-16 Mk. IIB	42-12501		(to RAF as FH114)	
				(to RDAF as 31-306)	
				Mr. J. Utzon, Hellebeek	31.5.61
				Dansk Veteranflysamlung, Skjern	79/85
14-764 •	AT-16 Mk. IIB	42-12517		(to RAF as FH130)	
				(to RNAF as B-165) : instructional use	.66/77
				Antony Fokker Scvhool, Den Haag	72/92
14-765 •	AT-16 Mk. IIB	42-12518		(to RAF as FH131)	
				(to RNAF as B-175)	
				Militaire Luchtvaart Museum, Soersterberg	77/85
14-770 •	AT-16 Mk. IIB	42-12523		(to RAF as FH136)	
				(to RNAF as B-193) : reported preserved	77
				Westerschouwen,Schelde Estuary, Holland	92
14-772 •	AT-16 Mk. IIB	42-12525		(to RAF as FH138)	
				(to RSwAF/Flyvapnet as Fv16033)	
				Svedinos Bil Och Flygmuseum, Ugglarp, Sweden	75/88
14-773 •	AT-16 Mk. IIB	42-12526		(to RAF as FH139)	
				(to RNAF as B-185) : reported preserved	77
14-787 •	AT-16 Mk. IIB	42-12540		(to RAF as FH153)	
				(to RNAF as B-158)	
			PH-PPS		
			PH-HTC		
			G-BBHK	Personal Plane Services, Booker	.73
				Bob Warner Aviation Exeter	87/92
14A-807 •	AT-16 Mk. IIB	43-12508		(to RAF as FS667)	
				(to RNAF as B-182)	
				P-47 mock up "A Bridge Too Far"	76
				remains only Gilze Rijenl	92
14A-808 •	AT-16 Mk. IIB	43-12509		(to RAF as FS668)	
				(to RNAF as B-182)	
				Aviodome Museum, Amsterdam-Schiphol	77/85
14A-868 •	AT-16 Mk. IIB	43-12569		(to RAF as FS728)	
				(to RNAF as B-104)	
			PH-SKL		
			G-BAFM	Hon. Patrick Lindsay, Booker	4.5.73
				John Parkes, Sandown IOW	87
				Neil Moffat, West Sussex	92
14A-927 •	AT-16 Mk. IIB	43-12626		(to RAF as FS787)	
				(to R Indian AF as HT291)	
				Indian Air Force Museum, Palam, New Delhi	79
14A-966 •	AT-16 Mk. IIB	43-12667		(to RAF as FS826)	
				(to RDAF as 31-309)	
				Flyvevabnet Museum, Vaerlose, Denmark	79/85
				Danmarks Flyvemuseum, Billund	14.10.86/92
14A-1020	AT-16 Mk. IIB	43-12721		(to RAF as FS880)	
				(to RNAF as B-135)	

			PH-BKT		
14A-1053•	AT-16 Mk. IIB	43-12754		(to RAF as FS913) (to RNAF as B-136) : to Dutch Navy/MLD reported preserved	 77
14A-1055	AT-16 Mk. IIB	43-12756		(to RAF as FS915) (to RNAF as B-41) : sold in USA	 .68
14A-1057•	AT-16 Mk. IIB	43-12758		(to RAF as FS917) (to RDAF as 31-310)	
			LN-BNN	Fjellfly S. Kjetilson, Skien canc. 14.6.71: stored: to playground Sweden High Chaparral Wild West Village, Sweden	5.1.61/71 71 85
14A-1100•	AT-16 Mk. IIB	43-12801		(to RAF as FS960) (to RNAF as B-184) Militaire Luchtvaart Museum, Soersterberg	 77/85
14A-1124	AT-16 Mk. IIB	43-12825		(to RAF as FS984) ZS-DMN (to Syrian AF as ....)	 reg. .55 6.56
14A-1184•	AT-16 Mk. IIB	43-12885		(to RAF as FT144) (to RNAF as B-59)	
			PH-KLU	Lelystad Museum	85/89
14A-1188•	AT-16 Mk. IIB	43-12889		(to RAF as FT148) (to RNAF as B-82) Leeuwarden Dump Badhoevedorp (Aviodome storage reduced to spares/scrapped	 63/82 83
14A-1203•	AT-16 Mk. IIB	43-12904		(to RAF as FT223) (to RNAF as B-69) Nederlands National Oorlogs en Verzetsmus.	 85
14A-1216 •	AT-16 Mk. IIB	43-12917		(to RAF as FT176) (to RNAF as B-56) (to Dutch Navy/MLD as 043)	
			PH-KMA	Skylight. J. Daams collision Spitfire AB910, Bex in store pending rebuild Nieuw Loosdrecht	 20.8.78 92
14A-1268•	AT-16 Mk. IIB	43-12969		(to RAF as FT228) (to RNAF as B-73) Aviodome Museum, Amsterdam-Schiphol Bevrijdende Vleugels, Veghel	 77/85 88/92
14A-1269•	AT-16 Mk. IIB	43-12970		(to RAF as FT229) (to RNAF as B-45)	
			PH-SKM		
			G-AZKI	Doug Arnold/Warbirds of GB Ltd, Blackbushe	24.2.72
			F-AZDS	based Montpellier	.84/89
14A-1273	AT-16 Mk. IIB	43-12974		(to RAF as FT233) (to RNAF as B-61) : to Dutch Navy/MLD as 12-3	
			PH-NGR		
			PH-NIE		
14A-1362	AT-16 Mk. IIB	43-13063		(to RAF as FT322)	
			ZS-DMK	reg. (to Syrian AF as ....)	.55 6.56
14A-1363•	AT-16 Mk. IIB	43-13064		(to RAF as FT323) (to RNAF as B-19)	
		PH-SKK			

			G-AZSC	Doug Arnold/Warbirds of GB Ltd, Blackbushe	23.6.72
				Gary Numan, White Waltham	85/88
				Gary Numan, White Waltham	85/88
				Gary Numan, Duxford	91/92
				(painted to represent 'Zero')	
14A-1365•	AT-16 Mk. IIB	43-13066		(to RAF as FT325)	
				(to RNAF as B-15)	
			PH-NIF	ret. to RNAF as B-15; wfu	64
14A-1368•	AT-16 Mk. IIB	43-13069		(to RAF as FT328)	
				(to RNAF as B-16)	
			PH-NIZ	ret. to RNAF as B-16; wfu	64
14A-1420•	AT-16 Mk. IIB	43-13121		(to RAF as FT380)	
				(to RDAF as 31-324)	
				Egeskov Veteranmuseum, Denmark	79/92
14A-1422	AT-16 Mk. IIB	43-13123		(to RAF as FT382)	
				(to RNAF as B-66) : sold in USA	.68
14A-1431 •	AT-16	43-13132		(to RAF as FT391)	
				(to RNAF as B-97)	
			PH-HON	Sir W. D. Roberts, Strathallan	.71
			G-AZBN	Sir W. D. Roberts, Strathallan	18.1.72
				Colt Executive Aviation, Staverton	86
				Tudor Owen/op. Old Flying Machine Company, Duxford	87
				Swaygate, Hove, West Sussex	92
14A-1432	AT-16	43-13133		(to RAF as FT392)	Mk. IIB
			ZS-DML	reg.	.55
				(to Syrian AF as ....)	6.56
14A-1444•	AT-16 Mk. IIB	43-13145		(to RAF as FT404)	
				(to RNAF as B-71)	
			PH-MLM	Militaire Luchtvaart Museum, Gilze-Rijen	85
14A-1459•	AT-16 Mk. IIB	43-13160		(to RAF as FT419)	
				(to RNAF B-103)	
				KLM Bedrijfsschool	72
				Valkenburg (restoration)	23.10.86
				MLM Kamp Zeist	86/92
14A-1462•	AT-16 Mk. IIB	43-13163		(to RAF as FT422)	
				(to RNAF)	
				Brasschaat, Belgium	
				Brussels Museum	.87
				stored Tieln, Belgium	92
14A-1467	AT-16 Mk. IIB	43-13168		(to RAF as FT427)	
				(to RNAF as B-118)	
			PH-TOO		
14A-1494 •	AT-16 Mk. IIB	43-13195		(to RAF as FT454)	
				(to RNAF as B-84) : to Dutch Navy/MLD as 098	
			OO-DAF	Eric Vormezeele, Brasschaat	4.8.72/92
14- •	AT-16 Mk.IIB	-		(to RAF as F.......)	
				(to RSwAF/Flyvapnet as Fv16028)	
				Svedinos Bil Och Flygmus., Sloinge, Sweden	79
14- •	AT-16 Mk.IIB	-		(to RAF as F.......)	
				(to RSwAF/Flyvapnet as Fv16030)	
				High Chaparral Wild West Village, Hillerstorp, Sweden	85

14- •	AT-16 Mk.IIB	-		(to RAF as F.......) (to RSwAF/Flyvapnet as Fv16033) Svedinos Bil Och Flygmus., Sloinge, Sweden	 79
14 - •	AT-16 Mk.IIB	-		(to RAF as F.......) (to RSwAF/Flyvapnet as Fv16126) Dansk Veteranflysamlung, Skjern, Denmark	 85
14A-1832	AT-16 Mk. IIB	KF132	ZS-DMF	reg. (to Syrian AF as ....)	.55 6.56
14A-2036	AT-16 Mk. IIB	KF336	ZS-DMM	reg. (to Syrian AF as ....)	.55 6.56
14A-2107	AT-16 Mk. IIB	KF407	ZS-DMI	reg. (to Syrian AF as ....)	.55 6.56
14A-2115•	Mk. IIB	KF415	 OO-GDO	(to RBAF as H52) COGEA Nouvelle, Ostende (to F. A. Portuguesa as ....)	 25.1.62 24.5.62
14A-2149	AT-16 Mk. IIB	KF449	ZS-DMO	reg. (to Syrian AF as ....)	.55 6.56
14A-2162	AT-16 Mk. IIB	KF462	ZS-DMJ	reg. (to Syrian AF as ....)	.55 6.56
14A-2268•	Mk. IIB	KF568	 OO-AAR D-FIBU LN-TEX	(to RBAF as H58) H. de Paepe, Borgerhout (to F. A. Portuguesa as 1794) J. Murer & Partners, Oslo	 1.10.58 11.9.59 3.8.79
14A-2415•	AT-16 Mk. IIB	KF715	 OO-GDP	(to RBAF as H67) COGEA Nouvelle, Ostende (to F. A. Portuguesa as ....)	 25.1.62 24.5.62
14A-2433	AT-16 Mk. IIB	KF733	ZS-DMG	reg. (to Syrian AF as ....)	.55 6.56
14A-2434•	AT-16 Mk. IIB	KF734	 OO-GDQ	(to RBAF as H73) COGEA Nouvelle, Ostende crashed rebuilt with parts of 14-724/PH-NIB) canc.	 25.1.62 .62 4.2.70
14A-2502	AT-16 Mk. IIB	KF802	ZS-DMH	reg. (to Syrian AF as ....)	.55 6.56
59-1938 •	AT-6	40-2112		Bradley Air Museum, Windsor Locks CT New England Air Museum, Windsor Locks CT (dismantled, outside storage) Conneticut Historical Aeronautical Assn	18.5.74 85/90 74/90 92
59-1945	AT-6	40-2119	N56737	George Pulse, Pendleton OR	76
65-1999•	SNJ-2	Bu2010	N52900	Stinis Air Service Inc, Cypress CA SNJ-2 Corporation	76 88/92
65-2000•	SNJ-2	Bu2011	N55729	Stinis Air Service Inc, Cypress CA Crossroads Air Ent. NY	76 92
65-2009	SNJ-2	Bu2020	N87613	Stinis Air Service Inc, Cypress CA	76
65-2014•	SNJ-2	Bu2025	N61563	National Diversified Svcs., AZ	92
65-2016•	SNJ-2	Bu2027	N40HS	SSS Inc., Cincinatti, OH	92
65-2021	SNJ-2	Bu2032	N60734	Stinis Air Service Inc, Cypress CA	76

				SNJ-2 Corporation	88
65-2023	SNJ-2	Bu2034		noted unconv., in USMC sc., Salisbury MD	73
65-2026 •	SNJ-2	Bu2037	N66082	Stinis Air Service Inc, Cypress CA Mark D. Dilullo, VA	76 92
65-2028	SNJ-2	Bu2039	N62382	SNJ-2 Corporation	88
65-2029 •	SNJ-2	Bu2040	N52033	Stinis Air Service Inc, Cypress CA SNJ 2 Corp	76 92
65-2032	SNJ-2	Bu2043	N61563	Stinis Air Service Inc, Cypress CA	76
66-2265 •	Mk.II	RCAF2532		Canadian National Collection, Rockliffe ONT	79
66-2313•	Mk.II	RCAF2580	N5848N	B & F Aircraft Supply, Oaklawn IL	76
66-2316	Mk.II	RCAF2583	C-GAYD	No further information	
66-2513 •	Mk.II	RCAF2780	N9785Z N88RT	Willis Webb, Fort Valley GA APEXXCo. Inc., Canby, OR	76 92
66-2517 •	Mk. II	RCAF2784	N203V N8BP	Robert B. Dilbeck, Keller TX Trapline Inc Boyne City, MI	76 92
66-2583 •	Mk.II	RCAF2850	N28500 N214RL	Michael Coutches, Hayward CA John Loerch, Tulsa, OK	76 92
66-2611	Mk.II	RCAF2878	N6558D	Robert Greacen, Merchantville NJ	76
66-2633	Mk. II	RCAF2900	N92871	Robert L. Younkin, Fayetteville AR	76
66-2637 •	Mk. II	RCAF2904	N8992	David Goodwin, Manchester NH Carl Best, Dallas, TX	76 92
66-2638 •	Mk. II	RCAF2905	N3270	William E. Riddle, Suffern NY James E. Kaylor, Ocala, FL	76 92
66-2647	Mk. II	RCAF2914	N194A	Sky Prints Corp., St Louis MO	76
66-2660	Mk.II	RCAF2927	N9786Z	Glenn T. Shaw, McCloud OK	76
66-2684 •	Mk. II	RCAF2951	N99839 C-GDJC	Hawkins & Powers Aviation, Greybull WY Canadian Warplane Heritage, Hamilton ONT	76 79
66-2689 •	Mk. II	RCAF2956	N2956	Frank J. Ciccolella, Tewksbury MA Ronald H. Gertsen, Kinnelon, NJ	76 92
66-2690	Mk. II	RCAF2957	N47079	Charles Landells, Kennewick WA	76
66-2703 •	Mk. II	RCAF2970	N97GM N97AW	Gary J. Meermans, Long Beach CA James Bennett, Euless, TX	76 92
66-2709 •	Mk. IIB	RCAF2976	N8993	Ryman Ennis Kay, Jackson MS Thomas R. Martin, Wasilla, AK	76 92
66-2757 •	Mk. II			(to RNZAF as NZ944) Museum of Transport & Technology, Auckland	 69/88
- •	Mk. II	RCAF3048	N9790Z	Confederate Air Force, Harlingen TX American Airpower Heritage Inc, Midland, TX	76/84 92
66-2788	Mk. II		N3647G	Norman H. Hatden, Kent WA	76
66-2814	Mk. II		N8994	Marylin Francis, Dawson GA	76

-•	AT-6C Mk.II	RCAF3275	CF-MGI	Canadian Warplane Heritage, Hamilton ONT (id. quoted as "144")	79
			N8994	John R. Smith, Greensboro, GA	92
-•	AT-6C Mk.II	RCAF3324	N3653G	Lance J. Johnson, Denver CO	76
				George Coombs TX	88
75-3048 •	Mk II		N9793Z	Brian G. Vooght, McLean, VA	92
75-3441	Mk. II	RCAF3617	CF-MEQ		
			C-GMEQ	Jeremy I. Milsom	82
75-3473 •	AT-6C		N16730	Edward Modes, Burbank CA	76
				Ray F. Schutte, Valencia, CA	92
75-3497•	AT-6C Mk II			To Flygvapnet as FV Nr 16145	
				Hilding Anderson, Ostersund, Sweden	92
76-3658 •	Mk.II	AJ688		(to RCAF as AJ688)	
			N3646G	Eugene F. Bowlin, Brookings OR	76
				Larry R. Thomas, San Mateo, CA	92
76-3701	Mk.II	AJ731		(to RCAF as AJ731)	
			N9789Z	Steve Fowler, Seattle WA	76
76-3802•	Mk.II	AJ832		(to RCAF as AJ832)	
			N832N	Barrie Simonson, Mercer Island WA	76
				Robert Coleman, Quincy, MA	92
76-3905•	Mk.II	AJ935		(to RCAF as AJ935)	
			N9796Z	Francis Moran, Franksville WI	76/92
76-3938•	Mk.II	AJ968		(to RCAF as AJ968)	
			N4802E	Robert Behrens, Council Bluffs IA	76
				David A. Fayman, Lawrence, KS	92
77-3962•	AT-6A	41-153	N94444	Paul Gaines, Salt Lake City UT	76
				Darrell Domann MO	88
77-4176•	AT-6A	41-217		(to F.A. Portuguesa as 1608)	
			G-BGGR	Euroworld Ltd	.79
			D-FOBY	reg.	.79
				Air Classik, Dusseldorf	87
77-4183 •	AT-6A	41-224	N57451	Alan G. Zabowski, Washington, NJ	92
77-4201	AT-6A	41-242	N57493	Ron Reed, Redwood City CA	76
77-4209•	AT-6A	41-250	N94506	Sale Reported	10.92
77-4259	AT-6A	41-500		(to RSwAF/Flygvapnet as Fv........)	
			SE-CAR		
			D-IBEC	Deutscher Luftfahrt Beratungsdienst	56/57
77-4396 •	AT-6A	41-437	N96208	Sale Reported	92
77-4601•	AT-6A	41-642	N78RN	Lone Star Flight Museum, TX	92
77-4607•	AT-6A	41-648		(to USN as Bu............)	
	SNJ-3		N48BC	Romaine A. Collins, Buckley WA	76
				Charles K. Theis Reno, NV	92
78-6394•	AT-6A	41-16116	N144KM	Kirk McKee, Sacremento, CA	92
78-6562	AT-6A	41-16184		(to RAF as ....: RBAF H48)	
	Mk. IIA		OO-GDN	COGEA Nouvelle, Ostende	25.1.62
				(to F. A. Portuguesa as ....)	24.5.62

78-6632•	AT-6A	41-16254	N18J	Earl C. Gibbs, Cleveland OH	76
				Donald J. Czapucki, Omaha, NE	92
78-6680•	AT-6A	41-16302	N57318	Randal Difani, Gardenia, CA	92
78-6696•	AT-6A	41-16318	N99293	Sale Reported	92
78-6698•	AT-6A	41-16320		(to F.A. Portugusesa as 1620)	
			G-TIDE		
			N77TX	William P. Lear, Los Altos Hills, CA	92
78-6851 •	AT-6A	41-16473§	N63631	Sale reported	10.92
78-6922 •	AT-6A	41-16544		(to RSwAF/Flygvapnet as Fv16291)	
	OY-AYE		D-IGAL	Deutscher Luftfahrt Beratungsdienst	56/57
			D-FGAL	Deutscher Luftfahrt Beratungsdienst	59
			PH-NKD		
78-6999 •	AT-6A	41-16621	N766CA	Lars Ljungqvist, Gasten, CA	92
78-7005	AT-6A	41-16627		(to FA Brasiliera as FAB T-6 1506)	
			PT-KVG	Jose Aurelia, Lima Redig, Belo Horizonte	83
78-7018 •	AT-6A	41-16640	N7991C	Rick Fernalld	92
78-7115	AT-6A	41-16737	CB-55	Direccion Aeronautica Civil, La Paz	
78-7211 •	AT-6A	41-16832	N96225	Sale reported	10. 92
78-7228 •	AT6A	41-16849	N7055D	John M. Foster, Alamagordo, NM	92
78-7375	AT-6A	41-16997	N90629	for sale	76
79-3988•	SNJ-2	Bu2553	N58224	Stinis Air Service Inc, Cypress CA	76
				SNJ-2 Corporation	88
79-3993•	SNJ-2	Bu2558	N60645	Stinis Air Service Inc, Cypress CA	76
				Classic Aviation Int'l, FL	92
79-3997•	SNJ-2	Bu2562	N52033	Stinis Air Service Inc, Cypress CA	76
			N65370	SNJ-2 Corporation	88/92
79-4003•	SNJ-2	Bu2568	N60833	Stinis Air Service Inc, Cypress CA	76
				Sale Reported, Miami, Fl.	92
81-4043	AT-6C Mk.II	RCAF3776	CF-PST	Canadian Warplane Heritage, Hamilton ONT	79
81-4099	AT-6C Mk.II	RCAF3832	N96281	Richard D. Benner, Anchorage AK	76
81-4107 •	AT-6C Mk.II	RCAF3840		Canadian National Collection, Rockliffe ONT	79
84-7412•	AT-6B	41-17034	N30HA	James Powell, Clarkesdale MS	76
				Warbirds of Arkansas, Pine Bluff, AR	92
84-7640 •	AT-6B	41-17262		(to R Saudi AF as 17262)	
				R. Saudi AF Museum Collection, Riyadh	79
84-7448•	AT-6B	41-17311	N57418	Richard T. Sykes, Toluca Lake, CA	92
84-7800•	AT-6B	41-17422	N11171	Confederate Air Force, Harlingen TX	76
-	SNJ-	Bu05599		noted unconv., in USN sc., Salisbury MD	73
-	SNJ-	Bu10046		noted unconv., in USN sc., Salisbury MD	73

-	SNJ-	Bu10106		noted unconv., in USN sc., Salisbury MD	73
-	SNJ-	Bu10136		noted unconv., in USN sc., Salisbury MD	73
-	SNJ-	Bu10176		noted unconv., in USN sc., Salisbury MD	73
-	SNJ-	Bu10205		noted unconv., in USN sc., Salisbury MD	73
-	SNJ-4	Bu26518		noted unconv., in USN sc., Salisbury MD	73
-	SNJ-4	Bu26554		noted unconv., in USN sc., Salisbury MD	73
-	SNJ-4	Bu26573		noted unconv., in USN sc., Salisbury MD	73
-	SNJ-4	Bu26578		noted unconv., in USN sc., Salisbury MD	73
-	SNJ-4	Bu26627		noted unconv., in USN sc., Salisbury MD	73
-	SNJ-4	Bu26687		noted unconv., in USN sc., Salisbury MD	73
-	SNJ-4	Bu26700		noted unconv., in USN sc., Salisbury MD	73
-	SNJ-4	Bu26704		noted unconv., in USN sc., Salisbury MD	73
-	SNJ-4	Bu26717		noted unconv., in USN sc., Salisbury MD	73
-	SNJ-4	Bu26764		noted unconv., in USN sc., Salisbury MD	73
-	SNJ-4	Bu26774		noted unconv., in USN sc., Salisbury MD	73
-	SNJ-4	Bu26781		noted unconv., in USN sc., Salisbury MD	73
-•	SNJ-4	Bu26808	N26808	Lee Groff, Jax TX	76
				Wings of Eagles, Readington, NJ	92
-	SNJ-4	Bu26822		noted unconv., in USN sc., Salisbury MD	73
-	SNJ-4	Bu26840		noted unconv., in USN sc., Salisbury MD	73
-	SNJ-4	Bu26841		noted unconv., in USN sc., Salisbury MD	73
-	SNJ-4	Bu26844		noted unconv., in USN sc., Salisbury MD	73
-•	SNJ-4	Bu26912	N9522C	D & D Aero Sparaying, Rantoul KS	76
				James Greeson, Lebanon, TN	92
-	SNJ-4	Bu26937		noted unconv., in USN sc., Salisbury MD	73
-	SNJ-4	Bu26978		noted unconv., in USN sc., Salisbury MD	73
•-	SNJ-4	Bu26992	N269WB	Ed Maslon, CA	92
-	SNJ-4	Bu27041		noted unconv., in USN sc., Salisbury MD	73
-	SNJ-4	Bu27071	N5850N	B & F Aircraft Supply, Oaklawn IL	76
-	SNJ-4	Bu27089		noted unconv., in USN sc., Salisbury MD	73
-	SNJ-4	Bu27132		noted unconv., in USN sc., Salisbury MD	73
-	SNJ-4	Bu27134		noted unconv., in USN sc., Salisbury MD	73
-	SNJ-4	Bu27160		noted unconv., in USN sc., Salisbury MD	73
-	SNJ-4	Bu27222		noted unconv., in USN sc., Salisbury MD	73
-	SNJ-4	Bu27233		noted unconv., in USN sc., Salisbury MD	73
-	SNJ-4	Bu27234		noted unconv., in USN sc., Salisbury MD	73
-	SNJ-4	Bu27258		noted unconv., in USN sc., Salisbury MD	73
-	SNJ-4	Bu27289		noted unconv., in USN sc., Salisbury MD	73
•-	SNJ-4	Bu27293	N9523C	John J. Stokes, San Marcos TX	76
				Paul Farbor, Great Neck, NY	92
-	SNJ-4	Bu27344		noted unconv., in USN sc., Salisbury MD	73
-	SNJ-4	Bu27352	N7058C	Cherokee Corp, Encampment WY	76
-	SNJ-4	Bu27414		noted unconv., in USN sc., Salisbury MD	73
-	SNJ-4	Bu27423		noted unconv., in USN sc., Salisbury MD	73
88-9260	AT-6C	41-33154		(to RAF as EX181)	
	Mk. IIA			(to RBAF as H18)	
			OO-GEQ	COGEA Nouvelle, Ostende	11.10.58
				(to FA Portuguesa as ....)	24.5.62
88-9272 •	AT-6C	41-33166		(to RAF as EX193)	
	Mk. IIA			(to RNZAF as NZ1015)	
				RNZAF Memorial Flight, RNZAF Wigram NZ	87
88-9351	SNJ-4	Bu	N9589C	Frank Howerton, Long Beach CA	76

88-9360	AT-6C		PT-KTH	Serrna SA de Aviacao, Agricola, Sao Paulo	83
88-9419 •	AT-6C		N211RF	Richard B. Ferguson, Chula Vista CA	76
				Richard B. Ferguson, Overrton, NY	92
88-9437 •	AT-6C		N5286N	Mid Continent Aircraft Corp, Hayti MO	76
				Tan Air AC Industries, No. Granby, CT	92
88-9450 •	SNJ-4	Bu	N101X	J. K. Kohlhaas, Corpus Christi TX	76
				American Airpower Heritage Inc	92
88-9544•	AT-6C		N55941	Walter R. Griffin, Summerfield NC	76
				Steven Miles, Carmel Valley, CA	92
88-9551•	SNJ-4	Bu	N5287N	Sabre Aviation Ltd, Hauppauge NY	76
				Firebrand Enterprises OH	88
				Frederick Hosking, Sedona, AZ	92
88-9589	AT-6C			(to FA Brasiliera as FAB T6D 1406)	
			PT-KVD	Fauzzi Faud Bunduck, Sao Paulo	83
88-9648	AT-6C			(to SAAF as 7142?)	
	Mk. IIA			(to F.A. Portuguesa as 1532)	
				stored, Portugal	80
88-9666	AT-6C			(to SAAF as 7103?)	
	Mk. IIA			(to F.A. Portuguesa as 1558)	
				stored, Portugal	80
88-9683	AT-6C	41-33240		(to SAAF as 7110)	
	Mk. IIA			(to F.A. Portuguesa as 1519)	
				stored, Portugal	80
88-9689	AT-6C	41-33246		(to RAF as EX273)	
	Mk. IIA			(to RBAF as H36)	
			OO-GES	COGEA Nouvelle, Ostende	11.10.58
				(to F. A. Portuguesa as ....)	24.5.62
88-9696•	AT-6C	41-33253		(to RAF as EX280)	
	Mk. IIA			(to SAAF as 7333)	
				(to F.A. Portuguesa as 1523)	
			G-TEAC	Euan English, Norfolk, UK	92
88-9723•	AT-6C	41-33260		(to RAF as EX287)	
	Mk. IIA			(to SAAF as 71...)	
				(to F.A. Portuguesa as 1560)	
			G-RCAF		6.3.79/80
			N42BA	William Arnot, Breckenridge, TX	14.4.80/92
88-9725 •	AT-6C	41-33262		(to RAF as EX289)	
	Mk. IIA			(to SAAF as 7183)	
				(to F.A. Portuguesa as 1535)	
			G-TSIX	Dan Taylor, Fritchley, Derbyshire	19.3.79/92
88-9728 •	AT-6C	41-33265		(to RAF as EX292)	
	Mk.IIA			(to RBAF as H-39)	
				Musee Royal de A'Armee, Brussels	79/87
				Brasschaat Belgian Army	92
88-9755 •	AT-6C	41-33275		(to RAF as EX302)	
	Mk. IIA			(to SAAF as 7084)	
				(to F.A. Portuguesa as 1545)	
			G-BICE	Colin Edwards, Ipswich	.80/92
88-9778•	AT-6C	41-33278		(to RAF as EX305)	
	Mk. IIA			(to RBAF as H37)	

			OO-GDK	COGEA Nouvelle, Ostende	25.1.62
				cancelled as sold in Congo	29.10.62
88-9796•	SNJ-4	Bu	N47040	Donald Marshall, Ferriday LA	76
				Sale reported Wilmington, DE	92
88-10014	AT-6C Mk. IIA	41-33344		(to RAF as EX371)	
				(to RBAF as H26)	
			OO-GEN	COGEA Nouvelle, Ostende	11.10.58
				(to F. A. Portuguesa as ....)	24.5.62
88-10177•	SNJ-4	Bu	N6411D	Airmen Inc, Norman OK	76
				Confederate Air Force, Abiline TX	88
88-10185•	SNJ-4	Bu	N90650	for sale	76
			N119DP	Daniel L. Petersen, MO	92
88-10188	AT-6C Mk. IIA	41-33365		(to RAF as EX392)	
				(to SAAF as 7185)	
				(to F.A. Portuguesa as 1554)	
			G-BGOU	Euroworld Ltd	28.3.79
				Peter Snell	85
				crashed and destroyed, Bourn (Snell k.)	7.9.85
88-10254 •	AT-6C Mk. IIA	41-33397		(to RAF as EX424)	
				(to RNZAF as NZ1025)	
			ZK-ENN	D. M. Diamond & J. M. Sullivan, Timaru NZ	87
88-10271 •	AT-6C	41-33415	N7093C	J.W. Duff, Denver, Co	92
88-10278 •	AT-6C	41-33421	N7413C	Peter Crown, Waianae, HI	92
88-10293 •	AT-6C	41-33436	N3747X	Paul Resse, Sissonville, WV	92
88-10554	AT-6C Mk. IIA	41-33434		(to RAF as EX461)	
				(to RBAF as H28)	
			OO-GEO	COGEA Nouvelle, Ostende	11.10.58
				(to F. A. Portuguesa as ....)	24.5.62
88-10560	AT-6C Mk. IIA	41-33440		(to RAF as EX467)	
				(to SAAF as 7039)	
				(to F.A. Portuguesa as 1551)	
			G-BGOT	Euroworld Ltd	28.3.79/80
			N37642	reg.	4.80
88-10569•	AT-6C Mk. IIA	41-33449		(to RAF as EX476)	
				(to RBAF as H-8)	
			F-BJBE	Soc. Air France, Toussous-le-Noble	
			F-AZDK	Aero Retro, St Rambert d'Albion	89
				(flies as "USN/9')	
88-10589 •	AT-6C Mk. IIA	41-33469		(to SAAF as 7223)	
				(to F.A. Portuguesa as 1538)	
				stored, Portugal	80
88-10633 •	AT-6C	41-33513	N7044J	NA50 Inc. c/o AVIREX, NY	92
88-10635	AT-6C Mk. IIA	41-33515		(to RAF as EX542)	
				(to RBAF as H17)	
			OO-GEM	COGEA Nouvelle, Ostende	11.10.58
				cancelled as sold in Congo	22.10.62
88-10677 •	AT-6C Mk. IIA	41-33557		(to RAF as EX584: SAAF as 7244)	
				(to F.A. Portuguesa as 1522)	
			G-RBAC		
			G-BHXF	ntu:	
			G-VALE		
			N36CA	Confederate Air Force (MI Wing), Gary IN	88

				Boa Limited IL	88
				Leslie J. Raffel, Gurnee, IL	92
88-10712 •	AT-6C	41-	N99292	USCAR	10.92
88-11017 •	AT-6C	41-	N6411D	American Heritage	92
88-11041 •	AT-6C	41-	N37477	Art Medore, Denville, NJ	92
88-11083 •	AT-6C	41-	N9530C	Robert McCoy, Inglewood CA	76
			N89015	Dennis Buehn, Carson City, NV	92
88-11447	SNJ-4	Bu	N7083C	Kent Jones, Dallas TX	76
88-11545	SNJ-4	Bu26861	NC58273		
			LN-MAN	Thor Solberg Flyveselskap, Bergen	10.1.48
				(to RNoAF as MB-G) canc. LN-reg 9.11.48	
				(to Turkish AF as ....)	
88-11850	SNJ-4	Bu	N6413D	H. L. Webb, Berkeley CA	76
88-11913			XB-PAB		77
88-11959 •	SNJ-4		N6514D	Sale Reported	10.92
88-11988•	SNJ-4	Bu	N5299N	Minnesota Air & Space Mus., Minneapolis MN	88
88-12018	AT-6C		N60380	Low Level Dusting Co., La Salle CO	76
88-12032•	AT-6C	41-33561		(to RAF as EX588)	
	Mk. IIA			(to RNZAF as NZ1033)	
			ZK-SGQ	NZ Sport & Vintage Avn. Soc., Masterton NZ	87
88-12033•	AT-6C	41-33562		(to RAF as EX589)	
	Mk. IIA			(to RNZAF as NZ1034)	
				RAAF Museum, Point Cook VIC	88/90
				(displayed as "NZ947")	
88-12036•	AT-6C	41-33565		(to RAF as EX592)	
	Mk. IIA			(to RNZAF as NZ1037)	
			ZK-ENA	J. Mathewson, Central Otago NZ	87
88-12044•	AT-6C	41-33573		(to RAF as EX600)	
	Mk. IIA			(to SAAF as 7382)	
				(to F.A. Portuguesa as 1559)	
			G-BGOV	Euroworld Ltd	28.3.79/80
				Aces High Ltd, North Weald	11.80/83
			N4434N	June Mourad, Merecedes, TX	17.5.83/92
88-........	AT-6C	41-33596		(to RAF as EX623)	
	Mk. IIA			(to RBAF as H-....)	
			OO-GDL	COGEA Nouvelle, Ostende	25.1.62
				(to F. A. Portuguesa as ....)	24.5.62
88-12122 •.......	AT-6C	41-33601		(to RAF as EX628)	
			N83598	Art Medore, Denville, NJ	92
88-12127•.......	AT-6C	41-33606		(to RAF as EX633)	
	Mk. IIA			(to RBAF as H-29)	
			F-BJBI	Soc. Air France, Toussous-le-Noble	
			F-WJBI	Soc. Air France, Toussous-le-Noble	
			F-AZBE	Salis Collection, La Ferte Alais	89
				(mod. flies as USN Wildcat "RM-27")	
88-12139	AT-6C	41-33618		(to RAF as EX645)	
	Mk. IIA			(to SAAF as 7570)	

				Atlas Aircraft Co., Apprentice School,	
				Jan Smuts Airport, Johannesburg	79
88-12150 •	SNJ-4	Bu27160	N7055H	Richard Fields, Fullerton, CA	92
88-12151 •	SNJ-4	Bu27161	N7054X	John M. Foster, Alamagordo, NM	92
88-12188 •	SNJ-4	Bu27193		(to F.A. Portuguesa as 1524)	
				stored, Portugal	80
88-12281•	SNJ-4	Bu	N24554	Banaire Enterprises Inc, Hemet CA	76
				Mid Atlantic Air Museum, Middletown PA	88
88-12289 •	SNJ-4	Bu	N48119	for sale	76
				Brandon D. Kunicki, Chino, CA	92
88-12291	SNJ-4	Bu	N86WW	Robert C. Forbes, Porterville CA	76
				Charles Beck, Los Angeles CA	77
88-12326•	AT-6C		F-BJBC	Aero Retro St Rambert D'Albon	86/89
88-12327	AT-6C	41-33634		(to RAF as EX661)	
	Mk. IIA			(to RBAF as H31)	
			OO-GER	COGEA Nouvelle, Ostende	11.10.58
				(to F. A. Portuguesa as ....)	24.5.62
88-12407	AT-6C	41-	N9525C	Richard Sykes, North Hollywood CA	76
88-12427•	AT-6C	41-	N2269N	Art Medore, CA	92
88-12472•	AT-6C	41-		(to FA Brasiliera as FAB T6D-1264)	
			PT-KTA	Caio Antonio dos Santos, Piracununga	83
			N310JH	MichaelHalem, NY	92
88-12507	AT-6C	41-	N9543C	Chester Siepiela, Hawley PA	76
				Clark Motor Co Inc, State College PA	77
88-12533•	SNJ-4	Bu	N6416D	Ernest Enos, Bridgewater MA	76
				George Baker, FL	92
88-12546	AT-6C	41-33653		(to RAF as EX680)	
	Mk. IIA			(to RBAF as H45)	
			OO-GEP	COGEA Nouvelle, Ostende	11.10.58
				cancelled as sold in Congo	22.10.62
88-12619•	AT-6C	41-	N2269S	Ray Sanders, Kalsipell, MT	10.92
88-12622•	AT-6C		N7061C	Intnl. Recruiting Services Inc, Van Nuys CA	76
				Furlong Gates Inc., Van Nuys, CA	92
88-12640	SNJ-4	Bu	N7412C	Wheeler Ridge Aviation, Bakersfield CA	76
88-12709	SNJ-4	Bu	N9536C	Rosie O'Grady Warehouse Inc, Pensacola FL	76
88-12817	SNJ-4	Bu	N48153	Banaire Enterprises Inc, Hemet CA	76
88-12827•	SNJ-4	Bu		(to Ejercito del Aire as C.6-............)	
			N127VF	Minter Field Air Museum, Bakersfield CA	88/92
88-12841•	SNJ-4	Bu	N2269T	Art Medore, Hemet, CA	92
88-12847•	SNJ-4	Bu	N3747Z	Art Medore, Denville, NJ	92
				Danny Kinker, Lawrence, KS	92
88-12850•	SNJ-4		N2269U	Charles Beck, Los Angeles, CA	92
88-12858•	SNJ-4		N934JT	Joe Tobul, Pittsburgh, PA	92

88-12929•	AT-6C		N6861C	Newton H. Smith, Edison NJ	76
				Har Ran Aircraft Sales, Tulsa OK	77
				Robert Beckman, Ashville, OH	92
88-12932	SNJ-4	Bu	N7038C	Dimitry V. Prian, Long Beach CA	76
88-12956•	SNJ-4	Bu27500	N30CE	Carl Schmeider, mod to NA-64 config.	
				Lone Star Flight Museum	91/92
88-12996	SNJ-4	Bu27540		noted unconv., in USN sc., Salisbury MD	73
88-13001•	SNJ-4	Bu27549	N80714	Seminole Air Center, OK	92
88-13037•	SNJ-4	Bu27581	N37474	Art Medore, Denville, NJ	92
88-13041•	SNJ-4	Bu27585	N7438C		
			N224X	Confederate Air Force, Harlingen TX	76/92
88-13059	SNJ-4	Bu27603		noted unconv., in USN sc., Salisbury MD	73
88-13061	SNJ-4	Bu27605		noted unconv., in USN sc., Salisbury MD	73
88-13067•	SNJ-4	Bu27611	N7437C	Harry Roth, Houma LA	76
				John Thigpen, Franklinton LA	77
				MGH Enterprises, Wilmington, DE	92
88-13072•	SNJ-4	Bu27616	N22KD	Coleman Warbird Museum, TX	92
88-13164•	SNJ-4	Bu	N7070C	Frank Land, Klamath Falls, OR	92
88-13166•	SNJ-4	Bu	N67003	Mary Salerno, Las Vegas NV	76
				Marvin Hetzel, Riverside, IL	92
88-13171•	SNJ-4		N7062C	Hugh C. Conley, College Park, GA	92
88-13243•	SNJ-4	Bu	N55A	Sierra Enterprises, Reno NV	76
				Har Ran Aircraft Sales, Tulsa OK	77
				James Thompson, Plainfield, NH	92
88-13345•	AT-6C		N7407C	Cinema Air, Carlsbad, CA	92
88-13364•	AT-6C		N10597	Livesays Flying Service, Weldon AR	76
				Lee Maples MO	88
				C.E. Schmidt, Vichy, MO	92
88-13369	SNJ-4	Bu	N6419D	for sale	76
88-13370•	SNJ-4	Bu	N7090C	Douglas Sellix, Springtown PA	76
				Harvey Gillman Aircraft, Brokkville OH	77
				Philip Robins, Minneapolis, MN	92
88-13372•	SNJ-4	Bu	N13372	Arvin Pliss, San Jose CA	76
				Paul Mace, Ashland, WA	92
88-13374	SNJ-4	Bu	N6420D	for sale	76
88-13376•	SNJ-4	Bu	N7077C	Lawrence B. Klaers, Fontana CA	76
				Eugene Zeiner, Los Angles, CA	92
88-13384•	AT-6C		N5208V	Frank G. Compton, Redondo Beach CA	76
			N101VT	Gary Anderson IL	88
				Dennis Jankowski, Elgin, IL	92
88-13386	SNJ-4	Bu	N6421D	Caprock Flying Service, Vega TX	76
88-13391	SNJ-4	Bu	N99DA	Wings of Yesterday, Santa Fe NM	76

88-13466•	SNJ-4	Bu	N33CC	Anthony Aguanno, Denville NJ Evergreen Ventures, McMinneville, OR.	76 92
88-13478•	SNJ-4	Bu	N6422D	Philip Ditillo, Oakville CT Tan Air Industries, Granby, CT	76 92
88-13517	SNJ-4	Bu	N7024C	Charles Tucker, Ferriday LA Confederate Air Force, Harlingen TX	76 88
88-13519	SNJ-4	Bu	N6423D	Fred Eiler, Tarentum PA	76
88-13583•	AT-6C		N4136A	Robert E. Wright, Brighton CO Sale Reported, Vernon, TX	76 92
88-13585•	AT-6C		N8540Z	Bruce Anderson Racing, Belgrade, MT	92
88-13586•	SNJ-7	Bu	N6436C	James M. Landeen, Laurel MS Normond B. McAllister, Mobile, AL	76 92
88-13587•	AT-6C		N97TR	Aero Enterprises Inc, Seattle WA William Lamberton, Mercer Island WA Royal Eagle Squadron, Bellvue, WA	76 77 92
88-13598	AT-6C Mk. IIA	41-33752	 OO-GDM	(to RAF as EX779) (to RBAF as H-43) COGEA Nouvelle, Ostende (to F. A. Portuguesa as ....)	 25.1.62 24.5.62
88-13625	SNJ-4	Bu	N4140A	Howard Bennett, Salisbury MD	76
88-13635•	SNJ-4		N29BS	Thomas Shelton, Ashville, NC	92
88-13627•	SNJ-4	Bu	N6424D	Jack Ivey, Albany GA Steven Hay, Prospect Heights, IL	76 92
88-13630•	SNJ-4	Bu	N22518	Tom Dodson, Tulsa, OK	92
88-13640	SNJ-4	Bu	N7034C	Roland J. Harrington, Abbeville LA	76
88-13763	SNJ-4	Bu51381	N6425D	Aerotech Inc, Pontiac MI Jerrold Wannemacher CO	76 88
88-13780	SNJ-4	Bu51398		NASM, Silver Hills MD	88
88-13784	SNJ-4	Bu51402	N7008C	D & D Aero Spraying Inc, Rantoul KS	76
88-13785	SNJ-4	Bu51403		noted unconv., in USN sc., Salisbury MD	73
88-13796	SNJ-4	Bu51414	N156	Leeroy Whitehead, Lacrascenta CA	76
88-13805	SNJ-4	Bu51423	N7011C	John Green, Grenada MS Courtesy Aircraft Inc, Rockford IL James Over CO	76 77 88
88-13892•	SNJ-4	Bu	N7013C	Phillip Godlewski, Newcastle, DE	92
88-13948	AT-6C		N630X	Dean Ortner, Wakeman OH	76
88-14124•	SNJ-4	Bu	N7404C	Brownings Inc, Roberts ID Jerry McDonald, San Joaquin, CA	76 92
88-14253•	SNJ-4	Bu	N22519	Gordon Pedron, Groveland, CA	92
88-14317•	SNJ-4	Bu	N6427D	Clifford Baker, Eudora AR Tee Six Inc., Casper, WY	76 92
88-14342•	SNJ-4	Bu	N7406C	Donald Ayers, Oklahoma City OK John Reynolds, Aspen, CO	76 92

88-14362•	AT-6C		N58917	Roy Sharp, Glendale CA	76
			N674N	Scott Morse, Plano, TX	92
88-14518	SNJ-5		N4745C	Joe Binder, Fremont OH	76
88-14552•	Mk. IIA			(to SAAF as 7424)	
				(to F.A. Portuguesa as 1506)	
			G-SUES		
			LN-LFW		92
88-14555	Mk. IIA			(to SAAF as 7426)	
				(to F.A. Portuguesa as 1513)	
				stored Portugal	80
88-14659•	Mk. IIA		N3770D	Pony Corp., Abilene, TX	92
88-14661	Mk. IIA			(to SAAF as 74...)	
				(to F.A. Portuguesa as 1504)	
			G-ELLY	Crashed and destroyed Malta (E. White & M. Campbell k.)	22.6.82
88-14672•	AT-6D	41-33878		(to RAF as EX905)	
	Mk. III			(to RNZAF as NZ1066)	
			ZK-ENE	G. M. Porter, R. J. Booth, P. J. Adams,	
				Ardmore NZ	87
88-14722•	AT-6D-	41-33888		(to SAAF as 7439)	
	Mk. III			(to F.A. Portuguesa as 1502)	
			G-JUDI	Anthony Hodgson, Clywd, Wales	92
88-14748	AT-6D	42-44554		(to RN FAA as FT971)	
	Mk. IIA			(to F.A. Portugusesa as 1661)	
			G-BGOW	Euroworld Ltd	28.3.79/80
			N.....	reg.	16.4.80
88-14863•	AT-6D	41-33908		(to RAF as EX935)	
	Mk. IIA			(to SAAF as ....)	
				(to F.A. Portuguesa as 1508)	
			G-BGOR	Euroworld Ltd	28.3.79
				Martin Sargeant, Rochester	87
88-14886•	AT-6D	41-33914		(to RAF as EX941)	
	Mk. III			(to RNZAF as NZ1062)	
			ZK-ELN	NZ Wing Confederate Air Force, Ardmore NZ	87
88-14889•	AT-6D	41-33917		(to RAF as EX944)	
	Mk. III			(to RNZAF as NZ1065)	
			ZK-ENF	M. R. Broadbent & R. F. Duncan, Ardmore NZ	87
88-14893 •	AT-6D	42-44629	N6983C	Paul Poberezny/EAA Aviation Foundation,	
				Oshkosh WI	76/88
88-14905	AT-6D	42-44641	N75342	Eldon P. Harvey, El Paso TX	76
				Sherwood Sublett VA	88
88-14939	AT-6D	42-44675	N83H	James L. Irwin, Mineral Wells TX	76
				Ozarks Auto Show, Branson, MO	92
88-14973•	AT-6D	42-44709	N4292C	Doug Goss, Topeka, KS	92
88-14948	AT-6D	41-33931		(to RAF as EX958)	
	Mk. III			(to RBAF as H-9)	
			F-BJBF	Soc. Air France, Toussous-le-Noble	
			G-AZJD	Sir W. D. Roberts, Strathallan	30.11.71
			F-AZDU	based, Laval	.84/89
88-	AT-6D	41-33959		(to RAF as EX976)	

	Mk. III			(to Portuguese AF as FAP 1657) Fleet Air Arm Museum, Yeovilton	
88•-	AT-6D Mk.III	41-34050	N111PB	(to RAF as EZ214) Gerald W. Morgan, Bedford, TX	92
88•-	AT-6D Mk.III	41-34073	N8539L	(to RAF as EZ237) Carl Penner, Salt Lake City, UT	92
88-14871• or 971?	AT-6D Mk. III	41-34117	ZK-ENB	(to RAF as EZ244) (to RNZAF as NZ1076) R. Brereton, Ohakea NZ	87
88-•-	AT-6D	41-34166	N14166	Charles Hall, Ramona, CA	92
88-15356•			N30CE	Gerald Walbrun, Neenah, WI	92
88-15726•	SNJ-5	Bu	N1043C	David Hooker, Huntington Beach, CA	92
88-15738	SNJ-5	Bu	N437S	Paul Taylor, Shakopee MN	76
88-15902	SNJ-5	Bu	N3687F	Gerald Walburn, King of Prussia PA Gerald Walburn WI	76 88
88-15950	AT-6D Mk.IIA	42-84169		(to RAF as EZ256) (to RBAF as H-21) Musee Royal de A'Armee, Brussels	79/88
88-16183•	AT-6D SNJ-5	42-84402	N3685F	(to USN as Bu...........) W. M. Branch, Dallas TX Paul Cash, Morganton, NC	76 92
88- •	AT-6C Mk. IIA	41-.........		(to RAF as EZ310) (to SAAF as 7625) : ret to RAF as EZ310 (to RBAF as H-15) (to SAAF as 7729) Fort Klapperkop Military Museum, Pretoria	79
88-•	AT-6C Mk. IIA	41-.........	VH-TEX	(to RAF as ....) (to RNZAF as NZ1006) C. Sperou, Adelaide SA	90
88-•	AT-6C Mk. IIA	41-.........	VH-HAR	(to RAF as ....) (to RNZAF as NZ1007) B. Simpson, Sydney NSW	90
88- •	AT-6C Mk. IIA	41-.........	VH-CRC	(to RAF as ....) (to RNZAF as NZ1023) G. Camage & Ptnrs, Canberra ACT	90
88- •	AT-6C Mk. IIA	41-.........		(to RAF as ....) (to RNZAF as NZ1024) Airworld Museum, Wangaratta VIC	90
88-•	AT-6C Mk. IIA	41-.........		(to RAF as ....) (to RNZAF as NZ1038) H. Brunton, Narromine NSW	90
88-•	AT-6C Mk. IIA	41-.........		(to RAF as ....) (to RNZAF as NZ1051) Rob Poynton, Cunderdin WA	87/90
88-•	AT-6C Mk. IIA	41-.........	VH-NAH	(to RAF as ....) (to RNZAF as NZ1056) A. Pay, Mount Beauty VIC	90
88-•	AT-6C Mk. IIA	41-.........		(to RAF as ....) (to RNZAF as NZ1058)	

				Ferrymead Historic Park, Christchurch NZ	79
88-•	AT-6C	41-.........		(to RAF as ....)	
	Mk. IIA			(to RNZAF as NZ1060)	
			VH-SFY	RAAF Museum, RAAF Point Cook VIC	90
				(flies as "NZ1060")	
88-•	AT-6C	41-.........		(to RAF as ....)	
	Mk. IIA			(to RNZAF as NZ1061)	
			VH-PEM	Walcha Air Service, Walcha NSW	90
88-•	AT-6C	41-.........		(to RAF as ....)	
	Mk. IIA			(to RNZAF as NZ1075)	
			VH-HVD	J. Barnes, Melbourne VIC	90
88-•	AT-6C	41-.........		(to RAF as ....)	
	Mk. IIA			(to RNZAF as NZ1085)	
			VH-SNJ	Guido Zuccoli, Darwin NT	90
88-•	AT-6D	41-34374		(to USN as Bu43639)	
	SNJ-5		N8151	Jerrome Libby, Lake Orion MI	76
				Byrne Aviation, Bloomfield Hills, Mi	92
88-	AT-6D	41-34377		(to USN as Bu43642)	
	SNJ-5		N2960T		
			F-AZDM	crashed and destroyed, Coulommiers	11.6.84
88-•	AT-6D	41-34378	N1049A	AVAG Inc., Richvale, CA	92
88-•	AT-6D	41-34382		(to USN as Bu43647)	
	SNJ-5		N3274G	James Mott, Long Beach CA	76
88-•	AT-6D	41-34404		(to USN as Bu43669)	
	SNJ-5			(to FA Brasiliera as FAB T-6 1703)	
			PT-KRD	Jose Angelo Simioni, Campo de Marte	83
88-	AT-6D	41-34408		(to USN as Bu43673)	
	SNJ-5		N3256G		
			VP-JBN	reg.	10.59
88-	AT-6D	41-34412		(to USN as Bu43677)	
	SNJ-5		N7999C	Harry Wright, Calipatria CA	76
				High Expectations, Evanston, WY	92
88-	AT-6D	41-34419		(to USN as Bu43684)	
	SNJ-5			(to FA Brasiliera as FAB T-6 1704)	
			PT-KSX	Silvio Teani Comenho, Jacarepagua	83
88-•	AT-6D	41-34418		(to USN as Bu43683)	
	SNJ-5		N2250	Neil Rose, Vancouver, WA	92
88-•	AT-6D	41-34424		(to USN as Bu43689)	
	SNJ-5		N502	Walter Ohlrich, Moore OK	76
				Walter Ohlrich VA	88/92
88-	AT-6D	41-34434		(to USN as Bu43699)	
	SNJ-5		N169D	David Robinson, Miami Springs FL	76
88-•	AT-6D	41-34465		(to USN as Bu43724)	
	SNJ-5		N1045C	Robert Gardner, Northampton MA	76
				T. Conlon, Massapequa Peak NY	77
			N62724	Camion Corporation IN	88/92
88-•	AT-6D	41-34466		(to USN as Bu43725)	
	SNJ-5B		N1666T	Gary Lund, Redwood Falls MN	76
				John Sandberg	

				'Stoney' Stonich WA	88/92
88-	AT-6D SNJ-5	41-34469	 TI-301C TI-301P	(to USN as Bu43728)	 c59
88-•	AT-6D SNJ-5B	41-34473	 N8214E	(to USN as Bu43732) John Stamer, Louisville KY Victor Krause IL	 76 88/92
88-•	AT-6D SNJ-5	41-34477	 N3259G	(to USN as Bu43736) W. C. Boldt & Co., Hammond IN Joseph N. Miller, Pocono Pines, PA	 76 92
88-•	AT-6D SNJ-5	41-34497	 N350HT	(to USN as Bu43756) Indiana Aircraft Sales, Indianapolis, IN	 92
88-•	AT-6D SNJ-5	41-34524	 N7300C	(to USN as Bu43763) Robert P. Mora, Grand Forks ND American Airpower Heritage Inc.	 76 92
88-•	AT-6D SNJ-5	41-34527	 N3242G	(to USN as Bu43766) Tallmantz Aviation Inc., Santa Ana CA John V. Rawson, Rocky Hill, NJ	 76 92
88-•	AT-6D SNJ-5	41-34532	 N43771	(to USN as Bu43771) Stanton C. Hoefler, Hermosa Beach CA	 76
88-•	AT-6D SNJ-5	41-34536	 N43775	(to USN as Bu43775) Raymond Houx, Ennis, TX	 92
88-	AT-6D SNJ-5	41-34537	 N82583	(to USN as Bu43776) George C. Borchin, Lewisville TX	 76
88-	AT-6D SNJ-5	41-34540	 N3645F	(to USN as Bu43779) Roy Mitchell, Cincinnati OH	 76
88-•	AT-6D	41-34571	N87H	Frederick Kohler, Los Angeles CA Andrew T. Gemellaro, Canoga Park, CA	76 92
88-	AT-6D SNJ-5	41-34585	 N7968C	(to USN as Bu43791) M. Leberman, Laceys Springs AL	 76
88-	AT-6D SNJ-5	41-34586	 N9065Z	(to USN as Bu43792) Glenn L. Schroeder, Reseda CA William Collins, Mansfield, TX	 76 92
88-•	AT-6D SNJ-5	41-34607	 N8541B	(to USN as Bu43793) John Vick, Longmont, CO	 92
88-•	AT-6D SNJ-5	41-34626	 N9824C N180NB	(to USN as Bu43812) James D. Slaney, Dallas TX Wayne Bullock, Warrington, PA	 76 92
88-•	AT-6D SNJ-5	41-34629	 N3630F	(to USN as Bu43815) Harry Anapo, Brewster NY Dickinson L. Morris, Wyckoff, NY	 76 92
88-	AT-6D SNJ-5	41-34632	 N6628C	(to USN as Bu43818) Sandford M. Graves, Columbia MO	 76/88
88-•	AT-6D SNJ-5	41-34649	 N9060Z	(to USN as Bu43835) Austin Gibbons, Elgin IL SNJ-5 Inc.. Bensenville, IL	 76 92
88-	AT-6D SNJ-5	41-34653	 N3258G	(to USN as Bu43839) for sale	 76

				Frederick Reynolds, Riverside CA	77
				Ray Diekman, OH	92
88-	AT-6D	41-34654		(to USN as Bu43840)	
	SNJ-5		N5598V	Aviation High School, Long Island NY	76
88-	AT-6D	42-84177		(to USN as Bu43846)	
	SNJ-5		N3326G	Aubrey King, Salinas CA	76
88-•	AT-6D	42-84211		(to USN as Bu43820)	
	SNJ-5		N42897	Richard Slaney, Eugene, OR	92
88-•	AT-6D	42-84246		(to USN as Bu43855)	
	SNJ-5		N3670F	Iowa Tech Area XV Community College,	
				Ottomwa IA	76
				Herbert Spector IL	88
88-•	AT-6D	42-84266		(to USN as Bu43875)	
	SNJ-5		N5199V	West Pacific Electric, Grants Pass OR	76
				Wilbert Mehrer, Portland, OR	92
88-•	AT-6D	42-84425		(to USN as Bu43924)	
	SNJ-5		N777AP	Charles T. Blaine, Phoenix AZ	76
				Jack Jordan, Phoenix AZ	77
				LaGrange Aero, GA	92
88-•	AT-6D	42-84437		(to USN as Bu43936)	
	SNJ-5		N3641F	John W. Hardy, Kansas City MO	76
			N241F	Charles Harmon, Lockport NY	76
				(NB: both listed in76 USCAR)	
				Del Marcotte FL	88
				Richard McNeil, North Wilkesboro, NC	92
88-•	AT-6D	42-84439		(to USN as Bu43938)	
	SNJ-5		N7980C	F. T. Brundrett, Chandler AZ	76
				Michael Christine, Memphis, TN	92
88-•	AT-6D	42-84443		(to USN as Bu43942)	
	SNJ-5			(to Ejercito del Aire as C6-134)	
				storage compound Museo del Aire	
				Cuatro Vientos, Spain	
			N3931Z	Ronald Kunny, Hinsdale IL	88
88-16300 •	AT-6D	42-84519		(to USN as Bu43958)	
	SNJ-5		N6644C	for sale	76
				John Schleich, Galway NY	77
				Aries Aviation, Brookfield, CT	92
88-16310	AT-6D	42-84529		(to USN as Bu43968)	
	SNJ-5		N8212E	Robert Henry, Atlanta GA	76
				Richard Maxwell PA	88
88-16314•	AT-6D	42-84533		(to USN as Bu43972)	
	SNJ-5		N7981C	Paul Schorn, Pompano Beach FL	76
				Randy Miller, Grays Lakes, IL	92
88-16316	AT-6D	42-84535		(to USN as Bu43974)	
	SNJ-5		N7969C	Richard T. Sykes, Toluca Lake GA	76
88-16336•	AT-6D	42-84555		(to RAF as EZ341)	
	Mk. II			(to FA Portuguesa as 1662)	
				Museu do Ar, Montijo, Alverca, Portugal	88/89
				(held in Museum store)	91
				AJD Engineering Suffolk	11.91
			G-ELMH	Mark Hammond, Eye,Suffolk	9.92

88-16341•	AT-6D	42-84560		USAFM, Randolph AFB, SDan Antonio TX	88
88-16371	AT-6D	42-84590	N6432D	Gerhard C. Rettberg, Champaign IL	76
88-16388•	AT-6D	42-84607	N6436D	Dan Caldarale NJ	88
88-16410•	AT-6D SNJ-5	42-84629		(to USN as Bu44008) San Diego Aerospace Museum, San Diego CA	 88
88-16411•	AT-6D SNJ-5	42-84630	 N30JF	(to USN as Bu44009) West Pacific Electrical Inc, Grants Pass OR Charles Foran, Dallas, TX	 76 92
88-16459 •	AT-6D	42-84678	N7095C	John Larsen, Minneapolis MN Paul M. Holman, Plymouth, MI	76 92
88-16461 •	AT-6D	42-84680	N7476C	Robert B. Willson, Martinsburg PA James McCabe, Markle, IN	76 92
88-16466 •	AT-6D SNJ-5	42-84685	 N3642F	(to USN as Bu44014) Robert Morrow, Salem OR James Elkins, Salem, OR	 76 92
88-16469	AT-6D SNJ-5	42-84688	 HK-2049P	(to USN as Bu44017) H. E. Valez	 .77/82
88-16472•	AT-6D SNJ-5	42-84691	 N14HB N43WB	(to USN as Bu44020) David Anderson, Scotch Plains NJ Haywood Bartlett, AL	 77 92
88-16472•	AT-6D SNJ-5	42-84696	 N2864D	(to USN as Bu44025) John Meyer, Seattle, WA	 92
88-16497 •	AT-6D SNJ-5	42-84716	 N3272G	(to USN as Bu84826) Herbert Taylor, Gallup NM Linda Finch, San Antonio, TX	 76 92
88-16498	AT-6D SNJ-5	42-84717	 N7979C	(to USN as Bu84827) Wilbert L. Mehrer, Portland OR	 76
88-16503	AT-6D SNJ-5	42-84722	 N7982C	(to USN as Bu84832) Williams Flying Service, Tutweiler MS	 76
88-16505•	AT-6D Mk. III	42-84724	 ZK-ENC	(to RAF as EZ360) (to RNZAF as NZ1091) W. J. & S. M. Williams, Mount Maunganui NZ	 87
88-16506•	AT-6D Mk. III	42-84725	 ZK-WAR	(to RAF as EZ361) (to RNZAF as NZ1092) T. T. Bland & E. J. Schroeder, Ardmore NZ	 87
88-16560	AT-6D	42-84779	N7RK	Ronald Klemm, Fairbanks AK	76
88-16570•	AT-6D SNJ-5	42-84788	 N590WW	(to USN as Bu84839) Wayne Witt, Wooddale, IL	 92
88-16574•	AT-6D SNJ-5	42-84793	 N3680F	(to USN as Bu84844) Lloyd P. Nolan, Mercedes TX Rudolph Perez, Valencia, CA	 76 92
88-16580•	AT-6D SNJ-5	42-84799	 N7988C	(to USN as Bu84850) Terramar Inc, Cape Canaveral FL John W. Kehoe, Lakeland, FL	 76 92
88-16582•	AT-6D SNJ-5	42-84801	 N11SH	(to USN as Bu84851) Raymond A. Rakers, Breeese IL Scott Johnson, Clarendon Hills, IL	 76 92

88-16640•	AT-6D	42-84859		(to USN as Bu...........)	
	SNJ-5		N4748C	Ferguson Flying Service, Pensacola FL	76
				Robert F. Wallin, Shell, WY	92
88-16676•	AT-6D	42-84895		(to USN as Bu84865)	
	SNJ-5		N89014	Confederate Air Force, Camarillo CA	88
88-16678•	AT-6D	42-84897		(to USN as Bu84867)	
	SNJ-5		N6900C	Michael Mockbee, Los Angeles CA	76
				Danny Summers, Sugar City, ID	92
88-16679•	AT-6D	42-84898		(to USN as Bu84868)	
	SNJ-5		N988E	Robert Shaver, Linwood NJ	76
				Simulated Automatic Weapons, Live Oak, FL	92
88-16686	AT-6D	42-84905		(to USN as Bu84875)	
	SNJ-5		N3725G	Eagle Aviation Inc, Tulsa OK	76
				Ronald Bryant, Springfield MO	77
				Confederate Air Force, Houston TX	88
88-16706•	AT-6D	42-84925		(to USN as Bu84895)	
	SNJ-5		N7055C	Gary Petersen, Lincoln, NE	92
88-16714	AT-6D	42-84933	N9103R	Robert L. Kimball, Ebensburg PA	76
88-16771	AT-6D	42-84990		(to USN as Bu84910)	
	SNJ-5		N3674F	City of New York, New York NY	76
88-16778 •	AT-6D	42-84997		(to USN as Bu84917)	
	SNJ-5		N3668F	Air Classics Inc, Lewisville TX	76
			N2023	William Rose, Barrington, Il	92
88-16791	AT-6D	42-84918		(to USN as Bu84930)	
	SNJ-5		N3665F	Don Rhynalds, Bealeton VA	76
				Sellersburg Aviation Museum, Sellersburg IN	88
88-16797•	AT-6D	42-84924		(to USN as Bu84936)	
	SNJ-5		N64KP	Kevin Larosa Enterprises, CA	92
88-16873	AT-6D	42-85092	N10605	Gary Boucher, Natchitoches LA	76
				Frank Nelson, Vicksburg MS	77
88-16923	AT-6D	42-85142		(to USN as Bu84912)	
	SNJ-5		N7211C	Richard Watson, Goleta, CA	92
88-16940 •	AT-6D	42-85159		(to USN as Bu84929)	
	SNJ-5		N8521K	Sale reported	92
88-16962•	AT-6D	42-85181		(to RAF as EZ407)	
	Mk. III			(to Portuguese AF as FAP1656)	83
				to Fleet Air Arm HF Yeovilton	
88-16973	AT-6D	42-85192		(to USN as Bu84962)	
	SNJ-5			USMC Air-Ground Mus., MCAS Quantico VA	88
88-16979 •	AT-6D	42-85198		(to USN as Bu84968)	
	SNJ-5		N65BL	Ben Lowell, Boulder CO	76
			N231H	Miles Biggs, Covington, LA	92
88-16980 •	AT-6D	42-85199		(to USN as Bu84969)	
	SNJ-5		N1040C	Stanley Gnesa, Modesto CA	76
			N6TF	Clancy Flanagan, Chowchilla, CA	92
88-16990 •	AT-6D	42-85209		(to USN as Bu84979)	
	SNJ-5		N7296C	for sale	76
				Samuel Saxton, Allentown, PA	92

88-16992•	AT-6D	42-85211		(to USN as Bu84981)	
	SNJ-5		N85169	Harold Rowe, Las Vegas, NV.	92
88-16994	AT-6D	42-85213		(to USN as Bu84983)	
	SNJ-5		XB-FOS		77
88-17002 •	AT-6D	42-85221		(to USN as Bu84991)	
	SNJ-5			(to Ejercito del Aire as ....)	
			N29940	Yankee Air Museum, Willow Grove MI	88
				Polish Flyers, Bellville, MI	92
88-17004•	AT-6D	42-85223		(to RAF as EZ449)	
	Mk. III			(to RNZAF as NZ1096)	
			ZK-END	W. S. Bell & R. D. Dahlberg, Mount Maunganui	87
88-17010•	AT-6D	42-85229		(to RAF as EZ455)	
	Mk. III			(to RNZAF as NZ1097)	
			ZK-ENJ	K. R. Brooking, Waitakere NZ	87
88-17011•	AT-6D	42-85230		(to RAF as EZ456)	
	Mk. III			(to RNZAF as NZ1098)	
			ZK-ENK	d'E. C. Darby, Ardmore NZ	87
88-17025	AT-6D	42-85244	4X-ARC	Marom Ltd, Tel Aviv	.63/72
88-17026•	AT-6D	42-85245	N6600C	Charles McFarland, Gig Harbour WA	76
				Hubert Mohr, Linwood, WA	92
88-17076•	AT-6D	42-85295		(to USN as Bu84995)	
	SNJ-5		N9813C	George W. Wrenn, Greensville TN	76
				Charles Lewis, Leadville, CO	92
88-17082	AT-6D	42-85301		(to USN as Bu85001)	
	SNJ-5		N3689F	Dennis K. Simpson, Anderson IN	76
88-17085•	AT-6D	42-85304		(to USN as Bu85004)	
	SNJ-5		N6437D	Sale reported, Wilmington, DE	92
88-17089•	AT-6D	42-85308		(to USN as Bu85008)	
	SNJ-5		N777HL	Donald Fowler, Fort Worth TX	76
				Andres Katz, Dallas, TX	92
88-17109•	AT-6D	42-85328	N3771M	George S. Morris, Dunedin FL	76
				Russell Turner, Panama City, FL	92
88-17155•	AT-6D	42-85374	N49961	Sale Reported, Irving, TX	92
88-17168 •	AT-6D	42-85387	N957ED	Eric Danfelt, Bellvue, WA	92
88-17181•	AT-6D	42-85400	N65555	George Madsen, Sylmar CA	76
				F.G. Kohler, Truckee, CA	92
88-17189 •	AT-6D	42-85408	N6979C	California Warbirds, San Jose CA	76/92
88-17197•	AT-6D	42-85416		(to USN as Bu85036)	
	SNJ-5		N9805C	Jack Flaherty, Hollister CA	76
				Robert Byrne, Detroit MI	77
				David Voglund, Radcliffe, KY	92
88-17199•	AT-6D	42-85418		(to USN as Bu85038)	
	SNJ-5			(to FA Brasiliera as FAB T-16 1706)	
			PT-KRC	Carlos Alberto Edo Palma, Jundiai	83
88-17208 •	AT-6D	42-85427		(to USN as Bu85047)	
	SNJ-5		N3640F	A. Castillo, Homestead FL	76
			N4LH	Bruce Moore, Canaan, NH	92

88-17237•	AT-6D	42-85456	N9649C	Tim Ehlies, Miami FL	76/92
88-17269	AT-6D	42-85488	N7213C		
			HP-304	Aeroquinca SA	.61
				withdrawn from use, by	65
88-17274 •	AT-6D	42-85493		(to USN as Bu85053)	
	SNJ-5		N8210E	Gorden Newell, Utica NY	76
			N777WS	Thersa Moretti RI	88
				Henri Moretti, Cranston, RI	92
88-17277	AT-6D	42-85496		(to USN as Bu85056)	
	SNJ-5		N164CL	Clay Lacey, Boise ID	76
88-17282 •	AT-6D	42-85501		(to USN as Bu85061)	
	SNJ-5		N9012Y	Ronald Paliughi, Visalia, CA	92
88-17284 •	AT-6D	42-85503		(to USN as Bu85063)	
	SNJ-5		N1047C	Grant L. Zickgraf, Franklin NC	76
				Stone Mountain Avn Museum,GA	92
88-17287 •	AT-6D	42-85506		(to USN as Bu85066)	
	SNJ-5		N666MC	William E. Henry, Ball Ground GA	76
			N2676P	Courtesy Aircraft, Rockford, IL	92
88-17301	AT-6D	42-85520		(to USN as Bu85080)	
	SNJ-5		N1046C	Don C. Barrett, Valley View TX	76
88-17307 •	AT-6D	42-85526		(to USN as Bu85086)	
	SNJ-5		N12377	Robert Richardson, Burbank CA	76/92
88-17308 •	At-6D	42-85527		(to USN as Bu85087)	
	SNJ-5		N25SS	Duane Potts, Marengo IA	76
				Campbell Barnett, Airy, NC	92
88-17311	AT-6D	42-85530		(to USN as Bu85090)	
	SNJ-5		N15090	Wilson C. Edwards, Big Spring TX	76
88-17331 •	AT-6D	42-85550	N7471C	Wellys Aircraft Sales, Delray FL	76
				Roger Henderson, El Sobrante, CA	92
88-17380 •	AT-6D	42-85599	N7421C	Gerald A. Swayze, Mesquite TX	76
				Edward J. Modes, Burbank, CA	92
				Gamma Holdings, Rockwall, TX	92
88-17400	AT-6D		N8213E	Sebring Simpson LA	88
88-17412	AT-6D	42-85631		(to USN as Bu90599)	
	SNJ-5		N3726G	Western State Aviation, Gunnison CO	76
88-17425•	AT-6D	42-85644		(to USN as Bu90612)	
	SNJ-5		N3261G	Keener S. White, Pembroke MA	76
				Robert Chisholm, Memphis, TN	92
88-17433 •	AT-6D	42-85652		(to USN as Bu90620)	
	SNJ-5		N5486V	James Odell, Sepulveda CA	76
				Thomas Payne, Leesburg, VA	92
88-17477	AT-6D	42-85696	N2864D	Ben Harrison, Seattle WA	76
88-17478•	AT-6D	42-85697	NN29947	Walter Newton, Lenoir, NC	92
88-17532 •	AT-6D	42-85751	N7214C	Don Harris, Fremont CA	76
				Connie Fleckenstein, Nacogdoches, TX	92
88-17551 •\	AT-6D	42-85770		(to USN as Bu90623)	

	SNJ-5		N89013	Jim Beasley PA	88
88-17552•	AT-6D	42-85771		(to USN as Bu90624)	
	SNJ-5		N13AA	Mechanical Systems, Silkeston MO	76
			VH-USN	G. Markey, Sydney NSW	90
88-17561 •	AT-6D	42-85780		(to USN as Bu90633)	
	SNJ-5		N3644F	Casimir Trelka, Libertyville IL	76
			VH-USS	Colin Rodgers, Sydney NSW	.89/90
			N3644F	Lan Dale Co., Reno, NV	92
88-17562•	AT-6D	42-85781		(to USN as Bu90634)	
	SNJ-5		N29965	WW II Enterprises NJ	88
				Danaire Corp. Bridgewater, NJ	92
88-17575•	AT-6D	42-85794	N991GM	T-6 Inc., Earle, AZ	92
88-17638 •	AT-6D	42-85857		(to USN as Bu90640)	
			N3257G	Sale reported	10.92
88-17647•	AT-6D	42-85866		(to USN as Bu90649)	
	SNJ-5		N7976C	I. N. Burchinall Jr, Paris TX	76
				Exec Aviation, Cincinatti, OH	92
88-17652•	AT-6D	42-85871		(to USN as Bu90654)	
	SNJ-5		N621BC	Bud Cashen CA	88
			N6438D	Douglas Peoples, Collierville, TN	92
88-17661	AT-6D	42-85880		(to USN as Bu90663)	
	SNJ-5B		N3633F	Phillip D. Bostwick, Bethesda DC	76
88-17662	AT-6D	42-85881		(to USN as Bu90664)	
	SNJ-5		N3682F	Ralph Parker TX	88
88-17667 •	AT-6D	42-85886		(to USN as Bu90669)	
	SNJ-5		N9801C	Ernest Bishop, Los Angeles CA	76
			F-AZBL	Aero Retro, St Rambert d'Albion	89/92
88-17668 •	AT-6D	42-85887		(to USN as Bu90670)	
	SNJ-5		N8215E	Thomas Faulkner, Oultewah TN	76/92
88-17670	AT-6D	42-85889		(to USN as Bu90672)	
	SNJ-5		N6643C	Pikes Peak Aviation, Fountain CO	76
88-17676 •	AT-6D	42-85895		(to USN as Bu90678)	
	SNJ-5		N830X	Frederick Krape, Wilmington DE	76
				Victor Norman, Staverton UK	1.90
			G-BRVG	Intrepid Aviation, North Weald	91/92
88-17678	AT-6D	42-85897		(to USN as Bu90680)	
	SNJ-5		N6972C	Harold Jolliff, Modesto CA	76
88-17716	AT-6D	42-85935	4X-ARB	Avitor Ltd, Tel Aviv	.63/72
88-17759	AT-6D	42-85978		(to USN as Bu90691)	
	SNJ-5		N3203G	Rodney Barnes WI	88
88-17767	AT-6D	42-85986		(to USN as Bu90699)	
	SNJ-5		N26862	Danaire Corp NJ	88
88-17780•	AT-6D	42-85999		(to USN as Bu90712)	
	SNJ-5		N7130C	John Larsen, Minneapolis MN	76
				Minnesota Air & Space Mus., Minneapolis MN	88
				Ingemar Holm, Bloomington, MI	92
88-17834•	AT-6D	42-86053	N117R	Stephen Roberts, Newark DE	76
				Richard T. Neil, Newark, DE	92

88-17873•	AT-6D	42-86092		(to USN as Bu90725)	
	SNJ-5		N3246G	Confederate Air Force, Mesa AZ	76/88
88-17883•	AT-6D	42-86102		(to USN as Bu90735)	
	SNJ-5		N1HZ	Hendrik Otzen, Granada Hills CA	76
			C-GPIN	Helair Enterprises BC	82
			N11HP	American Warbirds Collections, Chicago, IL	92
88-17923•	AT-6D	42-86142		(to Ejercito del Aire as C6-30)	
				storage compound Museo del Aire	
				Cuatro Vientos, Spain	84/86
			N4996M	David L. Tinker, Canton. MI	92
88-17960 •	AT-6D	42-86179		(to USN as Bu90752)	
	SNJ-5C		N3268G	Eugene O. Frank, Caldwell ID	76
			N964JD	Warbird Corp. Wichita, KS	92
88-17981 •	AT-6D	42-86200		(to USN as Bu90773)	
	SNJ-5		N3617F	Milton Leshe, Flanders NJ	76
				C.D. Clapper, Delray Beach, FL	92
88-18022•	AT-6D	42-86241	N7215C	Richard Ryerson, Middletown NY	76
			N817TX	Michael McCormick, Bay City, TX	92
88-18067•	AT-6D	42-86286		(to USN as Bu90789)	
	SNJ-5		N41BT	Wellesville Aviation Club, Wellesville NY	76
				Michael Scanlan, Huntingdon Beach CA	77
				Good Warbirds, Casper, WY	92
88-18068	AT-6D	42-86287		(to USN as Bu90790)	
	SNJ-5		N3275G	Ed Maloney/Planes of Fame Inc, Chino CA	76/88
88-18072	AT-6D	42-86291		(to USN as Bu90790)	
	SNJ-5		N7998C	Lawrence Donnerbert, Sand Point ID	76
88-18078•	AT-6D	42-86297		(to USN as Bu90810)	
	SNJ-5		N66JL	Charles Riley, Kansas City MO	76
			N810JF	Steve Afeman, Baton Rouge, LA	92
88-18079	AT-6D	42-86298		(to USN as Bu90811)	
	SNJ-5		N3634F		
			TI-260P		c55
88-18155	AT-6D	42-86374	N7216C		
			HP-330	P. Jansun/Aeroquimca SA	.62
				withdrawn from use, by	72
88-18171	AT-6D	42-86390	N6432D	Robert Elliot AZ	88
88-18205 •	AT-6D	42-86404		(to USN as Bu90837)	
	SNJ-5		N3724G	Chaytor D. Mason, Pomona CA	76/92
88-18215	AT-6D	42-86414		(to USN as Bu90847)	
	SNJ-5		XB-GEM		77
88-18286	AT-6D	42-86485		(to FA Brasiliera as FAB 1517)	•
				Museu Aerospacial do FAB, Rio de Janeiro	79
88-18304 •	AT-6D	42-86503		(to USN as Bu90866)	
	SNJ-5		N90866	Charlie Hammonds Flying Service, Houma LA	76
				USMC Air-Ground Mus., MCAS Quantico VA	88/92
				(displayed as "90866")	
88-18306 •	AT-6D	42-86505		(to USN as Bu90868)	
	SNJ-5		N9013A	Karen Grimm, CA	92

88-18328 •	AT-6D	42-86519		(to USN as Bu90882)	
	SNJ-5		N3148G	Lionel J. Caeton, Dos Palos, CA	92
121-41572	AT-6D	44-80850	N64577	Des Moines Technical School, Des Moines IA	76
121-41580	AT-6D	44-80858	N107FG	Frank Glover TX	88
121-41623	AT-6D	44-80901		(to USN as Bu90907)	
	SNJ-5		N3673F	Colonial Flying Corps Museum Inc, Toughkenamon PA	76
121-41628•	AT-6D	44-80905		(to USN as Bu90911)	
	SNJ-5		N73SL	Scott Rozell, Houston, TX	92
121-41634•	AT-6D	44-80911		(to USN as Bu90917)	
	SNJ-5		N1038A	John Collver, Lomita, CA	92
121-41634•	AT-6D	44-80912		(to USN as Bu90918)	
	SNJ-5		N8158H	Dennis G. Buehn, Long Beach CA	76
			N96RM	Russell Mayberry, Woodland Hills CA	77
			N26BT	Blue Thrailkill, Granada Hills, CA	92
121-41642•	AT-6D	44-80920		(to USN as Bu90926)	
	SNJ-5		N2266W	Jeffrey Perkins VA	88
				John Dankos, Ashland, VA	92
121-41732•	AT-6D	44-81010		(to USN as Bu90946)	
	SNJ-5		N125JD	John Darznieks, Dallas, TX	92
121-41736•	AT-6D	44-81014		(to USN as Bu90950)	
	SNJ-5		N3239G	Confederate Air Force, Harlingen TX	76/88
			N1689C	Clyde Barton, Clute, TX	92
121-41738•	AT-6D	44-81016		(to USN as Bu90952)	
	SNJ-5		N3204G	James E. Sullivan, Tarzana CA	76
				Joseph Chizmadia, Los Angeles, TX	92
121 41742•	AT-6D	44-81020		(to USN as Bu90956)	
	SNJ-5		N3631F	Brull Interstate Aircraft Co., Higginsville MO	76
				Rudy Blakey Inc. Perry, Fl	92
121-41757	AT-6D	44-81035		(to FA Brasiliera as FAB T-6D 1639)	
			PT-KUX	Luiz Raphael Vieiva Souta Costa, Rio de Jan.	83
121 41826 •	SNJ-5	44-81103		(to Ejercito del Aire as C6-124)	
				Escuela Superior de Ingenieros Aeronauticos nr Cuatro Vientos, Spain	82/88
121-41833 •	AT-6D	44-81111		(to USN as Bu90982)	
	SNJ-5			(to Ejercito del Aire as C.6-155)	
				Museo del Aire, Cuatra Vientos, Spain	85/92
121-41835•	AT-6D	44-81113		(to USN as Bu90984)	
	SNJ-5		N8223E	Raymond Karrels, Port Washington WI	76
				Haywood Bartlett, Pike Road, AL	92
121-41840•	AT-6D	44-81118		(to USN as Bu90989)	
	SNJ-5		N9804C	Verne J. Goodwin, Rutland VT	76
				Peter Pritchard, Amerhusrt, NH	92
121-41842	AT-6D	44-81120		(to USN as Bu90991)	
	SNJ-5		N73SL	Ben Lowell, Boulder CO	76
121-41846•	AT-6D	44-81124		(to USN as Bu90995)	
	SNJ-5		N8201E	Calvin R. Weier, Boca Raton FL	76
			N12KY	Classic Aviation International, Rosharon, TX	92

121-	AT-6D	44-81148	N10602	Earl R. Benedict, Fairfield CA	76
41870•				Novaro E. Nichols, Pleasant City, CA	92
121-	AT-6D	44-81210		(to USN as Bu90996)	
41932•	SNJ-5		N21JD	Larry Cogan, Melbourne FL	76
				Vern Raburn CA	88/92
121-	AT-6D	44-81219		(to USN as Bu91005)	
41941•	SNJ-5		N141SP	Susanne Parish, Kalamazoo MI	76
			N333SU	Kalamazoo Avn History Museum, MI	92
121-	AT-6D	44-81222		(to USN as Bu91008)	
41944•	SNJ-5		N144KM	Kirk McKee, Sacramento CA	77
			N29GK	Gordon Kibby CA	88/92
121-	AT-6D	44-81235		(to USN as Bu91021)	
41957•	SNJ-5		N6971C	Western State Aviation, Gunnison CO	76
				Lorren Kalish AZ	88
121-	AT-6D	44-81240		(to USN as Bu91026)	
4196•2	SNJ-5		N914DM	John J. Maney, Winsor, CA	92
121-	AT-6D	44-81248		(to USN as Bu91034)	
41970•	SNJ-5		N3262G	Sale Reported	92
121-	AT-6D	44-81223		(to USN as Bu91040)	
41945•	SNJ-5		N1944D	Bill McLeod, San Diego, Ca	92
121-	AT-6D	44-81232		(to USN as Bu91049)	
41954•	SNJ-5		N3265G	Thomas Hutchins, Advance, NC	92
121-	AT-6D	44-81265		(to USN as Bu91051)	
41987•	SNJ-5		N2686D	David O. Dodd, Denton, TX	92
121-	AT-6D	44-81346		(to USN as Bu91072)	
42068	SNJ-5		N6637C	Louis Heckelsberg, Bartlesville OK	76
121-	AT-6D	44-81356		(to USN as Bu91082)	
42078•	SNJ-5		N9823C	Lee Schaller, Sausalito CA	76
				Paul Beck, Gold Hill, OR	92
121-	AT-6D	44-81362		(to USN as Bu91088)	
42084•	SNJ-5			(to Ejercito del Aire as C6-132)	
				storage compound Museo del Aire	
				Cuatro Vientos, Spain	82
			N29930	Doug Clark, Glendale, CA	92
121-	AT-6D	44-81388		(to USN as Bu91094)	
42110•	SNJ-5		N8218E	Thomas Horne, Fort Worth TX	76
				David Hall, CT	92
121-	AT-6D	44-81453	N4983N	VFR Aero Inc, Kalamazoo MI	76
42175•				Jeff Neff, Seattle, Wa	92
121-	AT-6D	44-81468	N6984C	George Younghahs, Las Vegas NV	76
42190•				Mustang Enterprises NJ	88
				Hartzell Propeller In. OH	92
121-	AT-6D	44-81480	N6980C	P. M. Dusters Inc, Chico CA	76
42202•				John Herlihy, Mt. Shasta, CA	92
121-	AT-6D	44-81493	N7230C	Richard J. Bowers, Rockford IL	76
42215•			N36	Joe B. McShane, Monahans, TX	92
121-	AT-6D	44-81494	N7448C	Joseph. W. Quinn, Saugus CA	76

Continued on Page 350

Join the

North American Trainer Association

NOW!

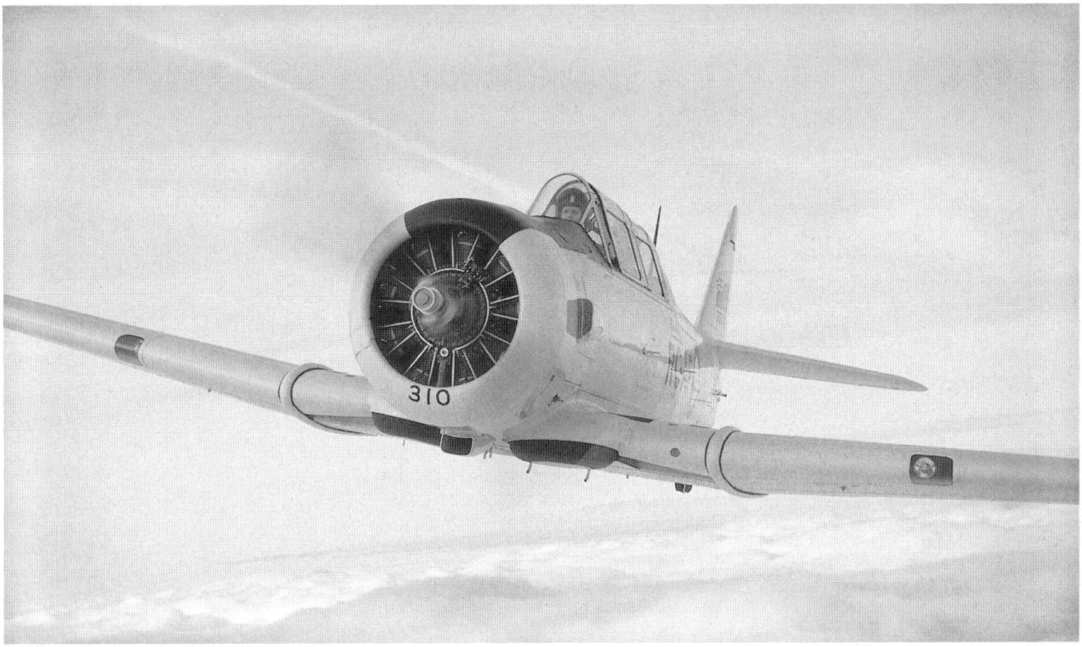

Enjoy membership of this international group of owners, pilots, crew members, performers, mechanics and enthusiasts of the Yale, AT-6, T-28, TF-51 and TB-25.
The popular quarterly magazine of the Association, "Texans & Trojans", includes articles dedicated to the preservation, restoration and safe flying of these airplanes.
Exclusive photos and articles in each issue

Dues are $40.00 (USA & CANADA), $50.00 all others. Visa/Mastercard accepted. Join Now for yourself or give a gift membership.

North American Trainer Association (NATA)
25801 NE Hinness Road, Brush Prarie, WA 98606, USA
206-256-0066 fax 206-896-5398

Continued from Page 348

North American T-6/SNJ & Canadian Car Foundry Harvard

42216•				Michael E. Jauregui, Newhall, CA	92
121-42228	AT-6D	44-81506	N7231C HP-331	 B. J. Norton & P. S. Shacklett, Paitilla	 .61
121-42239•	AT-6D	44-81517	N6496D N45GK	George Banjak, Webster Groves MO Gary Kohs, Birmingham, MI	76 92
121-42285	AT-6D	44-81563	N7231G	B & F Aircraft Supply, Oak Lawn IL	76
121-42318•	AT-6F SNJ-6	44-81596	 N211A	(to USN as Bu.............) Doug Champlin/Windward Aviation, Enid OK Robert Deford AZ	 76 88
121-42368•	AT-6F	44-81646	N4485	Greg Klassen, Bakersfield, CA	92
121-42372•	AT-6F	44-81650	N4486	John Gostomski, Omaha, NE	92
121-42378•	AT-6F	44-81656	N7461C	Sun Master Awnings, Mishawaka IN AVIREX Inc Long Island City, NY	76 92
121-42409•	AT-6F	44-81687	N164US	T64 US Incorporated VA	88
121-42412	AT-6F	44-81690	F-BJBT OO-JBT	Soc. Air France, Toussous-le-Noble COGEA Nouvelle, Ostende J. Theil, Wevelgem; later Monchengladbach Mr Honkoop, Veen, Netherlands to scrap yard, Bergen op Zoom, Neths.	 20.8.65 15.2.66 7.70 .71
121-42415 •	AT-6F	44-81693	N85593	Howard J. Crowe, Toledo OH Courtesy Aircraft Division, Rockford IL John Luther, San Antonio, Tx	76 77 92
121-42438	AT-6F	44-81716	OO-ABD N9752F N9852F	Automotive Industries Inc NV, Moorsele ntu: Henry Lloyd Knight, Eure, France Henry Lloyd Knight, Eure, France (reg. carried illegally) impounded, smuggling, Barcelona, Spain	31.5.61 5.6.61 6.61 8.64/7.71
121-42452	AT-6F	44-81730	F-BJBU OO-JBU	Soc. Air France, Toussous-le-Noble COGEA Nouvelle, Ostende J. Theil, Wevelgem; later Monchengladbach Mr Honkoop, Veen, Netherlands to scrap yard, Bergen op Zoom, Neths.	 .8.65 15.2.66 7.70 .71
121-42475•	AT-6F	44-81753	N2834D	Rudolph W. Hazuka, Wilmington CA John Dimmer, Tacoma, WA	76 92
121-42479•	AT-6F	44-81757	N6601C	Chan Stokes, Rosenburg OR Jefferson Flight Group, Grants Pass OR James Garemore, Ocala, FL	76 77 92
121-42480•	AT-6F	44-81758	F-BJBP OO-JBP	Soc. Air France, Toussous-le-Noble COGEA Nouvelle, Ostende J. Theil, Wevelgem; later Monchengladbach Mr Honkoop, Veen, Netherlands stored , Tyre-Firemat premises, Aalburg	 18.8.65 15.2.66 7.70 71-
121-42497•	AT-6F	44-81775	F-BJBS OO-JBS	Soc. Air France, Toussous-le-Noble COGEA Nouvelle, Ostende J. Theil, Wevelgem; later Monchengladbach Mr Honkoop, Veen, Netherlands	 10.8.65 15.2.66 7.70

Continued on Page 352

FORMATION FLYING

"the art"™

A New Professionally Produced Video

Two hours of airborne and classroom training in warbirds taught by former military pilots using actual military procedures and techniques. Included with each film is an original "Formation Flight Manual" *, a special pack of briefing forms, and a video table of contents.

- Recommended and endorsed by **Bob Hoover**
- You are in the cockpit!! See all airborne sequences performed from the wingman's viewpoint
- Full comprehensive classroom discussions and descriptions of each maneuver
- Learn how formation flying should be done correctly and safely
- Learn all the military terms and what they mean, "station keeping, acute, sucked..."
- A must video for **all** pilot's film libraries
- Standardized to the T-34 Association, Inc. "Formation Flight Manual©," 3rd edition, the official manual of:
  - T-34 Association®
  - EAA/Warbirds of America®
  - Valiant Air Command®
  - North American Trainer Association®
- Procedures described are applicable to all aircraft types, Cessna 150s to jets
- An excellent review video for all current and former military pilots

Available in all International Formats

Introductory Offer:

$49.95

plus shipping & handling

A New How-to Video Now Available

Produced and Distributed by Darton International, Inc.
Visa and Mastercard Accepted Call (619) 434-0701, FAX (619) 434-3919

Continued from Page 350

				to scrap yard, Bergen op Zoom, Netherlands	.71
121-42500	AT-6F	44-81778	D-IDEM D-FDEM	J. Hossl, Straskirchen	72
121-42502	AT-6F	44-81780	VR-HDC	Lee Kim Bun J. H. Fleming, Kai Tak, Hong Kong to CATC-14: restored: fate unknown	10.46 22.4.48
121-42506•	AT-6F	44-81784	VT-AVA	 Air Commodore Mehar Singh, Delhi-Palam	3.46 79
121-42509	AT-6F	44-81787	VT-AYR	Rusi Mistri, Bombay A.C.P. Wadia, Bombay	3.46 24.2.50
121-42511	AT-6F	44-81789	F-BJBV OO-JBV	Soc. Air France, Toussous-le-Noble COGEA Nouvelle, Ostende J. Theil, Wevelgem; later Monchengladbach Mr Honkoop, Veen, Netherlands to scrap yard, Bergen op Zoom, Neths.	 27.8.65 15.2.66 7.70 .71
121-42512	AT-6F	44-81790	F-BJBQ OO-JBQ	Soc. Air France, Toussous-le-Noble COGEA Nouvelle, Ostende J. Theil, Wevelgem; later Monchengladbach Mr Honkoop, Veen, Netherlands broken-up and. canc.	 24.8.65 11.10.66 7.70 8.70
121-42513	AT-6F	44-81791	F-BJBR OO-JBR	Soc. Air France, Toussous-le-Noble COGEA Nouvelle, Ostende J. Theil, Wevelgem; later Monchengladbach Mr Honkoop, Veen, Netherlands broken-up and. canc.	 20.8.65 15.2.66 7.70 8.70
121-42525•	AT-6F	44-81803	N7809B	Degado Trades & Tech. Inst., New Orleans LA State of Louisiana	76 92
121-42541•	AT-6F	44-81819	N7446C	Charles Gilbert, Rolling Hills CA Gerald Gabe	76 92
121-42548•	AT-6F	44-81826	N10434	City of New York, New York NY	76
121-42563•	AT-6F	44-81841	N10590 N578JB	Philip Bond, Irving TX John MacGuire Santa Teresa, NM	76 92
121-42579	AT-6F	44-81857	N81854	David C. Tallichet/ MARC, Chino CA	76
121-42583•	AT-6F	44-81861	N4503B	Clarke Hill, Wentworth, NH	92
121-42592	AT-6F	44-81870	N4708C	Robert L. Younkin, Fayetteville AR	76
121-42606	AT-6F	44-81884	N7460C	Charles B. Dulgerian, Monroe NY	76
121-42611•	AT-6F	44-81889	N999JP	Aero Enterprises Inc, Seattle WA Gerald Gale CA	76 88
121-42615	AT-6F	44-81893	N706F	Charles F. Saunders, El Paso TX	76
121-42642•	AT-6F	44-81920	N10490	Raymond J. Urmston, Kinnelon NJ	76/92

121-42650	AT-6F	44-81928	VT-CHW	G. D. Mukherjee, Calcutta	11.46
121-42698•	AT-6F	44-81976	N7464C	Clyde Wolf, Commerce City CO	76
				Kenneth Burham, Ft Collins, CO	92
121-42714	AT-6F	44-81992	N373N	Robert B. Spencer, Galena OH	76
121-42749•	AT-6F	44-82027	N7475C	Robert J. Richardson, Burbank CA	76
				Marvin Quaid, Monteroy, CA	92
121-42750•	AT-6F	44-82028	N66J	W. J. Reedy, South Pasadena CA	76
				William Leasure, Northridge, CA	92
121-42770•	AT-6F	44-82048	N4488	Art Medore, Hemet, CA	92
121-42776•	AT-6F	44-82054	VT-AXS	Maharaja Jam Sahib of Nawanagar, Jamnagar	2.46
				Maharaja of Jaipur, Jaipur	22.3.49/79
121-42823	AT-6F	44-82101		(to USN as Bu11..........)	
	SNJ-6		N8217E	William H. Mundhenk, West Alexandria OH	76
121-42854•	AT-6F	44-82132	N101BW	Jerry Rubin, Southampton PA	76
				Dean Edmonds, Weston, MA	92
121-43022	AT-6F	44-82300	N2867D	State of California, Tracy CA	76
121-43186•	AT-6F	44-82464		(to USN as ....)	
	SNJ-6		N186D	Jack C. Strother, Gastonburg AL	76
			N47LF	N. F. McGowin AL	88
121-43211	AT-6F	44-82489	N7462C	Merle B. Gustafson, Tallulah LA	76
• -	SNJ-5	Bu51429	N51428	B. Ashenfelter, Agincourt ONT	76
				Lynn Crouch, Whitehouse TN	77
				Clifford Ashenfelter, Hartford, WI	92
-	SNJ-5	Bu51503		noted unconv., in USN sc., Salisbury MD	73
-	SNJ-5	Bu51521		noted unconv., in USN sc., Salisbury MD	73
-	SNJ-5	Bu51584	N1395N	Brull Interstate Aircraft Co. , Higginsville MO	76
-	SNJ-5	Bu51585		noted unconv., in USN sc., Salisbury MD	73
-	SNJ-5	Bu51631		noted unconv., in USN sc., Salisbury MD	73
-	SNJ-5	Bu51677	N6975C	Ronald Montayne, Phoenix AZ	76
•-	SNJ-5	Bu51678	N3579	Dixon James Smith, Mercer, WA	92
-•	SNJ-5	Bu51686	N913D	Donald Alderson, Hidden Hills CA	76
				Gary Stearns, Camarillo, CA	92
-	SNJ-5	Bu51693		noted unconv., in USN sc., Salisbury MD	73
-•	SNJ-5	Bu51698	N7986C	Experimental Aircraft Association, Oskosh WI	76
				Rudy Frasca, Champaign, IL	92
-	SNJ-5	Bu51711		noted unconv., in USN sc., Salisbury MD	73
-•	SNJ-5	Bu51764	N15WS	Waldon D. Spillers, Versailles OH	76
				Georgia Historical Museum, GA	92

•-	SNJ-5	Bu51788	N3633F	James Ricks, Greenwood, MA	92
-	SNJ-5	Bu51789	N5488V	Cascade Ditching Co., Salem OR	76
-	SNJ-5	Bu51810	N3269G	Emillo Nervino, Santa Cruz CA	76
-	SNJ-5	Bu51811		(to Ejercito del Aire as C6-134) storage compound Museo del Aire Cuatro Vientos, Spain	83
			N3931S		
-•	SNJ-5	Bu51819	N7804B	Russell Boy, Plantation FL	76
				B.L. Smith, De Ridder, LA	92
-	SNJ-5	Bu51828	N711RA	Robert G. Abrams, Chula Vista CA	76
				Michael McCrae CA	88
-•	SNJ-5	Bu51875	N3JC	William J. Crone, Beach City, OH	92
-	SNJ-5	Bu51880	N7991C	Robert Ashworth, Farmer City IL	76
-	SNJ-5	Bu51882	N3676F	William Wobbe, Louisville KY	76
-	SNJ-5	Bu51892		noted unconv., in USN sc., Salisbury MD	73
-•	SNJ-5	Bu51903	N51903	Lester D. Friend, San Diego CA	76
				Joe Arnold, Eudora AR	77
				Clarence Rittelmeyer, Pine Bluff, AR	92
-•	SNJ-5	Bu51908	N44999	Michael Yannell, Lafayette NJ	76
			N446CM	Christopher Maier, Hope, NJ	92
-•	SNJ-5	Bu51952	N15HB	Dabob Inc, Bernardsville NJ	76
				Thomas Hatchell, NC	92
-	SNJ-5	Bu51965		noted unconv., in USN sc., Salisbury MD	73
-•	SNJ-5	Bu51971	N3267G	Thomas W. Henley, Emelle AL	76
				Alan Henley, Emelle, AL	92
-•	SNJ-5	Bu51974	N3264G	Darren L. Wall, Floresville TX	76
				James Engleman, Vanderpool, TX	92
-•	SNJ-5	Bu51979	N51979	Jerry D. King, Sand City CA	76
				Donald T. Bailey, CA	92
-	SNJ-5	Bu51985	N64L	James U. Lemke, Delmar CA	76
				B & S Enterprises, Sacramento CA	77
-	SNJ-5	Bu52006	N52006	C. J. Shirpser, North Hollywood CA	76
-•	SNJ-5	Bu52017	N543LB	Speedway Volkswagen, Indianapolis IN	76
				Lowell Blossom, Zionsville IN	77
				Albert Stix, St. Louis, MO	92
-	SNJ-5	Bu52020	N8211E	Carl Launderville, Rolling Hills CA	76
-	SNJ-5	Bu52026	N29941	David Fain IL	88
-	SNJ-5	Bu52031	N3666F	Air Repair Inc, Lewisville TX	76
				George Ceshker, Azle TX	77
-	SNJ-5C	Bu	N6438D	Challenge Publications Inc, Van Nuys CA (id. quoted as "39331")	76
-•	SNJ-6	Bu111957	N4RC	Triple S. Co, Bingen WA	76

				Robert Jones, Federal Way, WA	92
-	SNJ-6	Bu111966	N9828C	Amalio N. Polidori, Mundelein IL	76
-•	SNJ-6	Bu111974	N3169G	Carter Clark, Edwards AFB, CA	92
-•	SNJ-6	Bu111987	N9825C	Mid West Avn. Enterprises Inc, Champaign IL	76
				Rudy Frasca, Champaign, IL	92
-•	SNJ-6	Bu112007	N5485V	V. S. Sloan, Thomaston GA	76
				William Johnson, Fayetville, NC	92
•-	SNJ-6	Bu112023	N5500V	Edward A. Ray, Westlake Village CA	76
				Robert Thompson, Orange, CA	92
•-	SNJ-6	Bu112034	N3254G	Robert Heale, Warden WA	76
			N2129	Richard Clinton, Fairoaks, CA	92
- •	SNJ-6	Bu112047		noted stored unconv., Greybull WY	89
•-	SNJ-6	Bu112049	N9809C	Middletown Enterprises, Richmond CA	76
				Quarry Products, Richmond, CA	92
•-	SNJ-6	Bu112070	N68JS	Joe Speidel, Wheeling WV	76
				Joe Scogna, Yardley, PA	92
-•	SNJ-6	Bu112071	N3646F	Jim Malone, Oklahoma City OK	76
				Buck Bros, Joliet, IL	92
-•	SNJ-6	Bu112079	N1044C	James H. Bohlander, Marengo IL	76
				Robert Willard, Durango, CO	92
-•	SNJ-6	Bu112114	N58740	Crawford Deems, Leesburg FL	76
				Michael J, Cobb, Boston, MA	92
-•	SNJ-6	Bu112123	N7984C	Johnathan Staeling, Woodstock, IL	92
-	SNJ-6	Bu112124	N2857G	Thomas H. Jones, San Ramon CA	76
-•	SNJ-6	Bu112130	N2860G	Merrell Gossman, Van Nuys CA	.77
				Andrew Gemellaro, Canoga Pk CA	92
-•	SNJ-6	Bu112131	N73RR	Ralph Rina, Huntingdon Beach CA	76
				Morton Aviation, Shrewsbury, NJ	92
-	SNJ-6	Bu112148	N3639F	Robert W. Speed, Monroe LA	76
				William Albers, Fairfax, VA	92
-•	SNJ-6	Bu112157	N2861G	Donald H. Bontz, Buena Park CA	76/92
-•	SNJ-6	Bu112161	N2862G	Ronald T. Golan, Los Angeles CA	76
				sale reported, Mojave, CA	92
-•	SNJ-6	Bu112168	N3238G	Terry Adams, Libertyville, IL	92
-•	SNJ-6	Bu112169	N2864G	William G. Palank, Fair Oaks CA	76/92
-•	SNJ-6	Bu112178	N9820C	Wesley Y. Braggs, Virginia Beach VA	76
				American Airpower Heritage, Midland, TX	92
-•	SNJ-6	Bu112180	N9831C	Aero Enterprises Inc, Seattle WA	76
			N916DC	Jim Clevenger, Marion, NC	92
-•	SNJ-6	Bu112187		(to FA Brasiliera as FAB T6 1712)	
			PT-KVE	Armando Vianna Egreja, Penapolis	83
-•	SNJ-6	Bu112201	N6617X	Robert L Ferguson, MA	92

-	SNJ-6	Bu112204	N6515C	David H. Carnochan, Fort Wayne IN	76
	SNJ-6	Bu112208	N7970C	reg. pending	77
-•	SNJ-6	Bu112213	N9161 N969RH	Robert M. Harkey, Indianapolis IN John Booth, Aberdeen, NC	76 92
-•	SNJ-6	Bu112220	N21BA	Kelly Chevrolet Cadillac, Butler PA John Williams, IL	76 92
-•	SNJ-6	Bu112227	N9800C	Moore Aviation Inc, Tulare CA Jerry Borchin NC	76 88
-•	SNJ-6	Bu112237	N7985C	Jerry C. Marracola, Sparks NV Alfred Goss, Woodlands, CA	76 92
-•	SNJ-6	Bu112239	N6442D	Lanie S. Jones, Opa Locka FL Robert Button, Stevensville, MD	76 92
-•	SNJ-6	Bu112447	N7983C	Norman E. Goyer, Apple Valley CA Randolph Wilson, Dallas, TX	76 92
-•	SNJ-6	Bu112269	N269CB	A. C. Sears, Aurora OR Robert Lessman, CA	76 92
-•	SNJ-6	Bu112301	N9806C	Trissell Flying Service Inc, Clarksville TX Texas Air Museum, Harlingen, TX	76 92
-•	SNJ-6	Bu112314	N4135A	Ag Air, Los Fresnos, TX	92
-	SNJ-6	Bu112316	N6298C	Confederate Air Force, Harlingen TX	76
-•	SNJ-6	Bu112323	N611F	Colene Giglio, Long Beach CA Repatria, CA	76 92
-	SNJ-6	Bu112348	N3283G	Iowa Western Comm. Coll., Council Bluffs IA Steven Smith, Lincoln NE	76 77
168-1•	T-6G	49-2897	N7197C	Douglas W. Goss, Aurora CO Edward Huber, CO	76 92
168-2•	T-6G	49-2898	N3715G	William H. Sole, Midland TX Carl Payne, Katy TX Richard James WI	76 77 88
168-5	T-6G	49-2901		(to L'Armee de L'Air as 92901) Amicale Jean-Baptiste Salis, La Ferte-Alais	 79
168-14	T-6G	49-2910	N2813G	D. L. Shacklelette, Louisville KY	76
168-16•	T-6G	49-2912	N29936	Mike McIntyre, Aptos, CA	92
168-19•	T-6G	49-2915	N66JB	J. K. Biegger, Las Vegas NV Steven Harrison, Rolla, MO	76 92
168-32	T-6G	49-2928	N2886G	H & W Spraying Inc, Midland TX	76
168-40	T-6G	49-2936	N3717G	R. M. Hendrickson, Buffalo Grove IL	76
168-47•	T-6G	49-2943	N6253C	Maurice D. Birkholz, Minot MD Hal Darly, Griffin, GA	76 92
168-50	T-6G	49-2946	C-GBPL	Dennis J. Bradley ONT	82
168-51•	T-6G	49-2947	N6183C	W. Branch, Dallas TX K&M Aircraft Corp, Carroltown, TX	76 92

168-53•	T-6G	49-2949	N4QU	Michael Jeffery, Lexington NC (registered as 48-2949)	76/92
168-54•	T-6G	49-2950	N96143	Lloyd Freeman, Atlanta GA Adrian Blackmon, Atlanta GA James Ricks MO	76 77 88
168-61•	T-6G	49-2957	N2806G	C. H. Harvey, Berkeley CA Skarda Flying Service, Hazen, AR	76 92
168-66•	T-6G	49-2962	N12CC	C. G. Cox, Birmingham AL Southern Museum of Flight, AL	76 92
168-77•	T-6G	49-2974	N9670C	Louis Antonacci, Hampshire IL John Sucich, Chicago, IL	76 92
168-81•	T-6G	49-2977	N29963	Marion Gregory WI	88
168-87•	T-6G	49-2983		(To French Air Force as 92983) To Moroc AF as Y61501 Major Iran by Maroc. To Tunisia Recovered - at Etampes, France	88 10.61 10.92
168-91•	T-6G	49-2987	N2757G	Carl Schmeider AZ	88
168-92•	T-6G	49-2988	N7657C N584M	Thomas P. Kelly, Peoria IL John D. McCoy, Villa Park, CA	76 92
168-94•	T-6G	49-2990	N9035Z	Leroy A. Smith, Wichita Falls TX Glen Johnson TX	76 88/92
168-100•	T-6G	49-2996	N2879G	Edward O. Messick, San Antonio TX Bruce Grassfield, Aspen, CO	76 92
168-102•	T-6G	49-2998	 N128WK	(to F.A. Hondurenas as 211) William Speer, La Mesa, CA	 92
168-105	T-6G	49-3001	N9067Z	Claiton R. Jordan, Phoenix AZ	76
168-107•	T-6G	49-3003	 N39311	(to Ejercito del Aire as C6-186) storage compound Museo del Aire Cuatro Vientos, Spain Warbirds of Dayton, Dayton OH	 82/83 84
168-109•	T-6G	49-3005	N6FD N4313Z	James C. Bennet, Chestertown MD Robert Younkin, AZ	76 92
168-134•	T-6G	49-3030	N9871C	George D. Koren, Atlanta GA Gary Leggette, Atlanta, GA	76 92
168-138•	T-6G	49-3034	N	Wiley Sanders Truck Lines, AL	92
168-141•	T-6G	49-3037	 F-AZCQ F-AZCQ	(to Ejercito del Aire as E.16-193) Group Alcyons Lons/Le Saulnier based, Frontenas	 10.88
168-142•	T-6G	49-3038	N66TY	Jeppio Limited CO Glenn Jones, Littleton, CO	88 92
168-152•	T-6G	49-3048	N9890C N51987	James D. Scully, Jenkintown PA John Vandersluis, Fitzwilliam NH John Vandersluis CT	76 77 88
168-160•	T-6G	49-3056		(to Ejercito del Aire as C6-188) storage compound Museo del Aire Cuatro Vientos, Spain	 83/89

168-161•	T-6G	49-3057	N5296V	Atlantic Aero Inc, Greensboro NC	76
				Robert Phillips, NC	92
168-170•	T-6G	49-3066	N49388	Michael Hooper, Harvey, LA	92
168-175•	T-6G	49-3071	N2996Q	Victor Henry, Woodland, MS	92
168-176•	T-6G	49-3072	N2807G	Joseph Natoli, Nokesville VA	76
			G-BHTH	Jim Keen	.80
				Bryn Rossiter, Wellesbourne Mountford	87
				John Woodhouse, Hants	92
				(flies as "USN 2807/V-103")	
168-185•	T-6G	49-3081	N7771C	Trissell Flying Service, Clarksville TX	76
				Warbird Rides & Adv., Orlando, FL	92
168-189•	T-6G	49-3085	N2993S	Radial Runners, Silver Lake, MN	92
168-190	T-6G	49-3086	N5270V	Matthew Kibler, Balto MD	76
168-191•	T-6G	49-3087	N3173G	Maynard Lund, Ritzville WA	76
				Michael McMahon, NY	92
168-201•	T-6G	49-3097	N3HG	L. B. Johnson, East Wenatchee WA	76
				Ed Stringfellow, Cropwell, AL	92
168-204•	T-6G	49-3100	N6625C	Danny R. Dunagan, Atlanta GA	76
				Bert Zeller, New Bern, NC	92
168-241	T-6G	49-3137	N101GB	Lasalle Elect, Galesburg IL	76
168-242	T-6G	49-3138	N3748G	Robert Fleagane, Cadiz OH	76
168-243	T-6G	49-3139	N2805G	Robert J. Mejdrich, Lagrange IL	76
168-245•	T-6G	49-3141	N157DC	Donald Cassidy, Martinsville IN	76
				David Manire, KY	92
168-248•	T-6G	49-3144	N55897	Charles Feken, Bloomington IL	76
				Butch Schroeder, Danville, IL	92
168-249•	T-6G	49-3145	N9628C	Gregs Crop Care Co, Wilbur WA	76
				Topflight Aviation Inc, Imperial NB	77
				Don Anklin	92
168-252•	T-6G	49-3148	N9034Z	registered	10.92
168-255•	T-6G	49-3151	N151AT	John C. Williams, Tampa FL	76
				S.W. Muse, Westlaco, TX	92
168-256•	T-6G	49-3152	N3158G	Richard Churchill OR	88/92
168-257	T-6G	49-3153	N5557V	Chuck Easton, Greeley CO	76
168-259	T-6G	49-3155	N94155	Robert L. Wick, Worthington OH	76
				Robert L. Wick TX	88
168-262•	T-6G	49-3158	N444RB	John Johnson, Rexburg ID	76
			N6HC	Ted Contri, Reno, NV	92
168-264•	T-6G	49-3160	N6128C	John Becker, Dallas TX	76
				Classic Aviation International TX	88
			N5ZS	Hezca Inc. Pell City, AL	92
168-268	T-6G	49-3164	N5184V	Board of Cooperative Educational Service, Westbury NY	76

168-275•	T-6G	49-3171	N9043Z	George M. Staehling, Woodstock IL	76
			N36913	William Melamed CA	88
				Ed Shipley, CA	92
168-276•	T-6G	49-3172	N3172G	Arthur S. Kuchan, Hudson IL	76
				Kevin Batterton, Morton, IL	92
168-281•	T-6G	49-3177	N3753G	Emerson Davies, Davisburg, MI	92
168-283•	T-6G	49-3179	N5289V	Charles Feken, Bloomington IL	76
				Aero Dynamics, Wilmington, DE	92
168-290•	T-6G	49-3186	N1751	Steven Seghetti, Vacaville CA	76
			VH-HAJ	Col Pay, Scone NSW	90
168-293	T-6G	49-3189	N3142G	Board of Cooperative Educ. Serv., Verona NY	76
168-294•	T-6G	49-3190	N8399H	Woods Aviation Inc, East Prairie MO	76
				Gordon Swenson IA	88
168-295 •	T-6G	49-3191		(to Austrian AF as 4C-TE)	
				stored Heeresgeschichtliches Museum, Vienna	79/88
168-302•	T-6G	49-3198	N5188V	Walter R. Patten, Sacramento CA	76
				Air Share, Palo Alto, CA	92
168-306•	T-6G	49-3202		(to FA Brasiliera as FAB T-6D 1658)	
			PT-KVF	Luiz Rinaldo da Motta Rizental, Nova Igaucu	83
168-311•	T-6G	49-3207	N3100G	Keith Hilton, Oceanside CA	76
				Art Medore, Denville, NJ	92
168-312•	T-6G	49-3208	N7664C	Clayton J. Carriveau, Franksville WI	76/92
168-313•	T-6G	49-3209	G-DDMV	Elizabeth Morgan, Northants	92
168-314•	T-6G	49-3210	N8335H	Donald E. Murphy, Nelson CA	76/92
168-315•	T-6G	49-3211	N9893C	Philip Waterman, Reno NV	76
				Hans Christensen, Pahrump, NV	92
168-325•	T-6G	49-3221	N990JP	James Milliken, Narbeth PA	76
			N17498	Cinema Air, Houston, TX	92
168-326•	T-6G	49-3222	N9042Z	William A. Jeff, Dayton OH	76
			N22NA		92
168-336•	T-6G	49-3232	N2449	Ray Kinney, Gainesville, TX	92
168-340	T-6G	49-3236	N9MC	Melvin Craig, Crown Point IN	76
168-345•	T-6G	49-3241	N8203H	Bill Miller, Anaheim CA	76
				Robert Hall, Ocala, FL	92
168-346•	T-6G	49-3242	N51944	William D. Platero, Clifton NJ	76
				Donald Contant, Santee SC	77
				John Watson, Blackwood, NJ	92
168-347•	T-6G	49-3243	N7613C	Frank Sylvestri, Millbrae CA	76
				Mark Moody, Moreno Valley, CA	92
168-349•	T-6G	49-3245	N28955	Latshaw Drilling Company & Expl Co., Houston, TX	92
168-358•	T-6G	49-3254	N6889C	Joe Rankin, San Francisco CA	76
				Foreign Automotive Inc, Santa Rosa CA	77
				Air Bear Corp, Waukegan, IL	92
168-360•	T-6G	49-3256	N7487C	Everett Community College, Everett WA	76

				James Milliken, Narberth PA	77
				Owls Head Tr. Museum, ME	92
168-363•	T-6G	49-3259	N3168G	David Fain, Skokie IL	76
				Rodney Barnes, WI	92
168-370•	T-6G	49-3266	N9604C	Elmer F. Ward, Santa Ana CA	76
				Richard Foote, Andover CT	77
			N51KT	Dumfries Marine Corp, Dover, DE	92
168-373•	T-6G	49-3269		(to Ejercito del Aire as C6-170)	
				storage compound Museo del Aire	
				Cuatro Vientos, Spain	82/83
			N3931U		3.9.82
			N61MH	Northaire Inc., Wilmington, DE	92
168-376•	T-6G	49-3272	NN3167G	Albert Costa, Waban, MA	92
168-382	T-6G	49-3278	N165P	Paul Taylor, Shakopee MN	76
				(registered as 49-3536)	
168-383	T-6G	49-3279	N7704C	Chris Nelson, Wheatridge CO	76
				Al Trovinger Ford Inc, Mobile AL	77
168-388•	T-6G	49-3284	N8204H	Mustang Pilots Club, Beverley Hills CA	76
				Kenneth Dwelle, Auburn, CA	92
168-395•	T-6G	49-3291	N3166G	Skytypers, CA	92
168-396•	T-6G	49-3292	N9644C	for sale	76
			N426DB	Dorr Burns, Grand Junction, CO	92
168-401•	T-6G	49-3297	N9627C	Charles Feken, Bloomington IL	76
				American Airpower Heritage Museum, TX	92
168-404•	T-6G	49-3300	N3171G	Charles M. Dedrick, Vergennes VT	76
				Hampton Air, Griffin, GA	92
168-406•	T-6G	49-3302	N9609C	Stuart Schwartz, Southfield MI	76
			N666SS	Joe Kasperoff, Montebello, CA	92
168-407•	T-6G	49-3303	N5259V	Ronald G. Ellis, Miami FL	76
				Outlaw Aircraft Sales Inc, Clarksville TN	77
				Fred Keister, MD	92
168-409•	T-6G	49-3305	N332CA	Richard Hansen IL	88
168-410•	T-6G	49-3306	N7000S	for sale	76
				Richard Braky, Hubbs, NM	92
168-411•	T-6G	49-3307	N3307	Edward J. Mitchell, Hollister CA	76
				Earl Curtis, Phoenix, AZ	92
168-414•	T-6G	49-3310	N7679C	Richard Fields, Fullerton, CA	92
168-415•	T-6G	49-3311		(to Ejercito del Aire as C6-167)	
				storage compound Museo del Aire	
				Cuatro Vientos, Spain	82/83
			N3931Y	Linda E. Meyers, Miami, FL	3.9.82/92
168-417•	T-6G	49-3313	N7050C	Registered USCAR	10.92
168-424•	T-6G	49-3320		(to Ejercito del Aire as E16-67)	
				storage compound Museo del Aire	
				Cuatro Vientos, Spain	82/83
			N4996H	Warbird Leasing MD	88

168-430•	T-6G	49-3326		(to Ejercito del Aire as E16-69)	
				storage compound Museo del Aire	
				Cuatro Vientos, Spain	82/83
			N100XK	Charles Murray, KY	92
168-431•	T-6G	49-3327	N2205G	George Byard, Dayton, NV	92
168-434•	T-6G	49-3330		(to Ejercito del Aire as E16-85)	
				storage compound Museo del Aire	
				Cuatro Vientos, Spain	82/83
			N5115D	Forbes Matthews, Hampton, GA	92
168-440•	T-6G	49-3336		(to Ejercito del Aire as E16-79)	
				storage compound Museo del Aire	
				Cuatro Vientos, Spain	82/83
			N4993G		
			N25KP	Theodore Pitchell, Brielle, NJ	92
168-451 •	T-6G	49-3337		(to Ejercito del Aire as E.16-86)	
				Patrimoine Aeronautique Nat., Luxembourg	83/87
168-456	T-6G	49-3342		(to Ejercito del Aire as E.16-71)	
			I-TSEI	Mario Ferrari, Treviso	87
				Destroyed in flying accident (Ferrari k)	89
168-463•	T-6G	49-3349	N6G	Quivira Flyers, Olathe, KS	92
168-464•	T-6G	49-3350	N49RR	Ed Robinson TX	88
				David Webb, Dallas, TX	92
168-466•	T-6G	49-3352		(to Ejercito del Aire as E16-92)	
				storage compound Museo del Aire	
				Cuatro Vientos, Spain	82/83
			N49939	Peter Hunt, Marietta, GA	84/92
168-469•	T-6G	49-3356	N5443X	McNeeley Charter, Earle, AZ	92
168-470•	T-6G	49-3357	N6593D	Michael Hay, Newport Beach, CA	92
168-471•	T-6G	49-3358	N116NA	Danny Linkous, Mooresville, NC	92
168-472•	T-6G	49-3359		(to Ejercito del Aire as E16-92)	
				storage compound Museo del Aire	
				Cuatro Vientos, Spain	82/84
			N5830R	K&K Aircraft, Bridgewater, VA	84/92
168-477•	T-6G	49-3363	N44CT	Robert Tullius, Winchester, VA	92
168-479•	T-6G	49-3365		(to Ejercito del Aire as E.16-98)	
			N5380X		85
			N365TA	Don Keller IL	88
168-481•	T-6G	49-3367		(to Ejercito del Aire as C6-100)	
				storage compound Museo del Aire	
				Cuatro Vientos, Spain	82
			N4995C	John Kreuger, Redlands, CA	84/92
168-482•	T-6G	49-3368	N799MM	USAF Museum, Wright Patterson, OH	92
168-490•	T-6G	49-3376		(to Ejercito del Aire as E.16-84)	
			N49NA	Chrisboy Incorporated VA	88
				White Knuckles Inc. Long Island, NY	92
168-494•	T-6G	49-3380		(to FA Brisiliera as FAB T-16 1672)	
			PT-KQX	Aristedes de Araujo Leite, Nova Iguaca	83
168-496•	T-6G	49-3382	N5451E	Frank C. Nelson, Vicksburg, MS	92

168-498	T-6G	49-3384	N6900G	Adrian S. Kale, Lemars IA	76
168-500	T-6G	49-3386	N74DW	Elmer Reynolds, Whittier CA	76
168-500•	T-6G	49-3430		(to Ejercito del Aire as E.16-103)	
				storage compound Museo del Aire	
				Cuatro Vientos, Spain	
			N74DW	Elmer Reynolds, Whittier CA	76
			N45CT	John Morello, Mason, OH	92
168-502•	T-6G	50-1288	N7765C	Richard S. Drury, Woodland Hills CA	76
				Francis Elliot, Pasadena, CA	92
168-503•	T-6G	50-1289		(to L'Armee de L'Air as 01289)	
				Amicale Jean-Baptiste Salis, La Ferte-Alais	79
				Etampes	83
168-505•	T-6G	50-1291	N3518G	Michael Schloss, NY	92
168-507	T-6G	50-1293	N7767C	T. G. Saltonstall, Pacific Palisades CA	76
168-514•	T-6G	49-3390	N94922	John Booth, Whitehall, MT	92
168-515	T-6G	49-3391	N2878G	Stewart Nicolson, Mt Holly NJ	76
168-516•	T-6G	49-3392	N3746G	Commander Aviation Corp, Bismark ND	76
			N104DC	William Simons, Avery Island, LA	92
168-517•	T-6G	49-3393	N7767C	3 Plus 6, Cincinatti, OH	92
168-525•	T-6G	49-3401	N4995P	T.S. Bass, Griffin, GA	92
168-526•	T-6G	49-3402	N85JR	Robert Pond, Minneapolis, MN	92
168-528	T-6G	49-3404	N9883C	Henry Best, Theinsville WI	76
168-529•	T-6G	49-3405	N7618C	Sheldon Prudhomme, Dayton OH	76
				Scott Groh, Palm Beach, FL	92
168-571•	T-6G	49-3437	N8084G	Scott Morse, Plano, TX	92
168-583•	T-6G	49-3449	N29931	Classic Air Parts, Miami Lakes, FL	92
168-622•	T-6G	50-1306	N2760A	Robert Tobacco, Colts Neck NJ	76
				Victor Schilleci, Metairie, LA	92
168-636	T-6G	49-3492	N2897G	Paul R. Macy, Tulelake CA	76
168-644 •	T-6G	49-3500		(to Greek AF as 93500)	
				Polemico Mussio, Athens	79/88
168-653	T-6G	49-3509	N7057	Richard S. Vogler, Appleton WI	76
168-672	T-6G	49-3528	TG-JOM	C. Funjul, La Aurora, Colombia	4.64/77
				in store by	77
168-673	T-6G	49-3529	N717UP	Fromhagen Aviation Inc, Clearwater FL	86
				(see 168-674?)	
168-683•	T-6G	49-3270	N3166G	E. E. Burke, Galveston TX	.77
				Conservair, Conroe, TX	92
168-685	T-6G	49-3272	N3167G	Albert Costa, Newton MA	76
168-687•	T-6G	49-3274	N7689C	Hersey Trucking Co, Camarillo CA	76/88

182-1•	T-6G	51-14314		(to L'Armee de L'Air as 114314)	
				Institut Amaury de la Grange, Merville	79/85
				Metz; restored as ELA.12/72 marked ac	85/87
182-5•	T-6G	51-14318		(to L'Armee de L'Air as 114318)	
			N13842	Art Medore, Hemet, CA	92
182-20•	T-6G	51-14333		(to L'Armee de L'Air as 114333)	
			N5599L	Andrew Keenan, Gautier, MS	92
182-28•	T-6G	51-14341	N4434M	(to L'Armee de L'Air as 114341)	
				June Mourad, Mercedes, TX	92
182-29	T-6G	51-14342		(to L'Armee de L'Air as 114342)	
				(to FA Portugusesa as 1715)	
			G-BIHS	Aces High Ltd, Duxford	.80/83
			N4434M	reg.	5.83
182-30•	T-6G	51-14343		(to L'Armee de L'Air as 114343)	
			N8048E	Lee Maples CA	88
182-38•	T-6G	51-14351		(to L'Armee de L'Air as 114351)	
				Paris/Le Bourget Musee de l'Air	92
182-54•	T-6G	51-14367		(to L'Armee de L'Air as 114367)	
				Amicale Jean-Baptiste Salis, La Ferte-Alais	79
			F-BVQD	Amicale Jean-Baptiste Salis, La Ferte-Alais	
			F-AZBK	Amicale Jean-Baptiste Salis, La Ferte-Alais	89
182-61•	T-6G	51-14374		(to L'Armee de L'Air as 114374)	
				Amicale Jean-Baptiste Salis, La Ferte-Alais	79
				derelict	90
182-74•	T-6G	51-14387		(to L'Armee de L'Air as 114387)	
				Centre d'Instruction de Vilgenis, Paris	
			F-AZEF	based, Etampes with AMPAA	89
182-75•	T-6G	51-14388		(to L'Armee de L'Air as 114388)	
				To Moroc AF	
				Major Iran by Maroc.	10.61
				To Tunisia	
				Recovered - at Etampes, France	10.92
182-78	T-6G	51-14391		(to L'Armee de L'Air as 114391)	
				Institut Amaury de la Grange, Merville	79
182-81•	T-6G	51-14394		(to L'Armee de L'Air as 114394)	
				Andrew Michalak, Arnold, MD	92
182-88	T-6G	51-14401		(to L'Armee de L'Air as 114314)	
				Institut Amaury de la Grange, Merville	79/85
				Centre d'instruction de Vilgenis, Paris	86
182-115•	T-6G	51-14428	N51428	Clifford Ashenfetter WI	88
				(id. quoted as 51-428: pres correct?)	
			N8FU	Greg Speed, Monroe, LA	92
182-116•	T-6G	51-14429	N896WW	Ben Cunningham, Jackson, MS	92
182-141•	T-6G	51-14454		Derelict La Ferte Alais	77/92
182-143•	T-6G	51-14456		(to Ejercito del Aire as E.16-191)	
			F-AZCV	Group Alcyons Lons/Le Saulnier	10.88
182-156•	T-6G	-		(to Italian AF as MM54049)	
				Recovered from Sardinia	
				Old Flying Machine Co., Duxford	88
				Tim Routsis, Audley End	

			G-BRBC	Anthony Murphy, Chigwell, Essex	91
182-209•	T-6G	51-14522		(to L'Armee de L'Air as 114522)	
				Musee de L'Air et L'Espace, Le Bourget	79/92
				(displayed as "114915/RM")	
182-213•	T-6G	51-14526		(to L'Armee de L'Air as 114526)	
			G-BRWB	Aircraft Restoration Co, Duxford	9.89
182-361•	T-6G	51-14674		(to L'Armee de L'Air as 114674)	
				Centre d"instruction de Vilgenis, Paris	
			F-AZEZ	based, Chaveney	82/92
182-371	T-6G	51-14684		(to L'Armee de L'Air as 114684)	
				Amicale Jean-Baptiste Salis, La Ferte-Alais	79
182-375•	T-6G	51-14688		(to L'Armee de L'Air as 114688)	
				Amicale Jean-Baptiste Salis, La Ferte-Alais	79
				Escadrille de Souvenir, Etampes	82//87
				Amberieu base	.87
182-381•	T-6G	51-14694	N7865	Andres Katz, Dallas, TX	92
182-383•	T-6G	51-14696		(to L'Armee de L'Air as 114696)	
			F-BMJP		
				Air Classik, West Germany	79
				Vienna Airport	89/92
182-387•	T-6G	51-14700		(to L'Armee de L'Air as 114700)	
				Amicale Jean-Baptiste Salis, La Ferte-Alais	79
				derelict	90
182-394•	T-6G	51-14707		(to L'Armee de L'Air as 114707)	
				Amicale Jean-Baptiste Salis, La Ferte-Alais	79
				derelict	90
182-405•	T-6G	51-14718		(to L'Armee de L'Air as 114718)	
				Amicale Jean-Baptiste Salis, La Ferte-Alais	79
				derelict	90
182-407•	T-6G	51-14720		(to L'Armee de L'Air as 114720)	88
				To Moroc AF as Y61305	
				Major IRAN by Maroc.	10.61
				To Tunisia	
				Recovered - at Etampes, France	10.92
182-413•	T-6G	51-14726		(to L'Armee de L'Air as 114726)	
			N92761	Roy Douglas, Delhi, LA	92
182-421•	T-6G	51-14734		(to L'Armee de L'Air as 114734)	
			N9705W	Alicia Gummo, Valdosta, GA	92
182-427•	T-6G	51-14740		(to L'Armee de L'Air as 114740)	
				Amicale Jean-Baptiste Salis, La Ferte-Alais	79
				derelict	90
182-448•	T-6G	51-14761		(to L'Armee de L'Air as 114761)	
			N9739T	Clara Pyle, Seminole, FL	92
182-457	T-6G	51-14770		(to L'Armee de L'Air as 114770)	
				impounded Cascais, Portugal en route	
				Biafran Air Force.Last noted here	84
182-477	T-6G	51-14790		(to L'Armee de L'Air as 114790)	
				Amicale Jean-Baptiste Salis, La Ferte-Alais	79

Continued on Page 366

Continued from Page 364

North American T-6/SNJ & Canadian Car Foundry Harvard

182-478•	T-6G	51-14791	N8044H	Mark Henley, Birmingham, AL	92
182-481	T-6G	51-14794		(to L'Armee de L'Air as 114794)	
				impounded Cascais, Portugal en route	
				Biafran Air Force.Last noted here	84
				rear fuselage to Sintra (Museo do Aer)	
182-486•	T-6G	51-14799	N92778	John Crisi, North Eastham, MA	92
182-487	T-6G	51-14800		(to L'Armee de L'Air as 114800)	
				impounded Cascais, Portugal en route	
				Biafran Air Force.Last noted here coded 21	84
182-498•	T-6G	51-14811		(to L'Armee de L'Air as 114811)	
				Amicale Jean-Baptiste Salis, La Ferte-Alais	79
				derelict	90
182-506•	T-6G	51-14819	N7804B	B. L. Smith LA	88
182-514•	T-6G	51-14827		(to L'Armee de L'Air as 114827)	
				Amicale Jean-Baptiste Salis, La Ferte-Alais	79
			N92796	William Kyle NC	88
182-526•	T-6G	51-14839		(to L'Armee de L'Air as 114839)	
				Amicale Jean-Baptiste Salis, La Ferte-Alais	79
				derelict	90
182-535•	T-6G	51-14848		(to L'Armee de L'Air as 114848)	
				Institut Amaury de la Grange, Merville	79
			F-BOEO		
			F-AZBQ	Amicale Jean-Baptiste Salis, La Ferte-Alais	89/92
182-536•	T-6G	51-14849		(to L'Armee de L'Air as 114849)	
			N9701Z	Lance Toland, Griffin, GA	92
182-558	T-6G	51-14871		(to L'Armee de L'Air as 114871)	
				Amicale Jean-Baptiste Salis, La Ferte-Alais	79
182-560	T-6G	51-14873		(to L'Armee de L'Air as 114873)	
				Amicale Jean-Baptiste Salis, La Ferte-Alais	79
182-585	T-6G	51-14898		(to L'Armee de L'Air as 114898)	
				Institut Amaury de la Grange, Merville	79
182-591•	T-6G	51-14904		(to Ejercito del Aire as E16-198)	
				storage compound Museo del Aire	
				Cuatro Vientos, Spain	84/85
			EC-DUM		88/92
182-600•	T-6G	51-14913	N278DB	Thomas Dodson, Tulsa, OK	92
182-603•	T-6G	51-14916		(to FA Hondurena as '208')	
			N27817	Jack Lowry, Chino, CA	92
182-454	T-6G	51-14959		(to L'Armee de L'Air as 14959)	
				impounded Cascais, Portugal en route	
				Biafran Air Force.Last noted here coded KK	84
182-648	T-6G	51-14961	N1190	Richard O. Burns, Hinsdale IL	76
182-657•	T-6G	51-14970	N25WT	John Watson, Blackwood, NJ	92
182-666	T-6G	51-14979		(to L'Armee de L'Air as 114979)	
				Amicale Jean-Baptiste Salis, La Ferte-Alais	79
182-678	T-6G	51-14991		(to L'Armee de L'Air as 14991)	

				impounded Cascais, Portugal en route	
				Biafran Air Force.Last noted here	84
182-694 •	T-6G	51-15007		(to L'Armee de L'Air as 115007)	
				(to FA Portuguesa as 1681)	
				abandoned Maputo, Mozambique	.74
				recovered by Brian Zeederberg/Ian Popplewell,	
				Syferfontein, Johannesburg	.89
				Aerofab, Thruxton UK	.89
			G-BSBD	Aerofab, Thruxton UK	
182-704	T-6G	51-15017		(to L'Armee de L'Air as 115017)	
				Amicale Jean-Baptiste Salis, La Ferte-Alais	79
				derelict	90
182-720 •	T-6G	51-15033		(to L'Armee de L'Air as 115033)	
			G-BDZZ	Robs Lamplough, Duxford	15.6.76
				IDFAF/ Israeli AF Museum	.12.76
				(displayed as "001")	
182-729•	T-6G	51-15042		(to L'Armee de L'Air as 115042)	
				(to FA Portugusesa as 1707)	
			G-BGHU	Gladaircraft Ltd	.79
				Philip & Sheena Warner,	
				Wellesbourne Mountford	87
				Christopher. E. Bellhouse, Kent	87/92
182-733	T-6G	51-15046		(to L'Armee de L'Air as 115046)	
				impounded Cascais, Portugal en route	
				Biafran Air Force.Last noted here	84
182-735•	T-6G	51-15048	N42JM	Jerry Meadors, Indianapolis, IN	92
182-736•	T-6G	51-15049		(to L'Armee de L'Air as 115049)	
			F-AZAS	Amicale Jean-Baptiste Salis, La Ferte-Alais	79/92
				(flies as USN "3-F-1")	
182-747	T-6G	51-15060		(to L'Armee de L'Air as 115060)	
				Amicale Jean-Baptiste Salis, La Ferte-Alais	79
182-750•	T-6G	51-15063		(to FA Portugusesa as 1710)	
			G-SURF		
			N8048J	John Luther, San Antonio, TX	92
182-769	T-6G	51-15082		(to L'Armee de L'Air as 115082)	
				Amicale Jean-Baptiste Salis, La Ferte-Alais	79
182-770	T-6G	51-15083		(to L'Armee de L'Air as 115083)	
				impounded Cascais, Portugal en route	
				Biafran Air Force.Last noted here	84
182-792•	T-6G	51-15102		Musee Automobile de Cleres	87
182-792•	T-6G	51-15105	N66WP	William Pryor, Keego Harbour MI	76
				Joe Natoli, Nokesville, VA	92
182-800•	T-6G	51-15113		(to L'Armee de L'Air as 115113)	
			F-BNAU		
			F-AZAU	Escadrille du Souvenir, Etamps	79
				(flies as "USAF "MH-038")	92
188-90 •	T-6G	51-15227		(to MM/ Italian AF as MM53664/ RM-91)	
				to UK	11.81
			G-BKRA	Pulsegrove, Thruxton.	19.8.83/92
195-1 •	T-6G	51-17354		Korean War Museum, Seoul, South Korea	79
195-2 •	T-6G	51-17355	N4269P	Andrew Gemellaro, Canoga Pak., CA	92

197-2•	T-6G	52-8199	N1385B	Art Medore, Hemet, CA (kit?)	92
197-15•	T-6G	52-8211	N711AP	Omni Aviation Managers, Van Nuys CA	76
			N432RT	Ronald Thompson, Fullerton, CA	92
197-20•	T-6G	52-8216		(to Ejercito del Aire as E16-201)	
				storage compound Museo del Aire	
				Cuatro Vientos, Spain	83/85
			EC-DUN		88/92
197-22•	T-6G	52-8218	N5632V	John H. Weiser, Honolulu HI	76
				SSS Inc. Cincinatti, OH	92
197-35	T-6G	52-8231		(to L'Armee de L'Air as 28231)	
				Amicale Jean-Baptiste Salis, La Ferte-Alais	79
197-42•	T-6G	52-8238	N555Q	Patrick Connell, New York NY	76
				Yankee Flyers, Southfield, MI	92
197-54•	T-6G	53-4558	N4269Q	Claude Yew, Fairfax, VA	92
197-64•	T-6G	53-4568	N153NA	(to Spanish AF as E.16-200)	
				Cuatro Vientos Museo del Aire reserve collectn.	83/89
				James & Carol Shuttleworth IN	88/92
197-68	T-6G	53-4572		(to L'Armee de L'Air as 34572)	
				Amicale Jean-Baptiste Salis, La Ferte-Alais	79
197-73•	T-6G	53-4577	N2831D	John Brinkerhoff, Torrance CA	76
				Bowlin & Associates, Griffin, GA	88/92
197-75•	T-6G	53-4579		(to L'Armee de L'Air as 34579)	
				Amicale Jean-Baptiste Salis, La Ferte-Alais	79
				broken down for rebuild	10.92
197-88•	T-6G	53-4592		(to L'Armee de L'Air as 34592)	
				Amicale Jean-Baptiste Salis, La Ferte-Alais	79
				Warbirds Worldwide recovered airframe	88
			G-BTKI	Philip & Sheena Warner, Evesham, Worcs.	90
				restoration to concours Tewkesbury, Glos	92
197-89•	T-6G	53-4593		(to L'Armee de L'Air as 34593)	
				Amicale Jean-Baptiste Salis, La Ferte-Alais	79
197-97•	T-6G	53-4601		(to L'Armee de L'Air as 34601)	
			N4269E	James Morgan, Aumsville, OR	92
197-106•	T-6G	53-4610		(to L'Armee de L'Air as 34610)	
			N4269X	Gerald Giroux, Planation, FL	92
197-107	T-6G	53-4611		(to L'Armee de L'Air as 34611)	
				Amicale Jean-Baptiste Salis, La Ferte-Alais	79
197-114•	T-6G	53-4618		(to L'Armee de L'Air as 34618)	
				Institut Amaury de la Grange	79
			F-BGRA		
CCF4-1	Mk 4	RCAF20210	C-FPTP	National Aeronautical Establishment, Ottawa ONT	86
CCF4-4	Mk 4	RCAF20213	CF-UUU	Canadian Warplane Heritage, Hamilton ONT	79
CCF4-7•	Mk 4	RCAF20216	N7552U	Rodney E. Barnes, Oconomowoc WI	6.65/76
				James Michaels, Oconomowoc WI	92
CCF4-8•	Mk 4	RCAF20217	CF-VCM		
			N47217	Victor Stottlmyer, Wauwatosa, WI	92

CCF4-9•	Mk 4	RCAF20218	N4288C	Arlie P. Kelley, Euclid OH	76
			N91AM	Barrie Snowden, San Ramon, CA	92
CCF4-13	Mk 4	RCAF20222		in compound dismantled unconv., Mesa AZ	78
CCF4-16•	Mk 4	RCAF20225	N15796	Tallmantz Aviation, Santa Ana CA	77
				Zeke Inc.	92
CCF4-19•	Mk.4	RCAF20228	N24GB	George Baker, FL	92
CCF4-20•	Mk.4	RCAF20229	CF-UVN		
			N1264	Caroline Harms, Jetmore, KS	92
CCF4-22	Mk.4	RCAF20231	CF-RUV		12.64
CCF4-23	Mk 4	RCAF20232	N2048	Confederate Air Force, Harlingen TX	76
CCF4-27	Mk 4	RCAF20236	CF-GUY		
CCF4-31	Mk 4	RCAF20240	N20240	James Peterson, Homosassa Springs FL	77
CCF4-33	Mk 4	RCAF20242	CF-WPK		
CCF4-34	Mk 4	RCAF20243	CF-VYF		
CCF4-35	Mk 4	RCAF20244	CF-WPM		
CCF4-38 •	Mk 4	RCAF20247	CF-UZO		2.66
			N1811B	rep. stored unconv., Chino CA	64/78
				noted unconv., Chino CA	78
				Santa Monica CA	90
				Air SRV, Houston, TX	92
				Disp Lone Star Flight Museum	
CCF4-39•	Mk 4	RCAF20248	N1465	John Alden, Manhatten Beach CA	77/92
CCF4-42•	Mk 4	RCAF20251	N3544	Forrest Bennett, Milwaukee MI	77
			N10908	C. E. Slinger, Phoenix AZ	77
				Jeff Nelson, Scottsdale, AZ	92
CCF4-46•	Mk 4	RCAF20255	CF-WPS		7.67
			N305GS	Greg Shelton,	92
CCF4-47•	Mk 4	RCAF20256	N1381N	William Whisner	3.82/92
CCF4-48•	Mk 4	RCAF20257		in compound dismantled unconv., Mesa AZ	78
			N98474	John P. Vandersluis CT	88/92
CCF4-50	Mk 4	RCAF20259	CF-VTZ		13.5.63
CCF4-52	Mk 4	RCAF20261	CF-WWO		
CCF4-53	Mk 4	RCAF20262	CF-SWW		
CCF4-55	Mk 4	RCAF20264	CF-WLO		
CCF4-58	Mk 4	RCAF20267	N6TS	Thomas Short, Phoenix AZ	77
CCF4-61	Mk 4	RCAF20270	C-GRLR		70
CCF4-64	Mk 4	RCAF20273	CF-RUJ		
CCF4-66	Mk 4	RCAF20275	CF-WLA		
CCF4-71	Mk 4	RCAF20280	CF-UNB		
			N72375	Romaine A. Collins, Buckley WA	77
CCF4-74	Mk 4	RCAF20283	N14429	Clifford Baker, Eudora AR	77

				Joe Mabee, Midland, TX	92
CCF4-75•	Mk 4	RCAF20284	N711SS	Harvard Corp, Hartford CT	77/88
CCF4-77•	Mk 4	RCAF20286	N13631	Robert Philips, Phoenix AZ	77
			G-BKCK	Eric Webster & A.Haig-Thomas Dorking, Surrey	92
CCF4-83	Mk 4	RCAF20292	N2047	John Stokes, San Marcos TX	77
CCF4-85•	Mk 4	RCAF20294	CF-RUQ		
			N294CH	Combat Air Museum, Topeka KS	88/92
CCF4-88•	Mk 4	RCAF20297	N777BT	Arthur Sutherland, Ardmore, OK	92
CCF4-89	Mk 4	RCAF20298	CF-UAT		
CCF4-93	Mk 4	RCAF20302		in compound dismantled unconv., Mesa AZ	78
CCF4-97•	Mk 4	RCAF20306	N13595	Confederate Air Force, Harlingen TX	76/88
				American Airpower Heritage Museum, TX	92
CCF4-98	Mk 4	RCAF20307		in compound dismantled unconv., Mesa AZ	78
CCF4-104	Mk 4	RCAF20313	N15795	Roland Harrington, Abbeville LA	77
CCF4-109•	Mk 4	RCAF20318	CF-RQC		
			N161FE	Mark IV Aviation, Miami, FL	92
CCF4-110	Mk 4	RCAF20319	N44110	Aircraft & Equip. Components, Arcadia CA	77
CCF4-112	Mk 4	RCAF20321	CF-UFZ		
CCF4-114	Mk 4	RCAF20323		in compound dismantled unconv., Mesa AZ	78
CCF4-115•	Mk 4	RCAF20324	N4289C	S. F. Gripper, San Francisco CA	76
				Parker O'Mally Aeroplane Co. Ghent, NY	92
CCF4-116	Mk 4	RCAF20325	CF-RFS		
CCF4-117	Mk 4	RCAF20326	N15799	Confederate Air Force, Harlingen TX	77
CCF4-119	Mk 4	RCAF20328		in compound dismantled unconv., Mesa AZ	78
			N304GS	Gregory Shelton OK	88
CCF4-123•	Mk 4	RCAF20332	CF-RZP		
			N91264	William McHenry, Muskegon, MI	88/92
CCF4-124•	Mk 4	RCAF20333	N1466	Lee Donham CA	88
CCF4-125	Mk 4	RCAF20334	CF-VIR		
CCF4-128	Mk 4	RCAF20337	CF-UVQ		
CCF4-132•	Mk 4	RCAF20341	CF-RZQ	Canadian Warplane Heritage, Hamilton ONT	79
			N452CA	HH Avery, Morganton, NC	92
CCF4-133	Mk 4	RCAF20342		in compound dismantled unconv., Mesa AZ	78
			CF-WPK	Canadian Warplane Heritage, Hamilton ONT	79
CCF4-134	Mk 4	RCAF20343		in compound dismantled unconv., Mesa AZ	78
CCF4-136	Mk 4	RCAF20345		in compound dismantled unconv., Mesa AZ	78
CCF4-143	Mk 4	RCAF20352		in compound dismantled unconv., Mesa AZ	78
			C-GBQB		

CCF4-144•	Mk 4	RCAF20353	CF-WWQ	S.J. Roberts,Ottawa, Ontario	
			N4329J	Gerald Walbrun, WI	92
CCF4-145	Mk 4	RCAF20354	CF-SPC		
CCF4-153•	Mk 4	RCAF20362	N15798	John Silberman, Fl	92
CCF4-156•	Mk 4	RCAF20365	N7553U	Robert D. Staehling, Dubois ID	76
				Roger Christgau, Edina, MN	92
CCF4-157	Mk 4	RCAF20366	N16240	Gilbert H. Moyer, Coolidge AZ	76
CCF4-158	Mk 4	RCAF20367	N9097	Confederate Air Force, Harlingen TX	77
CCF4-164•	Mk 4	RCAF20373	CF-NSN		
			C-FNSN	Conair, Abbotsford	92
CCF4-167	Mk 4	RCAF20376	CF-RUL		
CCF4-168•	Mk 4	RCAF20377	CF-WGA	Canadian Warplane Heritage, Hamilton ONT	79
			C-FWGA	Aero Taxi, St. Hubert, PQ	92
CCF4-169	Mk 4	RCAF20378		in compound dismantled unconv., Mesa AZ	78
CCF4-171	Mk 4	RCAF20380	N7757	Challenge Publications, Canoga Park CA	77
CCF4-172•	Mk 4	RCAF20381	CF-NUQ		
			N514FS	Picacho Aviation, Fairacres, NM	92
CCF4-173	Mk 4	RCAF20382	CF-VIJ		
CCF4-175	Mk 4	RCAF20384	CF-UNL		
				in compound dismantled unconv., Mesa AZ	78
				(prob. wrongly identified)	
CCF4-176•	Mk 4	RCAF20385	N7520U	John Bell, Northridge CA	77
			N175JR		
			F-AZGB	based, Etamps	89
CCF4-178	Mk 4	RCAF20387	CF-GBV		
				Canadian National Collection, Rockliffe ONT	79
				(displayed as "20387")	
CCF4-179	Mk 4	RCAF20388	N2WS	Ramsten Construction Inc, Muncie IN	77
CCF4-181	Mk 4	RCAF20390		in compound dismantled unconv., Mesa AZ	78
CCF4-189	Mk 4	RCAF20398	CF-UAB		
CCF4-191•	Mk 4	RCAF20400	CF-SRJ		
			N600LM	James E. Smith, Fortine, MT	92
CCF4-192•	Mk 4	RCAF20401	CF-UZG		
			N5101W	Vincent Mancini, Salt Lake City, UT	92
CCF4-194•	Mk 4	RCAF20403		in compound dismantled unconv., Mesa AZ	78
			N90448		
			G-BRLV	Geraint Owens, North Weald	14.9.89
				Barbel Christa Abela, Oxford	92
CCF4-195	Mk 4	RCAF20404	CF-VFG		
CCF4-196	Mk 4	RCAF20405		in compound dismantled unconv., Mesa AZ	78
CCF4-199	Mk 4	RCAF20408	N15797	Confederate Air Force, Harlingen TX	77
CCF4-200	Mk 4	RCAF20409		in compound dismantled unconv., Mesa AZ	78

CCF4-201	Mk 4	RCAF20410	N6865	Edwards & Edwards, Big Spring TX	76
CCF4-203	Mk 4	RCAF20412	CF-VMG		
			C-FVMG	Canadian Warplane Heritage, Hamilton ONT	79
CCF4-204	Mk 4	RCAF20413	N7518U	Harvard Corp, Minneapolis MN	76
CCF4-206	Mk 4	RCAF20415	CF-VCJ		
			C-FVCJ	Canadian Warplane Heritage, Hamilton ONT	79
CCF4-211•	Mk 4	RCAF20420		in compound dismantled unconv., Mesa AZ	78
			N1046Y	Jay Stokely, Opelika, AL	92
CCF4-212•	Mk 4	RCAF20421	CF-UAD		
			N421QB	Carol Hunt, Anchorage, AK	92
CCF4-213	Mk 4	RCAF20422	CF-RZW		
CCF4-214	Mk 4	RCAF20423	N7522U	Donald W. Brunnell, Azusa CA	76
CCF4-215•	Mk 4	RCAF20424	N7754	Lone Star Flight Museum, TX	92
CCF4-216	Mk 4	RCAF20425	N20425	George Naphas, Pitman NJ	76
CCF4-217	Mk 4	RCAF20426	CF-UZH		
CCF4-219	Mk 4	RCAF20428	N7554U	Jonathon J. Steahling, Woodstock IL	76
CCF4-222	Mk 4	RCAF20431	CF-UZW	Canadian Warplane Heritage, Hamilton ONT	79
CCF4-227•	Mk 4	RCAF20436	CF-WWI		
			N436WL	William Lamon, Eugene, OR	92
CCF4-228	Mk 4	RCAF20437		in compound dismantled unconv., Mesa AZ	78
CCF4-230	Mk 4	RCAF20439	N1254	Robert Clopton, Windsor CA	77/87
CCF4-231	Mk 4	RCAF20440	CF-VTT		
CCF4-233•	Mk 4	RCAF20442		in compound dismantled unconv., Mesa AZ	78
			C-GNJM		92
CCF4-237•	Mk 4	RCAF20446	N7519U	David Schmitz, Spooner, WI	92
CCF4-240	Mk 4	RCAF20449		in compound dismantled unconv., Mesa AZ	78
CCF4-241	Mk 4	RCAF20450	N4447	Confederate Air Force, Harlingen TX	77
CCF4-242	Mk 4	RCAF20451		in compound dismantled unconv., Mesa AZ	78
CCF4-246•	Mk 4	RCAF20455		in compound dismantled unconv., Mesa AZ	78
			N45918	James Merrill, Chatsworth, CA	92
CCF4-250•	Mk 4	RCAF20459		in compound dismantled unconv., Mesa AZ	78
			N459JP	James Powers, CA	92
CCF4-252•	Mk 4	RCAF204461	N17400	George Sanders, Higley AZ	77
			N884TC	Thomas Clayton, Overland Pk. KS	92
CCF4-254	Mk 4	RCAF20463	CF-UAE		
CCF4-255	Mk 4	RCAF20464	CF-WXY	G. Nelson, Dinmore, Sask.	
CCF4-256	Mk 4	RCAF20465	C-GURP	Lawrence W. Mantie BC	82
CCF4-261•	Mk 4	RCAF20470		in compound dismantled unconv., Mesa AZ	78

			N202LD	Jack Rose, Spangle, WA	92
CCF4-264•	Mk 4	RCAF20473	N296W	William Childers, Temple TX	77
				J&R Investments, Wichita, KS	92
CCF4-265	Mk 4	RCAF20474	CF-XEX		
CCF4-266	Mk 4	RCAF20475	C-GYYO	Marjorie Duncan SASK	82
CCF4-270•	Mk 4	RCAF20479	N1467	Jacques Trudeau, Buckley WA	77
				Sherman Aircraft Sales, FL	92
CCF4-387•	Mk.4	RCAF	C-GJCJ	Jerry Janes	
			C-FCLJ		
			N52494	Don Monacco, Modesto, CA	92
CCF4-400•	T-6J	51-17103		(To Italian AF as MM53792/SC.65)	
				Castrette Scrapyard, Italy	
CCF4-288•	T-6J	51-17106		(To Italian AF as MM53785/SC.62)	
				Castrette Scrapyard, Italy	
			I-TSIX	Mario Ferrari on rebuild Treviso	89
CCF4-400•	T-6J	51-17218		(To Italian AF as MM53835/SC.74)	
				Castrette Scrapyard, Italy	
				Velentino Corsi furniture shop	87
CCF4-407•	T-6J	51-17225		(To Italian AF as MM53844/SL.30	
				Castrette Scrapyard, Italy	87
CCF4-410•	T-6J	51-17212		(To Italian AF as MM53847/SC.77)	
				Castrette Scrapyard, Italy	88
CCF4-442•	T-6J	52-8521		(to Luftwaffe as AA+652)	
				(to FA Portuguesa as 1730)	
				abandoned Maputo, Mozambique	.74
				recovered by Brian Zeederberg/Ian Popplewell,	
				Syferfontein, Johannesburg	.89
				Aerofab, Thruxton UK	.89
			G-BSBE	Pulsegrove Ltd., Thruxtion	92
CCF4-464•	T-6J	52-8543		(to Luftwaffe as AA+063)	
				(to FA Portuguesa as 1766)	
				AJD Engineering, Suffolk	11.91
			G-BUKY	P.R. Monk,Maidstone, Kent	9.92
CCF4-465•	T-6J	52-8544		(to Luftwaffe as AA+615)	
			D-FABU		
				Luftwaffen Museum, Uetersen	79
CCF4-483•	T-6J	52-8562		(to Luftwaffe as AA+053)	
				(to FA Portuguesa as 1753)	
				abandoned Maputo, Mozambique	.74
				recovered by Brian Zeederberg/Ian Popplewell,	
				Syferfontein, Johannesburg	.89
				Aerofab, Thruxton UK	.89
			G-BSBG	John James Woodhouse, Andover, Hants UK	92
CCF4-484	T-6J	52-8563		(to Luftwaffe as AA+678)	
			D-FACA	ntu	
CCF4-486•	T-6J	52-8565		(to Luftwaffe as BF+079)	
				(to FA Portuguesa as 1774)	
				Museu do Ar, Montijo, Portugal	79/89
				(flies as FAP 1774)	
CCF4-491•	T-6J	52-8570		(to Luftwaffe as AA+622)	

				Luftwaffen Museum, Uetersen	79
				Kongelige Norsk Luftforssvaret Coll. Oslo,Norway	83/89
				Painted as '8570'	
CCF4-499•	T-6J	52-8578		(to Luftwaffe as AA+624)	
			D-FABE	Federal Republic of Germany, Bonn	72
				KBB Flugdienst Josef Koch KG, Augsburg	86
CCF4-509•	T-6J	52-8588		(to Luftwaffe as AA+633)	
				derelict Munchengladbach	78
CCF4-511•	T-6J	52-8590		(to Luftwaffe as AA+058)	
				(to FA Portuguesa as 1736)	
				abandoned Maputo, Mozambique	.74
				recovered by Brian Zeederberg/Ian Popplewell,	
				Syferfontein, Johannesburg	.89
				Aerofab, Thruxton UK	.89
			G-BSBF	Pulsegrove, Thruxton UK	92
CCF4-514	T-6J	52-8593		(to Luftwaffe as AA+603)	
			D-FABO	Federal Republic of Germany, Bonn	72
CCF4-517•	T-6J	52-8596		(to FA Portuguesa as 1769)	
				Museu do Ar, Montijo, Portugal	79/89
				(held in Museum store)	
CCF4-524	T-6J	52-8603		(to Luftwaffe as AA+629)	
			D-FACE	ntu : Federal Republic of Germany, Bonn	
CCF4-537•	T-6J	53-4618		(to Luftwaffe as AA+628)	
			D-FABI	Federal Republic of Germany, Bonn	
			N73688		
			F-BRGA		
			F-AZFC	Escadrille Mercure, Le Castelet	89
CCF4-538•	T-6J	53-4619		(to Luftwaffe as AA+050; BF+050)	
				(to FA Portuguesa as 1747)	
			G-BGPB	Robs Lamplough/Alistair Walker, Duxford	4.4.79
				based, North Weald	87
				(flew as RCAF "20385")	
				The Aircraft Restoration Co., Duxford	15.9.89/92
CCF4-542	T-6J	53-4623		(to Luftwaffe as AA+682; AA+666)	
				reported preserved	79
CCF4-548•	T-6J	53-4629		(to Luftwaffe as AA+6....)	
				(to FA Portuguesa as 1741)	
				abandoned Maputo, Mozambique	.74
				recovered by Brian Zeederberg/Ian Popplewell,	
				Syferfontein, Johannesburg	.89
				Aerofab, Thruxton UK	.89
			G-BSBC	John Woodhouse, Thruxton UK	92
CCF4-550•	T-6J	53-4631		(to Luftwaffe as AA+635)	
			D-FABA	Federal Republic of Germany, Bonn	72
			N73687		
			F-BRGB		
			F-AZAT	based, Beauvais	89
CCF4-555•	T-6J	53-4636		(to Luftwaffe as AA+689)	
				(to FA Portuguesa as 1788)	
				abandoned Maputo, Mozambique	.74
				recovered by Brian Zeederberg/Ian Popplewell,	
				Syferfontein, Johannesburg	.89
				Aerofab, Thruxton UK	.89
			G-BSBB	Pulsegrove, Thruxton UK	92

1•	T-6	-		(to Luftwaffe / or L'Armee de L'Air) (to FA Portuguesa as 1.......) abandoned Maputo, Mozambique recovered by Brian Zeederberg/Ian Popplewell, Syferfontein, Johannesburg South African Airways, Apprentice Training School	 .74 .89
2•	T-6	-		(to Luftwaffe / or L'Armee de L'Air) (to FA Portuguesa as 1.......) abandoned Maputo, Mozambique recovered by Brian Zeederberg/Ian Popplewell, Syferfontein, Johannesburg South African Airways, Apprentice Training School	 .74 .89
3•	T-6	-		(to Luftwaffe / or L'Armee de L'Air) (to FA Portuguesa as 1.......) abandoned Maputo, Mozambique recovered by Brian Zeederberg/Ian Popplewell, Syferfontein, Johannesburg South African Airways, Apprentice Training School	 .74 .89
4•	T-6	-		(to Luftwaffe / or L'Armee de L'Air) (to FA Portuguesa as 1.......) abandoned Maputo, Mozambique recovered by Brian Zeederberg/Ian Popplewell, Syferfontein, Johannesburg Mark Kusters, South Africa	 .74 .89
5•	T-6	-		(to Luftwaffe / or L'Armee de L'Air) (to FA Portuguesa as 1.......) abandoned Maputo, Mozambique recovered by Brian Zeederberg/Ian Popplewell, Syferfontein, Johannesburg John Sawyers, South Africa	 .74 .89
6•	T-6	-		(to Luftwaffe / or L'Armee de L'Air) (to FA Portuguesa as 1.......) abandoned Maputo, Mozambique recovered by Brian Zeederberg/Ian Popplewell, Syferfontein, Johannesburg syndicate, Nelspruit, South Africa	 .74 .89
7•	T-6	-		(to Luftwaffe / or L'Armee de L'Air) (to FA Portuguesa as 1.......) abandoned Maputo, Mozambique recovered by Brian Zeederberg/Ian Popplewell, Syferfontein, Johannesburg	 .74 .89
-	AT-6F	-	CU-N635	no further information	
-	T-6J	-	D-FAMO	Luftwaffe; used in Portugal	
-	T-6J	-	D-FAMU	Luftwaffe; used in Portugal	
-	T-6J	-	D-FBEC	Luftwaffe; used in Portugal	
-	T-6J	-	D-FIBU	Luftwaffe; used in Portugal	
-	T-6J	-	D-FOTO	Luftwaffe; used in Portugal	
-•	T-6	-	N1363R VH-USR	 W. Waterton Snr, Melbourne VIC	 90
-•	T-6	-	N1364J	Charles Bivenour AZ (id. quoted as 53-655?)	88
-•	T-6	-	N3274G VH-OVO	 M. Falls, Melbourne VIC	 90

•-	T-6	-	N4995A VH-LJQ	flying in Australia D. Noonan, Oakey, Queensland	90
•-	T-6	-	N29944	M. English & Ptnr, Bathurst NSW	90
-	T-6	-	YS-172P	H. J. Kowalzeyk	77
-	T-6	-	YS-183P	H. J. Kowalzeyk	77
•-	AT-6	-		(to FA Brasiliera as FAB 1329) Museu do FAB, Rio de Janeiro, Brazil	79
•-	AT-6	-		(to FA Brasiliera as FAB 1339) Museu de Armas e Veiculos Motorizados Antigos, Bebeduoro, Brazil	79
•-	AT-6	-		(to FA Brasiliera as FAB 1390) Museu Aeronautica do Sao Paulo, Brazil	79
-•	AT-6	-		(to FA Brasiliera as FAB 1559) Museu do FAB, Rio de Janeiro, Brazil	79
•-	AT-6	-		(to FA Brasiliera as FAB 1575) Museu de Armas e Veiculos Motorizados Antigos, Bebeduoro, Brazil	79
•-	AT-6	-		(to FA Chile as 285) Museo Aeronautico, Santiago	79
- •	AT-6	-		(to FA Colombiana as FAC 772) Museo FAC, Bogota	79
- •	AT-6	-		(to FA Ecuatoriana as 20310) Museo Aero de FAE, Quito	79
- •	AT-6	-		(to FA Ecuatoriana as 43233) Museo Aero de FAE, Quito	79
- •	AT-6	-		(to FA Ecuatoriana as 53233) Museo Aero de FAE, Quito	79
- •	AT-6C/D	-		(to MM/Italian AF as MM53432) to UK - Staverton	3.82
- •	AT-6	-		(to MM/Italian AF as MM53652) P. Croser, Mt Eliza VIC	90
- •	T-6G	-		(to MM/Italian AF as MM53657) Castrete scrapyard	81/89
- •	AT-6	-		(to MM/Italian AF as MM53670) Preserved Castello Di Annone	90
- •	AT-6	-		(to MM/Italian AF as MM53679) Capua, Italy, Scuola Speciialisti	90
CCF4- •	T-6H Mk. 4	-		(to MM/Italian AF as MM53792) Castrette scrapyard	
CCF4- •	T-6H Mk. 4	-	G-BJST	(to MM/Italian AF as MM53795) reg. Robs Lamplough, London John Hawke, Coventry (Empire of the Sun movie) Vic Norman & Michael Lawrence	21.12.81 88 92
CCF4- •	T-6H Mk. 4	-		(to MM/Italian AF as MM53796) reg. Robs Lamplough, London	21.12.81

c/n		Type	ID	Reg	History	Date
CCF4-	•	T-6H	-		(to MM/Italian AF as MM53802)	
		Mk. 4			to UK	16.7.81
				G-BJMS	reg.	5.10.81
				F-AZCM	reg.	3.3.82/89
-	•	T-6H	-		(to MM/Italian AF as MM53818)	
					gate guard, Viterbo	.82
-	•	T-6H	-		(to MM/Italian AF as MM53823)	
					Museo Dell'Aria, Castello di San Pelagio	83
-	•	T-6H	-		(to MM/Italian AF as MM53825)	
					preserved, Guidonia	83
-	•	T-6H	-		(to MM/Italian AF as MM53835)	
					preserved, Cascino	83
-	•	T-6H	-		(to MM/Italian AF as MM53846)	
		Mk. 4		G-BIWX	Anthony Hutton, The Squadron, North Weald	85/92
-	•	T-6C/D	-		(to MM/Italian AF as MM53864)	
					preserved, Camp Darby, Italy	83
-	•	T-6G	-		(to MM/Italian AF as MM54097)	
					Museo Storico Dell Aeronautica, Vigna di Valle	79/83
-	•	T-6H	-		(to MM/Italian AF as MM54098/SL37)	
					Grazzanise	83/92
-	•	T-6G	-		(to MM/Italian AF as MM54106)	
					preserved, Cameri	.79/83
-	•	T-6G	-		(to MM/Italian AF as MM54114)	
					Museo Nazionale Della Scienza e Della Technica, Milan	79/83
-	•	T-6H	-		(to MM/Italian AF as MM54137)	
				G-CTKL	reg	22.11.83
					Tim Lane	84
					Gavin & Sandra Keegan	92
-	•	T-6H	-		(to MM/Italian AF as MM54139)	
					preserved, Viterbo	83
-	•	T-6H	-		(to MM/Italian AF as MM54143)	
					Gallarate - 2 Deposito Centrale It.AF	85
-	•	T-6H	-		(to MM/Italian AF as MM54149)	
					preserved, Castel del Rio	83
-	•	SNJ-5	-		(to MM/Italian AF as MM54292/SC79)	
					Conegliano D'Otranto	87
-	•	T-6G	-		(to Ejercito del Aire as E.16-106)	
					Patrimoine Aeronautique Nat., Luxembourg	85
					(additional to c/n 168-451/E.16-86)	
-	•	AT-6	RCAF........		(to RNEAF as B-416)	
		Mk.II			(to AURI/Indonesian AF as B-416)	
					Armed Forces Museum, Jakarta	79/88
-	•	AT-6	-		(to Pakistan AF as T4200)	
					Pakistan Air Force Museum, Peshawa	79/88
	•	T-6D	'413279'		(to Fuerza Aerea Paraguaya as 0101)	
				N3173L	World Wide Aeronautical Industries, Moorpark, CA	24.6.91

•	T-6D	'7083'	N3173N	(to Fuerza Aerea Paraguaya as 0104) World Wide Aeronautical Industries, Moorpark, CA	24.6.91
•	T-6D	'7699'		(to Fuerza Aerea Paraguaya as 0124) World Wide Aeronautical Industries, Moorpark, CA	24.6.91
•	T-6D	'7040'	N3171A	(to Fuerza Aerea Paraguaya as 0102) World Wide Aeronautical Industries, Moorpark, CA	24.6.91
•	T-6D	'7095'		(to Fuerza Aerea Paraguaya as 0103) World Wide Aeronautical Industries, Moorpark, CA	24.6.91
•	T-6D	'7094'		(to Fuerza Aerea Paraguaya as 0106) World Wide Aeronautical Industries, Moorpark, CA	24.6.91
•	T-6D	'412223'	N3171H	(to Fuerza Aerea Paraguaya as 0107) Worldwide Aeronautical Industries, Moorpark, CA	24.6.91
•	T-6D	'412227'	N3171K	(to Fuerza Aerea Paraguaya as 0108) World Wide Aeronautical Industries, Moorpark, CA	24.6.91
•	T-6D	'7500'	N3171N	(to Fuerza Aerea Paraguaya as 0109) World Wide Aeronautical Industries, Moorpark, CA	24.6.91
•	T-6D	'7320'	N3171P	(to Fuerza Aerea Paraguaya as 0116) World Wide Aeronautical Industries, Moorpark, CA	24.6.91
•	T-6D	'7229'	N3171R	(to Fuerza Aerea Paraguaya as 0119) World Wide Aeronautical Industries, Moorpark, CA	24.6.91
•	T-6D	'7234'	N3172H	(to Fuerza Aerea Paraguaya as 0123) World Wide Aeronautical Industries, Moorpark, CA	24.6.91
•	T-6D	'417250'	N3172J	(to Fuerza Aerea Paraguaya as 0143) World Wide Aeronautical Industries, Moorpark, CA	24.6.91
•	T-6D	'417233'	N3172M	(to Fuerza Aerea Paraguaya as 0147) World Wide Aeronautical Industries, Moorpark, CA	24.6.91
•	T-6D	'417210'	N3172N	(to Fuerza Aerea Paraguaya as 0148) World Wide Aeronautical Industries, Moorpark, CA	24.6.91

NAKAJIMA B5N

-	•	B5N1			NASM, Silver Hill MD	65/88

NAKAJIMA B6N TENZAN "Jill"

	-	B6N2			NAS Willow Grove PA	58/80
-		B6N2	5350		(to USAF as T2-1702)	
					NASM, Silver Hill MD	87/91

NAKAJIMA C6N SAIUN "Myrt"

4161		C6N-1S	4161		(to USA for evaluation as T2-1702)	
					NASM, Silver Hill MD	65/91

NAKAJIMA J1N GEKKO "Irving"

7334	•	J1N1-S	7334		(to USA for evaluation as T2-N700)	
					NASM, Silver Hill MD	65/91
					(rest. completed .87, displ. Silver Hill)	

NAKAJIMA Ki-43 HAYABUSA "Oscar"

5465	•	Ki-43			Australian War Memorial, Canberra ACT	.84/92
					(complete airframe recov. ex Alexishhafen	
					PNG .84: static rest. project)	
					AWM Mitchell Storage Facility ACT	
62387	•	Ki-43-IIb			NASM, Silver Hill MD	60/91
					loan: EAA Museum, Hales Corner WI	
					later Oshkosh WI	70/91
					(id. also rep. as 6430, c/n 6)	
-	•	Ki-43			forced landing on beach, Bathurst Island NT	.42
					RAAF: held by 2AD Richmond	49
					Australian War Memorial, Canberra ACT	3.8.49
					R. G. Curtis, Sydney NSW : sold for scrap	.53
					Sid Marshall, Bankstown Airport NSW	62/80
					Jack Davidson, The Oaks NSW	80/85
					Col Pay/Pays Air Service,Scone NSW	.85/92
					(rebuild to fly Scone)	
-	•	Ki-43			Indonesian Air Force Museum,	
					Adisucipo AB, Yogyakarta	88/91
-		Ki-43			Roy Worcester, Wewak PNG	72

NAKAJIMA Ki-84 HAYATE "Frank"

1446	•	Ki-84	62387		captured Philippines	.45
					(to US for evaluation by USN)	c45
					sold for scrap	
					Ed Maloney/The Air Museum, Claremont CA	c52/60
				N3385G	(rebuilt Claremont 58/63, ff .63 LAX)	
					Ed Maloney/The Air Museum, Ontario CA	64/73
					Ed Maloney/Planes of Fame Museum, Chino	.73
					(trucked to Chino .73, rest. to flying condition)	
					shipped to Japan for tour .73, flew in Japan	.73
					sold in Japan, displ. Iruma Japan	.73/91

NAKAJIMA KIKKA

91ST	•				NASM, Silver Hill MD	60/91
-	•				NASM, Silver Hill MD	60/91

NORTHROP P-61 BLACK WIDOW

		Type	Serial	Reg'n	History	Date
-	•	P-61B	42-39445		forced landed, 7000ft up Cyclops Mountain,	
					Dutch New Guinea (Irian Jaya)	10.1.45
					recov. commenced by MAAM, abandoned	.85
				N550NF	Mid Atlantic Air Museum, Middletown PA	5.88/92
					recov. completed, shipped to Reading PA	.91
					(rest. project)	
-	•	P-61C	43-8330		NASM, Silver Hill MD	65/92
-	•	P-61C	43-8353		Boy Scouts of America, Urbania OH	
					USAFM, Wright-Patterson AFB, Dayton OH	20.6.58/92
					(displ. as "239468/"Moonlight Serenade")	
-	•	P-61C	-		Beijing Aeronautical Institute, Beijing China	87
					(displ. as "7602")	

REGGIONE RE 2001

		Type	Serial	Reg'n	History	Date
-	•	Re 2001	MM8071		ditched in sea off Sardinia : recov.	23.11.91
					Italian Air Force Museum, Vigna di Valle AB	.91
					(static rest. project)	

REPUBLIC P-47 THUNDERBOLT

		Type	Serial	Reg'n	History	Date
-	•	P-47D	42-8066		William G. Chapman/PNG War Museum	.68/72
					(recov. ex swamp near Pt Moresby PNG .68)	
					Kokoda Track War Memorial Museum,	
					Port Moresby , PNG	.72
					Mus. of Transport & Technology, Auckland NZ	80/92
-	•	P-47D	42-8205		(to FA Boliviana as FAB.....)	
					gate guard, La Paz, Bolivia	
					Jim Cullen/Westair International Inc,	
					Monument CO : recov. ex La Paz	7.73
				N14519	Westair International, Monument CO	12.73
					Doug Champlin/Windward Aviation, Enid OK	2.76/79
					(rebuilt Carlsbad CA 76/81; ff .81)	
					Champlin Fighter Museum, Mesa AZ: del.	5.81/92
					(flies as "Big Stud/88")	
-	•	P-47D	42-8320		BOC USAAF 30.5.43; crashed Lake Kerr FL	12.8.43
					recov. from Lake Kerr by Jay Wisler	c84
					P-47 Heritage Commission, Evansville IN	87
					(rebuild,to be displ. as "222250"/Hoosier Spirit")	
-	•	P-47D	42-23278		USC Technical School, Santa Maria CA	.47
					Bob Bean Aircraft, Blythe CA (stored Blythe)	.53/61
				N5087V	Republic Aviation Corp, Farmingdale NY	4.61/64
					(displ. in UK and Europe .63)	
				N347D	USAFM Wright-Patterson AFB, Dayton OH	11.64/92
-	•	P-47G	42-25068		Oakland Technical School, Oakland CA	.46/52
		TP-47G			Jack P. Hardwick, El Monte CA	.52/75
					(used by Flying Tiger as ground engine test rig)	
					stored Hardwick's yard, El Monte CA	c55/75
					Eagle Aviation, Tulsa OK (rest. began)	.75
					Hurley Boehler/Sirrus Aviation, Tulsa OK	
					Ray Stutsman, Elkhart IN	7.12.79
				N42354	Ray Stutsman, Elkhart IN	5.81
				N47DG	Ray Stutsman, Elkhart IN	2.82/87
					(rest. Elkhart, ff 4.82 as "28476/Little Demon")	
					Robert L. Waltrip/ Lone Star Flight Museum,	
					Houston, later Galveston TX	5.87/92
-	•	P-47G	42-25234		Grand Central Aircraft Co, Glendale CA	.44
					Cal-Aero Technical Institute, Glendale CA	50/55
					The Air Museum, Claremont CA	10.55

			N3395G	The Air Museum, Ontario CA	63/71
				(rest. Kirtland AFB NM .58/63; flew as	
				"Roscoe's Retreat/MX-W",later"226387/NM-U")	
				crashed during airshow, NAS Point Mugu CA	23.10.71
				(rebuilt Chino CA, ff .76 as "28487/M-UN")	
				Planes of Fame, Chino CA	76/92
				(FAA quote id. 42-25254)	
- •	P-47D	42-26450		(to FA Brasileira as 4104)	
				Guararapes AB, Recife	67/87
				(displ. on pole as "226450/A1")	
- •	P-47D	42-26760		(to FA Brasileira as 4109)	
				Museum of Aeronautics, Sao Paulo, Brazil	70/87
- •	P-47D	42-26766		(to FA Brasileira as 41....)	
				arrived dism. Chino CA, from Brazil	c9.88
				Bill Destefani, Shafter CA : rest. project	10.90/91
				(rebuild to fly, Shafter CA)	
- •	P-47D	42-27385	NX4477N	Republic Aviation: retired, dismantled	46/47 Y
	P-47M			William Odom/Dallas Aero Service	7.47
				(Bendix racer #42/"Reynolds Bombshell")	
				Earl Reinert, Chicago IL	6.48/63
				(stored engineless, Oklahoma c50/63)	
				Victory Air Museum, Mundelein IL	.63/84
			N4477M	Yankee Air Corps, Chino CA	10.85/91
			N4464N	Yankee Air Corps, Chino CA	3.86/90
			N27385	Yankee Air Corps, Chino CA	92
				(rebuild to fly, Chino CA 85/92)	
				(FAA quote id. as "93-F-12000")	
- •	P-47D	44-20371		(to L'Armee de L'Air as 420371)	
				Musee de l'Air: stored St Cyr, Paris	74
				Musee de l'Air, Paris-Le Bourget	75/87
				(displ. in A de L'A markings "420371")	
- •	P-47D	44-32669		(to FA Brasileira as FAB....)	
				arr. dism. Chino CA, from Brazil	c9.88
- •	P-47D	44-32691		NASM, stored Silver Hill MD ("H-E")	65/90
- •	P-47D	44-32809		(to FA Venezuela as FAV 10B36)	.48
				Museo Aeronautico, Maracay AB	80/91
				(also quoted as ex 44-32814)	
- •	P-47D	44-33712		(to Turkish AF as TC-21)	
				Turk Hava Muzesi, Cumaovasi AB, Izmir	66
				Turkish Air Force Museum, Istanbul	82/87
539C1537•	P-47N	44-89320		Miguel Such Vocational School, San Juan PR	.54/67
				displ. PR ANG, Muniz ANGB, Isla Verde	.67/70
				(displ. as "489320/ PR ANG")	
			N345GP	Major Gabriel I. Penagarico/Thunderbolt Inc,	
				Santurce PR	.70/78
				(rest. San Juan, ff. 20.9.72, "489320/5A-Z")	
				dam., tipped on nose, Myrtle Beach AFB SC	10.6.77
				USAFM, Eglin AFB FL (displ. as "126")	11.78/91
- •	P-47N	44-89348		USAFM, Lackland AFB TX	.56/92
				(displ. as "489348/HV-A")	
- •	P-47N	44-89425		American Legion Post, Shortsville NY	
				USAFM, Stewart AFB NY	10.69
				USAFM, Perrin AFB TX	71
				USAFM, Peterson AFB, CO	5.71/87
				(displ. on pole as "489425/PE-425")	

- •	P-47N	44-89444		USAFM, Langley AFB VA	c56
				USAFM, Wright-Patterson AFB, Dayton OH	57/61
				USAFM, PA ANGB Greater Pittsburgh PA	73/78
				Cradle of Aviation Museum, Garden City NY	6.78/92
				(displ. as "489444/08/Cheek Baby")	
- •	P-47D	44-89746		(to Italian AF as MM4653)	1.3.51
				Pisa University Engineering School: del.	19.5.53/73
				Museo Storico Dell'Aeronautica Militare	
				Italiana, Vigna di Valle	.73/87
				(restored, displ. as "MM4653/51-19")	
- •	P-47D	44-90103		(to FA Brasileira as FAB....)	
				arrived dism. Chino CA, from Brazil	c9.88
- •	P-47D	44-90294		(to FA Brasileira as FAB....)	
				arrived dism. Chino CA, from Brazil	c9.88
- •	P-47D	44-90368		(to FA Venezuela as FAV.......)	
				Dr. Steve Schulke, Orlando FL	.71
				J-B Salis Collection, La Ferte Alais, France	85/86
				(noted stored unrest., La Ferte Alais 5.85)	
				Charles A. Osborne, Louisville KY	87
			N4747P	Blue Sky Aviation, Louisville KY	6.91/92
				(flies as "432773/4P-S/Big Ass Bird II")	
- •	P-47D	44-90438		(to Yugoslav AF as 13021)	2.52
				Yugoslav Aeronautical Museum, Belgrade	84
				Warbirds of GB Ltd, Bitteswell	.85
				John Whittington, Knoxville TN	.86/91
				(rebuild to fly, Knoxville TN)	
38955616•	P-47D	44-90471		(to FA Peruana as FAP114)	.52
			N47DA	Ed Jurist/Vintage Aircraft International Ltd,	
				Nyack NY	.69/75
				(arr. SS Rosaldina, Brownsville TX 5.9.69;	
				assembled by CAF, Harlingen TX, ff 26.8.71)	
				Military Aircraft Restoration Corp, Chino CA	4.75/92
				(stored Barstow-Daggett CA 75)	
				56th FG Restaurant, Farmingdale NY: del	4.83/87
				(displ. as "421175/"Zemke's Wolfpack/UN-Z")	
				loan: National Warplane Museum, Geneseo NY	4.87/90
				Air Heritage Inc, Beaver Falls PA	91/92
				(under rest. to fly, Beaver Falls PA)	
-	P-47N	44-95171		NASM, Silver Hill MD	71
				(rep. fuselage & tailplane only)	
39955690•	P-47D	45-49151		(to FA Brasileira as 4184)	53
				Quaratingueta AB, Sao Paulo	67/72
				Museu Aerospacial da FAB Rio de Janeiro	78/87
				(displ. as FAB "420339/D3")	
				under rest. to fly	87/89
39955706•	P-47D	45-49167		(to FA Peruana as FAP116)	.52
			N47DB	Ed Jurist/Vintage Aircraft International Ltd,	
				Nyack NY	69/75
				(arr. SS Rosaldina, Brownsville TX 5.9.69;	
				assembled by CAF, Harlingen TX: ff 2.12.71	
				as "353rd FG/226422/LH-E")	
				(raced at Reno as #13 by M. L. Gardner 9.74)	
				Military Aircraft Restoration Corp, Chino CA	4.75/81
				stored Barstow-Daggett CA	.75
				displ. Restaurant, St Petersburg FL	
				dam. by storm St.Petersburg, rebuilt Chino	.79
				USAFM, Wright-Patterson AFB, OH: del.	5.81/90

				(displ. as "432718")	
39955720•	P-47D	45-49181		(to FA Peruana as FAP115)	.52
			N47DC	Vintage Aircraft International Ltd, Nyack NY	69/75
				(arr. SS Rosaldina, Brownsville TX 5.9.69;	
				assembled by CAF, Harlingen TX: ff 28.8.72	
				as "420473/FT-L")	
				Military Aircraft restoration Corp, Chino CA	4.75/77
				(stored Barstow-Daggett CA .75/77)	
				Lester Friend, Carlsbad CA	4.77
			N159LF	Lester Friend, Carlsbad CA	.78/79
				(flew as "549181/LD-F")	
				Preston Parish, Kalamazoo MI	26.7.79
			N444SU	Preston Parish/ Kalamazoo Aviation History	
				Museum, Kalamazoo MI	3.83/92
				(flies as "226418/HV-A")	
39955731•	P-47D	45-49192		(to FA Peruana as FAP119)	.52
			N47DD (1	Vintage Aircraft International Ltd, Nyack NY	.69/75
				(arr. SS Rosaldina, Brownsville TX 5.9.69;	
				assembled by CAF, Harlingen TX: ff .73	
				as "86FG/Grumpy")	
				Military Aircraft restoration Corp, Chino CA	4.75/80
				(stored Barstow-Daggett CA 4.75/77)	
				Yesterdays Air Force Kansas Wing,	1.80
				crashed on take-off on del. flight, Tulsa OK	9.2.80
				(wreck trucked to Del Rio TX .80)	
				Jon Ward, Saugus CA	6.80/82
				Stephen Grey, Duxford UK	.85
				(basis of static rebuild: N47DD(2 resurrected as	
				composite with parts of 45-49192: see below)	
				Imperial War Museum, Duxford UK: arr.	11.85/92
				(long-term static rebuild Duxford)	
39955744•	P-47D	45-49205		(to FA Peruana as FAP122)	.52
			N47DE	Vintage Aircraft International Ltd,Nyack NY	.69/75
				(arr. SS Rosaldina, Brownsville TX 5.9.69,	
				assembled by CAF, Harlingen TX: ff .73)	
				Military Aircraft restoration Corp, Chino CA	4.75/79
				(stored Barstow-Daggett CA .75/79)	
				Warbirds of GB Ltd, Blackbushe	5.79/85
				(arr. Blackbushe on del. ex Chino CA 11.11.79)	
			G-BLZW	Warbirds of GB Ltd, Blackbushe	15.7.85
				Stephen Grey, Duxford	8.85
			N47DE	Planes of Fame East, Eden Prairie MN	17.12.85
				(shipped UK-Chino CA, ff Chino 6.86	
			N47RP	Robert J. Pond, Eden Prairie MN	3.86/92
				(flies as "228473/Big Chief/HV-P")	
				displ. EAA Museum, Oshkosh WI	91
39955834•	P-47D	45-49295		(to Yugoslav AF as 13064)	
				Yugoslav Aeronautical Museum, Belgrade	85
				Warbirds of GB Ltd, Bitteswell	.85
				RAF Museum store, RAF Cardington	.86/92
				(static rest., prev. rep. as 42-22936/13024)	
39955874•	P-47D	45-49335		(to FA Peruana as FAP127)	10.52
			N47DF	Vintage Aircraft International Ltd, Nyack NY	.69/74
				(arr. SS Rosaldina, Brownsville TX 5.9.69;	
				assembled by CAF, Harlingen TX: ff .73)	
				(flew as 354th FG "228790/Unadilla Killa")	
				Tom Friedkin, Palomar CA	74
				Military Aircraft restoration Corp, Chino CA	4.75/92
				(stored, Barstow-Dagget CA .75/80)	
				crashed on take-off, Barstow CA	3.7.80
				(rebuilt Tulsa OK, later Casper WY 80/86)	
				loan: Liberal Air Museum, Liberal KS	.86/90
				dam. forced landing nr Flagstaff AZ, during	

				ferry flight Topeka-Chino	10.90
				rebuild to fly, Chino CA	91
39955885•	P-47D	45-49346		(to FA Brasileira as FAB....)	
			N3152D	Yankee Air Corps, Chino CA	9.91/92
- •	P-47D	45-49406		(to FA Brasileira as FAB....)	
			N7159Z	Victor Haluska/Santa Monica Propeller Inc,	
				Santa Monica CA	7.90/92
39955997•	P-47D	45-49458		(to FA Peruana as FAP.....)	
				USAFM, loan Bradley Air Museum/New England	
				Air Museum, Windsor Locks CT	11.72/92
				(displ. as "420344/Norma/54")	
- •	P-47N	45-53436		(to GN Nicaraguana as GN....)	
			N478C	Lloyd P. Nolan/Thunderbolt & Co,	
				Mercedes TX : del. ex Managua	7.2.63/70
			N47TB	Confederate Air Force, Harlingen TX	.70/91
				crashed Vero Beach FL (rebuilt .76)	29.4.71
				American Airpower Heritage Flying Museum,	
				Midland TX	9.91/92
				(FAA quotes "45-3436", CAF quotes 44-53436,	
				other sources quote 44-88436 & 44-53456!)	
- •	P-47D	-			
				(incomplete fuselage P-47N ex trade school	
				(id incorrectly quoted as "44-95471")	
				Military Aircraft restoration Corp, Chino CA	75
				(stored Barstow CA 75/80)	
				Wayne Williams (adv. for sale as project)	.80
				Robin Collard, Del Rio TX	.80
				(composite rebuild, wing and parts of N47DD/	
				45-49192, and wing from South America	
				trucked to Tahoe NV)	80
				Jon Ward, Saugus CA	6.80/82
				(rebuild at Truckee CA & Agua Dulce CA 82/84)	
				Jim Kirby, Tahoe NV (rebuild 70% complete)	.84
			N47DD (2	Steven J. Hinton/Fighter Rebuilders Inc,	
				Chino CA: :	.85/92
				The Fighter Collection, Duxford	.85/92
				(rebuild completed at Chino, ff. 8.85; shipped	
				to UK, arr. Duxford 22.1.86)	
				(flies as "226671/MX-X")	
- •	P-47N	-		(to GN Nicaraguana as GN......) : retired	7.2.63
			N6148U	Glenn Martin/MACO Sales Financial Corp,	
				Chicago IL	9.63
				crashed on beach Mexico, on del. flight	26.9.64
				stripped for components by CAF	.64
				Confederate Air Force, Albuquerque NM	87
				(fuselage only)	
				(FAA quote id. "5496765C")	
- •	P-47N	-		(to FA Boliviana as FAB 007)	
				FA Bolivia Air Base, La Paz Airport, Bolivia	68/88
- •	P-47N	-		(to FA Boliviana as FAB 120)	
				La Paz FAB AB, Bolivia	72/88
- •	P-47D	-		(to FA Brasileira as FAB 4107)	
				Santa Cruz AB, Brazil	87
- •	P-47D	-		(to FA Brasileira as FAB 4181)	
				Fortaleza AB, Brazil	70/87

-	P-47D	-		(to FA Brasileira as FAB 4191) displ. in park, Sao Paulo City, Brazil: "C3"	68/72
- •	P-47D	-		(to FA Brasileira as FAB 4194) FAB Academy Museum, Pirassununga AB, Sao Paulo	87
- •	P-47D	-		(to FA Chile as 750) El Basque AB, Santiago, Chile	87
- •	P-47D	-		(to FA Colombiana as FAC 861) Museo FAC, Catam Air Base, El Dorado, Bogota	72/87
- •	P-47D	-		(to FA Cubana as ......) displ. Havana, Cuba	76/88
- •	P-47D	-		(to FA Mexicana as .....) Museo de la FAM, displ Santa Lucia AB	78/87
- •	P-47D			(to FA Mexicana as .....) rep. at Guadalajara, Mexico: derelict	87
- •	P-47D	-		(to FA Venezuala as FAV 8A36) displ. Fort Tiuna, Caracas	82
- •	P-47D	-		(to Yugoslav AF as 13056) Yugoslavian Aviation Museum, Belgrade	84/92
- •	P-47D	-		(to Yugoslav AF as 13109) Technical Museum, Zagreb, Yugoslavia	84/92
- •	P-47N	-		Earl Reinert, Chicago IL (recov. ex Republic: uncompleted airframe) Walter Soplata Collection, Newbury OH (fuselage and tailplane only)	85
- •	P-47	-		(to GN Nicaraguana as GN.....) displ. Managua Airport, Nicaragua Roy M. Stafford, Jacksonville FL	c87
- •	P-47D	-		Beijing Aeronautical Institute, Beijing China (displ. as "7601")	87

SAVOIA-MARCHETTI SM.82 MARSUPIALE

- •	SM.82PW	MM61187		Museo Aeronautico Caproni di Taliedo, Milan Italian Air Force Museum, Vigna di Valle (displ. as "MM61850")	75 84

SAVOIA-MARCHETTI SM.79

- •	SM.79	MM45508	LR-AMB L-112	 Lebanese Museo Aeronautico Caproni di Taliedo, Milan Italian Air Force Museum, Vigna di Valle	 75 84

SHORT SUNDERLAND

SB.2018 • (SH.32C)	Mk. 3 Mk. 5 Sandringham 4	JM715	ZK-AMH	Tasman Empire Airways Ltd - TEAL, Auckland NZ "Auckland"	10.47/50
			VH-BRC	Barrier Reef Airways, Brisbane QLD "Beachcomber"	.50/53
				Ansett Flying Boat Services, Sydney NSW "Beachcomber"	.53/74
			N158C	Antilles Air Boats, St Thomas USVI "Southern Cross"	11.74
			VP-LVE	Antilles Air Boats, St Thomas USVI	.75
			N158C	Antilles Air Boats, St Thomas USVI	78/81
				(del. San Juan PR to Calshot 10.80 - 2.2.81)	
				Science Museum, London	.82
				displ. Southampton Hall of Aviation	8.83/91
				(displ. as "VH-BRC/"Beachcomber")	
SB.2022 • (SH.57C)	Mk. 3 Sandringham 7	JM719	G-AKCO	British Overseas Airways Corp - BOAC "St. George"	18.3.48
			VH-APG	Capt. P. G. Taylor, Sydney "Frigate Bird III"	14.10.54
			F-OBIP	Reseau Aerien Interinsulaire - RAI, Papeete	5.58/65
				retired Papeete, abandoned	65/78
				Douglas Pearson Jnr	.75
				recov., shipped to France by French Navy	7.78
				Musee de l'Air, Le Bourget : handed over	3.11.78/91
- •	GR Mk. 3	ML796		(to Aeronavale as ML796/50-S-3)	51/60
				Robert Bertin : ex storage Brest	.65
				Maisden-La-Riviere, Hydrobase, Nantes (in use as bar/night club)	.66/69
				moved to La Baule France : night club	.69/76
				Imperial War Museum, Duxford	.76/92
SH.974 • (SH.55C)	Mk. 3 Sandringham	ML814		(to RNZAF as NZ4108)	
			VH-BRF	Ansett Flying Boat Services, Rose Bay "Islander"	.63/74
			N158J	Antilles Air Boats, St Thomas USVI "Excalibur VIII"	25.9.74/81
				Edward Hulton, Calshot : del.	5.81
			G-BJHS	Edward Hulton/Sunderland Ltd, Chatham	11.9.81/92
				damaged by gales, Chatham (repaired)	16.10.87
				For sale	10.92
- •	GR Mk. 5	ML824		(to Aeronavale as ML824) del. 28.8.50 wfu	.60
				Peter F. M. Thomas/Sunderland Trust, Pembroke Dock, Wales	24.3.61/71
				RAF Museum, Hendon	3.71/92
				(displ. as "ML824/NS-Z")	
-	GR Mk. 5	RN272		(VB881 also: to RNZAF as NZ4112 'L')	
				stored whole, RNZAF Hobsonville	71
				Ferrymead Historical Park, Christchurch NZ (major components only by	79
SH.1552 •	GR Mk. 5	SZ584	G-AHJR	British Overseas Airways Corp - BOAC	16.7.46
				returned to RAF as SZ584	4.48
				(to RNZAF as NZ4115 'Q')	
				Museum of Transport & Technology, Auckland NZ	71/91

WE ARE GOING STRAIGHT AHEAD
Your reliable partner for all propeller systems. Manufacturer of 2- to 5-blade variable pitch, fixed pitch, & constant speed propellers and accessories for General Aviation, Hovercraft, and special fans for Wind Tunnels.
HOFFMANN PROPELLER
POSTF. 10 03 39 · D-8200 ROSENHEIM
TEL. 0 80 31/3 20 11 · FAX 0 80 31/1 58 32

6S 30225 •	Mk. 1a	K9942		RAF Cardiff : for exhibition use	28.8.44
				RAF Newark : displ.	9.51
				RAF Bicester : travelling exhibit	60/71
				RAF Museum, Hendon: arr.	9.11.71/92
				(displ. as "K9942/SD-V")	
CBAF. 14 •	Mk. IIa	P7350		RAF Colerne : stored	24.7.44/47
				sold as scrap, John Dale & Sons Ltd	.47
				RAF Colerne Collection : displ.	.47/67
			G-AWIJ	Spitfire Productions Ltd, Elstree	25.4.68
				(flown in movie "Battle of Britain" .68)	
				(returned to RAF as P7350)	10.68
				RAF Battle of Britain Memorial Flight	10.68/92
- •	Mk. IIa	P7540		312 sqdn: crashed into Loch Doon, Ayrshire	15.10.41
				Dumfries & Galloway Aviation Group Museum,	
				Tinwald Downs : recov. and displ.	.82/88
CBAF 492 •	Mk. IIa	P7973		shipped to Melbourne VIC: display aircraft	7.45/50
				Australian War Memorial, Canberra ACT	3.50/92
CBAF 711 •	Mk. IIb	P8332		RAF presentation aircraft "Soebang (N.E.I.)"	20.3.41
				(to RCAF as P8332) BOC	1.4.42
				displ. various RCAF bases	47/64
				RCAF Museum Collection, Rockcliffe ONT	6.12.64
				Canadian National Aviation Mus., Rockcliffe	68/90
				loan: National Mus. of Science & Technology	83
- •	Mk. Ia	P9306		Museum of Science & Industry, Chicago IL	11.44/88
- •	Mk. Ia	P9374		recovered from beach, Calais, France	9.80
6S/ 30613 •	Mk. Ia	P9444		RAF : allocated for display purposes	28.8.49
				RAF Newark	.51
				Science Museum Store, Sydenham, London	16.12.54
				Science Museum, South Kensington, London	.63/89
6S/ 80914 •	Mk. Ia	R6915		Imperial War Museum, London	26.8.46/92
6S/ 81254 •	Mk. Ia	X4590		RAF Cardiff : for exhibition use	28.8.44
				RAF Air Historical Branch Collection	54
				RAF Bicester : travelling exhibit	60/66
				RAF Museum, RAF Cosford	.77/78
				RAF Museum, Hendon	.78/92
				(displ. as "X4590/PR-F")	
CBAF. 1061 •	LF Mk. Vb	AB910	G-AISU	Grp. Capt. Allen H. Wheeler	25.10.46
				Vickers-Armstrongs Ltd, Weybridge	59/65
				RAF Battle of Britain Memorial Flight	15.9.65/91
				(flew in movie "Battle of Britain .68)	
				(damaged landing, Duxford 6.76)	
				(badly dam. in ground collision with Harvard,	
				Bex, Switzerland 21.8.78: redel. BBMF 26.10.81)	
				BBMF Royal Air Force Coningsby	92
WASP/ 20/2 •	Mk. 1a	AR213	G-AIST	Gp. Capt. Allan H. Wheeler	25.10.46
				(stored Old Warden & Abingdon 46/67)	
				Allan H. Wheeler, Duxford & Booker	.67
				(flown in movie "Battle of Britain" .68)	
				The Hon. Patrick Lindsay, Booker	78/89
				Victor Gauntlett, Booker	4.89/92
WASP/ 20/223 •	LF Mk. Vc	AR501		Loughborough Technical College, Leics : del.	21.3.46/61
				Shuttleworth Collection, Old Warden	.61/67
				(stored dism., Old Warden 61/67)	

			G-AWII	Spitfire Productions Ltd, Duxford	25.4.68
				(flown in movie "Battle of Britain" .68)	
				Shuttleworth Trust, Old Warden	.73/92
WASP/ 20/	F. Mk. Vc 288	AR614		RAF Padgate : displ.	49
				RAF West Kirby	c52
				RAF Hednesford	58
				RAF Bridgnorth : displ.	.58/63
				RAF Dishforth: as scrap	c52
				The Air Museum of Calgary ALTA: shipped	.64
				Donald Campbell, Kapuskasing ONT	.70
			C-FDUY	Donald Campbell, Kapuskasing ONT	86/89
				Old Flying Machine Co. Duxford	10.92
- •	Mk. V	BL370		crashed in marshland near Humber Estuary	.44
				recov. by Julian Mitchell & Stephen Arnold,	
				Oxford Composite (static rest.)	88/92
CBAF 1646 •	Mk. Vb	BL614		RAF Credenhill : displ. as "AB871"	3.55/67
				(taxy scenes, movie "Battle of Britain" .68)	
				RAF Wattisham : stored	69
				RAF Colerne	75
				RAF St Athan	8.75/82
				Manchester Air & Space Museum, Manchester	.82/85
				Museum of Science & Industry, Manchester	.85/92
CBAF 1660 •	Mk. Vb	BL628		fuselage/cockpit section derelict on farm	
				St Merryn, Cornwall	77
				recov. by Peter Croser & Michael Aitchison,	
				Melbourne VIC (shipped to Australia)	.77/91
				(rebuild project, Melbourne & Adelaide,	
				using wings and parts ex UK scrapyards)	
				shipped to UK, rebuild by Dick Melton	.88/91
			G-BTTN	D. J. T. John/Aerofab Restorations, Thruxton	13.8.91
•	Mk. Vb	BL655		crashed near Spilsby, Lancs.	1.7.43
				Lincolnshire Aviation Heritage Centre,	
				East Kirkby	.90/92
				(wreck recov. 90; display unveiled 10.91)	92
CBAF 2461 •	Mk. Vb	BM597		RAF Hednesford : gate guard	
				RAF Bridgnorth : gate guard	60/62
				RAF Church Fenton : gate guard	66/75
				RAF Henlow	.67/68
				(static scenes, movie "Battle of Britain" .68)	
				RAF Linton-on-Ouse	.75/79
				RAF Church Fenton : gate guard	9.79/88
				Historic Flying Ltd, Cambridge	6.88
			G-MKVB	Historic Flying Ltd, Audley End	2.5.89/91
				(rebuild to fly, Audley End)	92
- •	F Mk. Vc	BR108		shot down by Bf109, in sea near Gozo, Malta	8.7.42
				recov. by RAF Luqua team	.73
				National War Museum, Fort St Elmo, Malta	5.75/92
				(forward fuselage and wing sections only)	
- •	F Mk. Vc	BR545		(to RAAF as A58-51)	10.42
				ditched, Prince Regent River WA	24.12.43
				RAAF Museum, Point Cook VIC : recov.	12.87/92
- •	F Mk. IX	BR601		(to SAAF as 5631)	13.3.49
				Harold Barnett/South African Metal &	
				Machinery Co, Salt River, Cape Town	10.3.55/87
				(displ. on pole scrapyard as "BR601", later rebuilt	
				by Atlas Aircraft Co, displ. as "PV260/DB-P")	
				auctioned London UK	31.10.87
				Warbirds of GB Ltd, Biggin Hill	10.87/89

- •	F Mk. Vc	BS164		(to RAAF as A58-63) BOC	11.42
				midair collision, crashed nr. Strauss Strip NT	1.44
				Peter Croser, Melbourne VIC	91
				(rest project, parts recov. ex crash site NT)	
6S/ 199407 •	F Mk. Vc	BS199		(to RAAF as A58-81) BOC	10.42
				crashed Millingimbi NT during combat	5.43
				Robert L. Eastgate, Melbourne VIC	88/92
				(composite rest. project, RAAF Point Cook VIC)	
CBAF 196667	Mk. IXb	BS464		(to French Air Force as BS464) del.	25.6.46
				Musee de l'Air, Chalais-Meudon, Paris	12.49/69
				Musee de l'Air, Paris-Le Bourget	78/90
				destroyed in hangar fire, Le Bourget	17.5.90
WWA. 2822	F Mk. Vc	EE606		(to RAAF as A58-106) BOC 11.42 SOC	11.48
				hulk recov. ex Darwin NT : rest. project	
			G-MKVC	Charles Church (Spitfires) Ltd, Winchester	18.5.88/89
				(ff 20.11.88: flew as "EE606/D-B")	
				crashed and dest., nr Blackbushe (Church k.)	1.7.89
				Warbirds of GB Ltd: wreck	91/92
WASP/ 20/484 •	F Mk. Vc	EE853		(to RAAF as A58-146)	4.43
				dam. landing, Kiriwina, Solomon Islands	28.8.43
				Langdon Badger, Adelaide SA : recov.	.73/92
				(static displ. as "EE853/UP-O")	
WWA. 3832 •	F Mk. Vc	EF545		(to RAAF as A58-149) BOC 5.43 SOC	12.43
				N. Monty Armstrong, Auckland NZ	c73
				(recov. ex Kiriwina , Solomon Islands)	
				J. Shivas, Ashburton NZ	84
			ZK-MKV	Don J. Subritsky, Auckland NZ	86/89
				(composite rebuild, Dairy Flat airfield NZ, using parts from various aircraft recov. ex PNG)	
				Chris Warrilow, Woburn Green UK	92
6S/ 240837 •	LF Mk. IXe	EN145		(to Italian AF as MM4116)	27.6.46
				(to IDFAF as 20-78)	
				Ramat David AB, Israel : displ.	60/85
				IDFAF Museum, Hatzerim AB	.90
6S/ 197707 •	F Mk. XII	EN224		College of Aeronautics, Cranfield	4.7.46/60
			G-FXII	Peter R. Arnold, Newport Pagnell	4.12.89
				(frame 5 and other parts form., rest. project)	
6S/ 171652 •	Mk. VIIc	EN474		(to USAAF as EN474: later FE-400)	3.43
				NASM: stored Park Ridge IL & Silver Hill MD	.47/69
				NASM, Washington DC	78/89
CBAF 2403 •	LF Mk. Vb	EP120		RAF Wilmslow	.55/60
				RAF Bircham Newton	62
				RAF Boulmer	.64/67
				RAF Henlow	67/68
				(static scenes, movie "Battle of Britain" .68)	
				RAF Wattisham	.68/89
				RAF St Athan (for disposal)	.89/91
- •	Mk. VIII	JF294		flown Cairo-Cape Town, for exhibition use	3.44
				(to SAAF as 5501) : exhibition use only	
				S. A. National War Museum, Saxonwold	11.48
				S. A. Museum of Military History, Saxonwold	55/89
				(displ. as "SAAF 5501")	
- •	LF Mk. VIII	JG267		(to RAAF as A58-377) BOC	1.44
				forced landing on reef, Point Blaze NT	3.11.44
				Darwin Aviation Museum, Darwin NT: recov.	.85/92

	Type	Serial	Reg.	History	Date
- •	LF Mk. VIII	JG355		(to RAAF as A58-359) BOC	1.44
				forced landing, near Daly Waters NT	6.44
				Robert L. Eastgate, Melbourne VIC	88/92
				(composite rest. project, RAAF Point Cook VIC)	
- •	F Mk Vc	JG891		(to RAAF as A58-178) BOC	4.43
				missing on ferry flight	1.44
				N. M. (Monty) Armstrong, Auckland NZ	.74
				(recov. from Kiriwina, Solomon Islands .74)	
			ZK-MVI	Don J. Subritzky, Dairy Flat, Auckland	88/92
				(rest. to fly, Dairy Flat NZ)	
CBAF/ •	F Mk. Vc	JK448		(to Yugoslav AF as 9489)	
4690				Military Museum, Kalemagden Park, Belgrade	c58/61
				Yugoslavian Aviation Museum, Belgrade	84/92
				(displ. as "9486" , later "JK808/B")	
SMAF	F. 21	LA198		Air Training Corps, Portiswell, Worcester	19.2.54/67
4338 •				RAF Henlow	.67/68
				(static scenes, movie "Battle of Britain" .68)	
				RAF Locking	.69/86
				RAF Leuchars	3.86/89
				RAF St Athan	.89
SMAF	F. 21	LA226		Air Training Corps, Albrighton, Staffs	.54/58
4371 •				RAF Little Rissington	9.2.58/67
				RAF Henlow: for movie "Battle of Britain"	.67/68
				Vickers Ltd, South Marston Works	.68/84
				RAF Memorial Chapel, Biggin Hill	.84/87
				RAF Shawbury	89
SMAF	F. 21	LA255		RAF Cardington	60/62
4388 •				RAF West Raynham	64/67
				RAF Henlow : for movie "Battle of Britain"	.67
				RAF Wittering	69/88
- •	Seafire F. 46	LA546		Daniel Clark & Co, Carlisle (as scrap)	c51/66
				recov ex scrapyard by J. D. Kay/Manchester	
				Tankers Ltd, Charnock Richard, Lancs	.66
				Neville Franklin & Peter R. Arnold	73
				Peter R. Arnold, Newport Pagnell	.73
				Craig Charleston	88/92
SMAF	Seafire F. 46	LA564		Daniel Clark & Co, Carlisle (as scrap)	c51/66
19985 •				recov. ex scrapyard by J. D. Kay/Manchester	
				Tankers Ltd, Charnock Richard, Lancs	.66
				Neville Franklin & Peter R. Arnold UK	12.71
				Peter R. Arnold, Newport Pagnell UK	.73/92
				(composite rebuild, to Seafire F.XVII standard)	
- •	Mk. IX	LZ842		(to SAAF as ....)	
				stored Lanseria AB, South Africa	78/86
				A. Dunkerley, Oxford, UK	89
- •	F Mk. Vc	MA353		(to RAAF as A58-232) BOC	8.43
				missing on testflight from Strauss Strip NT	4.44
				John Haslett, Darwin NT	c71/92
				(recov. from crash site near Darwin NT c71)	
				(rest. project, using parts recov. crash sites)	
- •	HF Mk.IXe	MA793		(to USAAF as MA793) BOC 31.10.43: SOC	5.44
				(to SAAF as 5601) : shipped, arr.	30.9.48
				Meerhof Hospital for Handicapped Children,	
				Pretoria: playground	27.4.54/67
				Larry Barnett & Alan Lurie, Johannesburg	.67/86
				(rebuilt, ff. Johannesburg-Jan Smuts 29.9.75	
				as "SAAF PT672/WR-RR")	
				loan: SAAF, Lanseria AB : displ. flying	.76/86

			N930LB	Larry Barnett International California Inc,	
				Los Angeles CA (shipped Chino, ff 1.1.87)	14.8.86/90
				David G. Price/Museum of Flying,	
				Santa Monica CA	8.86/92
				(flies as "EN398/JE-J")	
- •	F Mk Vc	MA863		(to RAAF as A58-246) BOC	10.43
				crash landing , Lake Tarang VIC	8.45
				Richard E. Hourigan/Moorabbin Air Museum,	
				Melbourne VIC : hulk recov. ex farm	
				Ian A. Whitney, Romsey VIC : rest. to fly	.75/92
CBAF.	LF Mk. IXe	MH350		(to RNoAF as BM-A: later FN-M) BOC	8.11.45
IX490 •				last flight 15.11.51; stored Vaernes AB	.51/61
				Bodo AB, Norway: displ. as "FN-T"	5.61/82
				Norwegian Armed Forces Museum,	
				Akershus Castle, Oslo	8.82/90
CBAF.	HF Mk.IXb	MH415		(to RNAF as H-108: later H-65)	6.47/53
IX533 •				shipped to Java N.E.I.	5.47/50
				(to RBAF as SM-40)	4.53/56
			OO-ARD	COGEA Nouvelle, Ostend	15.6.56/61
				Rousseau Aviation, Dinard, France	61/66
				(flew in movie "The Longest Day" .61)	
			G-AVDJ	Gp Capt T. G. Mahaddie/Film Aviation Services,	
				Elstree	12.66/68
				(flew in movie "Battle of Britain" .68)	
			N415MH	Wilson C. Edwards, Big Spring TX	11.68/90
				(shipped ex Bovington to USA, arr. Houston 1.69)	
CBAF.	HF Mk. IXc	MH434		(to RNAF as H-105: later H-68)	19.2.47/53
IX552 •				shipped to Java N.E.I.	5.47/50
				(to RBAF as SM-41)	9.10.53
			OO-ARA	COGEA Nouvelle, Ostend	26.3.56/63
			G-ASJV	Tim A. Davies, Elstree : del.	29.6.63
				Gp Capt T. G. Mahaddie/Film Aviation Services,	
				Elstree	11.67/68
				(flew in movie "Battle of Britain" .68)	
				Adrian Swire, Booker & Duxford	2.69/83
				Ray G. Hanna/Nalfire Aviation Ltd, Duxford	14.4.83
				The Old Flying Machine Co, Duxford	87/92
- •	Mk. IX	MH603		(to SAAF as ......)	
				John Sykes, Oxford, UK : parts for rebuild project	89/92
CBAF.	LF Mk. IXc	MJ143		(to RNAF as H-1: later 3W-1) del.	17.6.46
IX907 •				retired 4.6.54; stored Gizle-Rijen	7.54/60
				Aeroplanorama Museum, Amsterdam-Schipol	3.60/68
				Militaire Luchtvaart Museum, Soesterberg AB	6.68/91
CBAF.	LF Mk. IXc	MJ271		(to RNAF as H-8: later 3W-8) del.	25.11.46
IX970 •				Volkel AB : decoy use	10.54/57
				War Museum, Delfzijl	6.1.59/76
				War Museum/Anthony Fokker Technical	
				School, Den Haag, Holland (rest.)	5.4.73/78
				Aviodome Museum, Amsterdam-Schipol	22.3.78/91
				(displ. as "MH424/ H-53")	
CBAF.	LF Mk. IX	MJ627		(to Irish Air Corps as 158) del.	5.6.51
7722 •	Mk. Tr 9			J. Crewdson/Film Aviation Services,	.63
				(arr. dism. Biggin Hill 13.11.63, stored dism.)	
			G-ASOZ	Film Aviation Services Ltd, Elstree	19.2.64
				Tim A. Davies, Elstree (stored dism.)	9.64/67
				John Fairey, Stockbridge (stored dism.)	12.67/78
			G-BMSB	Maurice Bayliss, Kenilworth, Warwick	3.5.78/92
				(rebuild to fly, Coventry: engine runs 2.92)	

CBAF. 7243 •	HF Mk. IXe	MJ730		(to Italian AF as MM4094)	27.6.46
				(to IDFAF as 0606: later 20-66) del.	21.1.55
				hulk recov. ex kibbutz Kabri, Israel by	
				Robs Lamplough; arr. Nailsworth, Glos	6.78/80
				Guy Black (rebuild commenced)	10.80/83
			G-FEDX	ntu: Fred Smith/Federal Express, Memphis TN	4.82
			G-BLAS	Guy Black/Aero Vintage Ltd, St Leonards	11.83/88
				David W. Pennell, East Midlands	88/89
				(ff East Midlands 12.11.88)	
			G-HFIX	David W. Pennell, East Midlands Airport	22.8.89/92
- •	LF Mk. IXc	MJ755		(to R. Hellenic AFas MJ755)	27.2.47
				last flight 8.9.53; stored Hellenikon AB	
				Tatoi AB : displ.	72/78
				Hellenic War Museum, Athens	85/87
CBAF. 7269 •	LF Mk. IX Mk. Tr 9	MJ772		(to Irish Air Corps as 159) del.	5.6.51/63
				J. Crewdson/Film Aviation Services,	
				Biggin Hill : stored dism.	.63
				COGEA Nouvelles, Ostend Belgium	3.64/65
				(airfreighted to Ostend 1.4.64: stored dism.)	
				N. A. W. Samuelson, Elstree	.65
			G-AVAV	N. A. W. Samuelson, Elstree	8.11.66/70
				(shipped ex Belgium; rebuilt Elstree, ff 7.67)	
				(flown in movie "Battle of Britain" .68)	
				crashed, landing, Little Straughton (repaired)	9.7.68
				Sir W. J. D. Roberts, Shoreham	12.69/71
				Strathallan Collection, Auchterader, Scotland	12.71/74
			N8R (2	Doug Champlin/Windward Aviation, Enid OK	13.12.74
				Champlin Fighter Museum, Mesa AZ	81/92
				crashed Amarillo TX, on ferry flight to Mesa	.81
				(rebuilt Mesa; configured as single-seater, ff 10.85)	92
CBAF. 1301 •	LF Mk. IXc	MJ783		(to RBAF as SM-15) BOC	3.2.48
				Musee de l'Armee et d'Histoire Militaire/	
				Palais du Cinquantenaire, Brussels: stored	1.52/78
				Musee Royal de l'Armee, Brussels	80/91
				(displ. as "MJ360/GE-B")	
CBAF. IX1514 •	LF Mk. IXc	MK297		(to RNAF as H-116: later H-55)	6.47/52
				shipped to Java, N. E. I.	5.47/50
				(to RBAF as SM-43)	.52/56
			OO-ARB	COGEA Nouvelle, Ostend	5.5.56
				(flew in movie "The Longest Day" .61)	
			G-ASSD	J. Crewdson/Film Aviation Services Ltd,	
				Biggin Hill : del.	5.64
				R. A. Wale, London	4.65
				Confederate Air Force, Mercedes TX	5.65
				(remained in UK & France for filming work)	
				Film Aviation Services Ltd, Biggin Hill	5.66
				G. A. Rich, Henlow	10.66
				dam. North Weald, movie "Battle of Britain"	17.5.68
			N1882	Aerosmith Corp, Dallas TX/Confederate AF	12.68/73
				(shipped, Bovington to Houston TX 11.68)	
			N9BL	Confederate Air Force, Harlingen TX	20.6.73/90
			N11RS	ntu: Confederate Air Force, Harlingen TX	86
			N9BL	Confederate Air Force, Harlingen TX	86/91
				American Airpower Heritage Flying Museum,	
				Midland TX	9.91/92
CBAF. IX1561 •	LF Mk. IXc	MK356		RAF Hawkinge (displ. as "M5690","MK365")	.51/61
				RAF Bicester	.62
				RAF Locking	66/67
				RAF Henlow	.67/69
				(static scenes, movie "Battle of Britain" .68)	
				RAF Museum, RAF St Athan	18.8.69/90
CBAF. IX1732 •	LF Mk. IXc	MK732		(to RNAF as H-25 later 3W-17) del.	27.6.48
				Eindhoven AB: decoy use	30.6.54/56

				RAF Oldenburg, West Germany (displ.)	.56/57
				RAF Aldhorn WG	
				RAF Gutersloh, WG	60/69
				RAF Brize Norton : airfreighted	27.6.69
				RAF St Athan	10.7.69/70
				RAF Bicester	3.12.70/74
				RAF Coltishall : B of B Flight spares source	23.10.74
				RAF Coningsby	78
				RAF St Athan (stripped, dism.)	8.79
				RAF Abingdon	9.80
				RNAF 322 Sqdn, Gilzen-Rijen AB	30.8.83/86
				(arr. Schipol 13.4.84, displ. Schipol 84/85;	
				to Gilzen-Rijen for rest. 29.11.85)	
				Dutch Spitfire Flight	89/92
				(rebuild to fly at Deelen AB, mainplane in UK)	
			G-HVDM	DSF (Guernsey) Ltd, Guernsey	18.1.91
CBAF.	Mk. IX	MK805		(to Italian AF/AMI as MK805)	27.6.46
IX1780 •				(to AMI as MM4084)	19.12.47
				displ. in town, Nettuno, Italy	
				Foce Vered Artillery School, Nettuno: displ.	65/77
				Museu Storico Dell'Aeronautica Militaire	
				Italiana, Vigna di Valle, Italy	82/89
				(displ. as "MM4084/A-32")	
CBAF.	LF Mk. IXc	MK912		(to RNAF as H-119: later H-59)	7.46/53
IX1875 •				shipped to Java, N.E.I	5.47/50
				(to RBAF as SM-29)	.53
				RBAF Technical School, Saffraenberg (displ.)	8.55/88
				Brussels Military Museum	.88
				Historic Aircraft Collection Ltd, Jersey: arr.	22.6.89
			G-BRRA	Historic Aircraft Collection Ltd, Jersey	10.10.89
				(c/n also quoted as CBAF8185)	
CBAF.	HF Mk.IXc	MK923		(to RNAF as H-104: later H-61)	7.46
IX1886 •				shipped to Java, N.E.I.	5.47/50
				(to RBAF as SM-37)	c3.52
			OO-ARF	COGEA Nouvelles, Ostend	25.4.58/63
				(flown in movie "Longest Day", France .61)	
				Cliff Robertson, Santa Ana CA: airfreighted	17.11.63
			N93081	Cliff P. Robertson, Santa Ana CA	.64
				(displ. Tallmantz/Movieland of Air Museum)	67
			N521R	Clifford P. Robertson, Los Angeles CA	2.66/92
				(flies as "5J-Z")	
CBAF.	Mk. IXc	MK959		(to RNAF as H-15: later 3W-15) del.	26.9.46
8125 •				Volkel AB & Eindhoven AB : decoy use	54
				Eindhoven AB : displ.	.55/87
				(displ. as "MJ289", later "MK959/H-15")	
				Dutch Spitfire Flight	92
CBAF.	LF Mk. IXe	ML119		(to Czech AF as ML119)	6.12.46
IX1892 •				(to IDFAF as 20-20)	5.49
				(to Burmese AF as UB441)	2.55
				displ. Mingaladon AB, Rangoon	65/89
- •	Mk. IX	ML255		(to SAAF as 5563) del.	16.11.48
				dam. collision, Ysterplaat AB : SOC	22.1.54
				derelict hulk held Snake Valley,Pretoria	81
				SAAF Museum : static rest.	
				Museu do Ar, Alverca, Portugal	.89
				(displ. as "FAP ML255/MR-2")	
- •	LF Mk. IX	ML407		(to Irish Air Corps as 162) del.	30.7.51/68
	Mk. Tr 9			to inst. airframe; stored dism. Baldonnel AB	62/68
				N. A. W. Samuelson, Cricklewood, London	3.68/70

				(stored dism., Cricklewood, North London 68/70)	
				Sir W. J. D. Roberts, Shoreham, later	
				Strathallan Collection, Scotland (stored dism.)	4.70/79
				E. Nick Grace, St Merryn, Cornwall	9.8.79
			G-LFIX	E. Nick Grace/Island Trading Ltd, St Merryn	1.2.80
				(rebuilt, ff. St Merryn 16.4.85)	
				Nick Grace & Chris Horsely, Middle Wallop	.85/88
				(crashed landing, Southend 5.3.86: repaired)	
				Caroline S. Grace, Winchester	26.5.89/91
				(flies as "ML407/OU-V")	
6S/	LF Mk. IXe	ML417		(to Indian AF as HS543)	.48
730116 •	Mk. Tr 8			stored for IAF Museum, Palam AB	67
				Senator Norman E. Gaar, Fort Collins CO	4.71/80
				(shipped to USA 3.72, rebuild Ft.Collins CO)	
				B. J. S. Grey, Duxford UK	11.6.80
				(shipped to UK, arr. 7.8.80)	
			G-BJSG	The Fighter Collection, Duxford	29.1.81/92
				(rebuild completed Booker, conv. to Mk.IXc	
				single seater, ff 10.2.84 as "ML417/2I-T")	
				(new c/n 6S-735188 when conv. to Tr.8)	
CBAF.	LF Mk. IXc	ML427		Vickers Castle Bromwich : gate guard	8.54/58
IX2131 •				Museum of Science & Industry, Birmingham	.58/89
6S/	LF Mk. VIIIc	MT719		(to Indian AF as HS...)	29.12.47
479770 •				to instructional airframe "T17"/Code 87	
				hulk recov. ex Jaipur AB by Ormond & Wensley	
				Haydon-Baillie, Duxford UK	.78
				Franco Actis, Turin, Italy: shipped ex UK	12.79
			I-SPIT	Franco Actis, Turin	.82/88
				(rest. Vergiate, ff 27.10.82 as "MT719/YB-J")	
				Adrian Reynard/Reynard Racing Cars : del.	5.11.88/89
			G-VIII	Reynard Racing Cars Ltd, Bicester	27.4.89/91
				Peter Ray	7.92
6S/	LF Mk. VIIIc	MT818	G-AIDN	Vickers-Armstrong Ltd, Eastleigh	7.1.47/56
729058 •	Mk. Tr 8			(stored at Chilbolton 52/56)	
				Vivian Bellamy, Eastleigh	9.56/63
				John S. Fairey, Eastleigh, later Andover	9.63/67
				John S. Fairey & Tim Davies, Andover	.67/76
				Mike S. Bayliss, Baginton	.76/78
				(damaged landing, Baginton 6.2.78)	
				George F. Miller, Baginton, later Dinas Powis	.78/83
				(rebuilt .82 as "MT818/G-M", then shipped to TX)	
				George F. Miller, Houston TX	.83/86
			N58JE	Jack A. Erickson/ Erickson Skycrane Inc,	
				Central Point OR	7.86/92
				(rebuild completed, ff 4.87 as "MT818/G-M")	
- •	HF Mk. VIIIc	MT834		(to RAAF as A58-615) BOC 9.44 SOC	2.45
				recov. from station property QLD	c88
			VH-ZPY	Alec Wilson, Frome Downs Station, Yunta SA	88/92
				(rebuild to fly, Melbourne VIC)	
6S/	FR Mk. XIVe	MT847		RAF Warton : gate guard	5.52
643779 •				RAF Freckleton	.55/62
				RAF Middleton St. George	
				RAF Weston	c63
				RAF Cosford : displ. on pylon	.64/78
				RAF Henlow : for movie "Battle of Britain"	.67
				RAF Museum, RAF Cosford	79/87
6S/	HF Mk. VIIIc	MV154		(to RAAF as A58-671) BOC 9.12.44 SOC	6.10.48
583793 •				Sydney Technical College, Ultimo NSW	c49/61
				A. J. R. Oates, Sydney NSW	.61

				Sid Marshall, Bankstown NSW	63/75
				Jack P. Davidson, Bankstown NSW	75/77
				Brian A. Simpson, Sydney NSW	5.77
				Robs J. Lamplough, Duxford UK	9.79/82
				(shipped to UK ex Sydney 18.9.79)	
			G-BKMI	Fighter Wing Display Team Ltd, Duxford	23.12.82
				Robs J. Lamplough, North Weald	85/92
				(rebuild to fly, Huntingdon)	
6S/ 581740 •	HF Mk VIIIc	MV239		(to RAAF as A58-758) BOC	26.6.45
				Sydney Technical College, Ultimo NSW	9.49/61
				A. J. R. Oates, Sydney	.61
				Sid Marshall, Bankstown NSW	63/75
				Camden Museum of Aviation NSW : loan	7.72/82
				Jack P. Davidson, Bankstown NSW	75/82
			VH-HET	Col Pay, Scone NSW	6.83/92
				(rest. Scone, ff 29.12.85 as "A58-758")	
6S/ 649170 •	F Mk.XIV	MV246		(to RBAF as SG-55) BOC	24.8.48
				Musee Royal de l'Armee, Brussels	.49/91
				(composite: using parts ex SG-37, SG-46)	
- •	FR Mk. XIV	MV262		(to Indian AF as "42")	12.47
				National Air Cadet Corps, Calcutta	.77
				hulk recov. by Ormond & Wensley	
				Haydon-Baillie, Duxford UK	.78
				Warbirds of GB, Blackbushe	.78/85
				(arr. crated, Blackbushe 26.5.78: rebuild began)	
				The Fighter Collection, Duxford	.85
				Charles Church (Spitfires) Ltd, Winchester	8.86
			G-CCVV	Charles Church (Spitfires) Ltd, Winchester	18.5.88/89
				Weeks Aviation Museum	
				Miami, FL(rebuild to fly)	9.92
6S/ 649205 •	FR Mk. XIV	MV293		(to Indian AF as "48")	12.47
				to "T-20" IAF Technical College, Jalahalli	
				recov. from Bangalore by Ormond & Wensley	
				Haydon-Baillie, Duxford UK	.78
				Warbirds of GB Ltd, Blackbushe	.78
				(arr. crated, Blackbushe 26.5.78)	
			G-BGHB	Doug Arnold/Warbirds of GB Ltd	
			G-SPIT	Warbirds of GB Ltd, Blackbushe	2.3.79/85
				The Fighter Collection, Duxford	7.10.85/92
				(ff,14.8.92 Duxford)	
- •	HF Mk. VIII	MV321		(to RAAF as A58-642) BOC 11.44 SOC	11.48
				Bill Martin/Darling Downs Aviation Museum,	
				Oakey QLD	89/92
				(parts only, recov. ex farm Oakey QLD)	
- •	FR Mk. XIVc	MV370		(to Indian AF as HS.......)	12.47
				to instructional airframe "T44"	
				hulk recov. ex Nagpur AB by Ormond & Wensley	
				Haydon-Baillie, Duxford UK	.77
			G-FXIV	A. K. & K. W. Wickenden & M. Connor,	
				Hemel Hempstead	11.4.80/83
				Paul Raymond/Whitehall Theatre of War	6.83/85
				(static rest., displ. as "MV370/AV-L")	
				Robs Lamplough, North Weald	5.6.85/91
				Old Flying Machine Co, Duxford	.91/92
				(static rest., Duxford: for German museum)	
CBAF. IX2161 •	LF Mk.IXc	NH188		(to RNAF as H-109: later H-64)	5.47/52
				shipped to Java, N.E.I., arr. Batavia	22.7.47/50
				(to RBAF as SM-39)	3.52
			OO-ARC	COGEA Nouvelle, Ostend	25.5.56/61
			CF-NUS	John N. Paterson, Fort William ONT	8.61/64
				(shipped UK-Canada, ff 13.2.62: retired 7.6.64)	

				Canadian National Aviation Museum,	
				Rockcliffe ONT: displ. as "NH188/AU-H"	6.6.64/89
CBAF. IX2200 •	LF Mk.IXc	NH238		(to RNAF as H-103; later H-60)	30.5.47/53
				shipped to Java, N.E.I., arr. Batavia	22.7.47/50
				(to RBAF as SM-36) del.	10.3.53
			OO-ARE	COGEA Nouvelles, Ostend	8.9.56
				Beverley Snook/Trans Global Aviation Supply,	
				Southend UK : del.	27.5.61
				damaged, landing Elstree UK	2.6.61
				Taskers of Andover Ltd UK	18.7.61/69
				(displ. in company museum, on RAF transporter)	
				Thomas H. Pasteur, Eastleigh UK	22.2.69
			N238V	Ed Jurist & Bruce Farkas/CAF, Sugarland TX	3.7.69/75
				(shipped from UK, arr. Galveston TX 14.6.70)	
				David C. Tallichet/ MARG, Chino CA	4.75/79
				Douglas W. Arnold, Blackbushe UK	.79
			G-MKIX	Warbirds of GB Ltd, Blackbushe	12.12.83
				(shipped to UK, ff Blackbushe 6.5.84)	
				Warbirds of GB Ltd, Biggin Hill	88/91
- •	HF Mk. IXc	NH417		(to RDAF as 41-401) del. 11.1.49: SOC	13.4.51
				Tojhusmuseet, Copenhagen (stored)	.51/75
				Danish Technical Museum, Elsinore (displ.)	.75/76
				RDAF Historical Section : stored Vaerlose AB	78
				Egeskov Veteranmuseum, Kvaerndrup (loan)	c80/85
- •	LF Mk. VIIIc	NH631		(to Indian AF as NH631)	31.12.47
				IAF Museum, Palam AB, New Delhi	67/90
				(maintained airworthy, displ. as "NH631")	
6S/ 583887 •	FR Mk. XIV	NH749		(to Indian AF as ....)	31.12.47
				to instructional airframe "T3"/Code 54	
				hulk recov. ex Patna AB by Ormond & Wensley	
				Haydon-Baillie, Duxford UK	.77
				A. W. & K. W. Wickenden, Cranfield	.79
			G-MXIV	Keith W. Wickenden, Cranfield	11.4.80/85
				(rebuilt Cranfield, Craig Charleston ff .83)	
			N749DP	David G. Price, Portland OR	4.3.85/88
				(shipped to Chino CA 4.85 : ff Chino 24.7.85)	
				David G. Price/Museum of Flight,	
				Santa Monica CA (flies as RAF "H749/L")	88/92
- •	FR Mk. XIV	NH799		(to Indian AF as ....)	31.12.47
				recov. ex India by Doug Arnold/Warbirds of GB,	
				Blackbushe UK : arr. dism.	c81/85
				(stored dism., Blackbushe & Bitteswell 81/85)	
				The Fighter Collection, Duxford	.86/92
				(under rest, Duxford)	
6S/ 648206 •	FR Mk. XIVc	NH904		(to RBAF as SG108)	9.4.51
				Oscar Dewachter Scrapyard, Ostend Belgium	57/66
				(displ. on roof : wings axed off)	
				Bunny Brooks, Hoylake, Cheshire UK	.66
				(fitted wings RM694, static displ. at garage)	
				Gp Capt T. G. Mahaddie, Henlow : stored	68/71
				Sir W. J. D. Roberts/Strathallan Collection	8.71/79
				(stored dism. Flimwell,Sussex & Strathallan)	
			G-FIRE	Spencer Flack/Classic Air Displays, Elstree	1.79/88
				(rebuilt, ff Elstree 14.3.81)	
			N8118J	Planes of Fame East, Plymouth MN	1.89/91
			N114BP	Robert J. Pond, Plymouth MN	4.91/92
6S/ 417723 •	PR Mk.XI	PA908		(to Indian AF as M342)	
				offered for sale by IAF at Patna AB, India	.84
				Carl Enzenhofer, John Wilson & Jeet Mehal,	

				Vancouver BC : arr. by ship Vancouver	8.2.85
				USAFM, Wright-Patterson AFB, Dayton OH	86/89
				(under rest.by Ascher Ward, to be displ. as USAAF PR.XI)	92
SMAF 15826	F Mk. 22	PK350		(to Southern Rhodesian AF as SR64) del.	28.3.51
				(to Royal Rhodesian AF as RRAF64)	10.54
				New Sarum AB, Rhodesia : displ. on pole	69/77
				Capt. Jack Malloch/Air Trans Africa, Salisbury/Harare, Zimbabwe	.77/82
				(rebuilt Salisbury: ff 29.3.80 as "PK350/MJ-M")	
				crashed and dest., Goromorzi, near Harare, Zimbabwe (Malloch k.)	26.3.82
- •	F Mk. 22	PK355		(to Southern Rhodesian AF as SR65) del.	28.3.51
				(to Royal Rhodesian AF as RRAF65)	10.54
				displ. Bulawayo Museum	
				Thornhill AB, Rhodesia : displ. on pole	78
				AF of Zimbabwe Museum, New Sarum AB	83/86
				(rep. under rest. to fly .86)	
				rep. sold	.90
CBAF. 70 •	F Mk. 22	PK481		RAFA, Brighton & Hove Branch UK	9.55
				Air Training Corps, Shoreham	58
				RAAFA,WA Branch, Perth WA: arr. by sea	10.6.59
				displ. on pole, Perth; later Bullcreek WA	9.59/84
				(replaced by fibreglass replica .85)	
				RAAFA Aviation Museum, Perth WA	.85/92
CBAF. 189 •	F Mk. 22	PK624		RAF North Weald : gate guard	58
				RAF Uxbridge (displ. as "WP916")	60
				RAF Northolt	.63/68
				RAF Henlow : for movie "Battle of Britain"	.68
				RAF Abingdon	23.7.70/89
				RAF St Athan (for disposal)	.89/91
CBAF. 217 •	F Mk. 22	PK664		RAF Waterbeach : gate guard	
				RAF West Raynham	
				RAF Binbrook	.62/67
				RAF Henlow : for movie "Battle of Britain"	.67/68
				RAF Binbrook	.68/88
				RAF St Athan (for disposal)	.89/91
CBAF. 236 •	F Mk. 24	PK683		RAF Changi, Singapore : gate guard	54/70
				RAF Bicester : arr. by RAF Belfast	16.4.70/72
				RAF Kemble	30.6.72
				RAF Colerne	11.72/75
				RAF Shawbury	21.8.75
				R. J. Mitchell Museum, Southampton	7.2.76
				Hall of Aviation, Southampton	5.84/88
CBAF. 255 •	F Mk. 24	PK724		RAF Norton : gate guard	4.11.54/61
				RAF Gaydon	1.12.61/70
				RAF Henlow : for movie "Battle of Britain"	.67/68
				RAF Finningley	20.2.70
				RAF Museum, Hendon	2.4.71/92
- •	LF Mk. IXe	PL344		Anthony Fokker Technical School, Holland	
				(dism., Holland, various parts sold)	
				Charles Church (Spitfires) Ltd, Andover: hulk	.85/88
			G-IXCC	Charles Church (Spitfires) Ltd, Winchester	18.5.88/91
				(rebuild Micheldever, ff 11.3.91)	
				Weeks Aviation Museum, Miami FL	9.92
6S/ 504719 •	PR Mk. XI	PL965		(to RNAF) del.	8.7.47
				RNAF School of Technical Training, Deelen AB	22.7.47/52
				Deelen AB : displ.	.52/60
				National War & Resistance Museum, Overloon	11.60/87

				E. Nick Grace, Chichester	.87
				Chris Horsley/Medway Aircraft Preservation	
				Society : arr. Rochester for rebuild	2.87
			G-MKXI	Chris P. B. Horsley, Chichester	11.89/92
				(rebuild Rochester 87/92: due to fly 5.92)	
6S/	PR Mk. XI	PL979		(to RNoAF as PL979/A-ZB) del.	31.7.47
583719 •				last flew 25.3.54; stored Rygge AB	60/81
				RNoAF Collection, Gardermoen AB	7.81/90
6S/	PR Mk. XI	PL983		Vickers Armstrong Ltd, Eastleigh (loan)	22.7.47
583723 •			NC74138	US Embassy, Air Attache, Hendon UK : del.	27.1.48
				Vickers Armstrong Ltd, Eastleigh	.49
				Shuttleworth Trust, Old Warden : static displ.	50/75
				Shuttleworth Trust: to Duxford, rebuild to fly	30.8.75/83
				Roland Fraissinet, Marseilles, France	14.4.83
			G-PRXI	Roland Fraissinet, East Midlands Airport UK	6.6.83/87
				(rebuild completed, ff. East Midlands 18.7.84)	
				Warbirds of GB Ltd, Biggin Hill	1.10.87/91
6S/	PR. Mk. XIX	PM627		(to Indian AF as HS964)	.53
699626 •				Indian AF Museum, Palam AB, New Delhi	.67
				John Weir/Canadian Fighter Pilots Association,	
				Downsview ONT : arr. dism. in C-130	3.2.71
				Canadian National Exhib. Grounds, Toronto	.72/73
				Ontario Science Centre, Toronto ONT : displ.	11.73/78
				Canadian Warplane Heritage, Mount Hope ONT	
				David C. Tallichet/MARG, Chino CA	
				Flygvapenmuseum Malmem, Malmo, Sweden	10.82/89
				(taken on charge by RSwAF as Fv31051)	
6S/	PR Mk. XIX	PM630		(to R Thai AF as PM630)	8.54
683527 •				school playground, Trat, Thailand	60/86
6S/	PR Mk. XIX	PM631		RAF Memorial Flight, RAF Biggin Hill	14.6.57
683528 •				RAF Battle of Britain Memorial Flight	60/92
				(flew in movie "Battle of Britain" .68)	
6S/	PR Mk. XIX	PM651		Rolls-Royce Ltd, Hucknall : gate guard	.54
687107 •				RAF Andover	3.57/62
				RAF Benson	66/67
				RAF Henlow	.67/68
				(static scenes, movie "Battle of Britain" .68)	
				RAF Bicester : travelling exhibit	70
				RAF Benson : gate guard	.71/88
				RAF Museum, Hendon	.89/91
				RAF Museum, St.Athan	12.91/92
- •	Seafire LF. IIIc	PP972		(to Aeronavale as 12F.2 later 1F.9)	.48
				op. from carrier "Arromanches", Indo China	48/49
				retired to instruction use, Hyeres AB	.49
				recov. from scrap yard, Gavres, near	
				Lorient, by Jean Frelaut, Vannes-Meucon	.70/87
				(static rest. as "PP972/1.F.9")	
				displ. Musee de la Resistance, St Marcel	82/84
				Warbirds of GB Ltd, Biggin Hill	.88/92
				(rebuild to fly, Thruxton UK 88/91)	
				Rebuild to fly Trent Aero, East Midlands Airport	
			G-BUAR	Precious Metals Ltd, Bournemouth	21.1.92
- •	Seafire F. XV	PR376		(to Burma AF as UB409)	
				displ. Meiktila AB, Burma	70/89
CO	Seafire F. XV	PR451		(to RCN as PR451) BOC 1.6.46: SOC	25.5.49
9673 •				Southern Alberta Institute of Technology	c50
				HMCS Tecumseh, Calgary ALTA	.61/84

				(gate guard: displ. as "PR425/TG-B")	
				Aero Space Museum of Calgary ALTA	.84/85
				(rest., displ. as "VG-AA-N")	
				CAFB Tecumseh, Calgary (displ.)	88
- •	Seafire F. XV	PR503		(to RCN as PR503) BOC 1.6.46: SOC	5.4.50
				derelict hulk, Shearwater CFB NS	
				recov., Peter Myers Synd: stored Bedford NS	.58/64
				EAA/Dartmouth, NS Chapter	.66
				Dennis J. Bradley, Buttonville ONT	c70
			C-GCWK	Dennis J. Bradley/Canadian Warplane Heritage,	
				Mount Hope ONT : long-term rest.	87/92
				Mark Clark/Courtesy Aircraft, Rockford IL	.92
				(offered for sale, incomplete rest. project)	
6S/	PR Mk. XIX	PS836		(to R Thai AF as U14-27/97)	6.54
637129 •				stored dism. stripped, Chieng Mei, Thailand	80/86
				(rest. Chieng Mei AB, due to fly 8.92)	
				(RTAF serial also rep. as U14-30/93)	
6S/	PR Mk. XIX	PS853		RAF Memorial Flight, RAF Biggin Hill	.6.57
94677 •				RAF West Raynham : gate guard	.60/64
				RAF Battle of Britain Memorial Flight	14.4.64/90
				(flew in movie "Battle of Britain" .68)	
6S/	PR Mk. XIX	PS890		(to R Thai AF as U14-26/97)	6.54/62
585110 •				The Air Museum, Claremont CA	.62/70
				(donated by King Bhumibol of Siam, airfreighted	
				by Flying Tigers L-1049 to Burbank CA .62)	
				Planes of Fame Museum, Chino CA	70/90
				(rebuild to fly, Chino CA)	
6S/	PR Mk. XIX	PS915		RAF West Malling : gate guard	31.8.57/60
585121 •				RAF Leuchars	66/75
				RAF Henlow : for movie "Battle of Britain"	.67
				RAF Brawdy	.75/84
				(static scenes, movie "Battle of Britain" .68)	
				RAF Battle of Britain Memorial Flight	.84/92
				(rebuilt RAF Warton, ff 16.12.86)	
				(flies as "JF319")	
- •	HF Mk. IX	PT462		(to Italian AF as MM4100)	27.6.46
				(to IDFAF as 0607: later 20-67)	4.52
				hulk recov. from kibbutz Gaza Strip, Israel	
				by Robs Lamplough: arr. Fowlemere UK	5.83
				Charles Church, Winchester UK	7.84
			G-CTIX	Charles Church (Spitfires) Ltd, Winchester	9.4.85/92
				(rebuilt Winchester as Tr. 9 : ff 25.7.87)	
CBAF.	HF Mk. IXe	PT601		(to SAAF as 5573)	
2716 •				components stored Lanseria AB, South Africa	78/86
CBAF.	LF Mk. IX	PV202		(to Irish Air Corps as 161) del.	29.6.51/68
9590 •	Mk. Tr 9			N.A.W. Samuelson, Cricklewood	4.3.68
				(stored dism., Cricklewood, North London)	
				Sir W. J. D. Roberts/Strathallan Collection	4.70/79
				(stored dism., Flimwell & Strathallan 70/79)	
				E. Nick Grace, St. Merryn	9.8.79
			G-BHGH	ntu: Steve W. Atkins, Saffron Walden	10.10.79
			G-TRIX	Steve W. Atkins, Saffron Walden	2.7.80/89
				Richard Parker	.90/91
				(rebuild completed, ff Dunsfold 23.2.90)	
				Rick Roberts	.91/92
CBAF.	Mk. IX	PV270		(to Italian AF as MM4014)	27.6.46
IX3128 •				(to IDFAF as 20-..)	
				(to Burmese AF as UB424)	
				Hmawbi AB, Rangoon: displ. on pole: "UB425"	70/90

6S/ 432263	F Mk. XIVc	RM689	G-ALGT	Rolls-Royce Ltd, Hucknall (flown in movie "Battle of Britain" .68) Rolls-Royce PLC, Castle Donington (flew as "RM689/MN-E") crashed during airshow and dest., Woodford	9.2.49/73 76/92 29.6.92
6S/ 432268 •	F Mk. XIV	RM694		RAF Hornchurch RAF Bicester RAF Dishforth : for disposal as scrap A. H. 'Bunny' Brooks, Hoylake, Cheshire (wings used to rest. NH904 for static displ.) J. D. Kay/Manchester Tankers Ltd, Charnock Richard, Lancs. (fuse only) A. W. Francis, Southend John Lowe & Larry Matt, Chicago IL (rest project: wings from various sources: stored Victory Air Museum, Mundelein IL) Warbirds of GB Ltd, Bitteswell Don L. Knapp/DK Precision, Ft. Lauderdale FL	50/60 64 .66 .66/68 1.68 c72/78 .85 89
- •	F MK. XIVe	RM797	 VH-XIV	(to R Thai AF as U14-16/93) derelict, Surin AB, Thailand: recov. by Gary Cooper, Hong Kong airfreighted to Darwin NT : stored (damaged Cyclone"Tracy", Darwin 25.12.74) Gary Cooper, Sydney NSW (rebuild to fly, Albury & Sydney NSW)	.50 24.5.73 19.8.73/77 77/92
6S/ 432296 •	F Mk. XIV	RM873		(to R Thai AF as U14-6/93) display aircraft, central Thailand mainplane to P. Sledge, Australia for RR232 fuse. stored, Sanalok, Thailand	11.50 .81 85
6S/ 432331 •	FR Mk. XIVe	RM921		(to RBAF as SG-57) BOC Florennes AB, Belgium : displ. on pole	8.48 c55/85
6S/ 381758 •	FR Mk. XIVe	RM927		(to RBAF as SG-25) BOC Oscar Dewachter Scrapyard, Ostend, Belgium (displ. on roof : wings axed off) J. D. Kay/Manchester Tankers Ltd, Charnock Richard, Lancs : arr. by road A. W. Francis, Southend : arr. by road John Lowe & Larry Matt, Riverside IL (stored at Victory Air Museum, Mundelein IL) Larry Matt, Chicago IL (rebuild commenced, using wings ex IAF HS649) Don L. Knapp/DK Precision, Ft. Lauderdale FL	14.11.47 57/67 4.3.67/69 22.3.69 .69/78 82/85 87
6S/ 663417 •	F Mk. XIVe	RN201	 G-BSKP	(to RBAF as SG-31) del. Beauvechain AB, Belgium : displ. on pole Historic Aircraft Collection : del. by C-130 Historic Aircraft Collection Ltd, Jersey	19.2.48 c53/90 3.5.90 27.6.90
- •	HF Mk. IXc	RR232		(to SAAF as 5632) BOC 5.49 SOC South African Metal & Machinery Co, Salt River, Cape Town, South Africa recov. Larry Barnett & Alan Lurie, Jo'burg (tail section used to rebuild MA793) Peter Sledge, Sydney NSW (fuse. only) (static rebuild, Pt.Cook & Bankstown, using parts from various wartime crash sites and mainplane ex Thai AF Spitfire XIV RM873) rest. completed, rolled-out Bankstown NSW Peter Sledge/loan RAN Museum, Nowra NSW (shipped to UK, ex Nowra NAS 10.86) Charles Church, Micheldever UK	16.1.54 .54 .76/86 14.10.84 85/86 .86/89

			G-BRSF	Sussex Spraying Services Ltd, Shoreham	22.11.89
CBAF. IX3310 •	LF Mk. XVIe	RR263		RAF Kenley	55/67
				presented French Air Force: displ. Tours AB	5.67/77
				(arr. Tours AB in RAF Beverley 5.67,	
				displ. as "TB597": rep. flown at Tours 20.5.77)	
				Musee de l'Air et l'Espace, Paris-Le Bourget	.78/87
				(displ. as "TB597/B-GW")	
CBAF. IX4640 •	LF Mk. XVIe	RW382		RAF Leconfield : gate guard as "RW729"	.57/73
				RAF Henlow	.67/68
				(static scenes, movie "Battle of Britain" .68)	
				RAF Uxbridge: displ. on pole	4.4.73/88
				Tim Routis/Historic Flying Ltd, Cambridge	8.88/89
				(collected ex RAF Uxbridge 26.8.88)	
				Military Aircraft Restoration Corp, Chino CA	.89/92
			G-XVIA	Historic Flying Ltd, Audley End	2.7.91
				(ff Audley End 3.7.91 as "RW382/NG-C")	
				Military Aircraft Restoration Corp, Chino CA	91/92
				(c/n also quoted as CBAF.11581)	
CBAF. IX4644 •	LF Mk. XVIe	RW386		RAF Halton	30.8.57/67
				RAF St Athan	67/82
				Warbirds of GB Ltd, Blackbushe	.82
			G-BXVI	Warbirds of GB Ltd, Blackbushe	27.12.84
				Warbirds of GB Ltd, Bitteswell/Biggin Hill	85/89
				rebuild completed Historic Flying	92
CBAF. IX4646 •	LF Mk. XVIe	RW388		RAF Colerne	2.52/60
				RAF Benson	
				RAF Andover	63/67
				RAF Bicester	68/72
				Stoke-on-Trent City Museum, Hanley	15.2.72/88
- •	LF Mk. XVIe	RW393		RAF Turnhouse	8.56/89
				RAF Henlow: for movie "Battle of Britain"	.67/68
				RAF St Athan (for disposal)	.89/91
- •	Seafire L. III	RX168		(to Irish Air Corps as 157)	
				Chris Warrillow, Wooburn, UK	89/91
				(rebuild to fly, Dunsfold)	
CBAF. IX4656 •	LF Mk. XVIe	SL542		RAF Horsham St. Faith : gate guard	5.57
				RAF Coltishall : displ. on pole	66/88
				RAF St Athan (for disposal)	.89/91
CBAF. IX4688 •	LF Mk. XVIe	SL574		RAF Bentley Priory	11.61/86
				RAF Henlow"	.67/69
				(static scenes, movie "Battle of Britain" .68)	
				RAF Halton (for rebuild)	.86/89
				American Eagle Squadron/San Diego Air & Space Museum, San Diego CA	.86/89
				(still in UK awaiting shipment to USA 89)	
CBAF. IX4701 •	LF Mk. XVIe	SL674		RAF Memorial Chapel, Biggin Hill : del.	11.9.54/89
				RAF St Athan (for disposal)	3.89/91
CBAF. IX4756 •	LF Mk. XVIe	SL721		F. M. Wilcox, Worthing UK (displ. at garage)	2.55/65
				loaned to RAF Thorney Island: briefly flown	9.58
				loaned to Beaulieu Motor Museum	59/65
				Monty Thackray/M. D. Thackray Ltd UK	.65
				The Marquis of Headfort	.65
				Monty Thackray/M. D. Thackray Ltd UK	.65
				William D. Ross, Chicago IL	12.65
				(rebuilt Atlanta GA, ff 11.5.67)	
			N8R (1	William D. Ross, Du Page IL	.67/73
			G-BAUP	Fairoaks Aviation Services	4.4.73/77
				(shipped UK, assembled Leavesden .73)	

			N8WK	Woodson K. Woods, Scottsdale AZ	21.7.77/82
			N721WK	Aero Meridian Corp, Scottsdale AZ	2.82/92
				loan: San Diego Aerospace Museum CA	84/87
- •	LF Mk. XVIe	SM411		RAF Wattisham	8.55/67
				RAF Henlow	.67/70
				(taxy scenes, movie "Battle of Britain" .68)	
				RAF Bicester: travelling display exhibit	2.70
				RAF Abingdon	76/78
				Aviation & Space Museum, Krakow, Poland	.78/92
6S/ 663452 •	F Mk. XIV	SM832		(to Indian AF as ....)	7.47
				Indian Military Academy, Dehra Dun, India	72/78
				recov. from India by Ormond &	
				Wenseley Haydon-Baillie, Duxford UK	.78
			G-WWII	Warbirds of GB, Blackbushe	9.7.79/85
				(rest. begun to Mk. VIII, Blackbushe & Bitteswell)	
				The Fighter Collection, Duxford	8.86
				Charles Church (Spitfires) Ltd, Micheldever	11.88/91
				(rebuild continued,to Mk. XIV, Winchester)	
				The Fighter Collection, Duxford	11.91/92
6S/ 585092 •	FR Mk. XIVe	SM914		(to RThai AF as U14-1/93)	.50
				RTAF Museum, Don Muang AB, Thailand	.54/92
6S/ 663052 •	FR Mk. XVIIIe	SM969		(to Indian AF as HS877)	21.7.49
				Western Air Command HQ, Cantonment, Delhi	72/78
				recov. by Ormond & Wensley Haydon-Baillie,	
				Duxford UK	.78
				Doug Arnold, Blackbushe : arr crated	5.78
			G-BRAF	Warbirds of GB Ltd, Blackbushe	29.12.78
				(rebuilt Blackbushe, ff 12.10.85)	
				Warbirds of GB Ltd, Bitteswell/Biggin Hill	.85/91
6S/ 699526 •	FR Mk. XVIIIe	SM986		(to Indian AF as HS986)	30.6.49
				IAF Museum, Palam AB, New Delhi	.67/91
WASE1 • 4106	Seafire F XV	SR462		(to Burmese AF as UB414)	
				Hmawbi AB, Rangoon : gate guard	70/85
				Burmese AF Museum, Meiktila AB	88/89
				(displ. as "UB415")	
- •	F Mk. XV	SW800		Peter Croser, Melbourne VIC	91/92
				(rest. project)	
WASE1 • 5325	Seafire F XVII	SX137		RNAS Yeovilton : flying & static display	12.8.58/64
				Fleet Air Arm Museum, RNAS Yeovilton	.64/90
- •	Seafire F XVII	SX300		Peter R. Arnold, Newport Pagnell : fuse only	.73
				(recov. from scrapyard, Warrington .73)	
				John Berkeley, Warwick	82/85
				(long-term composite rest. project)	
FLWA/ 25488 •	Seafire F XVII	SX336		Peter R. Arnold, Newport Pagnell : fuse only .73	
				(recov. from scrapyard, Warrington .73)	
				Neville Franklin	.73
				Peter J. Wood, Twyford	80/89
			G-BRMG	Peter J. Wood, Twyford	19.9.89/92
				(long-term rest. project)	
- •	LF Mk. IX	TA805		Steve Atkins, Oxford, UK	89
				parts restoration to fly	
CBAF. IX3807 •	LF Mk. XVIe	TB252		RAF Odiham	12.9.55/59
				RAF Acklington	8.59/67
				RAF Boulmer	7.69

				RAF Leuchars	12.69/86
				RAF Bentley Priory	4.86/88
				Historic Flying Ltd, Cambridge	6.88/90
				(collected ex gate guard Bentley Priory 9.11.88)	
			G-XVIE	Historic Flying Limited Audley End	9.92
-	LF Mk. XVIe	TB287		RAF Martlesham Heath: spares recovery	c61
				RAF Bicester : for disposal	c62
				(existence rumoured: disposition unknown)	
- •	LF Mk. XVIe	TB382		RAF Thornaby	.55
				RAF Middleton St George	7.57/62
				RAF Hospital, Ely	66/67
				RAF Henlow	18.2.67/68
				(taxy scenes, movie "Battle of Britain" .68)	
				RAF Abingdon : travelling exhibit	77/90
- •	LF Mk. XVIe	TB752		RAF Kenley, for movie "Reach for the Sky"	55
				RAF Manston	28.9.55/89
CBAF. 10895 •	LF Mk. XVIe	TB863		Metro-Goldwyn-Meyer, Pinewood Studios UK	.55/68
				(used in movie "Reach for the Sky" .55)	
				(stored Pinewood Studios 56/67)	
				(dism. for spares, Henlow .68)	
				A. W. Francis, Southend (stored dism.)	12.68/77
			G-CDAN	J. Parkes & A. W. Francis, Booker	30.11.82
				The Fighter Collection, Duxford	.84/88
				Tim Wallis, Wanaka NZ	.87
				(ff Duxford 14.9.88: shipped to NZ 13.10.88)	
			ZK-XVI	Tim Wallis/Alpine Fighter Collection, Wanaka	17.1.89/92
				(flies as "TB863/FU-P")	
- •	LF Mk. XVIe	TB885		RAF Kenley : fire fighting practice	55
				background views, movie "Reach for the Sky"	9.55
				buried fire dump, RAF Kenley	.59/82
				recov. by Shoreham Aircraft Pres. Society	4.82
				Lashenden Air Warfare Museum, Sevenoaks	85
				Shoreham Aircraft Museum, Shoreham	91
				(long-term rest. for static displ.)	
CBAF. IX4218 •	LF Mk. XVIe	TD135		Air Training Corps, Tynemouth, Newcastle	51/63
				RAF Dishforth : for sale as scrap	63/64
				Percy Sheppard/The Spitfire Inn, Leominster	.64/75
				Worral Granger/Connie Motors	.75
				Larry Higgins/Thunderbird Aviation,	
				Deer Valley AZ	.75
				David Boyd & Hurley Bowler, Tulsa OK	.76
				Ray Stutsman, Elkhart IN	85/86
				William C. Anderson, Geneseo NY	20.1.86/91
				(long-term rebuild, Palmyra & Geneseo NY)	
CBAF. IX4262 •	LF Mk. XVIe	TD248		RAF Hooton Park	4.10.55/59
				RAF Sealand	8.4.59/67
				RAF Henlow : for movie "Battle of Britain"	.67/68
				RAF Sealand : displ. on pole	.68/88
				Tim Routsis/Historic Flying Ltd, Cambridge	6.88
				Eddie Coventry, Earls Colne	8.88
				(collected ex RAF Sealand 14.10.88)	
			G-OXVI	Eddie Coventry/BAC Aviation Ltd, Earls Colne	22.8.89/91
				(rebuild to fly, Audley End)	92
- •	Mk. IX	TD314		(to SAAF as ....)	12.5.48
				South African Metal & Machinery Co,	
				Salt River, Cape Town	c54
				recov. by Larry Barnett, Johannesburg	
				Pat Swonnell, Vancouver BC	.78/81
				(fuse. hulk arr. Vancouver by ship 11.4.79)	
				Matt Sattler, Carp ONT	85/91

				(long-term rest. project)	
CBAF. IX4394 •	LF Mk. XVIe	TE184		Air Training Corps, Royton, Lancs	.52/67
				RAF Bicester	2.67
				RAF Henlow : for movie "Battle of Britain"	67
				RAF Finningley Museum Collection	69
				RAF Aldergrove	.71/77
				Ulster Folk & Transport Museum,	
				Holywood, County Down, Northern Ireland	3.77/86
				E. Nick Grace, St Merryn	.86/88
			G-MXVI	Myrick Aviation Services, Castle Donington	17.2.89/90
				(rebuilt, ff East Midlands 23.11.90)	
- •	Mk. IXe	TE213		(to SAAF as 5518)	8.47
				Waterkloof AB : displ. on pole	.54/85
				(displ. as "5518","W5851", later "W5518")	
				SAAF Museum, Lanseria AB, Johannesburg	.85/86
CBAF 4424 •	LF Mk. XVIe	TE214		RAF Ternhill (displ. as "TE353")	56/60
				loaned RCAF: displ. Parliament Hill, Ottawa	.60
				RCAF Mountain View ONT, stored	.60/62
				RCAF: BOC, RCAF Trenton ONT	10.1.63
				Canadian War Museum, Ottawa ONT ("DN-T")	.66/90
				loan: Western Canada Avtn Museum, Winnipeg	12.88
				Canadian War Museum, Ottawa ONT	90
- •	LF Mk. XVIe	TE288		loaned for film "Reach for the Sky"	8.55
				RAF Rufforth	.55/59
				RAF Church Fenton	7.59/61
				RAF Dishforth	9.61/63
				Brevet Club, Canterbury NZ	.62/84
				(shipped to NZ, arr. 28.6.63: displ. on plinth	
				near Christchurch Airport as "AR251")	
				(replaced by fibreglass replica "TE283")	.84
				(to Woodbourne AB for rest. 84/86)	
				RNZAF Museum, Wigram AB (displ. as "DU-V")	90
- •	HF Mk. IX	TE294		(to SAAF as ....)	
				Mark de Vries, Bryanston, South Africa	81/89
				(rest. project at Honeydew, South Africa)	
CBAF. 4494 •	HF Mk. IXe Mk. Tr 9	TE308		(to Irish Air Corps as 163) del.	30.7.51/68
				instructional airframe, Baldonnel AB, Eire	.61/68
			G-AWGB	N. A. W. Samuelson/Samuelson Film Services	
				Elstree : del. ex Baldonnel	8.5.68
				(flown in movie "Battle of Britain" .68)	
				Sir W. J. D. Roberts, Shoreham	12.69/70
				Don Plumb, Windsor ONT	16.7.70
				(shipped to Toronto ONT, arr. 9.10.70)	
			CF-RAF	Don Plumb, Windsor ONT	12.70/73
			C-FRAF	Don Plumb, Windsor ONT	75
				(conv. to single seater by Don Plumb)	
			N92477	Thomas J. Watson/Owls Head Transport	
				Museum, Owls Head ME	.75/79
			N308WK	Woodson K. Woods, Scottsdale AZ	7.10.79
				(conv. back to two-seater, displ. Carefree	
				Aviation Museum, Scottsdale AZ)	
				Aero Meridian Corp, Scottsdale AZ	11.1.82
				William S. Greenwood, Aspen CO	.83/92
CBAF. IX4497 •	LF Mk. XVIe	TE311		RAF Tangmere : gate guard	11.8.55/67
				RAF Henlow	.67
				(taxy scenes, movie "Battle of Britain" .68)	
				RAF Benson	9.68/77
				RAF Abingdon : travelling display exhibit	77/90

- •	LF Mk.XVIe	TE330		RAF North Weald Station Flight	13.3.58
				USAF Academy, Colorado Springs CO	7.58
				(del. ex RAF Odiham by C-124 7.58)	
				USAFM Wright-Patterson AFB, Dayton OH	61/90
- •	LF Mk.XVIe	TE356		RAF Bicester	c52/67
				RAF Henlow	.67/68
				(taxy scenes, movie "Battle of Britain" .68)	
				RAF Kemble	5.69
				RAF Little Rissington	4.12.70/76
				RAF Cranwell	20.4.76/78
				RAF Leeming	.78/86
				Warbirds of GB Ltd, Bitteswell	.86
			G-SXVI	Warbirds of GB Ltd, Biggin Hill	25.2.87/90
				(rebuilt Trent Aero East Midlands : ff 16.12.87)	
			N356EV	Evergreen Ventures Inc, McMinnville OR	1.90/91
			N356TE	747 Inc., McMinnville OR	3.91/92
- •	LF Mk. XVIe	TE384		RAF Syerston : instructional airframe	11.57/67
				RAF Henlow	.67/68
				(taxy scenes, movie "Battle of Britain" .68)	
				RAFM Store, Henlow	10.68/72l
				Hockey Treloar, Sydney NSW	.72/92
				airfreighted to Australia by RAF Belfast	12.72
				(open storage, Canberra ACT 73/83)	
				H. Treloar/Jim Czerwinski, Toowoomba QLD	9.83/91
			VH-XVI	Jim F. Czerwinski, Toowoomba QLD	5.10.88/92
				(ff Toowoomba 6.10.88, flies as "TE384/XVI")	
- •	LF Mk. XVIe	TE392		RAF Wellesbourne Mountford	.52/60
				RAF Waterbeach	9.61/66
				RAF Kemble	3.66/70
				RAF Hereford	19.2.70/84
				Warbirds of GB Ltd, Blackbushe	.84/85
				Warbirds of GB Ltd, Bitteswell/Biggin Hill	.85/88
CBAF IX4590 •	LF Mk. XVIe	TE456		used in movie "Reach for the Sky"	8.55
				Domain War Memorial Museum, Auckland NZ	.56/87
CBAF IX4596 •	LF Mk. XVIe	TE462		RAF Ouston : gate guard	19.8.55/70
				Royal Scottish Museum/Museum of Flight, East Fortune, Lothian	19.2.71/91
CBAF. IX4610 •	LF Mk. XVIe	TE476		RAF Battle of Britain Flight	1.3.58/60
				RAF Neatishead : display duties	1.60/67
				RAF Henlow	2.67/68
				(taxy scenes, movie "Battle of Britain" .68)	
				RAF Northolt : gate guard	2.6.70/88
				Tim Routsis/Historic Flying Ltd, Cambridge	6.88
			G-XVIB	Tim Routsis/ Historic Flying Ltd, Cambridge	3.7.89/90
				Kermit A. Weeks, Tamiami FL (stored)	1.2.90
			N476TE	Weeks Air Museum,Tamiami FL	4.91/92
				(shipped FL to UK 5.92, for rest. at Booker)	
- •	LF Mk. IXe	TE517		(to Czech AF as TE517) del.	20.8.45
				(to IDFAF as 20-46)	.49
				hulk recov. from kibbutz, Gaaton, Israel by	
				Robs Lamplough : arr. Duxford	3.77
			G-BIXP	ntu: Robs Lamplough, Duxford	3.7.81/84
				Charles Church, Micheldever	8.84
			G-CCIX	Charles Church (Spitfires) Ltd, Winchester	9.4.85/90
				Weeks Air Museum, Miami, Florida	9.92
17-1351•	LF Mk. IXe	TE554		(to Czech AF as A708) del.	20.8.45/48
				(to IDFAF as 20-57)	.48/55
				retired, stored for displ. flying	.55
				IDFAF Museum, Ramat David AB	
			4X-FOG	IDFAF Museum, Be'er Sheva AB	76/85

				(flew 55/85, glossy black scheme "IDFAF 57")	
				IDFAF Museum, Hatzerim AB	90
- •	LF Mk. IXe	TE565		(to Czech AF as TE565)	.45
				Narodni Technicke Museum, Prague	22.5.50/70
				Military Museum, Kbely Airport, Prague	70/85
17-1363•	Mk. IX	TE566		(to Czech AF as TE566)	8.45
				(to IDFAF as 20-32)	.49
				hulk recov. from kibbutz at Alonim, Israel by	
				Robs Lamplough: arr. Duxford	12.76/81
				Guy Black/Aero Vintage Ltd, St Leonards	.81
			G-BLCK	Aero Vintage Ltd, Ludham	11.83/86
				Historic Aircraft Collection	.90/91
				rebuilt to fly by Historic Flying ff 2.7.92	
				(flies as "DU-A")	
6S/ 676368 •	FR Mk. XVIIIe	TP276		(to Indian AF as HS653)	31.12.47
				hulk recov. from Barakpor AB by Ormond &	
				Wensley Haydon-Baillie, Duxford UK	.77
				Rudy Frasca, Champaign IL	79/89
6S/ 676372 •	FR Mk. XVIIIe	TP280		(to Indian AF as HS654)	31.12.47
				hulk recov. from Kalaikunda AB by Ormond &	
				Wensley Haydon-Baillie, Duxford UK	.77
				Rudy Frasca, Champaign IL	79/92
				(rebuild to fly, Champaign IL & Audley End UK)	
			G-BTXE	Historic Flying Ltd, Audley End	23.10.91
				(shipped to US after rest. 9.92	
6S/ 676390 •	FR Mk. XVIIIe	TP298		(to Indian AF as HS66...)	31.12.47
				hulk recov. from Kalaikunda AB by Ormond &	
				Wensley Haydon-Baillie, Duxford UK	.77
				Marshall Moss/Dick Boolootian, Lancaster CA	c79
				Military Aircraft Restoration Corp, Chino CA	c81/91
				(rebuilt Tulsa OK, Casper WY, Colchester UK)	
			N41702	Military Aircraft Restoration Corp, Chino CA	7.91/92
				(final rest. Chino CA .91, as "TP298/T-UM")	
6S/ 676505 •	FR Mk. XIVe	TZ138		shipped to Canada for winterisation trials	16.11.45
			CF-GMZ	Imperial Oil Co, Edmonton ALTA	.48
				Flt. Lt. J. H. G. McArthur (Bendix race #80)	.49
			N20E	Fulgencio Batista, Hollywood FL	51
				damaged FL by Castro supporters	1.6.51
				U. S. Customs Service, Miami FL	
				Lloyd B. Milner, Minneapolis MN	.60
				John L. Russell	
				M. W. Fairbrother, Rosemont MN	.60
			N5505A	Harvey J. Ferguson, McAllen TX / CAF	.63/68
				Charles H. Leidal, Fergus Falls MN	69/70
				(stored/rest. 50/70: ff 5.70)	
				dam., forced landing, Mexico	5.70
				Jack Arnold, Brantford ONT	.71
				Max R. Hoffman, Fort Collins CO	.71
				Don Plumb, Windsor ONT	6.74
				Ray Jones, Pontiac MI	78
				Leonard A. Tanner, New Braintree CT	79/87
				loan: Bradley Air Museum, Windsor Locks CT	79/81
			N138TZ	Leonard A. Tanner, New Braintree CT	87
			N5505A	Don L. Knapp/DK Precision, Ft. Lauderdale FL	.88
			N180RB	rep. ntu: Don L. Knapp/DK Precision,	
				Ft. Lauderdale FL	11.88/90
			N5505A	Lone Star Flight Museum, Galveston TX	.90/91
				Bill Destefani, Bakersfield CA	.91/92
				(rest. project Galveston TX, trucked to CA 1.92)	

- •	F. 24	VN485		Royal Hong Kong Auxiliary AF, Kai Tak	31.5.52
				last flight 21.4.55; stored & displ. Kai Tak	7.55/89
				Imperial War Museum, Duxford UK	7.89/92
6S/	Seafire	VP441		Air Training Corps, Saltash, Devon	c55/65
73228 •	FR.47			recov. Malcolm D. N. Fisher/Historic Aircraft	
				Preservation Society: displ. RNAS Culdrose	65
				HAPS/Reflectair Museum, Blackpool	69/72
				Personal Plane Services, Booker	4.72
			N47SF	John J.Stokes/Rebel Aviation, San Antonio TX	75/77
				Confederate Air Force, Harlingen TX	4.12.80/91
				American Airpower Heritage Flying Museum,	
				Midland TX	9.91/92
				(stored dism. Midland TX, pending rest. to fly)	
- •	HF Mk. VIII	MV........		(to RAAF as A58-.....)	
				recov. from Kiriwina, Solomon Islands by	
				Monty Armstrong NZ (fuse. hulk only)	.73
				Barry Coran, Melbourne VIC	80/92
				(composite rest., RAAF Pt. Cook as "R6915/PR-U")	
- •	F Mk. IX	-		(to IDFAF as 20-..)	
				(to Burmese AF as UB421) del.	27.9.54
				Burmese Air Force Museum, Meiktila AB	88/90
				static rest., displ. Rangoon	3.89
- •	LF Mk. IXe	-		(to IDFAF as 20-..)	
				(to Burmese AF as UB425) del.	1.10.54
				displ. on pole, King Mindon's Palace, Mandalay	81/90
- •	F Mk. IX	-		(to Burmese AF as UB431)	.56
				Aung Sang Park, Royal Lakes, Rangoon, Burma	60/75
				dam. by storm, scrapped	c75
- •	Mk. XIV	-		(to Indian AF as HS365)	
				Ambala AB, Haryana, India	c68/78
6S/	FR Mk. XVIII	-		(to Indian AF as HS649)	
672268 •				hulk recov. from Kalaikunda AB by Ormond &	
				Wensley Haydon-Baillie, Duxford UK	.77
				Spencer Flack, Elstree	
				A. & K. Wickenden, Hemel Hampstead (stored)	
				Guy Black/Aero Vintage Ltd, St Leonards	
				S.W.Atkins/Vintage Airworks Ltd,St Leonards	85
				(wings to RM927 in USA; fuse. rebuilt as Mk.XIV)	
				E. Nick Grace & Chris Horsley, Chichester	86
				(composite rebuild: wings ex SAAF & USA)	
				Militaire Luchtvaart Museum, Overloon	.87
				(displ. as "NH649")	
- •	Mk. XVIII	-		(to Indian AF as HS669)	
				stored, India	79/89
- •	Mk. XVIII	-		(to Indian AF as HS674)	
				IAF Technical School, Chandigarh, Punjab	60/85
6S/ •	FR Mk. XVIIIe	-		(to Indian AF as HS687)	31.12.47
672224				hulk recov. from Kalaikunda AB by Ormond &	
				Wensley Haydon-Baillie, Duxford UK	.77
				Marshall Moss/Dick Boolootian, Lancaster CA	c79
				David C. Tallichet/MARC, Chino CA	c81/87
				(rebuilt at Tulsa OK and Casper WY)	
				Adrian Reynard, Kidlington UK	88
				(shipped UK-Chino CA for final rebuild .90)	
				Wings at Historic Flying for rebuild	
- •	Mk. XIV	-		(to Indian AF as ......)	
				Don L. Knapp/DK Precision, Ft. Lauderdale FL	
				Bill Destefani & Robert Converse, Shafter CA	.88

			(rebuild to fly, Shafter CA)	
SH/CBAF IX558 •	LF Mk. IXe	TE5..	(to Czech AF as TE5..) (to IDFAF as 20-38) Hatzor AB, Israel (displ. as "105")	 78/90
- •	Mk. V	-	Ross Campbell, Toowoomba QLD (incomplete, static restoration)	89

TACHIKAWA Ki-36 "Ida"

- •	Ki-36		(to R. Thai AF as ....) R.Thai AF Museum, Don Muang AB, Bangkok	.40 70/90

TACHIKAWA Ki-54 "Hickory"

•	Ki-54		Japanese surrender aircraft, Borneo Australian War Memorial, Canberra ACT fuselage in playground RAAF Canberra RAAF Museum, RAAF Point Cook VIC (fuselage only)	9.45 65/75 84/91
- •	Ki-54		Beijing Aeronautical Institute, China (fuselage only)	91

TACHIKAWA Ki-55

103/2•	Ki-55		(to Chinese Peoples Armed Forces AF as.....) Military Museum of the Chinese People's Revolution, Changping	 65/91

TACHIKAWA Ki-9 "Spruce"

62•	Ki-9		Indonesia Armed Forces Museum, Jakarta	70/91

TUPOLEV Tu-2

- •	Tu-2	-	(to Chinese AF as 20465) (still flying 81, then stored in cave China) John MacGuire/War Eagles Air Museum, Santa Teresa NM: arr. dism. (assembled Santa Teresa .91, rebuild to fly)	 12.8.91/92
- •	Tu-2S	-	(to Chinese AF as ....) Aero Trader, Chino CA arr. dism. Chino, green/grey camouflage Weeks Air Museum, Tamiami FL (cockpit section displ. in museum .92)	 .88 .88 .88/91
- •	Tu-2S	-	(to Chinese AF as ....) Aero Trader, Chino CA arr. dism. Chino, green/grey camouflage Weeks Air Museum, Tamiami FL	 .88 .88 .88/92
- •	Tu-2		(to Chinese AF as 44792) Military Museum of the Chinese People's Revolution, Beijing (displ. complete, under cover)	 75/87
- •	Tu-2		(to Chinese AF as 4-----) Military Museum of the Chinese People's Revolution, Beijing	 75/87
•	Tu-2		Army Aviation Museum, Krakow, Poland Aviation & Space Museum, Krakow	68/75 92

AV H
MH434
Z 
TP280

VICKERS WELLINGTON

- •	Mk. 1a	L7775		South Yorkshire Aircraft Museum, Firbeck	.86/89
				(recov. from crash site, Braemar, Scotland;	
				static rest. project)	
- •	Mk. 1a	N2980		crashed into Loch Ness, Scotland	31.12.40
				recov. from Loch Ness	21.9.85
				Brooklands Museum, Weybridge	86/92
				(long-term complete rest.)	
- •	T Mk. I0	MF628		flew in movie "The Dam Busters"	.54
				Vickers Armstrong Ltd, Weybridge	.55
				Royal Aeronautical Society/Nash Collection,	
				stored Heathrow	.56
				RAF Air Historical Branch, RAF Biggin Hill	60
				RAF Museum, Hendon	72/92

VOUGHT/GOODYEAR FG/F4U CORSAIR

- •	FG-1A	Bu13459		USMC Museum, MCAS Quantico VA	74/79
				(displ. as "13486/86")	.82/88
1871 •	FG-1D	Bu14862		(to Royal Navy FAA as KD431)	
		Mk. IV		College of Aeronautics, Cranfield	12.46/63
				Fleet Air Arm Museum, RNAS Yeovilton	.63/91
				(displ. as "KD431/EZ-M")	
- •	F4U-1A	Bu17799		unconv. derelict, MGM Studios CA	70
				The Air Museum, Ontario CA	.70
			N83782	The Air Museum, Chino CA	9.77/92
				(flies as USN "17799/WS-80")	
				(id. also quoted as 3884/Bu56198)	
- •	F4U-1A	Bu17995		derelict in junk yard, Provo UT	65
				Harry S. Doan, Daytona Beach FL	c66
			N90285	Doan Helicopters, Daytona Beach	82/89
				(rebuilt 65/82: ff 3.82 Daytona Beach)	
				crashed into sea, New Smyrna Beach FL	8.5.83
				(rebuilt 84/89 New Smyrna Beach: ff 11.3.89)	
				Roy M. Stafford, Jacksonville FL	.89
				D. K. Precision, Fort Lauderdale FL	7.89/90
			ZK-FUI	Alpine Fighter Collection, Wanaka	.90/92
				(shipped to NZ, ff 20.10.91 as RNZAF "NZ5201")	
- •	F4U-1D	Bu50375		NASM, Silver Hill MD ("Sun Setter")	65/92
- •	FG-1D	Bu67070		John Roxbury, Princeton MN	88
				(under rebuild 88)	
- •	FG-1D	Bu67087		rest. project, Rialto CA	88
- •	FG-1D	Bu67089		stored NAS Jacksonville FL	.53/58
				disposal, Queen City Salvage, Jacksonville FL	.58
			N4716C	Queen City Salvage Inc, Charlotte NC	66/69
				Earl Ware/Harran Aircraft Sales,	
				Jacksonville FL	.75/77
			N4715C	Knight Aircraft Corporation	1.77/81
				Don C. Davis/Tired Iron Racing Team,	
				Casper WY (race #82/"Wart Hog")	.81/86
				Denver International Bank, Denver CO	10.86
				Gary Meermans, Long Beach CA	.86/87
			N97GM	Gary Meermans, Chino CA	3.87/92
				(flies as "VF-53/"Sky Boss")	
- •	FG-1D	Bu76628		forced landed, Hawaii	
				Ted Darcy, Kailua HI : recov. ex crash site	.85/86
				Robert J. Odegaard, Kindred ND	.87

				Kevin M. Hooey, Corning NY (hulk)	5.90
			N7171K	Kevin M. Hooey, Corning NY (rest. project)	1.91/92
- •	XF4U-4	Bu80759		NAS Norfolk VA (stored)	65
				Bradley Air Museum, Windsor Locks CT	.65/81
				New England Air Museum, Windsor Locks CT	81/90
7889 •	F4U-4	Bu81164		crashed, NALF Charlestown RI	27.1.50
				wreck buried, NALF Charlestown RI	.50/77
				hulk recov. by New England Air Museum,	
				Windsor Locks CT	.77/87
				Gerald S. Beck/Tri-State Aviation,	
				Wahpeton ND	1.87
			N5014	Robert J. Odegaard, Kindred ND	17.3.87/90
				(rest. project) : sold	.90
8140 •	F4U-4	Bu81415	N5219V	Robert Bean, Hereford AZ	59/69
				Korean War Museum, Seoul, Korea	74/88
				(displ. as "Marines/WR-22")	
8423 •	F4U-4	Bu81698	N3763A	Joe Arnold, Mulberry AR	77
			N53JB	John MacGuire, Fort Hancock TX	10.80
				War Eagles Air Museum, Santa Teresa NM	84/92
				(flies as "Marines/JM")	
8582 •	F4U-4	Bu81857		crashed, NALF Charlestown RI	21.1.50
				wreck buried, NALF Charlestown RI	.50/77
				hulk recov. by New England Air Museum,	
				Windsor Locks CT	.77/87
			N5081	Robert J. Odegaard, Kindred ND	1.87/92
				(rebuild to fly, Kindred ND)	
7240 •	F4U-1D	Bu82811		War Memorial Museum of Virginia,	
				Newport News VA	79
				Confederate Air Force, Virginia Beach VA	88
				(rest. project)	
7279 •	F4U-1D	Bu82850		Walter Soplata Collection, Newbury OH	85
2840 •	FG-1D	Bu88026		Walter Soplata Collection, Newbury OH	65/88
				(unconv. USN "00")	
2900 •	FG-1D	Bu88086	NX63382	Vought Company (executive transport)	
				(Bendix racer #90/"Joe ; #99)	46/49
			N63382	Paul Mantz, Orange County CA	55/63
				Tallmantz Aviation, Santa Ana CA	.63
				Rosen Novak Auto Co, Omaha NE	66
				(remained displ. at Tallmantz Collection)	
				Jack M. Spanich, Livonia MI	.69/77
				Weeks Air Museum, Tamiami FL	3.84/92
				(rebuilt, ff .90 as "USN G5")	
				damaged Hurricane Andrew	24.8.92
2904 •	FG-1D	Bu88090		(to RNZAF as NZ5612)	
				Jack Asplin, Hamilton NZ (as scrap)	5.49
				displ. Asplin's Garage, Hamilton NZ	69/71
				Museum of Transport & Technology, Auckland	74
				Ross Jarratt, Ardmore NZ (stored)	74/92
3111 •	FG-1D	Bu88297		USN disposal, to scrap metal dealer	23.1.59
			N9154Z	Frank G. Tallman, Orange County CA	9.1.60
				Tallmantz Collection, Orange County CA	
				displ. unconv. "Columbus/C", Orange County	.60/68
				Rosen Novak Autos, Omaha NE	66
				sold at auction, Orange County CA	29.5.68
				Johan M. Larsen, Minneapolis MN	69/72

				Minnesota Aircraft Museum, Minneapolis MN	73/75
			N8297	Louis E. Antonacci, Hampshire IL	83/86
				The Fighter Collection, Duxford	3.86/91
				(shipped from US to Rotterdam: arr. 21.4.86)	
			G-FGID	The Fighter Collection, Duxford	1.11.91/92
				(flies as "88297/29")	
3117 •	FG-1D	Bu88303	N6594D	Gene Strine, Middletown PA	56/66
				William C. Whitesell, Medford NJ	.66
			N700G	Flying W Ranch Airpark, Mount Holly NJ	69/71
				Doug Champlin/Windward Aviation, Enid OK	.71/79
				Champlin Fighter Museum, Mesa AZ	81/84
				Larry D. Rose, Peoria AZ	87/92
				(flies as "VMF-115/WA-22")	
3181 •	FG-1D	Bu88368		Patriots Point Naval & Maritime Museum,	
				Charleston SC	87/90
				(displ. on USS Yorktown, Mt.Pleasant SC as "21")	
3196 •	FG-1D	Bu88382		midair collision, crashed Lake Washington WA	29.7.50
				recov. from lake, in good condition	8.83
				Museum of Flight, Seattle WA	.83/92
				(static rest., Twin Falls ID)	
3205 •	FG-1D	Bu88391		(to RNZAF as NZ5648) BOC 17.8.45: SOC	9.5.49
				Jack Asplin, Hamilton NZ (as scrap)	5.49
				displ. Hamilton Airport NZ	.53
				displ. Asplin's Garage, Hamilton NZ	54/c65
				Museum of Transport & Technology, Auckland	c65/71
				(displ. as "NZ5611/Josephine II")	
				Ed A. Jurist, Nyack NY	.70
				(shipped Auckland - Vancouver 10.71; impounded	
				by Canadian Customs, stored Vancouver 72/73)	
				Duane Egli, Harlingen TX	73
				Jim Landry & Pat Palmer, Seattle WA	.73/82
			N55JP	Jim Landry & Pat Palmer, Seattle WA	.82
				(rebuilt Paine Field WA, ff 17.7.82)	
				Sky Garden Centre Inc, Seattle WA	84
				Peter W. Thelen, Fort Lauderdale FL	85
				Lone Star Flight Museum, Houston-Hobby TX	7.85/88
				Warbirds of GB Ltd, Biggin Hill	.88/91
				(shipped to UK 4.89, flies as "17640/Big Hog")	
				Old Flying Machine Co, Duxford	.91/92
				(id. also rep. as Bu88439, FAA quotes "P32823")	
3274 •	FG-1D	Bu92013	N1978M	Robert Gardner/Damn Yankee Air Force,	
				Hartfield MA	65
				Arnold R. (Bob) Tefft, Wakeman OH	69
				USMC Museum, MCAS Quantico VA	
				USNAM, NAS Pensacola FL	75/77
				Patriots Point Dev. Authority, Charleston SC	79
				USNAM, NAS Pensacola FL	80/85
				(heli-lift NAS Pensacola-Smyrna TX 5.80 for	
				rebuild by Stones River Air Service)	
				USNAM, Washington Navy Yard DC	88
3311 •	FG-1D	Bu92050	N6604C	Aero Enterprises Inc, La Porte IN	63
				Robert Mitchum, Broomfield CO	66
			N194G	Robert Mitchum, Broomfield CO (race #94)	69
				Aero Inc, Broomfield CO	72
				James R. Axtell, Denver CO (race #94)	77/92
3342	FG-1D	Bu92081	N4719C	James T. Lambert, Clarksdale MS	63/65
				Lou Kaufman	65
				crashed racing, Lancaster CA	6.65
				James T. Lambert, Clarksdale MS	72
3346 •	FG-1D	Bu92085		USMC Training Center, Lincoln NE	

				Pima County Air Museum, Tucson AZ	73/76
				USMC Museum, Quantico VA : loaned to	
				Selfridge ANGB Museum, Selfridge ANGB MI	81/89
				(displ. as "92085/1.01/LE-09")	
3356 •	FG-1D	Bu92095		(to FA Salvadorena as FAS 220)	
				Terry Randal/ Har-Ran Aviation, Tulsa OK	.75
				(ferried Salvador - Tulsa .75)	
			N62344	John Stokes, San Marcos TX	.75/77
			N67HP	Howard E. Pardue, Breckenridge TX	9.77/90
				(flew as "VMF-111/HP-67")	
				Evergreen International Airlines/747 Inc,	
				McMinnville OR	19.5.90/92
3367 •	FG-1D	Bu92106		stored unconv., Brewster WA	74
			N6897	Military Aircraft Restoration Corp, Chino CA	75/88
				(flew as "VMF-214/WE/"Blacksheep")	
				struck-off reg.	4.89
				(stored Twin Falls ID, pending rest.)	
3393 •	FG-1D	Bu92132	N3466G	The Air Museum, Claremont CA	58/73
				Military Aircraft Restoration Corp, Chino CA	.73/92
3507 •	FG-1D	Bu92246	N8050E	James R. Spletstoser, Fort Pierce FL	66
			N766JD	Joseph T. Norris/Air & Space Museum,	
				Charlottesville VA	69
				Bentwing Aircraft, Plant City FL	72/77
				USNAM, NAS Pensacola FL	79/91
				(displ. as "92246/86")	
3660 •	FG-1D	Bu92399	N4717C		
			N448AG	Alvin T. George, Atlanta GA	66/69
				crashed on take-off, Norfolk VA	
				USMC Museum, MCAS Quantico VA	72
				Harry Doan, Daytona Beach FL	77/87
				John C. Hooper, Harvey LA	88/90
				William J. Hooper, Harvey LA	92
3694	FG-1D	Bu92433	N3440G	Frank. G. Tallman/Movieland of the Air Museum,	
				Orange County CA	60/69
				I. N. Burchinall Jr, Paris TX	72/77
				rep. destroyed in hangar fire, Addison TX	.79
				sale reported, Addison TX (USCR)	84/92
3697 •	FG-1D	Bu92436	N3470G	The Air Museum, Ontario CA	63/73
			CF-JJW	Canadian Warplane Heritage, Hamilton ONT	15.10.73
				(flew as "VMF-112/"Wolf Pack")	
			C-GCWX	Canadian Warplane Heritage, Mount Hope ONT	74/92
				(flies as "KD658/X-115")	
3721 •	FG-1D	Bu92460		(to FA Salvadorena as FAS 201) : del.	.57
				donated by FAS as Sikorsky Memorial	.69
				displ. on pole at airport, Bridgeport CT	.69/90
				(displ. as "USMC/217")	
3729 •	FG-1D	Bu92468		stored NAS Litchfield Park AZ	
				sold, towed to Buckeye AZ and stored until	60
			N9964Z	Marvin L. Gardner/CAF, Mercedes TX	.60/75
				crashed, Olathe KS	.74
				Confederate Air Force, Harlingen TX	8.5.75/91
				(rebuilt by LTV Corp 74/3.81)	
				cr., forced landing, Forney TX (repaired)	14.4.82
				American Airpower Heritage Flying Museum,	
				Midland TX (flies as "13/USS Essex")	9.91/92
3750 •	FG-1D	Bu92489		(to FA Salvadorena as FAS 409)	
				Frank Arrufat, Los Angeles CA	88
				(under rebuild)	92

3869 •	FG-1D	Bu92508	N7225C	H. A. Matteri, Santa Rosa CA	66
				Valley Air Service, Sunnyside WA	69
				C. J. Lutt, Hayward CA	c69
			N46WB	Whitington Bros, Fort Lauderdale FL	76
			N46LF	Louis E. Fischer, Miami FL	1.77
			N70RP	ntu: Robert P. Lammerts, Oklahoma City OK	5.79
			N46LF	Robert P. Lammerts, Oklahoma City OK	79/84
			N46RL	Robert P. Lammerts, Oklahoma City OK	4.84/90
				Dee Ring Inc, Dallas TX	92
				(flies as "Marines/L-46")	
3870 •	FG-1D	Bu92509	N9150Z	M. L. Miller, Carpinteria CA	63
				David W. Slica, Sylmar CA	66
			N92509	David W. Slica, Sylmar CA	69
				John H. Van Andel, Stanford CT	1.71/74
				Preston Parish/Kalamazoo Aviation History Museum, Kalamazoo MI	77
				David W. Slica, Sylmar CA (racer #86)	78
			N9PP	ntu: Preston Parish, Kalamazoo MI	4.78
			N3PP	Kalamazoo Aviation History Museum, Kalamazoo MI	8.79/92
				(flies as USN "92509/611")	
3890 •	FG-1D	Bu92529		(to FA Salvadorena as FAS-2....)	
			N62290	Har-Ran Aviation, Tulsa OK (dism.)	75
				John J. Stokes, San Marcos TX	.75/77
				(rebuilt, flew as "VF-53/USS Essex")	
				Robert Friedman, Waukegan IL	.77
				Wayne Williams, Garland TX	.79
				Ray Jones	82
				Planes of Fame East, Minneapolis MN	83/92
				(flies as "USS Essex/S-301")	
				(id also quoted as Bu92629)	
9039 •	F4U-4	Bu96885		Earl Ware, Jacksonville FL	81/92
				(rest. project)	
9149 •	F4U-4	Bu96995	N5221V	Robert Bean, Hereford AZ	
				(to FA Hondurena as FAH614)	.60
				recov. Hollywood Wings, Long Beach CA	.78
			N4908M	Robert L. Ferguson & Howard E. Pardue, Breckenridge TX	79
				J. K. Ridley, Abilene & Breckenridge TX	80/89
			OE-EAS	Siegfried Angerer/Tyrolean Jet Service, Innsbruck	1.90/91
				(shipped to Austria, flies as "USN/BR37")	
9296 •	F4U-4	Bu97142	N3771A	Robert Bean, Hereford AZ	59
				stored unconv., Moseley Field, Phoenix AZ	67/69
				stored dism., Tucson Airport AZ	73
				Arthur W. McDonnell, Mojave CA	78
				stored unconv., Mojave CA	78/80
				USMC Museum: loaned Pima County Air Museum, Tucson AZ	88
9297 •	F4U-4	Bu97143	N96042	sale reported	77
				Charles T. Unkle, Homestead FL	84
			N713JT	Joseph O. Tobul, Pittsburgh PA	3.85/92
9413 •	F4U-4	Bu97259	N3728A	probably Robert Bean, Hereford AZ	
			N6667	Eugene H. Akers, Lancaster CA	66/72
				(racer #100; #22/"Lancer Two")	
				Wilson C. Edwards, Big Spring TX	.74/82
				EAA Aviation Foundation, Oshkosh WI	12.81/92
9418 •	F4U-4	Bu97264	N5218V	Robert Bean, Hereford AZ (USN/"K11")	59

				stored unconv., Moseley Field, Phoenix AZ	67/69
				Pacific Warbirds Museum, Half Moon Bay CA	73
				Eugene H. Akers, San Diego & Ramona CA	77/90
				(rebuild to fly, Ramona CA)	
				H & H Aircraft Sales, Pinedale WY	92
9434 •	F4U-4	Bu97280	N52...V	Robert Bean, Hereford AZ	
				(to FA Hondurena FAH 615)	.61
				recov. Hollywood Wings, Long Beach CA	.78
			N49092	Robert L. Ferguson & Howard E. Pardue,	
				Breckenridge TX	79
				Robert F. Yancy, Klamath Falls OR : del.	4.7.80/88
				(flew as USN "S-101/"Old Blue")	
				Warbirds of GB Ltd, Biggin Hill	1.88/90
				(shipped to UK, arr. Biggin Hill 19.2.88)	
				ret. to Fort Lauderdale, USA; for sale	3.92
9440 •	F4U-4	Bu97286	N5215V	Robert Bean, Hereford AZ	59/72
				(stored Blythe CA 63/72)	
				Merle B. Gustafson, Tullahoma LA	.72/84
				Robby R. Jones, Minter City MS	87/88
				Weeks Air Museum, Tamiami FL	.90/92
				(painted as "Bu97286/G5/Angel of Okinawa")	
9442 •	F4U-4	Bu97288	N52...V	Robert Bean, Hereford AZ	59
				(to FA Hondurena as FAH 612)	.60
				recov. by Hollywood Wings, Long Beach CA	.78
			N4907M	Robert L. Ferguson & Howard E. Pardue,	
				Breckenridge TX	79
				Joseph J. Bellantoni, Bridgeport CT	80
				crashed, Stratford CT (repaired)	7.6.81
				Joseph J. Bellantoni, Port Chester NY	84/92
9456 •	F4U-4	Bu97302	N3764A	Bob Bean, Hereford AZ ("Seattle/T4")	
				stored unconv., Moseley Field, Phoenix AZ	67/69
				stored dism., Tucson Airport AZ	73
			N68HP	Howard E. Pardue, Breckenridge TX	2.79
				Breckenridge Aviation Mus., Breckenridge TX	84/92
				(flies as "VMF-223/HP68")	
9474 •	F4U-4	Bu97320	N52...V	Robert Bean, Hereford AZ	59
				(to FA Hondurena as FAH 616)	.60
				John Roxbury, Princeton MN	88
				(rebuild to fly, Wahpeton ND)	92
9484	F4U-4	Bu97330	N5222V	Robert Bean, Hereford AZ	59
				stored unconv., Moseley Field, Phoenix AZ	67/69
				stored dism., Tucson Airport AZ	73
				William Barnes, Lancaster CA	77
				Shouling M. Barnes, Lancaster CA	84
				Erickson Air Crane Co, Central Point OR	86/91
				crashed, dest., Chilquin OR (pilot baled out)	2.8.91
9503 •	F4U-4	Bu97349		Robert Bean, Hereford AZ	7.56
				stored unconv., Moseley Field, Phoenix AZ	67/69
				Tucson Inn, Tucson AZ : displ. on pole	73/76
				Arthur W. McDonnell, Mojave CA	78/79
				noted unconv., Mojave CA	10.78/9.79
				USMC Museum, Quantico VA	.79
				USMC Museum, loaned Pima County Air Museum,	
				Tucson AZ	.79/83
			N4802X	USNAM, NAS Pensacola FL	4.84/91
				(displ. as "97349/WR-18")	
9513 •	F4U-4B	Bu97359	N5213V	Robert Bean, Hereford AZ	59
				stored unconv., Moseley Field, Phoenix AZ	67/69
				stored dism., Tucson Airport AZ	73
			N97359	Thomas Friedkin/Cinema Air, Houston TX	76/77

				(flew in TV series " Ba Ba Black Sheep")	76
			N240CA	Cinema Air, Houston TX	4.80/88
				Merlin Aire Ltd, King City CA	88
				Classic Flying Machines Ltd, King City CA	90/92
				op: Old Flying Machine Co, Duxford	4.88/92
				(shipped to UK, arr. Duxford 17.4.88)	
				shipped to USA	3.92
				(flies as RNZAF "NZ5628")	
9523 •	F4U-4	Bu97369	N5214V	Robert Bean, Hereford AZ	59
				stored unconv., Moseley Field, Phoenix AZ	67/69
				stored dism., Tucson Airport AZ	73
				Arthur W. McDonnell, Mojave CA	74
				USMC Museum, MCAS Quantico VA	75/88
9542 •	F4U-4	Bu97388		Robert Bean, Hereford AZ	59
				(to FA Hondurena as FAH 610)	.60
				Earl Ware, Jacksonville FL	81
				noted in yard, ("FAH 610"), Jacksonville FL	81
				Gerald S. Beck, Wahpeton ND	.82/92
				(rebuild Wahpeton ND, due to fly .92)	
				(id. also rep. as 9492/Bu97338)	
9543	F4U-4	Bu97389		Robert Bean, Hereford AZ	59
				stored unconv., Moseley Field, Phoenix AZ	67/69
				stored dism., Tucson Airport AZ	73
9544 •	F4U-4B	Bu97390		Robert Bean, Hereford AZ	59
				stored unconv., Moseley Field, Phoenix AZ	67/69
				stored dism., Tucson Airport AZ	73
			N47991	Yankee Air Corps, Chino CA	4.84/92
				(rebuild to fly, Chino CA)	
- •	F4U-5	Bu121794		(to Argentine Navy as 0384)	.58
				displ. Bahia Blanca AB, Argentina	91
				(displ. as "3-A-211")	
- •	F4U-5	Bu121859	N4993V	reg. res.	11.78/92
- •	F4U-5	Bu121881		(to Argentine Navy as ......)	
				displ. in park, Argentina	
				Lone Star Flight Museum, Galveston TX	.90/92
				(recov. ex park, Argentina .90;	
				rest. to fly, Breckenridge TX)	
- •	F4U-5N	Bu122179		(to FA Hondurena as FAH 604)	.56
				recov., Hollywood Wings, Long Beach CA	.78
			N4903M	Robert L. Ferguson & Howard E. Pardue,	
				Breckenridge TX	79
				Barry A. Landy, Fairfield NJ	80
				Barry Lansing/ Mike Collier/ Jack Goulding	
				& Foy Midkiff/Banner Inc, Lubbock TX	.83/84
				(flew as "Marines/BL-13")	
				crashed near Houston TX	3.84
				Peter W. Thelen, Fort Lauderdale FL : rebuilt	87
			N179PT	Peter W. Thelen, Fort Lauderdale FL	10.87/88
			N179NP	Warbirds of GB Ltd, Biggin Hill	14.8.88/90
				(arr. Biggin Hill on del. ex USA 16.8.88)	
				(flies in UK as USN/NP-9")	
- •	F4U-5N	Bu122184		(USMC: VMF(N)-513 and VMF-212 in Korea)	
				stored NAS Litchfield Park AZ SOC	3.56
			N3764A	Bob Bean, Hereford AZ	.56
				(to FA Hondurena as FAH 605)	.56
			N49051	recov. by Hollywood Wings, Long Beach CA	.78
				Robert L. Ferguson & Howard E. Pardue,	

				Breckenridge TX	.79
			N65HP	Howard E. Pardue, Breckenridge TX	2.79/87
				Robert J. Ready/Exec Aviation, Cincinatti OH	11.87
			N65WF	Exec Aviation Inc, Cincinatti OH	2.88/92
				(dep. Breckenridge on del. to Ohio 21.7.88, flies as "VMF(N)-513/WF-6")	
-	•	F4U-5P	Bu122189	NTS Bainbridge	
				USNAM, NAS Pensacola FL	65/76
				USMC Museum, MCAS El Toro CA	88/92
-	•	F4U-5NL	Bu124447	(to FA Hondurena as FAH 602)	.56
				recov. as collection of components by Hollywood Wings, Long Beach CA	.78
				rebuild, Van Nuys later Chino CA	81/82
			N100CV	Glen Hyde, Dallas TX (ff. at Chino 21.1.87)	10.84/88
				dep. Breckenridge TX , on del. El Toro CA	20.7.88
				USMC Museum, MCAS El Toro CA	7.88
				IR3T Inc, Roanoke TX/Pahrump NV	.88/92
-	•	F4U-5NL	Bu124486		
			N52...V	Robert Bean, Hereford AZ	
				(to FA Hondurena as FAH 606)	.56
				recov. by Hollywood Wings, Long Beach CA	.78
			N49068	Robert L. Ferguson & Howard E. Pardue, Breckenridge TX	.79
				Phil Dear, Jackson MS	80/84
				McGhee Air Inc, McGhee AR	87
				Sherman Aircraft Sales, West Palm Beach FL	88
				Richard Bertea, Chino CA	.88/92
				(flies as "124453/NP-21/Annie Mo")	
-	•	F4U-5NL	Bu124541	(to Argentine Navy as 3-A-204) : del.	.56
				Museo Naval de la Nacion, Rio Parana Delta AB	72/91
-	•	F4U-5NL	Bu124569	(to FA Hondurena as FAH 601)	.56
				recov. by Hollywood Wings, Long Beach CA	.78
			N4901W	R. Ferguson & Howard E. Pardue, Breckenridge TX	.79
				Robert L. Ferguson, Wellesley MA	80/82
				Sherman Aircraft Sales, West Palm Beach FL	83
				Bruce Lockwood, Juneau AK	3.83
				Preston Air Museum, Dallas TX	.84/88
				David K. Burnap, Dayton OH	.88/92
				(flies as "RF-12/ Old Deadeye")	
				(FAA quote id. Bu124560)	
-	•	F4U-5N	Bu124692	(to FA Hondurena as FAH...)	
				Collings Foundation, Stowe MA	88/91
				(rebuild to fly, Kissimmee FL)	
-	•	F4U-5NL	Bu124724	(to FA Hondurena as FAH 600)	.56
				recov. by Hollywood Wings, Long Beach CA	.78
				crash landing on del. flight, Belize	.78
			N4901E	Robert L. Ferguson & Howard E. Pardue, Breckenridge TX	.79/80
				Ralph C. Parker, Wichita falls TX	.84/86
				Amicale Jean Baptiste Salis, La Ferte-Alais	3.86
				shipped to Amsterdam, Holland : arr.	21.4.86
			F-AZEG	Amicale Jean Baptiste Salis, La Ferte-Alais	12.86/91
				(flies as "124724/P-22")	
-	•	F4U-7	Bu133693	(to Aeronavale as 693)	
				ret. to USN, NAS Norfolk VA	
				The Air Museum of Canada, Calgara ALTA	67
			N693M	American Aerospace & Military Museum, Pomona CA	69/70
				Robert E. Guilford, Beverly Hills CA (race #3)	70/71
			N33693	Robert E. Guilford, Beverly Hills CA	.71/84

c/n		Type	Serial	Reg.	History	Dates
					(race #3 ; #93/"WR-93/Blue Max")	
					G & R Aviation Enterprises, Santa Monica CA	84/87
					crashed and dest., nr Brown Fd, San Diego CA (2K)	10.5.87
-	•	F4U-7	Bu133704		(to Aeronavale as 704)	
					USNAM, NAS Pensacola FL	65/72
					USS Alabama Memorial Comm., Mobile AL	77/88
					(displ. as "Marines/LD-15")	
-		F4U-7	Bu133710		(to Aeronavale as 710)	
					USMC Museum, Quantico VA	68
					Air & Space Museum, Charlottesville VA	69
					USMC Museum, Quantico VA	c70
-	•	F4U-7	Bu133714		(to Aeronavale as 714)	
				N33714	USMC Museum, Quantico VA	69
					Dean J. Ortner, Wakeman OH	71/72
					John Schafhausen, Hayden Lake WA	.73/77
					(flew as Aeronavale "965")	
				C-GWFU	Blain Fowler, Camrose ALTA	10.83/88
					(flies as "Alberta Blue")	
-	•	F4U-7	Bu133722		(to Aeronavale as 722)	
					retired .64, to inst. airframe Toulon	64/73
				N1337A	Gary L. Harris, Oakland CA	.74/84
					(shipped to San Francisco .74, rebuilt	
					Half Moon Bay CA, ff. 22.8.76)	
					Lindsey Walton, Duxford UK : del.	7.8.82/92
					(flies as Aeronavale "133722/15F.22")	
-	•	F4U-1D	-		used as movie prop., Hollywood CA	
		Super			Ed Maloney/The Air Museum, Ontario CA	c59/69
		Corsair			(displ. fuselage only, 7 Japanese victories)	
					(rebuild Chino .82 as racer, with P&W R4360)	
				N31518	James Maloney/Planes of Fame, Chino CA	11.82/84
					Steve Hinton/Fighter Rebuilders, Chino CA	
					(race #1)	84/92
					(FAA quote id. "0020"; type "F2G")	
6163	•	F2G-1D	Bu88454		USN storage container, NAS Norfolk VA	c48/66
					NASM, Washington DC: (listed)	
					Bradley Air Museum, Windsor Locks CT	65/66
					loan: MCAS Museum, MCAS Quantico VA	68/72
				N4324	Walter E. Ohlrich, Norfolk VA	73/74
					(res. race #50 : civil conv. at Newport News	
					not completed)	
					USMC Museum, Quantico VA	74
					Doug Champlin Collection, Enid OK	.74
					USS Intrepid Museum, New York NY	76
					ferried NAS Norfolk - Enid OK	c77
					Champlin Fighter Museum, Mesa AZ	.78/92
					(flies as "NATC/454")	
6166	•	F2G-1	Bu88457	NX5588N(2	Cook Cleland (Bendix racer #57)	.49
					Cook Cleland Air Svce, Willoughby OH: USCR	66/69
					dism. hulk stored, Van Sant PA	72/80
					Doan Helicopters, Daytona Beach FL (dism.)	1.83/88
					D. K. Precision, Fort Lauderdale FL	2.89/90
					Lone Star Flight Museum, Galveston TX	.90/92
					(stored dism., pending rebuild to fly)	
6172	•	F2G-2	Bu88463	NX5577N	Cook Cleland (Bendix racer#74)	.46/47
					Dick Beckler (Bendix racer#74)	.48/49
					Walter Soplata Collection, Newbury OH	65/88
-	•	FG-1D	-		Goodyear World of Rubber, Akron OH	c52/c74
					(displ. Goodyear blimp hangar "USN/6")	

				Arthur W. McDonnell, Mojave CA	.75
				arr. by road for rebuild, Mojave CA	2.75
-	FG-1D	-		Naval Reserve HQ, Lincoln NE	73
				held dism., recov. ex park display	
- •	F4U-5N	-		(to FA Hondurena as FAH 609)	
				Honduras Air Force Museum	.80/90
- •	F4U-4	-		(to FA Hondurena as FAH 611)	.60
				Earl Ware, Jacksonville FL	81
				hulk in yard, "FAH 611", Jacksonville FL	81
				Ray Adams, Melbourne FL	85/90
				(rebuild to fly, Titusville FL)	
- •	F4U-4	-		(to FA Hondurena as FAH 617)	.60
				Earl Ware, Jacksonville FL	81
				hulk in yard, "FAH 617", Jacksonville FL	81
- •	F4U-4	-		(to FA Hondurena as FAH 692)	.60
				Earl Ware, Jacksonville FL	81
				hulk in yard, "FAH 692", Jacksonville FL	81
- •	FG-1D	-		(to FA Salvadorena as ....)	
				displ. Ilopango AB, San Salvador	91
- •	F4U-5	-		recov. in FL, by Walt Disney Studios	
				(used in deal for use of RNZAF A-4s in film)	
				RNZAF Museum, Wigram (del. by sea)	9.87/91
- •	F4U-1	-		Ross Jarratt, Ardmore NZ	89
				(major components; restoration project)	
-	F4U-	-		rep. City Park, Overland KS	67/71
- •	F4U-5NL	-		(to Argentine Navy as ....)	
				displ. on pole, Trelew AB, Argentina	91
				(displ. as "2-A-202")	

WESTAND LYSANDER

- •	Mk. III	R9125		RAF Museum Store, RAF Henlow	69
				RAF Museum, Hendon	73/92
				(displ. as "R9125/LX-L")	
- •	Mk.IIIA	V9300		(to RCAF as 1558)	
				Don Bradshaw, Saskatoon SASK	
				(recov. ex farm, Harris SASK)	
			G-LIZY	Graham A. Warner/British Aerial Museum,	
				Duxford UK : arr. dism. Duxford	11.82/90
				Imperial War Museum, Duxford	91
				(static rest. Duxford, to be displ. as "V9300")	
Y1363 •	Mk.IIIA	V9312		(to RCAF as V9312) BOC 22.10.42 SOC	1.10.46
	Mk.IIITT			Harry Whereatt/Whereatt's Warbirds,	
				Assiniboia SASK	72/88
				(recov. derelict ex farm, Meyvoune SASK)	
			N3093K	Weeks Air Museum,Tamiami FL	9.91/92
				rest. project	
Y1399 •	Mk. IIIA	-		(to RCAF as ......)	
				Vince O'Connor, Uxbridge ONT	
				(fuse. only, wings from RCAF2404)	
				Peter Dimond UK	92
Y1530 •	Mk. IIIA	V9546		(to RCAF as V9546)	
	Mk. TTIIIA			Wes Agnew, Hartney MAN	

				(recov. from farm, Cabri SASK)	
				Musee Royal de l'Armee, Brussels : stored	.71/82
			OO-SOT	Sabena Old Timers, Brussels	7.82/92
				(rest. Brussels, ff 27.8.88 as "2442/MA-D")	
				(id. also quoted as RCAF 2442: small parts only)	
Y1536 •	Mk. IIIA	V9552		(to RCAF as 1582)	
				Wes Agnew, Hartney MAN	
				(recov. from farm, Stroughton SASK)	
			G-AZWT	Sir W. J. D. Roberts/Strathallan Aircraft	
				Collection, Auchterader, Scotland	9.6.72/92
				(rest Strathallan, ff 14.12.79 "V9441/AR-A")	
				(id. also quoted as RCAF 2355: small parts only)	
- •	Mk. IIIA	RCAF1589		Canadian National Aeronautical Collection,	
				Rockcliffe ONT	65/67
				Indian Air Force Museum, Palam, New Delhi	10.67/90
				(displ. as IAF "1589")	
1176 •	Mk. IIIA	RCAF....		Military Aircraft Restoration Corp, Chino CA	72/92
				Air Heritage Inc, Beaver Falls PA ; .	91/92
				(stored Beaver Falls PA, planned rest. to fly)	
1181 •	Mk. IIIA	RCAF2341		Ed Zalesky/Canadian Museum of Flight &	
				Transportation, Vancouver BC	79/88
				(hulk recov. ex farm, Riverhurst SASK)	
				Ed & Rose Zalesky, Surrey BC	88/92
1183 •	Mk. IIIA	RCAF2344		Ed Zalesky/Canadian Museum of Flight &	
				Transportation, Vancouver BC	79/88
				(hulk recov. ex farm, Gull Lake SASK)	
				Ed & Rose Zalesky, Surry BC	88/92
1185 •	Mk. IIIA	RCAF2346		Ernie Simmons, Tillsonburg ONT	.45/57
				F. D. Emmorey, Montreal QUE	
				Dolph Overton, Kenley NC (stored)	
			N7791	Dwight Brooks, Van Nuys CA	.73/75
				(rebuilt Van Nuys CA, using parts from	
				RCAF 2366: ff 3.7.74 as "N7791/AC-B")	
				NASM: loan USAFM, Wright-Patterson AFB OH	79/92
				(displ. as "N7791/AC-B")	
1194 •	Mk. IIIA	RCAF2349		Wes Agnew, Hartney MAN	
				(recov. from farm, Cabri SASK)	
				Tim Inman, Beasley TX/Confederate AF	80
				Ed Zalesky/Canadian Museum of Flight &	
				Transportation, Vancouver BC	5.80/92
				(basis of composite static rest. for "Expo 86")	
1202 •	Mk. IIIA	RCAF2363	C-GCWL	Canadian Warplane Heritage, Mount Hope ONT	83/88
			N1274	Friends of CWH, Tonawanda NY	4.89/92
				(rest. to fly, Niagara Falls NY)	
1205 •	Mk. IIIA	RCAF2364		Martin Riehl, Calgary ALTA	.72
				(recov. ex farm, Weyburn SASK .72)	
				Arny Carnegie, Edmonton ALTA	.72
				Dwight Brooks, Van Nuys CA	1.73/74
				(spare airframe for rebuild of RCAF 2346)	
				Friends of CWH, Tonaswanda NY	85
				(spare airframe for rebuild of RCAF 2363)	
			C-GCWW	Canadian Warplane Heritage, Hamilton ONT	85/92
				(rest. project: RCAF serial also poss. 2366)	
1206 •	Mk. IIIA	RCAF2365		Martin Riehl, Calgary ALTA	72/77
				(recov. ex farm, Weyburn SASK .72)	
				Harry Whereatt, Assiniboia SASK	.77/92

1209	•	Mk. IIIA	RCAF2367		Martin Riehl, Calgary ALTA	72/77
					(recov. ex farm, Weyburn SASK .72)	
					Harry Whereatt, Assiniboia SASK	.77/92
					(RCAF serial also poss. 2366)	
1216	•	Mk. IIIA	RCAF2374		Capt. Bernie M. Lapointe	67
					(rest. from three derelict airframes recov.	
					from MAN farms : ff 29.12.67)	
					Canadian National Aviation Museum,	
					Rockcliffe ONT (displ. as "R9003")	.68/90
1217	•	Mk. IIIA	RCAF2375		Wes Agnew, Hartney MAN	
					Commonwealth Air Training Plan Museum,	
					Brandon MAN	88/92
1218	•	Mk. IIIA	RCAF2376		G & M Aircraft, St. Albert ALTA	85
					Ed Zalesky/Canadian Museum of Flight &	
					Transportation, Vancouver BC : arr.	7.85/92
1222	•	Mk. IIIA	RCAF2381		G & M Aircraft, St. Albert ALTA	85
					Ed Zalesky/Canadian Museum of Flight &	
					Transportation, Vancouver BC : arr.	7.85/88
					fuse. only: dam. in truck crash during recov.	18.7.85
					Ed & Rose Zalesky, Surrey BC	88/91
					(id. also quoted as RCAF 2383)	
1223		Mk.IIIA	RCAF2382		E. S. Holmes, Edmonton ALTA	
				CF-FOA	Westland Spraying Services, High River ALTA	.48/55
					(converted for crop spraying)	
					sold as scrap : rep. used as landfill	
1244	•	Mk. IIIA	RCAF....		Wes Agnew, Hartney MAN	
					(recov. from farm, Nipiwan MAN)	
					Joe Gertler, New York NY	
					Philip A. Mann, Booker	71/75
				G-BCWL	Philip A. Mann, Booker	9.9.75/79
					(composite rebuild Booker, ff 1.3.74;	
					also using parts of 2341, 2349, 2391)	
					Doug Arnold/Warbirds of GB Ltd, Blackbushe	9.5.79/85
					forced landing, overturned, Whitchford	21.8.83
					Brian Woodford/Wessex Aviation & Transport,	
					Henstridge	2.85/89
					(rebuilt Booker, ff 18.9.87: flies as "V9281/RU-M")	
-		Mk. IIIA	RCAF....		Eric Vormezeele, Braaschaat, Belgium	84
					Musee de l'Air, Paris-Le Bourget	8.85/90
					destroyed in museum hangar fire, Le Bourget	17.5.90
					(id. rep. as "RCAF 1589": see above)	

YAKOLEV Yak-1

-	•	Yak-1	1342		recov. from forced landing site, Russia	c90
					Historic Aircraft Collection : imported to UK	8.91
				G-BTZD	Historic Aircraft Collection	10.12.91
					(rebuild to fly; fuselage at Historic Flying	
					wings at Skysport, Bedford)	92

YAKOLEV Yak-3

-	•	Yak-3	-		Museum of Flying, Santa Monica CA	8.91
					on loan from Yakovlev, arr. dism.	8.91
					("115450123" painted on fuselage)	
-	•	Yak-3	-		Musee de l'Air, Paris-Le Bourget	82/92
-	•	Yak-3UA	-		Patrick Harrison, Houston TX	10.91
					(reputedly to be built by Yakovlev, Moscow 91/92:	
					first of new production run of 20 Model 3UAs)	

102146 •	LET C.11	-		(to Egyptian AF as ....)	
				recov. by Jean-Baptiste Salis/Salis Collection,	
				La Ferte Alais, France	.84
			N2124X	Joseph R. Haley, El Segundo CA	8.89/92
				(rebuilt with R-2000, Chino CA .89;	
				race #111/"Defector")	
105022 •	LET C.11	-		(to Egyptian AF as ....)	
				recov. by Jean Salis, La Ferte Alais, France	.84
			N7030U	reg.	9.89
			N711JT	Vintage Wings, Anchorage AK	10.89/92
				(FAA quote type "Yak/Thomas-11")	
170101 •	LET C.11	-		(to Egyptian AF as 533)	
				recov. by Jean Salis, La Ferte Alais, France	.84
				Patina Ltd, Duxford Duxford	.88
			G-BTHD	The Fighter Collection, Duxford	7.3.91/92
				(to Russia .91 for rebuild in Yak-3U configuration)	
171101 •	LET C.11	1701		(to Egyptian AF as 590) : del.	.59
				(defected to Israel, to IDFAF as ....)	.64/78
				recov. by Robs Lamplough : shipped to UK	.78
			G-KYAK	Robs Lamplough, Duxford/North Weald	12.78/92
				(rest. Duxford, ff 29.4.81 in Soviet AF sc.)	
				sold to "Flying Legends" France: del. ex North Weald	1.92
171205 •	LET C.11	-	OK-KIH	Czech Government: reg. for del.	.64
				(to Egyptian AF as 705)	
				recov. by Jean Salis, La Ferte Alais, France	.84
			G-OYAK	Eddie Coventry, Earls Colne	2.88/92
				(rebuilt Earls Colne, ff 18.11.90 as Soviet "27")	
				(also rep. ex EAF 205, or 097: definitely 705)	
171304 •	LET C.11	171304		Czech AF: noted Chino CA	90
171312 •	LET C.11	-	OK-JIK	Czech Government: reg. for del.	.64
				(to Egyptian AF as ...)	
				recov. by Jean Salis, La Ferte Alais, France	.84
				Tony Bianchi, Booker : arr. dism. for rest.	5.5.89/92
			G-BTZE	Bianchi Aviation Film Services Ltd, Booker	11.2.92
				(under rest. Booker 92)	
171314 •	LET C.11	-		(to Egyptian AF as.........)	.55
				recov. by Jean Salis, La Ferte Alais, France	.84
				Paul Franceschi, Le Castellet, nr Marseille	.85/87
				(under rebuild 87/92)	
171521 •	LET C.11	-		(to Egyptian AF as ....)	
				recov. by Jean Salis, La Ferte Alais, France	.84
				John W. Houston, Harlingen TX	
				Ascher Ward, Van Nuys CA	88
			N134JK	Joe Kasparoff, Van Nuys CA	5.88/92
				(rebuilt Van Nuys as mod. racer with R-3350,	
				ff Mojave 11.8.88; race #97/"Mr Awesome")	
				Darryl Greenamyer, Van Nuys CA	8.89
				(further racing mods.,including T-33 tail)	
				crashed, Reno NV	11.8.89
172503 •	LET C.11	-		(to Egyptian AF as ....)	
				recov. by Jean Salis, La Ferte Alais, France	.84
				G. Chambert, La Ferte Alais	88/91
			F-AZOK	G. Chambert	.91
172521 •	LET C.11	-		(to Egyptian AF as ....)	
				recov. by Jean Salis, La Ferte Alais, France	.84
			N111YK	Robert G. Chinnery, Independence MO	5.90/92

172612 •	LET C.11	-		(to Egyptian AF as ....)	
				recov. by Jean Salis, La Ferte Alais, France	.84
				Don C.Talley & C.A.Barnes, Longview TX	88
			N9YK	Don C.Talley/Talleys Warbirds Inc, Longview TX	3.89/92
				(rebuilt as single-seater, ff 20.9.91; flies as Soviet AF "11")	
172623 •	LET C.11	-		(to Egyptian AF as 543)	
				recov. by Jean Salis, La Ferte Alais, France	.84
			G-BTUB	Mark & John Jeffries, Little Gransden	29.8.91/92
				(rest. Little Gransden, due to fly .92)	
				(id. also quoted as "039")	
172701 •	LET C.11	-	OK-KIE	Czech Government: reg. for del. Egyptian AF	.64
				forced landing on del., near Nicosia, Cyprus	27.3.64
				impounded by RAF Cyprus	3.64
			G-AYAK	Philip Mann, Booker	31.3.70
				Robs Lamplough, Duxford	
				Anthony E. Hutton,	.76/83
				(shipped to US for demo. tour: ret. UK)	.82/.83
				Guy Black/Aero Vintage Ltd, Lydd	11.2.83/84
			N11YK	Heliflight Inc, Fort Lauderdale FL	7.6.84
				Weeks Air Museum, Tamiami FL	88/92
				damaged Hurricane Andrew	24.8.92
				(flies as Soviet AF "14")	
458519 •	LET C.11	-		(to Egyptian AF as ....)	
				recov. by Jean Salis, La Ferte Alais, France	.84
			N11YH	Jim H. McKinstry, Longmont CO	1.86/92
1701231•	LET C.11	-		(to Egyptian AF as ....)	
				recov. by Jean Salis, La Ferte Alais, France	.84
			N11SN	Neil R. Anderson, Fort Worth TX	3.86/90
				The Old Flying Machine Company, Duxford	17.3.90/92
				(flies in Soviet AF sc.)	
				(to Russia .91 for conv. to Yak 3U configuration)	
2511103•	LET C.11	-		(to Egyptian AF as 539: unconf.)	
				recov. by Jean Salis, La Ferte Alais, France	.84
			F-YAKA	reg. for test flying	
			F-AZJB	Jacques Bourett/Aero Retro, St-Rambert	29.8.88/91
				(rebuilt as Yak-9T replica; flies as "Soviet AF 60")	
2511108•	LET C.11	-		(to Egyptian AF as ....)	
				recov. by Jean Salis, La Ferte Alais, France	.84
			F-AZPA	J. Salis, La Ferte Alais	5.9.90
2511120•	LET C.11	-		(to Egyptian AF as ....)	
				recov. by Jean Salis, La Ferte Alais, France	.84
			N18AW	Ascher Ward, Van Nuys CA	87/88
				Thomas L. Camp, San Francisco CA	90/91
				(rebuilt with R2800; race #58/"Maniyak")	
2511125•	LET C.11	-		(to Egyptian AF as ....)	
				recov. by Jean Salis, La Ferte Alais, France	.84
				Robert J. Pond, Minneapolis MN	.85
			N25YK	Robert J. Pond/Planes of Fame East, Plymouth MN	5.88/92
				(rebuilt Chino CA with R-1830 : ff 4.87)	
				(flies as "Soviet AF 27")	
8492250•	LET C.11	-		(to Egyptian AF as ....)	
				recov. by Jean Salis, La Ferte Alais, France	.84
			N5YK	Tom Everhart, Louisville KY	87/90
- •	LET C.11	-		(to Egyptian AF as ....)	

c/n		Type	Serial	Reg.	History	Date
					recov. by Jean Salis, La Ferte Alais, France	.84
				F-AZFB	based La Ferte Alais	89
-	•	LET C.11	-		(to Egyptian AF as ....)	
					recov. by Jean Salis, La Ferte Alais, France	.84
				F-AZFJ	Jean-Baptiste Salis Collection, La Ferte Alais	88/91
					(flies as Soviet AF "29")	
-	•	LET C.11	-		(to Egyptian AF as ....)	
					recov. by Jean Salis, La Ferte Alais, France	.84
				F-AZNN	Pierre Dague, La Ferte Alais ff.	5.87/91
					(rebuilt in single seat configuration by Dague & Gerry Marchadier;flies as "Soviet AF 14")	
-	•	LET C.11	-		(to Egyptian AF as ....)	
					recov. by Jean Salis, La Ferte Alais, France	.84
				N3YK	John W. Houston/Texas Air Museum, Harlingen TX	12.85/92
					(rebuilt Harlingen TX single seat configuration)	
					(FAA quote id. "Y337")	
-	•	LET C.11	-		(to Egyptian AF as ....)	
					recov. by Jean Salis, La Ferte Alais, France	.84
				N7YK	reg. res.	90/92
					(FAA quote id. "51-24")	
-	•	LET C.11	-		(to Egyptian AF as ....)	
					recov. by Jean Salis, La Ferte Alais, France	.84
				N5940	Robert F. Yancey, Klamath Falls OR	4.87/92
					(FAA quote id. "210")	
-	•	LET C.11	-		(to Egyptian AF as ....)	
					recov. by Jean Salis, La Ferte Alais, France	.84
				N5942	Robert F. Yancey, Klamath Falls OR	4.87/89
-	•	LET C.11	-		(to Egyptian AF as 407)	
					recov. by Jean Salis, La Ferte Alais, France	.84
				N5943	Robert F. Yancey, Klamath Falls OR	4.87/92
					(rebuilt with R-2800; race #101/"Perestroika")	
-	•	LET C.11	-		(to Egyptian AF as ......)	
					recov. by Jean Salis, La Ferte Alais, France	.84
				N5945	reg.	4.87
					(under rebuild 87/88)	
-	•	LET C.11	-		(to Egyptian AF as ....)	
					recov. by Jean Salis, La Ferte Alais, France	.84
				N21241	Daniel M. McCue, Somersworth NH	88/89
				N11MQ	Daniel M. McCue, Somersworth NH	7.89/92
					(rebuilt Live Oak FL with P&W R-2000, ff. c3.90)	
					(FAA quote id."Yak-11-O1M": flies in Soviet AF sc.)	
-	•	LET C.11	-		(to Egyptian AF as 079)	
					recov. by Jean Salis, La Ferte Alais, France	.84
					BAP Air, Charleroi, Belgium : del. dism.	.85
				OO-YAK	M. Adge	87/92
					(rebuilt Gosselies, Belgium, ff 12.5.88)	
					Philip Wolffe	
					(flies as "12")	
-	•	LET C.11	-		(to Egyptian AF as ....)	
					recov. by Jean Salis, La Ferte Alais, France	.84
				N........	Jean-Marie Garric, Mercedes TX	87/88
					(rebuilt as Yak-3 replica)	
172321	•	LET C.11	-		(to Egyptian AF as ....)	

Continued on Page 431

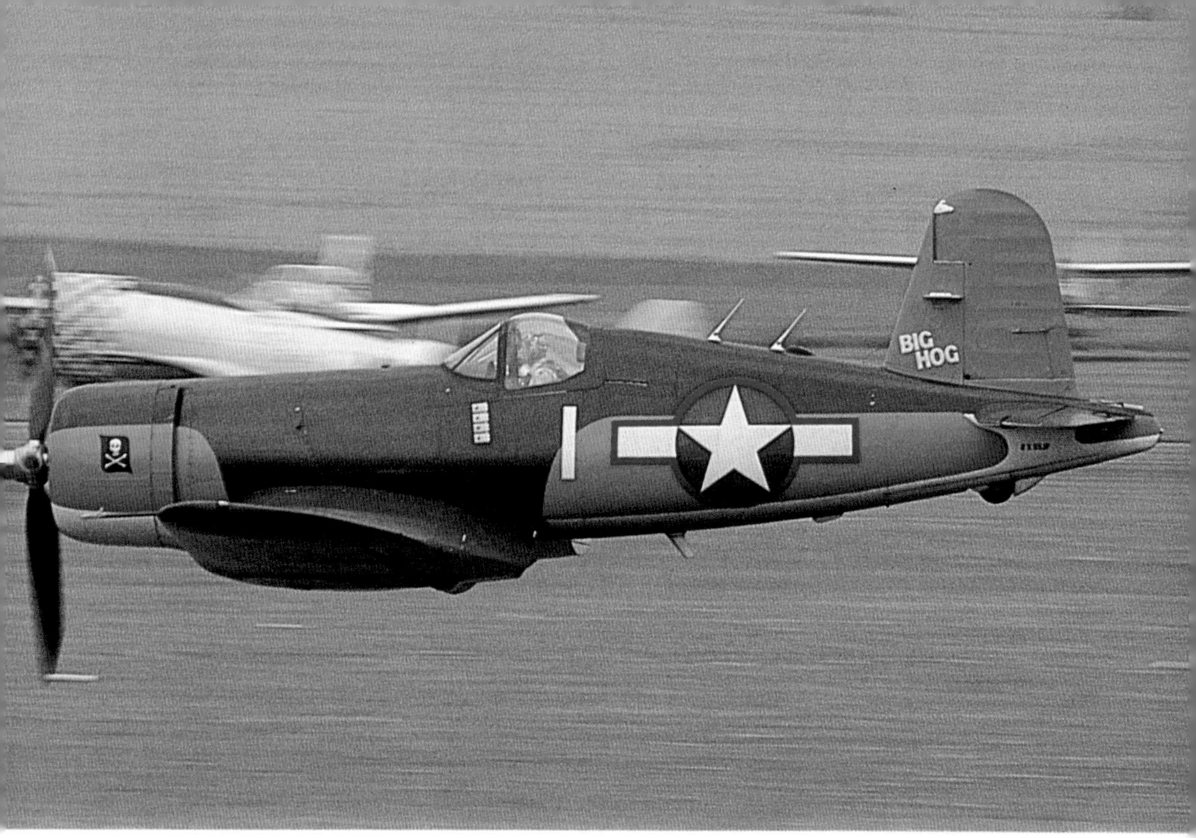
BIG
HOG

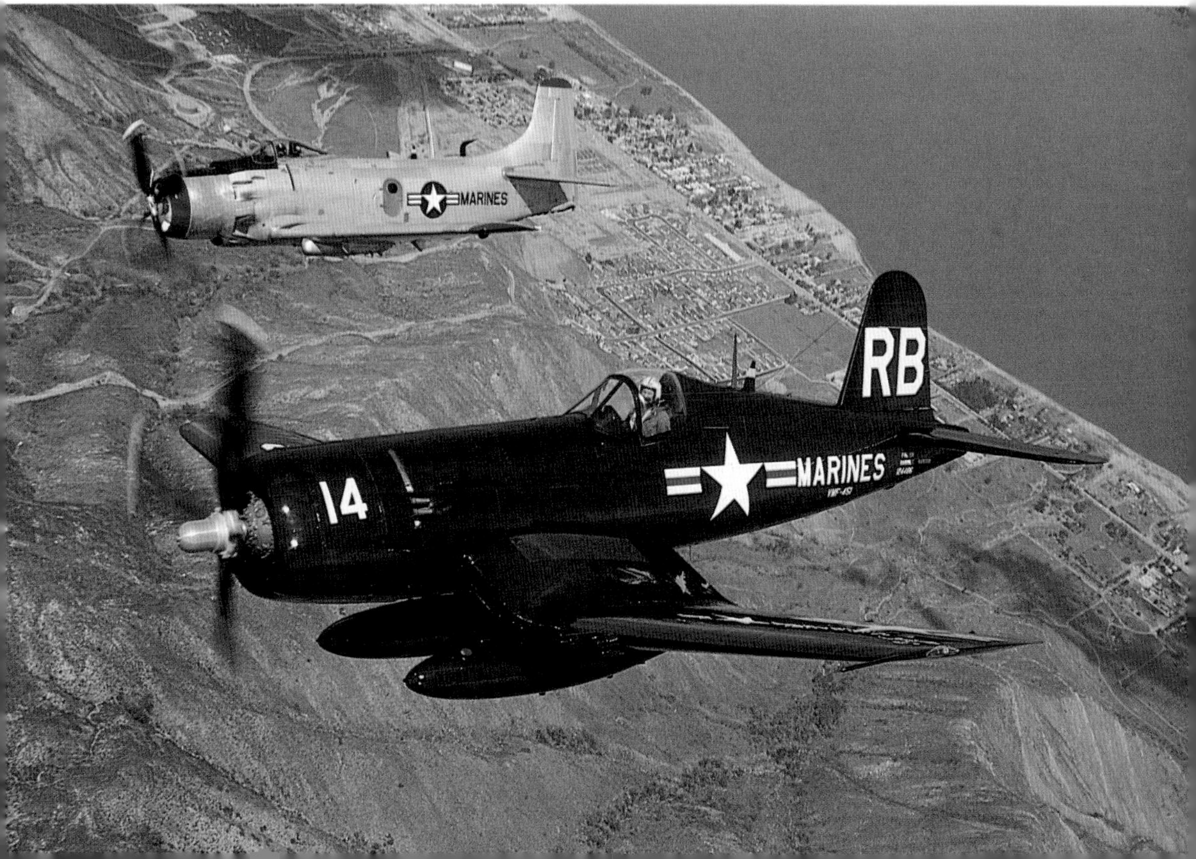
MARINES
RB
14
MARINES

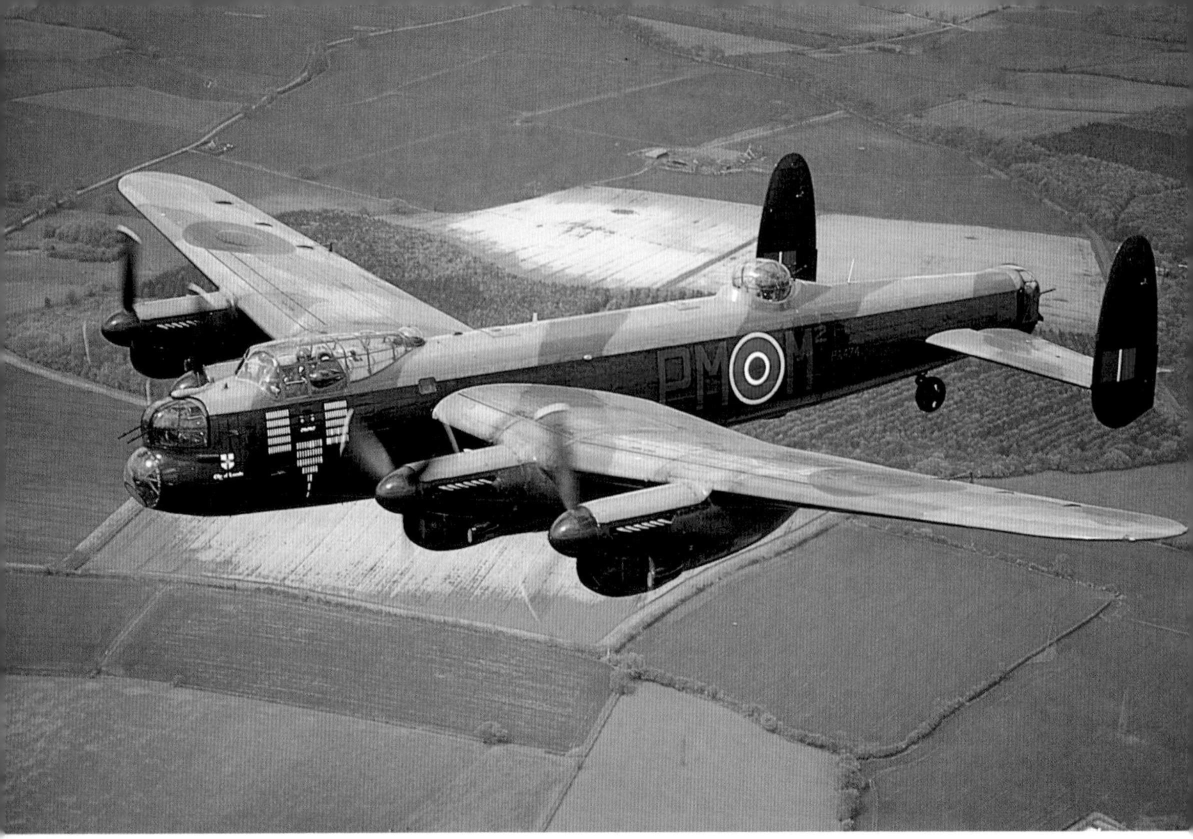
PM
M
PA474

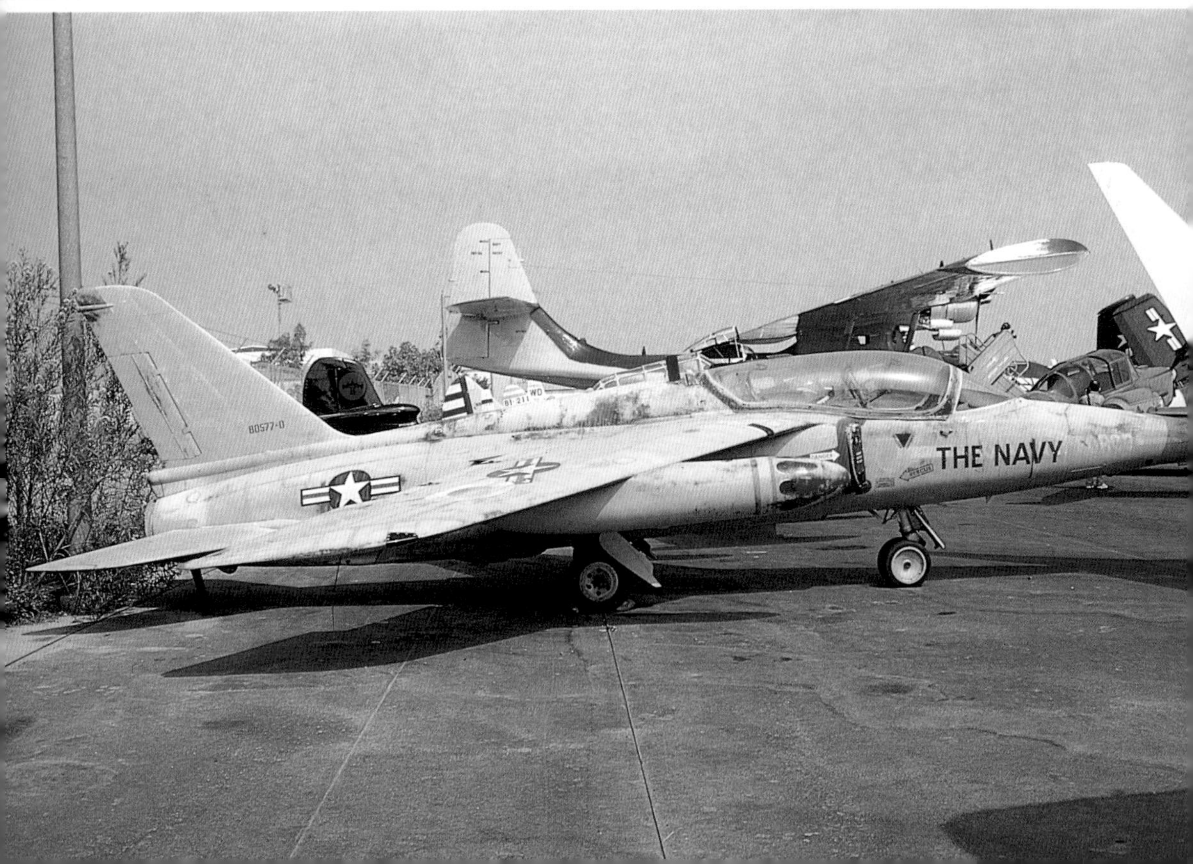
THE NAVY
80577-D

Continued from Page 428

					recov. by Jean Salis, La Ferte Alais, France	.84
				N........	Jean-Marie Garric, Mercedes TX	87/88
-	•	LET C.11	-		(to Egyptian AF as ....)	
					recov. by Jean Salis, La Ferte Alais, France	.84
					Jean-Baptiste Salis, La Ferte Allais (rebuild)	87
-	•	LET C.11	-		(to Egyptian AF as ....)	
					recov. by Jean Salis, La Ferte Alais, France	.84
					Aero Retro	87
-	•	LET C.11	-		(to Egyptian AF as ....)	
					recov. by Jean Salis, La Ferte Alais, France	.84
					Philip Joyet, Lausanne, Switzerland	87
					M. Perrin, Lausanne, Switzerland	88
-	•	LET C.11	-		(to Egyptian AF as ....)	
					recov. by Jean Salis, La Ferte Alais, France	.84
					Planes of Fame, Chino CA	88/91
					(displ. as "30")	
-	•	LET C.11	-		(to Egyptian AF as ....)	
					recov. by Jean Salis, La Ferte Alais, France	.84
					Dale Clark, Chino CA	88
-	•	LET C.11	-		(to Egyptian AF as ....)	
					recov. by Jean Salis, La Ferte Alais, France	.84
					Planes of Fame East, Minneapolis MN	.85
					(prob. the Yak.11 in open storage, complete,	
					Planes of Fame compound, Chino CA 89/91)	
-	•	LET C.11	-		(to Egyptian AF as ....)	
					recov. by Jean Salis, La Ferte Alais, France	.84
					Capel Aviation rebuild in Rumania	92
-	•	LET C.11	-	OK-JZE	Museum of Aviation & Cosmonautics, Kbely	89/91
					(rest. 89/91, ff 27.11.91)	
		Yak-11 (x10)			Ten airframes, ex Rumanian Air Force on rebuild	
					in Rumania for Capel Aviation, La Ferte Alais, France	92

YAKOLEV YAK-18/NANCHANG CJ-6

1432030	•	Yak-18 tailwheel	-		(to Chinese AF as .....)	
					Warren Sessler/China Technologies Inc, USA	
					Jim Gardner, Sacramento CA	.88
				N7013S	Jim Gardner, Sacramento CA	5.89
				N18YK	James A. Gardner, Windsor CA	8.89/92
					(id. also rep. as 18-1402030)	
1609	•	Yak-18U	-		(to Egyptian AF as 640)	
					recov. by Jean-Baptiste Salis, La Ferte Alais	.84
				F-AZFG	Aero Retro, St Rambert D'Albion	88/91
					(flies as "Soviet AF 7")	
-	•	Yak-18A	-		(to Egyptian AF as 607)	
					recov. by Jean-Baptiste Salis, La Ferte Alais	.84
					Alain Capel, La Ferte Alais	88
				F-AZFK	R. Capel, La Ferte-Alais	11.89/91
					(flies as "54")	
-	•	Yak-18U	-		(to Egyptian AF as 627)	
					recov. by Jean-Baptiste Salis, La Ferte Alais	.84
				G-BMJY	Robs Lamplough, North Weald	1.86/90

- •	Yak-18A	-		(to Egyptian AF as 710)	
				recov. by Jean-Baptiste Salis, La Ferte Alais	.84
			HB-RBD	J-F. Perrin, Yverdon	31.3.89/91
				(rebuilt Switzerland: ff. 11.4.89; flies as "18")	
- •	LAGG-11	-		Warren Sessler/China Technologies	
				Aero Trader, Chino CA: arr. dism.	1.89
				Weeks Air Museum, Tamiami FL	89
532007 •	CJ-6A	-		(to Chinese AF as .....)	
			N18YA	reg.	12.90
				Alan L. Buchner, Fresno CA	92
532021 •	CJ-6A	-		(to Chinese AF as .....)	
			N41845	Starfighter Aerospace Co, Mineral Wells TX	5.91/92
				Walter Davidson & Rolf Yri, BC, Canada	92
832602 •	CJ-6A	-		(to Chinese AF as .....)	
			N7144H	reg.	7.90
832604 •	CJ-6A	-		(to Chinese AF as .....)	
			N7144F	reg.	7.90
0232012•	CJ-6A	-		(to Chinese AF as ....)	
			N31513	Bob Kantner, San Rafael CA	7.91/92
0232019•	CJ-6A	-		(to Chinese AF as ....)	
			N31103	Starfighter Aerospace Co, Mineral Wells TX	7.91/92
1032022•	CJ-6A	-		(to Chinese AF as ....)	
			N3104D	reg.	7.91
				Monty R. Yancey, Klamath Falls OR	92
1232028•	CJ-6A	-		(to Chinese AF as ....)	
			N5182C	Starfighter Aerospace.	10.92
1332008•	CJ-6A	-		(to Chinese AF as .....)	
			N4184G	Starfighter Aerospace Co, Mineral Wells TX	5.91
				Mike A. Rhodes, Corbett OR	92
1332010•	CJ-6A	-		(to Chinese AF as .....)	
			N99YK	Variety Aircraft Inc, Los Animas CO	10.91/92
1332012•	CJ-6A	-		(to Chinese AF as ....)	
			N51800	Starfighter Aerospace.	10.92
1332013•	CJ-6A	-		(to Chinese AF as ....)	
			N3110S	Starfighter Aerospace Co, Mineral Wells TX	7.91/92
				Joal Holdings, BC Canada	
1332014•	CJ-6A	-		(to Chinese AF as ....)	
			N3110W	Starfighter Aerospace Co, Mineral Wells TX	7.91/92
1332043•	CJ-6A	-		(to Chinese AF as 63)	
			N4184W	Starfighter Aerospace Co, Mineral Wells TX	5.91
				Ivan O. Rasmussen, Glendale AZ	92
1432049•	CJ-6A	-		(to Chinese AF as ....)	
			N3104U	reg.	7.91
				Frank M. Land, Klamath Falls OR	92
1532006•	CJ-6A	-		(to Chinese AF as ....)	
			N3105M	reg. res.	7.91/92
1832039•	CJ-6A	-		(to Chinese AF as 78)	
			N4183E	Starfighter Aerospace Co, Mineral Wells TX	5.91

				Ivan O. Rasmussen, Glendale AZ	92
1832040•	CJ-6A	-		(to Chinese AF as ....)	
			N3110Q	Starfighter Aerospace Co, Mineral Wells TX	7.91/92
2032007•	CJ-6A	-		(to Chinese AF as ....)	
			N5180W	Starfighter Aerospace.	10.92
2032008•	CJ-6A	-		(to Chinese AF as ....)	
			N5183F	Starfighter Aerospace.	10.92
2032011•	CJ-6A	-		(to Chinese AF as 82)	
			N4182C	Starfighter Aerospace Co, Mineral Wells TX	5.91
				Ivan O. Rasmussen, Glendale AZ	92
2032015•	CJ-6A	-		(to Chinese AF as ....)	
			N31101	W. R. Laws, Placerville CO	7.91/92
2032018•	CJ-6A	-		(to Chinese AF as .....)	
			N41836	Starfighter Aerospace Co, Mineral Wells TX	5.91
				W. R. Laws, Placerville CO	92
2032020•	CJ-6A	-		(to Chinese AF as ....)	
			N3110U	Starfighter Aerospace, Mineral Wells TX	7.91
				Richard A. Cunningham, Pekin IL	92
2132048•	CJ-6A	-		(to Chinese AF as 24)	
			VH-NNA	Brian Chandler/Lampa Holdings,Canberra ACT	7.90/91
				(assembled Bankstown NSW, ff 11.90)	
2232012•	CJ-6A	-		(to Chinese AF as .....)	
			N31513	Aero Trader, Chino CA	8.91
2232013•	CJ-6A	-		(to Chinese AF as 61668)	
			N4350D	Starfighter Aerospace Co, Mineral Wells TX	2.92
				Ivan Rasmussen, Glendale, AZ	92
2232036•	CJ-6A	-		(to Chinese AF as ....)	
			N3210R	Barclay C. Imle, Spring TX	1.92
				Crashed and destroyed (Imle k.)	6.92
2332009•	CJ-6A	-		(to Chinese AF as ....)	
			N3210N	Milo S. Turner, Fort Myers FL	1.92
2432051•	CJ-6A	-		(to Chinese AF as ....)	
			N31107	Starfighter Aerospace, Mineral Wells TX	7.91
				David A. Rieder, Glendale AZ	92
2532044•	CJ-6A	-		(to Chinese AF as 71887)	
			N4184S	Starfighter Aerospace	5.91
				Ivan Rasmussen, Glendale, AZ	92
				John Crothers, Prescott Valley AZ	10.92
2532045•	CJ-6A	-		(to Chinese AF as .....)	
			N41839	Starfighter Aerospace Co, Mineral Wells TX	5.91
				Frank M. Land, Klamath Falls OR	92
2532049•	CJ-6A	-		(to Chinese AF as ....)	
			N3112A	Starfighter Aerospace Co, Mineral Wells TX	7.91/92
2532051•	CJ-6A	-		(to Chinese AF as .....)	
			N42952	Robert B. Caldwell, Williams CA	9.91/92
2532060•	CJ-6A	-		(to Chinese AF as .....)	
			N4294X	Robert B. Caldwell, Williams CA	9.91/92
2532061•	CJ-6A	-		(to Chinese AF as .....)	
			N4295C	Robert B. Caldwell, Williams CA	9.91/92

2632034•	CJ-6A	-		(to Chinese AF as ....)	
			N66YK	Variety Aircraft Inc, Los Animas CO	10.91/92
2751248•	CJ-6A	-		(to Chinese AF as 76)	
			VH-NNC	Brian Chandler/Lampa Holdings,Canberra ACT	7.90/92
				(stored dism., Bankstown NSW)	
2951207•	CJ-6A	-		(to Chinese AF as ....)	
			N3210M	Marcus L. Bates, Odessa TX	1.92
2951208•	CJ-6A	-		(to Chinese AF as 46)	
			VH-NNB	Brian Chandler/Lampa Holdings,Canberra ACT	7.90/91
				(assembled Bankstown NSW .91)	
3151207•	CJ-6A	-		(to Chinese AF as ....)	
			N3210G	Marcus L. Bates, Odessa TX	1.92
- •	CJ-6A	-		(to Chinese AF as .....)	
			N7039Y	Ron Weaver/Silverwest Aviation, Buckeye AZ	.91
				op: Yak USA Ltd, Buckeye AZ	.91
				(flies as Chinese AF "76")	

WARBIRDS WORLDWIDE DIRECTORY
JETS SECTION

AERO L-29 DELFIN

591238 •	L-29	N3159Y	Mira Slovak Aerobatics Inc, Santa Paula CA	9.91/92
591311 •	L-29		(to Indonesian AF as LL2901)	
		N7150M	Erickson Air Crane Co, Central Point OR	5.90/92
591312 •	L-29		(to Indonesian AF as LL2902)	
		N7150J	Erickson Air Crane Co, Central Point OR	5.90/92
591317 •	L-29		(to Indonesian AF as LL2907)	
		N7150D	Erickson Air Crane Co, Central Point OR	5.90/92
591318 •	L-29		(to Indonesian AF as LL2908)	
		N7150A	Erickson Air Crane Co, Central Point OR	5.90/92
591319 •	L-29		(to Indonesian AF as LL2909)	
		N7149Z	Erickson Air Crane Co, Central Point OR	5.90
			Robert F. Yancey, Klamath Falls OR	92
591322 •	L-29		(to Indonesian AF as LL2912)	
		N7149X	Erickson Air Crane Co, Central Point OR	5.90/92
591324 •	L-29		(to Indonesian AF as LL2914)	
		N7149J	Erickson Air Crane Co, Central Point OR	5.90
			Robert F. Yancey, Klamath Falls OR	92
591328•	L-29		(to Indonesian AF as LL2918)	
		N7149E	Erickson Air Crane Co, Central Point OR	5.90/92
792405 •	L-29		(to Czech AF as 2405)	
		N29AD	Aero Taxi Inc, New Castle DE	7.91/92
892813 •	L-29		(to Czech AF as 2813)	
		N31088	Mira Slovak Aerobatics Inc, Santa Paula CA	7.91/92
892814 •	L-29		(to Czech AF as 2814): storage Vodochody	91
		N12DN	Aero Taxi Inc, New Castle DE	3.92
892815 •	L-29		(to Czech AF as 2815)	
			Mira Slovak Aerobatics Inc, Santa Paula CA	.90/91
892817 •	L-29		(to Czech AF as 2817)	
		N3098E	Mira Slovak Aerobatics Inc, Santa Paula CA	8.91/92
- •	L-29		(to Czech AF as ....)	
		OH-XXA	Mira Slovak Aerobatics Inc, Santa Paula CA	.90/91
			(testflown Vodochody, Czechoslovakia .90)	
- •	L-29	N3939L	Mira Slovak Aerobatics Inc, Santa Paula CA	4.90/92
			(FAA quote id. "0902")	
- •	L-29	N5959L	Delfin Group Inc, Santa Paula CA	4.90/92
			(FAA quote id. "0909")	

AERO L-39 ALBATROS

2314 •	L-39ZO			(to Libyan AF 2314) : captured by Chad AF	.87
			N4313Y	ntu	
			N162JC	Avstar Inc, Seattle WA	4.91
				Robs Lamplough, North Weald UK : del.	6.6.91
				sale rep., Zurich, Switzerland	11.91/92
232337 •	L-39ZO			(to Libyan AF 2337) : captured by Chad AF	.87
			N4312X	ntu	
			N159JC	Avstar Inc, Seattle WA	4.91
				Robs Lamplough, North Weald UK : del.	7.91
				sale rep., Zurich, Switzerland	92
..3549 •	L-39ZO			(to Libyan AF 3549)	
				captured by Chad AF at Ouadi Doum, Libya	.87
			N4312C	ntu	
			N157JC	Avstar Inc, Seattle WA	4.91/92
				(noted at Paris-Le Bourget 8.91)	
..8201 •	L-39ZO			(to Libyan AF 8201) : captured by Chad AF	.87
			N4312E	ntu	
			N158JC	Avstar Inc, Seattle WA	4.91/92
				Robs Lamplough, North Weald UK : del.	6.6.91
..8211 •	L-39ZO			(to Libyan AF 8211)	
				captured by Chad AF at Ouadi Doum, Libya	.87
			N43129	ntu	
			N160JC	Avstar Inc, Seattle WA	4.91/92
				(noted at Paris-Le Bourget 8.91)	
..8212 •	L-39ZO			(to Libyan AF 8212)	
				captured by Chad AF at Ouadi Doum, Libya	.87
			N4313T	ntu	
			N161JC	Avstar Inc, Seattle WA	4.91/92
				(noted at Paris-Le Bourget 8.91)	
..8229 •	L-39ZO			(to Libyan AF 8229)	
				captured by Chad AF at Ouadi Doum, Libya	.87
			N4313Z	ntu	
			N163JC	Avstar Inc, Seattle WA	4.91/92
				(noted at Paris-Le Bourget 8.91)	
533216 •	L-39ZO			(to Czech AF as ....)	
			OK-186	del. Prague to USA, via Prestwick	29.7.91
			N92JJ	Avstar Inc, Seattle WA	2.92
- •	L-39ZO			(to Czech AF as ....)	
			OK-GXA	noted La Ferte Alais, France	8.91
- •	L-39ZO			(to Libyan as .....) : captured by Chad AF	.87
			F-ZVLS	Michel Bidoux : arr Toussus-le Noble	7.91

BAC JET PROVOST

P84/6 •	T Mk. 1		G-AOBU	Hunting Aircraft Ltd, Luton	.56
				Shuttleworth Trust, Old Warden	70/91
				Loughborough University: loan	88/91
				stored, Old Warden : arr dism.	1.91
				T.J. Manna, London	9.92
P84/12 •	T. Mk.2		G-AOHD	(to RAAF as A99-001)	.59
				Sydney Technical College, Ultimo NSW	63/80
				Richard E. Hourigan, Melbourne VIC	83
				RAAF Museum, RAAF Point Cook VIC	85/92
K84-03/ 6523/4 •	T Mk.3A	XM405	G-TORE	Butane Buzzard Aviation, North Weald	14.6.91

K-84-03/ 6579/4 •	T.Mk. 3A	XM461		Lance Toland Associates, Griffin, GA	9.92
				rebuild to fly	
PAC/W 13901 •	T Mk. 3	XN637	G-BKOU	Vintage Aircraft Team, Cranfield	17.2.83/91
PAC/W 17635 •	T Mk. 52A	XP666		(to South Arabian AF as 107)	.67
				(to South Yemen AF as 107)	
				(to Singapore ADC as 355)	.78
			G-JETP	Brencham Historic Aircraft Co, Hurn	12.83/87
				(recov. ex Singapore, shipped to UK 11.83)	
				LGH Aviation Ltd, Hurn	1.10.87/91
				op. Jet Heritage/Hunter Wing, Hurn	
PAC/W 23905 •	T. 4 T Mk. 52A	XS228		British Aircraft Corp	18.1.67
				(to South Arabian AF as 104) : del.	16.10.67
				(to South Yemen AF as 104)	
				(to Singapore ADC as 352) BOC 2.75 last flt.	14.10.81
			G-PROV	Brencham Historic Aircraft Co, Hurn	12.83/87
				(shipped ex Singapore 11.83, ff Hurn 23.11.84)	
				LGH Aviation Ltd, Hurn	1.10.87/91
				op. Jet Heritage/Hunter Wing, Hurn	
29 • Mk. 84	Mk. 81		G-AXFX	British Aircraft Corporation, Preston	21.5.69
				(to South Yemeni AF as 504)	7.69
				(to Singapore ADC as 323)	
				International Air Parts, Sydney NSW	.89
				Wally Fisk/Amjet Services Int'l, St Paul MN	90/92
31 •	Mk. 82 Mk. 84			(to Oman AF as 402)	1.69
				(to Singapore ADC as 327)	
				International Air Parts, Sydney NSW	.89
				Wally Fisk/Amjet Services Int'l, St Paul MN	90/92
33 •	Mk. 82 Mk. 84			(to Oman AF as 404)	3.69
				(to Singapore ADC as 328)	
				International Air Parts, Sydney NSW	.89
				Wally Fisk/Amjet Services Int'l, St Paul MN	90/92
36 •	Mk. 82 Mk. 84			(to Oman AF as 407)	6.69
				(to Singapore ADC as 329)	
				Intyernational Air Parts, Sydney NSW	.89
				Wally Fisk/Amjet Services Int'l, St Paul MN	90/92
41 •	Mk. 84			(to Singapore ADC as 304)	
				International Air Parts, Sydney NSW	.89
				Wally Fisk/Amjet Services Int'l, St Paul MN	90/92
42 •	Mk. 84			(to Singapore ADC as 305)	
				International Air Parts, Sydney NSW	.89
				Wally Fisk/Amjet Services Int'l, St Paul MN	90/92
45 •	Mk. 84			(to Singapore ADC as 308)	
				International Air Parts, Sydney NSW	.89
				Wally Fisk/Amjet Services Int'l, St Paul MN	90/92
47 •	Mk. 84			(to Singapore ADC as 310)	
				International Air Parts, Sydney NSW	.89
				Wally Fisk/Amjet Services Int'l, St Paul MN	90/92
48 •	Mk. 84			(to Singapore ADC as 311)	
				International Air Parts, Sydney NSW	.89
				Wally Fisk/Amjet Services Int'l, St Paul MN	90/92
49 •	Mk. 84			(to Singapore ADC as 312)	
				International Air Parts, Sydney NSW	.89
				Wally Fisk/Amjet Services Int'l, St Paul MN	90/92

BAC Jet Provost/Strikemaster

51 •	Mk. 84		G-AYHS	British Aircraft Corporation, Preston	22.7.70
				(to Singapore ADC as 314)	10.70
				International Air Parts, Sydney NSW	.89
				Wally Fisk/Amjet Services Int'l, St Paul MN	90/92
52 •	Mk. 84		G-AYHT	British Aircraft Corporation, Preston	22.7.70
				(to Singapore ADC as 315)	10.70
				Steve Ferris/International Air Parts, Sydney NSW	.89/92
				(rest. to fly, Bankstown Airport NSW)	
53 •	Mk. 82			(to Oman AF as 408)	12.69
				(to Singapore ADC as 330)	
				International Air Parts, Sydney NSW	.89
				Wally Fisk/Amjet Services Int'l, St Paul MN	90/92
54 •	Mk. 82			(to Oman AF as 409)	12.69
				(to Singapore ADC as 331)	
				International Air Parts, Sydney NSW	.89
				Wally Fisk/Amjet Services Int'l, St Paul MN	90/92
- •	Mk. 81			(to S. Yemen AF as 50...)	c69
				(to Singapore ADC as 322)	
				International Air Parts, Sydney NSW	.89
				Wally Fisk/Amjet Services Int'l, St Paul MN	90/92

BELL P-59 AIRACOMET

27-10 •	YP-59A	42-108777		to instructional airframe at trade school	
				The Air Museum, Claremont CA	3.58/60
				The Air Museum, Ontario/Chino CA	60/90
				(rebuild to fly) Chino, CA	92
- •	XP-59A	42-108784		NASM, Washington DC	65/88
				displ. as "Miss Fire/1"	
BE-6 •	P-59A	44-22614		Hancock College Aeronautics, Santa Maria CA	.48
				noted Van Nuys CA: USAF sc. "88"	3.50
				Los Angeles Trade Technical School	
				Jack P. Hardwick, El Monte CA: stored yard	.60/76
				Ascher Ward, Van Nuys CA	.76
				USAFM, March AFB CA	.77/90
- •	P-59B	44-22633		displ. on pole at Edwards AFB CA	69/90
				Flight Test Historical Museum, Edwards AFB	88/92
- •	P-59B	44-22650		stored Kirtland AFB NM	55/56
				USAFM, Wright-Patterson AFB, Dayton OH	2.56/90
- •	P-59B	44-22656		(to USN as Bu64108)	
				Harold Warp Pioneer Village, Minden NB	65/88

CONVAIR F-102 DELTA DAGGER

-	F-102A	56-0998	N617NA	NASA, Lewis Research Center	78
- •	F-102A	56-1116	N8970	School District 1, Helena MT	10.70/91
				Helena Vocational Tech. College, Helena MT	6.91
-	F-102A	57-0835	N300	FAA, Oklahoma City OK	70
				stored MASDC, Davis Monthan AFB AZ by	8.71

CANADAIR CL-41 TUTOR

1072	CL-41A	CAF114072	C-GVQX	Canadair Ltd, Montreal QUE	81/82
				(Challenger chase plane, based Mojave CA)	
2201 •	CL-41G			(to R. Malaysian AF as 2208)	
			N21527	Avstar Inc, Seattle WA	12.89
			N401AG	Aero Flight Services Inc, Ypsilanti MI	1.91/92
2202 •	CL-41G			(to R. Malaysian AF as 2209)	
			N2153R	Avstar Inc, Seattle WA	12.89
			N402AG	Aero Flight Services, Ypsilanti MI	1.91/92
2205 •	CL-41G			(to R. Malaysian AF as FM2211)	
			N2153V	Avstar Inc, Seattle WA	1.90
				Aero Flight Services Inc, Ypsilanti MI	91/92
-	CL-41A		CF-OUM	*no further information*	

CESSNA A-37

40046 •	T-37B	56-3474		Thunderbird Aviation Inc, Deer Valley AZ	92
				(noted under conv., Phoenix-Deer Valley AZ 92)	
40053	T-37B	56-3480		(to FA Panama as FAP.......)	
				recov. Panama by David Brady	c85
			N120DB	David Brady, Cartersville GA	8.87/91
				(flew as USAF "63480/Georgia Tweet")	
				crashed after mid-air collision with A-26,	
				near Cartersville GA (Brady k.)	7.6.91
40055 •	T-37B	56-3482		Lone Star Flight Museum, Galveston TX	91/92
	A-37A	67-14534		(rest. to fly, Phoenix AZ)	
40056 •	T-37B	56-3483	N3757U	Thunderbird Aviation Inc, Deer Valley AZ	83/92
	A-37A	67-14535			
40059 •	T-37B	56-3486	N3757Z	Thunderbird Aviation Inc, Deer Valley AZ	83/90
	A-37A	67-14537			
40087 •	T-37B	56-3515		(to F.A. Peru as ....)	
			N7154Y	Air Acres Museum, Cartersville GA	13.9.91
				(FAP446,458,492,494 at Cartersville 12.90)	
				Reva J. Brady, Cartersville GA	92
40152 •	T-37B	56-3580		(to F.A. Peru as ....)	
			N6528G	Air Acres Museum, Cartersville GA	13.9.91
				Reva J. Brady, Cartersville GA	92
-	T-37B	60-0084	N807NA	NASA	
40974 •	T-37C	66-13618		(to F.A. Peru as ....)	
			N7154W	Air Acres Museum, Cartersville GA	13.9.91
				Reva J. Brady, Cartersville GA	92
40976 •	T-37C	66-13620		(to F.A. Peru as ....)	
			N6527M	Air Acres Museum, Cartersville GA	13.9.91
				Reva J. Brady, Cartersville GA	92
41049 •	T-37C	-	N7081C	E. H. Wachs, Harrison MT	92
41221 •	T-37C	-	N3127M	E. H. Wachs, Harrison MT	92
43156 •	A-37B	68-10805		(to SVNAF as 68-10805)	
				(recov. from Bien Hoa, Vietnam by Col Pay,	
				Scone NSW : arr. Sydney by ship 11.89)	
				David Lowy, Sydney NSW	.89/92
			VH-DLO	David Lowy/DL Aviation, Sydney NSW	29.4.92

				(rest. Scone NSW, ff 1.5.92)	
43158 •	A-37B	68-10807		(to SVNAF as 68-10807) (recov. from Bien Hoa, Vietnam by Col Pay, Scone NSW : arr. Sydney by ship 11.89) Hugh Farris, Narrabri NSW	 90/92
43255 •	A-37B	69-6410		(to SVNAF as 69-06410) (recov. from Bien Hoa, Vietnam by Col Pay, Scone NSW : arr. Sydney by ship 11.89 Col Pay/Pays Air Service, Scone NSW (id. quoted as "70-69410")	 .89/92
43328 •	A-37B	71-0790		(to SVNAF as 71-0790) M. Perrin, La Ferte Alais, France: arr dism.	 5.90
43372 •	A-37B	71-0834		(to SVNAF as 71-0834) M. Perrin, La Ferte Alais, France: arr dism.	 5.90
43392 •	A-37B	71-0854		(to SVNAF as 71-0854) Bruce Black, Auckland, New Zealand	 .91/92
- •	A-37A	-		(to SVNAF as ....) (recov. from Bien Hoa,Vietnam by Col Pay, Scone NSW : arr. Sydney by ship 11.89) Noel R. Vinson/Australian Aviation Salvage, Bankstown Airport, Sydney NSW	 .89/92
- •	A-37A	-		(to SVNAF as ....) (recov. from Bien Hoa,Vietnam by Col Pay, Scone NSW : arr. Sydney by ship 11.89) Noel R. Vinson/Australian Aviation Salvage, Bankstown Airport, Sydney NSW	 .89/92
- •	T-37C	-		(to F.A. Brasileira as 0897) FAB Museum Stacy Prineas, Redmond OR (shipped to US via Honduras, offered at auction, dism. unconv., Santa Monica CA 10.91) (built 22.7.68; also rep. ex F.A. Guatamala)	 .91 .91

CONVAIR F-106 DELTA DART

- •	NF-106B	57-2507	N607NA N607NM	NASA, Lewis Research Center, Cleveland OH NASA, Lewis Research Center, Cleveland OH struck-off USCR	11.9.72 8.83/87 8.87
- •	NF-106B	57-2516	N616NA N816NA	NASA, Lewis Research Center, Cleveland OH NASA, Edwards AFB, CA VA Air & Space Museum, Hampton VA : del.	15.7.69 5.79/91 30.4.91

DASSAULT MYSTERE IVA

No. 315	Mk.1VA	No.315	F-AZDF	Roland Fraissinet/Ailes Anciennes, Marseilles	9.83/89

DE HAVILLAND DH-110 SEA VIXEN

110145 •	FAW. 2TT	XS587	G-VIXN	Brencham Historic Aircraft Ltd, Hurn Peter G. Vallance/Vallance By-Ways Museum, Charlwood : displ.	5.8.85/90 6.9.90/92

NOTED AN ERROR OR OMISSION? PLEASE TELL US ABOUT IT BY WRITING TO:

WARBIRDS WORLDWIDE, P.O. Box 99, Mansfield, Notts NG19 9GU ENGLAND,

EEP	F Mk.3	RCAF17018	N6881D	Merle C. Zuehlke/Fliteways Inc, West Bend WI	.57/58
42310 •				Dave White, Carpenteria CA	63
				William H. Boyce, Pomona CA	66
				(stored, derelict, Santa Barbara CA 66)	
				Roland G. Holmes Company, Long Beach CA	69
				Ed Maloney/The Air Museum, Chino CA: dism.	77/92
EEP	F Mk.3	RCAF17020	N6863D	Merle C. Zuehlke/Fliteways Inc, West Bend WI	.57/58
42312 •				James Cook, Milwaukee WI	66/69
				Gateway Technical Institute, Kenosha WI	75/77
				Crosby Enterprises Inc, Milwaukee WI	
				Canadian Warplane Heritage, Hamilton ONT	81/84
				(stored dism., Hamilton ONT)	
				Reynolds Aviation Museum, Wetaskiwin ALTA	88/92
- •	F Mk.3	RCAF17031	N41J	Stinson Field Aircraft, San Antonio TX	.56/59
				W. H. Boyce, Ramona CA	66
				Roland G Holmes, Long Beach CA	69
				(open storage, derelict, Long Beach CA 69/72)	
				Western Aerospace Museum, Lancaster CA	73
				Al Hansen, Mojave CA	77/82
				Bill Lamberton/Pacific Flying Service,	
				Everett-Paine Field WA	.82/92
				(8 year rebuild, ff Arlington WA 12.4.91,	
				flies as "17031/SL-031")	
EEP	F Mk.3	RCAF17058	N6860D	Merle C. Zuehlke/Fliteways Inc, West Bend WI	4.3.58
42376 •				Dewey-Shepard Boiler Co, Peru IN	
				George D. Arnold, Peru IN	66/69
				Calgary Air Museum, Calgary ALTA : dism.	c68
				Don Campbell, Kapuskasing ONT : dism.	.70/82
				Canadian Museum of Flight & Transportation	
				Vancouver BC : arr. dism.	19.9.82/92
EEP	F Mk.3	RCAF17062	N6885D	Merle C. Zuehlke/Fliteways Inc, West Bend WI	.57/58
42380 •				E. H. Roybal, Livermore CA	66/69
				(noted derelict, Santa Ana CA 6.73)	
				Letcher & Associates, Lancaster CA	.73/81
				stored dism., Mojave CA	74/81
EEP	F Mk.3	RCAF17069	N6877D	Merle C. Zuehlke/Fliteways Inc, West Bend WI	.57/59
42387 •				Ken Cook Publishing Co, Milwaukee WI	63
			CF-RLK	Milt Harradance, Calgary ALTA	.64/65
				Centennial Planetarium, Calgary ALTA	72/88
				Aero Space Museum of Calgary ALTA	88/92
EEP	F Mk.3	RCAF17071	N6883D	Merle C. Zuehlke/Fliteways Inc, West Bend WI	.57/58
42389 •				E. H. Roybal, Livermore CA	66/69
				(noted derelict, Santa Ana CA 6.73)	
				Letcher & Associates, Lancaster CA	.73/77
				(stored dism., Mojave CA 74/79)	
				Flight Research Inc, State College MS	86
				Reynolds Aviation Museum, Wetaskiwin ALTA	92
EEP	F Mk.3	RCAF17072	N6878D	Merle C. Zuehlke/Fliteways Inc, West Bend WI	.57/58
42390 •				John E. Morgan, Pittsburg PA	.58
				(flew as "Johny Rocket")	
				Frank G. Tallman, Orange County CA	.59
				displ. Movieland of the Air : "Golden Eagle"	59/68
				Rosen Novak Auto Co, Omaha NE	66/68
				(sold at Tallmantz auction 29.5.68)	
				James F. Brucker, Somis CA	29.5.68/69
				Jet Craft Inc , Las Vegas NV	70
				(planned conv. to 8 passenger "Mystery Jet")	

				Pete Regina, Van Nuys CA : del.	12.70/73
				(rebuilt Van Nuys, ff 8.4.72 as "VN68/YG")	
				Al Letcher & Associates, Lancaster CA	.73/81
				John T. Downing, Cumming GA	86
				Greater Leasing Inc, Marietta GA	12.87
				Randall K. Hames, Gaffney SC	4.88/89
				John Travolta/Atlo Inc, Studio City CA	10.89/92
-	FB. Mk.9	-		(to R. Rhodesian AF: Zimbabwe AF as R1378)	
				retired, stored ZAFB Gwelo	80/88
				Hosking/Judy Pay syndicate, Melbourne VIC	.88/92
				(shipped dism., arr. Melbourne VIC 12.88)	
-	FB. Mk.9	-		(to R. Rhodesian AF: Zimbabwe AF as R1829)	
				retired, stored ZAFB Gwelo	80/88
				Hosking/Judy Pay syndicate, Melbourne VIC	.88/92
				(shipped dism., arr. Melbourne VIC 12.88)	
-	FB. Mk.9	-		(to R. Rhodesian AF: Zimbabwe AF as R1832)	
				retired, stored ZAFB Gwelo	80/88
				Hosking/Judy Pay syndicate, Melbourne VIC	.88/92
				(shipped dism., arr. Melbourne VIC 12.88)	
-	FB. Mk.9	-		(to R. Rhodesian AF: Zimbabwe AF as R1835)	
				retired, stored ZAFB Gwelo	80/88
				Hosking/Judy Pay syndicate, Melbourne VIC	.88/92
				(shipped dism., arr. Melbourne VIC 12.88)	
-	FB. Mk.9	-		(to R. Rhodesian AF: Zimbabwe AF as R1828)	
				retired, stored ZAFB Gwelo	80/88
				Hosking/Judy Pay syndicate, Melbourne VIC	.88/92
				(shipped dism., arr. Melbourne VIC 12.88)	
				(also rep. as ZAF R8128)	
22100 •	FB. Mk.9	WL505		RAF Museum, RAF St Athan	87/89
				D. G. Jones : sold at auction	21.4.89
			G-FBIX	D. G. Jones, Bridgend, Wales	24.7.91/92
				(rest. to fly, Cranfield)	
15127 •	T Mk. 11	WZ507	G-VTII	J. Turnbull & S. Topen, Duxford	9.1.80
				Vintage Aircraft Team, Cranfield	85/92
				(flies as "WZ507")	
- •	T Mk. 11	XD538	N70877	Laub America Corp, Carmel CA	84/86
				(noted Marana AZ as "N77087" 10.84)	
				Wesley D. O'Dell, Dana Point CA	8.87
				William G. Dilley/Spectra Sonics, Ogden UT	2.88/92
			N675LF	ntu: Gregory Dilley, Ogden UT	7.88
			N70877	William G. Dilley, Ogden UT	90/92
15641 •	Sea Vamp. T Mk. 22	XG766		(to RAN as XG766; N6-766) ex NAS Nowra	16.9.71
				Chewing Gum Field Air Mus.,Tallebudgera QLD	.72/89
			VH-RAN	Kim Rolph-Smith, Brisbane QLD	.89
				Ian Aviation, Bankstown NSW : stored	90/92
15679 •	T Mk. 55	XH271		(to RNZAF as NZ5709)	
			ZK-TII	G. S. Smith, Auckland New Zealand	84/89
- •	T Mk. 11	XK623	G-VAMP	Brencham Historic Aircraft, Hurn	84
				(planned rest. to fly)	84
				Snowdon Mountain Aviation Mus., Caernarfon	90
15765 •	T Mk. 55			(to Irish AC as 186)	
				noted stored, Tucson AZ	11.81
			N4861K	Laub America Corp, Carmel CA	84/87

				Wesley D. O'Dell, Dana Point CA	8.87
				William G. Dilley/Spectra Sonics, Ogden UT	7.88/92
4123 •	T Mk. 35	A79-602		disposal ex RAAF Laverton VIC (TT 2925)	17.6.70
			N11920	Westair International, Broomfield CO: USCR not imported to USA	8.70/90
				Pearce Dunn/Warbirds Aviation Museum, Mildura VIC	80/83
				Lincoln Nitschke/Military & Historic Aircraft Collection, Parafield/Greenock SA	9.83/92
4135 •	T Mk. 35	A79-613		disposal ex RAAF Laverton VIC (TT2894)	17.6.70
			N11921	Westair International, Broomfield CO	8.70/71
				Arthur W. McDonnell, Mojave CA	.72
				Ascher Ward, Van Nuys CA	82/83
				Alan G. Preston, Dallas TX	7.83
				Preston Air Museum, Dallas TX	3.86
				J. Duncan/Microjet Airshows, Miami FL	86
				William G. Dilley/Spectra Sonics, Ogden UT	2.87/90
4138 •	T Mk. 35	A79-616		disposal ex RAAF Laverton VIC (TT1945)	17.6.70
			N11922	Westair International, Broomfield CO	8.70/71
				Curtis Everett, Gretra LA	76
				stored unconv. dism., Tucson AZ	76/78
				James F. Moody, Atascadero CA	86/90
4139 •	T Mk. 35	A79-617		disposal ex RAAF Laverton VIC (TT2809)	17.6.70
			N11923	Westair International, Broomfield CO	8.70/72
				Arthur W. McDonnell, Lancaster CA	76
				Firebird Enterprises, Middlefield OH	6.84/88
				Ohio Associated Enterprises, Painesville OH	.88/90
4140 •	T Mk. 35	A79-618		disposal ex RAAF Laverton VIC (TT2605)	17.6.70
			N11924	Westair International, Broomfield CO	8.70/72
				Robert A. Mitchum, Broomfield CO	.72
				Crosby Enterprises Inc, Wauwatosa WI	76
				Vampire Mk.35W Inc, Miami FL	3.84
				Preston Air Museum Inc, Dallas TX	2.85/86
				J. Duncan/Microjet Airshows, Miami FL	4.86/88
				Sherman Aircraft Sales, West Palm Beach FL	2.88
				Red Stevenson, Haskell OK	5.89
				Ernest J. Saviano, Arlington TX : "Shamu"	1.90
4146 •	T Mk. 35	A79-624		disposal ex RAAF Laverton VIC (TT2475)	17.6.70
			N11925	Westair International, Broomfirld CO	8.70/72
				(noted under assembly, Oakland CA 2.71)	
				Mercer Aviation Inc, Kalamazoo MI	72
				Lawrence W. Borret, Las Vegas NV	76
				(noted derelict, Van Nuys CA 78)	
				(conv. Las Vegas to 8-seater "Mystery Jet")	
				Don Bateman, Las Vegas NV	86/90
				(open storage, Las Vegas 90)	
4153 •	T Mk. 35	A79-631		disposal ex RAAF Laverton VIC (TT2636)	17.6.70
			N11926	Westair International, Broomfield CO	8.70/72
				Edwin Dye, Devine TX	76
				Wayne Dye Inc, Helotes TX	18.8.78/87
				Charles R. Parnell/Mission Motors, Universal City TX	1.87/90
				Combat Jets Flying Museum, Houston TX (flies in Zimbabwe AF sc.)	.90/92
				EAA Aviation Foundation, Oshkosh WI	.92
4157 •	T Mk. 35	A79-635		disposal ex RAAF Laverton VIC (TT1964)	17.6.70
			N11927	Westair International, Broomfield CO	8.70/72
			N35DS	Dennis M. Sherman, West Palm Beach FL	72

				Country Club Investment Co, Fairmont WV	76/90
4158 •	T Mk. 35	A79-636		RAAF Museum, RAAF Point Cook VIC	75/88
			VH-HLF	RAAF Heritage Flight, RAAF Point Cook VIC	25.2.88/92
				(ff RAAF Laverton VIC 28.2.88 as "A79-636")	
4159 •	T Mk. 35	A79-637		disposal ex RAAF Laverton VIC (TT1944)	17.6.70
				Arnold J. Glass, Bankstown NSW	8.70
				Jeremy Flynn/Jecani Pty Ltd, Bankstown	80/92
				(stored Bankstown, rest. project)	
4161 •	T Mk. 35	A79-639		disposal ex RAAF Laverton VIC (TT2627)	17.6.70
			N11928	Westair International, Broomfield CO	8.70/76
				Patrick Donovan, Seattle WA	84
				Museum of Flight, Seattle WA : stored dism.	.84/88
4166 •	T Mk. 35	A79-644		disposal ex RAAF Laverton VIC (TT2514)	17.6.70
			N11929	Westair International, Broomfield CO	8.70/72
				Dayton Air Taxi, Dayton OH	76/87
				Indiana Museum of Military History, Indianapolis IN	.87/90
4167 •	T Mk. 35	A79-645		disposal ex RAAF Laverton VIC (TT2716)	17.6.70
			N11930	Westair International, Broomfield CO	8.70/72
				Age Leasing Corp	25.3.74
				John O. Sheeran, Plum City WI	76
				Edward C. Stead, Bedford & Manchester NH	1.83/91
				(flies as RAF "WH930/ES930")	
4168 •	T Mk. 35	A79-646		disposal ex RAAF Laverton VIC (TT1024)	17.6.70
			N11931	Westair International, Broomfield CO	8.70/72
				Robert R. Redding, Houston TX	72
				Redding International Inc, Houston TX	84/86
				Rick E. Sharpe, Manvel TX	87/88
				FOAG Inc, Breckenridge TX	6.89/92
4171 •	T Mk. 35	A79-649		disposal ex RAAF Laverton VIC (TT2536)	17.6.70
				Arnold J. Glass, Bankstown NSW	8.70/80
			VH-ICP	Jeremy Flynn/Jecani Pty Ltd, Bankstown	26.9.86/90
				(rest. Bankstown, ff 19.9.86)	
			ZK-VAM	Ross Ewing/Vampire Syndicate, Ardmore NZ	11.90/92
				(del. via Brisbane 20.11.90)	
4176 •	T Mk. 35	A79-654		disposal ex RAAF Laverton VIC (TT1998)	17.6.70
			N11932	Westair International, Broomfield CO	8.70/71
				Mercer Aviation, Kalamazoo MI	72
				Jimmie Moe	22.7.74
				Don Bateman, Las Vegas NV	74/84
				Mark E. Foster, Aurora CO	86
				Bill Lamberton, Mercer Island WA	2.87/89
				Bill Lamberton/Jet Jockey Squadron Inc., Mercer Island WA	5.89/91
				Bill Lamberton/Pacific Flying Services, Mercer Island WA	7.91
4179 •	T Mk. 35	A79-657		disposal ex RAAF Laverton VIC (TT1948)	17.6.70
			N11933	Westair International, Broomfield CO	8.70/72
				Bradley Air Museum, Windsor Locks CT	74/84
				New England Air Museum, Windsor Locks CT	.84/89
				Louis Alex, Rockland ME	.89
			N6528Z	reg.	11.90
- •	T Mk. 55	-		(to Indian AF as BY385)	

				N172LA	Lance Aircraft Supply Inc, Dallas TX	12.86/90
					Allen Dunn & Frank Kirchoff/	
					A & F Entertainment Inc, Wilmington DE	2.90/92
-	•	T Mk. 55			(to Indian AF as IB882)	
				N173LA	Lance Aircraft Supply Inc, Dallas TX	12.86/89
					Reid Moorhead, Alhambra CA	7.89/90
					sale rep. (rebuild to fly, Chino CA 92)	92
-	•	T Mk. 55			(to Indian AF as IB1686)	
				N174LA	Lance Aircraft Supply Inc, Dallas TX	12.86/88
					Donald L. Fitzgerald, Aloha OR	4.88/92
-	•	T Mk.11	-		(to R. Rhodesian AF: Zimbabwe AF as R2424)	
					Hosking/Judy Pay syndicate, Melbourne VIC	.88/92
					(shipped dism., arr. Melbourne VIC 12.88)	
-	•	T Mk.11	-		(to R. Rhodesian AF: Zimbabwe AF as R4221)	
					Hosking/Judy Pay syndicate, Melbourne VIC	.88/92
					(shipped to Melbourne 12.88; rebuilt Tyabb,	
					due for ff .92 as "RRAF119/4221")	
				VH-ZVZ	Judy Pay/Mount Sherman Pty Ltd, Melbourne	4.5.92
993	•	FB Mk.6	J-1082		sold at auction, Dubendorf AB	23.1.91
				HB-RVE	E. Wildhaber AG, Altenrhein	30.8.91/92
610	•	FB Mk.6	J-1101		sold at auction, Dubendorf AB	23.1.91
				F-AZHY	B. Vuraillot	.91
611	•	FB Mk.6	J-1102		sold at auction, Dubendorf AB	23.1.91
					H. Weisskopff, Switzerland	23.1.91
					(del. to North Weald UK 3.10.91: then crated)	
					Kermit A. Weeks, Tamiami FL	.91
					(shipped ex UK to Fort Lauderdale FL 10.91)	
				N100VJ	Vampire Aeronautic Corp, Delray Beach FL	12.91/92
612	•	FB Mk.6	J-1103		sold at auction, Dubendorf AB	23.1.91
					to USA	.91
624	•	FB Mk.6	J-1115		sold at auction, Dubendorf AB	23.1.91
					Jean Salis, La Ferte-Alais France	23.1.91
				F-AZHX	B. Vuraillot	.91
636	•	FB Mk.6	J-1127		sold at auction, Dubendorf AB	23.1.91
				F-AZOO	Aero Dimat, Nantes	.91
638	•	FB Mk.6	J-1129		sold at auction, Dubendorf AB	23.1.91
					(del. Dubendorf to Duxford UK 28.8.91)	
					Worldwide Jet Management, Chino CA	91
					sold to USA, crated ex Duxford	20.9.91
				N4024S	Ray Dieckman/Air Museum, Cincinatti OH	2.92
-	•	FB Mk.6	J-1140		sold at auction, Dubendorf AB	23.1.91
					Weeks Air Museum, Tamiami FL	23.1.91
					(del. North Weald UK 11.9.91: crated to USA)	
652	•	FB Mk.6	J-1143		sold at auction, Dubendorf AB	23.1.91
				F-AZHI	Yves Duval, Rennes	.91/92
-	•	FB Mk.6	J-1146		sold at auction, Dubendorf AB	23.1.91
					Oyvind Ellingsen/Warbirds of Norway, Oslo	23.1.91
					(del. Dubendorf AB - Oslo 3.7.91)	
658	•	FB Mk.6	J-1149		sold at auction, Dubendorf AB	23.1.91
					Jet Heritage/Hunter Wing Ltd, Hurn	23.1.91
				G-SWIS	Hunter Wing Ltd, Hurn : del.	10.5.91/92

661	•	FB Mk.6	J-1152		sold at auction, Dubendorf AB	23.1.91
					(del. Dubendorf to Duxford UK 28.8.91)	
					sold to USA, crated ex Duxford	20.9.91
				N152RD	Ray Dieckman/Air Museum, Cincinatti OH	2.92
					(shipped to Chino CA, ff 21.3.92 as "J-1152")	
668	•	FB Mk.6	J-1159		sold at auction, Dubendorf AB	23.1.91
				F-AZHJ	Gerald Marie-Berger/Assoc. Varoise Avions	
					de Collection, Cuers	9.91/92
					(flies as French AF "VZ221/4-LF)	
673	•	FB Mk.6	J-1164		sold at auction, Dubendorf AB	23.1.91
				SE-DXY	Scandinavian Historic Flight	.91/92
676	•	FB Mk.6	J-1167		sold at auction, Dubendorf AB	23.1.91
					Sandy Topen, Cranfield UK	23.1.91/92
					(del. to Cranfield 8.8.91)	
682	•	FB Mk.6	J-1173		sold at auction, Dubendorf AB	23.1.91
					Don Woods, Southampton UK	23.1.91
				G-DHXX	Lindsay Woods Promotions Ltd, Cranfield: del.	7.8.91/92
687	•	FB Mk.6	J-1178		sold at auction, Dubendorf AB	23.1.91
					Michael Pont/Savigny Les Beaunes Museum,	
					Dijon France : maintained airworthy	.91/92
-	•	FB Mk.6	J-1184		sold at auction, Dubendorf AB	23.1.91
				SE-DXY	Scandinavian Historic Flight, Norrkopping	23.1.91/92
					(arr. Duxford UK 8.9.91)	
-	•	FB Mk.6	J-1191		sold at auction, Dubendorf AB	23.1.91
					del. to Nimes-Garons, France	.91
-	•	FB Mk.6	J-1192		sold at auction, Dubendorf AB	23.1.91
					del. to Sion, Switzerland : rest. to fly	.91
-	•	FB Mk.6	J-1196		sold at auction, Dubendorf AB	23.1.91
					del. to Nimes, France	.91
708	•	FB Mk.6	J-1199		sold at auction, Dubendorf AB	23.1.91
				F-AZHH	Messrs Langeard & deRanieri/	
					Association Atlantic, Caen	.91/92
-	•	T Mk.55	U-1204		sold at auction, Dubendorf AB	23.3.91
					Gilbert Villa/Nimes-Garons, France	.91
866	•	T Mk.55	U-1206		sold at auction, Dubendorf AB	23.3.91
					(del. to North Weald UK 11.9.91: then crated)	
					Kermit Weeks, Tamiami FL	.91
					(shipped to Fort Lauderdale FL ex UK 11.11.91)	
				N115DH	Vampire Aeronautic Corp, Delray Beach FL	12.91/92
868	•	T Mk.55	U-1208		sold at auction, Dubendorf AB	23.3.91
				HB-RVF	A-Jet Ltd, Altenrhein	3.9.91/92
870	•	T Mk.55	U-1210		sold at auction, Dubendorf AB	23.3.91
				F-AZHU	Yves Duval, Rennes-St. Jaques	12.91/92
772	•	T Mk.55	U-1212		sold at auction, Dubendorf AB	23.3.91
				SE-DXT	NFZ-Flyg AB, Eskilstuna	25.10.91
973	•	T Mk.55	U-1213		sold at auction, Dubendorf AB	23.3.91
				N935HW	Paul McMinn/IMP Inc, Coatesville PA	8.91/92

Continued on Page 448

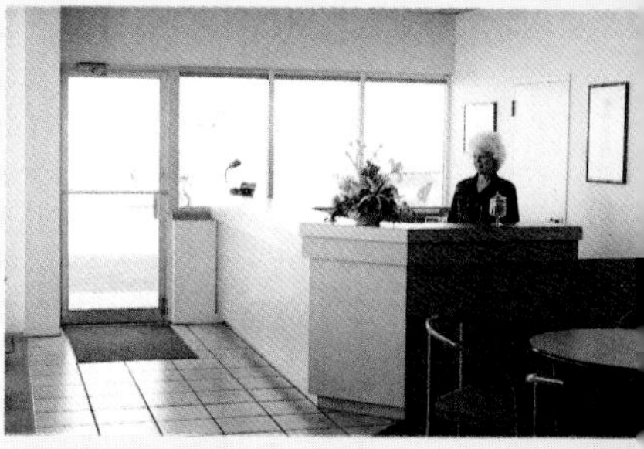

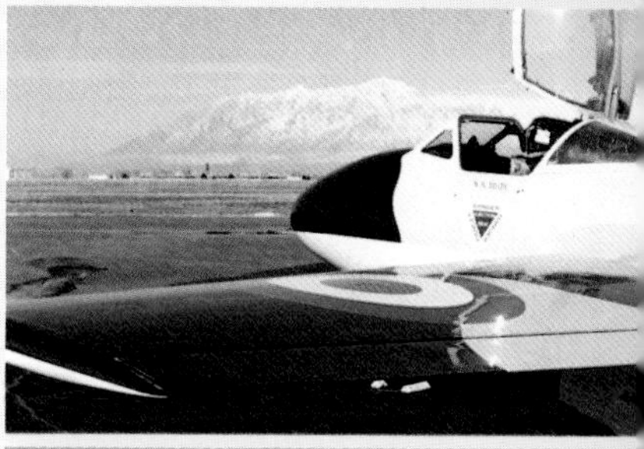

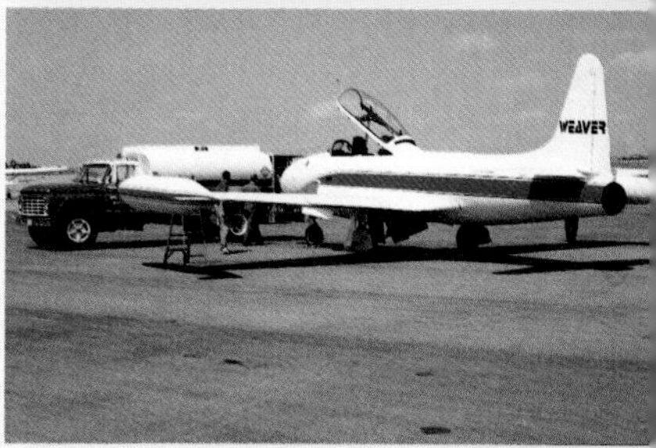

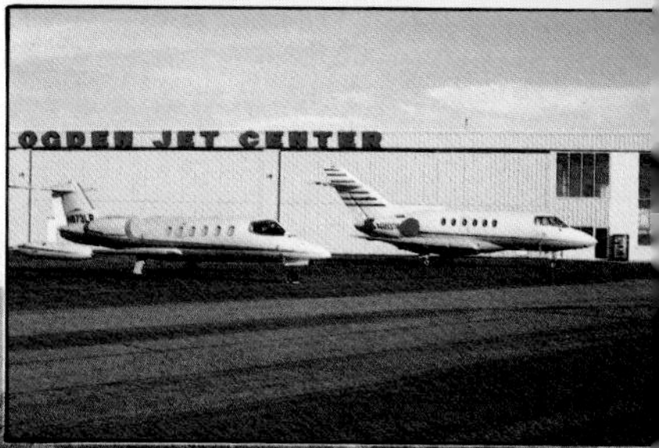

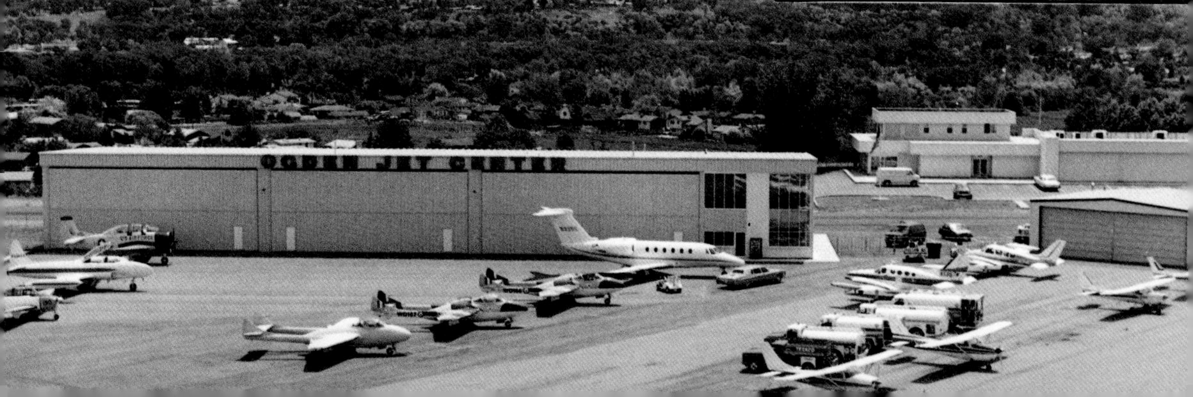

Continued from Page 446

				(del. to USA, ex Cranfield UK 16.9.91)	
55092 •	T Mk.55	U-1214		sold at auction, Dubendorf AB	23.3.91
				Don Woods, Southampton	23.3.91
			G-DHVV	Lindsay Woods Promotions Ltd, Cranfield	5.9.91/92
975 •	T Mk.55	U-1215		old at auction, Dubendorf AB	23.3.91
				Jet Heritage/Hunter Wing Ltd, Hurn	23.3.91
			G-HELV	Hunter Wing Ltd, Hurn : del.	28.8.91/92
- •	T Mk.55	U-1216		RAF Benevolent Fund	.90/92
				(stored RAF Boscombe Down as "ZH563": for sale)	
- •	T Mk.55	U-1218		sold at auction, Dubendorf AB	23.3.91
				Monte Tamaro SA, Rivera, Switzerland	.91/92
979 •	T Mk.55	U-1219		sold at auction, Dubendorf AB	23.3.91
				Don Woods, Southampton	23.3.91
			G-DHWW	Lindsay Woods Promotions Ltd, Cranfield	5.9.91/92
980 •	T Mk.55	U-1220		sold at auction, Dubendorf AB	23.3.91
				Randall K. Hames, Cliffside NC	23.3.91
			N391RH	Randall K. Hames, Gaffney SC	16.9.91/92
				del. to USA, ex Cranfield UK 16.9.91	
981 •	T Mk.55	U-1221	SE-DXV	Swedish Air Force Museum	.91/92
983 •	T Mk.55	U-1223		sold at auction, Dubendorf AB	23.3.91
			F-AZHV	Yves Duval, Rennes	.91
987 •	T Mk.55	U-1227		sold at auction, Dubendorf AB	23.3.91
				Gilbert Villa, Nimes-Garons, France : del.	.91
988 •	T Mk.55	U-1228		sold at auction, Dubendorf AB	23.3.91
			HB-RVJ	Custox AG, Bern	.91
989 •	T Mk.55	U-1229		sold at auction, Dubendorf AB	23.3.91
			F-AZGU	Y. Descamps, Cannes-Mandelieu	.91/92
990 •	T Mk.55	U-1230		sold at auction, Dubendorf AB	23.3.91
				Don Woods, Southampton	23.3.91
			G-DHZZ	Lindsay Woods Promotions Ltd, Cranfield: del.	7.8.91/92
994 •	T Mk.55	U-1234		sold at auction, Dubendorf AB	23.3.91
				H. Weisskopff, Switzerland	.91
				Aces High Ltd, North Weald UK : del.	3.10.91
DHP/ •	T Mk.55	U-1235		sold at auction, Dubendorf AB	23.3.91
44352			HB-RVI	Air Vampire SA, Sion	9.9.91/92
- •	T Mk.55	U-1236		sold at auction, Dubendorf AB	23.3.91
			SE-DXX	Flygexpo, Vasteras	.91/92
22277 •	T Mk.55	U-1237		sold at auction, Dubendorf AB	23.3.91
			LX-...	del. to Charleroi, Belgium	28.8.91
				(rest. to fly, Gosselies 10.91)	
40279 •	T Mk.55	U-1238		sold at auction, Dubendorf AB	23.3.91

Notes

15

Ex Swiss Air Force DH-100 Vampire J-1152 became N152 with Ray Dieckman. Being prepared for paint at Chino, July 1992. (Thierry Thomassin)

DE HAVILLAND DH115 VENOM

12364 • J-33	NF Mk.51		SE-DCA	(to R SwAF/Flygvapnet as Fv33015) Svensk Flygtjanst AB, Visdel, Sweden Flygvapenmuseum, Malmslatt, Sweden	 .58/69 84
12374 • J-33	NF Mk.51		SE-DCD	(to R SwAF/Flygvapnet as Fv33025) Svensk Flygtjanst AB, Visdel, Sweden Flygvapenmuseum, Malmslatt, Sweden	 .58/69 69/84
12760 •	Sea Venom FAW. 53	WZ903		(to RAN as WZ903) Pearce Dunn/Warbirds Aviation Museum, Mildura VIC Dennis Sanders/Sanders Aircraft, Chino CA	 72/90 90/91
12786 •	Sea Venom FAW .53 TT.53	WZ944		(to RAN as WZ944) Pearce Dunn/Warbirds Aviation Museum, Mildura VIC Dennis Sanders/Sanders Aircraft, Chino CA on rebuild to fly Sanders Aircraft, Chino, CA	 72/90 90/91 92
12752 •	Sea Venom FAW. 53	WZ895	VH-NVV	(to RAN as WZ895) Naval Aviation Museum, Nowra NAS NSW RAN Historic Flight, Nowra NAS NSW (under rebuild to fly, Nowra)	 86/92
733 •	FB Mk.50 Mk. 1	J-1523	G-VENI	Don Woods/Source Premium & Promotional Consultants Ltd, Weybridge (stored Cranfield 90)	8.6.84/87
737 •	FB Mk.50 Mk. 1	J-1527	N9196M	Westair International USA Inc, Monument CO M & M Aircraft Sales, Broomfield CO	11.87/90 92
749 - •	FB Mk.50 Mk. 1	J-1539	G-BMOD	ntu : stored Locarno, Switzerland	90

752	•	FB Mk.50	J-1542	G-GONE	Philip Meeson & Elsdon Davies/Glylynn Ltd,	
		Mk. 1			Hurn UK	17.9.84/89
					op. by Jet Heritage Collection Ltd, Hurn	
					Venom Jet Promotions Ltd, Hurn	20.2.89
					J. E. Davies, Bournemouth	22.2.91/92
783	•	FB Mk.50	J-1573	G-BMOB	ntu	
		Mk. 1		HB-RVB	Tarmac Aviation Gordold, Altenrhein	4.89
811	•	FB Mk.50	J-1601	G-VIDI	Don Woods/Source Premium & Promotional	
		Mk. 1			Consultants Ltd, Weybridge	8.6.84/87
					Sandy Topen/Vintage Aircraft Team,Cranfield	89/90
					(flies as RAF "WE402")	
815	•	FB Mk.50	J-1605	G-BLID	Aces High Ltd, Duxford	13.7.84/86
		Mk.1			Peter F. A. Hoar, Duxford	89
					Peter G. Vallance/Vallance By-Ways Museum,	
					Charlwood : static displ., arr.	1.90/92
-	•	FB Mk.50	J-1611	G-BMOC	ntu : stored Locarno, Switzerland	90
		Mk. 1				
824	•	FB Mk 50	J-1614	G-BLIE	Aces High Ltd, Duxford	28.2.85
		Mk.1			R. Everett/Air Charter Scotland,Glasgow:del.	27.2.85/91
826	•	FB Mk.50	J-1616	G-BLIF	Aces High Ltd, Duxford	28.9.84
		Mk.1			(del. Dubendorf-Duxford 5.7.84; loaned	
					Imperial War Museum, Duxford 84/85)	
				N202DM	Dean Martin/Warplanes Inc, Burlington VT	4.86/88
					Red Stevenson, Haskell OK	2.89/90
					CATS Inc, Eugene OR	1.90
					Dolphin Oil Ltd, Eugene OR	5.90
					ACE Ltd, Houston TX	92
840	•	FB Mk.50	J-1630	HB-RVA	Halos AG/Foundation Pour Le Maintien du	
		Mk. 1R			Patrimoine Aeronautique, Lausanne : del.	14.7.84/89
					(ff 22.6.88 Altenrhein : flies as "J-1630")	
841	•	FB Mk.50	J-1631	HB-RVC	FMPA - Association pour le Maintien	
					du Patrimoine Aeronautique	88/90
					(rest Sion, ff 20.4.90)	
842	•	FB Mk.50	J-1632	G-VNOM	A. Topen/Vintage Aircraft Team, Cranfield	13.7.84/91
		Mk. 1R			(del. Dubendorf-Cranfield 5.7.84)	
					stored unconv. Cranfield: struck-off reg.	25.3.91
844	•	FB Mk.50	J-1634		Aces High Ltd, Duxford UK : del.	27.2.85
		Mk. 1R		ZK-VNM	Trevor Bland/NZ Warbirds Inc, Ardmore	8.11.87/91
					(shipped NZ, ff Whenuapai 29.8.87 as RAF "WE434")	
					crashed Ardmore NZ	17.12.91
846	•	FB Mk.50	J-1636	HB-RVC	Association pour le Maintien du Patrimoine	
		Mk. 4			Aeronautique - FMPA, Sion	88/90
					(rebuilt Sion, ff 20.4.90)	
-	•	FB Mk.54	J-1730	G-BLIA	Aces High Ltd, Duxford	8.6.84
		Mk. 4		N402DM	Dean Martin/Warplanes Inc, Burlington VT	1.11.84/86
					Gene F. Fisher, Boiling Springs PA	.86/92
					(flies as "J-1730")	
917	•	FB Mk.54	J-1747	G-BLIB	Aces High Ltd, Duxford	8.6.84
		Mk. 4		N5471V	Warplanes Inc, East Middlebury VT	31.8.84/86
					James W Goodwin, Rutland VT	.86
				N747J	James W Goodwin, Rutland VT	12.86/87
					Venom Partners Inc, Campbell CA	1.89
					Ernest J. Saviano, Arlington TX	5.90
					David L. Vanliere, Huntington IN	1.92

- •	FB Mk.54	J-1758	G-BLSD	Aces High Ltd, Duxford	20.5.85
	Mk. 4		N203DM	Dean Martin/Warplanes Inc, Burlington VT	4.4.86
				(held in store, North Weald)	86/88
			G-BLSD	Aces High Ltd, North Weald	22.4.88/91
- •	FB Mk.54	J-1763	G-BLSE	Aces High Ltd, Duxford	20.5.85
	Mk. 4		N902DM	Warplanes Inc, East Middlebury VT	8.85/86
				Classic Fighters Inc, Argyle TX	6.86
				Ernest J. Salviano, Arlington TX	4.90
				crashed, dest., Muskogee OK (Saviano k.)	8.6.90
- •	FB Mk.54	J-1790	G-VENM	ntu: del. Dubendorf AB to Cranfield	5.7.84
	Mk. 4		G-BLKA	A. Topen/Vintage Aircraft Team, Cranfield	13.7.84/90
				(ff Cranfield 1.12.85: flies as RAF "WR410")	
- •	FB Mk.54	J-1799	G-BLIC	Aces High Ltd, Duxford	13.7.84
	Mk. 4			(del. Dubendorf - Duxford 5.7.84)	
			N502DM	Dean Martin/Warplanes Inc, Burlington VT	7.6.85
				Maintenance One, Essex Junction VT	1.86
				sale rep., Klamath Falls OR	90
				reg. pending, Visalia CA	92

DOUGLAS A-4 SKYHAWK

11366 •	A-4B	Bu142112	N3E	Combat Jets Flying Museum, Houston TX	1.87/92
				(ex tech. school, rebuilt Chino CA, ff 12.4.89)	
				(flies as "148609/USS Bon Homme Richard")	
				EAA Aviation Foundation, Oshkosh WI : del.	5.92
11370	A-4B	Bu142116	N116MD	US Navy, Long Beach CA	77
11420 •	A-4B	Bu142166	N5548	George T. Baker Aviation School, Miami FL	.72/92
				(FAA quote id. "A11-32")	
11967	A-4B	Bu142905	N905MD	US Navy, Long Beach CA	77
12764 •	A-4C	Bu148571	N53996		76
			N401FS	US Navy/Flight Systems Inc, Mojave CA	1.77/81
				retired to MASDC, Davis-Monthan AFB AZ	23.10.81
				Pima County Air Museum, Tucson AZ	.82/92
12841	A-4C	Bu149516	N402FS	US Navy/Flight Systems Inc, Mojave CA	1.77/86
	A-4L			retired .84, struck-off USCR	1.86
12997	A-4C	Bu150586	N403FS	US Navy/Flight Systems Inc, Mojave CA	1.77/86
	A-4L			struck-off USCR	1.86
-	TA-4J	Bu158128	N3203Z	reg. res: Stacy Prineas, Redmond OR	90/91
			N128TA	reg. res.	11.91/92
- •	TA-4J	Bu158471		Tom Reilly Vintage Aircraft, Kissimmee FL	90/91
				(rebuild to fly)	
14219	A-4A	-		Pascal Mahvi, Chino CA	c78/84
				(recov. ex gate guard USN Base, rebuilt	
				Chino 82/86, flew as "A-4A 14219")	
			N444AV	Pascal Mahvi/Aeronautical Test Vehicles Inc,	
				Newport Beach CA	10.84
				Guy Neeley/Advanced Aero Enterprises Inc,	
				Newport Beach CA	86/87

				crashed, California City CA (Neeley k.)	4.6.87
- •	A-4D	-	N21NB	Dave Straight/Sierra Hotel Inc, Addison TX	88/89
				(flies as "RAN 011")	
-	A-4	-	N115MD	US Navy, Long Beach CA	
			N900MD	US Navy, Long Beach CA	75
- •	TA-4J	-	N91KD	John Dilley/Fort Wayne Air Service,	
				Fort Wayne IN	90/92
				(FAA quote id. "921001")	

ENGLISH ELECTRIC CANBERRA/MARTIN B-57

71591	PR Mk.57	-	VT-EEM	National Remote Sensing Agency, Secundrabad	6.76/80
- •	T Mk.4		A84-502	RAAF Wagga NSW: instructional airframe	70/89
				Robert Greinert/Historic Aircraft	
				Restoration Society, Sydney NSW	9.89
				(trucked Wagga-Sydney 9.89: rebuild to fly)	
				Bob Delahunty, Sydney NSW	91/92
- •	B Mk.20	A84-229		stored RAAF Amberley QLD : last flight	20.5.85/90
				Jim Ricketts/Aero Nostalgia Inc, Stockton CA	7.88/90
			N20AN	Steve Picatti, Hayward CA	8.90/91
				(arr. Hayward on del. ex Australia 14.8.90)	
			N229CA	Steve Picatti, Hayward CA	.91/92
				(returned to Australia for airshows 11.91/3.92)	
- •	B-57A	52-1419	N1005	Department of Commerce/ NOAA, Miami FL	.60/71
	WB-57A			George T. Baker Aviation School, Miami FL	5.74/81
-	RB-57A	52-1447	N97	FAA, Oklahoma City OK	1.4.57/71

ENGLISH ELECTRIC LIGHTNING

95207 •	F Mk. 6	XR724	G-BTSY	Barry Pover/Lightning Association, Callington	25.7.91
B1/ •	T Mk. 5	XS451		Peter F. A. Hoare/Militair, Cranfield	.87/88
95011				Vintage Aircraft Team, Cranfield	88/89
			G-LTNG	Barry J. Pover/Lightning Flying Club,	
				Plymouth ; arr. dism., rest. to fly	12.9.89/92
95012 •	T Mk.5	XS452		Ruanil Investments Ltd, Cranfield	29.6.88
			G-BPFE	Ruanil Investments Ltd, Cranfield	10.88/92
95113 •	F Mk. 2A	XN734		BAC Ltd, Saudi Support School, Warton: del	26.6.73/86
	F Mk. 3A		G-BNCA	Aces High Ltd, North Weald UK	10.12.86
				Peter F. A. Hoare/Militair, Cranfield: arr.	31.10.87
				A. Topen/Vintage Aircraft Team, Cranfield	10.87/91

FOLLAND GNAT/HINDUSTAN ADJEET

- •	F Mk. 1	IE-1076		del. to Indian AF	.59
				Military Aircraft Restoration Corp, Chino CA	86/88
				stored dism., Chino CA	88
				USAFM, March AFB CA	90/92
- •	F Mk. 1	IE-1214		Military Aircraft Restoration Corp, Chino CA	86/88
				stored dism., Chino CA	88
- •	F Mk. 1	IE-1222		Military Aircraft Restoration Corp, Chino CA	86/88
				stored dism., Chino CA	88
FL.507 •	T Mk. 1	XM697		Air Training Corps, Woking UK	
			G-NAAT	Jet Heritage Ltd/Hunter Wing, Hurn	27.11.89
FL.508 •	T Mk. 1	XM698		RAF Museum, RAF Cosford	86
			N698XM	James E. Thompson, St Cloud FL	2.87/92

FL.510 •	T Mk. 1	XM705	N705XM	James E. Thompson, St Cloud FL	2.87/92
FL.519 •	T Mk. 1	XP504		Ambrion Aviation, Leavesden : arr.	16.1.92
			G-TIMM	T. J. Manna, Leavesden	19.2.92
FL.528 •	T Mk. 1	XP513	N513XP	Morey Darzniek/Lance Aircraft Supply Inc, Dallas TX	3.85
			N513X	Lance Aircraft Supply Inc, Dallas TX	8.86/92
FL.529 •	T Mk. 1	XP514		Ruanill Investments, Cranfield	12.88
				(shipped to USA, ex Felixstowe 2.8.89)	
			N22394	ntu	
			N7HY	Morgan Merrill/Jet 1 Inc, Alexandria VA	4.90
FL.537	T Mk. 1	XP535		School of Aircraft Handling, RNAS Culdrose	87
			G-BOXP	Ruanil Investments, Cranfield	3.8.88
				(arr. Leavesden by road 11.87; ff 5.8.88)	
			N1CW	Morgan Merrill/Jet 1 Inc, Alexandria VA	9.89/90
				(shipped to USA, ex Felixstowe 2.8.89)	
				crashed dest., Mojave CA (Merrill k.)	29.9.90
FL.542 •	T Mk. 1	XP538		sold at Sotheby's auction	9.3.90
			N19GT	Pyramid Aerospace Inc, Houston TX	3.90
				Cinema Air Jet Centre Inc, Carlsbad CA	1.91/92
FL.545 •	T Mk. 1	XP541		Warbirds of GB Ltd, Biggin Hill	.86/89
			N8130Q	Robert F. Yancey, Klamath Falls OR	5.89
				Andrew J. McCarthy, Merrimack NH	1.92
FL.546 •	T Mk. 1	XR535		Warbirds of GB Ltd, Biggin Hill	.86/89
			N8130N	Robert F. Yancey, Klamath Falls OR	8.5.89
				John Dilley/Fort Wayne Air Service IN	2.91/92
				(rest. California City CA, ff 2.92)	
FL.548 •	T Mk. 1	XR537		Sold at Sotheby's auction	9.3.90
			G-NATY	Jet Heritage Ltd, Hurn	19.6.90/91
FL.562 •	T Mk. 1	XR572		Michael W. Bertz, Broomfield CO	87
			N572XR	Michael W. Bertz, Broomfield CO	3.89/92
FL.568 •	T Mk. 1	XR951		Warbirds of GB Ltd, Biggin Hill	.86/89
			N81298	Robert F. Yancey, Klamath Falls OR	8.5.89
				Andrew J. McCarthy, Merrimack NH	1.92
- •	T Mk. 1	XR955		Glenn Hyde, Dallas TX	90
				(under rest. Chino CA 90)	
FL.585 •	T Mk. 1	XR991	G-BOXO	Ruanil Investments, Cranfield	3.8.88
				(arr. Leavesden for rest. 11.87)	
				(shipped to USA, ex Felixstowe 2.8.89)	
			N1CL	Morgan Merrill/Jet 1 Inc, Alexandria VA	7.89/92
FL.587	T Mk. 1	XR993		RAF Museum storage: offered for disposal	.86
				purchased by Canadian dealer	2.87
			N3XR	Gnati Inc, Wilmington DE	11.90/91
				Gary Thompson, St. Cloud FL	91
				crashed dest., Shreveland LA (Thompson k.)	9.1.91
FL.594 •	T Mk. 1	XS100	N7CV	Morgan Merrill/Jet 1 Inc, Alexandria VA	4.90
				McDonnell Enterprises, Mojave CA	3.92
FL.595 •	T Mk. 1	XS101	G-GNAT	Stephen Grey, Duxford	14.4.82
				Ruanil Investments, Cranfield	29.8.83/92
FL.596 •	T Mk. 1	XS102		sold at Sotheby's auction	9.3.90
			G-MOUR	Intrepid Aviation, North Weald	16.5.90/92

				(ff Leavesden 6.91, flies as Yellowjacks "XR991")	
FL.598 •	T Mk. 1	XS104		Ruanil Investments, Cranfield	12.88
			G-FRCE	Butane Buzzard Aviation Corp, North Weald	11.89/91
				(rebuilt Cranfield, ff 2.12.90)	
FL.599 •	T Mk. 1	XS105		sold at RAF auction	9.3.90
			N18GT	Pyramid Aerospace Inc, Houston TX	3.90
				Cinema Air Jet Centre Inc, Carlsbad CA	1.91/92
FL.604 •	T Mk. 1	XS110		sold at RAF auction	9.3.90
			N7152Z	Jim Cullen/Westair Int'l, Broomfield CO	.90
				International Jet Centre, Miami FL	8.90
			N110XS	Duncan Young Partnership, Miami FL	10.90/92
- •	HF.24	IE-276		Military Aircraft Restoration Corp, Chino CA	86/88
				(stored Chino CA 88/91)	
- •	HF.24	IE-296		Military Aircraft Restoration Corp, Chino CA	86/88
				(stored Chino CA 88)	
				George Perez, Reno NV	.89/92
- •	HF.24	E-299		Military Aircraft Restoration Corp, Chino CA	86/88
				(stored Chino CA 88/91)	
- •	HF.24	E-315		Military Aircraft Restoration Corp, Chino CA	86
				Unlimited Aircraft Limited, Chino CA	87

FOUGA CM-170 MAGISTER

2	•	CM.170	No 2		(Armée de l'Air as2 coded BH-CEAM)	
				F-WDXH	Air Memorial Lons Le Saulnier	4.86
					Aero Retro, Ste Rambert D'Albion, near Lyon	.87
30	•	CM.170	No 30	F-WDHG	(Armée de l'Air as 30 coded 3-KC)	
					Musee de l'Aeronautique et des Ailes Lorraines,	
					Nancy/Essey	84
31	•	CM.170	No 31	F-....	(Armée de l'Air as 31 coded 30-QG)	
					J. C. Lutringer	89
45	•	CM.170	No.45		(Armée de l'Air as 45 coded 312-TD)	
				G-BSCT	Aces High Ltd, North Weald	20.3.90
				G-FUGA	Royalaire Services Ltd, Nottingham	12.4.90/91
					(rest. North Weald, ff 19.9.91)	
61		CM.170	No 61		(French AF - Patrouille de France Aerobatic Team)	
				G-BKSY	Stephen Grey, Duxford	7.6.83/85
					sold to USA	11.1.85
69	•	CM.170	No 69		(Armée de l'Air as 69 coded TG)	
					Israeli Air Force	
				F-GELI	Salis Aviation, La Ferte Alais	9.91
79	•	CM.170 R/ (Flugzugunion-Sud)	AA+179		(to Luftwaffe coded /SC603/SB202/93+02))	
					German Navy apprentice school	71
				D-IFCC	Claus Colling, Gammesdorf, Germany	89/92
102	•	CM.170	No 102		(Armée de l'Air as 102 coded 7GE)	
				F-GELH	Salis Aviation, La Ferte Alais	9.91/92
					(due for del. Bordeaux AB to Veronne 3.92)	
182	•	CM.170	FM-2		(Finnish Air Force as FM-2)	
				N903DM	Dean Martin/Warplanes Inc, Burlington VT	5.86
					John C. Bennett/Warbirds West,	
					Klamath Falls OR	.87/89

					James Oliver, Visalia CA "The Screamer"	88/92
201		CM.170R (Mess.)	YA+203		(later Luftwaffe 93+20)	
				D-IBYZ	*no further information*	
206	•	CM.170	No.206		(Armée de l'Air as 206 coded 315-QX)	
				F-WDJD		
				F-WMOM	Aero Retro, Ste Rambert D'Albion	12.86
240	•	CM.170	No.240		(Armée de l'Air as 240 coded 315-QE)	
				N301FM	Basler Flight Service Inc, Oshkosh WI	12.85/92
251		CM.170R	FM-26		(Finnish AF as FM26)	
				N16FM	Exotic Aircraft Inc, Coraopolis PA	3.87/88
					noted, Port Charlotte FL	7.87
					struck-off USCR	1.89
256	•	CM.170R	FM-18	N805DM	(Finnish AF as FM26)	
					Dean Martin/Warplanes Inc, Burlington VT	3.87
					Sacramento Aviation Inc, Sacramento CA	9.88/89
					Bradley Flight Service, Wethersfield CT	92
259	•	CM.170R	MT2		(Belgium Air Force as MT2)	
					Israel Aircraft Industries, Tel Aviv: stored	
					Aces High Ltd, North Weald UK	.88
				N906DM	Dean Martin/Warplanes Inc, Burlington VT	3.89
					Falcon Aircraft Conversions, San Antonio TX	5.90/92
262	•	CM.170R	MT5		(Belgium Air Force as MT5)	
					Israel Aircraft Industries, Tel Aviv: stored	80
					Aces High Ltd, North Weald UK	.88
				N216DM	Dean Martin/Warplanes Inc, Burlington VT	1.89
					James W. Goodwin, Middlebury VT	89
268	•	CM.170R	MT11		(Belgium Air Force as MT11)	
					Israel Aircraft Industries, Tel Aviv: stored	.80
					Aces High Ltd, North Weald UK	.88
				N219DM	Dean Martin/Warplanes Inc, Burlington VT	1.89
					Vintage Aircraft Team, Cranfield	6.89
					Militair, Cranfield	8.89
				G-BRFU	Aces High Ltd, North Weald	7.8.89
269	•	CM.170R	MT12		(Belgium Air Force as MT12)	
					Israel Aircraft Industries, Tel Aviv: stored	.80
					Aces High Ltd, North Weald UK	.88
				N907DM	Dean Martin/Warplanes Inc, Burlington VT	3.89/92
272	•	CM.170R	MT15		(Belgium Air Force as MT15)	
					Israel Aircraft Industries, Tel Aviv: stored	.80
					Aces High Ltd, North Weald UK	.88
				N908DM	Dean Martin/Warplanes Inc, Burlington VT	3.89
					Sam J. Kademenos, Pittsburgh PA	92
273	•	CM.170R	MT16		(Belgium Air Force as MT16)	
					Israel Aircraft Industries, Tel Aviv: stored	.80
					Aces High Ltd, North Weald UK	.88
				N909DM	Dean Martin/Warplanes Inc, Burlington VT	3.89/92
275	•	CM.170R	MT18		(Belgium Air Force as MT18)	
					Israel Aircraft Industries, Tel Aviv: stored	.80
					Aces High Ltd, North Weald UK	.88
				N312DM	Dean Martin/Warplanes Inc, Burlington VT	1.89
					Universal Aviation Corp Inc., Kent DE	89
284	•	CM.170R	MT27		(Belgium Air Force as MT27)	
					Israel Aircraft Industries, Tel Aviv: stored	
					Aces High Ltd, North Weald UK	.88

				N313DM	Dean Martin/Warplanes Inc, Burlington VT	1.89
					Jon Galt Bowman, Seattle WA	89
325	•	CM.170R	No.325		(Armée de l'Air as 325 coded 315-PU)	
				N325FR	Basler Flight Service Inc, Oshkosh WI	6.88
					Frank J. McIntosh, San Francisco CA	89/92
328	•	CM.170R	No.328	N304FM	(Armée de l'Air as 328 coded 315-QX)	
					Basler Flight Service Inc, Oshkosh WI	9.86
					Robert J. Farrell, Sacramento CA	12.86/92
354	•	CM.170R	No.354	N302FM	(Armée de l'Air as 354 coded 315-XF)	
					Basler Flight Service Inc, Oshkosh WI	6.87
					First Options Inc, Kalamazoo MI	88
					Jim R. Porter, Hinsdale IL	88/90
					(flew in Patrouille de France scheme)	
					crashed, Oshkosh WI	8.90
					sale rep., Xenia OH: USCR	92
471	•	CM.170R	No.471	F-WFPK	(Armée de l'Air as 325 coded 312-TD)	
					M. Piazzola	.88
494	•	CM.170R	No.494		(Armée de l'Air as 494 coded 312-AB)	
				N300FM	Basler Flight Service Inc, Oshkosh WI	6.87/89
					John J. Mark/MA Inc, Oshkosh WI	92
522	•	CM.170R	No.522		(Armée de l'Air as 522 coded 313-DZ)	
				F-WHCF	del. to Brive, France ex storage Chateaudun	12.91
576	•	CM.170R	No.576	F-WFTX	(Armée de l'Air as 576 coded VN/PdF)	
					AG du Haut-Comtat-Visan	11.88
					G. Guillaumaund	1.92
-	•	CM.170R	FM-27		(Finnish Air Force as FM27)	
				N604DM	Dean Martin/Warplanes Inc, Burlington VT	3.87
					Which Way Is Up Aerobatics Inc., Miami FL	88
					International Jet Centre, Miami FL	4.91/92
-	•	CM.170R	FM-28		(Finnish Air Force as FM28)	
				N18FM	Exotic Aircraft Inc, Coraopolis PA	3.87/88
					noted, Port Charlotte FL	7.87
				EI-BXO	Gerry W. Connolly, Shannon, Eire	.88/90
					(airfreighted to Shannon by C-130 16.11.88)	
-	•	CM.170R	FM-29		(Finnish Air Force as FM29)	
				N403DM	Dean Martin/Warplanes Inc, Burlington VT	3.87
				N403PF	Air Armco Inc, Middletown DE	2.89/92
-	•	CM.170R	FM-30		(Finnish Air Force as FM30)	
				N204DM	Dean Martin/Warplanes Inc, Burlington VT	5.86
					Dennis R. Demers, Essex Junction VT	.87/91
				N101TD	Dennis R. Demers, Essex Junction VT	3.91/92
					(flies gloss black "FM30/The Dog Whistle")	
-		CM.170R	FM-31		(Finnish Air Force as FM31	
				N19FM	Exotic Aircraft Inc, Coraopolis PA	3.87/88
					struck-off USCR	1.89
-	•	CM.170R	FM-32		(Finnish Air Force as FM32)	
				N305DM	Dean Martin/Warplanes Inc, Burlington VT	2.87/88
					Condor Aviation, Teterboro NJ	92
-	•	CM.170R	FM-35		(Finnish Air Force as FM35)	
				N405DM	Dean Martin/Warplanes Inc, Burlington VT	2.87
					Dario Taquechel, Hilton Head Island SC	87/92
-	•	CM.170R	FM-36		(Finnish Air Force as FM36)	

				N505DM	Dean Martin/Warplanes Inc, Burlington VT	2.87
					John Galt Bowman, Seattle WA	87/92
-	•	CM.170R	FM-39	N19JV	Exotic Aircraft Inc, Coraopolis PA	3.87
					Firebird Enterprises, Middlefield OH	10.87
					Ohio Associated Enterprises, Painesville OH	7.88/92
-	•	CM.170R	FM-47	N605DM	Dean Martin/Warplanes Inc, Burlington VT	3.87
					Richard F. Korff, Lewiston NY	88/92
-	•	CM.170R	FM-49	N804DM	Dean Martin/Warplanes Inc, Burlington VT	3.87
				N101DD	Dennis R. Demers, Essex Junction VT	6.89/92
-	•	CM.170R	FM-72	N404DM	Dean Martin/Warplanes Inc, Burlington VT	5.86
					David H. Willis Leasing Co., Manchester MA	12.86/92
-	•	CM.170R	FM-73	N504DM	Dean Martin/Warplanes Inc, Burlington VT	5.86
					John P. Silberman, Tampa FL	.87/92
					(flies in camouflage as "IDFAF 73")	
-	•	CM.170R	FM-76	N705DM	Dean Martin/Warplanes Inc, Burlington VT	3.87
					Air Classics Foundation Ltd, Lincoln MA	10.88/92
-	•	CM.170R	FM-80	N904DM	Dean Martin/Warplanes Inc, Burlington VT	3.87
					Coleman Warbird Museum, Coleman TX	8.89/92
-	•	CM.170R	FM-81	N303DM	Dean Martin/Warplanes Inc, Burlington VT	2.87
					Rick E. Sharpe, Arcola TX	87
					James Wickersham, Oakland CA	88
					Sonoma Valley Aircraft Inc, Sacramento CA	92

GLOSTER METEOR

	•	F Mk.4	VT229		Newark Aircraft Museum, Winthorpe	4.83/91
				N229VT	Weeks Air Museum, Tamiami FL (ex UK)	9.91
G5-361641	•	F Mk.8	VZ467		RAF last flight 22.10.82, then stored	
				G-METE	Air Support Aviation Services Ltd, London	5.11.91/92
					(rest. to fly, Cranfield)	
-	•	T Mk.7	VZ638		Historic Aircraft Museum, Southend : arr.	12.1.72/83
				G-JETM	Brencham Historic Aircraft Ltd, Hurn	10.5.83/87
					Aces High Ltd, North Weald	1.10.87/89
					Peter G. Vallance/Vallance By-Ways Museum, Charlwood	.89/92
-	•	NF Mk.11 TT Mk.20	WD592	N94749	Al Letcher & Associates, Mojave CA	12.74/88
					(del. Biggin Hill to Mojave 18-22.6.75)	
					Al Hansen & Ascher Ward, Mojave CA	.88/90
G5-1496		T Mk.7	WF833	SE-CAS	Svensk Flygtjanst AB, Bromma, Sweden: del.	29.7.55
					withdrawn, stored, Bromma	4.59/74
					Flygvapnets Flygmuseum, Malmslatt : del.	29.7.74/79
-	•	T Mk. 7	WF877		Flight Refuelling Ltd, Tarrant Rushton	6.66
					Torbay Aircraft Museum, Higher Blagdon	2.74
					Aces High Ltd, North Weald	19.10.88
				G-BPOA	Aces High Ltd, North Weald	16.3.89/90
G5-1525		T Mk. 7		G-ANSO	Gloster Aircraft Ltd	12.6.54
					retired Moreton Valence	9.56/58
				SE-DCC	Svensk Flygtjanst AB, Bromma, Sweden : del.	11.8.59
					rep. del. to museum Malmslatt	16.9.74
G7-146		T Mk.7	WH128	SE-CAT	Svensk Flygtjanst AB, Bromma, Sweden	9.55
					crashed at Visby Airport	21.1.59
-	•	F Mk. 8	WK914		RAF Manston : fire dump	77/82

				Medway Aircraft Pres. Society, Rochester	83
				The Old Flying Machine Co, Duxford UK	.88/92
				(arr. Duxford by road 8.8.88, for rest.)	
S4/U/	NF Mk.11	WM167		Warbirds of GB Ltd, Blackbushe	83
2342 •	TT Mk.20		G- LOSM	Brencham Historic Aircraft Ltd, Hurn	8.6.84
				(del. Blackbushe - Hurn 6.7.84)	
				Hunter One Collection, Hurn	86/87
				LGH Aviation Ltd/Jet Heritage Collection,Hurn	1.10.87/89
				Hunter Wing Ltd, Hurn	3.5.89/91
				(long-term rebuild Hurn, ff 8.91)	
AW.	NF Mk.14	WM261	G-ARCX	Ferranti Ltd, Turnhouse	8.9.60/69
2163 •				withdrawn from use	12.69
				Museum of Flight, East Fortune, Scotland	76/91
AW. •	NF Mk.13	WM334		(to IDFAF as 157/4X-FNB)	
5582			4X-BET	Israel Aircraft Industries, Tel Aviv-Lod	.71/72
				Hatzerim Air Base Museum	81/90
AW.	NF Mk.11	WM391		(to RDAF as 51-508: later TT.20 H-508)	
5549 •	TT Mk.20		SE-DCH	Svensk Flygtjanst AB, Bromma, Sweden	6.8.62/69
			D-CAKU	ntu: Flugzeughandelsgesellchaft Karlsruhe	29.10.69
				(del. Malmo-Germany 15.3.69, sale to Biafra	
				aborted; abandoned Gosselies, Belgium 69/75)	
				Musee Royal de l'Armee, Brussels	84
AW.	NF Mk.11	WM395		(to RDAF as 51-512: later TT.20 H-512)	
5562 •	TT Mk.20		SE-DCF	Svensk Flygtjanst AB, Bromma, Sweden	27.8.62
			D-CAKY	ntu: Flugzeughandelsgesellchaft Karlsruhe	29.10.69
				(del. Malmo-Germany 15.3.69, sale to Biafra	
				aborted; abandoned Gosselies, Belgium 69/75)	
				Musee Royal de l'Armee, Brussels	84
AW.	NF Mk.14	WS804	G-AXNE	reg.	28.8.69
5803				abandoned Bissau, Portuguese Guinea	9.69/72
-	F Mk.8			(to RBAF as EG162)	
			OO-ARU	COGEA Nouvelle, Ostend	27.8.58
				sold to Belgian Congo	2.3.61
				(returned to RBAF as EG162)	
				displ. Dinart AB, Belgium	79

GRUMMAN F9F PANTHER/COUGAR

- •	F9F-3	Bu123072		Air Service & Supply Co, Tulsa OK : scrap	73
			N72WP	Jack Levine & Bill Pryor, Pontiac MI	1.79/85
				(rebuilt Pontiac MI, using parts from hulk of	
				Bu137180 ex Philadelphia Navy yard, ff 30.7.83)	
				Arthur A. Wolk, Philadelphia PA	10.85/89
				Flying Warbirds Foundation, Philadelphia PA	90/92
				(flies as USN "123072/806V")	
- •	F9F-2	Bu123078	N9525A	reg.	4.78
				Mark E. Foster, Aurora CO	12.84
				Harry S. Doan/Doan Helicopter Inc,	
				New Smyrna Beach FL (flies in USN scheme)	4.87/92
				auctioned	30.10.92
- •	F9F-2	Bu123526	N3456G	John D. Moore, North Hollywood CA	66/69
				John D. Moore, Lancaster CA	72
- •	F9F-5	Bu125467		(reserialled Bu125434)	
			N1332F	Van Dusen Airport Services	8.81
				Thomas E. Wright, Snyder TX	84/90
				Roger A. Christgau, Edina MN	92

- •	F9F-6P	Bu127487	N7993A	John G. Johnson, Dallas TX	65/69
	RF-9F		N9FP	George Perez, Reno NV	77
				I. N. Burchinall Jnr, Paris TX	80
				Le Tourneau College, Longview TX	84
				Condor Enterprises Inc	84
				Howard Pardue/Breckenridge Aviation Museum, Breckenridge TX	87
				David H. Turlington, Greensboro NC	88
				struck-off USCR	4.89
				(FAA quote id. as "15")	
- •	F9F-8P	Bu141675	N9256	Sergio Tomassoni, Buckeye AZ	78
				noted unconv. derelict, Buckeye AZ	78
				rep. aircraft noted Phoenix-Deer Valley AZ	92
-	F9F-8T	Bu142498	N24WJ	(to Argentine Navy as ....)	.62
	TF-9J			Don Whittington/World Jet Inc, Fort Lauderdale FL	7.89/91
				(flew as "Marines 142498/YU")	
				crashed in sea off Louisiana coastline	31.10.91
				(id. assumed, FAA quotes "A-20-60")	

HAWKER HUNTER

41H/ 679948 •	F Mk.6	XE587	N587XE	Andrew N. McNeil, Augusta NJ	3.92
				(ex RAE, Farnborough : shipped to US 3.92)	
HABL/ 003020 •	F Mk.4	XE677		Hawker Siddeley Aircraft Ltd, Dunsfold	7.4.61/62
				Loughborough College : inst. airframe : arr.	9.1.62/89
			G-HHUN	Jet Heritage Collection/Hunter Wing Ltd, Hurn	30.10.89
HABL/ 003080 •	F Mk.4	XF319		RAF Halton : inst. airframe	90
			G-BTCY	Gray Tuplin Ltd, Southall	22.1.91
				sold to USA	.91
- •	F Mk.6	XF375		Old Flying Machine Co, Duxford	.91/92
			G-BUEZ	Old Flying Machine Co, Duxford	3.4.92
				(rest. to fly)	
HABL/ 003129 •	F Mk.4	XF974		RAF Halton : inst. airframe	90
			G-BTCX	Gray Tuplin Ltd, Southall	22.1.91
				sold to USA	.91
HABL/ 003311 •	T Mk.7	XL572	G-HNTR	Hunter Wing Ltd/Jet Heritage, Hurn	7.7.89/91
				(rebuild to fly, BAe Brough 91)	
- •	T Mk.7	XL576		Edward C. Stead, Manchester NH	.88
			N576NL	Northern Lights Aircraft Inc, Montgomery AL	4.89/91
- •	T Mk.7	XL595	G-BTYL	Judith E. Cubitt/Cubitt Aviation, Foulsham, Norfolk	29.11.91
41H/ 695449 •	T Mk.7	XL617	G-HHNT	Hunter Wing Ltd/Jet Heritage, Hurn	7.7.89
			N617NL	Northern Lights Aircraft Inc, Montgomery AL	11.89/91
- •	F Mk. 51			(to RDAF as E-403)	
				Hawker Siddeley Aircraft Ltd, Dunsfold	.76
			N72602	Al Letcher & Associates, Mojave CA	.77/85
				(shipped Mojave CA: ff 23.5.78)	
				Al Hansen & Ascher Ward, Mojave CA	89/90
41H/ 680277 •	F Mk. 51			(to RDAF as E-418) : del. 22.6.56 : wfu	.74
				Hawker Siddeley Aircraft Ltd, Dunsfold	12.75/78
				Surrey & Sussex Aviation Society	.78
			G-HUNT	Spencer Flack, Elstree	5.7.78/81
				(rebuilt Elstree, ff 20.3.80)	
				Mike Carlton/Brencham Historic Aircraft Ltd/ Hunter One Collection, Hurn	9.81/87

			N50972	Jim Robinson, Houston TX	12.87
			N611JR	Jim Robinson/Combat Jets Flying Museum, Houston TX	2.88/92
				(flies as Neville Duke's "WB188")	
				EAA Aviation Foundation, Oshkosh WI	.92
41H/ 693749 •	T Mk.7 T Mk 53			(to RNAF as N-307)	
				(to RDAF as ET-274)	
				Hawker Siddeley Aircraft Ltd, Dunsfold	.76
			G-BOOM	Brian Kay/Ambrion Aviation, Leavesden	6.10.80/82
				(rebuilt Leavesden, ff 24.4.81)	
				Brencham Historic Aircraft Ltd, Hurn	29.9.82/87
				LGH Aviation Ltd/Jet Heritage, Hurn, UK	1.10.87/91
41H/ 693833 •	T Mk.54			(to RDAF as 35-271: later ET-271)	
				Hawker Siddeley Aircraft Ltd, Dunsfold	.76
				arr. Blackbushe, stored	7.79
				loan: Booker Aircraft Museum, Booker	86/87
			G-BNFT	Peter F.A. Hoare/Militair, Cranfield	27.2.87
			N10271	Edward C. Stead, Bedford NH	3.87/92
41H/ 695432 •	T Mk.7	XM126		(XM126 ntu: to RNAF as N-320)	
			PH-NLH	Stichting Nat. Lucht-en-Ruimtevaart Lab./ Dutch National Air Laboratory, Schipol	72
				Staravia Ltd, Exeter UK : del.	22.1.80/86
				rep. sold in USA	.86
- •	F Mk. 50			(to Swedish AF/Flygvapnet as Fv34006)	
				Military Aircraft Restoration Corp, Chino CA	.83/87
				Jim Robinson/Combat Jets Flying Museum, Houston TX	11.87
				Ed Stead, Manchester NH	1.88/91
				(mod. to T. Mk. 8 with nose of WT745)	

HAWKER SEA HAWK

6032 •	FB Mk. 3 FB Mk. 5	WM994		College of Aeronautics, Cranfield	
				Webborn Air Museum, Swansea : stored dism	.77/83
			G-SEAH	Nobleair Ltd, Southend	5.4.83
				Brencham Historic Aircraft Co, Hurn	16.3.84/87
				Jet Heritage Collection, Hurn	1.10.87
				Sark International Airways/Jet Heritage	25.1.88
6385 •	FGA Mk.6	XE489		British Historic Aircraft Museum, Southend	20.5.67/83
				(del. Southend 20.5.67, displ. as "XE364/485J")	
			G-JETH	Brencham Ltd, Hurn	10.5.83/87
				(civil conv. not completed, displ. Hurn 86/87)	
				Peter G. Vallance/Vallance By-Ways Museum, Charlwood : static displ. as "XE364"	1.10.87/92
-	Mk.			Bernie Vajdi, Winnipeg MAN	.84

LOCKHEED F-80 SHOOTING STAR

1258 •	P-80A F-80A	44-85235		(to USN as Bu29689)	
				Walter Soplata Collection, Newbury OH	85
				Rick Ropkey, Longview TX (rest. to fly)	91
- •	P-80C F-80C	47-215		(to FA Colombia as 2058)	
			N10DM	Richard W. Martin, Van Nuys CA	71/78
				(arr. dism. Van Nuys 3.71 for rebuild using parts of T-33 N156 : not completed)	
				stored, stripped Whiteman Air Park CA by	84
				Kulis ANGB, Anchorage AK	86/90
				(for rebuild as static displ.): struck-off USCR	4.87
- •	P-80C F-80C	48-868	N80PP	reg. res.	90/92

20/42 •	HA.200A	AE.10B-42	N3178N	Sierra Warbirds Corp, Truckee CA	11.91/92
20/43 •	HA.200A	A10B-43	N2741P	Combat Aircraft Inc, Elkhart IN	9.82
				Southeast Whirly Birds Inc, New Canaan CT	88
				Classic Aircraft Inc, Albertville AL	92
20/44 •	HA.200A	-	N9108R	Combat Aircraft Inc, Elkhart IN	7.87/89
				Tim Bacci/Sierra Warbirds Corp, Truckee	90/92
20/46 •	HA.200A	AE.10B-46	N3179K	Sierra Warbirds Corp, Truckee CA	11.91/92
20/48 •	HA.200A	E.14A-13	N613HA	Nathaniel A. Kalt, San Antonio TX	6.85
				Dean Martin/Warplanes Inc, Dover DE	2.89
			N2000G	Dean Martin/Warplanes Inc, Burlington VT	7.89/92
			N20036	Warplanes Inc, Dover DE	8.90/92
20/53 •	HA.200A	AE.10B-53	N3179U	Sierra Warbirds Corp, Truckee CA	11.91
			N390WW	re reg.	1.92
20/57 •	HA.200A	AE.10B-57	N3179W	Sierra Warbirds Corp, Truckee CA	11.91/92
20/60 •	HA.200A	-	N4551W	Combat Aircraft Inc, Elkhart IN	11.83
				James C. Parham, Greenville SC	88/92
20/61 •	HA.200A	AE.10B-61	N3179Z	Sierra Warbirds Corp, Truckee CA	11.91/92
20/62 •	HA.200A	AE.10B-62	N31792	Sierra Warbirds Corp, Truckee CA	11.91/92
20/64 •	HA.200A	-	N553GA	General Aviation Services, Wheeling IL	9.90/92
20/69 •	HA.200A	-	N9123E	Combat Aircraft Inc, Elkhart IN	9.87
				David Van Liere, Huntington IN	89
				Five Star Aviation, Columbus City IN	92
20/72 •	HA.200A	-	N554GA	General Aviation Services, Wheeling IL	9.90/92
20/74 •	HA.200A	AE.10B-74	N31793	Sierra Warbirds Corp, Truckee CA	11.91/92
20/80 •	HA.200A	AE.10B-80	N31798	Sierra Warbirds Corp, Truckee CA	11.91/92
20/83 •	HA.200A	AE.10B-83	N3180G	Sierra Warbirds Corp, Truckee CA	11.91
			N212AM	Sierra Warbirds Corp, Truckee CA	2.92
20/87 •	HA.200A	AE.10B-87	N3180J	Sierra Warbirds Corp, Truckee CA	11.91
20/89 •	HA.200A	-	N9108Q	Combat Aircraft Inc, Elkhart IN	7.87/89
				Sierra Warbirds Corp, Truckee CA	92
20/91 •	HA.200A	AE.10C-91	N3180T	Sierra Warbirds Corp, Truckee CA	11.91/92
20/94 •	HA.200A	AE.10C-94	N3180X	Sierra Warbirds Corp, Truckee CA	11.91/92
20/96 •	HA.200A	-	N9123N	Combat Aircraft Inc, Elkhart IN	9.87
				David Van Liere, Huntington IN	89
				Classic Aircraft Inc, Albertville AL	92
•	HA.200	C.10B-50	EC-DXR	Fundacion Infante de Orleans Museum, Cuatro Vientos	90
- •	HA.200	E.14A-2	N602HA	Nathaniel A. Kalt, San Antonio TX	6.85
				rep. sold to Panama	6.87
				Airfleet Corp, Omaha NE	88
				Skyway Sales Inc, Omaha NE	92
- •	HA.200	E.14A-4	N604HA	Nathaniel A. Kalt, San Antonio TX	6.85
				rep. sold to Panama	6.87
				Charles J. Cavnaday, Blue Ridge VA	92

	-	•	HA.200	E.14A-5	N5486Y	Nathaniel A. Kalt, San Antonio TX	9.84
						Avstar Inc, Seattle WA	85
						Rick E. Sharpe, Houston TX	86
						Flight Research Inc, Hattiesburg MS	88/92
	-	•	HA.200	E.14A-6	N606HA	Nathaniel A. Kalt, San Antonio TX	6.85
						W. Scott Kidwell, Redmond WA	2.87
						rep. sold to Panama	6.87
						Airfleet Corp, Omaha NE	88
						Bill Russell/Russair Ltd, Hillsboro OR	90/92
	-	•	HA.200	E.14A-7	N607HA	Nathaniel A. Kalt, San Antonio TX	6.85
						Joseph B. Clark/Avstar Inc, Seattle WA	88/92
	-	•	HA.200	E.14A-10	N3951G	Nathaniel A. Kalt, San Antonio TX	6.83/86
						(assembled, San Antonio TX: ff 29.11.84)	
						Rick E. Sharpe, Arcola TX	88
						Rolf F. Brunckhorst, Oxford OH	92
	-		HA.200A	E.14A-11	N611HA	Nathaniel A. Kalt, San Antonio TX	6.85
						W. Scott Kidwell, Redmond WA	2.87
						rep. sold to Panama	6.87
						Airfleet Corp, Omaha NE	88
						Whistlin Dixie Corp, Jacksonville FL	
92	-	•	HA.200A	E.14A-14	N614HA	Nathaniel A. Kalt, San Antonio TX	6.85
						Regis Herbst, Pittsburgh PA	89/92
	-	•	HA.200A	E.14A-15	N5486J	Nathaniel A. Kalt, San Antonio TX	9.84
						Joseph B. Clark/Avstar Inc, Seattle WA	86
						Fred J. Garrison, Angleton TX	88
						Hoffman Aircraft Inc, Texico NM	
92	-	•	HA.200A	E.14A-16	N616HA	Nathaniel A. Kalt, San Antonio TX	6.85
						W. Scott Kidwell, Redmond WA	2.87
						rep. sold to Panama	6.87
						Air Technics Inc, Houston TX	89
					N232DS	Donald H. Schlueter, Genesee ID	1.90/92
	-	•	HA.200A	E.14A-17	N617HA	Nathaniel A. Kalt, San Antonio TX	6.85
						Joseph B. Clark/Avstar Inc, Seattle WA	89/92
	-	•	HA.200A	E.14A-19	N619HA	Nathaniel A. Kalt, San Antonio TX	6.85
						W. Scott Kidwell, Redmond WA	2.87
						James E. Johnson, Salina KS	89
						Joseph B. Clark/Avstar Inc, Seattle WA	92
	-	•	HA.200A	E.14A-20	N620HA	Nathaniel A. Kalt, San Antonio TX	6.85
						W. Scott Kidwell, Redmond WA	2.87
						rep. sold to Panama	6.87
						Shepard Aircraft Corp, Corvaillis OR	89/92
	-	•	HA.200A	E.14A-22	N622HA	Nathaniel A. Kalt, San Antonio TX	6.85
						W. Scott Kidwell, Redmond WA	2.87
						Joseph Clark/Avstar, Seattle WA	89
						Morgan Aviation, Arlington WA	90
					N9107J	Katharine S. Gray, Simi CA	3.92
	-	•	HA.200A	E.14A-26	N626HA	Nathaniel A. Kalt, San Antonio TX	6.85
						Joseph B. Clark/Avstar Inc, Seattle WA	89
	-	•	HA.200A	E.14A-27	N5485G	Nathaniel A. Kalt, San Antonio TX	9.84
						America In Motion Inc, Sherman Oaks CA	88
						(unconv., auctioned Santa Monica CA 10.91)	
						OK Aircraft Accessories, Monterey CA	92
	-	•	HA.200A	E.14A-28	N128HA	Nathaniel A. Kalt, San Antonio TX	6.85
						Joseph B. Clark/Avstar Inc, Seattle WA	88/92

- •	HA.200A	E.14A-29	N629HA	Nathaniel A. Kalt, San Antonio TX	6.85
				Joseph B. Clark/Avstar Inc, Seattle WA	89/92
- •	HA.200A	E.14A-31	N631HA	Nathaniel A. Kalt, San Antonio TX	6.85
				Wayne E. Cozad, Xenia OH	89/92
- •	HA.200A	E.14A-32	N632HA	Nathaniel A. Kalt, San Antonio TX	6.85
				rep. sold to Panama	6.87
				Guy Morgan, Whitestone NY	92
-	HA.200A	E.14A-33	N633HA	Nathaniel A. Kalt, San Antonio TX	6.85
				W. Scott Kidwell, Redmond WA	2.87
				rep. sold to Panama	6.87
				crashed, dest. Tuskegee AL	2.6.90
- •	HA.200A	E.14A-34	N634HA	Nathaniel A. Kalt, San Antonio TX	6.85
				W. Scott Kidwell, Redmond WA	2.87
				Scott W. Kidwell, Redmond WA	88
				Western Wings Inc, Oakland OR	90
				Rhett E. Woods, Roseburg OR	92
-	HA.200A	E.14A-35	N635HA	Nathaniel A. Kalt, San Antonio TX	6.85
				W. Scott Kidwell, Redmond WA	2.87
				sold to Panama	6.87
22/113 •	HA.220	-	N9122F	Combat Aircraft Inc, Elkhart IN	9.87/92
22/114	HA.220	-	N5831Z	Combat Aircraft Inc, Elkhart IN	4.85
				struck-off USCR	5.85
220/100•	HA.220	AE.10C-100	N3110P	Combat Aircraft Inc, Elkhart IN	7.91/92
220/112•	HA.220	AE.10C-112	N4280X	Combat Aircraft Inc, Elkhart IN	7.91/92

LOCKHEED F-104 STARFIGHTER

1007 •	F-104A	55-2961	N818NA	NASA, Edwards AFB CA	72/76
				NASM, Washington DC	78/90
1021	F-104A	56-0733	N104RB	Darryl Greenamyer/Red Baron Flying Service, Tonopah NV	76/79
				crashed & dest. (Greenamyer ejected)	c79
1066 •	F-104A	56-0778		(to R. Jordanian AF as 907)	
			N66305	Air International Corp, Dallas TX	11.90/92
				(stored unconv. dism., Montgomery AL 6.91)	
1068 •	F-104A	56-0780		(to R. Jordanian AF as 908)	
			N66342	Air International Corp, Dallas TX	11.90/92
				(stored unconv. dism., Montgomery AL 6.91)	
1074 •	F-104A	56-0786		(to R. Jordanian AF as 909/G)	
			N66328	Air International Corp, Dallas TX	11.90/92
				(stored unconv. dism., Montgomery AL 6.91: stored unconv., Mojave CA 92)	
1078 •	F-104A	56-0790	N820NA	NASA, Edwards AFB CA	72/78 NF-104E
				Flight Test Historical Museum, Edwards AFB	88/91
4045 •	NF-104A		N811NA	NASA, Edwards AFB CA	71/89
				struck-off USCR	12.89
4053 •	NF-104A		N812NA	NASA, Edwards AFB CA	71/89
				struck-off USCR	12.89
5008 •	F-104B	57-1296		(to R. Jordanian AF as 901)	
			N65354	Air International Corp, Dallas TX	11.90

				(stored unconv. dism., Montgomery AL 6.91)	
				Northern Lights Aircraft, Minnetonka MN	92
5015	F-104D	57-1303	N819NA	NASA, Edwards AFB CA	78
				USAFM, McClellan AFB CA	90
5042	F-104D	57-1330		Letcher & Associates, Mojave CA	84
				Al Hansen & Ascher Ward, Mojave CA	89/90
5302 •	CF-104D	104632		(to RNoAF as 4632)	
				Norwegian Armed Forces Museum	
			N104NL	Northern Lights Aircraft Inc, Montgomery AL	1.89/92
				(flies in civil scheme, "Renee")	
5303 •	CF-104D	104633		(to RNoAF as 4633)	
				Norwegian Armed Forces Museum	
				S. Bruce Goessling/Combat Jet & Aerospace Museum, Chino CA	.86/87
			N104JR	Jim Robinson/Combat Jets Flying Museum, Houston TX (rebuilt Chino, ff 11.11.87)	8.87/92
				EAA Aviation Foundation, Oshkosh WI	.92
5307 •	CF-104D	104637		(to RNoAF as 4637)	
				S. Bruce Goessling/Combat Jet & Aerospace Museum, Chino CA	87
5419 •	F-104DJ	36-5019		(to JSDFAF as 36-5019)	
				noted at Mojave CA	11.87
5735 •	TF-104G	61-3064		(to Luftwaffe as KF+234; 27+33)	
			N825NA	NASA, Edwards AFB CA	2.7.75/78
			N824NA	NASA, Edwards AFB CA	8.84/92
5939 •	TF-104G	66-13628		(to Luftwaffe as 28+09)	
			N826NA	NASA, Edwards AFB CA	2.7.75/78
			N825NA	NASA, Edwards AFB CA	8.84/92
7161 •	F-104G	KE+461		(to Kreigsmarine as VA+137: later 22+79)	
				stored unconv., Mojave CA	92
8213 •	RF-104G	KG+313		(to Luftwaffe as ED+114; 24+64)	
			N824NA	NASA, Edwards AFB CA	.75/78
			N826NA	NASA, Edwards AFB CA	8.84/92
9094 •	F-104G	FX-51		stored Koksijde AB, Belgium	80/88
				Warren Sessler Inc, Chino CA	6.90
				Tom Reilly, Kissimee FL	19.5.90/91
				(stored, unconv. Kissimmee FL)	
9140 •	F-104G	FX-82		stored Koksijde AB, Belgium	80/88
				stored unconv., Chino CA	.89/90
- •	F-104G	FX-84		stored Koksijde AB, Belgium	80/88
				noted unconv., Mineral Wells Airport AL	10.89
				noted unconv., Mojave CA	3.90/92
				(same owner as c/n 7161)	
-	F-104	-	N40GL	Enright Co	77
-	F-104	-	N90500	*no other information*	

Notes

5034 •	T-33A	49-0884		(to RNAF as M-48)	
			N652	Consolidated Aero Export Corporation,	
				North Hollywood CA	7.4.72
				(del. Holland to US, via Shannon 7.4.72)	
				Jim Cullen, Monument CO	76/92
5223 •	T-33A	50-0370		(to RNAF as M-49) BOC	5.2.64
			N651	Consolidated Aero Export Corporation,	
				North Hollywood CA	7.4.72
				(del. Holland to US, via Shannon 7.4.72)	
				(to F.A. Mexicana as JE-017)	
				Forbes Bigbee Manufacturing, San Ramon CA	84
				Cameron Wilke, Lubbock TX	5.84
				Allied Bank of Marble Falls, Marble Falls TX	12.86
				Courtesy Aircraft Inc, Rockford IL	1.87/88
				T Bird Partners, Van Nuys CA	9.88
				Museum of Flying, Santa Monica CA	1.92
5313 •	T-33A	51-4019		(to USN as Bu126583)	
	TV-2		N151	FAA, Oklahoma City OK	
	T-33B		N1519	Schilling Institute, Salina KS	66
				Kansas Technical Institute, Salina KS	69/92
5315	T-33A	51-4021		(to USN as Bu126585)	
	TV-2		N9126Z	reg. res	84/92
	T-33B				
5327 •	T-33A	51-4033		(to USN as Bu126591)	
	TV-2		N335V	E. D. Weiner, Los Angeles CA	66/69
	T-33B		N6633D	E. D. Weiner, Los Angeles CA	.69
				Leroy B. Penhall, Balboa CA	72/74
				Edward O. Messick, San Antonio TX	10.74/86
				G. A. Smith, Long Beach CA	9.86/87
				Shooting Star Productions, Reno NV	6.87/92
5435 •	T-33A	51-4141		(to USN as Bu126617)	
	TV-2			FAA, Oklahoma City OK	.61
	T-33B		N1118U	Westair Inc, Broomfield CO	72
				General Industrial Supply, Muskegee OK	76
				AG Central Aircraft Inc, TX	3.83
				Stanley W. Cameron, Lubbock TX	7.83/84
				Allied Bank of Marble Falls, Marble Falls TX	12.86
				Courtesy Aircraft Inc, Rockford IL	1.87
				Lawrence S. Green, New Castle NH	87/91
				GAE Inc, Manchester NH	92
5565	T-33A	51-4271	N8682E	Chicago Board of Education, Chicago IL	66/76
5587	T-33A	51-4293		(to USN as Bu128671)	
	TV-2		N152	FAA, Oklahoma City OK	63/73
	T-33B			crashed and dest., Elk City OK	24.1.73
5603 •	T-33A	51-4309	N8683E	Chicago Board of Education, Chicago IL	66/76
				still extant but off USCR	89
5677	T-33A	51-4383		(to l'Armee de l'Air as 14383)	
			F-GBEX	reg. for delivery to R. Thai AF	2.83
5860	T-33A	51-6528		(to RNAF as M-51)	
			N650	Consolidated Aero Export Corporation,	
				North Hollywood CA	7.4.72
				(del. Holland to US, via Shannon 7.4.72)	
5863	T-33A	51-6531		(to RNAF as M-55)	
			N649	Consolidated Aero Export Corporation,	
				North Hollywood CA	3.72

				(del. Holland to US, via Shannon 7.4.72)	
				Aero Systems Inc, Boulder CO	76/83
				struck-off USCR	4.83
5912 •	T-33A	51-6580		(to USN as Bu128705)	
	TV-2		N156	FAA, Oklahoma City OK	66/69
	T-33B			(crash landing : hulk noted Van Nuys 4.71)	
			N156Y	Richard W. Martin, Van Nuys CA	72
				(parts used to rebuild Martin's F-80 N10DM, Van Nuys .72)	
				Thunderbird Aviation Inc, Phoenix AZ	76/92
5913 •	T-33A	51-6581		(to USN as Bu128706)	
	TV-2		N9124Z	Ward E. Duncan, Satellite Beach FL	69/76
	T-33B			T-Birds Three Inc, Lubbock TX	84/92
6003	T-33A	51-6671		(to USN as Bu128719)	
	TV-2		N154	FAA, Oklahoma City OK	
	T-33B				
6285 •	T-33A	51-6953		(to RNAF as M-52)	
			N648	Consolidated Aero Export Corporation, North Hollywood CA	7.4.72
				(del. Holland to US, via Shannon 7.4.72)	
				Samuel Reed, Zachary LA	76
				GHS Flying Inc, Bakersfield CA	84
				Preston Air Museum, Dallas TX	9.86
				Morris Cannan, San Antonio TX	12.86/87
				I. N. (Junior) Burchinall, Brookston TX	88/92
6289	T-33A	51-6957	N224NA	NASA (ex NASA 224)	
				stored MASDC by	75
6350 •	T-33A	51-8566		(to RDAF as 18566: later DT-566)	
			G-TJET	Aces High Ltd, Duxford	8.1.82/86
				Nigel Brendish, Cranfield	.86
				Ipswich Airport Ltd, North Weald	12.5.86
				A. S. Topen/Vintage Aircraft Team, Cranfield	88/91
				(flew as "USAF 91007/TR-007")	
			G-NASA	A. S. Topen/Vintage Aircraft Team, Cranfield	3.6.91
6460	T-33A	51-8676	N31040	Greg Forbes, San Jose CA	10.75/77
				(FAA quote "aircraft constructed from parts")	
6518 •	T-33A	51-8734		(to USN as Bu131770)	
	TV-2		N59TW	Thomas E. Wright, Snyder TX	84/88
	T-33B		N59TM	Thomas G. McCoy, Snyder TX	10.91/92
6536	T-33A	51-8752		(to L'Armee de L'Air as 18752)	
			F-GBEY	reg. for delivery to R. Thai AF	2.83
6544	T-33A	51-8760		(to RNAF as M-53)	
			N647	Consolidated Aero Export Corporation, North Hollywood CA	16.3.72/76
				(del. Holland to US, via Shannon 16.3.72)	
				Roger Wolfe, Lovelock NV	.77
				sale rep.	84/92
6608 •	T-33A	51-8824		(to RNAF as M-56)	
			N646	Consolidated Aero Export Corporation, North Hollywood CA	16.3.72
				(del. Holland to US, via Shannon 16.3.72)	
				Northrop University, Inglewood CA	76/87
				struck-off USCR	8.87
6638	T-33A	51-8854		(to USN as Bu131804)	
	TV-2		N155	FAA Oklahoma City OK	
	T-33B		N15511	Canadian Valley Area School, El Reno OK	76

				sale rep.	84/92
6807	T-33A	51-9023	N7507U	Noblesville School Corp, Noblesville IN	66/69
6808	T-33A	51-9024	N651P	Purdue University, Lafayette IN	66/69
6821	T-33A	51-9037		(to Italian AF as MM51-9037)	
			N.........	filed for reg. with FAA	8.86
6882	RT-33A	51-9098	N7490C	Robert V. Kamensky Co, Hollywood CA	.57/61
				(built up from components of several aircraft at Phoenix AZ 57/58)	
			N233Y	Mechanical Products Inc, Jackson MI	63
				Florida Airmotive Sales Inc, Ft Lauderdale FL	66/69
				sale rep.	84/92
6890 •	T-33A	51-9106	N11987	Lewis College, Lockport IL	72/76
				Donald R. Sharp, Pauls Valley OK	6.3.85
				Chester Dubaj, Bedford OH	87/88
				Harry W. Caplan, Pepper Pike OH	92
6911 •	T-33A	51-9127	N123MJ	Ralph Johnson, Richmond CA	69
				American Air Museum, Oakland CA	72/76
				Archie Baldocchi, San Francisco CA	77
				A. H. Massey, West Palm Beach FL	84
				Thunderbird Aviation, Deer Valley AZ	11.86/88
			N9127	Louis Antonacci, Hampshire IL	6.90
				Rolf F. Brunckhorst, Oxford OH	92
6912 •	T-33A	51-9128	N11988	Lewis College, Lockport IL	72/76
				Donald R. Sharp, Pauls Valley OK	6.3.85/92
6952	T-33A	51-9168		(to l'Armee de l'Air as 19168)	
			F-GBEP	reg. for delivery to R. Thai AF	12.82
7047 •	T-33A	51-9263		displ. in park, Brookpark OH	84
			N8042M	reg. res.	92
7055	T-33A	51-9271	N16697		
			N1452	Utah University of Agriculture, Logan UT	.72/84
				struck-off USCR	3.84
7086 •	T-33A	51-9302	N48097	Clark County School Dist, Las Vegas NV	66/92
			N13182	Arizona State University, Tempe AZ	66/69
				(FAA quote same id. for both aircraft)	
7108 •	T-33A	51-16989	N989MS	D. N. Rounds : reg. reserved	6.86
				Michael J. Sohnly, Grand Forks ND	1.87/92
7138 •	T-33A	51-17445		(to RBAF as FT-15)	
			N1180C	Valiant Air Command, Titusville FL	9.81
				AG Central Aircraft Inc TX	83
				Stanley W. Cameron, Lubbock TX	7.83/84
				Allied Bank of Marble Falls, Marble Falls TX	12.86
				Courtesy Aircraft Inc, Rockford IL	1.87
			N410GH	Victor Haluska, Santa Monica CA	11.87/89
				Connie Kalitta Services, Lakeview OR	11.89
			N133CK	Connie Kalitta Services, Lakeview OR	3.92
7254 •	T-33A	51-17463	N533CB	Norman E. Hibbard, Oakland OR	6.90
				Connie Bowlin/Bowlin & Assoc., Griffin GA	92
7362 •	T-33A	51-17468	N125AT	reg.	7.90
				David E. Clayton, San Ramon CA	92
7364	T-33A	51-17470		(to Italian AF as MM51-17470)	

			N.........	filed for reg. with FAA	8.86
7418 •	T-33A	52-9333		Bradley Air Museum, Windsor Locks CT	9.83/84
				New England Air Museum, Windsor Locks CT	.84/88
				Gerald Butterworth/Rhode Island Aircraft,	
				West Kingstown RI (rebuild to fly)	.88/90
7423	T-33A	52-9338	N942NA	NASA, Lyndon B. Johnson Space Center,	
				Houston TX	
				(ex NASA 942) stored MASDC by	75
7477	T-33A	51-17497		(to L'Armee de L'Air as 17497)	
			F-BKXM	reg. for delivery to R. Thai AF	3.82
7571 •	T-33A	52-9461	N4698T	University of Illinois, Urbana IL	66/92
7584 •	T-33A	51-17524		(to RBAF as FT-22)	
			N1180D	AG Central Aircraft Inc, TX	9.81
				Stanley W. Cameron, Lubbock TX	7.83/84
				Red Stevenson, Jenks OK	87/92
7594	T-33A	51-17534		(to Italian AF as MM51-17534)	
			N.........	C. H. Midkiff	8.86
				(id. quoted as "51-17624": above bel. correct)	
7689	T-33A	51-17544		(to l'Armee de l'Air as 17544)	
			F-GBEZ	registered for delivery to R. Thai AF	2.83
7807	T-33A	52-9622	N86905	Winona Area Technical School, Winona MN	.73/92
8149	T-33A	52-9843	N58417	Detroit Education Board, Detroit MI	66/76
8162	T-33A	52-9856	N49892	South Illinois University, Carbondale IL	.73/76
8229	T-33A	53-4890	N12270	Independent School District, Watertown SD	69/76
8245	T-33A	53-4906	TG-LAY	S. Perez, La Aurora, Guatamala	2.75
				C of A expired	7.8.75
8306 •	T-33A	53-4967	N47799	Delgado Junior College, Lakefront Airport,	
				New Orleans LA	.73/88
				State of Louisiana, New Orleans LA	6.90/92
8336 •	T-33A	53-4997	N73680	SFO Community College, San Francisco CA	.73/92
8349	T-33A	53-5010	N13006	reg. res.	.73
8459	T-33A	53-5120		(to l'Armee de l'Air as 35120)	
			F-GBEO	reg. for delivery to R. Thai AF	12.82
8471	T-33A	53-5132		(to l'Armee de l'Air as 35132)	
			F-GBEN	reg. for delivery to R. Thai AF	12.82
8486	T-33A	53-5147		(to l'Armee de l'Air as 35147)	
			F-BJNO	reg. for delivery to R. Thai AF	3.82
8511	T-33A	53-5172	N510NA	NASA, Langley Research Center, Hampton VA	78
8536	T-33A	53-5197	TG-LAX	S. Perez, La Aurora, Guatamala	2.75
				C of A expired	7.8.75
8554 •	T-33A	53-5215	N8361	Honolulu Community College, Honolulu HI	5.73/88
				Jack A. Myers, Half Moon Bay CA	11.88
				sale rep., Coleman TX	90/92
				Dixie Air Parts, San Antonio TX: stored dism.	91/92
8558	T-33A	53-5219	N1040Z	Western Michigan University, Kalamazoo MI	63/69

8577	T-33A	53-5238		(to Italian AF as MM53-5238)	
			N.........	filed for reg. with FAA	8.86
8586	T-33A	53-5247	N64351	St Louis University, Cahokia IL	76
8621	T-33A	53-5282		(to l'Armee de l'Air as 35282)	
			F-GBEQ	reg. for delivery to R. Thai AF	12.82
8739 •	T-33A	53-5400		(to NASA as NASA 945)	
			N715NA	NASA, Ames Research Center, NAS Moffet Field CA	71/72
			N94481	Peralta Comm. College, Oakland Airport CA	76/92
8926	T-33A	53-5587		(to Italian AF as MM53-5587)	
			N.........	filed for reg. with FAA	8.86
9149	T-33A	53-5748		(to l'Armee de l'Air as 35748)	
			F-BJXM	reg. for delivery to R. Thai AF	3.82
9195	T-33A	53-5794		(to l'Armee de l'Air as 35794)	
			F-BJGY	reg. for delivery to R. Thai AF	3.82
9216	T-33A	53-5815	N4980	Delta Air Parts Co, Sun Valley CA	72/76
9251 •	T-33A	53-5850	N1453		
			N4605B	San Diego Community College, Montgomery Field, San Diego CA	76/92
				(FAA quotes id. "9291")	
9424 •	T-33A	53-5948	N62519	Southwest Michigan College, Dowagiac MI	.73/92
9518 •	T-33A	55-3021	N3497F	Solano City College, Suisun City CA	1.10.76/92
9522	T-33A	55-3025	N512NA	NASA	
9543	T-33A	53-6011		(to NASA as NASA 940)	
			N940NA	NASA, Houston TX : stored MASDC by	75
				reg. pending	76/88
				noted stored Tulsa OK	4.82
9594	T-33A	55-3053		(to USN as Bu141538)	
	TV-2		N13007	New York City Education Board NY	66/72
	T-33B			Sea-Air-Space Museum, New York NY	91/92
				(displ. on carrier USS Intrepid as "141538/538")	
9605 •	T-33A	55-3064		(to USN as Bu141549)	
	TV-2		N99472	Helena Vocational Tech School, Helena MT	76/92
	T-33B				
9618	T-33A	55-3077		(to Italian AF as MM55-3077)	
			N.........	filed for reg. with FAA	8.86
9658 •	T-33A	53-6055	N99095	School of the Ozarks, Point Lookout MO	76/92
9712 •	T-33A	53-6091	N11989	Lewis College, Lockport IL	72/76
			N8077X	Gerald N. Butterworth/Rhode Island Aircraft, West Kingston RI	5.88
			N32GB	Gerald N. Butterworth, West Kingston RI	8.89/92
				(rest. to fly, flies as "USAF 36091")	
9779 •	T-33A	55-4335	N9979Q	Tech. College, Spokane WA : del. ex MASDC	10.12.76
				sale rep., Spokane WA	84/88
				Steve L. Picatti, Boise ID	4.91/92
9795 •	T-33A	55-4351	N815NA	NASA, Edwards AFB CA	69/72
				Shasta Tehama Trinity, Redding CA	76/92

9830	T-33A	55-4386	N938NA	NASA	
9835	T-33A	55-4391	N1058	Sowella Technical Institute, Lake Charles LA	69/72
9843 •	T-33A	55-4399	N87912	Academy of Aeronautics, La Guardia Airport NY : del. ex MASDC K & K Aircraft Inc, Bridgewater VA	 23.2.77/84 6.88
9923 •	T-33A	56-1573	N97477 N7477	Honolulu Community College, Honolulu HI Jack A. Myers, Half Moon Bay CA sale rep., Coleman TX	69/88 11.88 92
9924 •	T-33A	56-1574	N8362	Honolulu Community College, Honolulu HI Jack A. Myers, Half Moon Bay CA	73/88 11.88/92
9939	T-33A	56-1589	N948NA	NASA	
1019 •	T-33A	56-1669	N391P	Trustees Purdue University, Lafayette IN sale reported, Vincennes IN	.73/76 84/92
1080	T-33A	56-1730	N1449	US Dept of Interior Geological Surveys, Water Resources Division: stored MASDC by	 75
1097 •	T-33A	56-1747	N43856	Board of Education, Westbury NY	12.76/92
1099 •	T-33A	56-1749	N61749 N155SF	 Aviation Consultants Inc, Tulsa OK Richard F. Bohannon, McAllen TX	 76/77 84/92
1102 •	T-33A TV-2 T-33B	56-1752	 N40186	(to USN as Bu143040) Lansing Community College, Lansing MI	 76/92
1150	T-33A	56-3666	 N941NA	(to NASA as NASA 941) NASA, Houston TX : to MASDC Allied Aircraft, Tucson AZ : del. ex MASDC	 3.9.70 2.8.78
1145	T-33A	56-3661	N83615	reg. res.	.73
1151 •	T-33A	56-3667	N51SR	Leroy Penhall/Fighter Imports Inc, Chino CA David C. Tallichet/ MARC, Chino CA (FAA quote 57-0451, "1451" & "0451"; 51-17416 also quoted!)	74 76/92
1155	T-33A	56-3671	 N937NA	(to NASA as NASA 937) NASA, Houston TX : retired to MASDC Allied Aircraft, Tucson AZ : del. ex MASDC	 20.11.70 19.1.76
1173 •	T-33A	56-3689	N939NA	NASA, Houston TX Golden Triangle Votec School, Columbus OH George W. Lancaster, Wilmington NC (flies as "USAF 63689")	.73/76 76/87 11.87/92
1282	T-33A	57-0553	N57553	South Illinois University, Carbondale IL	.73/76
1294 •	T-33A	57-0565	N22ES	Western Michigan University MI reg. res. E. J. Saviano, Portage WI James E. Smith, Boulder CO/Fortine MT	2.85 4.85 87/92
1297	T-33A	57-0568	N41839	Victor Valley College, Victorville CA struck-off USCR	76/88 5.90
1298 •	T-33A	57-0569	N64274	George T. Baker Aviation School, Miami FL	.75/92
1302 •	T-33A	57-0573	N99152	Cincinnati Technical College, Cincinnati OH sale rep., Chesterfield MO	.73/88 89/92
1337 •	T-33A	57-0598	N23745	Area Vocational Tech. School, Tallahassee FL	76/92

1348 •	T-33A	57-0609	N82852	Sowela Technical Institute, Lake Charles LA	76/92
1412	T-33A	57-0683		(to l'Armee de l'Air as 70683)	
			F-GBEV	reg. for del. to R. Thai AF	2.83
1417	T-33A	57-0688	N942NA	NASA, Houston TX	
1449	T-33A	57-0720	N943NA	NASA, Houston TX	
1450	T-33A	57-0721	N934NA	NASA, Houston TX	
1451	T-33A	57-0722	N935NA	NASA, Houston TX	
1480 •	T-33A	57-0751	N17076	Los Angeles School District, Mission Hills CA	76/92
1519 •	T-33A	58-0470	N63313	Area Vocational Tech. School, Tallahassee FL	76/92
1520 •	T-33A	58-0471	N94498	Le Tourneau College, Longview TX	76/87
				Fred N. Ropkey, Longview TX	87/92
				(rebuilt, ff .90 as "USAF 80471")	
				(FAA quote id. "1441")	
1529 •	T-33A	58-0480	N63311	George T. Baker Aviation School, Miami FL	75/92
1540 •	T-33A	58-0491	N94484	Los Rios Community College, Sacramento CA	.73/92
1541 •	T-33A	58-0492	N24837	Montcalm Community College, Sidney MI	76
				sale reported, Dowagiac MI	84/92
1546	T-33A	58-0497	N87778	State Board for Education, Columbia SC	76
1558 •	T-33A	58-0509	N57969	Kirtland Community College, Roscommon MI	.73/92
1588 •	T-33A	58-0539		Trident College, Charleston SC (ex MASDC)	8.6.77
			N37998	Trident Technical College, Charleston SC	.78/92
				(FAA quote id. "1508")	
1591 •	T-33A	58-0542	N10265	Texas State Technical Institute, Waco TX	75/92
1595 •	T-33A	58-0546	N93224	Tarrant City Junior College, Fort Worth TX	.73/84
				Eagles Nest Of The Ozarks Inc, Springfield MO	4.86/92
1685	T-33A	58-0636	N83737	Warren High School, Gurnee IL	76
				sale rep., Chicago IL	84/92
1700 •	T-33A	58-0651	N88769	Southwest Tech. Institute, East Camden AR	.73/92
1714 •	T-33A	58-0665		imported by Aero Technical Services Inc	5.88
			N658W	Jack A. Myers, Half Moon Bay CA	10.88
			N556RH	Randall Hames/Hames Aviation, Cliffside NC	4.91/92
1720	T-33A	58-0671		(to NASA as NASA 936)	
			N936NA	NASA, Houston TX : retired to MASDC by	75
1746 •	T-33A	58-0697	N49239	Florence School District, Florence SC	76/84
				sale reported, Jacksonville FL	88
				Doan Helicopters, New Smyrna Beach FL	7.91/92
				(rebuilt, flies in USAF scheme)	
1749 •	T-33A	58-0700	N88812	Florida Academy of Aerospace Technology,	
				St. Petersburg-Clearwater Airport FL	.73/92
24 •	Mk.3	RCAF21024	N157X	Omni Investment Group, Long Beach CA	3.65/73
			N302FS	Flight Systems Inc, Mojave CA	5.77/89
				T-Bird Aviation, Mojave CA	3.90/92

15		Mk.3	RCAF21015		(to l'Armee de l'Air as 21015)	
				F-WEQB	ferry to Dinard, ex storage Chateaudun AB	.85
				F-ZVLH (1	dep. Dinard, France on del. to Bolivia	12.7.85
					(to F.A. Boliviana as ....)	
27		Mk.3	RCAF21027		(to l'Armee de l'Air as 21027)	
				F-WEQA	ferry to Dinard, ex storage Chateaudun AB	.85
				F-ZVLC (1	dep. Dinard, France on del. to Bolivia	19.6.85
					(to F.A. Boliviana as ....)	
42		Mk.3	RCAF21042		(to l'Armee de l'Air as 21042)	
				F-WEQE	ferry to Dinard, ex storage Chateaudun AB	.85
				F-ZVLI (1	dep. Dinard, France on del. to Bolivia	19.6.85
					(to F.A. Boliviana as ....)	
50		Mk.3	RCAF21050		(to l'Armee de l'Air as 21050)	
				F-WEQC	ferry to Dinard, ex storage Chateaudun AB	.85
				F-ZVLJ (1	dep. Dinard, France on del. to Bolivia	12.7.85
					(to F.A. Boliviana as ....)	
81		Mk.3	RCAF21081		(to l'Armee de l'Air as 21081)	
				F-WEQF	ferry to Dinard, ex storage Chateaudun AB	.85
				F-ZVLK (1	dep. Dinard, France on del. to Bolivia	12.7.85
					(to F.A. Boliviana as ....)	
88		Mk.3	RCAF21088		(to l'Armee de l'Air as 21088)	
				F-WEQQ	ferry to Dinard, ex storage Chateaudun AB	.85
				F-ZVLN (2	dep. Dinard, France on del. to Bolivia	10.85
					(to F.A. Boliviana as ....)	
98	•	Mk. 3	RCAF21098	N99184	Flight Systems Inc, Mojave CA	2.77/88
					T-Bird Aviation, Mojave CA	3.89
					Fort Wayne Air Service, Fort Wayne IN	6.89
					Rick Brickert/Red Knight Airshows Inc,	
					Fort Wayne IN : flies as "Red Knight"	.90/92
118	•	Mk. 3	RCAF21118	N99192	Flight Systems Inc, Mojave CA	2.77/88
					T-Bird Aviation, Mojave CA	3.89/92
129	•	Mk. 3	RCAF21129	N64776		
				N84TB	Creature Enterprises, Bridgehampton NY	9.77
					Thunderbird Aviation Inc, Deer Valley AZ	86/92
132		Mk.3	RCAF21132		(to l'Armee de l'Air as 21132)	
				F-WEQK	ferry to Dinard, ex storage Chateaudun AB	.85
				F-ZVLJ (2	dep. Dinard, France on del. to Bolivia	10.85
					(to F.A. Boliviana as ....)	
150		Mk. 3	RCAF21150		(later CAF 133150)	
				C-GWHM	Arnie Carnegie, Edmonton ALTA	7.75
					(to FA Boliviana as FAB615)	
					crashed and dest., Punata, Bolivia	21.2.80
152		Mk.3	RCAF21152		(to l'Armee de l'Air as 21152)	
				F-WEQP	ferry to Dinard, ex storage Chateaudun AB	.85
				F-ZVLC (3	dep. Dinard, France on del. to Bolivia	11.85
					(to F.A. Boliviana as ....)	
157	•	Mk. 3	RCAF21157	N155X	Omni Investment Group, Long Beach CA	3.65/66
					Jim Cullen, Broomfield CO	69
					Flight Systems Inc, Mojave CA	76
					Creature Enterprises, Bridgehampton NY	77
					Centurion Airways CA	84
					Aeronautical Test Vehicles,Newport Beach CA	5.84
				N133AT	Aeronautical Test Vehicles,Newport Beach CA	7.85
					Advanced Aeronautical Enterprises Inc,	
					Newport Beach CA	3.86

					Barron Thomas Aviation Inc, Dallas TX	6.88/92
159	•	Mk.3	RCAF21159		(to RCN as 21159)	
				N96186	Flight Systems Inc, Mojave CA	9.76
				N305FS	Flight Systems Inc, Mojave CA	9.77/89
					Tracor Flight Systems, Austin TX	92
160	•	Mk. 3	RCAF21160	N12414	Leroy Penhall/Fighter Imports Inc, Chino CA	.73
					Murray McCormick Aerial Surveys	75
					Consolidated Leasing, Sacramento CA	77
				N221SF	Flight Test Research Inc, Englewood CO	8.83/92
162		Mk. 3	RCAF21162	CF-FIF	Northwest Industries Ltd, Edmonton ALTA	1.73
					(del. to South America, via Miami 13.1.73)	
182		Mk.3	RCAF21182		(to l'Armee de l'Air as 21182)	
				F-WEQO	ferry to Dinard, ex storage Chateaudun AB	.85
				F-ZVLK (2	dep. Dinard, France on del. to Bolivia	10.85
					(to F.A. Boliviana as ....)	
192	•	Mk. 3	RCAF21192	N156X	Omni Investment Group, Long Beach CA	3.65
					Flight Test Research Inc, Long Beach CA	68/72
					Flight Systems Inc, Mojave CA	73/76
				N304FS	Flight Systems Inc, Mojave CA	79/90
					Arthur W. McDonnell/McDonnell Enterprises Inc, Mojave CA	2.90
					T-33 Inc, Winter Park FL	8.90/92
195		Mk.3	RCAF21195		(to l'Armee de l'Air as 21195)	
				F-WEQR	ferry to Dinard, ex storage Chateaudun AB	.85
				F-ZVLM	dep. Dinard, France on del. to Bolivia	11.85
					(to F.A. Boliviana as ....)	
200		Mk. 3	RCAF21200	N12420	Leroy Penhall/Fighter Imports Inc, Chino CA	.73
					Winchester Meteorology Division, New Haven CT	73/75
					(based Torino, Italy, del. via Prestwick 10.5.73)	
					dam. by hailstorm, Torino, Italy	22.6.73
					struck-off USCR : "sold for salvage"	7.10.75
					Ormond Haydon-Baillie, Duxford UK	.76
					del. to USA, via Prestwick	25.11.77
211		Mk.3	RCAF21211		(to l'Armee de l'Air as 21211)	
				F-WEQL	ferry to Dinard, ex storage Chateaudun AB	.85
				F-ZVLI (2	dep. Dinard, France on del. to Bolivia	30.9.85
					(to F.A. Boliviana as ....)	
221		Mk. 3	RCAF21221	N12424	Leroy Penhall/Fighter Imports Inc, Chino CA	72/74
231	•	Mk. 3	RCAF21231	N134AT	Advanced Aeron. Ent. Inc, Mojave CA	
				N10018	E. Duke Vincent, Los Angeles CA	86
				N134AT	Aeronautical Test Vehicles,Newport Beach CA	1.87
				N333DV	Duke E. Vincent, Los Angeles CA	2.87/92
236	•	Mk. 3	RCAF21236		(to RCN as 21236)	
				N99195	Flight Systems Inc, Mojave CA	2.77/89
					T-Bird Aviation, Mojave CA	3.89
					Neil J. McClain, Strathmore ALTA/Mojave CA	92
247		Mk.3	RCAF21247		(to l'Armee de l'Air as 21247)	
				F-WEQG	ferry to Dinard, ex storage Chateaudun AB	.85
				F-ZVLN (1	dep. Dinard, France on del. to Bolivia	26.8.85
					(to F.A. Boliviana as ....)	
261	•	Mk. 3	RCAF21261		(later CAF133261)	
				CF-IHB	Ormond Haydon-Baillie, Cold Lake ALTA	8.72/73

				(del. Canada to UK, arr. Southend 9.11.73)	
			G-OAHB	Ormond Haydon-Baillie, Duxford	9.5.74/80
				Brotway Ltd: dism. Duxford & Baginton	.80/82
			G-JETT	Anvil Aviation Ltd, Blackbushe	4.6.82
				Aces High Ltd, Duxford	83/85
				Patina Pty Ltd, Baginton	30.1.85
				(del. to USA, via Prestwick 14.7.85)	
			N33VC	Bruce Goessling/Combat Jet & Aerospace Museum, Chino CA	11.85
				Pacifica Investments Inc, Las Vegas NV	87
				Grob Aviation Inc, Wilmington DE	88
				(del. US to Switzerland, arr. Zurich 29.4.88)	
				John V. Crocker, Herndon VA	90/92
				op: Old Flying Machine Co,Duxford	5.90/92
				(del. Switzerland-Duxford 1.5.90, flies as "USAF 54-21261")	
265	•	Mk. 3	RCAF21265	N12418	Leroy Penhall/Fighter Imports Inc, Chino CA	.73/74
					Jack Ormes, Los Angeles CA	77
					Raymond F. Mabrey, Coon Rapids MI	82/92
273	•	Mk. 3	RCAF21273	N12413	Leroy Penhall/Fighter Imports Inc, Chino CA	.73/74
					Richard Doebler, Milwaukee WI	77
					John R. Sandberg, Robstown TX	.82/88
					Rick Brickert & Dennis Sanders, Chino CA	.88/90
				N233RK	Frank C. Sanders, Chino CA	9.89/90
					Red Knight Air Shows, Chino CA	5.90
					crashed, dest., Roswell NM (Sanders k.)	4.5.90
288		Mk. 3	RCAF21288	N106D	Flight Test Research, Long Beach CA	3.65/68
					crashed near Mojave CA : pilot ejected	19.9.68
295	•	Mk. 3	RCAF21295	N4TM	Thomas McMullen, Fullerton CA	76
				N33EL	Ed P. Lunken, Cincinnati OH	10.81
				N72JR	Jim Robinson, Houston TX	7.85/86
					Combat Jets Flying Museum, Houston TX	12.86/92
					EAA Aviation Foundation, Oshkosh WI	.92
298	•	Mk. 3	RCAF21298	CF-SSZ	rep. Malton ONT	65
				N109X	Flight Test Research Inc, Long Beach CA	3.65
					Aeronautical Specialties Inc, Long Beach CA	66
					Flight Test Research Inc, Long Beach CA	72
					Boeing Equipment Holding Co, Seattle WA	76/92
306	•	Mk. 3	RCAF21306	N99173	Flight Systems Inc, Mojave CA	2.77
				N306FS	Flight Systems Inc, Mojave CA	1.78/89
					T-Bird Aviation, Mojave CA	3.89/92
					(flies as USAF "21306")	
307		Mk.3	RCAF21307		(to l'Armee de l'Air as 21307)	
				F-WEQN	ferry to Dinard, ex storage Chateaudun AB	.85
				F-ZVLD (3	dep. Dinard, France on del. to Bolivia	11.85
					(to F.A. Boliviana as ....)	
325		Mk. 3	RCAF21325	CF-ADY	Lester Addie/Addie & Assoc. Ltd, Moncton NB	10.72
				N325DS	reg.	6.76
329		Mk. 3	RCAF21329		(later CAF 133329)	
				C-GWHO	Arnie Carnegie, Edmonton ALTA	7.75
					(to FA Boliviana as FAB619)	.75
333		Mk. 3	RCAF21333	N1355Q		
				N4345F	reg.	7.82
341	•	Mk. 3	RCAF21341	N12422	Leroy Penhall/Fighter Imports Inc, Chino CA	.73/74
					Kay J. Eckhardt, Salt Lake City UT	9.75/92
342	•	Mk. 3	RCAF21342	N144M	Omni Investment Corp, Washington DC	12.64/66

					Flight Test Research Inc, Long Beach CA	69/72
					Paul B. McCready, New Haven CT	72
					Flight Systems Inc, Mojave CA	76/77
				N303FS	Flight Systems Inc, Mojave CA	3.77/89
					Tracor Flight Systems, Austin TX	92
369	•	Mk. 3	RCAF21369	N12416	Leroy Penhall/Fighter Imports Inc, Chino CA	.73/74
					Ed Fisher, Kansas City KS	77
					Boeing Equipment Holding Co, Seattle WA	86/92
375	•	Mk. 3	RCAF21375	N12430	Leroy Penhall/Fighter Imports Inc, Chino CA	.73/74
				N33WR	Walter Rye, Cincinnati OH	76
					Harrah Corporation Unlimited, Portland OR	
				N33HW	Harrah Corporation Unlimited, Portland OR	4.85/86
					Jet I Inc, Alexandria VA	88
					ISRMS Inc, Land-o-Lakes FL	92
379	•	Mk. 3	RCAF21379	CF-SKH	National Research Council, Ottawa ONT	70
				C-FSKH-X	National Aeronautical Estab., Ottawa ONT	83/86
400		Mk.3	RCAF21400		(to l'Armee de l'Air as 21400)	
				F-WEQD	ferry to Dinard, ex storage Chateaudun AB	.85
				F-ZVLD	dep. Dinard, France on del. to Bolivia	19.6.85
					(to F.A. Boliviana as ....)	
420		Mk.3	RCAF21420		(to l'Armee de l'Air as 21420)	
				F-WEQI	ferry to Dinard, ex storage Chateaudun AB	.85
				F-ZVLC (2	dep. Dinard, France on del. to Bolivia	26.8.85
					(to F.A. Boliviana as ....)	
439		Mk. 3	RCAF21439		(to l'Armee de l'Air as 21439)	
				N4249R	Vince Clothier Corp, Phoenix AZ	5.81
					not del., struck-off USCR	1.85
				F-WEQJ	ferry to Dinard, ex storage Chateaudun AB	.85
				F-ZVLD (2	dep. Dinard, France on del. to Bolivia	30.9.85
440	•	Mk. 3	RCAF21440	N12417	Leroy Penhall/Fighter Imports Inc, Chino CA	74
					Douglas Clark/Clark Aviation, Allandale FL	77/92
					(flies in "Thunderbirds" scheme)	
456	•	Mk. 3	RCAF21456	N158X	Mount Union Airport, Mount Union PA	3.65/66
					Playboy Missile Systems, Amarillo TX	69
					Playboy Missile Systems, Las Vegas NV	72
				N333MJ	Matt Jackson, Portland OR	2.82/84
					(flew in movie"The Right Stuff" as "11808")	
				N333JM	Jimmy McMillan, Breckenridge TX	.84
				N333MJ	Don H. Novas, Blackfoot ID	87/92
464		Mk. 3	RCAF21464		(later CAF 133464)	
				N21464	reg.	.73
				C-GPEG	Arnie Carnegie, Edmonton ALTA	7.75
					(to FA Boliviana as FAB618)	.75
485		Mk. 3	RCAF21485		(to L'Armee de L'Air as 21485)	
				N4249R	Vince Clothier Corp, Phoenix AZ	5.81/85
					not del., struck-off USCR	1.85
				F-WEQM	ferry to Dinard, ex storage Chateaudun AB	.85
				F-ZVLH (2	dep. Dinard, France on del. Bolivia	30.9.85
					(to FA Boliviana as ....)	
488		Mk. 3	RCAF21488		(later CAF 133488)	
				C-GWHL	Arnie Carnegie, Edmonton ALTA	7.75
					(to FA Boliviana as FAB617)	.75
489		Mk. 3	RCAF21489		(to L'Armee de L'Air as 21489)	
				N4249V	Vince Clothier Corp, Phoenix AZ	5.81/85

				not del., struck-off USCR	1.85
			F-WEQH	ferry to Dinard, ex storage Chateaudun AB	.85
			F-ZVLM	dep. Dinard, France on del. Bolivia	26.8.85
				(to FA Boliviana as ....)	
535 •	Mk. 3	RCAF21535	N35RV	Robert M. Vuksanovic, Dover NH	7.86/88
				Robert M. Vuksanovic, Caledonia WI	89/92
555 •	Mk. 3	RCAF21555	N96178	Flight Systems Inc, Mojave CA	.76
			N301FS	Flight Systems Inc, Mojave CA	9.77/89
				Tracor Flight Systems, Austin TX	92
556 •	Mk. 3	RCAF21556	N99179	Flight Systems Inc, Mojave CA	2.77/89
				T-Bird Aviation, Mojave CA	3.89
				(open storage, faded RCAF sc., Mojave 80/90)	
				PLR Aircraft Leasing Co, Los Angeles CA	92
557 •	Mk. 3	RCAF21557	N99175	Flight Systems Inc, Mojave CA	2.77/89
				T-Bird Aviation, Mojave CA	3.89
				Neil J. MacLain,Strathmore ALTA/Mojave CA	91/92
				(flies as "RCAF 21557 Golden Hawks")	
559 •	Mk. 3	RCAF21559	N3370		
			N83TB	Thunderbird Aviation, Deer Valley AZ	76/92
566 •	Mk. 3	RCAF21566	N99193	Flight Systems Inc, Mojave CA	2.77/85
			N307FS	Flight Systems Inc, Mojave CA	5.85/89
				Tracor Flight Systems, Austin TX	92
580	Mk. 3	RCAF21580		(later CAF 133580)	
			C-GWHN	Arnie Carnegie. Edmonton ALTA	7.75
				(to FA Boliviana as FAB616)	.75
590 •	Mk. 3	RCAF21590		(later CAF 133590)	
			CF-WIS	National Aeronautical Estab., Ottawa ONT	70
			C-FWIS-X	National Aeronautical Estab., Ottawa ONT	72/86
582 •	Mk. 3	RCAF21582	N99202	Flight Systems Inc, Mojave CA	2.77
			N92JB	John McGuire, Santa Teresa NM	2.84/92
640	Mk. 3	RCAF21640		(to RCN as 21640)	
			CF-EHB	Ormond Haydon-Baillie, Toronto ONT	11.73
				(flown Canada to UK : arr. Southend 30.11.73)	
			G-WGHB	Ormond Haydon-Baillie, Duxford	9.5.74/80
				Brotway Ltd : dism. Duxford & Baginton	.80/83
				Anvil Aviation Ltd	6.82
				moved by road to Southampton	3.8.85
-	Mk. 3	RCAF21...	CP-1045	ferry reg. for flight Edmonton - FA Boliviana	

LOCKHEED TV-2 SEASTAR

- •	T2V-1 T-1A	Bu144735	N447TV	Museum of Alaska Transport and Industry, Palmer AK	1.86/92

Notes

McDONNELL F-101 VOODOO

- •	F-101A	53-2418		Fred E. Wiesbrod Aircraft Museum, Pueblo CO	87
			N9250Z	Dennis E. Kesley, Lind WA	90/92
- •	F-101A	54-1443	N7006K	Rick E. Sharpe/Warbirds Unlimited, Rosharon TX	8.88
				Dean Martin/Warplanes Inc, Burlington VT	9.88/92
- •	F-101B	57-0410	N8234	Colorado State University, Denver CO	75/76
				(flew as "Severe Storm Research/Grey Ghost")	
				sale rep., Topeka KS	90/92
- •	TF-101B	59-0400	N37647	Florida Exhibitions Inc, Orlando FL	31.3.80/92
				displ. Wings & Wheels Museum, Orlando FL	81
				EAA Museum, Lakeland FL	88/91

McDONNELL F-4 PHANTOM II

- •	F-4C	63-7545	N421FS	USAF/Flight Systems Inc, Mojave CA	8.87/92
- •	F-4C	63-7564	N422FS	USAF/Flight Systems Inc, Mojave CA	11.87/92
- •	F-4C	63-7567	N402FS	USAF/Flight Systems Inc, Mojave CA	4.86/92
- •	F-4C	63-7607	N423FS	USAF/Flight Systems Inc, Mojave CA	11.87/92
- •	F-4C	63-7689	N420FS	USAF/Flight Systems Inc, Mojave CA	8.87/92
- •	F-4C	64-0741	N403FS	USAF/Flight Systems Inc, Mojave CA	4.86/92
				(static displ., Mojave CA 90/92)	
- •	F-4D	64-0952	N401AV	USAF/Flight Systems Inc, Mojave CA	90/92
- •	F-4D	64-0964	N403AV	USAF/Flight Systems Inc, Mojave CA	90/92
- •	F-4D	64-0965	N424FS	USAF/Flight Systems Inc, Mojave CA	1.91/92
- •	F-4D	65-0694		USAF/Flight Systems Inc, Mojave CA	92
				(stored unconv., Mojave CA 92)	
- •	F-4D	65-0696	N402AV	USAF/Flight Systems Inc, Mojave CA	90/92
- •	F-4D	65-0704	N404AV	USAF/Flight Systems Inc, Mojave CA	90/92
				(stored unconv., Mojave CA 92)	
- •	F-4D	65-0763	N426FS	USAF/Flight Systems Inc, Mojave CA	1.91/92
- •	F-4D	66-7483	N430FS	USAF/Flight Systems Inc, Mojave CA	10.91/92
- •	F-4D	66-7505	N427FS	USAF/Flight Systems Inc, Mojave CA	1.91/92
- •	F-4D	66-7759	N428FS	USAF/Flight Systems Inc, Mojave CA	1.91/92
				struck-off USCR	1.92
644	F-4C	-	N3933N	struck-off USCR	2.90

MESSERSCHMITT Me163 KOMET

Nr120370 •	Me163B-1a	Nr120370	(to RAF for trials as AM.210)	
			RAF Air Historical Branch Collection	62/64
			Deutsches Museum, Munich	11.64/88
Nr191060 •	Me163B-1	Nr191060	(to RAF for trials as VF241)	
			RAF Air Historical Branch, RAF Biggin Hill	62
			Imperial War Museum, Lambeth	73
			Imperial War Museum, Duxford	84/92
			(id. also rep. as Nr191660)	

Nr191095 •	Me163B-1	Nr191095	Canadian National Aviation Museum, Rockcliffe ONT	 65/90
Nr191190 •	Me163B-1	Nr191190	captured, Husum (to USA for trials as FE-500; T2-500) Smithsonian Institute, stored Park Ridge IL NASM Silver Hill MD	 .46 65/90
Nr191316 •	Me163B-1	Nr191316	The Science Museum, London	65/89
Nr191614 •	Me163B-1a	Nr191614	Ministry of Transport Rocket Propulsion Establishment, Westcott RAF Museum, RAF Cosford	 69/73 79/89
Nr191659 •	Me163B-1	Nr191659	(to RAF for trials as AM.215) College of Aeronautics, Cranfield Royal Scottish Museum, East Fortune	 63/73 .75/91
Nr191904 •	Me163B-1a	Nr191904	JG400, captured Husum (to RAF for trials as AM.217) RAF Museum, RAF Colerne RAF Museum, RAF St. Athan Aviation Heritage Centre, Oldenburg WG	.45 64/73 .75/88 5.5.88
Nr191907 •	Me163B-1	Nr191907	JG400, captured Husum (to RAF for trials as AM.81) Australian War Memorial, Canberra ACT loan: RAAF Museum, RAAF Point Cook VIC	.45 .49/92 71/76
Nr191916 •	Me163B-1	Nr191916	Canadian National Aviation Museum, Rockcliffe ONT loan: Canadian War Museum, Ottawa ONT (displ. as "JG1/400: 191916/26")	 65/90 78/90
-	Me163		Victory Air Museum, Mundelein IL	76

MESSERSCHMITT Me262 VOLKSJAEGER

Nr110305 • / U-1	Me262B-1a	Nr110305	(10 / NJG 11 Red 8: to RAF as AM.50) del. Schleswig - Farnborough National Museum of Military History, Saxonwold, South Africa : arr. by ship	 .45 7.3.47/88
Nr110639 •	Me262B-1a /U-1	Nr110639	(III / EGJ2 White 35) shipped to USA for USN trials as FE-101 NAS Willow Grove PA (displ. as "13")	 .45 58/90
Nr111617 •	Me262A-1a /U-3	Nr111617	(Komm. Braunegg, White 25) shipped to USA on HMS Reaper (to USAAF for trials as FE-4012;T2-4012) flight tests Hughes Aircraft, Culver City CA Cal Aero Technical Institute, Glendale CA The Air Museum, Claremont/Ontario CA (rest. 69, displ. as "13") Planes of Fame Museum, Chino (planned rest. to fly, Chino)	 7.45 .48 c49/55 c55/70 74/92
Nr112372 •	Me262A-1a	Nr112372	(3/JG7 Yellow 7): to RAF as AM.51; VK893 RAF Gaydon RAF Museum, RAF Cosford RAF Museum, RAF St. Athan RAF Museum, RAF Cosford	 72/73 77/84 86/88 89/91
Nr121442 •	Me262A-1a	Nr121442	flight tested at NAS Patuxent River MD USAFM Wright-Patterson AFB, Dayton OH	.45 .58/90

Messerschmitt Me262

Nr500071 •	Me262A-1a	Nr500071	(9 / JG7 White 3)	
			interned by Swiss at Dubendorf, Switzerland	25.4.45
			Deutsches Museum, Munich	.75/86
Nr500210 •	Me262A-1a	Nr500200	(11/ KG51 Black X): to RAF as AM.81, VH519	
			Australian War Memorial, Canberra ACT	50/92
			loan: RAAF Museum, RAAF Point Cook VIC	71/92
			(prev. incorrectly quoted as Nr500210)	
Nr500491 •	Me262A-1a /U-3	Nr500491	(11/ JG7 Yellow 7: to USAAF as FE-111)	
			shipped to USA on HMS Reaper	7.45
			Smithsonian Institute, stored Park Ridge IL	.46
			NASM, Silver Hill MD	65/68
			NASM, Washington DC	88/90
- •	Me262A		Victory Air Museum, Mundelein IL	76
			Don Knapp, Abilene TX (rest. project)	87/90
51104 •	Avia CS.92		Vojenske Muzeum, Kbely AB, Czechoslovakia	79/86
			(displ. as "V-31")	
4 •	Avia S.92	V-34	Narodni Technicke Muzeum , Prague	79
			Vojenske Muzeum, Kbely AB, Czechoslovakia	84

MIKOYAN GUREVICH MiG-15

3804 •	SBLim-2		(to Polish Air Force as 3804)	
			Randal W. McFarlane, Brisbane QLD	.89
			(arr. by ship Melbourne VIC 6.89 : TT 155hrs	)
			Barry Batagol & Bruce Alexander/	
			Rivolta Investments, Melbourne VIC	.89
		VH-DIE	Barry Batagol, Melbourne VIC	18.1.91/92
			(ff Essendon 7.91, flies as Soviet AF "15")	
			Barry Hempel & Greg Schweikert,	
			Archerfield QLD : del.	14.3.92
81072 •	MiG-15		(to Chinese AF as 81072)	
		N7013L	Warren Sessler/China Technologies Inc	6.88/90
			(noted at Chino CA .88)	
81676 •	MiG-15UTI		(to Chinese AF as 81676)	
		N7013N	Warren Sessler/China Technologies Inc	6.88
			(noted assembled at Chino CA .88)	
122073 •	F-2		(to Chinese Navy as ....)	
			Unlimited Aircraft Ltd, Chino CA : arr. dism.	10.86
		N90601	Paul Entrekin, Pensacola FL	6.87
		N15PE	Paul Entrekin, Pensacola FL	9.87/92
			(ff Chino CA 29.7.87: flies as Soviet AF "15")	
137077 •	MiG-15		(to Chinese Navy as ....)	
			Unlimited Aircraft Ltd, Chino CA	3.87
242271 •	SBLim-2		(to Polish AF as 2271)	
			Ian McGregor/LBA Systems, Retford UK	9.86
			(shipped Poland to Tees-side UK 10.86, then	
			shipped to USA; assembled Reno NV)	
		N271JM	John MacGuire, Santa Teresa NM	3.87
			Al Reddick/Classics in American Aviation,	
			Reno NV	6.87
			Howard Torman/Aviation Classics Ltd,	
			Reno NV	8.89
612782 •	SBLim-2		(to Polish AF as 2782)	
			Randal W. McFarlane, Brisbane QLD	.89
			(arr. by ship, Melbourne VIC 6.89 : TT 170)	

			Geoff Milne & John Rayner, Melbourne VIC	.89
			John Weymouth, Darwin NT	8.89
		VH-XIG	John Weymouth/Heli-Muster Pty Ltd, "Victoria River Downs" Station, NT	27.7.90/92
			(ff Essendon 1.11.90, as Soviet AF "15")	
622055 •	SBLim-2		(to Polish AF as 655)	
			Ian Kenny, Brisbane QLD	.90/92
			(stored Brisbane, pending rest.)	
712277 •	SBLim-2		(to Polish AF as 777)	
			Randal W. McFarlane, Brisbane QLD	.89
			(arr. by ship, Sydney NSW .89)	
		VH-LJP	Hockey Treloar, Bankstown NSW	.90/92
			(stored dism. Bankstown, pending rest.)	
1A06007•	MiG-15bis SBLim-2A		(to Polish AF as 607)	
			Randal W. McFarlane, Brisbane QLD	.89
			(arr. by ship, Melbourne VIC 6.89 : TT 255)	
			F. W. (Bill) Pike, Sydney NSW	6.89
			Hockey Treloar, Sydney NSW	.89
		VH-BPG	Hockey Treloar, Bankstown NSW	7.2.91/92
			(ff Bankstown 4.91, flies as Polish AF "607")	
1A06015•	SBLim-2		(to Polish AF as 015)	
			Randal W. McFarlane, Brisbane QLD	.89
			(arr. by ship Sydney NSW .89)	
		VH-LSN	Gordon Glynn, Bankstown NSW	.89/92
			(ff Bankstown 14.3.92)	
1A06036•	SBLim-2		(to Polish AF as 636)	
			Randal W. McFarlane, Brisbane QLD	.89
		VH-LKW	Hockey Treloar, Bankstown NSW	.89/92
			(stored dism. Bankstown, pending rest.)	
1A06038•	Lim-1		(to Polish AF as 638)	
			Ian McGregor/LBA Systems, Retford UK	9.86
			(shipped Poland to Tees-side UK 10.86, then shipped to USA; assembled Reno NV)	
		N38BM	John MacGuire, Santa Teresa NM	2.87
			Al Reddick/Classics in American Aviation, Reno NV	6.87
			struck-off USCR	10.89
1A06040•	Lim-1		(to Polish AF as 640)	
			Ian McGregor/LBA Systems, Retford UK	9.86
			(shipped Poland to Tees-side UK 10.86, then shipped to USA; assembled Reno NV)	
		N40BM	John MacGuire/War Eagles Air Museum, Santa Teresa NM	2.87/90
			(ass. Reno NV, flies as Soviet AF "640")	
1A08017•	SBLim-2		(to Polish AF as 8017)	
			Ian McGregor/LBA Systems, Retford UK	9.86
			(shipped Poland to Tees-side UK 10.86, then shipped to USA; assembled Reno NV)	
		N17KM	John MacGuire, Santa Teresa NM	2.87/90
			Al Reddick/Classics in American Aviation, Reno NV	6.87/90
			Howard Torman/Aviation Classics Limited, Reno NV	91
			Tacair Systems Inc, Reno NV	6.91
			(flies as Soviet AF "17")	
1A09006•	SBLim-2		(to Polish AF as 906)	
			Randal W. McFarlane, Brisbane QLD	.89
			(arr. by ship, Melbourne VIC 6.89 : TT 100)	
			Greg Lovett, Essendon VIC	89/92

			(rest. Essendon, due to fly .92)	
1A09012•	SBLim-1		(to Polish AF as 012)	
			Lusso Service, Duiven Holland : arr.	8.10.91
			(stored Duiven : airworthy condition)	
1A09015•	SBLim-2		(to Polish AF as 015)	
			Ian Kenny, Brisbane QLD	.90/92
			(stored Brisbane, pending rest.)	
1A12002•	SBLim-2		(to Polish AF as 202)	
			Randal W. McFarlane, Brisbane QLD	.89
			(arr. by ship, Melbourne VIC 6.89 : TT 265)	
			Ray Ekinci, Sydney NSW : arr. by road	7.7.89/90
			Kay Williamson, Sydney NSW	90/92
			(rest. to fly, RAAF Richmond & Bankstown NSW)	
1B00822•	SBLim-2		(to Polish AF as 0822)	
			Ian McGregor/LBA Systems, Retford UK	9.86
			(shipped Poland to Tees-side UK 10.86, then shipped to USA; assembled Reno NV)	
		N822JM	John MacGuire, Santa Teresa NM	2.87/90
			op: Al Reddick/Classics in American Aviation, Reno NV (flies as Soviet AF "822")	6.87/90
1B01013•	SBLim-2		(to Polish AF as 1013)	
			Ian McGregor/LBA Systems, Retford UK	9.86
			(shipped Poland to Tees-side UK 10.86, then shipped to USA; assembled Reno NV)	
		N13KM	John MacGuire/War Eagles Air Museum, Santa Teresa NM	2.87/90
1B01016•	SBLim-2		(to Polish AF as 1016)	
			Ian McGregor/LBA Systems, Retford UK	9.86
			(shipped Poland to Tees-side UK 10.86, then shipped to USA; assembled Reno NV)	
		N15YY	Donald R. Young, Santa Barbara CA	8.88/90
1B01120•	SBLim-2		(to Polish AF as 1120)	
			Ian McGregor/LBA Systems, Retford UK	9.86
			(shipped Poland to Tees-side UK 10.86)	
			RAF Museum, Hendon : arr. dism.	11.86/90
			Imperial War Museum, Lambeth, London	90/92
			RAF Museum, Hendon : arr.	2.92
1B01205	SBLim-2		(to Polish AF as 1205)	
			Ian McGregor/LBA Systems, Retford UK	9.86
			(shipped Poland to Tees-side UK 10.86, then shipped to USA; assembled Reno NV)	
		N205JM	John MacGuire, Santa Teresa NM	2.87
			Al Reddick/Classics in American Aviation, Reno NV	6.87
			struck-off USCR	10.89
1B01416•	SBLim-2		(to Polish AF as 1416)	
			Ian McGregor/LBA Systems, Retford UK	9.86
			(shipped Poland to Tees-side UK 10.86, then shipped to USA; assembled Reno NV)	
		N416JM	John MacGuire/War Eagles Air Museum, Santa Teresa NM	2.87/90
1B01420•	SBLim-2		(to Polish AF as 1420)	
			Ian McGregor/LBA Systems, Retford UK	8.86
			arr. dismantled, Retford	9.86
		G-BMZF	Aces High Ltd, North Weald : arr. dism.	22.12.86
			Fleet Air Arm Museum, RNAS Yeovilton	.87/89

c/n	Type	Regn	History	Date
1B01606•	SBLim-2		(to Polish AF as 1606)	
			Ian McGregor/LBA Systems, Retford UK	9.86
			(shipped Poland to Tees-side UK 10.86, then shipped to USA; assembled Reno NV)	
		N606BM	John MacGuire/War Eagles Air Museum, Santa Teresa NM	2.87/90
1B01614•	SBLim-2		(to Polish AF as 1614)	
			Ian McGregor/LBA Systems, Retford UK	9.86
			(shipped Poland to Tees-side UK 10.86, then shipped to USA; assembled Reno NV)	
		N614BM	John MacGuire/War Eagles Air Museum, Santa Teresa NM	2.87/90
1B01621•	SBLim-2		(to Polish AF as 1621)	
			Ian McGregor/LBA Systems, Retford UK	9.86
			(shipped Poland to Tees-side UK 10.86, then shipped to USA; assembled Reno NV)	
		N621BM	John MacGuire/War Eagles Air Museum, Santa Teresa NM	2.87/90
1B01629•	SBLim-2		(to Polish AF as 1629)	
			Ian McGregor/LBA Systems, Retford UK	9.86
			(shipped Poland to Tees-side UK 10.86, then shipped to USA; assembled Reno NV)	
		N629BM	John MacGuire/War Eagles Air Museum, Santa Teresa NM	2.87/90
1B01979•	SBLim-2		(to Polish AF as ....)	
			Fighter Rebuilders Inc, Chino CA	88
			(noted under rebuild, Chino 8.88)	
- •	MiG-15UTI		(to Chinese AF as 83238)	
			stored as '3238', Phoenix-Deer Valley AZ	92
910-51 •	MiG-15		(to Chinese AF as 83277)	
		N87CN	Tom Freidkin/Cinema Air, Carlsbad CA	6.91/92
- •	MiG-15		(to Chinese AF as 83177)	
			J. Curtiss Earl, Phoenix AZ	.89/90
			loan: Champlin Fighter Museum, Mesa AZ	.90
			stored, Phoenix-Deer Valley AZ	92
- •	Shenyang F-2		(to Chinese Navy as 0245)	
			Unlimited Aircraft Ltd, Chino CA	3.87
- •	Shenyang F-2		(to Chinese Navy as 0411)	
			Unlimited Aircraft Ltd, Chino CA	3.87
- •	Shenyang F-2		(to Chinese Navy as 1301)	
			Planes of Fame Museum, Chino CA	.88/90
			(arr. Chino dism. ex ship Long Beach CA .88)	
- •	Shenyang F-2		(to Chinese Navy as 1411)	
			Unlimited Aircraft Ltd, Chino CA	3.87/90
		N15MG	Jim Robinson/Combat Jets Flying Museum, Houston TX	10.87/92
			(flies as Soviet AF "4115")	
			EAA Aviation Foundation, Oshkosh WI	.92
- •	Shenyang F-2		(to Chinese Navy 1301)	
			arr. Chino dism. ex ship Long Beach CA	.88
- •	Shenyang F-2		(to Chinese Navy 1961)	
			Unlimited Aircraft Ltd, Chino CA	3.87
		N51MG	James E. Beasley, Philadelphia PA	3.89/92
			(flies as Soviet AF "23")	

- •	F-2		(to Chinese Navy 1986)	
			Unlimited Aircraft Ltd, Chino CA	3.87
			(noted outside MARC hangar, Chino CA 8.88)	
- •	F-2		(to Chinese Navy 2292)	
			Unlimited Aircraft Ltd, Chino CA	3.87
		N90589	First City Air Charter Ltd, Los Angeles CA	6.87/90
			(ff Chino 29.7.87; flies as Soviet AF "1170")	
			James K. Wickersham, Danville CA	92

MIKOYAN GUREVICH MiG-17

508	Lim-5		(to Polish AF as ....)	
			rep. imported into UK	.88
0704 •	MiG-17		(to Chinese AF as ......)	
			China Ocean Helicopter Corp	
		N306DM	Consolidated Aviation Enterprises Inc,	
			Burlington VT	1.88
			Dean Martin/Warplanes Inc, Burlington VT	90
			(FAA quote id. as "0714")	
0613 •	MiG-17		(to Chinese AF as ....)	
			China Ocean Helicopter Corp	
		N406DM	Consolidated Aviation Enterprises Inc,	
			Burlington VT	1.88
			Dean Martin/Warplanes Inc, Burlington VT	90
1321 •	MiG-17		(rep. to Polish AF as .....)	
		LN-MIG	Bjorn Bostad, Norway	17.2.92
1327 •	JJ-5		(to Chinese AF as ....)	
		N69PP	Peter Franks, Angel Fire NM	90
2507 •	F-4		(to Chinese AF 2507)	
		N1VC	Morgan Merrill/Jet 1 Inc, Alexandria VA	88/90
			(civil conv. Chino CA, ff 5.4.89)	
			Stephen M. Rosenberg, Novato CA	92
			(FAA quote id. as "2705")	
551604 •	MiG-17		(to Chinese AF as ......)	
			China Ocean Helicopter Corp	
		N905DM	Consolidated Aviation Enterprises Inc,	
			Burlington VT	1.88
			Dean Martin/Warplanes Inc, Burlington VT	90
10003 •	Lim-5		(to Polish AF as 003)	
			Lusso Service, Duiven Holland : arr.	8.10.91
			(stored Duiven, airworthy condition)	
1C1228 •	Lim-5		(to Polish AF as ....)	
			rep. imported into UK	.88/92
1C1617 •	Lim-5		(to Polish AF as 1617)	
			Planes of Fame Museum, Chino CA	.88
			(arr. Chino dism. ex ship Long Beach CA .88)	
1G1619 •	MiG-17F		(to Polish AF as 619)	
			Ian Kenny, Brisbane QLD	.90/92
			(stored Brisbane, pending rest.)	
1F0102 •	Lim-5		(to Polish AF as 102)	
			Randal W. McFarlane, Brisbane QLD	.89
			Jack McDonald, Caboolture QLD	.90/92
			(rest. to fly, Caboolture QLD)	

1J0434 •	Lim-5m		(to Polish AF as 434)	
			Randal W. McFarlane, Brisbane QLD	.89
			Hockey Treloar, Bankstown NSW	.90/92
			(rest. Bankstown, due to fly .92)	

MIKOYAN GUREVICH MiG-19

- •	MiG-19		(to Chinese AF as 0301)	
			Military Aircraft Restoration Corp, Chino CA	.88
			(shipped, assembled Chino .88)	

MIKOYAN GUREVICH MiG-21

- •	MiG-21PF		(to Hungarian AF as 501)	
			RAF Benevolent Fund: auctioned London	13.9.90
			(airfreighted to UK by Belfast 8.90)	
			Arnold J. Glass, Monaco	9.90/92
			loan: RAF Museum, RAF St.Athan : arr. dism.	6.6.91/92
- •	MiG-21PF		(to Hungarian AF as 503)	
		G-BRAM	Aces High Ltd, North Weald	22.5.89
- •	MiG-21PF		(to Hungarian AF as 506)	
		G-BRAN	Aces High Ltd, North Weald	22.5.89/90
			N316DM	
			Dean Martin/Warplanes Inc, Burlington VT	1.90/92
- •	MiG-21PF		(to Hungarian AF as 1603)	
		G-BRAO	Aces High Ltd, North Weald UK	22.5.89
		N213DM	Dean Martin/Warplanes Inc, Burlington VT	1.90/92
PF1683 •	F-7		(to Chinese AF as 905)	
		N515DM	Dean Martin/Warplanes Inc, Burlington VT	9.89/92
- •	F-7		(to Chinese AF as 1603)	
		N610DM	Dean Martin/Warplanes Inc, Burlington VT	1.90
		N21MG	Jim Robinson/Combat Jets Flying Museum,	
			Houston TX	3.90/92
			(shipped to Houston, ff Houston-Hobby 6.90,	
			flies as NVNAF "4603")	
			EAA Aviation Foundation, Oshkosh WI	.92
761811 •	MiG-21PF		(to Polish AF as 1811)	
		N21PF	EDF Associates, Camarillo CA	6.91/92
			stored dism. unconv., Mojave CA	92
762410 •	MiG-21PF		(to Polish AF as 2410)	
		N21MF	EDF Associates, Camarillo CA	6.91/92
			stored dism. unconv., Mojave CA	92
- •	MiG-21		(to Polish AF as 408)	
			Classics in American Aviation , Reno NV	89
4418 •	MiG-21U	N315DM	Dean Martin/Warplanes Inc, Burlington VT	92
5068 •	MiG-21U		(to Egyptian AF as 5068)	
		N4318W	Amanda Corp, Wilmington DE	7.91/92
- •	MiG-21U	N317DM	Dean Martin/Warplanes Inc, Burlington VT	3.92
			(id. quoted as "516913056")	
- •	MiG-21U		(to Polish AF as 7505)	
			(shipped to Australia 6.92 : TT1275)	
			Dick McIntosh, Sydney NSW	6.92
			(Russian built, id. quoted as "05695175")	
- •	MiG-21PF		(to Czech AF as 1304)	
			RAF Benevolent Fund : auctioned London	13.9.90

c/n		Type	Serial	Reg	History	Date
					(arr. RAF Abingdon on del. 10.9.90)	
					Arnold J. Glass, Monaco	9.90/92
-	•	MiG-21			noted Reno NV, nose code "2313"	9.88
-	•	MiG-21UM			(to Egyptian AF as ....)	
					Arnold J. Glass, Monaco	.91/92
					stored, Burlington VT	

NORTH AMERICAN F-86/CANADAIR CL-13 SABRE

c/n		Type	Serial	Reg	History	Date
151-38433	•	F-86A	47-606	N7793C	Reedley Joint Union High School, Reedley CA	66/69
				N57965	Ben W. Hall, Seattle WA	72/89
					(used for spares for rest. of 48-0178)	
					Museum of Flight, Seattle WA (static rest.)	.89/91
151-43547	•	F-86A	48-0178	N68388	Ben W. Hall, Seattle WA	.73/78
					(recov. ex scrapyard, Fresno CA .70;	
					rest. Paine Field WA, ff 24.5.74)	
				N178	Ben W. Hall, Seattle Wa	10.83/88
					John E. Dilley/Fort Wayne Air Service,	
					Fort Wayne IN	6.89/91
					Golden Apple Trust, UK : rest. Ft. Wayne IN	.90/91
				G-SABR	Golden Apple Operations Ltd, Stamford	10.91/92
					(shipped to UK, assembled Bournemouth 3.92,	
					flies as USAF "8178/FU-178")	
151-43609		F-86A	48-0240	N196B	noted, Chino CA	10.84
161-318	•	F-86A	49-1324	N57964	Ben W. Hall, Seattle WA	78/92
170-75		F-86E	50-0653	N5637V	Hawaii Public College of Trade Instruction,	
					Honolulu Airport HI	66/69
					USAFM, Hickam AFB HI	79/90
172-167	•	F-86F	51-2884	N57966	Ben W. Hall, Seattle WA	78/92
172-271		F-86F	51-2988	N86Z	Dave Zeuschel Racing Engines, Chino CA	3.8.82/87
					(recov. ex storage in CA orchard, rebuilt	
					Van Nuys, flew as USAF "24513/FU-513")	
					crashed & dest., Shafter CA (Zeuschel k.)	25.4.87
173-215	•	F-86D	51-6071		Sergio Tomassoni, Buckeye AZ	F-86L
					(noted unconv., derelict at Buckeye AZ .78)	
				N3280U	Sergio Tomassoni, Buckeye AZ	82
					S & T Aerial Contractors, Buckeye AZ	16.8.82
				N86RJ	Robert A. Kemp, Reno NV	3.83/92
176-348	•	F-86F	51-13417		(to Ejercito del Aire as C5-....): del. ex USAFE	.58
				N51RS	Mid Atlantic Air Museum, Middletown PA	11.87/92
					(rest. to fly)	
187-84	•	F-86H	52-2058	N205P	Purdue University, Lafayette IN	66/69
					Happy Hollow Park IN	
					noted derelict, Halsmer Airport, Lafayette IN	86
					Civil Air Patrol, Lafayette IN	86
190-594		F-86L	52-4191	N2401H	Hawaii Education Dept, Honolulu HI	66/69
					USAFM, Hickam AFB	73
190-804		F-86L	52-10079	N59303	Idaho State University, Pocatello ID	66/69
					Ricks College Corp, Rexburg ID	72
191-304	•	F-86F	52-4608		(test bed for Rocketdyne AR2-3 motor)	
				N57963	Robert D. Scott, San Martin CA	78/92

191-655•	F-86F	52-4959	N105BH	World Wide Aircraft, Miami FL (flies in camouflage scheme)	9.90/92
191-658•	F-86F	52-4962		(to FA Argentina as C-111)	
			N7006G	Rick E. Sharpe/Warbirds Unlimited, Rosharon TX (FAA quote id. "SA111")	8.88
191-682•	F-86F	52-4986		Coleman Warbird Museum, Coleman TX	
			N188RL	D K Precision Inc, Fort Lauderdale FL (id. assumed, FAA quote id. "524986CW")	6.90/92
191-708•	F-86F	52-5012		Rick E. Sharpe/Warbirds Unlimited, Rosharon TX	
			N4TF	Tom Friedkin/Cinema Air, Carlsblad CA	4.90/92
191-812•	F-86F	52-5116		(to FA Argentina as C-119)	
			N7006J	Rick E. Sharpe/Warbirds Unlimited, Rosharon TX	8.88
				Bill Woods/Western Wings Aircraft Sales, Oakland OR	5.89
			N30CW	Western Wings Aircraft Sales, Oakland OR (flew as "Marines 25012/FU-012") (FAA quote id. "SA119", struck-off USCR 4.90)	11.89/90
			N3145T	Coleman Warbird Museum, Coleman TX	1.92
191-835•	F-86F	52-5139		(to FA Peruana as FAP.......)	
				recov. by Dave Zeuschel, Van Nuys CA (arr. dism. Chino CA 2.81, ff Chino 8.81)	2.81
			N86F	Dave Zeuschel Racing Engines, Reno NV	6.81
				John R. Sandberg, Robstown TX	.81/86
				Don Young/Exotics Leasing Corp, Santa Barbara CA	86/88
				Tom Wood/Heritage Aircraft Sales, Indianapolis IN (flies as USAF "12849/FU-849")	2.89/92
191-839•	F-86F	52-5143	N25143	William Simone, Fountain Valley CA	78
				Lesley L. Crowder, Sunland CA	84/92
201-25	F-86D F-86L	53-0581	N64803	Dixie College, St George UT	72/78
201-99	F-86D	53-0655	N1364J	reg. res.	11.81
201-186	F-86D F-86L	53-0742	N4959	Cochise College, Douglas AZ	72/78
201-260	F-86D	53-0816	N1363W	reg. res.	11.81
201-273	F-86D	53-0829	N13636	reg. res.	11.81
201-277	F-86D	53-0833	N1364R	reg. res.	11.81
201-484•	F-86D	53-1040	N74062	Aircraft Engine Enterprises Inc, Moore OK	66
				Tuxhorn Aviation, Phoenix AZ	69
				Aircraft Surplus Co, Tucson AZ	72/86
				AMCEP Inc, Tucson AZ	87/92
202-25	F-86F QF-86E	53-1096	N306X	Flight Systems Inc, Mojave CA	78
				shot down, White Sands Missile Range NM	22.7.78
203-52 •	F-86H	53-1250		Rock Valley College, Rockford IL : del.	28.5.70/87
			N31250	Spirit Fighters Inc, Chesterfield MO	5.91/92
203-168	F-86H	53-1396	N9047	Board of Trustees School District, Helena MT	72/78
203-283•	F-86H	53-1511	N5585	Columbus Technical Institute, Columbus OH	72
				USAFM, Robins AFB GA	88

244-83 •	FJ-4B Fury	Bu143575	N9255	Flight Systems Inc, Long Beach CA	.71/78
			N400FS	Flight Systems Inc, Mojave CA	.78/90
				(stored Mojave, last flew 82)	
507 •	Mk. 4	RCAF19607		(to RAF as XB546)	
				(to Italian AF as MM19607)	
			G-ATBF	Malcolm D. N. Fisher/Historic Aircraft Preservation Society, Biggin Hill UK	24.3.66
				(arr. dism. Biggin Hill .66 : never flown)	
				Reflectaire Ltd Museum, Blackpool, UK	69/72
				T. Bracewell, Preston, Lancs : stored dism.	4.72/88
				(arr. dism. Duxford 8.84 for auction: not sold)	
811	Mk. 5 QF-86E	RCAF23021		Maritime Aircraft Repair & Overhaul/ Targetair Ltd, Moncton NB	
			N1046D	Flight Systems Inc, Mojave CA	5.79/80
				crashed, White Sands Missile Range NM	1.2.80
818	Mk. 5 QF-86E	RCAF23028		Maritime Aircraft Repair & Overhaul/ Targetair Ltd, Moncton NB	
			N99605	Flight Systems Inc, Mojave CA	78
				shot down, White Sands Missile Range NM	12.10.78
824	Mk. 5 QF-86E	RCAF23034		Maritime Aircraft Repair & Overhaul/ Targetair Ltd, Moncton NB	
			N1046G	Flight Systems Inc, Mojave CA	5.79/82
				struck-off USCR	11.82
826	Mk. 5 QF-86E	RCAF23036		Maritime Aircraft Repair & Overhaul/ Targetair Ltd, Moncton NB	
			N1046P	Flight Systems Inc, Mojave CA	5.79
				shot down during unmanned trials	
848	Mk. 5 QF-86E	RCAF23058		Maritime Aircraft Repair & Overhaul/ Targetair Ltd, Moncton NB	
			N1046S	Flight Systems Inc, Mojave CA	5.79/82
				struck-off USCR	11.82
886	Mk. 5 QF-86E	RCAF23096		Maritime Aircraft Repair & Overhaul/ Targetair, Moncton NB	20.9.67
			N8686F (1	Boeing Equipment Co, Seattle WA	.67/74
				(del. to Seattle ex Moncton 21.12.67)	
				Targetair Ltd, Moncton NB	.74
			N74180 (2	Flight Systems Inc, Mojave CA: del.	26.7.74/80
				sale rep.	86/92
887	Mk. 5 QF-86E	RCAF23097		Maritime Aircraft Repair & Overhaul/ Targetair Ltd, Moncton NB	
			N5591C	Flight Systems Inc, Mojave CA	2.80/83
				struck-off USCR	6.83
892	Mk. 5 QF-86E	RCAF23102		Maritime Aircraft Repair & Overhaul/ Targetair Ltd, Moncton NB	
			N65331	Flight Systems Inc, Mojave CA : del.	8.76/78
				(rep. shot down, missile trials)	
				noted dism. in compound, Mojave CA	10.84
896	Mk. 5 QF-86E	RCAF23106		Maritime Aircraft Repair & Overhaul/ Targetair Ltd, Moncton NB	
			N5591F	Flight Systems Inc, Mojave CA	2.80/83
				struck-off USCR	11.83
918	Mk. 5 QF-86E	RCAF23128		Maritime Aircraft Repair & Overhaul/ Targetair Ltd, Moncton NB	
			N96123	Flight Systems Inc, Mojave CA	9.76/80
				shot down, White Sands Missile Range NM	29.8.80

923	Mk. 5 QF-86E	RCAF23133		Maritime Aircraft Repair & Overhaul/ Targetair Ltd, Moncton NB	
			N96120	Flight Systems Inc, Mojave CA	9.76/78
				crashed, White Sands Missile Range NM	18.5.78
925	Mk. 5 QF-86E	RCAF23135		Maritime Aircraft Repair & Overhaul/ Targetair Ltd, Moncton NB	
			N92426	Flight Systems Inc, Mojave CA	12.76/79
				crashed, White Sands Missile Range NM	22.5.79
936	Mk. 5 QF-86E	RCAF23146		Maritime Aircraft Repair & Overhaul/ Targetair Ltd, Moncton NB	
			N5591K	Flight Systems Inc, Mojave CA	2.80
				shot down, missile trials	
937	Mk. 5 QF-86E	RCAF23147		Maritime Aircraft Repair & Overhaul/ Targetair Ltd, Moncton NB	
			N72491	Flight Systems Inc, Mojave CA	12.77/79
				damaged, White Sands Missile Range NM	16.10.79
941	Mk. 5 QF-86E	RCAF23151		Maritime Aircraft Repair & Overhaul/ Targetair Ltd, Moncton NB	
			N5591L	Flight Systems Inc, Mojave CA	2.80/83
				damaged, White Sands Missile Range NM	23.8.83
950	Mk. 5 QF-86E	RCAF23160		Maritime Aircraft Repair & Overhaul/ Targetair Ltd, Moncton NB	
			N5591M	Flight Systems Inc, Mojave CA	2.80/82
				shot down, White Sands Missile Range NM	21.8.82
980	Mk. 5 QF-86E	RCAF23190		Maritime Aircraft Repair & Overhaul/ Targetair Ltd, Moncton NB	
			N98230	Flight Systems Inc, Mojave CA	12.77/80
				(rep. flying at Mojave .80 as "US Army 23190")	
				shot down, White Sands Missile Range NM	8.1.80
985 •	Mk. 5	RCAF23195		Maritime Aircraft Repair & Overhaul/ Targetair Ltd, Moncton NB	
			N5591N	Flight Systems Inc, Mojave CA	2.80/86
				sale rep., Orlando FL	87/92
988	Mk. 5 QF-86E	RCAF23198		Maritime Aircraft Repair & Overhaul/ Targetair Ltd, Moncton NB	
			N5591S	Flight Systems Inc, Mojave CA	2.80/83
				struck-off USCR	6.83
992	Mk. 5 QF-86E	RCAF23202	N55911	Flight Systems Inc, Mojave CA	2.80/84
				shot down, missile trials	
				struck-off USCR	7.84
993	Mk. 5 QF-86E	RCAF23203		Maritime Aircraft Repair & Overhaul, Moncton NB	
				Oshawa Chamber of Commerce, Oshawa ONT	69
				(planned display in park)	
			N201X	Spectrum Air Inc, San Francisco CA	.71
				(civil conv., Toronto Island Airport ONT .71)	
				Robert Love, Oakland CA	73
				Jerry Brassfield/Pacific Military Museum CA	c75/77
				Flight Systems Inc, Mojave CA	.77/83
				struck-off USCR	6.83
996	Mk. 5 QF-86E	RCAF23206		Maritime Aircraft Repair & Overhaul/ Targetair Ltd, Moncton NB	
			N5592D	Flight Systems Inc, Mojave CA	2.80/83
				(flying Mojave CA .80 as "US Army 23206")	
				shot down missile trials : struck-off USCR	11.83
997	Mk. 5	RCAF23207		Maritime Aircraft Repair & Overhaul/	

	QF-86E			Targetair Ltd, Moncton NB	
			N5592K	Flight Systems Inc, Mojave CA	5.80/84
				struck-off register	7.84
998	Mk. 5	RCAF23208		Maritime Aircraft Repair & Overhaul/	
	QF-86E			Targetair Ltd, Moncton NB	
				Flight Systems Inc, Mojave CA	1.11.83
			N4688J	ntu: Flight Systems Inc, Mojave CA	
			N46869	Flight Systems Inc, Mojave CA	2.84/88
				struck-off USCR	4.88
999	Mk. 5	RCAF23209		Maritime Aircraft Repair & Overhaul/	
	QF-86E			Targetair Ltd, Moncton NB	
			N4688J	Flight Systems Inc, Mojave CA	2.84/86
				US Army, Redstone Arsenal AL : USCR	88/92
1005	Mk. 5	RCAF23215		Maritime Aircraft Repair & Overhaul/	
	QF-86E			Targetair Ltd, Moncton NB	
			N2291B	Flight Systems Inc, Mojave CA	7.78/79
				shot down, White Sands Missile Range NM	27.4.79
1012	Mk. 5	RCAF23222		Maritime Aircraft Repair & Overhaul/	
	QF-86E			Targetair Ltd, Moncton NB	
			N46882	Flight Systems Inc, Mojave CA	2.84
				sale rep.	86/92
1013	Mk. 5	RCAF23223		Maritime Aircraft Repair & Overhaul/	
				Targetair Ltd, Moncton NB	
				Flight Systems Inc, Mojave CA	21.11.84
			N86EA	Southern Cal. Aviation Inc, Corona Del Mar CA	1.85/86
				USAFM : struck-off USCR	12.86
1016 •	Mk. 5	RCAF23226		Maritime Aircraft Repair & Overhaul/	
	QF-86E			Targetair Ltd, Moncton NB	
			N46883	Flight Systems Inc, Mojave CA	2.84
				Southern Cal. Aviation Inc, Corona Del Mar CA	86
				struck-off USCR	12.86
1017	Mk. 5	RCAF23227		Maritime Aircraft Repair & Overhaul/	
	QF-86E			Targetair Ltd, Moncton NB	
			N2290R	Flight Systems Inc, Mojave CA	7.78/83
				struck-off USCR	6.83
1021 •	Mk. 5	RCAF23231		Maritime Aircraft Repair & Overhaul,	
				Moncton NB	
			N231X	Bankers Leasing Inc, Washington DC	72
				Ronald Reynolds, Kansas City KS	78
				Flight Systems Inc, Mojave CA	.81/82
			N91FS	Tracor Flight Systems Inc, Mojave CA	6.82/92
1028 •	Mk. 5	RCAF23238		Maritime Aircraft Repair & Overhaul/	
				Targetair Ltd, Moncton NB	
				Flight Systems Inc, Mojave CA	21.11.84
				(noted dism. FSI compound, Mojave 10.84)	
			N86EB	Southern Cal. Aviation Inc, Corona Del Mar CA	1.85/86
				USAFM : struck-off USCR	12.86
1031	Mk. 5	RCAF23241		Maritime Aircraft Repair & Overhaul,	
				Moncton NB	20.10.70
			N8544	Lockheed California Co, Palmdale CA	72
				(chase plane, L1011 programme)	
				crashed Mojave CA	c74
1042	Mk. 5	RCAF23252		Maritime Aircraft Repair & Overhaul/	
	QF-86E			Targetair Ltd, Moncton NB	
			N96122	Flight Systems Inc, Mojave CA	9.76/79

				shot down, White Sands Missile Range NM	8.11.79
1049	Mk. 5 QF-86E	RCAF23259		Maritime Aircraft Repair & Overhaul/ Targetair Ltd, Moncton NB	
			N98250	Flight Systems Inc, Mojave CA	11.77/78
				US Army, Redstone Arsenal AL : USCR	88/92
1058	Mk. 5 QF-86E	RCAF23268		Maritime Aircraft Repair & Overhaul/ Targetair Ltd, Moncton NB	
			N96125	Flight Systems Inc, Mojave CA	9.76/78
				damaged, White Sands Missile Range NM	16.8.78
1065	Mk. 5	RCAF23275		Oshawa Chamber of Commerce, Oshawa ONT	22.6.70
				(planned displ. in park)	69
			N275X	Spectrum Air Inc, San Francisco CA	.71/72
				(civil conv., Toronto Island Airport ONT .71)	
				crashed on take-off, Sacramento CA	24.9.72
				(struck icecream parlour, 22 killed, 28 hurt)	
1070	Mk. 5 QF-86E	RCAF23280		Maritime Aircraft Repair & Overhaul/ Targetair Ltd, Moncton NB	
			N2290V	Flight Systems Inc, Mojave CA	7.78/83
				(noted Mojave 10.79 as "US Army 23280")	
				struck-off USCR	6.83
1073	Mk. 5 QF-86E	RCAF23283		Maritime Aircraft Repair & Overhaul/ Targetair Ltd, Moncton NB	
			N2290Z	Flight Systems Inc, Mojave CA	7.78/84
				(noted Mojave 80/84 as "US Army 23283")	
1075 •	Mk. 5	RCAF23285	CF-BKG	Maritime Aircraft Repair & Overhaul, Moncton NB	
			N8686D	Leroy Penhall/Fighter Imports Inc, Chino CA	73
				Flight Systems Inc, Mojave CA	77/78
			N87FS (1	Flight Systems Inc, Mojave CA	82
			N92FS	Tracor Flight Systems Inc, Mojave CA	6.82/92
1079	Mk. 5 QF-86E	RCAF23289		Maritime Aircraft Repair & Overhaul/ Targetair Ltd, Moncton NB	
			N99594	Flight Systems Inc, Mojave CA	78
				shot down, White Sands Missile Range NM	16.8.78
1081	Mk. 5 QF-86E	RCAF23291		Maritime Aircraft Repair & Overhaul/ Targetair Ltd, Moncton NB	
			N70726	Flight Systems Inc, Mojave CA	9.77/83
				(noted Mojave 10.79 as "US Army 23291")	
				struck-off USCR	6.83
1083 •	Mk. 5	RCAF23293		Maritime Aircraft Repair & Overhaul/ Targetair Ltd, Moncton NB	
			N4689H	Flight Systems Inc, Mojave CA	2.84
				Southern Cal. Aviation Inc, Corona del Mar CA	86/88
				Morgan Merrill/Jet I Inc, Alexandria VA	4.89/90
				John Dilley/Fort Wayne Air Service, Fort Wayne IN	2.91/92
1090	Mk. 5 QF-86E	RCAF23300		Maritime Aircraft Repair & Overhaul/ Targetair Ltd, Moncton NB	
			N4724A	Flight Systems Inc, Mojave CA	2.84/85
				shot down, White Sands NM: struck-off USCR	12.85
1096	Mk. 5 QF-86E	RCAF23306		Maritime Aircraft Repair & Overhaul, Moncton NB	
			N306X	Flight Systems Inc, Mojave CA	73/78
				(noted as "US Army 23306", Mojave CA .77)	
				shot down, White Sands Missile Range NM	22.7.78
1098	Mk. 5	RCAF23308		Maritime Aircraft Repair & Overhaul/	

	QF-86E			Targetair Ltd, Moncton NB	
			N4724N	Flight Systems Inc, Mojave CA	2.84
				struck-off USCR	10.84
1099	Mk. 5	RCAF23309		Maritime Aircraft Repair & Overhaul/	
	QF-86E			Targetair Ltd, Moncton NB	
			N92473	Flight Systems Inc, Mojave CA	12.76/83
				struck-off USCR	6.83
1104 •	Mk. 5	RCAF23314	CF-BKH	Maritime Aircraft Repair & Overhaul,	
				Moncton NB	
			N8687D	Leroy Penhall/Fighter Imports Inc, Chino CA	73
				Flight Systems Inc, Mojave CA	76
				Whittington Brothers/Air Sabre Inc,	
				West Palm Beach FL	.76/78
				Military Aircraft Restoration Corp, Chino CA	80/86
				Jim Robinson/Combat Jets Flying Museum,	
				Houston TX	10.87/92
				EAA Aviation Foundation, Oshkosh WI	.92
				(flies as USAF "12897/The Huff/FU-897")	
1105	Mk. 5	RCAF23315		Maritime Aircraft Repair & Overhaul/	
	QF-86E			Targetair Ltd, Moncton NB	
			N72492	Flight Systems Inc, Mojave CA	12.77/79
				(noted Mojave 10.79 as "US Army 23315")	
1110	Mk. 5	RCAF23320	CF-CLM	Maritime Aircraft Repair & Overhaul,	
	QF-86E			Moncton NB	
			N74170	Flight Systems Inc, Mojave CA ("Bessy")	.73/80
				(noted Mojave 10.79 as "US Army 23320",	
				shot down, White Sands Missile Range NM	29.8.80
1113	Mk. 5	RCAF23323		Maritime Aircraft Repair & Overhaul/	
	QF-86E			Targetair Ltd, Moncton NB	
			N98279	Flight Systems Inc, Mojave CA	11.77/78
				(rep. in fire dump, Mojave CA 84)	
				US Army, Redstone Arsenal AL : USCR	88/92
1120 •	Mk. 5	RCAF23330		Maritime Aircraft Repair & Overhaul/	
				Targetair Ltd, Moncton NB	
			N86FN	Flight International Inc, Atlanta GA	11.84/85
				Flight International of Florida, Jacksonville FL	1.85/86
			N86JR	Combat Jets Flying Museum, Houston TX	12.86/92
				EAA Aviation Foundation, Oshkosh WI	.92
1121	Mk. 5	RCAF23331		Maritime Aircraft Repair & Overhaul/	
	QF-86E			Targetair Ltd, Moncton NB	
			N46901	Flight Systems Inc, Mojave CA	2.84
				(noted Mojave 10.84 as "23331")	
				struck-off USCR	10.84
1128 •	Mk. 5	RCAF23338		Maritime Aircraft Repair & Overhaul/	
	QF-86E			Targetair Ltd, Moncton NB	
			N4689N	Flight Systems Inc, Mojave CA	2.84/86
				USAFM, Chanute AFB IL	88
1129	Mk. 5	RCAF23339		Maritime Aircraft Repair & Overhaul/	
	QF-86E			Targetair Ltd, Moncton NB	
			N46791	Flight Systems Inc, Mojave CA	78/81
				shot down, White Sands Missile Range NM	25.7.81
1134	Mk. 5	RCAF23344		Maritime Aircraft Repair & Overhaul/	
				Targetair Ltd, Moncton NB	
				Flight Systems Inc, Mojave CA	21.11.84
			N86EC	Southern Cal. Aviation Inc, Corona del Mar CA	1.85/86
				USAFM : struck-off USCR	12.86

1137 •	Mk. 5	RCAF23347		Maritime Aircraft Repair & Overhaul/ Targetair Ltd, Moncton NB	
			N93FS	Flight Systems Inc, Mojave CA (based Kadena AFB, Japan .88)	6.82/88
				Tracor Flight Systems, Mojave CA	89
1141	Mk. 5	RCAF23351		Maritime Aircraft Repair & Overhaul/ Targetair Ltd, Moncton NB	
				Flight Systems Inc, Mojave CA (noted unconv., FSI compound, Mojave 10.84)	21.11.84
			N86ED	Southern Cal. Aviation Inc, Corona del Mar CA	1.85/86
				USAFM : struck-off USCR	12.86
1142	Mk. 5 QF-86E	RCAF23352		Maritime Aircraft Repair & Overhaul/ Targetair Ltd, Moncton NB	
			N98270	Flight Systems Inc, Mojave CA	11.77/83
				struck-off USCR	6.83
1148	Mk. 5 QF-86E	RCAF23358		Maritime Aircraft Repair & Overhaul/ Targetair Ltd, Moncton NB	
			N4690J	Flight Systems Inc, Mojave CA	2.84/86
				struck-off USCR	4.88
1153	Mk. 5 Mk. 6	RCAF23363	N74180(1	Maritime Aircraft Repair & Overhaul, Moncton NB (conv. to Mk. 6 for Pakistan AF project: ff Mojave CA 30.1.72)	.69/74
			N8686F(2	Boeing Equipment Co, Seattle WA	.74/91
				Museum of Flight, Boeing Field, Seattle WA	12.91/92
1157	Mk. 5 QF-86E	RCAF23367		Maritime Aircraft Repair & Overhaul/ Targetair Ltd, Moncton NB	
			N8549	Lockheed California Co, Palmdale CA	75
			N92402	Flight Systems Inc, Mojave CA	9.76
			N86FS	Flight Systems Inc, Mojave CA (rep. on fire dump, Mojave 84)	9.77/84
				US Army, Redstone Arsenal AL : USCR	88/92
1244	Mk. 6	RCAF23454		(ex RCAF Golden Hawks Aerobatic Team)	
			CF-AMH	Milt Harradence/Air Museum of Canada, Calgary ALTA	9.8.65
			N186F	Flight Test Research Inc, Long Beach CA	8.65/73
				Flight Systems Inc, Mojave CA	73/78
				dam. beyond repair, White Sands NM	17.5.78
1294 •	Mk. 6	RCAF23504		Age of Flight Museum, Niagara Falls ONT	11.65/67
				Brian Baird, Toronto ONT (stored Mesa AZ 69/74, stored dism. Chino 77)	69/77
			N86CD	S. Bruce Goessling/Combat Jet & Aerospace Museum, Chino CA	8.86
				Corporate Jets Inc, Scottsdale AZ	12.87
			N30CJ	Corporate Jets Inc, Scottsdale AZ (based Deccimomanuu, Sardinia : mil. contract .89) (based Soesterberg, Netherlands: mil. contract .91)	4.88/92
1459 •	Mk. 6	RCAF23669		(to SAAF as 350)	
			N3841V	Flight Systems Inc, Mojave CA	3.83/92
1461 •	Mk. 6	RCAF23671		(to SAAF as 352)	
			N38301	Flight Systems Inc, Mojave CA (noted stored unconv., Mojave 90)	3.83/90
				Corporate Jets Inc, Scottsdale AZ	7.91/92
1468 •	Mk. 6	RCAF23678		(to SAAF as 359)	
			N3831B	Flight Systems Inc, Mojave CA	3.83/89
				rep. sold to Cayman Islands	3.91
				M. D. Aire Co, Encino CA	92

1472 •	Mk. 6	RCAF23682		(to SAAF as 363)	
			N3842H	Flight Systems Inc, Mojave CA	3.83/90
				(noted stored unconv., Mojave 90)	
				Corporate Jets Inc, Scottsdale AZ	92
1474 •	Mk. 6	RCAF23688		(to SAAF as 365)	
				Flight Systems Inc, Mojave CA	21.3.83
			N106JB	John MacGuire, Fort Hancock TX	4.83
				John MacGuire/War Eagles Air Museum, Santa Teresa NM (flies as SAAF "365")	88/92
1480 •	Mk. 6	RCAF23690		(to SAAF as 371)	
			N3842J	Flight Systems Inc, Mojave CA	3.83/90
				(noted stored unconv., Mojave 90)	
				rep. sold to Cayman Islands	3.91
				National Airshows Inc, New Bern NC	8.91/92
1482 •	Mk. 6	RCAF23692		(to SAAF as 373)	
			N3844E	Flight Systems Inc, Mojave CA	3.83/90
				(noted stored unconv., Mojave 90)	
				Darryl G. Greenamyer, Ocala FL	92
1487 •	Mk. 6	RCAF23697		(to SAAF as 378)	
			N38453	Flight Systems Inc, Mojave CA	3.83/90
				Tracor Flight Systems, Austin TX	91/92
				(noted stored unconv., Mojave 90/92)	
1489 •	Mk. 6	RCAF23699		(to SAAF as 380)	
			N3846J	Flight Systems Inc, Mojave CA	3.83/90
				(noted stored unconv., Mojave 90)	
				Tracor Flight Systems, Austin TX	92
1490 •	Mk. 6	RCAF23700		(to SAAF as 381)	
				to SAAF Museum	
			N50CJ	Corporate Jets Inc, Scottsdale AZ	12.87/92
				based Soesterberg, Netherlands: mil. contract	91
1491 •	Mk. 6	RCAF23701		(to SAAF as 382)	
			N3847H	Flight Systems Inc, Mojave CA	3.83
			N87FS (2	Tracor Flight Systems Inc, Mojave CA	4.84/92
1593	Mk. 6	S6-1593		(to Luftwaffe as YA+043; BB+163; 01+02)	
			D-0113	Dornier, Oberpfaffenhofen WG	70/77
				Ormond Haydon-Baillie, Duxford UK	.77/79
				(stored dism., Wroughton UK .78/79)	
			N1039B	Flight Systems Inc, Mojave CA	4.79
			N81FS	Flight Systems Inc, Mojave CA	6.80/83
				struck-off USCR	8.83
1600 •	Mk. 6	S6-1600		(to Luftwaffe as BB+170)	
			D-9538	Dornier, Oberpfaffenhofen WG	70/77
				Ormond Haydon-Baillie, Duxford UK	.77/79
				(stored dism., Wroughton UK .78/79)	
			N1039C	Flight Systems Inc, Mojave CA	4.79
			N82FS	Flight Systems Inc, Mojave CA	10.81/92
1666	Mk. 6	S6-1666		(to Luftwaffe as BB+185)	
			D-9540	Dornier, Oberpfaffenhofen WG	70/77
				Ormond Haydon-Baillie, Duxford UK	.77/79
				(stored dism., Wroughton UK .78/79)	
			N1039D	Flight Systems Inc, Mojave CA	4.79
			N83FS	Flight Systems Inc, Mojave CA	
				crashed while target towing, Tampa Bay FL	.83
				struck-off USCR	4.84

1675 •	Mk. 6	S6-1675		(to Luftwaffe as BB+284; KE+104)	
				MBB, Manching WG	70/77
				Ormond Haydon-Baillie, Duxford, UK	.77
				(stored dism., Wroughton UK .78/79)	
			N1039K	Flight Systems Inc, Mojave CA	4.79/81
			N80FS	Tracor Flight Systems Inc, Mojave CA	10.81/92
1710 •	Mk. 6	S6-1710		(to Luftwaffe as JB+240)	
			D-9541	Dornier, Oberpfaffenhofen WG	70/77
				Ormond Haydon-Baillie, Duxford, UK	.77/79
				(stored dism., Wroughton UK .78/79)	
			N1039L	Flight Systems Inc, Mojave CA	4.79/81
			N89FS	Flight Systems Inc, Mojave CA	5.81/92
1711	Mk. 6	S6-1711		(to Luftwaffe as JC+239; 01+08)	
			D-FADE	H. C. Janus, Frankfurt	12.5.70
				crashed landing, Reichelsheim airfield	6.70
CA27-9 •	Mk.30	A94-909		RAAF Wagga NSW : inst. airframe	86
				RAAF Richmond NSW: spares for A94-983	88
				Lang Kidby/Transcorp, Redcliffe QLD : dism.	.88/89
				Sanders Aviation, Chino CA	.89/91
				(rest. to fly, Chino CA)	
CA27-14 •	Mk.30	A94-914		Les Arthur/Toowoomba Aero Museum QLD	84/86
				Gold Coast War Museum, Coolangatta QLD	.86/89
				sold at museum auction, incomplete	10.6.89
				Sanders Aviation, Chino CA	.89/91
				(rest. project)	
CA27-16 •	Mk.30	A94-916		Sanders Aviation, Chino CA	.90
				Doug Schultz/Stallion 51, Kissimmeee FL	.90/92
				(stored Kissimmee, rest. to fly)	
CA27-70 •	Mk.32	A94-970		(to TNI-AU/Indonesian AF as inst. airframe)	
				RAAF Wagga NSW : inst. airframe	87/88
				RAAF Richmond NSW : rest. to fly	.88/91
CA27-83 •	Mk. 32	A94-983		(to R. Malaysian AF as FM1983)	11.71
				retired Butterworth AB, Malaysia	.76/78
				(rest. Butterworth, ff 7.7.78; to Australia by	
				C-130; rebuilt RAAF Richmond NSW: ff 26.3.81)	
				RAAF Museum, RAAF Point Cook VIC	.81/92
			VH-PCM	RAAF Museum (flies as RAAF "A94-983")	2.5.88/92
CA27-94	Mk.32	A94-354		(to R. Malaysian AF as FM1354)	10.69
				Sanders Aviation, Chino CA	.89/91
				displ. Combat Jets Air Museum, Chino CA	91
				offered at auction, Santa Monica CA: not sold	10.91
CA27-109	Mk.32	A94-369		(to R. Malaysian AF as FM1369)	8.69
				Jeff Trappett, Morwell VIC (rest. to fly)	82/91
-	F-86E	-		I. N. Burchinal Jr, Paris TX	
			N190NB	reg. res.	10.85/92
				(FAA quote id. "190")	
- •	F-86D	-	N9202Z	Cal Northrop Institute Tech., Inglewood CA	63/86 F-86L
				(FAA quote id. "2568") : struck-off USCR	10.87
				San Jose State College Aero School,	
				San Jose Municipal Airport CA	.72/86

SUPERMARINE SWIFT

VA9597 •	F Mk.7	XF114		North East Wales Institute of Education	.67/89
				Jet Heritage Collection, Hurn	1.89
				(arr. by road Hurn 19.1.89, rebuild to fly)	
			G-SWIF	Jet Heritage Ltd, Hurn	1.6.90/91

192-22	F-100A	52-5777	N1453	reg. res.	.73
214-1 •	F-100C	53-1709	N703NA	NASA, Moffet Field CA	70/72
				San Jose State College Aero School,	
				San Jose Municipal Airport CA	.72/86
217-352•	F-100C	54-2091		(to Tukish AF as 3-091)	
			N2011M	Tracor Flight Systems Inc, Mojave CA	.89/92
				(del. Conya AB,Turkey to US, via PIK 9.8.89)	
				(stored unconv., Mojave CA 90/92)	
223-35 •	F-100D	54-2155		displ. on pole in Arizona	
			N100X	Flight Test Research Inc, Long Beach CA	.68
				Flight Systems Inc, Mojave CA	72
				static displ., Mojave CA	77/81
224-155•	F-100D	55-2888		(to Tukish AF as 3-888)	
			N2011U	Tracor Flight Systems Inc, Mojave CA	.89/92
				(del. Conya AB,Turkey to US, via PIK 9.8.89)	
				(stored unconv., Mojave CA 90)	
225-120•	F-100D	56-3022	N8056S	Flight Systems Inc, Mojave CA	12.79
			N405FS	Flight Systems Inc, Mojave CA	80/86
				USAF/Flight Systems Inc, Mojave CA	86/90
243-102•	F-100F	56-3826		(to RDAF as GT-826)	
			N32511	ntu:	
			N3252B	Flight Systems Inc, Mojave CA	10.82
				(del. Denmark to Filton UK 28.1.83)	
			N414FS	Flight Systems Inc, Hurn/Deccimomanu	26.3.83/92
243-118•	F-100F	56-3842		(to RDAF as GT-842)	
			N32511	Flight Systems Inc, Mojave CA	10.82
				(del. Denmark to Filton UK 27.1.83)	
			N417FS	Flight Systems Inc, Hurn/Deccimomanu	3.83/92
243-120•	F-100F	56-3844		(to RDAF as GT-844)	
			N32511	ntu:	
			N3251X	Flight Systems Inc, Mojave CA	10.82
				(del. Denmark to Filton UK 27.1.83)	
			N415FS	Flight Systems Inc, Hurn/Deccimomanu	15.3.83/92
243-175•	F-100F	56-3899	N8056Y	Flight Systems Inc, Mojave CA	10.79/80
			N404FS	Flight Systems Inc, Mojave CA	.80/86
				USAF/Flight Systems Inc, Mojave CA	86/92
243-192•	F-100F	56-3916		(to RDAF as GT-916)	
			N3251X	ntu:	
			N3251W	Flight Systems Inc, Mojave CA	10.82
				(del. Denmark to Filton UK 27.1.83)	
			N416FS	Flight Systems Inc, Hurn/Deccimomanu	3.83/92
243-224•	F-100F	56-3948		(to Tukish AF as 3-948)	
			N2011V	Tracor Flight Systems Inc, Mojave CA	.89/91
				(del. Conya AB,Turkey to US, via PIK 9.8.89)	
				Global Aerospace Inc, Newport Beach CA	11.91/92
				(stored unconv., Mojave 90/92)	
243-247•	F-100F	56-3971		(to RDAF as GT-971)	
			N3251U	Flight Systems Inc, Mojave CA	10.82
				(del. Denmark to Filton UK 27.1.83)	
			N419FS	Flight Systems Inc, Hurn/Deccimomanu	3.83/88
				Tracor Flight Systems Inc, Mojave CA	89/92
243-272•	F-100F	56-3996		(to RDAF as GT-996)	
			N3251S	Flight Systems Inc, Mojave CA	10.82

				(del. Denmark to Filton UK 28.1.83)	
			N418FS	Flight Systems Inc, Hurn UK	3.83/89
				crashed landing, Hurn	18.7.89
- •	F-100A	-	N2206Z	Robert A. Kemp, Sparks NV	12.89/92
				(FAA quote id. "ATL-F100-A01")	

NORTHROP F-5 FREEDOM FIGHTER

N.6001 •	YF-5A	59-4987	N156F	Northrop Aircraft, Hawthorne CA	
				Museum of Flight, Boeing Field, Seattle WA	88/90
N.6296 •	F-5A	66-9188		(to CNAF as 69188)	
				noted at Mojave CA	11.87
N.7068 •	F-5A	67-14905		(to R Norwegian AF as 905)	
			N91011	Jerry Westphal/Tacair Systems : del. to US	7.87
				S. Bruce Goessling/Combat Jet & Aerospace	
				Museum, Chino CA	7.87
				US Aviation Museum, Tulsa OK	8.87/92
N.8064 •	F-5B	68-9086		(to Imperial Iranian AF as 3-7007)	
				(to R. Jordanian AF as 233)	
			N7169P	Tom Friedkin/Cinema Air, Houston TX	9.90
				(del. Jordan to US, via Gatwick 26.7.90)	
			N5SF	Cinema Air, Houston TX/Carlsbad CA	10.90/92
RF.1009•	RF-5A	67-21227		(to R. Norwegian AF as ....)	
			N75FT	Flight International of Florida Inc,	
				Jacksonville FL	8.88
			N685TC	Chuck Thornton/Thornton Corp, Van Nuys CA	1.90/92
R.1057 •	F-5E	73-876		(to S. Vietnam AF as 73-876)	
			N9020H	reg. res.	.90/92
IH.1008	F-5F	-	N3139Y	Northrop Aircraft, Hawthorne CA	
				struck-off USCR	10.87
4003	NF-5B	-		(to Netherlands AF as K-4003 .) wfu	10.86
			N3206Y	US Aviation Museum, Tulsa OK	1.92
- •	F-5E	-	N300FG	reg. res.	.90/92
				(FAA quote id. "GG1003")	

NORTHROP T-38 TALON

N.5228 •	T-38A	61-0862	N538TC	Chuck Thornton/Thornton Corp, Van Nuys CA	6.89/91
				(crash hulk recov. ex scrapyard, rebuilt using	
				spare parts Chino CA : ff 11.6.90)	
			N38FT	Boeing Equipment Holding Co, Seattle WA	9.91/92
N.5518 •	T-38A	63-8141		Chuck Thornton, Van Nuys CA	.81
				(crash hulk recov. ex scrapyard, rebuilt using	
				spare parts Chino CA : ff 8.10.84)	
			N638TC	Chuck Thornton/Thornton Corp, Van Nuys CA	12.83/92
				(id. 63-8171 & 68-8171 also quoted)	

WSK-PZL MIELEC TS-11 ISKRA

1H0201	TS-11			(to Polish AF as 0201)	
				noted stored, Mierzecice, Poland	8.91
			N42GS	Greg Shepard, Fort Myers FL	2.92
1H0304	TS-11			(to Polish AF as 0304)	
				noted stored, Mierzecice, Poland	8.91
			N304WV	Jeffrey E. Roberts, Wheeling WV	92
1H0307	TS-11			(to Polish AF as 0307)	
			N307J	International Jets Inc., Gadsden, AL	92

1H0313	TS-11		(to Polish AF as 0313)	
			noted stored, Mierzecice, Poland	8.91
		N313TS	Helicopters West Inc, Provo UT	2.92
1H0314	TS-11		(to Polish AF as 0314)	
			noted stored, Mierzecice, Poland	8.91
		N66EN	Edgar T. Newberg, Hector MN	2.92
1H0316	TS-11		(to Polish AF as 0316)	
		N316BC	International Jets, Gadsden, AL	92
1H0409	TS-11		(to Polish AF as 0409)	
		N409J	International Jets, Albertville, AL	92
1H0415	TS-11		(to Polish AF as 0415)	
		N415J	International Jets, Albertville, AL	92
1H0501	TS-11		(to Polish AF as 0501)	
			noted stored, Mierzecice, Poland	8.91
		N501SH	R. H. Sulgrove, Henderson NV	2.92
1H0502	TS-11		(to Polish AF as 0502)	
			noted stored, Mierzecice, Poland	8.91
		N24ZR	reg. res.	92
1H0509	TS-11		(to Polish AF as 0509)	
		N509J	International Jets, Albertville, AL	92
1H0520	TS-11		(to Polish AF as 0520)	
		N520J	International Jets, Albertville, AL	92
1H0521	TS-11		(to Polish AF as 0521)	
		N44ZR	Valerie Franklin, Lovington, NM	92
1H0524	TS-11		(to Polish AF as 0524)	
			noted stored, Mierzecice, Poland	8.91
		N524SH	D. W. Smith, Henderson NV	2.92
1H0816	TS-11		(to Polish AF as 0816)	
			Gordon Glynn, Sydney NSW	.92
			(shipped to Australia, arr. Sydney 5.92)	
1H0603	TS-11		(to Polish AF as 0603)	
		N21HW	Wilke & Associates, Dallas, TX	92
1H0604	TS-11		(to Polish AF as 0604)	
		N604J	International Jets, Albertville, AL	92
1H0619	TS-11		(to Polish AF as 0619)	
		N619JR	J.R. Rudd, Mukilteo, WA	92
1H0718	TS-11		(to Polish AF as 0718)	
		N718JR	International Jets, Albertville, AL	92
1H1019	TS-11		(to Polish AF as 1019)	
		N101TS	Yankee Spark Flyers Inc., Warren MI	10.92

THE END